MW01054361

COMBAT GUNS

COMBAT GUNS

CHARTWELL
BOOKS, INC.

Published by Chartwell Books Inc.
A division of Book Sales, Inc.
110 Enterprise Avenue
Secaucus, NJ 07094

Produced by David Donald and Chris Bishop
Aerospace Publishing Ltd
179 Dalling Road
Hammersmith
London W6 0ES

© Aerospace Publishing Ltd

First published in book form 1987 by Temple Press
an imprint of The Hamlyn Publishing Group
Bridge House
69 London Road
Twickenham
Middlesex TW1 3SB
England

ISBN 1-55521-161-5

All rights reserved. No part of this publication may be
reproduced, stored in a retrieval system, or transmitted,
in any form or by any means, electronic, mechanical,
photocopying, recording or otherwise, without the
permission of the Publisher and the copyright owner.

Printed in Hong Kong by Mandarin Offset

CONTENTS

PISTOLS 7
Pistols of the Great War 9
Pistols of World War II 23
Modern Combat Pistols 41

SUB-MACHINE GUNS 59
Sub-Machine Guns of World War II 61
Modern Sub-Machine Guns 79

RIFLES 95
Rifles of the Great War 97
Rifles of World War II 113
Post-War Infantry Weapons 137
Modern Assault Rifles 153
Modern Sniping Rifles 173

MACHINE-GUNS 189
Machine-Guns of World War I 191
Machine-Guns of World War II 209
Modern Machine-Guns 227

SHOTGUNS AND RIOT CONTROL EQUIPMENT 251
Combat Shotguns 253
Riot Control Weapons 271

INDEX 282

PISTOLS

Pistols of the Great War

It was a pistol shot that led to the start of World War I, and once the conflict had engulfed the world, pistol production accelerated. Carried by officers, specialists and airmen, they were used on every front; some weapons stayed in service until after World War II, and a couple are still in production.

An officer of the Worcesters holds a service 0.455 Webley revolver during the battle of the Aisne, May 1918.

World War I was probably the last major conflict in which the pistol was involved as a major weapon of war. Most of the pistol's drawbacks (such as lack of useful range, lack of stopping power at other than close quarters and so forth) were all rendered void by the very nature of the conflict in the trenches. Most soldiers suffered from long-range weapons such as artillery, but often had to fight within the close confines of trenches or in hand-to-hand fighting. Here the pistol retained its combat effectiveness to a greater extent than many other weapons, including the rifle, and it was only when the sub-machine gun came on the scene in 1918 that the days of the combat pistol were numbered.

The number of types of pistol in use during World War I was remarkable. With the introduction of the automatic pistol, small-arms inventors used their considerable ingenuity to produce all manner of automatic self-loading mechanisms. Sometimes the ingenuity was used to get round existing patents while at other times sheer inventiveness won through. The revolver was still around in many forms, some of them getting rather long in the tooth, even by contemporary standards, but such was the state of development of many automatic pistols of the period that revolvers were frequently preferred to the automatic on grounds of reliability.

Some 'classic' pistols will be found in this study, some of them to be just as famous during World War II. The P '08 Luger is included along with the Mauser C/96 and such stalwarts as the Webley revolvers. Oddities such as the Webley Fosbery automatic revolver are also included, along with more orthodox weapons such as the first Beretta automatic pistol.

All these weapons had their part to play in World War I. On the whole they were large and heavy weapons that fired heavy bullets, often with considerable man-stopping power and the ability to produce dreadful wounds. Most of them have now passed from the scene, apart from those in the hands of collectors, but they were formidable weapons during the 'Great War'.

Royal Navy officers use a dangerous combination of weapons: Webley and Scott automatics and Webley revolvers. The mighty 0.456 bullet fired by the automatics was propelled by a fast-burning 7-grain charge, and it fitted the 0.455 revolver. If loaded by mistake it would blow the cylinder out.

Savage Model 1907 and 1915

The **Savage Model 1907** pistol was produced by the Savage Arms Corporation of Chicopee Falls, Massachussets, and other than some commercial sales it was acquired by only one military customer, the Portuguese armed forces. This has led to the Savage pistols being virtually identified with the Portuguese though their origins were definitely American.

The Savage Model 1907 was originally designed to take part in the US Army trials that led to adoption of the Colt M1911 automatic. The Model 1907 showed up well in the trials, and although the decision went elsewhere the Savage Corporation attempted to sell the design abroad. It was not successful until 1914, when the Portuguese found themselves cut off from their usual suppliers in Germany who were selling them versions of the Pistole '08 (the Luger). The Portuguese thus decided to adopt the Savage pistol in its original US Army competition form (as the **M/908**) and in a slightly modified version (as the **M/915**), both rechambered from their original 0.45 in (11.43 mm) to 7.65 mm (0.315 in).

The Model 1907 used a retarded blowback mechanism, an operating system rarely used in pistols. On the Model 1907 this involved the barrel turning through lugs before the slide was allowed to move to the rear after firing, but the system adopted by Savage was only marginally more effective than a simple blowback. It was effective enough with the 7.65-mm cartridge employed but would probably have been less successful with anything heavier over a prolonged period

of firing.

The Portuguese found the Savage pistols effective enough, but the pistol had one unfortunate safety problem. It was possible to rest the striker attached to the cocking spur (the design featured a concealed hammer) in such a way that the striker touched the base of a round in the chamber. Any sudden jar could therefore fire the weapon, often to the user's disadvantage (at best). This led to drills that ensured the pistol was cocked only

when required and if no firing was carried out the pistol had to be unloaded again. This was obviously not a good feature for a combat pistol, so as soon as they could the Portuguese reverted to procuring 9-mm Parabellum pistols of various types; they also used the British 0.455-in Webley revolvers.

Specification
M/908
Calibre: 7.65 mm (0.315 in)
Weight: 0.568 kg (1.252 lb)

This Savage Automatic belongs to the Weapons Museum at the School of Infantry, Warminster. The Savage design originated from the 1904 patent of E.H. Searle and was an entry to the US Army pistol trials of 1907, which were won by Colt.

Lengths: overall 165 mm (6.5 in); barrel 95 mm (3.75 in)
Muzzle velocity: 290 m (950 ft) per second
Magazine capacity: 10 rounds

0.45-in M1917 revolvers

By 1916 the demands for all types of war materials and weapons were outstripping the production capabilities of British and Commonwealth industries, so orders for various items were placed in the USA. Among these items were revolvers, and to save time it was decided to adopt American designs rechambered to accept the British 0.455-in (actually 0.441-in/11.2-mm) pistol cartridge. Many thousands of these pistols were accordingly placed into production by Smith & Wesson and the Colt Firearms Company, and were duly delivered to the British and Commonwealth armed forces.

Then in 1917 the USA entered the war and found itself even shorter of weapons to equip its expeditionary force than the British had ever been. It was time for yet another hasty rearrangement of production priorities and the British 0.455-in revolvers were quickly altered to accommodate the standard American 0.45-in (11.43-mm) pistol cartridge. This caused some problems, not in the pistol designs which remained unchanged (and virtually identical to each other) but in the loading. The British cartridge case had a distinct rim at its base while the American case, intended for use in automatic pistols, did not. Therefore as the cartridges were placed in the cylinder chambers they slipped through. This was avoided by loading the American rounds in 'half-moon' pressed steel clips, each holding three rounds. The clips allowed the rounds to be loaded quickly and held the cases in place for firing and unloading.

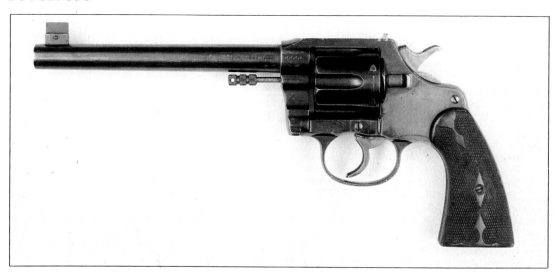

Both revolvers were provided with the designation **M1917**, the maker's name being appended to denote the different models. Although the two pistols were virtually identical to the users, there were in fact slight differences. The Colt revolver was based on the 'New Service' model dating from 1897, while the Smith & Wesson pistol was a 'new' design based on the company's existing range of models. Both used swing-out cylinders which, on the M1917 versions, had recesses in their rear face to accommodate the half-moon clips. Both were large and heavy revolvers.

Once in US Army service both pistols proved rugged and reliable. The three-round clip system gave no trouble and proved so successful that it was even adopted for service by other nations such as Brazil, which made large-scale purchases of the Smith & Wesson M1917 in 1938. Both pistols were still in service during World War II, although by then most were used by the British armed forces.

Specification
M1917
Calibre: 11.43 mm (0.45 in)
Weight: (Colt M1917) 1.134 kg (2.5 lb);

The US Army adopted several revolvers in 1917 chambered for 0.45 Auto, like the M1911 Automatic. US enthusiasm for 0.45 calibre stemmed from the failure of 0.38s like this Colt M1892 to stop charging Filipino tribesmen.

(Smith & Wesson M1917) 1.02 kg (2.25 lb)
Lengths: overall 274 mm (10.8 in); barrel 140 mm (5.5 in)
Muzzle velocity: 253 m (830 ft) per second
Cylinder capacity: 6 rounds in two 3-round clips

Pistola Automatica Beretta modello 1915

The **Pistola Automatica Beretta modello 1915** was the first of the Beretta automatic pistols, but it lacked the degree of manufacturing finesse that became the hallmark of later Beretta models. This was mainly because it was produced in a great hurry. When Italy entered World War I in 1914 it did so at a time when the levels of all kinds of weapons were very low, and pistols were no exception to this failing. Italian industry was rushed into production to churn out as many weapons as quickly as possible, and the Beretta modello 1915 was one result of this policy.

For all the rush with which it was placed into production, the modello 1915 showed all the basic features of the Beretta designs. The slide had the cut-away section over the barrel that was to become an instant recognition feature, but the overall appearance lacked the degree of balance and class that were to appear later. Modello 1915s were initially issued in 7.65-mm (0.301-in) calibre, but some were later produced to fire the 9-mm (0.354-in) special Glisenti cartridge; these versions had a more powerful return spring. A relatively small number were also produced to fire the 9-mm Short round, a round much less powerful than the 9-mm Parabellum. The mechanism was simple blowback and the firing mechanism used a concealed hammer. The 7.65-mm version did not use an ejector to force the spent cartridge cases from the weapon after firing: the cases were pushed out by coming into contact with the firing pin that had been forced through the breech block by the hammer at full recoil; the larger 9-mm cartridge versions used a conventional ejector stop.

As was to be expected under wartime conditions, there were several detail variations between models. A large safety catch with differing shapes and locations was one, and there were also changes in butt grip materials and finish. One thing these modello 1915s shared with all users was a general appreciation of the weapon's reliability and good handling. The modello 1915 introduced the basic pattern of what were later to become some of the finest automatic pistols ever produced. Even now the name Beretta stands for sound design and good finish, but examining a modello 1915 today few of these attributes are obvious, due mainly to the rapidity with which they were placed in mass production. But the seeds were there.

Specification
Beretta modello 1915
Calibre: 7.65 mm (0.301 in) or 9 mm (0.354 in) Short
Weight: 0.57 kg (1.25 lb)
Lengths: overall 149 mm (5.87 in); barrel 84 mm (3.31 in)
Muzzle velocity: (9-mm Short) 266 m (873 ft) per second
Magazine capacity: 8 rounds

An Italian 'Deathshead' pioneer, in full trench raiding kit, has a medieval appearance. In the savage close-quarter fighting in the trenches, the entrenching tool and pistol were more sensible weapons than a bulky rifle; the body armour was heavy, but provided good protection. Note the wirecutters carried on the belt.

Pistola Automatica Glisenti modello 1910

The **Pistola Automatica Glisenti modello 1910** was often known just as the **Glisenti**, but an essentially similar pistol was also issued to the Italian army and known as the **Brixia**. The initial pistol, the Glisenti, was designed in Switzerland but initial production was started in Italy in 1905 at the Societa Siderurgica Glisenti at Turin. In 1910 the pistol was accepted for Italian army use. Two years later, a **modello 12** produced by the Brixia concern, appeared. This modello 1912 was almost identical to the modello 1910 but lacked the grip safety. For simplicity's sake these two pistols will be treated as one and the same.

The Glisenti modello 1910 used a mechanism that employed a locked-breech system, but for various design reasons this system was not very effective. Therefore it could not use full-power cartridges such as the 9-mm (0.354-in) Parabellum, but instead had to fire its own special cartridge with a less powerful charge. The difficulty with this special cartridge was that it was virtually identical in shape and appearance to the Parabellum round, and that use of the Parabellum round in the Glisenti pistol could, and often did, cause trouble. Some of these troubles could be very hazardous to the firer. Under normal circumstances this potential problem could be avoided but under combat conditions the two types of cartridge could be easily mixed up.

When firing the correct cartridge the modello 10 proved to be reliable enough, but suffered from one basic design weakness. The designers had ensured good maintenance access by allowing almost the entire left-hand side of the pistol frame to be removable. This certainly made for good cleaning and repair, but the removable plate made the entire pistol weak on that side. Under combat conditions the pistol frame could become distorted to an unacceptable degree causing jams and other more potentially severe problems, or the access plate could simply fall off. Thus the modello 1910 was increasingly regarded with suspicion, and whenever possible knowledgeable users plumped for other types of side-arm.

This did not prevent the Glisenti pistols from being carried and used throughout World War I and even during World War II. If looked after and not subjected to too much hard use, the Glisenti/Brixia pistols were sound enough, but under severe combat conditions they often proved to be less than satisfactory.

Specification
Glisenti modello 1910
Calibre: 9 mm (0.354 in)
Weight: 0.8 kg (1.76 lb)

Lengths: overall 211.2 mm (8.315 in); barrel 95 mm (3.74 in)
Muzzle velocity: 258 m (846 ft) per second
Magazine capacity: 7 rounds

The Glisenti was not as popular as the Beretta: the left-hand side of the frame detaches, reducing its strength, and the breech accepted 9-mm Parabellum – far more powerful than the 9-mm Glisenti cartridge, and able to shatter the weapon.

Webley & Scott self-loading pistols

The Webley & Scott self-loading pistols must rank as among the most awkward-looking pistols ever designed, but in use they were reliable. The first of them was accepted for government service in 1912, mainly for police use, and by 1914 the **Webley Self-Loading Pistol Mk I** was in use by Royal Navy and Royal Marine landing or boarding parties. Later more were issued to the newly-formed Royal Flying Corps and to some Royal Horse Artillery battery personnel.

The basic design used a very positive locking system that ran in a series of angled grooves and lugs. This was just as well for the pistol continued to use the 0.455-in (actually 0.441-in/11.2-mm) cartridge but in a much more powerful form, so much so that for many years it remained the world's most powerful pistol cartridge. This cartridge had a charge so heavy that it could cause serious damage to pistol and user if fired from any of the 0.455-in revolvers. Some pistols were produced to fire the 0.38-in (9.65-mm) Super Auto and 9-mm (0.354-in) Browning long cartridges, but few of these appear to have been used by the British military.

The pistol had a a few odd design features all of its own, one being that it was possible to partially withdraw and lock the box magazine to allow single rounds to be fed into the chamber through the ejection slot, leaving the full magazine topped up for emergency use. There was provision on most versions for a flat wooden shoulder stock to be fitted to the butt for more accurate shooting at longer ranges.

These Webley & Scott self-loaders (the term 'automatic' was disliked by the British at the time) were massive pistols that took a lot of careful handling even at short combat ranges. They were well-built with a distinctive 'straight-line' appearance that was not helped by the almost square-set angle of the butt. This butt angle made the pistol rather difficult to fire instinctively, but deliberate shooting by a fully-trained user could be quite accurate. If all else failed the pistols could be used as clubs as even when unloaded each weighed 1.13 kg (2.5 lb). They were not generally liked. The Royal Horse Artillery got rid of theirs as soon as they could and the Royal Flying Corps were no more enthusiastic. As a result the Webley & Scott self-loaders were never accepted for full military service but the British armed forces continued to use the revolver for many years, officially until well after World War II.

Specification
Webley Self-loading Pistol Mk I
Calibre: 11.2 mm (0.441 in)
Weight: 1.13 kg (2.5 lb)
Lengths: overall(216 mm (8.5 in); barrel 127 mm (5 in)
Muzzle velocity: 236 m (775 ft) per second
Magazine capacity: 7 rounds

Adopted by the Royal Navy in 1914 and later by the artillery and RFC, the ungainly Webley & Scott 0.455 was not wildly popular.

Naval aviation pioneer commander Samson and his Nieuport 10 prepare for another sortie over the Turkish lines at Gallipoli. Pistols were initially carried by airmen for personal defence in case of a forced landing.

Webley 0.455-in revolvers

The 0.455-in cartridge fired by the Webley revolvers had an actual calibre of 0.441 in (11.2 mm), and its design reflected experience gained in colonial warfare. The cartridge was designed to be a certain 'man-stopper' for close-range use against charging native hordes, and the heavy bullet and powerful charge were certainly adequate for the task. The pistol intended for use with this powerful cartridge was produced by Webley & Scott Limited of Birmingham, which produced its first 0.455-in pistol in late 1887.

The **Webley & Scott Mk I** was the forerunner of a host of similar models, many of which are still around. The Mk I had a top-opening frame with an automatic ejecting device that pushed out spent cartridge cases as the frame opened. The butt had a distinctive shape that was termed a 'bird's head', and a lanyard ring was considered essential. A 102-mm (4-in) barrel was used, but later marks also used 152-mm (6-in) barrels.

After the Mk I came a large number of other marks and submarks with detail improvements and/or barrel length changes. The overall mechanism and design did not change much, although by the time the main World War I model appeared in 1915 the butt shape had changed and there had been some alterations to the sights. The Mk VI may be taken as typical of the World War I Webley 0.455-in revolvers, but many of the earlier marks remained in use.

The Mk VI was a very well made and solid revolver. It was also large and something of a handful to tote and fire. The powerful cartridge produced an equally powerful recoil and it was considered to have a useful combat range of only a few metres. For trench warfare this was ideal, and the Webleys were a preferred weapon for trench raids and close-quarter fighting. Under such circumstances the Webleys had one major advantage and that was that they were very forgiving of the dirty and muddy conditions under which they were often used. Even if a Webley jammed or ran out of ammunition it could still be used as an effective club. This attribute was developed by the introduction of the Pritchard-Greener revolver bayonet, a spike-type bayonet/trench knife that fitted over the muzzle with the metal hilt resting against the revolver frame. This fearsome pistol/bayonet combination appears to have been little

Still in service around the world, Webley revolvers are arguably the toughest and most accurate handguns ever made. Their calibre is 0.441 (11.2 mm) but, curiously, they have always been referred to as 0.455 (11.6 mm). Below is the Mk 1, introduced in 1887; above is the Mk 5 of 1913.

used as it was never approved officially. A more useful device was a charger that held six cartridges ready for instant loading into the opened cylinder.

Specification
Webley Mk VI
Calibre: 11.2 mm (0.441 in)
Weight: 1.09 kg (2.4 lb)
Lengths: overall 286 mm (11.25 in); barrel 152 mm (6 in)
Muzzle velocity: 189 m (620 ft) per second
Cylinder capacity: 6 rounds

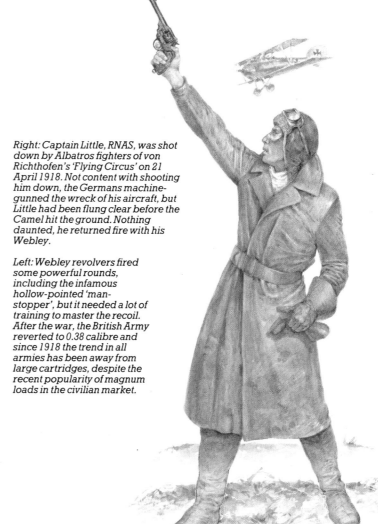

Right: Captain Little, RNAS, was shot down by Albatros fighters of von Richthofen's 'Flying Circus' on 21 April 1918. Not content with shooting him down, the Germans machine-gunned the wreck of his aircraft, but Little had been flung clear before the Camel hit the ground. Nothing daunted, he returned fire with his Webley.

Left: Webley revolvers fired some powerful rounds, including the infamous hollow-pointed 'man-stopper', but it needed a lot of training to master the recoil. After the war, the British Army reverted to 0.38 calibre and since 1918 the trend in all armies has been away from large cartridges, despite the recent popularity of magnum loads in the civilian market.

UK
Webley Fosbery revolver

The **Webley Fosbery** revolver was designed by Colonel G.V. Fosbery VC, and is in a class of its own as it is an automatic revolver. The original patent was taken out in 1896 and production was taken up by Webley & Scott shortly after that, the resultant pistols being chambered for the standard 0.455-in (actually 0.441-in/11.2-mm) cartridge.

The action of the Webley Fosbery was unique. On firing the recoil drove back the barrel, cylinder and top frame along a slide over the butt. This cocked the hammer and a return spring inside the butt then drove the whole assembly back to its initial position. As it did so a stud in the slide ran through an angled groove machined into the cylinder to turn it to the next cartridge position. The system had its attractions to those who thought that they had only to keep pulling the trigger to keep firing rapidly. In practice it was not that simple. One immediate drawback was that the action required a great deal of handling: the entire top frame moving back and forth added to the already considerable movement caused by the heavy recoil, and so made the pistol something of a brute to fire. Another drawback was that the firer had to hold the butt very firmly indeed or the entire system would not function, for the user's grip acted as the anchor for the entire mechanism.

Nevertheless the Webley Fosbery was sold in considerable numbers to British officers who had to supply their own side-arms. Many were sold to Royal Flying Corps personnel who thought that the automatic feature would be of considerable advantage when engaging enemy aircraft from the confines of their cockpits: they soon learned that the considerable

firing movements made in-flight shooting even more difficult than it might otherwise have been.

For all this the Webley Fosbery was never adopted officially, which was just as well for when used in the trenches the type's major drawback became all too obvious. This was that the action relied upon smooth movement through carefully-machined grooves, any clogging of those grooves by dirt or mud resulted in a jam. As most of the grooves involved were fully exposed

they soon became full of all manner of trench debris and it took constant attention to keep them clean. Many officers gave up the task and took up other less troublesome pistols.

Specification
Webley Fosbery
Calibre: 11.2 mm (0.441 in)
Weight: 1.25 kg (2.755 lb)
Lengths: overall 279 mm (11 in); barrel 152 mm (6 in)

The unique Webley Fosbery is an automatic revolver. The barrel and cylinder go back over the frame, cocking the hammer and returning by spring power; the stud on the frame engaged in the prominent grooves in the cylinder rotates it, so completing the action.

Muzzle velocity: 183 m (600 ft) per second
Cylinder capacity: 6 rounds

BELGIUM
Browning pistols

The Belgian Fabrique Nationale d'Armes de Guerre (FN) was formed in association with John M. Browning after the latter left Colt, and the association produced many excellent weapon designs. The first pistol produced by the Browning/FN combination was the **Browning Modèle 1900**, a fairly straightforward pistol with few frills and chambered in 7.65 mm (0.301 in). The Modèle 1900 was a pistol that was never officially adopted as a standard service pistol, but it was produced and used in thousands, usually by officers who had to supply their own side-arms. It was also copied in even larger numbers in China and Spain, usually unofficially.

The **Modèle 1903** was the Belgian version of a Browning-designed Colt pistol produced to use an European cartridge known as the 9-mm (0.354-in) Browning Long. The Modèle 1903 employed a straightforward blowback mechanism that could be used because of the relatively low power of the cartridge. The Modèle 1903 was adopted by the Belgian army and was also licence-produced in Sweden. Other user nations were Turkey, Serbia, Denmark and the Netherlands. Some versions could use a shoulder stock that doubled as a holster.

Perhaps the most important of the World War I Browning pistols was the attractive **Modèle 1910**. It was placed on the market in 1912 and was immediately recognized as an ideal

officer's side-arm. It was also accorded the accolade of being copied widely, often without any form of licence agreement. Produced to fire either the 7.65-mm or 9-mm Short (0.354-in, also known as the .380 ACP) cartridge, the Modèle 1910 is still in limited production. The mechanism of the Modèle 1910 is conventional blow-back with the return spring coiled around the barrel. The pistol is still a delight to handle and is easy to aim and fire, having a grip safety. The Modèle 1910 is another pistol that has never been officially adopted as a service weapon, other than by the Belgian army, but it was used in large numbers throughout World War I by many officers who had to purchase their own side-arms. Many Modèle 1910s were still around during World War II. After World War I a slightly enlarged version, the Modèle 1922, was produced but it never replaced the Modèle 1910.

Specification
Modèle 1900
Calibre: 7.65 mm (0.301 in)
Weight: 0.625 kg (1.378 lb)
Lengths: overall 162.5 mm (6.4 in); barrel 102 mm (4.02 in)
Muzzle velocity: 290 m (951 ft) per second
Magazine capacity: 7 rounds

Specification
Modèle 1903
Calibre: 9 mm (0.354 in)

Weight: 0.91 kg (2 lb)
Lengths: overall 203 mm (8 in); barrel 127 mm (5 in)
Muzzle velocity: 320 m (1,050 ft) per second
Magazine capacity: 7 rounds

Specification
Modèle 1910
Calibre: 7.65 or 9 mm (0.301 or 0.354 in)
Weight: 0.57 kg (1.26 lb)

The Modèle 1900 has the distinction of being the first Browning design to be made by FN of Herstal, the beginning of a long and successful association.

Lengths: overall 154 mm (6.06 in); barrel 88.5 mm (3.48 in)
Muzzle velocity: 299 m (981 ft) per second
Magazine capacity: 7 rounds

Austro-Hungarian pistols

The basic pistol of the Austro-Hungarian armies was the **8-mm Rast und Gasser Revolver M.1898**. This was a very robust and well made revolver, and was issued in large numbers to officers and NCOs of the imperial armies. But it was unusual on two counts: one was that it fired its own special 8-mm (0.315-in) cartridge, and the other was the unusual method of stripping. This was carried out by pulling down the trigger guard. In this way the entire interior workings were exposed for cleaning and repair, not that repairs had to be carried out very often for the M.1898 was extraordinarily tough. In fact the standard of production was so high that many were still in use during World War II.

Despite the widespread issue of the M.1898 revolver in 1907, the Austro-Hungarian army decided also to adopt an automatic pistol. This was the **8-mm Repetierpistole M.07** (also known as the **Roth-Steyr**), a pistol that used a unique mechanism that no one has seen fit to copy. The M.07 used a long bolt that initially moved backwards with the barrel on firing and continued to travel to the rear once the barrel was held by stops. A complicated process of ejection and feeding the next round then commenced, ceasing only when the bolt and the barrel were back in their initial position. The process involved a straight travel and at one point rotary movement. Despite all this complexity the M.07 was a sound service pistol but it was never produced for anything other than Austro-Hungarian military service. It too had a cartridge all of its own that was not adopted elsewhere.

The M.07 was difficult to produce and in 1912 the **9-mm Repetierpistole M.12** was introduced. Widely known as the **Steyr-Hahn**, the M.12 used what was probably the strongest pistol action ever made, with a locked-breech mechanism operated by a rotating barrel. The 9-mm (0.354-in) cartridge was again special to the weapon and was used by no other, and another distinction was that the magazine was fixed and had to be reloaded through the top using a charger clip.

The M.12 was officially the standard Austro-Hungarian side-arm of World War I and many were still around during World War II, by then in German

Superficially similar to the Mauser C/96, the Mannlicher M1903 was a rival weapon produced with the military market in mind, but was rejected as a service pistol as it was not sufficiently reliable.

hands. However, the official status did not prevent the earlier M.1898 and M.07 remaining in widespread use.

Specification
M.07
Calibre: 8 mm (0.315 in)
Weight: 1.03 kg (2.27 lb)

The Steyr M1912 was a first-class gun but was adopted only by the Austro-Hungarian army, perhaps because it fired a unique 9-mm cartridge that was more powerful than the increasingly popular 9-mm Parabellum. It was called 'Steyr-Hahn' ('Steyr-Hammer') to distinguish it from the Roth-Steyr.

Lengths: overall 233 mm (9.17 in); barrel 131 mm (5.16 in)
Muzzle velocity: 332 m (1,089 ft) per second
Magazine capacity: 10 rounds

Specification
M.12
Calibre: 9 mm (0.354 in)
Weight: 1.02 kg (2.25 lb)
Lengths: overall 216 mm (8.5 in); barrel 128 mm (5.1 in)
Muzzle velocity: 340 m (1,115 ft) per second
Magazine capacity: 8 rounds

Right: Having begun the Hussar style in the first place, it was only natural that Hungarian hussar uniforms in 1914 retained all the panache of traditional light cavalry, despite the addition of modern weaponry. This officer holds a Steyr-Hahn M12 automatic in classic duelling stance.

Japanese pistols

During World War I the Japanese armed forces used two types of sidearm: the **Pistol revolver Type 26** and the **Pistol Automatic Type 4**.

The 9-mm (0.354-in) Type 26 revolver was adopted in 1893, initially for cavalry use. It was a Japanese design that was typical of its era for it was produced at a time when the Japanese were still studying Western technology to bring their nation forward from the state of generally medieval backwardness. Unfortunately for the small-arms designers they did not know which particular Western designs to follow and so produced an amalgam of several different designs. The overall appearance owed much to the Nagant revolvers, the cylinder swing-out system was borrowed from the Smith & Wessons, the ability to swing open the lock mechanism came from the French Lebel and the action was derived from several European designs. The Japanese decided to add a touch of their own and made the pistol a double-action only weapon. To this they added their own 9-mm ammunition that was not then, or ever since, used by any other weapon. The result was an odd revolver that was at least serviceable and strong enough to last through two world wars.

The Type 4 automatic pistol was de-signed by one Kijiro Nambu and was never officially accepted for Imperial service. However, so many were purchased and used by Japanese officers from the late 1900s onwards that the design was provided with the Type 4 designation. To the West it became known as the **Nambu** and was so widely used that all subsequent Japanese pistols were called Nambus. The Type 4 fired an 8-mm (0.315-in) cartridge, and used an action not unlike that of the Italian Glisenti but mechanically stronger. This action gave the Type 4 a distinctive appearance. There were several variations of the basic Type 4, the most drastic of which was a special 7-mm (0.276-in) **'Baby Nambu'** version intended for use by staff officers. Despite its widespread use the Type 4 was apparently not a very satisfactory pistol. One constant source of troubles was the striker spring which sometimes became too weak to fire a cartridge. Another was the generally low standard of steel used for some components which often broke under anything other than light use. But the Type 4 remained in service for many years. Many were still in use during World War II despite the provision of a generally-improved design known as the Type 14 (introduced in 1937).

The 8-mm Nambu automatic was purchased by many Japanese officers although it was never adopted as a service pistol. It had a breech-lock similar to that of the Glisenti but suffered from a weak striker spring.

Specification
Type 26
Calibre: 9 mm (0.354 in)
Weight: 0.9 kg (1.98 lb)
Lengths: overall 239 mm (9.4 in); barrel 119 mm (4.7 in)
Muzzle velocity: 277 m (909 ft) per second
Ammunition capacity: 6 rounds

Specification
Type 4
Calibre: 8 mm (0.315 in)
Weight: 0.9 kg (1.98 lb)
Lengths: overall 229 mm (9 in); barrel 120 mm (4.7 in)
Muzzle velocity: 325 m (1,066 ft) per second
Ammunition capacity: 8 rounds

Nagant Model 1895

The **Nagant Model 1895** revolver was originally a Belgian design produced as early as 1878. From then onwards the basic design was procured by Belgium, Argentina, Brazil, Denmark, Norway, Portugal, Rumania, Serbia and Sweden, usually from Belgium and in various calibres (although copies were produced in Spain). However, the number of Nagant revolvers produced in Russia (initially under licence) dwarfed all output carried out elsewhere, to the extent that the Nagant is now regarded as a Russian weapon.

The first Russian production of the Nagant was carried out at the Tula Arsenal in 1895 and continued until 1940. The version involved was the Nagant Model 1895, a model designed to improve the overall efficiency of the basic revolver concept. It was an unusual revolver in many respects, not the least being the unique 7.62-mm (0.30-in) ammunition that used a brass cartridge case with a fully recessed bullet. The idea of this was that as the pistol was fired the cylinder was rammed forward into close contact against the end of the barrel, with the case forming a complete gas seal between the two assemblies. The idea behind this was supposedly to make the cartridge more efficient by minimizing the loss of propellant gases through the small gap between the cylinder and the barrel, but it was a feature of doubtful value that added a degree of complexity to the requirement for a special cartridge, although the Russians thought much of it and retained the feature unchanged until production ceased.

For some reason the Tsarist army decided to perpetuate the differences between the ranks by issuing enlisted men with single-action revolvers while officers received double-action versions. There was also a noticeable dif-

ference between the finish of the two models, the single-action models often being left as bare metal while the officers' versions were plated or blued. Both were extremely sturdy and reliable weapons: they had to be to last under the conditions in which the Russian army usually fought. The frame was solid and the cylinder was fixed, with loading taking place through a gate on the right. A rod was used to eject spent cases.

The Nagant Model 1895 revolvers were produced in hundreds of thousands over the years. The type was used throughout World Wars I and II, and it is possible to encounter some today in odd corners of the world. A few ammunition manufacturers still find it worth their while to produce the special recessed ammunition, although most sales must now be to collectors.

Specification
Nagant Model 1895
Calibre: 7.62 mm (0.3 in)
Weight: 0.795 kg (1.75 lb)

The Nagant was a Belgian design adopted by many different armies but so many were produced under licence in Russia that the revolver is regarded as Russian. It incorporated an unusual gas-seal mechanism which added needless complication for little real benefit.

Lengths: overall 230 mm (9.055 in); barrel 110 mm (4.33 in)
Muzzle velocity: 272 m (892 ft) per second
Cylinder capacity: 6 rounds

9-mm Pistole '08

The **9-mm Pistole '08** remains one of the 'classic' pistols and it is still almost universally known as the **Luger** after its designer, Georg Luger. The basic design was based on that of a previous pistol, the **Borchardt**, but Luger tidied up that design and developed it into the form manufactured by Deutsche Waffen und Munitionsfabriken (DWM) starting in 1898.

The first Luger pistols were sold to Switzerland in 1900, chambered for the 7.65-mm (0.301-in) cartridge. By 1904 the pistol was being re-chambered for the 9-mm (0.354-in) Parabellum cartridge, and this version was accepted for German navy use. In 1908 a slightly revised model was accepted by the German army and thereafter the P '08 was fabricated in hundreds of thousands. These early models were produced in a variety of barrel lengths, the shortest being 103 mm (4.06 in)

long. Other barrel lengths were 152 mm (6 in), 203 mm (8 in) and even 305 mm (12 in). These long-barrelled versions were usually issued with combined wooden shoulder stock/holster kits and were known as **Artillery Models**. They were frequently used with a 32-round 'snail' magazine.

All the variations of the P '08 used the same mechanisms with its upward-opening toggle lock mechanism. As the pistol was fired all the hinge elements of the toggle were in line to lock the breech. The recoil forces had to overcome the mechanical advantage of the toggle mechanism before it would open, and once open the ejection and reloading processes could be carried out. A return spring in the butt reset everything ready to fire the next round.

The toggle device gave the P '08 a distinctive appearance, and the rake

of the butt made the pistol a good one to aim and fire. The P '08 soon became a prized front-line weapon and war trophy, and throughout World War I there were never enough P '08s being produced to meet the ever-growing demands. It was here that the disadvantages of the P '08 became apparent, for it was a difficult weapon to produce in quantity as virtually all its components had to be hand-made. By 1917 much of the excellent pre-war detail finish had been omitted and the original grip safety was deleted altogether, never to return even after 1918. There was one other drawback to the P '08, and that was the fact that the toggle mechanism was not very tolerant of trench conditions. Mud and dirt could all too easily clog the workings, often at the worst possible times, so the pistols demanded a lot of care.

The soldiers did not seem to mind.

They liked the P '08, and after 1918 the model was kept in service. It was still in production in 1943 and even today many manufacturers find it well worth their while to produce 'look-alike' or direct copies for a seemingly unsatiable market.

Specification
P '08
Calibre: 9 mm (0.354 in)
Weight: 0.876 kg (1.93 lb)
Lengths: overall 222 mm (8.76 in); barrel 103 mm (4.06 in)
Muzzle velocity: 320 m (1,050 ft) per second
Magazine capacity: (box) 8 rounds

A standard Luger P '08 is shown beneath an 'Artillery' Model, thought to have been introduced in 1917. The latter had a 192-mm (7.5-in) barrel and a flat board-like stock.

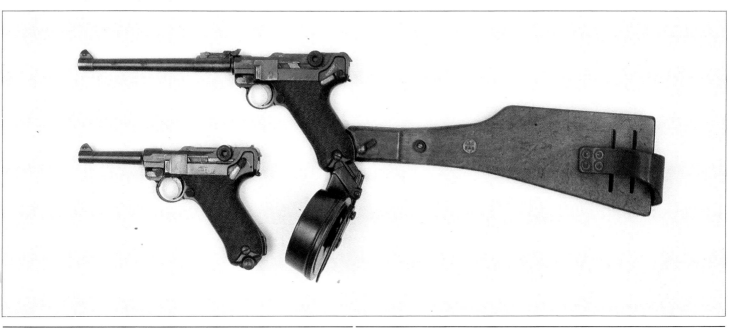

Other German pistols

When trench warfare had set in with a vengeance by the end of 1914, the armies of both sides demanded ever-growing quantities of weapons and war materials. Pistols were no exception to this situation, and as most service pistols then in use had virtually to be hand-made, it was not easy to meet these demands in a hurry. Consequently something else had to be found to equip the soldiers, and many storerooms were examined.

In some of them large numbers of **Reichs-Commissions-Revolver Modell 1879** were found. In fact some of them were still in reserve use by many units, despite their age. They fired an odd and low-powered 10.6-mm (0.417-in) cartridge, but were sturdy weapons as they had solid frames and a gate-load-

One of the first commercial pistols to be produced in 9-mm Parabellum was the RM & M 'Dreyse', which was manufactured only in limited numbers but saw active service nevertheless. The weapon was closely based on this earlier Dreyse Automatic, chambered for the 7.65-mm cartridge.

Other German pistols (continued)

ing system that required a rod to eject spent cartridge cases. These ancient revolvers were still around in 1918 and for many years after as they did not wear out. There was also a **Modell 1883** with a shorter (126-mm/4.96-in) barrel.

Another typical wartime expedient was the 7.65-mm (0.301-in) **Belholla-Selbsladepistole**. This was really a commercial automatic pistol of undistinguished design, but was available in some numbers and was fairly easy to make. Many were issued to staff officers who had to carry a pistol and for whom the Belholla would be quite sufficient, freeing more useful combat pistols for front-line units. Thousands of Belhollas were made and issued, often under an array of sub-contractor names. The design was so simple that little thought was given to maintenance and the pistol could not be stripped without recourse to a trained armourer with a substantial tool kit.

These two pistols were typical of the mix of commercial and ancient sidearms with which a great deal of the German army (and other services) had to conduct their war. Demand constantly outstripped pistol supply, so a wide range of odd pistols were collected into the German army net. Pistols with such names as the **Dreyse** and the **Langenham** were pressed into service in quantities that ensured that their names would not be entirely forgotten, as they would probably otherwise have been, but few of them were designed for front-line service of the

kind they often had to encounter, so many were less than satisfactory.

Specification
Modell 1879
Calibre: 10.6 mm (0.417 in)

Weight: 1.04 kg (2.29 lb)
Lengths: overall 310 mm (12.2 in); barrel 183 mm (7.2 in)
Muzzle velocity: 205 m (673 ft) per second
Cylinder capacity: 6 rounds

An automatic 7.65-mm pistol designed for the commercial market, the Langenhan was adopted by the German army during the war as demand for weapons exceeded the production capacity of existing guns.

GERMANY
Mauser C/96

The original design of the **Mauser C/96** range of pistols was produced by three brothers named Feederle, who worked on the basic design until 1896 when it was placed in production by Mauser at Oberndorf-Neckar. Thereafter the C/96 and its derivatives were produced in a bewildering array of models to the extent that it is still a veritable minefield for the unwary historian.

The first C/96 pistols were hand guns, but it was not long before later models began to sprout shoulder stocks and other such appendages. Barrels started to increase in length until the weapons became virtual carbines rather than pistols, and some models of the C/96 became very complex pieces of kit together with their shoulder stock/holsters that also carried cleaning tools, spare clips and so on. Only one model needs to be considered at this stage to explain most models.

The **Military Model** was first produced in 1912 and was widely used throughout World War I. It had a 140-mm (5.51-in) barrel and was one of the pistol/carbine versions that used a combination shoulder stock and holster. Originally these pistols were produced to fit a special 7.63-mm (3.01-in) cartridge but during World War I the demand was such that some were issued to fire the 9-mm (0.354-in) Parabellum cartridge: these had a large red number 9 engraved into their butts. Using both these cartridges the

The Mauser C/96 has one of the best known profiles of any pistol, and this elegant weapon, already popular at the turn of the century, is today a favourite for collectors.

Military Model had a mechanism that can only be described as complicated. Rounds were fed into the magazine situated in front of the trigger using clips fed in from above. At the moment of firing the breech was locked by a locking piece underneath the bolt that moved to and fro in a barrel extension. After firing, a system of tongues and bolt movement delayed the action until the chamber pressure had dropped to a safe level, after which the bolt was allowed to move back to carry out the reloading and recocking operations. The barrel also moved back, but only

to a limited extent. A return spring returned everything for the next round. The mechanism depended on careful machining and exact tolerances, two factors that made the C/96 series difficult to manufacture and which led to its eventual military demise.

The C/96 pistols were certainly formidable military weapons with a certain aura about them that survives to this day, for it seems that every pistol collector wants at least one C/96 in his collection. Such collectors have a wide choice, for the pistols were made in large numbers, not only in Germany

but in Spain and many other nations, including China where the quantities involved were prodigious. Most of this 'overseas' production was entirely unofficial.

Specification
Military Model
Calibre: 7.63 or 9 mm (3.01 or 0.354 in)
Weight: 1.22 kg (2.69 lb)
Lengths: overall 308 mm (12.125 in); barrel 140 mm (5.51 in)
Muzzle velocity: (7.63 mm) 433 m (1,420 ft) per second
Magazine capacity: 10 rounds

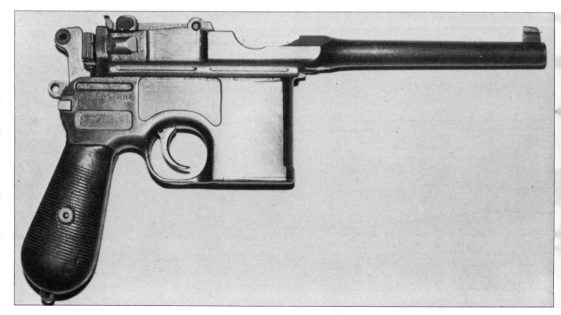

Mauser: the story continues

Designed in 1894 with a hammer intended to be cocked against a horseman's saddle, the Mauser C/96 was carried by Winston Churchill during his army days. Subsequently copied in arsenals around the world, a modified version is today marketed by the Chinese as a machine pistol.

The story of the Mauser C/96 'Broomhandle' pistols may have started back in the 1890s, but it is far from over. The C/96 was the world's first truly automatic self-loading pistol, and over the decades has gained a following that has yet to be lost.

The C/96 was first produced in 1896 and immediately became a much desired weapon. The main attraction was its self-loading feature, but many buyers were drawn to the weapon just by its appearance. Simply carrying the weapon seemed to impart some sense of importance to the carrier, but this was offset by the fact that the C/96 was not easy to maintain. It had a complicated mechanism and took some time to understand. The bystander never saw these 'off-stage' requirements, and thus remained impressed.

Anyone on the receiving end was also impressed. The 7.63-mm (0.301-in) cartridge fired by the C/96 was a high-velocity round that could inflict serious damage at quite long ranges compared with other pistols of the era, and Mauser took advantages of this by supplying some models with leaf rearsights calibrated up to as much as 1000 m (1,094 yards), which was rather optimistic. To take advantage of this long-range feature there emerged the use of wooden holsters that could also double as shoulder stocks for more accurate aiming. Originally these accessories were produced for wealthy commercial customers, but it was not long before they attracted the attentions of the military who then decided to take the idea one stage further and add cleaning tools, spare ammunition clips and other items to the holster. In the end the wooden holster was in turn carried in a leather holster with all the extras enclosed.

By the time World War I started the C/96 was in widespread use. Many sales were made to officers of diverse nations, for at that time an officer had to purchase his own side-arm. Many were attracted by the C/96, and many British officers sported them: Winston Churchill carried one during his spell in the World War I trenches. Most of the C/96s used by the German army during the war were a model known as the 'neue Sicherung 1912', this being a simplified variant compared with previous models, and having as standard a barrel 139.7 mm (5.5 in) long. Many were issued with the wooden stock/holsters.

It was with the introduction of this model 1912 that the company made increasingly feasible the use of the C/96 as a specialist assassination weapon by the introduction of a powerful 9-mm (0.354-in) cartridge known as the Mauser Export. This fired a bullet similar to that used in the Parabellum cartridge but at a higher muz-

Right: A German Uhlan sports a Mauser C/96 modified to fire the standard 9-mm Parabellum cartridge instead of the original 7.63-mm round. The weapons were marked on the grip with either a red or (less commonly) a black figure '9'. A few early models made for the army were chambered for the longer-cased 9-mm Mauser Export cartridge.

Below: Most Mauser C/96s were capable of being fitted with the Mauser hollow wooden shoulder stock, which doubled as a holster and carried the cleaning kit. The magazine was an integral part of the pistol and was loaded through the top of the action with the 10 round charger illustrated. Note the figure 9 on the grip of the lower pistol.

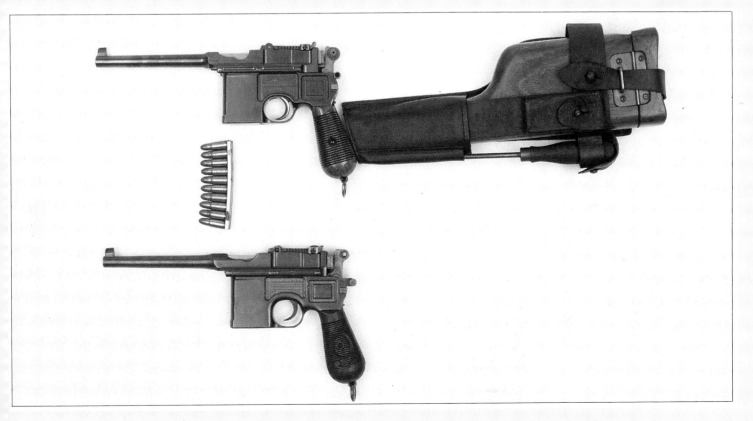

Mauser: the story continues

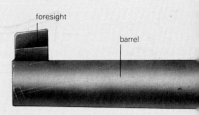

zle velocity (415 m/1,362 ft per second as opposed to 344 m/1,129 ft per second). This made the pistol/cartridge combination an excellent long-range weapon that could be relatively easily concealed and used at distances well above normal pistol ranges. Thus the Mauser Export pistols were often used for clandestine and assassination missions all around the world, especially in the Balkans where the C/96 was much favoured. The importance of this special cartridge must not be overemphasized, however, for the standard Mauser 7.63-mm cartridge was no mean performer in its own right.

During World War I the C/96 in its various forms did not fare as well as some other pistols when used in the trenches. The complex mechanism did not cope well with mud or dirt getting in its workings, so the C/96s were generally used by second-line units such as the artillery. They were also used with some degree of success by the newly-formed German air arm. It was almost certainly one of the first weapons ever used in air-to-air warfare when German pilots in their otherwise unarmed scout aircraft attempted to shoot at Allied pilots and aircraft flying close by. The C/96 was perhaps better than most pistols in this form of uncertain warfare and promoted Allied pilots to retaliate with pistols or rifles. It was not long before machine-guns were in use and the era of pistols in air-to-air combat passed almost as soon as it had began.

9-mm Parabellum

In World War I Mauser churned out C/96s (mainly the model 1912) in thousands to meet ever-growing demands. The standard of many of these war-time models suffered, and a change was made in 1916 to enable the pistol to fire 9-mm Parabellum ammunition. These pistols were issued with a large '9' burned into the broomhandle butt and painted red.

Emperor Haile Selassie sits pensively on a log after his epic march back to Ethiopia. His bodyguard carried an extraordinary variety of weapons, including the Mauser C/96 sported by the man on the right.

After the war Mauser was prevented by the Allies from supplying the German army, and so looked around for new customers. Many commercial sales were made by assembling pistols from spare parts, but the largest post-war customer was the USSR, for which Mauser produced a 7.63-mm model known as the 'Bolo', supposedly after 'Bolshevik'. This version had a barrel 99 mm (3.9 in) long and used a shortened six-round magazine. The overall appearance was cleaned-up and was much smoother than that of earlier models. These Bolos were used extensively by both sides during the Russian Civil War of the early 1920s, and more were purchased in 1926.

Far Eastern version

By the late 1920s Mauser was losing trade to a number of overseas producers of Mauser look-alikes. The attractions of the C/96 were not confined to World War I combatants, and numbers of C/96s were produced before the war for Persia and China, who took to the design with a will. Thus it was not long before nations other than Germany were producing C/96 copies for the market. Spain especially produced direct copies for sales to China and other Far East nations. The Chinese also began to produce Mauser C/96s of all types. Some were direct copies, others were simply look-alikes with differing mechanisms, and still others were produced that were downright dangerous to fire. These Chinese copies were usually liberally sprinkled with Chinese markings to denote their source of origin, and were produced in thousands for local markets.

The Spanish and Chinese also introduced an innovation. By some slight alterations to the trigger mechanism the C/96 could be converted into a form of sub-machine gun, or more correctly a machine pistol, providing fully automatic fire. The value of a weapon the size of the C/96 firing on fully automatic was dubious but its effects could be dramatic, especially at close ranges; the 10-round magazine capacity was soon exhausted and the recoil caused the barrel to climb rapidly away from the target. This did not appear to be any problem to the Chinese, who again took to these new Spanish and locally-produced automatics with a will. The weapons soon became considerable symbols of personal importance, and war lords often equipped their personal bodyguards with the guns in an effort to ensure that the men commanded respect wherever they went. The violent barrel climb was easily overcome by the Chinese: they simply turned the weapons on their side to produce a wide horizontal fan of fire.

New model

Mauser was alarmed by these inroads into its market and soon (1930) produced its own model to meet the situation. The company altered the basic C/96 mechanism slightly to produce the Model 712, almost always known as the 'Schnellfeuer'. This was a more sophisticated firearm than many of the foreign models, with an elongated magazine holding up to 20 rounds and a much superior standard of manufacture; most were produced with fittings for shoulder stocks. This model became just as much a success as many of the earlier models, despite its apparent lack of combat value. It certainly demanded respect for its carrier, and was soon found to be a formidable assassination weapon: King Alexander II of Yugoslavia was killed by one in 1934.

The German military were not so impressed, but nevertheless some were procured for the German armed forces. A few went to the Luftwaffe, more to the Waffen-SS and others to various Hitler Youth units. The German navy also received a number from a batch ordered by the Chinese but not delivered. In German use the Schnellfeuers were not widely used in combat but were generally retained for Waffen-SS activities behind the lines, largely against resistance fighters and partisans.

The C/96 and the Schnellfeur went out of production before the end of World War II. Both were too expensive to produce in large quantities, and other weapons had higher priorities. But the C/96 story did not end there. The Chinese still maintained the production of their various copies and continued to use them all through the campaigns that led to the eventual communist victories of 1948-9. Even then the C/96 was still retained by some, who used it more as a badge of rank rather than a combat weapon.

Mauser C/96 `Broomhandle'

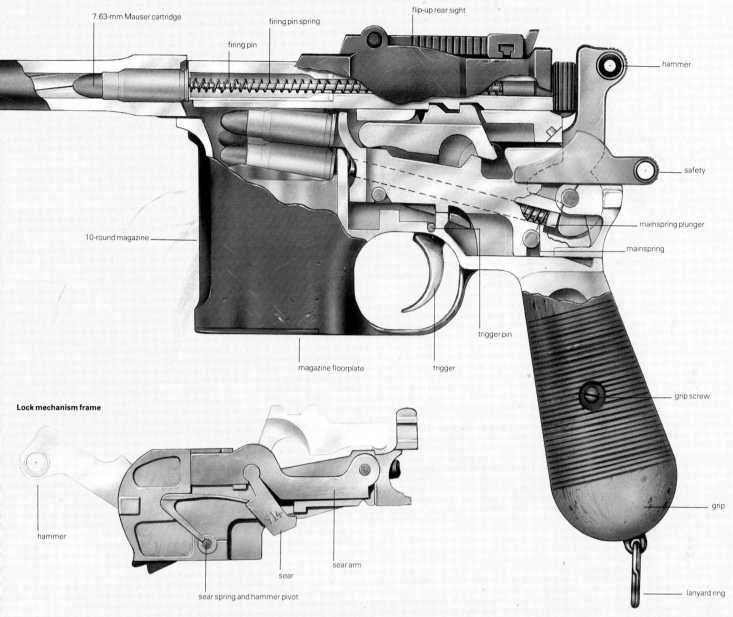

7.63-mm Mauser cartridge

firing pin

firing pin spring

flip-up rear sight

hammer

safety

mainspring plunger

mainspring

10-round magazine

trigger pin

magazine floorplate

trigger

grip screw

grip

Lock mechanism frame

hammer

sear spring and hammer pivot

sear

sear arm

lanyard ring

Even now the C/96 lives on. The Chinese still produce a version known as the Type 80. This bears no immediate resemblance to the old C/96, but the seeds are still there. The Type 80 fires a 7.62-mm (0.3-in) pistol round from a 10- or 20-round magazine in front of the trigger guard. The slide appears to be more of a simple blowback type than the complex Mauser mechanism, but without actually examining an example one cannot be sure. The pistol fires semi- or fully-automatic, and there is even a form of stock, no longer the old holster/stock but a thin telescopic device that clips onto the butt. The Type 80 even has a bayonet.

So the Mauser C/96 survives, far from its land of origin but still liable to be used in any action that comes its way. Exactly where that might be is difficult to say for the Chinese are offering the Type 80 for sale to anyone who will buy.

The Chinese are today offering for export the Type 80 machine pistol, which is a version of the Mauser C/96 modified for fully automatic fire. It evolved from the Chinese copies of the C/96 produced in the 1920s, when it was a favourite weapon with Chinese warlords.

Lebel revolver

The first French military revolvers were the **Modèle 1873** and **Modèle 1874**. When they were first issued they fired an 11-mm (0.433-in) cartridge that used black powder, although after 1890 a more modern propellant was substituted and some were even converted to fire the new 8-mm (0.315-in) cartridge. The only visual differences between the mles 1873 and 1874 was that the mle 1874 had cylinder flutes while the mle 1873 did not.

These two revolvers with their fixed frames and gate-loaded cylinders were still in use during World War I (indeed, many survived until World War II), but were largely replaced by a more modern design known officially as the **Pistol Revolveur Modele 1892** or the **Modèle d'Ordnance**. To most soldiers it was simply the **Lebel**. The Lebel had evolved via an interim design that fired a new 8-mm cartridge, but this interim model was not considered satisfactory and was redesigned to the mle 1892 standard by the design staff of the Saint Etienne arsenal. The Lebel was the first European revolver to incorporate a swing-out cylinder that considerably assisted rapid reloading: the cylinder swung out to the right and spent cases were ejected using a central hand-operated rod that was normally situated under the barrel.

The Lebel fired a special 8-mm cartridge using a double-action trigger mechanism. The action was very robust and heavy, which was good enough for short-range work but not forgiving enough for target-range accuracy. To clean and repair the action the Lebel had what must be one of the best mechanism access systems of any revolver. A plate at the lower left-hand side of the frame could be hinged open in a forward direction to expose the entire trigger and cylinder operating systems. Changing or cleaning any part was then very simple.

The main drawback to the Lebel when used in close-quarter action was the cartridge. It was seriously underpowered and even at short ranges inflicted wounds that only rarely knocked down an enemy. Unless a bullet found a vital spot an enemy could still continue to function – after a fashion. This drawback did not detract from the in-service popularity of the Lebel during World War I, for many front-line soldiers valued its reliability under adverse conditions more than its hitting power.

Being the first of its kind in Europe the Lebel was copied in both Spain and Belgium.

Specification
Modèle 1892
Calibre: 8 mm (0.315 in)
Weight: 0.792 kg (1.75 lb)
Lengths: overall 235 mm (9.25 in); barrel 118.5 mm (4.665 in)
Muzzle velocity: 225 m (738 ft) per second
Cylinder capacity: 6 rounds

Left: Their catastrophic losses in 1870 notwithstanding, the French cuirassier regiments went to war in 1914 in virtually Napoleonic uniforms, the only difference being that the glittering breastplate and helmet were covered and they carried modern pistols.

Below: The Lebel was the first European revolver to sport a swing-out cylinder for rapid re-loading. Inconveniently, it swung out to the right.

Above: A French officer delivers the coup de grâce to a German prisoner of war, executed by firing squad for fatally knifing one of the guards. This was perhaps the only situation in which the lack of stopping-power of the French 8-mm round was not a problem.

Pistols of World War II

Pistols are very close to the heart of fighting soldiers, and in World War II one of the most prized trophies on the Allied side was a captured German or Italian pistol. Yet as a weapon of war the hand gun seems of very little value, so what is the explanation for the retention of the sidearm in the armies of the 20th century?

December 1944, and the Battle of the Bulge is at its height. SS men pose in front of a captured American armoured car, captured Camels hanging from their lips. The pistol is a Browning, made in Belgium for the occupying Germans. The same pistol design was manufactured in Canada for the Allies!

The pistol, be it a revolver or an automatic, has long had an attraction for the soldier. Quite apart from the intrinsic attraction of the weapon, it is one that is very often a highly personal possession and one in which he usually takes great pride, for after even a very short time in service the soldier learns to appreciate its value to his well-being and chances of survival, especially when he is carrying out an operational role where no other weapon is available.

This attraction is difficult for the layman to appreciate, for even limited firing of any service pistol will reveal that it is inaccurate, difficult to use effectively and possesses only a very limited range. It is somewhat tricky to reconcile these two completely accurate conclusions, but the plain fact is that the pistol was used on a scale during World War II that overshadowed its employment in any previous conflict. On all fronts demands for pistols, more pistols and still more pistols were made throughout the conflict, and as a result the range of models and types was immense, those mentioned here being only a general indication of some of the more important types.

Despite the many advances in pistol design and development made in this century, it should be noted that the revolver was still in use between 1939 and 1945; and this remains true to this day, for the automatic pistol has not been able fully to oust the strong and reliable revolver. But the automatic pistol was in widespread use all the same, employing a large number of operating systems and an equally diverse range of calibres, despite the fact that the 9-mm Parabellum cartridge had emerged as the clear all-round leader. And quite apart from other factors, the study of the pistol is rewarding for its revelation of the great degree of ingenuity that designers have been able to bring to pistol design. World War II brought with it innovations and oddities, but what may be regarded as antiques were still in the field. Some of these will be found here, but the reader is asked to use these entries only as a general guide.

The pistol in its classic role as the weapon carried by a leader: in this case an officer in command of an infantry unit during one of the Alamein battles of 1942. The pistol is an Enfield No. 2 Mk 1, the 'standard' British and Commonwealth service pistol of World War II, with safety lanyard.

Enfield No. 2 Mk 1 and Webley Mk 4

UK

During World War I the standard British service revolver was one variant or other of the Webley 0.455-in (11.56-mm) pistol. These were very effective pistols, but their weight and bulk made them very difficult to handle correctly without a great deal of training and constant practice, two commodities that were in short supply at the time. After 1919 the British army decided that a smaller pistol firing a heavy 0.38-in (9.65-mm) bullet would be just as effective as the larger-calibre weapon but would be easier to handle and would require less training. So Webley and Scott, which up to that time had been pistol manufacturers of a virtually official status for the British armed forces, took its 0.455-in (11.56-mm) revolver, scaled it down and offered the result to the military.

To the chagrin of Webley and Scott, the military simply took the design, made a few minor alterations and then placed the result in production as an 'official' government design to be produced at the Royal Small Arms Factory at Enfield Lock in Middlesex. This procedure took time, for Webley and Scott offered its design in 1923 and Enfield Lock took over the design in 1926. Webley and Scott was somewhat nonplussed at the course of events but proceeded to make its 0.38-in (9.65-mm) revolver, known as the **Webley Mk 4**, all over the world with limited success.

The Enfield Lock product became the **Pistol, Revolver, No. 2 Mk 1** and was duly issued for service. Once in service it proved sound and effective enough, but mechanical progress meant that large numbers of these pistols were issued to tank crews and other mechanized personnel, who made the unfortunate discovery that the long hammer spur had a tendency to catch onto the many internal fittings of tanks and other vehicles with what could be nasty results. This led to a redesign in which the Enfield pistol had the hammer spur removed altogether and the trigger mechanism lightened to enable the weapon to be fired double-action only. This revolver became the **No. 2 Mk 1***, and existing Mk 1s were modified to the new standard. The double action made the pistol very difficult to use accurately at all except minimal range, but that did not seem to matter too much at the time.

Webley and Scott re-entered the scene during World War II, when supplies of the Enfield pistols were too slow to meet the ever-expanding demand. Thus the Webley Mk 4 was ordered to eke out supplies, and Webley and Scott went on to supply thousands of its design to the British army after all. Unfortunately, although the two pistols were virtually identical in appearance there were enough minor differences between them to prevent interchangeability of parts.

Both pistols saw extensive use between 1939 and 1945, and although the Enfield revolvers (there was a **No. 2**

The Webley Mk 4 revolver was used as the basis for the Enfield No. 2 Mk 1 but was passed over in favour of the government-sponsored development. In time the call for more revolvers was so great that the Mk 4 was placed in production for the British armed forces and used alongside the Enfield pistols.

Mk 1** which embodied wartime production expedients) were the official standard pistols, the Webley Mk 4 was just as widely used among British and Commonwealth armed forces. Both remained in service until the 1960s and both are still to be encountered as service pistols in various parts of the world.

Specification
Revolver No. 2 Mk 1*
Cartridge: 0.380 SAA ball (9.65 mm)
Length overall: 260 mm (10.25 in)
Length of barrel: 127 mm (5 in)
Weight: 0.767 (1.7 lb)
Muzzle velocity: 183 m (600 ft) per second
Chamber capacity: 6 rounds

Specification
Webley Mk 4
Cartridge: 0.380 SAA ball (9.65 mm)
Length overall: 267 mm (10.5 in)
Length of barrel: 127 mm (5 in)
Weight: 0.767 (1.7 lb)
Muzzle velocity: 183 m (600 ft) per second
Chamber capacity: 6 rounds

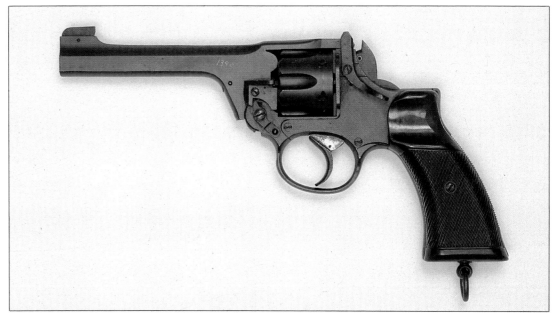

Above: The Enfield No. 2 Mk 1* revolver was the most widely used of all the British and Commonwealth armed forces. Firing a 0.38-in (9.65-mm) ball cartridge, it was an efficient combat pistol but lacked any finesse or frills; yet it was able to withstand the many knocks of service life.

Below: An airborne soldier stands guard on a house in Holland during Operation 'Market Garden'. The pistol is an Enfield No. 2 Mk 1* with the hammer removed to prevent snagging on clothing or within the close confines of vehicles or aircraft. They were issued to airborne soldiers such as glider pilots.

Tokarev TT-33

The first Tokarev automatic pistol to see extensive service was the **TT-30**, but not many of these pistols had been produced before a modified design known as the **TT-33** was introduced in 1933. This pistol was then adopted as the standard pistol of the Red Army to replace the Nagant revolvers that had served so well for many years. In the event the TT-33 never did replace the Nagant entirely until well after 1945, mainly because the revolver proved so reliable and sturdy under the rough active service conditions of the various fronts.

The TT-33 was basically a Soviet version of the Colt-Browning pistols, and used the swinging-link system of operation employed on the American M1911. However, the ever practical Soviet designers made several slight alterations that made the mechanism easier to produce and easier to maintain under field conditions, and production even went to the length of machining the vulnerable magazine feed lips into the main receiver to prevent damage and subsequent misfeeds. The result was a practical and sturdy weapon that was well able to absorb a surprising amount of hard use.

By 1945 the TT-33 had virtually replaced the Nagant revolver in service and as Soviet influence spread over Europe and elsewhere so did TT-33 production. Thus the TT-33 may be found in a variety of basically similar forms, one of which is the Chinese **Type 51**. The Poles also produced the TT-33 for their own use and for export to East Germany and to Czechoslovakia. The Yugoslavs still have the TT-33 in production and are still actively marketing the design as the **M65**. North Korea has its own variant in the form of the **M68**. The most drastic producer of the TT-33 is Hungary, which rejigged the design in several respects and recalibred it for the 9-mm Parabellum cartridge. The result was known as the **Tikagypt** and was exported to Egypt, where it is still used by the local police forces.

The Tokarev TT-33 was a sturdy and hard-wearing pistol that was used throughout World War II, but it never entirely replaced the Nagant.

Above: The Soviet Tokarev TT-33 in action in a well-posed propaganda photograph dating from about 1944. The officer is leading a section of assault infantry and has his pistol on the end of the usual lanyard. Snipers on all sides came to recognize these 'pistol wavers' as prime targets.

The TT-33 is now no longer used by the Soviet armed forces, who use the Markarov automatic pistol, but the TT-33 will be around for a long while yet. Despite the introduction of the Makarov many second-line and militia units within the Warsaw Pact are still issued with the TT-33 and as the type's overall standard of design and construction was sound there seems to be no reason why they should be replaced for many years.

Right: A Red Army military policeman, for whom the Tokarev TT-33 would have been the primary weapon. Military policemen of all nations still carry the pistol as the nature of their duties often precludes the use of any type of larger weapon, and they have no actual combat role.

Specification
TT-33
Cartridge: 7.62 mm Type P (M30)
Length overall: 196 mm (7.68 in)
Length of barrel: 116 mm (4.57 in)
Weight: 0.830 kg (1.83 lb)
Muzzle velocity: 420 m (1,380 ft) per second
Magazine: 8-round box

Pistole P 08 (I____r)

The pistol that is now generally, but misleadingly, known as the **Luger** had its design origins in a pistol design first produced in 1893 by one Hugo Borchardt. A George Luger further developed this design and produced the weapon that bears his name to this day. The first Lugers were manufactured in 7.65-mm (0.301-in) calibre and were adopted by the Swiss army in 1900. Thereafter the basic design was adopted by many nations and the type is still to be encountered, for by now well over two million have been produced by various manufacturers and at least 35 main variants are known to exist, together with a host of sub-variants.

The **Pistole P 08** was one of the main variants. It was taken into German army service in 1908 (hence the 08) and remained the standard German service pistol until the Walther P 38 was introduced in 1938. The main calibre encountered on the P 08 was 9 mm, and the 9-mm (0.354-in) Parabellum cartridge was developed for this pistol. However, 7.65-mm (0.301-in) versions were made as well. The P 08 is and probably always will be one of the 'classic' pistols, for it has an appearance and aura all of its own. It handles well, is easy to 'point' and is usually very well made. It has to be well made for it relies on a rather complicated action using an upwards-hingeing toggle locking device that will not operate correctly if the associated machined grooves are out of tolerance. In fact it is arguable that this action is undesirable in a service pistol for as it operates it allows the ingress of dust and debris to clog the mechanism. In practice this was often not the case for the pistol proved to be remarkably robust. It was only replaced in service and production for the simple fact that it was too demanding in production resources, took too long to produce and required too many matched spare parts. It was late 1942 before the last 'German' examples came off the production lines and it was never replaced by the P 38 in German service. Since 1945 it has reappeared commercially from time to time and will no doubt continue to be manufactured for years to come.

The standard P 08 had a barrel 103 mm (4.055 in) long, and earlier variants such as the **P 17 Artillerie** model with a 203 mm (8 in) or longer barrel and a snail-shaped magazine holding 32 rounds were no longer service weapons between 1939 and 1945. Lugers were among the most prized of all World War I and II trophies, and many still survive as collector's pieces.

Above: The Pistole P 08, commonly known as the Luger, was one of the classic pistol designs of all time. It still has a definite aesthetic appeal in the slope of the butt and the general appearance, and is a pleasant pistol to fire. However, it was expensive to produce and was destined to be replaced.

Right: The P 08 in service with a section of house-clearing infantry during the early stages of the advance into Russia during 1941. The soldier with the pistol is armed with Stielgranate 35 grenades and is festooned with ammunition belts for the section MG 34 machine-gun.

The type continues to attract the eye and attention of all pistol buffs throughout the world, and the P 08 was and still is a classic.

Specification
Pistole P 08
Cartridge: 9 mm Parabellum
Length overall: 222 mm (8.75 in)
Length of barrel: 103 mm (4.055 in)
Weight: 0.877 kg (1.92 lb)
Muzzle velocity: 381 m (1,250 ft) per second
Magazine: 8-round box

Below: A Stug 111 with a short 75-mm (2.95-in) gun supports advancing infantry during an attack on the Voronez front during January 1943. Although the pistol being carried by the soldier on the right is blurred, it appears to be a P 08.

What use is a pistol in combat?

The pistol has been a factor in warfare almost from the invention of the firearm. In the early days, its use was confined to officers and cavalrymen, and with longer ranges between opponents becoming the norm it seemed that the inherent short range of the weapon meant that the use of the pistol in battle was coming to an end. Paradoxically, however, more and more soldiers were turning to the pistol as a personal weapon. Clearly it is of some use after all.

An easy answer to the often-posed question 'What use is a pistol in combat?' is 'not much.' The pistol, be it a revolver or automatic, has only a very limited range and at best (and in the hands of a trained marksman) it has very little other than nuisance value beyond a range of 40-50 m (45-55 yards). It is also a weapon that is very prone to be pointed in the wrong direction – it is relatively easy to keep a long weapon such as a rifle pointed towards an enemy, but all too easy to point a pistol at a friend in the heat of the moment. For such a small weapon, the pistol is quite demanding of industrial potential and skills, and even a simple example is not cheap when compared with, say, a much more lethal weapon such as a hand grenade. Another factor in combat is that the average projectile fired from a pistol has only a limited lethality and, although it may have a terrific impact at short ranges, it is not as lethal as a high-velocity projectile.

For all that, the handgun is still a much favoured combat weapon and even today soldiers venture into battle wearing pistols about their persons. There are two main reasons for this, and they can be oversimplified by being labelled 'convenience' and 'morale'.

The convenience factor is brought about by the simple fact that for many personnel on active service there is no alternative. There are numerous combat roles carried out by all manner of soldiers, airmen and sailors where it is quite simply impractical to carry any form of weapon larger than a pistol. Categories that come to mind without difficulty include tank crews, aircrew, frogmen and men carrying heavy equipment such as radio sets. They have no hands free to carry a weapon and very little space about the person or place of operations to stow anything larger than a pistol. On larger vehicles such as tanks or trucks it is possible to carry a sub-machine gun or carbine but on smaller vehicles this is not possible. Even so, at some stage or other of combat operations it may be necessary to leave the sheltering confines of the vehicle, and some sort of weapon is still required for self-defence or survival. The latter factor is particularly important for aircrew who may be forced down behind enemy lines. Under such circumstances there is no alternative to the pistol.

The morale factor may be subdivided into two aspects. One is that wearing or flourishing a pistol gives an air of authority. The other aspect relates to morale alone: the carrying of a weapon such as a pistol imparts a measure of self-confidence to the carrier. The air of authority aspect is easily understood, for anyone such as a military or other policeman pointing or holding a pistol is immediately regarded by most persons as someone in authority who should be obeyed. Thus a pistol becomes an important symbol when dealing with an unarmed or demoralized enemy, such as prisoners of war. The self-confidence factor is less easily explained but is one that is understood by anyone who is operating or travelling in an unknown or hostile environment. This fact was well understood by the German forces who had to live and work in the occupied territories during World War II; every servicemen had to be armed for virtually his entire waking existence. Pistols were an easy way to interpret armed status, and consequently the servicemen had the secure knowledge that some form of weapon was always to hand should it become necessary. This self-confidence factor may perhaps be overstated but it is a factor that is well known to anyone who has ever had to operate in an unknown territory or situation, and in modern war combat is very often not confined to an easily defined front line. Soldiers in rear areas are just as likely to come under attack from partisans or SAS-type units as their front-line counterparts are to come under attack from a known enemy.

There is one further reason why the pistol is still carried in combat, and that is perhaps an offshoot of the two factors already described. This is the carrying of pistols as a symbol of status, and perhaps this is the reason why so many staff officers far from the battle area strap pistols to themselves. Even so, many pistols carried by officers of staff rank are small-calibre weapons of very limited combat value and a far cry from the relatively large-calibre pistols carried by combat personnel.

There is one factor that has further limited the use of the pistol in combat, and that is that the factors listed above are as recognizable to an enemy as they are to the user. This was particularly true during World War I, when marksmen in the front-line trenches learned that attacking soldiers carrying pistols were more likely to be officers or senior NCOs and thus unit leaders. Picking them off first tended to reduce the combat efficiency of the unit concerned; it was not long before even the most hidebound officers learned to carry rifles that rendered them indistinguishable from their men. Their trouble was that once in the trench system the rifle was too cumbersome for the dangerous task of trench clearing. Close-quarter combat tasks such as trench clearing are to this day one aspect of combat where the pistol still has an important role to play. House clearing in urban warfare is a very similar situation. Here the short and handy barrel of a pistol can be rapidly turned in any direction and the small heavy bullets need little aiming at short ranges. If they strike a target at short range they are usually enough to disable, if not kill. It is true that a sub-machine gun would be better under such circumstances, but a sub-machine gun is not always available when needed, and if a soldier carries a pistol he has at least a weapon.

There is little room inside the confines of a tank for the crew to carry any personal weapon larger than a pistol, so when the time came to dismount following the disabling of a vehicle it was a pistol or nothing. Here a Panzer Leutnant fires his P 38 against enemy tank-killing infantry squads as he bails out.

Walther PP and PPK

The **Walther PP** was first produced in 1929 and was marketed as a police weapon (PP standing for Polizei Pistole), and during the 1930s it was adopted by uniformed police forces throughout Europe and elsewhere. It was a light and handy design with few frills and a clean outline but was intended for holster carriage. Plain clothes police were catered for by another model, the **Walter PPK** (K standing for *kurz*, or short). This was basically the PP reduced in overall size to enable it to be carried conveniently in a pocket or under a jacket.

Although intended as civilian police weapons, both the PP and the PPK were adopted as military police weapons and after 1939 both were kept in production for service use. Each model was widely used by the Luftwaffe, and was often carried by the many German police organizations. Both were also widely used by staff officers as personal weapons. Both types could also be encountered in a range of calibres, the two main calibres being 9 mm short and 7.65 mm, but versions were produced in 5.56 mm (0.22 LR) and 6.35 mm. All these variants operated on a straightforward blowback principle, and more than adequate safety arrangements were incorporated. One of these safeties was later widely copied, and involved placing a block in the way of the firing pin when it moved forward, this block only being removed when the trigger was given a definite pull. Another innovation was the provision of a signal pin above the hammer which protruded when a round was

actually in the chamber to provide a positive 'loaded' indication when necessary. This feature was omitted from wartime production, in which the general standard of finish was lower. Production resumed soon after 1945 in such countries as France and Turkey. Hungary also adopted the type for a while but production is now once more by the Walther concern at Ulm. Production is still mainly for police duties but purely commercial sales are common to pistol shooters who appreciate the many fine points of the basic design.

One small item of interest regarding the PP centres on the fact that it is now a little-known and rarely seen pistol used by the British armed forces as the

XL47E1. The weapon is used for undercover operations where civilian clothing has to be worn and it is often issued to soldiers of the Ulster Defence Regiment for personal protection when off duty.

Specification
Walther PP
Cartridge: 9 mm short (0.38 ACP), 7.65 mm (0.32 ACP), 6.35 mm (0.25 ACP), 0.22 LR
Length overall: 173 mm (6.8 in)
Length of barrel: 99 mm (3.9 in)
Weight: 0.682 kg (1.5 lb)
Muzzle velocity: 290 m (950 ft) per second
Magazine: 8-round box

The Walther PP pistol was, and still is, one of the best small pistol designs ever produced. In German service it was used by various police organizations and by Luftwaffe aircrew.

Specification
Walther PPK
Cartridge: 9 mm short (0.38 ACP), 7.65 mm (0.32 ACP), 6.35 mm (0.25 ACP), 0.22 LR
Length overall: 155 mm (6.1 in)
Length of barrel: 86 mm (3.39 in)
Weight: 0.568 kg (1.25 lb)
Muzzle velocity: 280 m (920 ft) per second
Magazine: 7-round box

Walther P 38

The **Walther P 38** was developed primarily to replace the P 08, which was an excellent weapon but expensive to produce. After the National Socialists came to power in Germany in 1933 they decided upon a deliberate programme of military expansion into which the old P 08 could not fit. What was wanted was a pistol that could be quickly and easily produced but one that embodied all the many and various design features such as a hand-cocked trigger and improved safeties that were then becoming more common. Walther eventually received the contract for this new pistol in 1938, but only after a long programme of development.

Walther Waffenfabrik produced its first original automatic pistol design back in 1908 and there followed a string of designs that culminated in the PP of 1929. The PP had many novel features but it was intended to be a police weapon and not a service pistol. Walther consequently developed a new weapon known as the **Armee Pistole** (or **AP**) which did not have the protruding hammer of the PP but was calibred for the 9-mm (0.354-in) Parabellum cartridge. From this came the **Heeres Pistole** (or **HP**) which had the overall appearance of the pistol that would become the P 38. But the German Army requested some small changes to facilitate rapid production. Walther obliged and the P 38 was taken into German service use, the HP being kept in production in its original form for commercial sales. In the event Walther was never able to meet de-

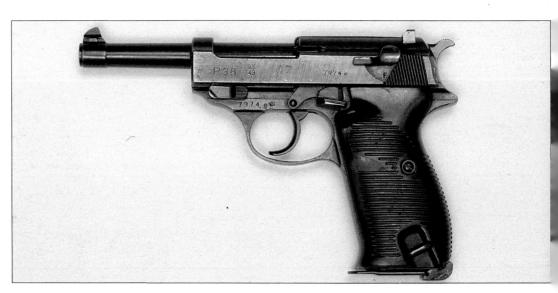

mand for the P 38 and the bulk of the HP production also went to the German armed forces.

The P 38 was (and still is) an excellent service pistol which was robust, accurate and hard wearing. Walther production versions, which were later supplemented by P 38s produced by Mauser and Spreewerke, were always very well finished with shiny black plastic grips and an overall matt black plating. The weapon could be stripped easily and was well equipped with safety devices, including the hammer safety carried over from the PP along

with the 'chamber loaded' indicator pin. It was a well-liked pistol and became a war trophy only slightly less prized than the Luger P 08.

In 1957 the P 38 was put back into production for the Bundeswehr, this time as the **Pistole 1** (or **P1**) with a dural slide in place of the original steel component. It is still in production and has been adopted by many nations.

Specification
Walter P 38
Cartridge: 9 mm Parabellum

Even today one of the best service pistols available, the Walther P 38 was developed to replace the P 08 Luger but by 1945 had only supplemented it. It had many advanced features including a double-action trigger mechanism.

Length overall: 219 mm (8.58 in)
Length of barrel: 124 mm (4.88 in)
Weight: 0.960 kg (2.12 lb)
Muzzle velocity: 350 m (1,150 ft) per second
Magazine: 8-round box

The Walther P 38 in Action

Arising out of a Wehrmacht requirement for a modern replacement for the Parabellum system P 08 (the well-known Luger), the Walther P 38 first saw service in 1938. In modified form, the pistol is still in production for West German service nearly 50 years later.

When the first Walther P 38s were issued to their recipients during late 1938 it was something of a change from the elderly but well-liked P 08, Although one of the main reasons the P 38 had been accepted for service was the fact that it had been designed for ease of production, it was still full of good modern features that immediately attracted the attention of the troops who were trained to fire the pistol. One of the main attractions was the combination of an external hammer and the various safety mechanisms. The use of the external hammer meant that the weapon could be loaded, the safety applied and the hammer could then be lowered onto a block that prevented the firing pin striking the cartridge housed in the chamber. The only way to remove the block was by a deliberate pull on the trigger. Thus a fully loaded pistol could be carried in complete safety and when required the weapon was ready for use without the need to fumble with receiver slides or awkward safety catches. The 'loaded' indicator above the hammer was also much appreciated, for if a round was chambered the user could rapidly confirm the fact by feeling for the protruding pin above the hammer. This meant that the pistol did not have to be unloaded to check if the weapon was empty. Unfortunately this feature was regarded as something of a luxury, and was later removed when wartime production had to be increased to meet an ever-expanding demand for P 38s.

The P 38 was issued to the troops with its own leather holster for fixing to the standard service-issue leather belt. The holster carried not only the pistol but a spare magazine and a cleaning rod.

Service introduction

The first pistols were issued mainly to the new Panzer arm. In 1938 these men were the apple of Hitler's eye and he was expecting much from them. They had already seen a limited form of action in the take-overs of Austria and the Sudetenland, but they were not to be fully blooded until the September of 1939 when the Germans demolished the Polish forces in a matter of weeks. By that time the P 38 had been issued to other arms of the German forces. The main problem then was that there were quite simply insufficient numbers coming off the production lines. In the short term the production lines for the esssentially similar Walther HP was taken over for German military use. The HP had been the final development model for the P 38, but the P 38 had some of the finer points of the HP left off for ease of produc-

tion. (Walther had plans to market the HP commercially and in fact managed to sell a batch of 2,000 to Sweden in 1939. These pistols were for long used by the Swedish army as the P/39.) But this short-term measure was somewhat overtaken by events. Instead of rounding off, the demands for more pistols and yet more pistols increased. The HP production line continued to operate alongside the P 38 line until well into 1944. By then new production lines had been set up by Mauser at Obendorf and the Spreewerke at Grottau. Even this was not enough, and component production lines were set up in the sequestered weapon factory at Brno in Czechoslovakia and the Fabrique Nationale plant at Liège in Belgium.

Production rises

As the production quantities expanded the general standard of manufacture declined when production short-cuts were introduced to speed up output. Items such as the loaded chamber indicator were left off, and markings were limited to the coded manufacturer's markings only (480 and ac were used for Walther production, byf and svw for Mauser output, and cyq for the Spreewerke examples). But even with these limitations the P 38 was still widely regarded as an excellent service pistol to the extent that the usual political infighting endemic within the Nazi war machine led to the Waffen SS attempting to take over the entire

Above: The P 38 was introduced into service to replace the P 08 which, although an excellent pistol to fire and 'point' (as seen here in this photograph of a Luftwaffe officer on the firing range), was too expensive and slow to produce, whereas the P 38 could be manufactured quickly using modern production techniques.

The Luftwaffe officer shown visiting the scene of the crash of his 80th victim (a Short Stirling) displays a notable difference between Allied and German practice in the wearing of pistols. German officers wore their weapons attached to the left of their service belts, drawing the pistol across the body. Allied service dress had pistols worn on the right, with the butt to the rear.

The Walther P 38 in Action

barrel

Left: May 1945, and soldiers of the Red Army celebrate the raising of the Red Flag over the Reichstag using an assortment of weapons including (from left) a PPS 1943 sub-machine gun, a P 38, a Mauser C/96 pistol and some PPSh sub-machine guns. Use of the captured pistols by Red Army Units was unusual.

Above: An Afrika Korps military policeman of the Feldgendarmerie, armed with a P 38 pistol, wears the distinctive gorgette that identified the wearer as a policeman.

Right: A Walther P 38 together with its leather holster, which carried a spare magazine and sometimes a cleaning rod. The holsters were carried on the belt with the butt forward, in contrast to the usual Allied practice.

production for its own requirements. This it was never able to do, but at times whole batches earmarked for the army or navy were diverted to Waffen SS units.

The P 38 was never able to replace the P 08 in service before the war ended: the production lines quite simply could not meet the constant demands made for pistols. One reason for this state of affairs was that troops in all the occupied territories had to be armed whenever they were not actually on a military base or establishment. As the bulk of the troops involved had to travel to and from their billets or had to carry out various missions away from the security of a base they had to carry some form of weapon. In many cases this meant pistols, but in quantities the war planners had been unable to foresee. The only way out of this was to issue stockpiles of captured pistols or to take into use numbers of requisitioned civilian pistols. The result was a quartermaster's nightmare. Everyone wanted a P 38 or a P 08 but had to make do with what they got, and they got some very odd pistols. Troops found themselves carrying ancient ex-Russian Nagant revolvers, shiny little Mauser pocket pistols, imported Spanish automatics of dubious reliability and ancient French and Belgian revolvers with obsolete calibres.

Valued by the troops

Those troops that did get P 38s valued them highly. In action they proved to be very reliable, handy to hold and point, and when called upon to be accurate they were accurate. Two reasons for this accuracy were that the P 38 tended to sit well in the hand, and that the weight of the weapon was such that when aimed the pistol remained steady just tha much more than a lighter pistol would have done. The trigger action was crisp and clean so there was no undue drag between trigger finger pressure and the actual shot. The actio proved to be proof against the ingress of dus and dirt but when used on the Eastern Fron one problem that was not confined to the P 38 came to light. This was partially the result of the thorough German maintenance training giver to all recruits. They were taught to strip and clean their personal weapons every day. Be fore reassembly the moving parts were provided with a film of gun oil. During the winte months, however, temperatures were often so low that the oil froze solid, even when the pisto was inside a holster. The only solution was to leave the gun clean but free of oil, and to the credit of its manufacturers the P 38 continued to operate even in this condition.

Still in production

In 1945 numerous P 38s became wa trophies, and large numbers were often take over by the victorious powers for their own use Thus French army and Foreign Legion units i action in Indo-China often found themselve issued with P 38s, but this state of affairs did no last beyond the mid-1950s. By then the P 38 wa once more being prepared for production, anc in 1957 it was once more in production unde Walther auspices, but this time slightly up dated by the adoption of a dural receiver slid and the new designation Pistole 1 or P 1. Thi pistol is now the standard service pistol of th new Bundesheer, the West German army, an the type has even been exported for use b other armies such as Chile.

The P 38 and P 1 are both excellent servic pistols and have been rated by many autho ities as the best service pistol designs to hav been produced in recent years, and certain during the years of World War II. Some recer innovations on the pistol scene may well hav dented that reputation somewhat, but the P 3 and the P 1 are both firm military favourites

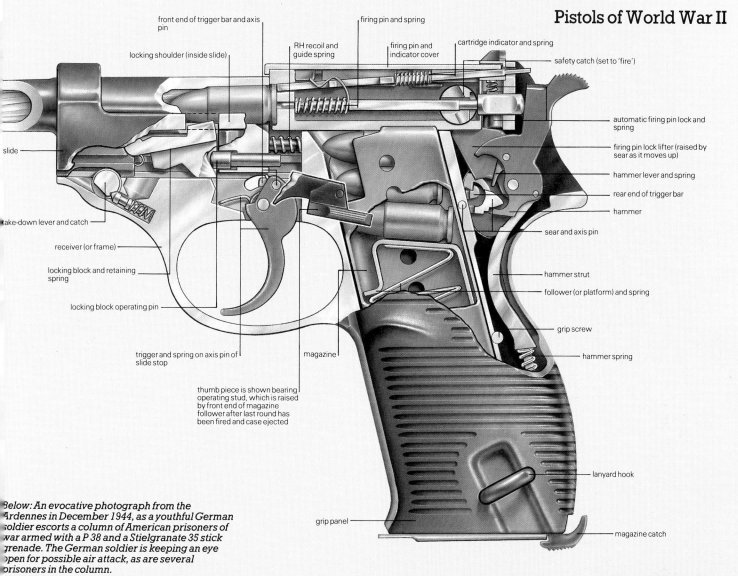

front end of trigger bar and axis pin

locking shoulder (inside slide)

RH recoil and guide spring

firing pin and spring

firing pin and indicator cover

cartridge indicator and spring

safety catch (set to 'fire')

automatic firing pin lock and spring

firing pin lock lifter (raised by sear as it moves up)

hammer lever and spring

rear end of trigger bar

hammer

sear and axis pin

hammer strut

follower (or platform) and spring

grip screw

hammer spring

lanyard hook

magazine catch

slide

take-down lever and catch

receiver (or frame)

locking block and retaining spring

locking block operating pin

trigger and spring on axis pin of slide stop

magazine

thumb piece is shown bearing operating stud, which is raised by front end of magazine follower after last round has been fired and case ejected

grip panel

Below: An evocative photograph from the Ardennes in December 1944, as a youthful German soldier escorts a column of American prisoners of war armed with a P 38 and a Stielgranate 35 stick grenade. The German soldier is keeping an eye open for possible air attack, as are several prisoners in the column.

Pistole Automatique Browning modèle 1910

The **Pistole Automatique Browning modèle 1910** is something of an oddity among pistol designs, for although it has remained in production virtually nonstop since 1910, it has never been officially adopted as a service weapon. Despite this it has been used widely by many armed forces at one time or another and the basic design has been widely copied and/or plagiarized by other designers.

As the name implies, this automatic pistol was yet another product of the fertile mind of John Moses Browning. Nearly all the model 1910s have been produced at the Fabrique Nationale d'Armes de Guerre (commonly known simply as FN) at Liège in Belgium. The type is still in production in Belgium for commercial sales. The reason why this particular pistol should have achieved such longevity is now not easy to determine, but the overall design is clean enough, with the forward part of the receiver slide having a tubular appearance. This results from the fact that the recoil spring is wrapped around the barrel itself instead of being situated under or over the barrel as in most other designs. This spring is held in place by a bayonet lug around the muzzle, providing the model 1910 with another recognition point. Grip and applied safeties are provided.

The model 1910 may be encountered in one of two calibres, either 7.65 mm or 9 mm short. Externally the

two variants are identical, and each uses a detachable seven-round box magazine. As with all other FN products the standard of manufacture and finish is excellent but copies made in such places as Spain lack this finish. The excellent finish was continued with one of the few large-scale production runs for the model 1910. This occurred after 1940 when the German forces occupying Belgium required large numbers of pistols. The model 1910 was kept in production to meet this demand, the bulk of the output

being issued to Luftwaffe aircrew who knew the type as the **Pistole P 621(b)**. Before that the model 1910 had been issued in small numbers to the Belgian armed forces, and many other nations obtained the type for small-scale use for their own military or police service. The numbers of model 1910s produced must by now be running into the hundreds of thousands.

Specification
Browning modèle 1910
Cartridge: 7.64 mm (0.32 ACP) or 9 mm

The Browning modèle 1910 was never officially adopted as a service pistol, but was nonetheless widely used and many of its design features were later incorporated in other pistol designs.

short (0.380 ACP)
Length overall: 152 mm (6 in)
Length of barrel: 89 mm (3.5 in)
Weight: 0.562 kg (1.24 lb)
Muzzle velocity: 299 m (980 ft) per second
Magazine: 7-round box

Pistole Automatique Browning, modèle à Grande Puissance (Browning HP)

The **Browning HP** may be regarded as one of the most successful pistol designs ever produced. Not only is it still in widespread service, in numbers that must surely exceed those of all other types combined, but it has also been produced at many locations in many countries. It was one of the last weapon designs produced by John Browning before he died in 1925, but it was not until 1935 that the HP was placed in production by FN at Liège. From this derives the name which is generally given as the HP (High Power) or **Pistole Automatique Browning GP 35** (Grand Puissance modèle 1935). Numerous versions may be encountered, but they all fire the standard 9-mm Parabellum cartridge. Versions exist with box fixed and adjustable rear sights, and some models were produced with a lug on the butt to enable a stock (usually the wooden holster) to be fitted, allowing the pistol to be fired as a form of carbine. Other versions exist with light alloy receiver slides to reduce weight.

One factor that is common to all the numerous Browning HP variants is strength and reliability. Another desirable feature that has often proved invaluable is the large-capacity box magazine in the butt, which can hold a useful 13 rounds. Despite this width the grip is not too much of a handful, although training and general familiarization are necessary to enable a firer to get the best out of the weapon. The weapon uses a recoil-operated mechanism powered by the blowback forces produced on firing and has an external hammer. In many ways the action can be regarded as the same as

that on the Colt M1911 (also a Browning design), but it was adapted to suit production and to take advantage of the experience gained in the design.

Within a few years of the start of production the Browning HP had been adopted as the service pistol of several nations including Belgium, Denmark, Lithuania and Romania. After 1940 production continued, but this time it was for the Germans who adopted the type as the standard pistol of the Waffen SS, although other arms of the German forces also used the weapon. To the Germans the Browning HP was known as the **Pistole P620(b)**. However, the Germans did not have the Browning

HP all to themselves, for a new production line was opened in Canada and from there the Browning HP was distributed to nearly all the Allied nations as the **Pistol, Browning, FN, 9-mm HP No. 1**, large numbers being sent to China to equip the nationalist forces. After 1945 the type was put back in production in Liège, and many nations now use the weapon as their standard pistol. Various commercial models have been developed, and the type has even been adapted to produce a target-shooting model. The British army still uses the Browning HP as the **Pistol, Automatic L9A1**.

The Browning GP 35 has been adopted by so many nations since its first appearance in 1935 that it must now be the most widely used of all pistols. It is remarkably robust, hard hitting and reliable in use.

Specification
Browning GP 35
Cartridge: 9-mm Parabellum
Length overall: 196 mm (7.75 in)
Length of barrel: 112 mm (4.41 in)
Weight: 1.01 kg (2.23 lb)
Muzzle velocity: 354 m (1,160 ft) per second
Magazine: 13-round box

USA
Liberator M1942

This very odd little pistol had its origins in the committee rooms of the US Army Joint Psychological Committee, who sold to the Office of Strategic Service the idea of a simple assassination weapon that could be used by anyone in occupied territory without the need for training or familiarization. The OSS took up the idea and the US Army Ordnance Department then set to and produced drawings. The Guide Lamp Division of the General Motors Corporation was given the task of producing the weapons, and the division took the credit for churning out no less than one million between June and August 1942.

The 11.43-mm (0.45-in) weapon was provided with the covername **Flare Pistol M1942**, but it was also known as the **Liberator** or the **OSS** pistol. It was a very simple, even crude device that could fire only a single shot. It was constructed almost entirely of metal stampings and the barrel was smoothbored. The action was just as simple as the rest of the design: a cocking piece was grasped and pulled to the rear; once back a turn locked it in place as a single M1911 automatic cartridge was loaded, and the cocking piece was then swung back for release as the trigger was pulled. To clear the spent cartridge the cocking piece was once more moved out of the way and the case was pushed out from the chamber by poking something suitable down the barrel from the muzzle.

Each pistol was packed into a clear plastic bag together with 10 rounds, and a set of instructions in comic strip form provided, without words, enough information for any person finding the package to use the pistol. There was space in the butt to carry five of the rounds provided but the pistol was virtually a one-shot weapon and had to be used at a minimal range to be effective. Exactly how effective it was is now difficult to say, for there seems to be no record of how these numerous pistols were ever employed or where they were distributed. It is known that some were parachuted into occupied Europe, but many more were used in the Far East and in China. The concept was certainly deemed good enough to be revived in 1964 when a much-modernized equivalent to the Liberator, known as the **'Deer Gun'**, was produced for possible use in Vietnam. In the event several thousands were made but were never issued, maybe because assassination weapons have a nasty tendency to be double-edged. Each Liberator pistol cost the American government just $2.40.

Specification
Liberator M1942
Cartridge: .45 ball M1911
Length overall: 140 mm (5.55 in)
Length of barrel: 102 mm (4 in)
Weight: 0.454 kg (1 lb)
Muzzle velocity: 336 m (1,100 ft) per second
Magazine: none, but space for five rounds in butt

The little Liberator M1942 was an assassination weapon pure and simple, and was produced as cheaply and easily as possible. The barrels were unrifled, there was no spent case ejector and the mechanism was crude to a degree. But they worked, and were used mainly in the Far East and in China.

USA
Colt M1911 and M1911A1

The **Colt M1911** vies with the Browning HP as being one of the most successful pistol designs ever produced, for it has been manufactured in millions and is in widespread service all over the world some 70 years after it was first accepted for service in 1911. The design had its origins well before then, however, for the weapon was based on a **Colt Browning Model 1900** design. This weapon was taken as the basis for a new service pistol required by the US Army to fire a new 11.43-mm (0.45-in) cartridge deemed necessary, as the then-standard calibre of 9.65 mm (0.38 in) was considered by many to be too light to stop a charging enemy. The result was a series of trials in 1907, and in 1911 the **Pistol, Automatic, Caliber .45, M1911** was accepted. Production was at first slow, but by 1917 was well enough under way to equip in part the rapid expansion of the US Army for its new role in France.

As the result of that battle experience it was decided to make some production changes to the basic design and from these came the **M1911A1**. The changes were not extensive, and were confined to such items as the grip safety configuration, the hammer spur outline and the mainspring housing. Overall the design and operation changed only little. The basic method of operation remained the same, and this mechanism is one of the strongest ever made. Whereas many contemporary pistol designs employed a receiver stop to arrest the backwards progress of the receiver slide the M1911 had a locking system that also produced a more positive stop. The barrel had lugs machined into its outer surface that fitted into corresponding lugs on the slide. When the pistol was fired the barrel and slide moved backwards a short distance with these lugs still engaged. At the end of this distance the barrel progress was arrested by a swinging link which swung round to pull the barrel lugs out of the receiver slide, which was then free to move farther and so eject the spent case and restart the loading cycle. This robust system, allied with a positive applied safety and a grip safety, make the M1911 and M1911A1 very safe weapons under service conditions. But the pistol is a bit of a handful to handle and fire correctly, and a good deal of training is required to use it to full effect.

The M1911 and M1911A1 have both been manufactured by numerous companies other than Colt Firearms and have been widely copied direct in many parts of the world, not always to very high levels of manufacture.

Specification
Colt M1911A1
Cartridge: .45 ball M1911
Length overall: 219 mm (8.6 in)

This pistol is the M1911 (the M1911A1 had several detail changes) and it is still the standard US Army service pistol after over 70 years in service. Firing a 0.45-in ball cartridge, it is still a powerful man-stopper, but is a bit of a handful to fire and requires training to use to its full potential.

Length of barrel: 128 mm (5.03 in)
Weight: 1.36 kg (3 lb)
Muzzle velocity: 252 m (825 ft) per second
Magazine: 7-round box

The Colt M1911 and M1911A1

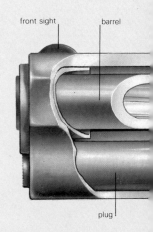

Developed from Browning's 1900 design, the M1911 Colt pistols are among the most successful combat pistols ever invented. Incredibly sturdy, with a stopping power unmatched by other semi-automatic pistols, the Colt has armed the US forces for more than 70 years.

At the turn of the century the US Army was equipped with a revolver that fired a 9.65-mm (0.38-in) cartridge that seemed effective enough for its task until the Americans became embroiled in operations in the Philippines. During the operations among the many islands they came up against a band of guerrillas known as the Moros who achieved some success in their limited action by mass charges at short ranges. Against such enemies the Americans found their pistol bullets were of little use, for even a Moro with two or three bullets in him could still continue his fanatical charge to the discomfort of his opponent. The soldiers called for a new and heavier projectile to stop such opponents.

For once the soldiers' requests were heeded at a high level. Starting in 1903 a series of trials was launched to discover the most suitable service calibre. The result was a new cartridge firing a 230-grain bullet with a calibre of 11.43 mm (0.45 in). By 1905 a Savage pistol was used for more trials, and in 1907 a Colt pistol appeared. In time this Colt pistol was taken into service (along with the new cartridge), and the M1911 was on the scene.

The M1911 was well blooded in action along the Mexican border before World War I started in 1914 and proved to be an excellent weapon. As the M1911 was an automatic pistol it took a little time for the more conservative soldiers to accept it, but once they appreciated the stopping power of the heavy bullet they took to it so much that even now many serving American soldiers still deem it the best service pistol in the world and will accept nothing else

in its place. By the time the United States entered World War I in 1917 the M1911 was a firm favourite, but that was among the serving and long-term trained personnel. New recruits who encountered its weight and bulk took time to become accustomed to the M1911's lively recoil and took even longer to become proficient in its use. Service in France revealed the need for some slight improvements and these were incorporated into the M1911A1 introduced in 1921. Subsequent production models were based on the M1911A1 but the older M1911 continued in service and the model can still be encountered in service to this day.

Between the wars

After World War I appropriations for more pistols fell away somewhat, and as there were no funds for further development and no call for any replacement weapon, by 1941 the M1911A1 was still the standard weapon in the US armed forces. However, as had been the case in 1917 there were not enough in the stockpiles to meet expected demand. Once again, as in 1917, numbers of converted revolvers with special clips to hold the rimless 11.43-mm (0.45-in) cartridges were pressed into use and various trials were made to improve the training of raw recruits to handle the weapon. Once again many recruits found the M1911A1 difficult to handle and all manner of training methods were tried in an attempt to overcome the problem. In the end it had to be accepted that the great bulk of the wartime recruits would never be able to use the pistol at ranges much over 18 m (20 yards), and that this was too short to make it worth retaining the M1911A1 as a service weapon. This fact led directly to the development of the 7.62-mm (0.3-in) M1 carbine, which was widely issued in place of M1911A1s to many front-line second-line personnel. Well over six million M1 carbines were produced, and this would under normal circumstances have led to an overall condemnation of the service pistol in general and the M1911A1 in particular. Despite this the M1911A1 soldiered on, no longer as a general

front-line US Army weapon but more and more as a weapon carried by aircrew and for general military police duties.

It was for US Army Air Force use that one of the more unusual cartridges was developed for the M1911A1. The usual cartridges for the pistol were the 0.45 Ball M1911, the blank M9, the dummy M1921 and the tracer M26. To these was added the 0.45 High Density Shot M261, which was originally developed to allow the M1911A1 to be used as an aircrew survival weapon. It was loaded with a number of steel-shot projectiles that were meant to be fired at fish, so providing downed aircrew with a food supply. What happened before very long was that these cartridges were fired against personnel, proving to be so effective that the survival function took a back seat.

Other developments relating to the M1911A1 included a series of long barrels that were intended to improve the pistol's accuracy at increased ranges. They were never adopted for service but were involved in a rather odd

US Marines with guns ready board a half-submerged Japanese landing barge following an engagement at Peleliu. By 1944, troops had learned to be very wary when approaching apparently overcome Japanese positions.

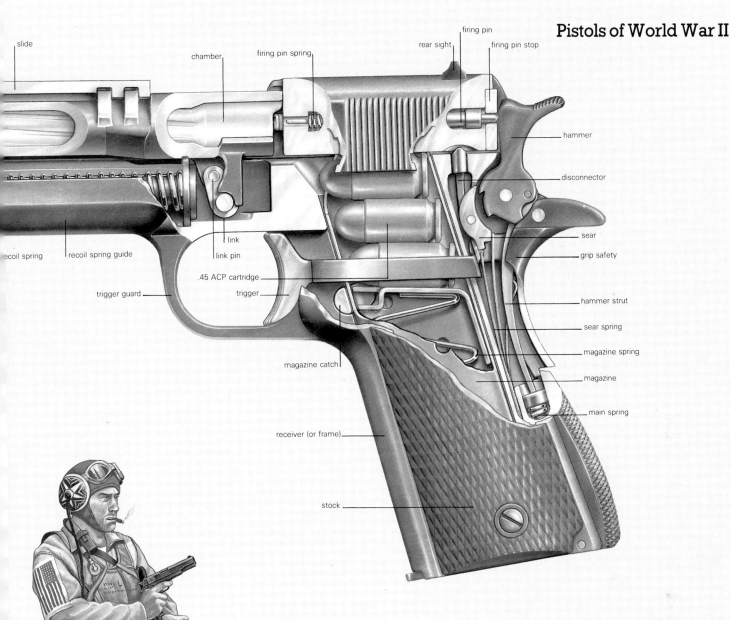

slide

chamber

firing pin spring

rear sight

firing pin

firing pin stop

hammer

disconnector

link

link pin

sear

grip safety

.45 ACP cartridge

hammer strut

recoil spring

recoil spring guide

trigger guard

trigger

sear spring

magazine spring

magazine

main spring

magazine catch

receiver (or frame)

stock

Standard issue to US Navy pilots in the Pacific in 1944, the government Colt .45 would be the only firearm available to a downed flier in hostile territory, and could mean the difference between life and death.

attempt to convert the M1911A1 into a submachine gun. This project used a barrel 240 mm (9.45 in) long and an extended magazine holding 20 rounds. A butt was fitted to the pistol grip and a cooling device was added to the barrel. Changes were made to the internal mechanism to permit fully automatic fire, but although successful the whole project was terminated during 1942 when the M3 submachine gun was adopted.

Into the 1980s

After World War II the M1911A1 continued in service despite all the limitations that had been demonstrated. These limitations were largely ignored as the US armed forces wanted a pistol and the M1911A1 was ready to hand. The soldiers continued to sing its praises and largely chose to ignore the performance of the 9-mm (0.354-in) Parabellum pistols in use elsewhere. In fact the M1911A1 is still a fully established weapon in America and elsewhere, for over the years it has been adopted by many nations, mainly those who have come under American influence such as Nationalist China.

The last M1911A1 was produced in 1945, so stocks still in US Army use are now getting somewhat elderly. A recent survey revealed that of the 418,000 M1911A1s still in stock, every one had been overhauled extensively or rebuilt at least three times. Despite the favour

bestowed upon the M1911A1 by the US military this is a situation that cannot be extended indefinitely, so the US Army now has a requirement for a new service pistol to be known as the XM9. This pistol will incorporate all the many innovations since the time that the M1911 was designed, and at long last the requested calibre is 9 mm (0.354 in). Between 1977 and 1980 a whole string of designs was used in a protracted series of trials to determine the new pistol, but the result was inconclusive. Several observers have stated that this might have been due to the fact that many of the pistols involved in the trials were not American in origin, but no doubt there was more to the outcome than that. One concrete result of the trials was that the existing M1911A1s should be rebuilt as 9-mm (0.354-in) pistols, but this proposal appears to have progressed little.

So, in the foreseeable future at least, the loved or hated M1911A1 will remain in American use. One day the XM9 will come, but for the foreseeable future the large number of companies that find it worthwhile to produce spares and components for the M1911 series will continue to prosper. The M1911A1 will no doubt continue to frighten the tyro with its hefty recoil and to alarm all at whom it is pointed, for the power of the 11.43-mm (0.45-in) projectile is as formidable today as it was when it was developed to stop the charging Moros.

UK/USA
Smith & Wesson 0.38/200 Revolver

In 1940 the British army was in a desperate plight, with few men trained and even fewer weapons with which to arm them. Fortunately the United States, although not yet actually in the war, were at least sympathetic to the point where that nation would produce weapons for the British, and to British designs. The British planned huge increases in armed manpower levels and had to obtain weapons to match, and among these weapons were pistols. Smith & Wesson was willing to produce revolvers to a British specification, and the result was the pistol known either as the **Revolver .38/200** or the **Revolver No. 2 Cal.380**.

Whatever its designation, the pistol was a strictly orthodox design that was conventional in every respect. It was straightforward in design and operation, and embodied not only Smith & Wesson craftsmanship but British requirements, the resulting weapon being robust to an extreme. It was just as well, for the British pistol production lines were never able to catch up with demand and the British/American design more than filled the gap. These pistols were issued to all arms of the British forces, went to many Commonwealth forces as well, and were even handed out to various European resist-

ance movements. Between 1940 and the time production ended in 1946 over 890,000 had been produced and issued. Many are still in service to this day, and it was well into the 1960s before some British units replaced them with the Browning HP.

The Revolver .38/200 fired a 200-grain bullet and used the classic Smith & Wesson chamber release to the left. Once the weapon was open, fired cartridge cases could be cleared with a sprung plunger rod. The trigger action could be either single- or double-action. The finish of the pistols was plain, and at times was neglected in order that the numbers required could be churned out. But the standard of manufacture never wavered: it was always good, and only the finest materials were used. Normally the pistol was carried in a closed leather or webbing holster which masked the hammer, so the snagging problem encountered with the Enfield revolver was not so acute, but a typical British touch was that the revolver was usually fitted to a waist or neck lanyard to prevent an enemy taking the pistol away from the firer at close quarters. The weapon appears never to have gone wrong, even when subjected to the worst possible treatment.

Below: A New Zealand officer armed with a Smith & Wesson 0.38/200 revolver during one of the campaigns in the desert. The revolver is being worn with the lanyard in the 'correct' position around the neck, but many preferred to wear it around the waist to prevent strangulation by an enemy in close-quarter combat.

Specification
0.38/200 Revolver
Cartridge: 0.380 SAA ball (9.65 mm)
Length overall: 257 mm (10.125 in)
Length of barrel: 127 mm (5 in)
Weight: 0.880 kg (1.94 lb)
Muzzle velocity: 198 m (650 ft) per second
Chamber capacity: 6 rounds

Above: A Canadian sergeant loads a Smith & Wesson 0.38/200 revolver. Empty cartridge cases were ejected by moving out the cylinder to the left and pressing a plunger normally under the barrel. All six spent cases were ejected together to allow each chamber to be reloaded one at a time, as seen here.

Below: The Smith & Wesson 0.38/200 revolver was an alliance of American workmanship and British combat experience that produced a robust and reliable pistol with no frills. Made from the very finest materials the finish was sometimes neglected to speed production, but manufacturing standards were never lowered.

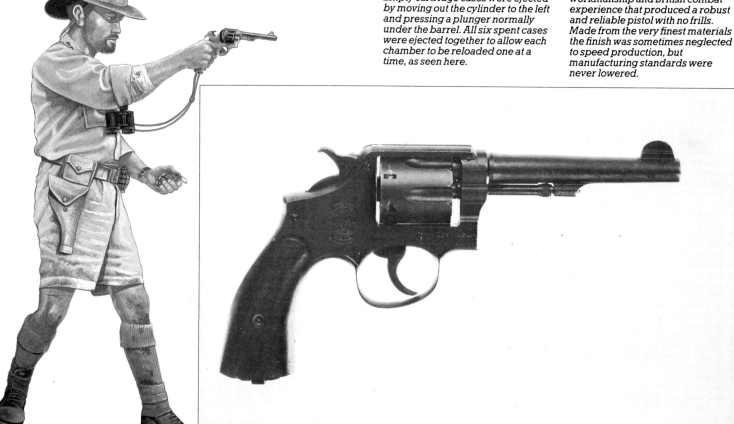

A batch of Smith & Wesson 0.38/200 revolvers is seen being unpacked, counted and checked by members of the ATS. Almost 900,000 examples of this sturdy design were produced.

Smith & Wesson M1917

During World War I the United Kingdom placed sizable orders in the United States for weapons of all types, and among these was one placed with Smith & Wesson of Springfield, Illinois, for the supply of military revolvers with a calibre of 11.56 mm (0.455 in), the then-standard British pistol cartridge. Large numbers of these were supplied, but after the USA had entered the war in 1917 it was realized that large numbers of pistols would be needed to arm the enlarged US Army, and that the output from the Colt M1911 production line would be insufficient to meet the requirements. As a direct result the Smith & Wesson contract was taken over for the American forces, only for a new problem to crop up once the pistol production had been adapted to the American 11.43-mm (0.45-in) calibre.

Nearly all pistol ammunition produced in 1917 was for the M1911 automatic pistol and was thus rimless. Using rimless ammunition in a revolver chamber posed several problems as revolver cartridges are normally rimmed. Hence a compromise solution was adopted in the form of three M1911 cartridges being held in 'half-moon' clips to keep the cartridges from slipping too far into the revolver chambers when loaded. After firing the spent cartridges could be ejected in the normal way together with their clips and the clips would be reused if necessary. This solution was taken into US Army service and the pistols subsequently saw service in France and elsewhere.

The **Revolver, Caliber .45, Smith & Wesson Hand Ejector, M1917**, as the pistol was subsequently designated,

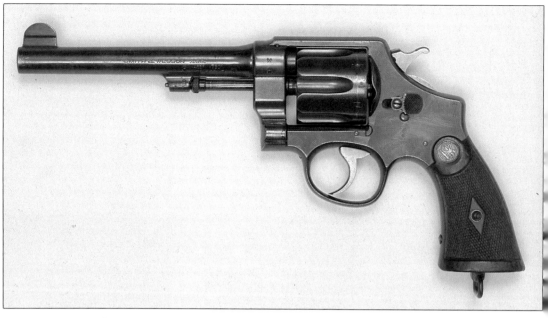

was a large robust weapon that was completely orthodox in design, operation and construction, apart from the use of the three-round clips. The revolving chambers swung out to the left for loading and case ejection, and the action was either single or double. Like many other pistols of its type, the M1917 was extremely robust and had already been well accepted by the British army before the US Army took over the type. The British were to use it again in 1940 when large numbers were sent over for Home Guard and Royal Navy use.

Colt Firearms also produced a very similar revolver to the Smith & Wesson weapon, as the **Revolver, Caliber .45, Colt New Service, M1917**. Total production of both was over 300,000 and Brazil purchased a further 25,000 in 1938. Many US military police units were still using the type as late as 1945.

Specification
Smith & Wesson M1917
Cartridge: .45 ball M1911
Length overall: 274 mm (10.8 in)

When the United States entered the war in 1917 there were not enough pistols to arm the gathering throngs of recruits. The Smith & Wesson M1917 was rushed into production after being adapted to fire the standard 0.45-in cartridge and was produced in large numbers.

Length of barrel: 140 mm (5.5 in)
Weight: 1.02 kg (2.25 lb)
Muzzle velocity: 253 m (830 ft) per second
Chamber capacity: 6 rounds

Pistolet Radom wz.35

By the early 1930s the Polish army had a large number of pistol types in service, and wished to standardize on one particular type. Consequently an all-Polish design emerged and was put into production at the Fabryka Radom. This weapon became the standard Polish service pistol as the 9-mm **Pistolet Radom wz.35** (wz. stands for *wzor*, or model).

The Radom wz.35 was a combination of Browning and Colt design features with a few local Polish touches. In operation and use it was entirely conventional, but it lacked an applied safety and used only a grip safety, what appeared to be the applied safety catch on the left-hand side of the receive being only a catch used when stripping the pistol. The ammunition used was the 9-mm Parabellum, but firing this rather powerful round from the Radom was no great problem as the bulk and weight of the pistol was such that the firing stresses were absorbed to a remarkable degree. This weight and bulk made the Radom a better-than-average service pistol as it was able to cope with all manner of hard use, a fact improved by the high standards of manufacture, materials and finish employed until 1939.

In 1939 the Germans overran Poland and took over the Radom arsenal complete with the pistol production line. Finding the Radom wz.35 a thoroughly serviceable weapon the Germans adopted the design as a service pistol and kept it in production for their own

use under the designation **Pistole P 35(p)**. However, the Germans' requirement for pistols was so great that to speed production they eliminated some small features and reduced the overall standard of finish to the extent that 'German' Radoms can be easily identified from the earlier 'Polish' versions by their appearance alone. The Germans kept the Radom in full-scale production until 1944 when the advancing Red Army destroyed the factory.

When the new Polish army was re-established after 1945 it adopted the Soviet TT33 as its new standard pistol and the Radom passed into history. Many are still around as collector's items, for the bulk of the German production went to the Waffen SS and was marked appropriately. Thus these pistols have an added collection value for many pistol buffs. Quite apart from this, the Radom wz.35 was one of the better service pistols of the war years and would continue to make a very serviceable sidearm to this day.

Specification
Radom wz.35
Cartridge: 9-mm Parabellum
Length overall: 197 mm (7.76 in)
Length of barrel: 121 mm (4.76 in)
Weight: 1.022 kg (2.25 lb)
Muzzle velocity: 351 m (1,150 ft) per second
Magazine: 8-round box

The Radom wz.35 was a sound and reliable pistol of entirely conventional design that was first produced in Poland in 1935. After 1939 it was produced in some numbers for the German forces and thus many now seen carry German markings. Featuring some of the best Colt and Browning features plus a few Polish touches, the Radom was an excellent service pistol.

CZECHOSLOVAKIA

Automaticky Pistole vz.38 (CZ 38)

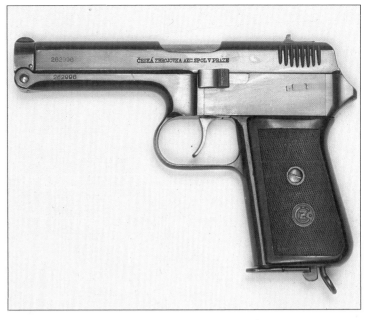

By the time that the German army marched into Czechoslovakia in 1938 and 1939 the Czech nations had evolved into one of the most industrious and innovative armaments manufacturers in all Europe. Pistols were one of the many weapon types produced, mainly at the Ceska Zbrojovka (CZ) in Prague, and from there emanated a string of excellent designs that included the vz.22, 24, 27, and 30 (vz. stands for *vzor*, or model). These pistols all fired the 9-mm (0.354-in) short cartridge and had many features in common with the Walther pistols of the period, but in 1938 came a pistol that bore no relation to anything that had been produced before.

The new pistol was the **CZ 38** (otherwise known as the **Automaticky Pistole vz.38**), and by all accounts this was not one of the better service pistols of the time. It was a large automatic weapon using a simple blowback mechanism, but it fired the 9-mm (0.354-mm) short cartridge even though its size and weight could have accommodated a more powerful round. One feature that was unusual and outdated even at that time was that the trigger mechanism was double-action only (it could be fired only by using the trigger to cock and release the hammer) while most

other actions of the time used an external hammer that could be cocked by hand. This double action required a long and heavy trigger pull, so accurate aiming of the weapon was very difficult. One good feature of the design was that the pistol could be stripped very easily, simply by releasing a catch to allow the barrel to be cleaned once the slide was clear.

Not many of these pistols were produced for the Czech army before the Germans moved in, but the type was kept in production for some time. To the Germans the CZ 38 was known as the 9 mm **Pistole P 39(t)**, but most of the production went to police forces and some second-line units. Few survived after 1945. It is one of the few pistol designs that has not contributed some points to later designs.

Specification
CZ 38
Cartridge: 9 mm short (0.380 ACP)
Length overall: 198 mm (7.8 in)
Length of barrel: 119 mm (4.69 in)
Weight: 0.909 kg (2 lb)
Muzzle velocity: 296 m (970 ft) per second
Magazine: 8-round box

Generally regarded as a less than successful design, the Czech CZ 38 was a large and cumbersome 9-mm pistol. It could be stripped very easily but the stiff and slow double-action made accurate shooting difficult.

JAPAN

94 Shiki Kenju

In the 1930s the Japanese armed forces had in service a sound design of automatic pistol known to most Westerners as the 'Nambu' (8-mm Pistol Type 14), but following the large-scale Japanese incursions into China in the mid-1930s the demand for more pistols for the expanding Japanese forces could not be met. An easy solution appeared on the scene in the shape of an 8-mm (0.315-in) automatic pistol that had been commercially produced in 1934, but sales of this pistol had been few, as a result mainly of the odd and clumsy appearance of the weapon. The armed forces were then able to purchase existing stocks of these pistols and took over the production of more. The resultant weapons were initially issued to tank and air force personnel, but by the time production ended in 1945 (after more than over 70,000 had been made) its use had spread to other arms.

By all accounts this pistol, known as the **94 Shiki Kenju** (or **Pistol type 94**), was one of the worst service pistols ever produced: for a start the basic design was unsound in several respects, and then the overall appearance was wrong and the weapon handled badly, but allied to this was the fact that it was often unsafe. One reason for this last factor was that part of the trigger mechanism protruded from the left side of the frame, and if this was pushed when a round was in the chamber the pistol would fire. Another bad feature was the device to

ensure that only single shots would be fired each time the trigger was pulled, for this was so arranged that a cartridge could be fired before it was fully in the chamber. When these faults were allied to poor manufacture and poor quality materials the result was a weapon that was unsafe to an alarming degree. The problem for the Japanese personnel who had to use the gun was that production was often so rushed that the product was badly made, and troops had to use the Type 94 simply because Japanese industry could produce nothing better at that time. Examples have been found that still bear file or other machine tool marks on the outside, and the degree of 'slop' in the mechanisms of some should signify that the Type 94 is a pistol that should not be carried or fired: it is a collector's piece only.

Despite the fact that this Japanese captain is a tank officer, he is armed with a traditional sword as well as a Type 94 pistol. The sword must have been rather unwieldy in the confines of a tank turret.

Specification
Pistol Type 94
Cartridge: 8 mm Taisho 14
Length overall: 183 mm (7.2 in)
Length of barrel: 96 mm (3.78 in)
Weight: 0.688 kg (1.52 lb)
Muzzle velocity: 305 mm (1,000 ft) per second
Magazine: 6-round box

The 94 Shiki Kenju was one of the worst pistol designs ever produced, for it was cumbersome, awkward to use and basically unsafe as the firing sear projected from the side and could be easily knocked to fire the pistol inadvertently. But it was all the Japanese had and it was kept in production until 1945.

An Alpini officer of the Italian army aims his Beretta Modello 34. This was the standard sidearm of the Italian infantry and was issued to all front line units.

ITALY

Pistola Automatica Beretta modello 1934

The little **Pistola Automatica Beretta modello 1934** is one of the joys of the pistol collector's world, for it is one of those pistols that has its own built-in attraction. It was adopted as the standard Italian army service pistol in 1934, but it was then only the latest step in a long series of automatic pistols that could be traced back as far as 1915. In that year numbers of a new pistol design were produced to meet the requirements of the expanding Italian army, and although the **Pistola Automatica Beretta modello 1915** was widely used it was never officially accepted as a service model. These original Beretta had a calibre of 7.65 mm, although a few were made in 9 mm short, the cartridge that was to be the ammunition for the later modello 1934.

After 1919 other Beretta pistols appeared, all of them following the basic Beretta design. By the time the modello 1934 appeared the 'classic' appearance had been well established with the snub outline and the front of the cutaway receiver wrapped around the forward part of the barrel to carry the fixed foresight. The short pistol grip held only seven rounds and thus to ensure a better grip the characteristic 'spur' was carried over from a design introduced back in 1919. The operation used by the mechanisms

Beretta automatics (right) were amongst the most sought after of war trophies. Although of excellent design, they were really too light to be effective service pistols, but as personal weapons to officers such as the colonel depicted (left), they were highly prized.

was a conventional blowback without frills or anything unusual, but although the receiver was held open once the magazine was empty it moved forward again as soon as the magazine was removed for reloading (most pistols of this type keep the receiver slide open until the magazine has been replaced). The modello 1934 did have an exposed hammer which was not affected by the safety once applied, so although the trigger was locked when the safety was applied the hammer could be cocked either by hand or by accident, an unfortunate feature in an otherwise sound design.

The modello 1934 was almost always produced to an excellent standard of manufacture and finish, and the type became a sought-after trophy of war. Virtually the entire production run was

taken for use by the Italian army, but there was a modello 1935 in 7.65 mm which was issued to the Italian air force and navy. Apart from its calibre this variant was identical to the modello 1934. The Germans used the type as the **Pistole P671(i)**. Despite its overall success the modello 1934 was technically underpowered, but it is still one of the most famous of all pistols used during World War II.

Specification
Beretta modello 1934
Cartridge: 9-mm short (0.380 ACP)
Length overall: 152 mm (6 in)
Length of barrel: 90 mm (3.4 in)
Weight: 0.568 kg (1.25 lb)
Muzzle velocity: 290 m (950 ft) per second
Magazine: 7-round box

Modern Combat Pistols

Pistols remain in widespread military service, despite their limited range and the increasing handiness of sub-machine guns. In the USA their design is a matter of national pride but, surprisingly, the Italian firm of Beretta won the competition to supply a new pistol for the US Army.

For many years military prophets have forecast the demise of the military pistol in both automatic and revolver forms. Such prophets have a case: in an era dominated by the ever-increasing firepower of assault rifles and machine-guns it would appear that this weapon no longer has a viable combat role and indeed, when the operational requirement is considered objectively, it is difficult to find one. Yet the pistol continues to flourish.

The short answer to the question of why this should be the case is that although there is no longer an operational field requirement for the pistol, there are still many other roles it can cover. Many military personnel, even in the front line, are unable by the very nature of their duties to carry any other weapon. Personnel in this category include tank crew, signallers, commanders and many others who would have to venture into battle areas unarmed unless they carried a pistol.

Thus the military pistol survives and continues to be produced in as wide a variety of forms and shapes as ever. As will be seen in this study the revolver continues to make its presence felt, although many of the potent Magnum rounds (rounds with a particularly heavy propellant load) have yet to have any marked effect on the front-line combat scene, for reasons that will be unfolded in the various entries. The automatic pistol continues to make use of all the technological innovations that arrive, and while it would seem that the whole spectrum of changes that could be effected to the automatic were made long ago, a short perusal of the contents of these pages will reveal that changes are still possible.

Two Portuguese soldiers demonstrate that carrying a side-arm is still no guarantee of personal safety. Given their lack of range and accuracy, pistols often serve as much in a symbolic as in a practical role; nevertheless, manufacturers strive to improve their design with larger magazines and more reliable safety devices.

Most of them involve the ever-increasing use of a safety mechanism to prevent the pistol firing when dropped or other mischances of this type. Modern trigger mechanisms can now be called upon to control limited bursts of fully automatic fire (usually three rounds) as a means of converting ordinary automatic pistols into powerful close-range weapons. Weight can be saved by using light alloys or plastics to replace steel components, and so on.

The importance that the pistol still possesses can be gauged from the great interest and investment in the American military pistol trials held over the last few years. The US armed forces have made a considerable allocation of defence capital to ensure they have a pistol suitable for their requirements into the next century. If the Americans are thinking in such terms it is certain that others are too, so it seems that the military pistol will be with us for some time to come.

The Browning High-power is one of the world's most widely used pistols; today it is in service with over 50 countries. Its 13-round magazine capacity gives the weapon a bulky butt grip which does not detract from the handiness of the gun. Introduced by Fabrique Nationale in 1935, it remains one of the most successful pistol designs ever produced.

FRANCE
French automatic pistols

The most important of the post-war French automatic pistols has been the mle 1950 MAS which was manufactured at both St Etienne and Chatellerault. It is no longer in production, but is still a standard pistol of the French armed forces and it has also been sold to many ex-French colonial forces.

The MAS uses a standard swinging-link locking mechanism and a virtually standard trigger system with all the usual safeties. The trigger mechanism uses an external hammer and the hammer can be lowered without firing if the safety catch is set to 'Safe'. When the pistol is in the firing condition a red dot appears next to the safety catch. Nine rounds can be loaded into the box magazine. All in all the MAS is a fairly straightforward pistol with few frills or items of particular note.

Another post-war French automatic

pistol is the **Model D MAB**. Unlike the MAS, which fires the 9-mm (0.354-in) Parabellum cartridge, the Model D MAB fires either the 7.65-mm (0.301-in) or 9-mm Short (also known as 0.380-in Auto). These less powerful rounds are used as the Model D MAB was originally designed for police use where more powerful ammunition such as the 9-mm Parabellum is not normally needed. Some military sales of the Model D MAB have been made, however, as it is a handy little pistol with good accuracy. It has no external

The 9-mm PA15 MAB is the current service pistol of the French army, in production at Manufacture d'Armes Automatiques in Bayonne. The bulky grip of this delayed blowback design holds up to 15 Parabellum rounds.

hammer, and this allows the weapon to be carried in a pocket without any danger of the hammer catching in clothing. Despite its small size the Model D MAB still uses a nine-round box magazine, and a feature of this pistol is that it can be converted from 7.65-mm to 9-mm Short simply by changing the barrel, no other alterations being necessary. The cartridge fired by the Model D MAB is the 7.65-mm Longue, which is used only by the French.

The Model D MAB is still in production.

Specification
MAS
Calibre: 9 mm (0.354 in)
Weights: empty 0.86 kg (1.896 lb); loaded 1.04 kg (2.3 lb)
Lengths: overall 195 mm (7.677 in);

barrel 112 mm (4.4 in)
Muzzle velocity: 354 m (1,161 ft) per second
Magazine capacity: 9 rounds

Model D MAB
Calibre: 7.65 mm (0.301 in)
Weights: empty 0.725 kg (1.6 lb); loaded 0.825 kg (1.82 lb)
Lengths: overall 176 mm (6.93 in); barrel 103 mm (4.05 in)
Muzzle velocity: 365 m (1,197 ft) per second
Magazine capacity: 9 rounds

The post-war 9-mm Model 1950 MAS self-loading pistol (made by Chatellerault as the MAC) used the basic M1911 Colt mechanism with modifications to its safety mechanism. It remains in French service.

SWITZERLAND
SIG-Sauer P220

For very many years the Schweizerische Industrie-Gesellscahft (SIG) has been producing excellent weapons at its Neuhausen Rhinefalls factory, but has always been restricted by the strict Swiss laws governing military exports from making any significant overseas sales. By joining up with the West German J P Sauer und Sohn concern, SIG was able to transfer production to West Germany and gain access to more markets, and thus SIG-Sauer was formed.

One of the first military pistols developed by the new firm was the **SIG-Sauer P220**, a mechanically-locked single- or double-action automatic pistol. When dealing with the P220 it is difficult to avoid superlatives, for this is a truly magnificent pistol in many ways. Its standards of manufacture and finish are superb, despite the extensive use of metal stampings and an aluminium frame to keep down weight and cost. The pistol handles very well, being one of those weapons that immediately feels right as soon as it is picked up. It is accurate, and the overall design is such that it is difficult for dirt or dust to find its way into the interior and cause stoppages. Despite this the pistol is easy to strip and maintain, and has all the usual pistol safeties.

One design feature of the P220 is that it can be supplied in any one of four calibres. These are the usual 9-mm (0.354-in) Parabellum, 7.65-mm (0.301-in) Parabellum, 0.45-in ACP (11.27-mm, ACP standing for Automatic Colt Pistol) and 0.38-in Super (9-mm not to be confused with 9-mm Parabellum). It is possible to convert any pistol from one calibre to another and kits can be provided to convert any pistol to fire 0.22-in Long Rifle (5.59-mm) for training purposes. Using 9-mm Parabellum the magazine holds nine rounds, but when firing 0.45-in ACP only seven rounds can be accommodated.

The excellence of the P220 has rewarded SIG-Sauer with a stream of orders. To date well over 100,000 have been produced, one of the largest orders coming from the Swiss government who ordered a batch of 35,000 weapons. The P220 is now in service with the Swiss army, which knows it as the 9-mm **Pistole 75**, a designation which sometimes provides the P220 with the name **Model 75**.

There is a later version of the P220 known as the **P225** which is slightly smaller and chambered only for the 9-mm Parabellum cartridge. This version has been selected for Swiss and West German police use as the **P6**.

Specification
Pistole 75
Calibre: 9 mm (0.354 in)
Weight: empty 0.83 kg (1.83 lb)
Lengths: overall 198 mm (7.8 in); barrel 112 mm (4.4 in)
Muzzle velocity: 345 m (1,132 ft) per second
Magazine capacity: 9 rounds

The magnificent SIG-Sauer P220 resulted from a collaborative venture between the Swiss SIG company and JP Sauer und Sohn to produce a pistol for export, unfettered by Swiss government restrictions. It is available in 0.45 ACP, 9-mm Parabellum, 7.65-mm Parabellum and even .22 LR.

The Automatic Choice?

The pros and cons of self-loading (automatic) pistols and revolvers have become less notable since World War II as the reliability of automatics has steadily increased. Police forces require unfailing reliability, which has led many to favour the revolver, whereas the military generally prefers the large magazine capacity of an automatic.

Ever since the automatic pistol arrived on the small-arms scene there has been a constant battle between the advocates of the revolver and the advocates of the automatic pistol. Apparently endless reams of paper have been devoted to the arguments produced by both sides, and no doubt more will be consumed in the future, but the simple fact is that the finer points of both arguments have been lost in the reality that on the military scene at least the automatic pistol reigns virtually supreme.

The word 'almost' has to be used, for even today in an era when virtually every armed force now makes use of automatics the revolver is still around: it seems that the type will not go away. So rather than go into all the old arguments as to the merits of one type of pistol against the other it might be as well to see how both weapons have reached the position in which they are today.

The automatic pistol has long since passed the point in its development where it had an inherent lack of reliability in comparison with the revolver. At one time the automatic pistol used a bewildering array of mechanisms to make it work, and these often went wrong or broke. This no longer applies. The modern automatic is a robust and reliable weapon, if properly looked after, something that also applies to the revolver. (Generally speaking revolvers take less maintenance skill and training than automatics.) Then there is the magazine capacity factor. Most modern military automatics can carry more ready-to-use ammunition than revolvers. It is difficult to find a large-calibre revolver that can accommodate more than six rounds, while some modern automatics can accommodate up to 19 (such as in the Austrian Steyr GB), and in action those extra rounds can be a definite advantage. As far as handling is concerned the automatic again scores, for the ammunition stowage in the butt usually makes the automatic a more manageable weapon to aim and handle as most of the weight balances securely in the hand; on the revolver it is usually forward, making the weapon muzzle-heavy. Another factor in favour of the automatic is that it is now an inherently safe weapon, some designs having built-in safeties to

Below: Pistols have been carried by airmen as side-arms since the beginning of military aviation, and the Vietnam War proved no exception, with the wide variety of regulation service pistols carried by helicopter crew supplemented by guns from the commercial market.

Right: In many countries the pistol remains an instrument of law enforcement. Here a member of a Californian SWAT (Special Weapons and Assault Team) unit snatches a child to safety as her kidnapper is dealt with by his colleagues.

The Automatic Choice?

the extent that nothing will fire them apart from a deliberate pull of the trigger, and that only comes when the weapon has to be used. The same cannot be said of many revolver designs (and some of the older automatic pistol designs) for they have an unfortunate tendency to fire if dropped or if a hammer gets snagged in clothing or something such as undergrowth.

How then does the revolver survive in military hands? The main reason is quite simply that it is inherently much stronger in design terms. The basic frame of a revolver can be much more solid and sturdy than that of nearly all automatics, enabling it to take not only much heavier knocks but heavier ammunition loads such as the potent Magnum ammunition. Ensuring that automatics can fire such loads introduces the problems of positive locking mechanisms that add both complication and weight, whereas most revolver frames only require a bit more beefing up, if that.

The argument against this is that most military users do not require the Magnum loads as they are too powerful to employ to their full advantage without the devotion of an inordinate amount of training time to their use; and indeed most combat soldiers have enough training obligations already without having to learn how to handle pocket artillery. Some soldiers consider that the considerable recoil and muzzle blast produced by the 9-mm Parabellum pistol is quite enough to handle, and even the smaller and lighter Magnum loads produce considerably more blast and recoil, making aiming and handling difficult under combat conditions.

But for security and military police personnel the Magnum loads are ideal, for such personnel can devote the necessary training time, and they can use their considerable weapon power to good effect. The combat soldier needs something that is generally handier and less trouble to use. One added bonus for police and similar users is that the Magnum revolvers are unmistakable in appearance, giving rise to the 'Dirty Harry' syndrome where even hardened felons or subversives are unwilling to consider the consequences of what might happen when a Magnum round is fired at them. Thus the revolver remains in military hands, not normally in front line use but behind the lines on important security and guard duties, where it will remain for many years to come.

An officer of the French Foreign Legion brandishes a 9-mm PA 15 MAB automatic, a distinctive weapon identified by the very prominent spur at the back of the receiver and a burr-type hammer. The PA 15 carries 15 9-mm Parabellum cartridges, which give it a very bulky grip and, unusually for an automatic pistol, it has a delayed blowback action.

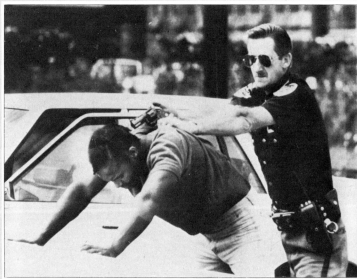

Below: The revolver may lack the magazine capacity of modern automatics, but in trained hands this is not a problem. Here a New Orleans policeman takes cover behind a car during a shoot-out.

Above: 'You have the right to remain silent' – a Magnum to the back of the neck is a powerful argument for surrender. This bank robber was arrested after stalling the getaway car at a junction.

Left: The 5.45-mm PSM is currently being introduced to the police and internal security forces of the Warsaw Pact countries. A small, notably slim pistol, it fires a round with low stopping power (unless it has been designed to tumble in flight).

Right: The weapon made famous by Clint Eastwood's 'Dirty Harry' films was the mighty 0.44 Magnum, made by Smith and Wesson. The fashion for revolvers of incredible stopping-power was followed by many armed forces at the beginning of the century; it remains to be seen whether modern military services will do so once again.

Below: A drugs raid in Miami involves an impressive demonstration of police firepower. Revolvers remain perhaps the best armament for regular police and paramilitary work, where ruggedness of design and reliability are more important than the ability to carry a large number of rounds.

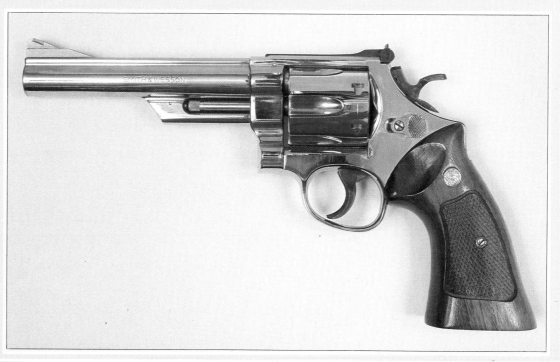

The Automatic Choice?

Above: A Luger automatic and a silenced revolver form part of the personal armament of French gangster Jacques Mesrine, killed by police in 1979.

Left: A bank security camera in Cologne records the shooting of a policeman (centre).

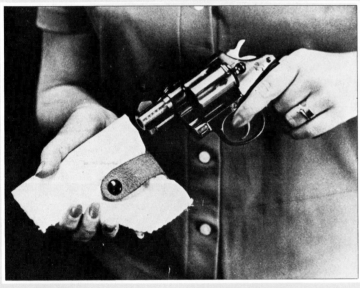

Smaller automatics make suitable weapons for female personnel, although the 6.35-mm 'Baby Berettas' held by these Italian policewomen are hardly noted for their stopping power. To defeat an armed enemy with such a light cartridge would demand a high standard of shooting.

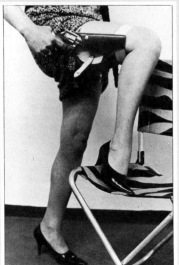

Above: South African women apparently take a more businesslike attitude to firearms; this curious-shaped holster was designed to accommodate a snub nosed 0.38 revolver in a woman's bra. In a timing test conducted by the manufacturer a woman drew and fired in three seconds.

Left: The bra holster proved unpopular due to its interesting effect on the figure; this is the replacement. The recent upsurge in urban violence in South Africa led to a rise in demand for ammunition, but not guns.

Right: Heckler & Koch designed the P7 automatic specifically with police use in mind; first issues to the West German army are going to the military police. The gun features a recoil-braking system which allows steadier shooting.

IMI Desert Eagle

The automatic pistol produced by Israel Military Industries and known as the **IMI Desert Eagle** was originally an American design proposed by M.R.I. Limited of Minneapolis, Minnesota. The basic concept has been developed in Israel to the point where the Desert Eagle is an extremely advanced and powerful weapon.

The Desert Eagle can be converted to fire either the 0.357-in Magnum (9-mm) cartridge or the even more powerful 0.44-in Magnum (10.92-mm) round; the latter cartridge is one of the most powerful pistol rounds available. All that is required to convert the pistol from one calibre to the other is the replacement of a few parts. To ensure complete safety when using these large rounds the Desert Eagle uses a rotating bolt for a maximum locking action. The safety catch can be engaged by either the right or left hand, and when in position on 'Safe' the hammer is disconnected from the trigger and the firing pin is immobilized.

The pistol uses a 152-mm (6-in) barrel as standard, but this basic barrel is interchangeable with barrels 203 mm (8 in), 254 mm (10 in), and 356 mm (14 in) long. The extended barrels are intended for long-range target shooting and may be used with a telescopic sight fitted to a mounting on top of the receiver. No special tools are required to change the barrels.

Several other options are available for the Desert Eagle. The trigger can be made adjustable and several different types of fixed sight can be fitted. The trigger guard is shaped to be used with a two-handed grip, although special grips can be fitted if required. The normal construction is of high quality

steels, but an aluminium frame can be supplied.

To date the Desert Eagle has been marketed with the civilian target shooter or enthusiast in mind, but it could also make a very powerful military or police weapon. However, most military authorities usually frown upon the use of Magnum cartridges as they are really too powerful for general military or police use and require a great deal of careful training for their best capabi-

lities to be realised. Thus pistols such as the Desert Eagle seem destined to remain in the hands of special police units and enthusiast who simply want the best and most powerful hand-guns available.

Specification
Desert Eagle
Calibre: 0.357 in or 0.44 in Magnum
Weight: empty 1.701 kg (3.75 lb)
Lengths: overall with 6-in barrel

IMI have entered the pistol field with the 'Desert Eagle', an automatic chambered for the ever-popular 0.357 Magnum cartridge. Military interest remains speculative.

260 mm (10.25 in); barrel 152.4 m (6 in)
Muzzle velocity: 0.357 Magnum 436 m (1,430 ft) per second; 0.44 Magnum 448 m (1,470 ft) per second
Magazine capacity: 0.357 Magnum 9 rounds; 0.44 Magnum 7 rounds

Beretta Model 1951

Pietro Beretta SpA has been making high-quality automatic pistols at Brescia for decades, and as over the years it has made its mark on pistol development in a number of ways it came as something of a surprise when in 1951 Beretta developed a pistol that did away with the company's former use of simple blowback mechanism in favour of a locked breech. In this system the breech and barrel are locked together for an instant after firing until they are unlocked by contact with the frame after a short recoil movement.

This pistol became known as the **Beretta Model 1951**, and it was also known at one time as the **Model 951** or **Brigadier**. It retained the usual Beretta trademark of an open-topped slide, but early hopes that this slide could be made from aluminium did not materialise and most production models use an all-steel unit. The first examples of the Model 1951 did not appear until 1957 as a result mainly of attempts to develop a satisfactory light slide. In more recent years the aluminium slide has become available as an option.

As always on Beretta weapons, the standard of finish of the Model 1951 was excellent and the pistol proved to be rugged and reliable. It was not long before overseas sales were made, and the Model 1951 became the standard service pistol of Israel and Egypt. In fact a production line was established in Egypt to manufacture the Model 951: that was during the 1960s, and the Model 1951 is known in Egypt as the

Helwan. The Model 1951 is also used in Nigeria and some other countries. The Italian armed forces also use large numbers of this pistol.

The Model 1951 continues to use the basic Beretta layout, despite the adoption of the locked breech system. The recoil rod and spring are still located under the largely open barrel, and the well-sloped butt holds the box magazine containing eight rounds. A very hard type of black nylon-based plastic

is used for the butt grips. There is an external hammer and the safety catch engages the sear when in use. Both rear and fore sights are adjustable on most versions of the Model 1951.

Specification
Model 1951
Calibre: 9 mm (0.354 in)
Weight: empty 0.87 kg (1.918 lb)
Lengths: overall 203.2 mm (8 in); barrel 114.2 mm (4.45 in)

The Beretta Model 1951 is the standard pistol of the Italian armed forces and has been exported to a number of countries, including Israel and Egypt. This is an example manufactured in Egypt, where the locally produced model is called the Helwan.

Muzzle velocity: 350 m (1,148 ft) per second
Magazine capacity: 8 rounds

ITALY

Beretta 9-mm Model 92 series

During 1976 Beretta placed in production two new families of automatic pistols, the Model 81 which used a blowback operating system and was chambered for calibres such as 7.65 mm (0.301 in), and the much larger **Beretta Model 92** which fires the usual 9-mm (0.354-in) Parabellum cartridge and accordingly uses a short recoil system very like that used on the earlier Model 1951. Since its introduction the Model 92 series has grown into a considerable range of weapons and it also seems certain to be one of Beretta's most successful designs for one of its variants, the **Model 92F**, has been selected as the US armed force's new standard automatic pistol.

Starting from the basic Model 92, the **Model 92 S** has a revised safety catch on the slide rather than below it as on the basic Model 92. This allows the hammer to be lowered onto a loaded chamber with complete safety as the firing pin is taken out of line with the hammer. The **Model 92 SB** is essentially similar to the Model 92 S, but the slide-mounted safety catch can be applied from each side of the slide. The **Model 92 SB-C** is a more compact and handier version of the Model 92 SB.

The Model 92F was a development of the Model 92 SB for the US Army pistol contest, which it won. The main changes from the Model 92 SB are a revised trigger guard outline to suit a two-handed grip (much favoured by the military), an extended magazine base, revised grips and a lanyard ring. The bore is chrome-plated and the exterior is coated in a Teflon-type material to resist wear and act as a non-glare surface.

Following on from the Model 92F there is a **Model 92F Compact** along the same lines as the Model 92 SB-C but using the features of the Model 92F, and also produced along the same lines is the **Model 92 SB-C Type M** which has an eight-round magazine instead of the 15-round magazine used on all the models mentioned above. To cap all these variants there are also two more models based on the Model 92 series but in a smaller calibre. They are the **Model 98** and **Model 99**, both in 7.65-mm calibre and based on the Model 92 SB-C and Model 92 SB-C Type M respectively.

This array of Model 92 pistols should be enough to satisfy just about every military or police requirement likely to arise. The selection of the Model 92 for the American armed forces has already led to a number of orders from other sources, including one from a police force in the UK, and more such orders can be expected. The original Model 92 is now no longer in production, but the Model 92 S still is and are the other variants are available. Apart from the American order various forms of the Model 92 are in service with the Italian armed forces and some of the 'compact' versions are used by various police forces in Italy and elsewhere.

Used extensively by the Italian armed forces, the Beretta Model 92 forms part of the equipment of the Italian army's 'Folgore' parachute brigade. Based at Pisa, the brigade incorporates a parachute battalion of the Carabinieri (who function as military police and as an internal security force).

Specification
Model 92F
Calibre: 9 mm (0.354 in)
Weight: loaded 1.145 kg (2.524 lb)
Lengths: overall 217 mm (8.54 in); barrel 125 mm (4.92 in)
Muzzle velocity: about 390 m (1,280 ft) per second
Magazine capacity: 15 rounds

Introduced in 1976, the Model 92 has proved a logical successor to the Modello 1951. This has a frame-mounted safety catch (later models have the catch on the slide).

ITALY

Beretta 9-mm Model 93R

With the **Beretta Model 93R** one is back in that no-man's land between true machine pistols and selective-fire pistols, for the Model 93R is another modern pistol design intended to fire three-round bursts. Derived from the Beretta Model 92, the Model 93R can be handled and fired as a normal automatic pistol, but when the three-round burst mode is selected the firer has to use both hands to hold the pistol reasonably steady during the burst. To do this Beretta has designed a simple and compact grip system on which the right hand carries out its normal function of operating the trigger and grasping the butt. For the left hand a small forehand grip is folded down from in front of the elongated trigger guard. The left thumb is inserted into the front of the trigger guard and the rest of the fingers grasp the forehand grip. For additional assistance in holding the pistol steady during firing the end of the protruding barrel is equipped with a muzzle brake that also acts as a flash hider.

To provide even more firing stability it is possible to fix a metal folding stock to the butt. When not in use this can be carried in a special holster, and when mounted on the pistol can be extended to two lengths to suit the firer.

Two type of box magazine can be used with the Model 93F, one holding 15 rounds and the other holding 20. The usual 9-mm (0.354-in) Parabellum cartridge is used.

The design detail incorporated into the Model 93R is considerable and one item that will no doubt be seen on future designs is the use of the foregrip in front of the trigger guard. This is so arranged tht the two-handed grip derived from its use is much steadier than the usual two-handed grip with both hands wrapped around what is often a bulky pistol butt. Using this foregrip it is quite possible to provide reasonably accurate burst fire as both hands are 'spaced' to produce a longer holding base and yet are close enough to prevent either hand wavering. It is possible to fire bursts without using the metal extending stock, but for really accurate rate fire (even with single shots) its use is recommended.

As yet the Model 93R is not on the open market and is still under development. One problem seems to be that the three-round burst mechanism is rather complicated and at present requires the services of a trained technician to carry out maintenance and repairs. Once this difficulty has been ironed out the Model 93R will no doubt attract a great deal of attention from many sources. It would certainly make a formidable close-quarter self-defence weapon.

Specification
Model 93R
Calibre: 9 mm (0.354 in)
Weights: loaded with 15-round magazine 1.12 kg (2.47 lb); loaded with 20-round magazine 1.17 kg (2.58 lb)
Lengths: pistol 240 mm (9.45 in); barrel 156 mm (6.14 in)
Muzzle velocity: 375 m (1,230 ft) per second
Magazine capacity: 15 or 29 rounds

Replacing a Legend

For many years, the United States Army stood aloof from the trend that has seen the 9-mm Parabellum round adopted as an almost universal military cartridge. Recently, however, the unthinkable has happened; a successor to the legendary Colt 0.45 has been chosen, it does not use the 0.45-in (11.43-mm) Colt cartridge, and it is not even American!

The Americans have always been highly individual when it comes to hand guns. Not only do they have a clause in their constitution that (when taken out of context) allows them to carry firearms, but they have devoted a great deal of their national technological expertise over the years to designing and developing some superlative pistols, many of which are still regarded as world leaders. This has been particularly true of the pistol that has been in US service for well over 75 years, the 0.45-in (11.43-mm) Colt M1911 and M1911A1 automatic.

This venerable pistol was developed during the first decade of this century to provide American troops with a weapon that would knock over any attacker at short range, the unfortunate but fanatical Moro tribesmen from the Philippines being the specified targets. The Colt M1911 with its heavy bullet was the outcome, and after World War I slight changes were introduced to produce the M1911A1. Many of the original M1911s remain in use to this day. Thereafter, despite technological innovations introduced elsewhere the M1911 has been the standard service pistol of the American armed forces, including the US Coast Guard, and it has been produced in hundreds of thousands.

The M1911 has also made a considerable impression on many generations of American servicemen. To them it has come almost to epitomize American military service, and so attached to the M1911 have many serving and ex-serving officers and men become that the mere idea of replacing the pistol was unthinkable. Even when the rest of the military world adopted the 9-mm (0.354-in) Parabellum cartridge as an almost universal round the Americans looked away and retained their M1911 with its big and powerful round.

To many observers the attachment of the Americans to the M1911 was understandable but wrong, especially when NATO standardization of calibres and weapons became one of the priorities of the post-war alliance. At a time when all the NATO nations except the United States were adopting the 9-mm cartridge the Americans stuck to their nonstandard 0.45-in round. There were other questions being asked as well. One was that training with the large and powerful M1911 took much longer than with the equivalent 9-mm pistols, for the 0.45-in cartridge in some ways heralded the objections to the later Magnum rounds in that it produced a violent recoil and was so noisy that many recruits were quite frankly terrified of it and thus took much longer to train. The other objection was that by the 1970s the M1911 was outdated as a design. It

The Beretta Model 92 was thoroughly adapted to meet US requirements. The safety catch has a lever on both sides of the slide, to allow left- or right-handed firing, and the magazine release catch can be fitted facing either left or right immediately beneath the trigger guard.

The Beretta is much less of a handful to fire than the venerable Colt, and the smaller round allows a much larger magazine capacity.

has none of the safety features introduced into the modern pistols and it can be used only by right-handed firers. Then there was the matter of the magazine capacity, for the M1911 holds only seven of the bulky 0.45-in rounds while most 9-mm pistols can carry far more (often twice as many).

What finally decided the US military authorities to seek a new pistol was none of these technicalities but a practicality, for many of the old M1911s were worn out. Many had been virtually rebuilt from spare parts several times over during their service lives, and the time was well past for many to be rebuilt yet again. The M1911 has not been manufactured for many years, and although numerous firms in the USA and elsewhere can make a good living churning out M1911 spares and conversions, a point was being reached where the pistols were simply too worn to be renovated.

New selection

When the decision to select a new pistol was announced during the early 1980s a storm of protest rose from the assembled ranks of the armed forces and veterans. All manner of alternatives were proposed from putting the M1911 back into production to converting existing pistols to 9-mm calibre. It did not take long for the authorities to overcome those arguments, but having said that it immediately became apparent that the Americans' once-over-whelming lead in handgun design had been

lost to the Europeans. Since World War II many European small-arms manufacturers have devoted a great deal of effort to developing modern materials for the design of pistols well in advance of anything the Americans had been making. Employing high-grade steels and light metals, and introducing hard plastics to functions where once they had been unthinkable, the Europeans had been able to manufacture pistols that seemed ahead of their time by comparison with American contemporaries.

Sensing large contracts the Europeans rushed to enter the American selection contest for what was tentatively named the XM9 programme (although that designation now appears to have lapsed). From the USA both Smith and Wesson and Colt put forward designs they felt sure would win. Smith and Wesson were particularly confident for their entry, the Model 469, had already been selected by the US Air Force. Colt entered a model known as the SSP.

Unfortunately for all the entrants, none of the pistols offered was selected as all failed to satisfy at least one of the criteria it was thought necessary they should meet. The paper requirements were fairly straightforward and although some were slightly changed at one stage or another, they came down to the following: the weight of each pistol was not to exceed 1.3 kg (2.866 lb) fully loaded; length was not to exceed 221 mm (8.3 in); height with magazine inserted was not to exceed 147 mm (5.787 in); the barrel had to have a minimum length of

Although the Colt and Beretta are of similar size, a[s] seen above, the difference between a gun introduced in 1911 and one developed in 1976 becomes evident when performance and durability are tested under extreme conditions.

102 mm (4 in); the magazine had to hold at leas[t] 10 rounds, the magazine baseplate being re[-] movable for cleaning and maintenance; th[e] rear sight was to be fixed but with some capa[-] bility for fine adjustment; after the last roun[d] had been fired the slide had to remain open and a manual slide stop feature had to be in[-] corporated; ambidextrous operation would b[e] an advantage; and 9-mm Parabellum ammuni[-] tion was to be used.

What the entrants were not told was wha[t] form the tests would take. The usual firing an[d] stripping tests were indeed carried out, but [a] number of others were also introduced. One o[f] these involved clamping the pistol in [a] machine that then vibrated at a high rate. An[y] parts that came loose or fell off were deeme[d] faults and any protest was met with the answe[r] that the old M1911 could pass this test: the fac[t] that the M1911 had none of the ambidextrou[s] operating levers and extra safeties was simpl[y] ignored. Ammunition stoppages were also re[-] garded as faults.

The results of this first series of tests le[ft] many of the Europeans with the impression tha[t] the well-known American NIH (Not Invente[d] Here) syndrome had been invoked: they fe[lt]

Beretta Model 92

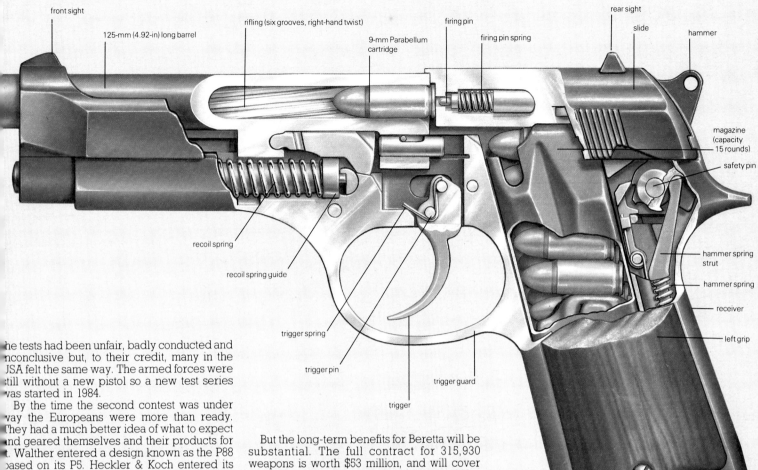

front sight

125-mm (4.92-in) long barrel

rifling (six grooves, right-hand twist)

9-mm Parabellum cartridge

firing pin

firing pin spring

rear sight

slide

hammer

magazine (capacity 15 rounds)

safety pin

hammer spring strut

hammer spring

receiver

left grip

grip screw

recoil spring

recoil spring guide

trigger spring

trigger pin

trigger guard

trigger

magazine bottom

magazine release button

lanyard loop

he tests had been unfair, badly conducted and nconclusive but, to their credit, many in the USA felt the same way. The armed forces were still without a new pistol so a new test series was started in 1984.

By the time the second contest was under way the Europeans were more than ready. They had a much better idea of what to expect and geared themselves and their products for it. Walther entered a design known as the P88 based on its P5. Heckler & Koch entered its P7A13, a version of the P7M13. Steyr entered its GB, and FN offered a version of the High-power known as the DDA. High in the list of favourites, SIG-Sauer entered its P226 and Beretta entered a version of the Model 92 S known as the Model 92F. It was noticeable that many of the Europeans had made changes to their submissions to cater for the American test criteria.

Legal disputes

By contrast Smith and Wesson submitted its Model 459M, a variant of the previously-favoured Model 469, while Colt once more put forward its SSA; a rumoured entry from Sturm, Ruger did not materialize. To everyone's surprise the two American entries were the first to be eliminated, leading almost immediately to legal action by Smith and Wesson. For a while the SIG-Sauer P226 seemed to be the clear favourite, but when the final result was announced in January 1985 it emerged that Beretta had won with the Model 92F.

Once again legal actions followed but got nowhere. All sorts of claims as to the conduct and findings of the tests were aired, and at the time of writing all legal submissions have been unsuccessful, though it is doubtful if the last of them has been heard. It seems that the SIG-Sauer P226 was indeed in the final running, but in the end costs won the day and one authority was claimed that all that the directors of Beretta will get out of the American contract is enough for a good lunch.

A gun cannot serve for three-quarters of a century without arousing much devotion and imitation. In spite of being replaced in US service, the Colt has inspired weapons such as the Spanish-built Star automatic pistol.

But the long-term benefits for Beretta will be substantial. The full contract for 315,930 weapons is worth $53 million, and will cover five years. In the first year 52,930 pistols will be produced in Italy. In the second year 57,000 pistols will be assembled and tested in the United States at the Beretta USA plant at Accokeek, Maryland. During the third year frames, slides and barrels will start to be manufactured in the United States to the tune of 72,000 pistols. For the final two years all production will take place in America, 72,000 pistols being produced in the fourth year and 62,000 in the fifth.

Smith and Wesson revolvers

Smith and Wesson has been making revolvers for well over 100 years, and during that time it has produced just about every type of revolver it is possible to make. Among the company's prolific output have been many military revolvers, but today Smith and Wesson do not make any revolver specifically for military use. This does not prevent many armed forces from using Smith and Wesson revolvers for many roles, but from the outset it has to be said that it is unlikely that any armed forces are likely to use Smith and Wesson revolvers in a front-line capacity. Instead they are to be found with military and security police and other such military agencies.

Top of the current list come the Magnums. For reasons explained elsewhere in this study such weapons are usually confined to special purpose units, one of them being very special for it is one of the most powerful revolvers available today. This is the **No. 29** 0.44-in Magnum (10.92-mm) which was first introduced in 1955. The No. 29 is too much of a handful for most users since its recoil is prodigious, so the **No. 57** was introduced in 1964 to use the less potent 0.41-in Magnum (10.41-mm). This has the same overall dimensions as the No. 29, is rather more manageable yet still retains its massive striking power.

But to most observers of the pistol scene Smith and Wesson means 0.38-in (9-mm) revolvers. There are many of these still on the Smith and Wesson marketing lists, a typical example being the **No. 38 Bodyguard**. This small snub-nosed revolver has a shrouded hammer to allow it to be concealed on the person without too much danger, but a stud over the hidden hammer allows the pistol to be cocked for single-action shooting. The cylinder holds only five rounds, and the No. 38 uses an aluminium body; the otherwise similar No. 49 uses an all-steel body.

Pistols such as the No. 38 and No. 49 are not likely to be used in front-line combat, but they can still be found on the inventories of many armed forces. Pilots carry them (or pistols very similar to them) on missions over enemy territory, and the weapons are often issued to military personnel operating in plain clothes in areas where the local population is hostile to their presence. It seems that there will always be a need for weapons such as the small Smith and Wesson revolvers.

Specification
No. 38 Bodyguard
Calibre: 0.38 in (9 mm)
Weight: 0.411 kg (0.9 lb)
Lengths: overall 165 mm (6.5 in); barrel 51 mm (2 in)
Muzzle velocity: 260 m (853 ft) per second
Chamber capacity: 5 rounds

Smith and Wesson 0.38-in (9-mm) revolvers are in common use with police and military forces worldwide. The typical snub-nosed, double-action weapon (top) is most widely seen, but the more specialized No. 38 Bodyguard has no external hammer and can be brought rapidly into action from a pocket or holster without danger of snagging.

Colt revolvers

To many the very name Colt means revolvers since it was the Colt's Firearms Company that produced the first successful commercial revolvers, including the famous single-action Colts such as the 'Peacemaker', the gun enshrined in the legends of the Old West. Gradually Colt moved away from producing revolvers (to leave the field open to others, as it was to learn to its cost) and concentrated on automatics. But Colt still continued to make some revolver designs apart from its various well-known and attractive commemorative models.

The modern Colt military revolvers are now all double-action designs, and although most models are produced with police use in mind many are still used by various military agencies in the USA and elsewhere. Many are used by military police units who can obtain the special training needed to handle the powerful Magnum rounds now in use. Thus although many present-day Colt revolvers have names such as **Trooper, Lawman, Police Positive** and so on, they may well be used in military hands.

One particular Colt revolver that comes into this category is the **Python**. First introduced in 1955, this weapon has a shrouded barrel with a distinctive appearance and is chambered for one cartridge only, the 0.357-in Magnum (9-mm). The Python is a very powerful weapon, but to absorb some of the effects of the heavy cartridge load it has to be constructed in an equally heavy fashion. It is thus very heavy (1.16 kg/2.56 lb) but this weight makes the revolver a very steady weapon to aim and fire, and also makes it very strong, so strong in fact that it can withstand the very worst rigours of a long military life. The Python is available in two barrel lengths, 102 mm (4 in) and 152 mm (6 in).

One advantage of the revolver is its capacity to remain in operation after harsh treatment. Powerful weapons such as the Colt Python would be extremely valuable to a Central American guerrilla, with guns, rounds and spares provided in many cases by interested parties in the USA.

Colt revolvers (continued)

Another Colt revolver is the Trooper. Although no longer available, the Trooper first appeared in 1953, again in a variety of barrel lengths and in various calibres, most of them tending to the heavy side, and with many ending up in military use, although mostly in security rather than combat roles. The Trooper has now been replaced by the **Lawman Mark III**, which is produced only in 0.357-in Magnum and with barrels as short as 51 mm (2 in). Again, many of these are in military use all over the world.

Specification
Lawman Mark III
Calibre: 0.357-in Magnum (9-mm)
Weight: 1.022 kg (2.253 lb)
Lengths: overall 235 mm (9.25 in); barrel 2 or 4 in (51 or 102 mm)
Muzzle velocity: about 436 m (1,430 ft) per second
Chamber capacity: 6 rounds

Colt revolvers are available in a number of calibres, with the .357 Magnum round (actually of 9-mm calibre) being used in the powerful Lawman Mk III. The Colt Cobra (bottom) is similar to the Python, but is chambered for the 0.38 Special round instead of the Magnum.

USA
Ruger revolvers

The armaments concern of Sturm, Ruger and Company Inc. of Southport, Connecticut, produced its first pistol, an automatic, in 1949 and thereafter has never looked back. The company owe a great deal of its success to the astute observation that there was still a large market for single-action revolvers in the USA but that Colt, the obvious choice for such a weapon, was no longer interested in making them. Sturm, Ruger and Co. decided to fill the gap and have been making revolvers (among other types of weapon) ever since.

Before simply copying the old Colt designs, William B. Ruger decided to examine the fundamental design aspects of the revolver in all its forms and soon came up with what was a very modern version of a weapon that had been around for nearly a century. New types of steel and other materials (especially springs) were introduced and the manufacture was gradually developed into a modular system where components could be added or subtracted to form any particular model. The point has now been reached where Sturm, Ruger and Co. produces a very wide range of modern revolvers to meet just about any requirement, military or civil.

Ruger revolvers are today produced in various barrel lengths and in varying finishes, including stainless steel. The revolvers are also available in a wide range of calibres from 0.38-in Special (9-mm) up to the Magnums, although the Magnums are not usually selected for ordinary military use. Typical of the service revolvers currently on offer is the **Service-Six** chambered for either the 0.38 Special or 0.357-in Magnum (again 9-mm) cartridges. The Service-Six can be fitted with either a 70-mm (2.75-in) or 102-mm (4-in) barrel, while the generally similar **Security-Six**, intended for police use, can have even longer bar-

rels. The trigger actions of both are single- and double-action. Some Ruger revolvers fire rimless 9-mm Parabellum ammunition, so for loading these rounds special 'half moon' clips, each holding three rounds, have to be used.

One particular Ruger revolver caused quite a stir when it was first introduced in 1955. This was the famous **Ruger Blackhawk** that could fire the very powerful 0.44-in Magnum (10.92-mm) round, making the Blackhawk one of the most powerful revolvers obtainable. This was too much of a handful for most users, so the Blackhawk range has now been extended to include other less potent cartridges and it is still in great demand by many pistol enthusiasts.

Specification
0.38-in Service-Six
Calibre: 0.38-in Special (9 mm)

Above: Ruger's Speed-Six is known to the US Army as the GS-32N. It is made in two versions: one for 0.357 Magnum/0.38 Special and one for 9-mm Parabellum. The 9-mm is rimless so three round half-moon clips are used to ensure ejection.

Weight: 0.935 kg (2.06 lb)
Lengths: overall 235 mm (9.25 in); barrel 102 mm (4 in)
Muzzle velocity: 260 m (853 ft) per second
Chamber capacity: 6 rounds

Most Ruger pistols in US military use are in the hands of military police or security forces. These roles require familiarity with and training in handling powerful handguns so that the capability of Magnum or Special calibre pistols is not wasted.

9-mm FN High-power

The **Browning High-power** pistols were first designed in 1925 by J.M. Browning, the famous weapons designer, but they are still in production and service to this day. The main producer is still the Belgian Fabrique Nationale (FN) of Herstal, although spares are being made in Canada following World War II production in that country.

FN now makes several variants of the High-power in addition to the basic military version. All use the same basic Browning short recoil method of operation, and can easily be recognized as coming from the same stable. One variant is the **High-power Mk 2**, which can be regarded as an updated version of the original with more modern finish and grip shape but still unchanged inside. There are also three versions of the standard military model.

The basic military model is now known to FN as the **BDA-9S**. The smaller **BDA-9M** uses the same frame as the BDA-9S but it is combined with a shorter slide and barrel, also used on the compact version of the family, the **BDA-9C**. The BDA-9C is a very small pistol for its calibre, and has a much shortened butt holding only seven rounds instead of the usual 14 of the other models. It is intended to be a 'pocket pistol' for use by plain clothes police units and for specialist roles such as VIP protection.

In recent years other versions of the High-power have appeared, some with specially-lightened slides to reduce weight and some with components made from light alloys, again to reduce weight. All these versions fire the 9-mm (0.354-in) Parabellum cartridge and all have found ready buyers, even in a world market sated with more modern pistol designs.

One factor that has consistently sold the FN High-power pistols has been the series' extreme robustness. The pistols are capable of accepting very hard use and will fire under the most adverse conditions, always providing that (as with any weapon) they are properly maintained and are loaded with decent ammunition. The High-power can be a bit awkward to handle as on all but the BDA-9C Compact

Above: Many of the great J.M. Browning's designs have proven exceptionally long-lived, with the Browning High-power pistol being no exception. This example has an advanced 'red spot' sighting device, and custom non-slip grips.

model the butt is rather wide to accommodate the double-stack box magazine. However, this has not prevented the High-power being used as a target pistol by some enthusiasts.

Specification
FN High-power
Calibre: 9 mm (0.354 in)
Lengths: overall 200 mm (7.874 in); barrel 118 mm (4.645 in)
Weights: empty 0.882 kg (1.944 lb); loaded 1.04 kg (2.29 lb)
Muzzle velocity: 350 m (1,148 ft) per second
Magazine capacity: 14 rounds

Above: Developed from the High-power to provide a genuine pocket pistol capable of firing full-power rounds, the Browning Compact has a very short butt, although the shortened slide is less obvious.

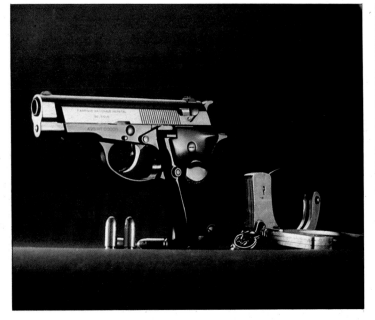

Left: Latest development from FN is the 7.65-mm or 9-mm short DA 140. Years of experience with the High-power and a collaboration with Beretta of Italy have produced a light, effective pistol.

Above: The 'Grande Puissance' remains in production after 45 years and is in use in 55 countries. It was the first of the large-capacity pistols, and remains one of the most popular.

Heckler & Koch pistols

Since the early 1950s Heckler & Koch GmbH of Oberndorf-Neckar has been one of the major European small-arms manufacturers, and although best known for its range of rifles and submachine guns the firm has also produced a range of advanced automatic pistol designs.

One of the first of these was the **Heckler & Koch HK4** intended as a small pistol firing a variety of light ammunition varying from 9-mm Short (0.380-in), through 7.65-mm (0.301-in) to 6.35-mm (0.25-in) and even 0.22-in Long Rifle (5.59-mm). All that has to be done to change the ammunition fired is the replacement of the barrel, the springs and the magazine. The HK4 is no longer in production.

The much larger **P7 K3** pistol uses 9-mm Parabellum ammunition and is one of the West German 'super safety' pistols with various built-in safety features to meet police requirements. It uses a prominent grip safety to prevent firing if the pistol is dropped accidentally and the same grip safety also acts as a cocking device for complete one-handed operation. Locking is carried out using a gas-operated delayed-blowback method similar to that used on the Steyr GB pistol and the German Volkspistole of World War II. The P7 K3 has been adopted by the West German army and many police forces.

By contrast a third Heckler & Koch pistol, the **P9S**, uses a small version of the roller and block delay locking device used on the Heckler & Koch G3

assault rifle. This system uses the recoil forces to force the bolt-body to the rear but at the same time two rollers are forced into barrel extensions to prevent further movement until the pressure on the bolt body has dropped to a safe level. This safe locking system allows the 9-mm Parabellum cartridge to be fired from a relatively light pistol, and to add to the locking safety there are numerous others including the usual feature that allows the pistol to be carried safely with a round already in the chamber; this safety can be released by operating a small cocking lever. The P9S has been sold to many armed and police forces worldwide. At one time an 11.43-mm (0.45-in) ver-

sion was produced for the American market, and a special version with a magazine holding 13 rounds, the **P7M13**, can be supplied. The P9S is licence-manufactured in Greece as the **EP9S**.

Specification
HK4
Calibre: 9 mm Short*
Weight: loaded 0.6 kg (1.32 lb)
Lengths: overall 157 mm (6.18 in); barrel 85 mm (3.35 in)
Muzzle velocity: 299 m (981 ft) per second
Magazine capacity: 7 or 8 rounds*
(* also other smaller calibres, all using an 8-round magazine)

P9S
Calibre: 9 mm (0.354 in)
Weight: loaded 1.065 kg (2.348 lb)
Lengths: overall 192 mm (7.56 in); barrel 102 mm (4.015 in)
Muzzle velocity: 351 m (1,152 ft) per second
Magazine capacity: 9 rounds

P7 K3
Calibre: 9 mm (0.354 in)
Weight: loaded 0.95 kg (2.09 lb)
Lengths: overall 171 mm (6.73 in); barrel 105 mm (4.13 in)
Muzzle velocity: 351 m (1,152 ft) per second
Magazine capacity: 8 or 13 rounds

Above: Conceived as a military pistol, the Heckler & Koch P9 is unusual in that it employs a version of the roller and block delayed-locking system (as used in the well-known Heckler & Koch family of rifles).

Below: Of rugged and simple construction, the Heckler & Koch P7 (PSP) self-loading pistol has been adopted as standard by the West German police and army. It has been designed as a police pistol.

An increasingly important element in any nation's armed forces is that of counter-terrorist warfare. Many nations have formed paramilitary units within the police forces; amongst the most effective of such groups is West Germany's GSG-9, ostensibly a branch of the Border Police.

Heckler & Koch 9-mm VP70M

The 9-mm (0.354-in) **Heckler & Koch VP70M** is a rather unusual pistol that at one time might have been placed in the machine pistol category, but for various reasons it cannot be called that for it has only a limited automatic-fire capability. A true machine pistol can fire in fully automatic mode, but the VP70M can fire only three-round bursts and then only when the carrying holster is attached to the butt to form a shoulder stock.

As a conventional pistol the VP70M uses a blowback action allied to an unusual trigger design. It uses a double-action mechanism and requires a pronounced first pressure when pulled back. Further pressure causes the trigger bar to slip off a spring-loaded firing pin to fire the loaded cartridge. There is thus no additional safety catch as it requires a definite pressure to fire the weapon.

Much of the receiver is made from hard plastics and there are only four moving parts, a number that has been kept to a minimum, for when the pistol is firing three-round bursts the cyclic rate of fire is equivalent to 2,200 rounds per minute which sets up considerable internal forces. The three-round bursts can only be fired when the holster/shoulder stock is fitted as the selector for the burst mode is in the holster. The stock engages in grooves on the pistol receiver and butt, and to take full advantage of the burst mode the magazine holds 18 rounds. Single shots can still be selected when the stock is attached.

A special version of the VP70M known as the **VP70Z** was produced. This version did not have the holster/shoulder stock capability and could not be used to fire bursts. It was produced for civilian sales only.

The VP70M caused quite a stir when it first appeared, and sales were made to several police and armed forces in Asia and Africa. But both the VP70M and VP70Z are now no longer manufactured. The VP70M in particular was viewed with deep suspicion by security forces in several European nations who had visions of these pistols falling into the wrong hands, but for all that the design features of the VP70M are almost certain to reappear in future pistols.

Specification
VP70M
Calibre: 9 mm (0.354 in)
Weights: empty 0.823 kg (1.814 lb); pistol loaded 1.14 kg (2.5 lb); pistol and stock loaded 1.6 kg (3.53 lb)
Lengths: pistol 204 mm (8.03 in); barrel

Heckler & Koch's VP-70 represents one of the most successful compromises between handling and rate of fire.

116 m (4.57 in); pistol and stock 545 mm (21.45 in)
Muzzle velocity: 360 m (1,181 ft) per second
Magazine capacity: 18 rounds
Rate of fire: 3-round burst (cyclic) 2,200 rpm

Walther P1 and P5

One of the most widely-admired and respected pistol designs that emerged from World War II was the 9-mm (0.354-in) **Walther Pistole 38**, or **P38**. This is still in production to this day at the Carl Walther Waffenfabrik at Ulm, but is now known as the **Walther P1**, though versions produced for civilian sales are still marked as the P38.

The main change in the P1 from the wartime version is that the modern weapon uses a lighter frame rather than the all-steel frame of World War II. Otherwise the only differences are the markings. The P1 remains an excellent combat pistol and it is still used by the West German armed forces and by those of a number of other nations, including Portugal and Chile.

The **Walther P5** is a much more modern design that was originally produced to meet a West German police specification that called for a double-action trigger mechanism combined with a high standard of safety. The resultant weapon emerged as a very compact and neat design with the required double action but with no less than four inherent safety features. The first is that the firing pin is kept out of line with the hammer unless the trigger is physically pulled. Another is that even if the hammer is released by any other means than the trigger the firing pin will not be struck. The hammer itself has a safety notch to form the third safety feature, and to top it all the pistol will not fire unless the slide is fully closed with the barrel locked to it.

Getting all these safeties into a pistol as small as the P5 has been a major design accomplishment, but the P5 is an easy weapon to use and fire, and as far as the user is concerned there are no extra features to worry about. The P5 is easy to aim and shoot, and its smooth lines ensure that it is unlikely to be caught on clothing when being handled. It continues to use the same well-tried 9-mm Parabellum ammunition as the P1 and many other pistols. To date some West German regional police forces have adopted the P5 and it has been adopted as the standard police pistol for the Netherlands police force.

Specification
P1
Calibre: 9 mm (0.354 in)
Weight: loaded 0.96 kg (2.11 lb)
Lengths: overall 218 mm (8.58 in);

Walther's P5 pistol has been adopted by several European police forces, and has been built to a very high safety specification.

The Walther P1 is still produced commercially as the P.38. This is the P.38K, or short version of the pistol.

barrel 124 mm (4.88 in)
Muzzle velocity: 350 m (1,148 ft) per second
Magazine capacity: 8 rounds

P5
Calibre: 9 mm (0.354 in)
Weight: loaded 0.885 kg (1,95 lb)
Lengths: overall 180 mm (7.09 in); barrel 90 mm (3.54 in)
Muzzle velocity: 350 m (1,148 ft) per second
Magazine capacity: 8 rounds

Weapons fitted with suppressors are much in demand for clandestine purposes. This version of the P1, known as the P4, was among a batch seized by Customs to forestall an attempt to export them illegally to Libya.

USSR
9-mm Makarov

The **Makarov** automatic pistol was developed in the USSR during the late 1950s and was first noticed by various Western intelligence agencies during the early 1960s. In design terms it is an enlarged version of the German Walther PP, a pistol first introduced in 1929 and ever since acknowledged to be one of the best of its type. However, the Makarov uses a different 9-mm (0.354-in) cartridge to any other in use, for it is intermediate in power between the 9-mm Parabellum and the 9-mm Short. This allows the Makarov to use a straightforward blowback operating mechanism without the complications that would be needed with a more powerful cartridge. The Makarov cartridge appears to have been based on a World War II design known as the Ultra which was not accepted for German war-time service, but which attracted some attention in the West for a while. The Ultra has not been produced in the West in any form, but the Soviets took to it and also use the Makarov round in the Stechkin machine pistol.

The Soviets know the Makarov as the **PM (Pistole Makarov)**. As well as being used by the Soviet armed forces

the Makarov is also used by virtually all other Warsaw Pact forces and by a great many of the Eastern bloc police forces as well. It is a sound, rugged and simple weapon that can be relied upon to operate even under severe conditions. Most accounts state that the pistol is rather awkward to handle as the butt is rather thick, but this is presumably no problem for Eastern bloc soldiers, many of whom have to wear heavy gloves during most of the year.

The Makarov has been manufactured outside the USSR. One of the largest producers is China, where it is known as the **Type 59** and from where it is being offered for export in opposition to the Soviets who often hand out Makarovs as part of their military aid packages. The East Germans produce a pistol almost identical to the Makarov known as the **Pistole M**, while the Poles turn out yet another Makarov 'lookalike' known as the **P-64**. The special Makarov ammunition is also manufactured in all three of these countries.

Below: The Makarov is a straightforward blowback pistol apparently derived from the pre-war Walther PP and PPK designs.

Specification
Makarov
Calibre: 9 mm (0.354 in)
Weight: empty 0.663 kg (1.46 lb)
Lengths: overall 160 mm (6.3 in); barrel

91 mm (3.58 in)
Muzzle velocity: 315 m (1,033 ft) per second
Magazine capacity: 8 rounds

An officer of the Soviet Naval Infantry prepares to fire his Makarov 9-mm pistol. The Naval Infantry is small in comparison with most Soviet arms, but for its size is regarded as one of the most effective fighting forces possessed by the Soviet Union.

SUB-MACHINE GUNS

Sub-machine guns of WW11

The sub-machine gun was born out of the trenches of World War I. In the confined, close-quarter fighting troops began to feel the need for some form of compact automatic weapon that would be less awkward to handle than a bayonetted rifle. Faced with this demand, manufacturers turned their hands to producing such a weapon.

Armed with the MP40 sub-machine gun, members of the Waffen SS pose for a propaganda photograph. These are French volunteers, as indicated by the tricolour arm patch.

The Italians were the first to introduce what might be termed a sub-machine gun. This was the Villar-Perosa which, while often quoted as being the first sub-machine gun, was in many ways a blind alley, for the Villar-Perosa was used only as a light machine-gun. The first true example of what was to be termed the machine-pistol or sub-machine gun was thus the German MP18. This appeared in front-line service during 1918 and to this day the MP18 remains the best example of all the attributes of the sub-machine gun.

The MP18 used a pistol cartridge (a small, relatively low-powered charge firing a small but heavy bullet). If a hand-held weapon was to be used to fire fully automatically the round fired had to be light and the pistol cartridge was the obvious choice. The MP18 fired the 9-mm Parabellum cartridge and in the years that followed this became an almost universal choice for most designs. Using a pistol cartridge also allowed the employment of an operating principle that had long been used on automatic pistols, the blow-back principle.

The blow-back principle is very simple. On the MP18 the magazine was fitted and the gun cocked by using a side-mounted lever in a slot. When the trigger was pulled it released the breech block to move forward under the energy from a large spring. As it moved forward the breech block picked up a cartridge from the feed, pushed it into the barrel chamber and once the round and breech block were in position the firing pin fired the cartridge. The recoil forces produced by the cartridge were initially overcome by the forward energy produced by the mass of the breech block and the spring, but the block remained in place long enough to 'lock' the system until the recoil forces were able to push back the breech block and its spring to their original condition. If the trigger was still pulled, the cycle began again and went on until the trigger was released.

If this simple operating principle was ever abandoned, the result was usually less than satisfactory, for the mechanism would be over-complex and would have more pieces to break or jam. But if the operating system could be kept basic and light, and the MP18 was light enough to be carried and used by one man, the overall concept could be kept simple. At first this was not always realized as gunsmiths lavished their considerable skills on many of the early sub-machine gun types. When the needs of World War II arrived it did not take long for the frills to be ditched in the rush to produce serviceable weapons rapidly. Things reached the point where the resultant sub-machine guns were horrible to look at, the obvious examples being the British Sten and the American M3. But these types lent themselves to rapid and simple mass production. Welding took the place of machining from solid metal, pins took the place of time-consuming jointing methods, rivets took the place of screws and so on. At first the front-line soldiers looked askance at such products but they soon learned that they worked. Those crude weapons could produce as lethal a stream of lead as many of the more refined designs from the arsenals, they were easy to learn how to use, they were easy to maintain and their ammunition was usually easy to procure, often from the enemy.

The sub-machine gun is still with us, now in many refined forms; but close examination will usually reveal the shadow of the basic MP18 lurking in its interior. From the MP18 came all the others that followed, even including the famous Thompson Gun. Designs such as the Sten, the M3, the German MP38 and the Soviet PPSh-41 all had their part to play during World War II, and their impact will be with us for years to come.

A Thompson gunner in action during the battle for Cassino. Firepower and ease of handling made the sub-machine gun ideal in the confinement of street fighting.

Owen Gun

It took some time and some fairly desperate measures before Lieutenant Evelyn Owen was able to persuade the Australian military authorities to adopt his design of sub-machine gun in 1940. At the time the Australian army had little or no interest in the weapon and by the time they realized the importance of the weapon they expected to receive all the Sten guns they required from the United Kingdom. It took some time before they appreciated the fact that they were going to receive no Sten guns as the British army wanted all that could be produced. So they decided after much procrastination to adopt the **Owen Gun**, but even then they were not sure in what calibre. Consequently the first trials batches were produced in four calibres before the universal 9-mm was adopted.

The Owen Gun can be easily recognized by the magazine, which points vertically upwards over the tubular gun body. This odd-seeming arrangement was apparently chosen for no other reason than that it worked, and it must be said that it worked very well to the extent that once the Australian soldiers got their hands on the type they preferred it to all others, and the Owen Gun was kept in service until well into the 1960s and its successor, the X-3, still retains the overhead magazine. The rest of the gun was fairly conventional and very robust to the point where it seemed to be able to take all manner of punishment and withstood being dropped in mud, dust, water and just about anything else. As production increased various changes were introduced to the design. The early fins around the barrel were removed and some changes made to the butt, which could be found in versions with just a wire skeleton, an all-wood design, and one version that was half-outline and half wood. One feature of the Owen that was unique to it, apart from the overhead magazine, was that the barrel could be quickly removed for changing. Exactly why this feature was incorporated is uncertain, for it would have taken a long period of firing for the barrel to become unusably hot, but the feature was retained through the design life of the weapon. Another odd point regarding the Owen was that once in service they were often painted in camouflage

Above: The Owen sub-machine gun was a sturdy and reliable weapon that soon gained itself a high reputation. The example has a camouflage paint scheme.

Right: The Australian Owen sub-machine gun's most prominent recognition feature was the vertically-mounted box magazine. The example shown here is one of the early production models.

schemes to suit the local terrain. For the Australian army (and the Owen was used by no other forces) that meant the hot and sweaty jungles of New Guinea, where the Australian soldiers found the Owen ideal for the close-quarter combat that the jungles enforced. It was true that the Owen was rather heavier than most comparable models but the forward-mounted grip and the pistol grip made it easy to handle.

The top-mounted magazine had one slight disadvantage for the firer as the magazine position meant that the sights had to be off-set to the right side of the body, an awkward arrangement but one that mattered little once the weapon was used in action for, like most sub-machine guns, the Owen was almost always fired from the hip.

Production of the Owen ceased in 1945 but in 1952 many were virtually rebuilt and provision was made for a long bayonet to be fitted to the muzzle; some versions made in 1943 used a much shorter bayonet that fitted over the muzzle with an almost unique tubular mount but they were not widely issued.

Specification:
Calibre: 9 mm
Length: 813 mm (32 in)
Length of barrel: 250 mm (9.84 in)
Weight loaded: 4.815 kg (10.6 lb)
Magazine: 33-round vertical box
Rate of fire, cyclic: 700 rpm
Muzzle velocity: 420 m (1,380 ft) per second

ZK 383

The Czech **ZK 383** is one of those sub-machine guns that is now little known in the West for the simple reason that it was little used outside Eastern Europe and its combat use was mainly limited to the war against the Soviet Union. However, the ZK 383 was a very important weapon type for its time and it was considered good enough to stay in production from the late 1930s until 1948.

First designed during the early 1930s, the ZK 383 went into production

The Czech ZK 383 was very well made from machined parts and had such luxuries as a bipod and a variable rate of fire. There was even a quick-change barrel. The bulk of these weapons were later produced for the German Waffen SS, who found it a heavy but reliable weapon.

at the famous Czech Brno arms plant, known for the later introduction of what was to be the Bren gun. The ZK 383 was a relatively large and heavy weapon for the sub-machine gun class, a feature emphasized by uncommon application of a bipod under the barrel on some models. This bipod was the result of the Czech army's tactical philosophy, for it regarded the weapon as a form of light machine-gun, in direct contradiction of the usually accepted role of a close-quarter combat weapon. This odd approach was further emphasized by the use of what was one of the ZK 383's oddest features in the form of a capability for two rates of fire. The ZK 383 could fire at the rate of 500 or 700 rpm, the fire rate being altered by the addition or subtraction of a small 0.17-kg (0.37-lb) weight to the breech block – with the weight removed the breech block could

move faster and thus the rate of fire could be increased. The slower rate of fire was used when the ZK 383 was used with its bipod as a light machine-gun, and the faster fire rate when the ZK was carried as an assault weapon.

But that was only the Czech army's point of view, and the feature does not appear to have been used much by the other customers for the weapon. The Bulgarian army adopted the type as their standard sub-machine gun (it used the ZK 383 until at least the early 1960s), but by far the largest number of ZK 383s were produced after 1939 for the German army. When they took over Czechoslovakia in 1939 the Germans found the ZK 383 production line still intact, and it was a sensible move as far as they were concerned to keep it intact for their own uses. The Brno factory was taken over for SS weapon production and thus the ZK 383 output

was diverted to the Waffen SS, who used the weapon only on the Eastern Front. The Waffen SS examples were all known as the **vz 9** (vz for vzor, the Czech for model) and the Waffen SS found it effective enough for it to become one of their standard weapons. Numbers were kept in Czechoslovakia for use by the Czech civil police who had their own version, the **ZK 383P** which was produced without the bipod.

The only nations other than Czechoslovakia, Bulgaria and Germany that purchased the ZK 383 were Brazil and Venezuela, and even then the numbers involved were not large. Apart from the use in Eastern Europe the ZK 383 had few points to attract attention and in many ways it was too complicated for the role it was called upon to play. The Czech army's predilection for the design as a light

machine-gun led to all manner of detail extras that the weapon did not need. The dual rate of fire feature has already been mentioned, as has the bipod, but the sub-machine gun does not really need a complex barrel-change mechanism, an all-machined mechanism made from the finest steels available or an angled breech block return spring angled into the butt. The ZK 383 had all these, making it a very reliable sound weapon but one that was really too complex for its role.

Specification:
Calibre: 9 mm
Length: 875 mm (34.45 in)
Length of barrel: 325 mm (12.8 in)
Weight loaded: 4.83 kg (10.65 lb)
Magazine: 30-round box
Rate of fire, cyclic: 500 or 700 rpm
Muzzle velocity: 365 m (1,200 ft) per second

 FINLAND

Suomi m/1931

The **Suomi m/1931** is now little known but in its day it was one of the most sought-after and admired sub-machine guns produced anywhere. The design of this weapon went back to the early 1920s and was almost certainly influenced by some German weapon designers who used Finland as a means of escaping the turmoil and uproar of post-war Germany. Using the influence and advice of such Germans the Finns gradually produced a series of very sound and effective sub-machine guns that resulted in the m/1931.

As sub-machine gun designs go there is little remarkable with the m/1931, for it used a conventional blow-back action and an orthodox layout. Where it did score over many existing designs was that it was extremely well made, almost to the point of lavishness in the quality of material used and the excellence of the machining, and the other point was the feed systems employed. These feed systems used a number of magazines that were so effective that they were extensively copied later, even by the Soviets who normally preferred their home-produced designs. There were two main versions, one a 50-round vertical box magazine and the other a 71-round drum magazine. In the box magazine the normal lengthy bulk of 50 rounds of ammunition was overcome by having the magazine split into two vertical columns. Rounds were fed from one column and then the other. In action this feed system was much favoured as it enabled a soldier to carry into action far more ready rounds than would be possible with a conventional magazine (despite this there was a normal 30-round box magazine for the Suomi).

The m/1931 was produced for the Finnish army in some numbers and it proved itself in action during the 1940 Russian invasion of Finland. There were several export models of the m/1931, some of them with small bipods under the barrel or body, and these were purchased by Sweden and Switzerland, who both set up their own production lines, as did a company in Denmark. The type was adopted by the Polish police before 1939, and examples popped up during the Spanish Civil War on both sides. Since then the

Above: The Suomi m/1931 was one of the most well-manufactured sub-machine guns ever made, for practically every part was machined from solid metal.

Right: The Suomi m/1931 in action, fitted with the 71-round magazine. Unlike many other sub-machine guns the m/1931 had a long barrel that was accurate enough for aimed fire at most combat ranges.

m/1931 has kept appearing up all over the place whenever conflicts arise. It is still in limited service in Scandinavia to this day and this longevity can be explained by two simple factors. One is that the m/1931 is so well made that it just will not wear out. The same sound manufacture also explain the reliability, for the m/1931 is one of those weapons that will work under any conditions without ever seeming to go wrong, and as mentioned above the feed system for the ammunition is almost legendary in its reliability. These two factors alone explain the high regard shown to the m/1931 in the past, but there was another factor. When the m/1931 was produced no pains were spared on detail machining and such care was taken on this that the whole of the gun, the body and bolt included, were machined from the solid metal. Consequently the gun was,

and still is, very accurate for its type. Most sub-machine gun types are accurate only to a few yards and most are almost useless at range over 50 m (55 yards). The m/1931 can be used accurately at ranges up to 300 m (330 yards). In relative numbers few were used during World War II but the influence of the design can be detected in many war-time models. The design was licence-produced in Switzerland for the Swiss army during 1943.

Specification:
Calibre: 9 mm
Length (butt extended): 870 mm (34.25 in)
Length of barrel: 314 mm (12.36 in)
Weight loaded (drum magazine): 7.04 kg (15.52 lb)
Magazine: 30- or 50-round box, or 71-round drum
Rate of fire, cyclic: 900 rpm
Muzzle velocity: 400 m (1,310 ft) per second

Sten sub-machine guns

After the Dunkirk evacuation of mid-1940 the British army had few weapons left. In an attempt to re-arm quickly the military authorities put out an urgent request for simple sub-machine guns that could be produced in quantity, and using the concept of the MP38 as an example the designers went to work. Within weeks the results were adopted. It was the product of two designers, Major R.V. Shepherd and H.J. Turpin who worked at the Enfield Lock Small Arms Factory, and from these three names came the universally-accepted name **Sten** for the new weapon.

The first result was the **Sten Mk I**, which must be regarded as one of the unloveliest weapon designs of all time. It was designed for production as quickly and cheaply as possible using simple tools and a minimum of time-consuming machining, so the Sten was made up from steel tubes, sheet stamping and easily produced parts all held together with welds, pins and bolts. The main body was a steel tube and the butt a steel framework. The barrel was a steel drawn tube with either two or six rifling grooves roughly carved. The magazine was again sheet steel and on the Sten Mk I the trigger mechanism was shrouded in a wooden stock. There was a small wooden foregrip and a rudimentary flash hider. It looked horrible and caused some very caustic comments when it was first issued, but it worked and the troops soon learned to accept it for what it was, a basic killing device produced in extreme circumstances.

The Sten Mk I was produced to the tune of about 100,000 examples all delivered within months. By 1941 the **Sten Mk II** was on the scene and this was even simpler than the Mk I. In time the Sten Mk II became regarded as the 'classic' Sten gun and it was an all-metal version. Gone was the wooden stock over the trigger mechanism, replaced by a simple sheet-metal box. The butt became a single tube with a flatt buttplate at its end. The barrel was redesigned to be unscrewed for changing and the magazine housing, with the box magazine protruding to the left, was designed to be a simple unit that could be rotated downwards once the magazine was removed to keep out dust and dirt. The butt could be easily removed for removing the breech block and spring for cleaning. By the time all these parts (barrel, magazine and butt) had been removed, the whole weapon occupied very little space and this turned out to be one of the Sten's great advantages. When the initial needs of the armed forces had been met, from several production lines, including those set up in Canada and New Zealand, the Sten was still produced in tens of thousands for paradrop into occupied Europe for use by resistance forces and partisans. There it found its own particular place in combat history, for the very simplicity of the Sten and the ease with which it could be broken down for hiding proved to be a major asset and the Germans came to fear the Sten and what it could do. The Germans learned, as did many others, that the bullet from a Sten was just as lethal as a bullet from something more fancy.

A silenced version of the Sten Mk II was produced in small numbers for Commando and raiding forces as the **Sten Mk IIS**, and then came the **Sten**

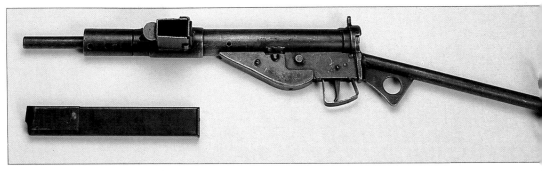

Above: The Sten Mk II was one of the most widely-used of all the Allied sub-machine guns. It looked crude but it worked, it could be stripped down for easy concealment, and it was available in quantity.

Right: The Sten was one of the first weapons issued to the newly-formed airborne troops of the British army, and this example is unusual in being fitted with a small spike bayonet.

Mk III. This was basically an even simpler version of the original Mk I as its barrel could not be removed and it was encased in a simple steel-tube barrel jacket. Again, tens of thousands were produced and were widely used.

The **Sten Mk IV** was a development model intended for parachute troops but it was not placed into production. By the time the **Sten Mk V** was on the scene things were going better for the Allies and the Mk V could be produced with rather more finesse. The Mk V was easily the best of the Stens for it was produced to much higher standards and even had such extras as a wooden butt, forestock and a fitting for a small bayonet. It had the foresight of the Lee-Enfield No. 4 rifle and the metal was even finished to a high degree, whereas the earlier marks had their metal left in a bare state with a minimum of fine finish. The Mk V was issued to the Airborne Forces in 1944, and after World War II it became the standard British army sub-machine gun.

The Sten was a crude weapon in nearly every way, but it worked and it

Right: Street fighting in the Mediterranean. This example has had a non-standard foregrip added to enhance handling.

Below: By the time the Sten Mk V was produced there was time for some finesse to be added to the basic design. While the original outline was retained a wooden butt and pistol grip and a No. 4 rifle foresight had been added.

could be produced in large numbers at a time when it was desperately needed. In occupied Europe it was revealed as an ideal resistance weapon and all over the world underground forces have been busy copying the design almost direct. The Germans even produced their own copies in 1944 and 1945. It was one of the more remarkable weapons of World War II.

Specification:
Sten Mk II
Calibre: 9 mm
Length: 762 mm (30.00 in)
Length of barrel: 197 mm (7.75 in)
Weight loaded: 3.7 kg (8.16 lb)
Magazine: 32-round box
Rate of fire, cyclic: 550 rpm
Muzzle velocity: 365 m (1,200 ft) p second

A patrol of British paratroopers is seen in the village of Oosterbeek during the ill-fated Arnhem operation. They are armed with early Sten Mark V sub-machine guns, which have had fore pistol grips added.

Lanchester sub-machine gun

In 1940, with the Dunkirk evacuation completed, the Royal Air Force decided to adopt some form of sub-machine gun for airfield defence. With no time to spare for the development of a new weapon it decided to adopt a direct copy of the German MP28, examples of which were to hand for the necessary copying. The period was so desperate that the Admiralty decided to join the RAF in adopting the new weapon; by a series of convoluted happenings the Admiralty alone actually took the resultant design into service.

The British MP28 copy was given the general designation **Lanchester** after one George Lanchester, who was charged with producing the weapon at the Sterling Armament Company at Dagenham, the same company that later went on to produce the Sterling sub-machine gun that is now the general standard weapon for so many armed forces. The Lanchester emerged as a sound, sturdy weapon that in many ways was ideal for the type of operations required of it by boarding and raiding parties. It was a very solid weapon, in many ways the complete opposite of its direct contemporary the Sten, for the Lanchester was a soundly engineered piece of weaponry with all the trimmings of a former era. Nothing was left off from the gunsmith's art. The Lanchester had a well-machined wooden butt and stock, the blow-back mechanism was very well made of the finest materials, the breech block well machined, and, to cap it all, the magazine housing was made from solid brass. A few typical British design details were added, such as a mounting on the muzzle for a long-bladed British bayonet (very useful in boarding party situations) and the rifling differed from the German original in details to accommodate the different types of ammunition the Lanchester had to use.

The magazine for the Lanchester was straight and carried a useful load of 50 rounds. Stripping was aided by a catch on top of the receiver and the very first models could fire either single-shot or automatic. That model was the **Lanchester Mk I** but on the Lan-

Above: Obviously based on the German MP 28, the Lanchester was ideally suited to the rough-and-tumble of shipboard life. It had a one-piece wooden stock based on the outline of the Lee-Enfield No. 1 Mk 3 rifle and there was a bayonet lug under the muzzle. The brass magazine housing can be seen.

Right: Lanchesters in a typical naval environment as captured U-boat personnel are escorted ashore in a Canadian port – the blindfolds were a normal procedure. The Lanchesters are carried using Lee-Enfield rifle slings.

chester Mk I* this was changed to full automatic fire only, and many Mk Is were converted to Mk I* standard at RN workshops.

The Lanchester was an unashamed copy of a German design but it gave good service to the Royal Navy throughout the war and for many years after. Many old sailors still speak of the Lanchester with respect; not with affection, for it was a heavy weapon and it had one rather off-putting feature: if the butt was given a hard knock or jar while the gun was cocked and loaded it would fire. The last example left Royal Navy use during the 1960s and the type is now a collector's item.

Specification:
Calibre: 9 mm
Length: 851 mm (33.50 in)
Length of barrel: 203 mm (8.00 in)
Weight empty: 4.34 kg (9.57 lb)

Magazine: 50-round box
Rate of fire, cyclic: 600 rpm
Muzzle velocity: about 380 m (1,245 f per second

MAS Model 1938

Often quoted as the **MAS 38**, this French sub-machine gun was first produced at St Etienne in 1938, hence the model number. The MAS 38 was the outcome of a long period of development, and was the follow-on from a model produced in 1935. But it must be stated that the development period was well spent, for the MAS 38 proved to be a sound enough weapon well in advance of its period. There were some rather odd features about the MAS 38, however. One was that it was rather complicated and another that it fired a cartridge produced only in France. Both these features can be explained by the period when it was designed. At that time there appeared to be no reason to make the weapon as simple as possible for existing production methods seemed adequate to churn out the numbers required, and at the time such numbers were not very high. The calibre can be explained by the fact that it was available at the time and so the MAS 38 had a calibre of 7.65 mm and used a car-

tridge available only in France, the 7.65-mm Long. While this cartridge was accurate it was not very powerful, and had the disadvantage that no-one else was likely to adopt it once the 9-mm calibre had been universally

adopted.

The MAS 38 has a complex mechanism with a long bolt travel that was partially off-set by having the gun body sloping down into the solid wooden butt. The cocking handle was separate

The MAS Model 1938 was a sound, advanced weapon. Unfortunately fc its future prospects, it fired an underpowered cartridge available only in France, and was complicate to manufacture.

MAS Model 1938 (continued)

Sub-Machine Guns of World War II

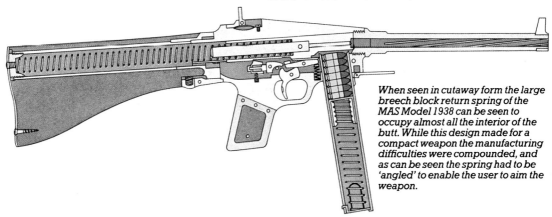

from the bolt once firing started, a good feature but one which introduced complexity into the design and manufacture. Another good point was a flap over the magazine housing that closed as the magazine was withdrawn. While this kept out dust and dirt very few other designs had this feature and most of them managed to work perfectly well without it.

In fact the MAS 38 turned out to be rather too good for the customer, who at first decided that it did not want a sub-machine gun after all. The French army turned down the weapon when it was first offered, and the first production examples went to some of the more para-military members of one of the French police forces. When hostilities did start in 1939, the French army soon changed its mind and ordered large quantities, but the complex machining that went into the MAS 38 resulted in a slow rate of introduction into service, and the French army was driven to ordering numbers of Thompson sub-machine guns from the USA. These arrived too late to make any difference to the events of 1940 and the

When seen in cutaway form the large breech block return spring of the MAS Model 1938 can be seen to occupy almost all the interior of the butt. While this design made for a compact weapon the manufacturing difficulties were compounded, and as can be seen the spring had to be 'angled' to enable the user to aim the weapon.

French army capitulated. When the French forces rearmed under the Vichy regime the MAS 38 was kept in production, and in fact the weapon was kept in production until 1949, and it was used in the Indo-China War.

The MAS 38 never got the recognition it deserved. It was rather too complicated, fired an odd cartridge and it was never possible to produce it in

quantity when it was required. Consequently it is now little known outside France and few, if any, modern weapon designs owe anything to its influence. The only armies to use the MAS 38, other than some of the ex-French colonies, were the Germans who captured enough in 1940 to issue them to their garrison force stationed in France.

Specification:
Calibre: 7.65 mm
Length: 623 mm (24.53 in)
Length of barrel: 224 mm (8.82 in)
Weight loaded: 3.356 kg (7.40 lb)
Magazine: 32-round box
Rate of fire, cyclic: 600 rpm
Muzzle velocity: 350 m (1,150 ft) per second

SWITZERLAND
Steyr-Solothurn S1-100

Although the Steyr-Solothurn is described as a Swiss weapon, for it was mainly produced in Switzerland, it was originally an Austrian design produced by Steyr who took over the Swiss Solothurn concern to produce weapon designs at a time when they were forbidden to do so by the terms of the 1919 Versailles Treaty. Even then the design was originally German (actually a Rheinmetall product) but had been switched to Austria for full development during the 1920s.

In its full production form this sub-machine gun was known as the **Steyr-Solothurn S1-100** and by 1930 the design was being produced mainly for export purposes. As with so many other designs of the period, it was based on the general outlines and principles of the German MP18 but by the time the Swiss manufacturers had finished with their development the design had reached a high point of refinement and detail manufacture. The S1-100 was an excellent product that was robust, reliable and adaptible, for the export market meant that the model had to be produced in a whole host of calibres and with a seemingly endless string of accessories and extras.

The S1-100 was produced in no less than three separate variations of the 9-mm calibre. Apart from the usual 9-mm Parabellum, the weapon was produced in 9-mm Mauser and 9-mm Steyr, the latter specially produced for the S1-100. Exports to China, Japan and South America were produced in 7.63-mm Mauser calibre, and the Portuguese purchased a large batch chambered for the 7.65-mm Parabellum cartridge. The extras were many and varied, with perhaps the most outlandish being a tripod to convert the weapon into what must have been a rather ineffective light machine-gun, though some of these were sold to China during the mid-1930s. There were also various forms of bayonet-securing devices and several barrel lengths were produced, some of them very long indeed for what were only pistol

cartridges. Another Steyr-Solothurn selling ploy was to present the S1-100 to a customer packed in individually-fitted chests containing not only the weapon but all manner of special magazines, special cleaning tools, spare parts, etc.

By the mid-1930s the S1-100 was the standard sub-machine gun of the Austrian army and police force, and when the Germans took over the state in 1938 they also took over the Austrian army armoury. Thus the S1-100 became the German **MP34(ö)**, which must have caused some confusion with the previously mentioned Bergmann MP 34. After a short period of front-line German service the confusion of no less than three types of 9-mm ammunition to be supplied for the type was too much even for the adaptable German army supply network and the MP34(ö) was relegated to German military police use; it was also retained by what was left of the Austrian police forces.

Today the S1-100 is still used in odd corners of the world, but only in very small numbers. Perhaps the most combat seen by the type was in China where at one point the S1-100 was in use by both the Chinese and Japanese armies. The latter even produced their

Above: The Steyr-Solothurn S1-100 was an Austrian version of the German MP18 produced during the 1920s and 1930s mainly for commercial sale on the export market. The type was well made and could be supplied with a range of accessories including tripods, bayonets and oversize magazines.

Right: The Steyr-Solothurn S1-100 is seen here in a drill-book position, mainly because the picture has been taken from a German manual produced for the type after the Germans had taken over Austria and its arsenal during 1938.

own copy at one point and used some of the design's features as the basis for their own 8-mm Type 100.

Specification:
S1-100 (9-mm Parabellum version)
Calibre: 9 mm
Length: 850 mm (33.46 in)
Length of barrel: 200 mm (7.87 in)
Weight loaded: 4.48 kg (9.88 kg)
Magazine: 32-round box
Rate of fire, cyclic: 500 rpm
Muzzle velocity: 418 m (1,370 ft) per second

Type 100

This Japanese private first class is armed with the Type 100 sub-machine gun. He is equipped for jungle fighting, typical of 1942.

The Japanese were surprisingly late on the sub-machine gun design scene, a fact made all the more remarkable considering their experience gained in the protracted campaigns in China before 1941 and the number of different overseas designs imported for service use or examination. It was not until 1942 that the first example of what had been several years of low-priority development left the Nambu production lines in the form of the **Type 100**, a sound but unremarkable design that was to be the only sub-machine gun the Japanese produced and used in any numbers.

The Type 100 was moderately well made but had several rather odd features. One was the use of a complex ammunition feed device that ensured that a round was fully chambered before the firing pin would operate. The exact purpose of this feature is rather uncertain (other than the safety aspect for the firer) for the cartridge used by all the Type 100 variants was the underpowered 8-mm Japanese pistol round, a rather weak and ineffective choice that was not aided by its being a bottle-shaped round that must have added its own feed complexities. The Type 100's barrel was chrome-plated to aid cleaning and reduce wear, and to add to such niceties the design had

complex sights and a curved magazine. Other oddities were the use of a complicated muzzle brake on some models and the use of a large bayonet-mounting lug under the barrel. Some versions also had a bipod.

There were three different versions of the Type 100. The first is described above. The second had a folding butt stock for use by paratroops: the stock was hinged just behind the gun body to fold along the side of the weapon. While this no doubt made the weapon handy for carrying and paradropping, it also weakened the weapon in combat situations and relatively few were made. The third version of the Type 100 appeared in 1944 at a time when demands for sub-machine guns were coming from all fronts. In order to speed up manufacture, the basic Type 100 was greatly simplified and in the result the design was lengthened slightly. The wooden stock was often left roughly finished and the rate of fire was increased from the early 450 rpm to 800 rpm. The sights were reduced to little more than aiming posts and the large muzzle lug for a bayonet was replaced by a simpler fitting. At the muzzle, the barrel protruded more from the perforated jacket and had a simple muzzle brake formed by two ports drilled in the barrel. Welding,

The Type 100 was not designed for ease of production and despite some production 'short cuts' such as spot welding and stampings there were never enough to meet demands.

often rough, was used wherever possible. The result was a much cruder weapon compared with the earlier version, but one that was sound enough for its purpose.

The main problem for the Japanese by 1944 lay not so much in the fact that the Type 100 was not good enough, but that the Japanese lacked the industrial capacity to turn out the huge numbers demanded. Consequently the Japanese troops had to fight their last ditch defensive campaigns at a permanent disadvantage against the better armed Allied troops.

Specification:
Type 100 (1944 version)
Calibre: 8 mm
Length: 900 mm (35.43 in)
Length of barrel: 230 mm (9.06 in)
Weight loaded: 4.4 kg (9.70 lb)
Magazine: 30-round curved box
Rate of fire, cyclic: 800 rpm
Muzzle velocity: 335 m (1,100 ft) per second

UD M'42

In accounts of the American sub-machine gun scene between 1939 and 1945 one weapon is often not mentioned at all, and that is the sub-machine gun known under a number of names but usually called the **UD M'42**. This weapon was designed in the days just prior to World War II as a commercial venture in 9-mm calibre. It was ordered under rather odd circumstances by an organization known as the United Defense Supply Corporation, a US government body that ordered all manner of items for use overseas, but the main point of its existence was that it was an American secret service 'front' for all forms of underground activities.

Exactly why the United Defense (hence UD) concern ordered the de-

sign that was produced by the Marlin Firearms Company is now not known, but the name 'Marlin' was subsequent-

ly often given to the weapon that became the UD M'42. The general impression given at the time was that the

weapons were to be shipped to Europe for use by some underground organizations working for the US in

The UD M'42 was not accepted as an official US service weapon, but numbers were purchased for issue to some odd undercover and special mission units. It was a very well made and finished weapon and was popular with its users.

terest, but events in Europe overtook the scheme. Some UD M'42s were certainly sent to the Dutch East Indies before the Japanese invasion of the area, but they vanished without trace.

Most of the UD M'42s did find their way to Europe but in some very odd hands. Most were handed out to some of the numerous resistance and partisan groups that sprang up around and in the German- and Italian-occupied areas of the Mediterranean Sea. There

they took part in some very odd actions, the most famous of which was when British agents kidnapped a German general on Crete. Other actions were just as dramatic but often took place so far from the public gaze that today these actions and the part the UD M'42 took in them are virtually forgotten.

This is perhaps a pity for many weapon authorities now regard the UD M'42 as one of the finest sub-machine

gun types used in World War II. Being made on a commercial and not a military basis it was well machined and very strong. The action was smooth and the gun very accurate, and by all accounts it was a joy to handle. It could withstand all manner of ill-treatment (including immersion in mud and water) and still work.

After all these years it now seems very unlikely that the full service record of the UD M'42 will ever be told,

but at least the very existence of the weapon should be better known.

Specification:
Calibre: 9 mm
Length: 807 mm (31.75 in)
Length of barrel: 279 mm (11.00 in)
Weight loaded: 4.54 kg (10.00 lb)
Magazine: 20-round box
Rate of fire: 700 rpm
Muzzle velocity: 400 m (1,310 ft) per second

USA
M3 and M3A1

By the beginning of 1941, although the United States was not yet directly involved in World War II, the American military authorities had acknowledged that the sub-machine gun had a definite role to perform on the modern battlefield. They already had to hand numbers of Thompson guns and more were on their way, but the appearance of the German MP38 and the British Sten indicated the production methods that could be employed in future mass-produced designs. Using an imported Sten, the US Army Ordnance Board initiated a design study to produce an American Sten-type weapon. The study was handed over to a team of specialists who included the same George Hyde who had developed the Hyde M2 and to executives from General Motors, to whom the mass-production aspects were entrusted. In a very short time they had designed a weapon and development models were produced for trials.

Unpopular with its users in Europe, the 'Grease Gun' gained acceptance in the Pacific, where there was no alternative weapon.

The first of these models was handed over for trials just before Pearl Harbor brought the United States into World War II. As a result the project got a higher priority and it was not long before the design was issued with the designation **M3**. The M3 was just as unpleasant-looking as the Sten. Construction was all-metal with most parts simple steel stampings welded into place. Only the barrel, breech block and parts of the trigger mechanism required any machining. A telescopic wire butt was fitted and the design was simple to the point that there was no safety system fitted and the gun could fire fully-automatic only. The main gun body was tubular and below it hung a long 30-round box magazine. An awkwardly placed and flimsy cocking handle was placed just forward of the trigger on the right-hand side, and the cartridge ejection port was under a hinged cover. The barrel screwed into the tubular body. Sights were very rudimentary and there were no luxuries such as sling swivels.

The M3 was rushed into production and once issued to the troops it soon ran into acceptance troubles. The very appearance of the weapon soon provided it with the nickname of 'Grease Gun' and it was regarded with about as much affection. But once in action it soon showed itself to be effective, but the rush into production on lines that were more used to producing motor car and lorry components led to all manner of in-service problems. The cocking handles broke off, the wire

stocks bent in use, some important parts of the mechanism broke because they were made of too soft a metal, and so on. Consequently the M3 received more than its fair share of in-service development and modification, but what was more important at the time, it rolled off the production lines in huge numbers for issue to the troops at the front.

The M3 never overcame the initial reception its appearance engendered. Whenever possible the troops in the front line opted for the Thompson M1 or used captured German MP38s and MP40s, but in the Pacific there was often no choice other than to use the M3 and when this happened the design often gained grudging acceptance. For some arms of the US forces the M3 became a virtual blanket issue. These arms included the drivers in the many transport units and tank crews. For both the M3 was easy to stow and easy to handle in close confines.

From the outset the M3 had been designed to have the capability of being rapidly converted to 9-mm calibre by simply changing the barrel, magazine and breech block. This facility was sometimes employed in Europe when the M3 was dropped to resistance forces. A silenced variant of the M3 was produced in small numbers.

Simple as the M3 was to produce it was decided in 1944 to make it even simpler. The result of combat experience allied with production know-how resulted in the **M3A1**, which followed the same general lines as the M3 but with some quite substantial changes. For the soldier the most important item was that the ejection cover was enlarged to the point where the full

The American M3 'Grease Gun' was the equivalent of the British Sten and the German MP40, for it was designed for mass production. It was a sound enough weapon but the American troops never really took to the type, preferring the Thompson.

breech block travel was exposed. This enabled the firer to place his finger into a recess in the block to pull the block to the rear for cocking, thus doing away with the awkward and flimsy cocking handle. A flash hider was added to the muzzle and some other minor changes were incorporated. The M3A1 was still in production when the war ended, by which time it had been decided to phase out the Thompson guns in favour of the M3 and M3A1.

Apart from the appearance problem, the M3 guns were not perfect weapons. They were rather prone to breakages, the ammunition feed was often far from perfect and the lack of a safety often gave rise to alarm. But it worked and it was available, and in war those two factors are more important than hankering after the something that might be better. Thus the M3 and M3A1 were used wherever the US Military went, and that was all over the world.

Specification: M3
Calibre: 0.45 in (11.43 mm) or 9 mm
Length, butt extended: 745 mm (29.33 in)
Length, butt retracted: 570 mm (22.44 in)
Weight loaded: 4.65 kg (10.25 lb)
Magazine: 30-round box
Rate of fire: 350-450 rpm
Muzzle velocity: 280 m (920 ft) per second

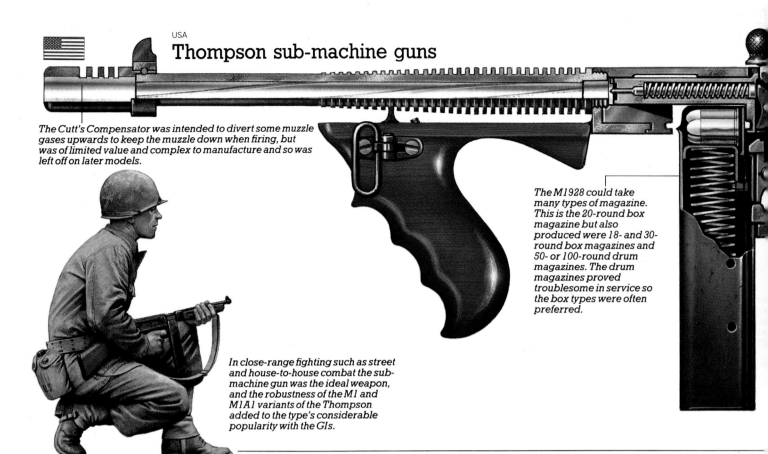

The Cutt's Compensator was intended to divert some muzzle gases upwards to keep the muzzle down when firing, but was of limited value and complex to manufacture and so was left off on later models.

The M1928 could take many types of magazine. This is the 20-round box magazine but also produced were 18- and 30-round box magazines and 50- or 100-round drum magazines. The drum magazines proved troublesome in service so the box types were often preferred.

In close-range fighting such as street and house-to-house combat the sub-machine gun was the ideal weapon, and the robustness of the M1 and M1A1 variants of the Thompson added to the type's considerable popularity with the GIs.

There can be very few who have not heard of or seen some pictures of the **Thompson** sub-machine gun at some time or another. Known universally as the 'Tommy Gun' the Thompson has even provided the sub-machine gun with a nickname, for to the lay public all sub-machine guns are Tommy Guns. Hollywood has done much to administer this fame but the story of the Thompson guns goes back to 1918.

In that year the US Army was embroiled in the trench warfare of the Western Front, a need becoming apparent for some form of 'trench broom' to sweep the trenches clear of an enemy. Since this 'sweeping' had to be carried out at short ranges a powerful cartridge was not necessary and a pistol cartridge was all that was deemed necessary. The German army had drawn the same conclusions and produced the MP18, but on the American side one General John Thompson initiated the development of an automatic weapon using the standard 0.45-in pistol cartridge. The first examples used a belt feed but this was later changed to a two-hand weapon of the

type soon known as a sub-machine gun, and with a box magazine.

By the time the first examples were produced World War I was over and all development for the next two decades was carried out on a commercial basis. The Thompson Gun, as it was soon labelled, went through a long chain of different models. Military sales were few, other than small batches to the US Army and US Navy, but it was with the coming of Prohibition in the USA that the weapon gained its public notoriety. The gang warfare that mushroomed throughout the American underworld soon found the Thompson a most useful weapon, and when Hollywood started to make gangster films the gun became famous overnight. Gradually police forces started to purchase Thompson guns, and the type became more generally accepted. Even then, military sales were few until 1928 when the US forces started to purchase some large batches.

The **Thompson M1928** was a complex piece of gunsmithing with a complicated blow-back mechanism and a

choice of a large 50-round drum magazine and 20- or 30-round vertical box magazines. Just maintaining the M1928 was quite a task. There were many variations between different models, which did nothing to endear the type to the military supply systems, and it was not until 1940 that sales really started to build up.

In 1940 several European nations were clamouring for Thompson guns. The unexpected employment by the Germans of sub-machine guns on a large scale produced requests for similar weapons from all the European combatants, and the Thompson was

Above: In 1939 and 1940 the UK had to purchase large numbers of Thompson sub-machine guns. This soldier is holding an M1928 complete with the 50-round drum magazine, a device that soon proved to be too complex for service use and too noisy due to the 0.45 calibre rounds moving about inside. Consequently these were issued to either the Home Guard or second-line units.

Left: The Thompson M1928 was the 'classic' model of the famous Thompson sub-machine gun, the weapon that was used by gangsters and American soldiers alike. For all its notoriety it was not a great commercial success until 1940.

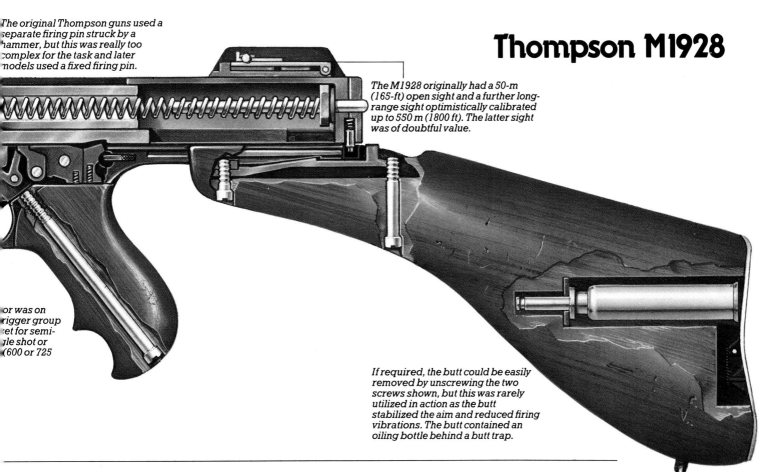

The original Thompson guns used a separate firing pin struck by a hammer, but this was really too complex for the task and later models used a fixed firing pin.

Thompson M1928

The M1928 originally had a 50-m (165-ft) open sight and a further long-range sight optimistically calibrated up to 550 m (1800 ft). The latter sight was of doubtful value.

...or was on ...rigger group ...et for semi-...le shot or ...(600 or 725

If required, the butt could be easily removed by unscrewing the two screws shown, but this was rarely utilized in action as the butt stabilized the aim and reduced firing vibrations. The butt contained an oiling bottle behind a butt trap.

...he only example on offer. Large-scale production of the Thompson commenced for France, the UK and Yugos-avia, but these orders were overtaken by events as the Thompson was an awkward weapon to mass-produce because of the large number of complex machining processes involved.

In the event the French and other orders were diverted to the United Kingdom, where the M1928 was used until the Sten became available, and even then many were issed for Commando raids and the later jungle fighting in Burma. When the USA entered the war the US Army also decided that it wanted sub-machine guns but the Thompson had to be redesigned to meet US Army requirements for mass production. After redesign the Thompson became a far simpler weapon with a straightforward blow-back action with no frills and the old large, noisy and awkward drum magazine so beloved by Hollywood was replaced by the simple vertical box. The new design became the **M1** and a later version with some extra simplifications added became the **M1A1**.

The M1 still used a wooden stock, pistol grip and foregrip (this was later replaced by a straight foregrip), but the body was machined as were many other parts. In service the M1 proved to be a well-liked weapon that was usually preferred to the unlovely M3. Again, exactly how much of this preference was due to the Hollywood image is now almost impossible to determine, for compared with many of its contemporaries the M1 was heavy and not so easy to strip and maintain. This did not deter the M1928 and the M1 from being widely copied in many back-yard workshops in the Far East where

the Thompson was regarded with great favour.

Over the years the Thompson underwent many changes and modifications. With time most of the more complex extras were removed. Out went the complex breech-locking mechanism, out went the Cutt's Compensator on the muzzle that was supposed to restrict the barrel 'climb' when firing, and out went the bulky drum magazine. The end result in the M1 form was a good sound weapon and one that is still as famous as it was in the days when the Tommy Gun was the symbol of the IRA and the Hollywood gangster era.

Specification:
Thompson M1
Calibre: 0.45 in (11.43 mm)
Length: 813 mm (32.00 in)
Length of barrel: 267 mm (10.50 in)
Weight loaded: 4.74 kg (10.45 lb)
Magazine: 20- or 30-round box
Rate of fire: 700 rpm
Muzzle velocity: 280 m (920 ft) per second

Above: A New Zealander armed with an M1928 during the Cassino campaign. This particular model is the M1928A1, a military version fitted with a horizontal foregrip in place of the original forward pistol grip. The M1928A1 also had some of the commercial refinements removed as well, and the 20- or 30-round box magazine was used instead of the larger drum magazine.

Right: The M1A1 was essentially the same weapon as the M1 but had a fixed firing pin and hammer, making the type a virtual blow-back design. It was the last production version of the famous Thompson family of weapons and retained the overall appearance and aura of the original.

Reising Model 50 and Model 55

USA

The **Reising Model 50** and the later **Model 55** are two more examples of how things can go wrong when the basic blow-back action used on the sub-machine gun is ignored and replaced with something that seems to offer a better action. On the Reising Model 50, which was first produced in 1940, the basic action was altered so that instead of the breech block moving forward to the chamber when the trigger was pulled, the action operated when the bolt was forward with a round in the chamber. This action can work quite well but it needs a system of levers to operate the firing pin in the breech block and these levers have to disconnect once the breech block moves. This all adds complexity and cost and adds something to the system which can break.

Thus it was with the Reising Model 50. The design was the result of a commercial venture and was thus not so influenced by military considerations as would have been the case a few years later, but the Model 50 was a well-made design with an unusual system of cocking the weapon by means of a small catch sliding in a slot under the fore-stock. This left the top of the gun body free of many of the usual hazards such as the cocking slot that usually provides an ingress for dirt to clog the system. But on the Model 50 all that happened was that the dirt got into

the slot underneath and was difficult to clean out, thus providing one source of potential bother. From the outside the Model 50 looked a fairly simple weapon but the internal arrangements were complex to the point where there was too much to go wrong, hence there were more stoppages and general unreliability.

When the Reising Model 50 was first offered to the US forces the US Marine Corps was some way down the list of priorities, a position it was later dramatically to reverse, so in the absence of any other source of sub-machine guns it obtained numbers of the Model 50. Once the USMC had the Model 50 it soon found the weapon wanting and

obtained other weapon types. Some Model 50s were obtained by a British Purchasing Commission but few were involved and some others went to Canada. Yet more were sent to the Soviet Union and by 1945 the Model 50 was still in production and over 100,000 had been made, a modest enough total but well worthwhile as far as the manufacturers were concerned.

Some of this total was made up by the Model 55 which was the same as the Model 50 other than that the all-wood stock of the Model 50 was replaced by a folding wire butt for use by airborne and other such units. The Model 55 was no more successful than the Model 50.

The Reising Model 50 was one of the least successful of all American sub-machine guns to see service, for it employed a complex mechanism that allowed ingress of dirt and other debris to jam the weapon to an unacceptable extent.

Specification:
Model 50
Calibre: 0.45 in (11.43 mm)
Length: 857 mm (33.75 in)
Length of barrel: 279 mm (11.00 in)
Weight loaded: 3.7 kg (8.16 lb)
Magazine: 12- or 20-round box
Rate of fire, cyclic: 550 rpm
Muzzle velocity: 280 m (920 ft) per second

MP18 and MP28

GERMANY

Although it was preceded in the time scale by the Italian Villar Perosa, the **MP18** can be considered as the father of the modern sub-machine gun. In both the general concept, operating principle and all-round appearance the MP18 embodied all the features that have become commonplace, and even today many sub-machine gun designs are no more than gradual improvement results of the basic MP18.

The design of the MP18 began on a low priority in 1916 to provide front-line troops with some form of rapid-fire low-range weapon. The designer was the man whose name later came to be synonymous with the sub-machine gun, namely Hugo Schmeisser. It was not until 1918 that large numbers of the new weapon, known to the Germans as a *Maschinen-Pistole* (hence MP) or machine pistol were issued to the troops on the Western Front to be used in the gigantic offensives that were intended to win the war for the Germans. The offensives were unsuccessful, and the MP18 had little more than local impact, the lessons to be learned from the design being largely ignored outside Germany and the few troops who had come into contact with the weapons.

The MP18 was a simple blow-back weapon firing the classic 9-mm Parabellum round that was to become the prototype for nearly all weapons to come. Considering later designs the MP18 was very well made, with a solid wooden stock and a 32-round 'snail' magazine (intended originally for the famous Luger pistol) mounted in a housing on the left of the gun body. The barrel was covered by a prominent perforated jacket to aid barrel cooling after firing, and the weapon fired on full automatic only. In its intended role of trench fighting it was a great suc-

cess, but too many front-line commanders attempted to use it as a form of light machine-gun and were thus disappointed with the MP18's performance. Consequently the MP18 had a mixed reception other than with the storm-troopers in the front assault waves, who found it invaluable at close quarters.

When Germany was disarmed after 1919 the MP18 was passed to the German police in an attempt to keep the concept alive. Numbers were also handed over to the French army who used them (but so little) that they were still 'on the stocks' in 1939. In German police service they were also modified during the 1920s to replace the Luger 'snail' magazine with a simple inline box magazine that again became the virtual prototype of what was to follow. In 1928 the MP18 was placed back into limited production in Germany, this time as the **MP28**, with new sights, a

single-shot fire feature, some small internal changes on the breech block and all manner of extras such as the mounting for a bayonet. The MP28 had the new box magazine as standard and the type was produced in Belgium, Spain and elsewhere for export all over the world, with China being one of the largest markets. Others went to South America and one batch, produced in the 7.65-mm calibre, was sold to Portugal.

By 1939 there were still appreciable numbers of MP18s and MP28s around, and the design went to war in Europe once again. By 1945 the weapons were still being encountered not only in the hands of the Germans but also in the hands of resistance forces and the many partisan forces.

Perhaps the greatest importance of the MP18 and the MP28 was not in their use as weapons, although they were successful enough in that, but in their

The German MP28 was a revised model of the original MP18. It retained the general outline of the MP18 but was able to fire either single shot or full automatic.

example for other designers to follow. With the MP18 the sub-machine gun design was virtually 'frozen' and the basic concept remains unchanged to this day.

Specification:
MP18
Calibre: 9 mm
Length: 815 mm (32.09 in)
Length of barrel: 200 mm (7.87 in)
Weight loaded: 5.245 kg (11.56 lb)
Magazine: 32-round 'snail', later 20- or 32-round box
Rate of fire, cyclic: 350-450 rpm
Muzzle velocity: 365 m (1,200 ft) per second

MP34 and MP35

At first sight the **MP34** and **MP35** appeared to be direct copies of the MP18 and MP28, but there were in reality many differences. Easily missed at first glance was that on the MP34 and MP35 the magazine protrudes from the right hand side of the gun body instead of on the left as with the MP18 and MP28. Another detail difference was the trigger mechanism, which on the MP34 and MP35 relied on a double-pressure system for control of rate of fire. A simple light pressure on the trigger produced single shots, while a full pressure on the trigger provided automatic fire.

The MP34 was designed by the Bergmann brothers, who almost undoubtedly used the MP18 as a basis on which to improve. As they had few facilities in Germany the brothers pro-

duced their first example in Denmark and only later was production switched to Germany. The first models were the MP34 but later improvements led to the MP35, which was produced in considerably greater numbers. At first production was slow, with sales being made to such nations as Ethiopia and Sweden, but with the Spanish Civil War sales really picked up to boost the company to a major position in the sub-machine gun market. The MP35 was produced in both long- and short-barrelled versions, and niceties such as bayonet attachments and even light bipods were introduced. One very noticeable point on the MP35 was the use of a rear-mounted bolt for cocking the weapon instead of the usual side-mounted cocking lever. This meant that the interior of the weapon body

along which the breech had to travel was kept clear of the dust and dirt that usually finds its way into open side-lever actions and the MP34 and MP35 were certainly reliable weapons, even if they were a little heavier than some of their rivals.

It was this reliability that brought the MP35 to the attention of what was to be the biggest customer for the weapon, namely the Waffen SS which was looking for its own weapons procurement separate from that of the German army, and after late 1940 all MP35 production went to the Waffen SS, continuing until the war ended in 1945. But MP34s and MP35s still cropped up elsewhere, and many can still be found in use with South American police forces, while small numbers can still be encountered in the Far East. The

reason for this longevity is quite simply that the MP34 and MP35 were very well manufactured, with nearly all parts machined from the solid metal. But in most countries today the MP35 is a much prized collector's piece as the bulk of the production carried the stamp of the Waffen SS.

Specification:
MP35
Calibre: 9 mm (plus many others in export models)
Length (standard model): 840 mm (33.07 in)
Length of barrel: 200 mm (7.87 in)
Weight loaded: 4.73 kg (10.43 lb)
Magazine: 24- or 32-round box
Rate of fire, cyclic: 650 rpm
Muzzle velocity: 365 m (1,200 ft) per second

MP38, MP38/40 and MP40

When the **MP38** was first produced in 1938 it revolutionized weapon design not by any particular feature of the design but by the method of manufacture employed. Gone was the accurate machine tooling of yesteryear, along with the finely-produced wooden fittings, and the standard of finish upon which gunsmiths so prided themselves. With the introduction of the MP38 came rough and simple metal stampings, die-cast parts, plastic instead of wood, and a finish that lacked any finesse or even plating of any kind. The MP38 looked what it was, a weapon mass-produced to meet a precise military need, namely a simple and cheap weapon that would work when called upon to fire, and nothing more. On the MP38 there was no wooden butt, just a bare folding heavy wire framework that folded under the body for use in close confines such as the back of a vehicle. The body was produced from simple sheet metal stampings that could be churned out in

Two German army Panzergrenadiers armed with MP40s occupying a shell hole on the outskirts of Stalingrad. As will be understood, the MP40 was at a slight disadvantage in such positions, for the long downward-pointing magazine was no assistance when firing over the lip of such a shell hole.

any metal workshop anywhere and the breech block was provided with only a minimum of machining. Most of the outer surfaces were left in their bare-metal state and at the best they were painted. Despite all these apparently cheap and cost-cutting measures the MP38 had an immediate impact out of all proportion to its design attributes, for in the years after 1938 more and more weapons adopted similar mass-production techniques first introduced on the MP38.

The MP38 was quite orthodox so far as operation went. It had a conventionally-functioning blow-back bolt and the vertical magazine under the

Above: This MP38 was the original production version. Although the design was intended for mass production the receiver and many parts were machined – these were later replaced by the pressings and welds of the MP40.

Right: The MP40, as used by this corporal during the invasion of the USSR, was almost identical to the MP38 except that it was much simpler to manufacture.

body fed 9-mm Parabellum rounds into a conventional feed system. A cocking handle along the left-hand side of the body operated in an open slot but although dust and dirt could enter the internal workings the weapon could absorb an appreciable amount of foreign bodies before it jammed. Under the barrel muzzle there was an odd projection that was designed to catch on the edge of vehicles to act as a firing rest but the same item also acted as a muzzle cover to keep out dirt.

Once in action in 1939 one rather nasty habit of the MP38 came to light. The gun operated from the open-breech position (the bolt was cocked to the rear before the trigger could release it to fire) but if the gun was jarred or knocked the bolt jumped forward and started the firing cycle by itself. This nasty fault caused many casualties before it was modified out by the machining of a slot over the

breech block 'home' position, through which a pin could engage and lock after being pushed through a hole on the other side of the body; it could be released when required for firing. With this modification fitted the MP38 became the **MP38/40.**

During 1940 the simple manufacture of the MP38 was taken one stage further with the introduction of even more metal stampings and even simpler manufacturing methods. The new version was called the **MP40**: to the soldier in the field it was little different from the MP38/40, but for the German economy it meant that the MP40 could be easily manufactured anywhere with sub-assemblies being produced in simple workshops and assembled only at central workshops. It was churned out in tens of thousands and in the field it proved a most popular and handy weapon with Allied troops using any examples they could find or capture. The MP38/40 was often used by resistance forces and partisans as well.

The only major change to the MP40 after 1940 was the introduction of a twin-magazine feature with the **MP40/2.** This was not a success and was little used. But the MP40 is still used today in odd corners of the world, especially by guerrilla forces.

One odd word about this weapon: It is often known as the 'Schmeisser'. Ex-

Above: This cutaway drawing shows the simple 'in-line' layout of the MP38. The compact design employs the blow-back principle, but the main return spring is housed in a telescopic tube that kept out dirt and foreign objects to ensure reliability. Note also the simple trigger mechanism.

Left: An MP40 in action during the Stalingrad fighting. Although many German propaganda photographs tend to give the impression that the MP38 and MP40 were in widespread use, their issue was largely restricted to front-line divisions only and the Panzergrenadiers in particular.

actly where this name came from is not known, but it is incorrect; Hugo Schmeisser had nothing to do with the design, which originated with the Erma concern.

Specification:
MP40
Calibre: 9 mm
Length, stock extended: 833 mm (32.80 in)
Length, stock folded: 630 mm (24.80 in)
Length of barrel: 251 mm (9.88 in)
Weight loaded: 4.7 kg (10.36 lb)
Magazine: 32-round box
Rate of fire, cyclic: 500 rpm
Muzzle velocity: 365 m (1,200 ft) per second

USSR
PPD-1934/38

The Soviet Union had enough troubles during the 1920s and 1930s without worrying too much about weapon design, but when things settled down enough for the re-equipment of the Red Army to be contemplated, sub-machine gun design was not very high on the list of priorities. Rather than make any innovations in sub-machine gun design the first Soviet sub-machine gun was a combination of existing designs. This was the **PPD-1934/38.**

When it was first produced in 1934, the weapon was a combination of features from the Finnish Suomi m/1931 and the German MP18 and MP28. It remained in production until 1940 by which time some modifications had been introduced to justify the use of the full designation of PPD-1934/38. There was nothing very remarkable about the PPD-1934/38. The mechanisms was almost the same as that used on the German sub-machine gun originals and, after a short attempt to produce a Soviet-designed component, the magazine was a direct take-off from the Suomi magazine. This was the Suomi 71-round drum magazine that was to become the virtual norm for later Soviet sub-machine guns, but there was also a curved 25-round box magazine issued on occasion. This box magazine had to be curved as the cartridge used for all the Soviet sub-machine guns was the 7.62-mm Tokarev (Type P) cartridge which had a bottle-necked shape and would not therefore lie completely flat for feeding from the magazine lips into the gun body.

There was one variant of the PPD-1934/38 that was placed in production in 1940. This was the **PPD-1940**, which was a general all-round improvement on the earlier design. It did have one very noticeable recognition feature in

that the drum magazine fitted up into the gun through a large slot in the stock. Very few other sub-machine gun designs used this magazine fixing system.

When the Germans and their allies invaded the USSR in 1941 the PPD-1934/38 and PPD-1940 were in relatively short supply among Red Army units and they had little impact on the course of events. Any the Germans captured they issued to their own second-line units, but the numbers involved were never very large. By the

end of 1941 even the PPD-1940 had passed out of production for the simple reason that the Germans had overrun the arsenals concerned and there was no time to set up the extensive machine-shops and production lines elsewhere. The Red Army had to resort to newer and more easily produced sub-machine gun models.

Specification:
PPD-1934/38
Calibre: 7.62 mm
Length: 780 mm (30.71 in)

The Soviet PPD-1934 introduced one feature later used on all Soviet sub-machine gun designs: the chromed barrel to reduce wear and ease cleaning.

Length of barrel: 269 mm (10.60 in)
Weight loaded: 5.69 kg (12.54 lb)
Magazine: 71-round drum or 25-round box
Rate of fire, cyclic: 800 rpm
Muzzle velocity: 488 m (1,600 ft) per second

In many ways the **PPSh-41** was to the Red Army what the Sten was to the British and the MP40 to the Germans. It was the Soviet equivalent of the mass-produced sub-machine gun, using simple methods and a minimum of complicated machining operations. But unlike the Sten and the MP40 the PPSh-41 was the result of a more measured and involved development process than was possible with, say the British Sten and thus the end result was a much better all-round weapon.

The PPSh-41 was designed and developed starting in 1940 but it was not until early 1942, in the wake of the upheavals of the German invasion, that the first examples were issued to the Red Army on a large scale. As it had been designed from the outset for ease of production the PPSh-41 was churned out in the tens of thousands in all manner of workshops ranging from properly-equipped arsenals to shed workshops in rural areas. By 1945 it has been estimated that over five millions had been produced.

Considering that it was a mass-produced weapon, the PPSh-41 was a well-made design with a heavy solid wooden butt. It used the conventional blow-back system but it had a high rate of fire and to absorb the shock of the recoiling breech block a buffer of laminated leather or felt blocks was provided at the rear of the breech block travel. The gun body and the barrel jacket were simple shaped steel stampings and the muzzle had a downward sloping shape that doubled as a rudimentary muzzle brake and a device termed a compensator that was intended to reduce the amount of muzzle climb produced by the recoil forces when the gun was fired. The barrel was chrome-plated, a standard Soviet practice to ease cleaning and reduce barrel wear, but at one time the need for weapons was so great that the barrels were simply old Mosin-Nagant rifle barrels cut to size. The

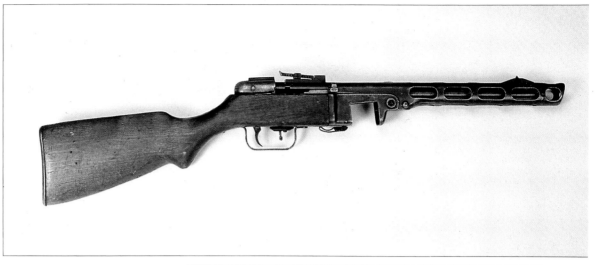

Above: The PPSh-41 was one of the 'classic' Red Army weapons of World War II, and it was produced in millions. It was an emergency design born out of the disruption of the German invasion of 1941.

Right: Involvement in the fighting extended throughout the population, for during some of the many sieges, such as those at Leningrad, Sevastopol and Stalingrad, even the women and children took up weapons.

drum magazine used was the same as that used on the earlier Soviet sub-machine guns. Fire selection (single-shot or full automatic) was made by a simple lever just forward of the trigger. Construction of the PPSh-41 was welding, pins and seam stampings. The overall result was a tough, reliable weapon.

The PPSh-41 had to be tough, for once the Red Army started to receive the type in appreciable numbers it adopted the weapon in a way that no other army even attempted to consider. Quite simply the PPSh-41 was doled out to entire battalions and regiments to the virtual exclusion of any other type of weapon other than hand grenades. These units formed the vanguard of the shock assault units that were carried into the attack on the backs of T-34/76 tanks, from which they only descended for the attack or for food and rest. They carried only enough ammunition for their immediate needs, their general life standards were low, and their combat lives were very short. But in their thousands these hordes armed with the PPSh-41 swept across eastern Russia and across Europe, carrying all before them. They were a fearful force and their PPSh-41s became a virtual combat symbol of the Red Army.

Under such circumstances the PPSh-41 (known to their users as the Pah-Pah-Shah) received virtually no maintenance, or even cleaning. Under Eastern Front conditions it soon became apparent that the best way to keep the weapon going under dust or ice conditions was to keep it completely dry and free from any sort of oil, otherwise it clogged or froze.

So many PPSh-41s were produced that the type became a virtual standard weapon for the Germany Army as well as the Red Army, the Germans even

The German army was much impressed with the Soviet PPSh-41, and when supplies of their own MP40s were lacking they took to using large numbers of captured PPSh-41s. If Soviet 7.62-mm ammunition was in short supply the weapon could fire the German 7.63-mm Mauser pistol round, and by 1945 numbers of PPSh-41s were being adapted to fire German 9-mm ammunition.

going to the extent of recalibring some of their captured hoard to their own 9 mm. Partisans found the PPSh-41 an ideal weapon for their purposes, and after the war the type was used by virtually every nation that came within the Soviet sphere of influence. It still turns up in the hands of 'freedom fighters' all over the world and it will no doubt be around for a long time yet.

Specification:
Calibre: 7.62 mm
Length: 828 mm (32.60 in)
Length of barrel: 265 mm (10.43 in)
Weight loaded: 5.4 kg (11.90 lb)
Magazine: 71-round drum or 35-round box
Rate of fire, cyclic: 900 rpm
Muzzle velocity: 488 m (1,600 ft) per minute

Soviet Sub-Machine Guns

eft: A Wehrmacht NCO beckons his men forwards during the fighting for ?ostov in the summer of 1942. He has equipped himself with a captured PPSh '1 sub-machine gun.

Above: Sailors of the Soviet Black Sea Fleet pose with their weapons. Note the 30-round box magazine on the PPSh 41 carried by the sailor in the centre.

USSR
PPS-42 and PPS-43

ew weapons can have been de-gned and produced under such de-erate conditions as those that sur-und the advent of the Soviet **PPS-42** b-machine gun. In 1942 the city of eningrad was surrounded by the erman army and the besieged Red rmy units were short of everything, cluding weapons. Leningrad con-ined a large number of manufactur-g facilities and machine shops, so hen it came to producing their own eapons the soldiers were relatively ell off, but they needed weapons uickly. Under such conditions the b-machine gun provides a basis on hich to work and so an engineer, A.I. darev, set to work.

Sudarev was limited in his choice of esign by the materials to hand and e type of machines with which he uld work. By sheer pragmatic trial nd error he developed a sub-achine gun that embodied all the fea-res to be found in other emergency esigns such as the British Sten and merican M3. The result was a simple, bust sub-machine gun manufactured om sheet metal stampings, most of em heavy for that was the only mate-al to hand. The gun was held together y welds, rivets and pins, and a simple lding butt was provided. The 35-und magazine used on earlier Soviet b-machine guns was adopted almost ichanged as production of a drum agazine would have proved too dif-:ult.

The firing trials of the new design ere carried out quite simply by hand-g out examples straight from the pro-duction shops to soldiers in the front line. Their comments and results were fed straight back to the assembly shops where any changes were made on the spot. One of these changes in-volved the use of a curved steel plate over the muzzle to act as a partial com-pensator and muzzle brake, and this crude and simple device was re-tained. In time the new weapon was provided with an official designation, becoming the PPS-42. In action around Leningrad it proved to be a thoroughly sound design and one that could be produced quickly and cheaply, so it was not long after the siege of Lening-rad was lifted that the design became official and adopted for general Red Army service. When this took place there was opportunity to remove some of the more rushed and crude features of the weapon. The folding butt was revised so that it could be folded up-wards to clear the ejection port, and the original rough wooden pistol grip was replaced by a hard rubber type. The general standard of finish was generally improved, and in this form the weapon became the **PPS-43**. In time the PPS-43 took its place with the Red Army alongside the PPSh-41, but never in quite the same numbers. Con-sidering the inauspicious beginnings of the design it proved to be an excel-lent weapon in service wherever it was taken, and in 1944 it was adopted by the Finns as their standard sub-machine gun once they came into the Soviet sphere of influence. To this day it remains in service with many armies and like the British Sten, it has been accorded the distinction of being copied in many backyard workshops for numerous subversive reasons.

The Soviet PPS-43 was the full production version of the emergency-produced PPS-42 designed during the siege of Leningrad. The PPS-43 introduced some finesse, but it was essentially a simple weapon.

Specification:
PPS-43
Calibre: 7.62 mm
Length, butt extended: 808 mm (31.81 in)
Length, butt folded: 606 mm (23.86 in)
Length of barrel: 254 mm (10.00 in)
Weight loaded: 3.9 kg (8.60 lb)
Magazine: 35-round curved box
Rate of fire, cyclic: 700 rpm
Muzzle velocity: 488 m (1,600 ft) per second

ITALY

Beretta sub-machine guns

The first of the Beretta series was the **Beretta Model 1938A**, which was produced in Brescia. The first examples were produced in 1935 but it was not until 1938 that the first mass-produced examples appeared for issue to the Italian armed forces. The term 'mass production' is perhaps rather misleading for the Berettas, as although they were produced on normal production lines, the care and attention that went into each example was such that they can almost be regarded as handmade. In fact the Berettas are still regarded as some of the finest examples of the sub-machine gun that it is possible to obtain, and the early Model 1938As were destined to become among the most prized of all.

In design terms the Berettas had little enough of note. They had a well-finished wooden stock, a tubular body, a downwards-pointing box magazine and a perforated barrel jacket, some of them with provision for a folding bayonet at the muzzle. There was nothing really remarkable in these points, but what was very noticeable was the way in which the weapon was balanced and the way it handled in action. It turned out to be a truly remarkable sub-machine gun. The superb finish endeared it to all who used the type, and one result of the painstaking assembly and finishing was a weapon that proved reliable and accurate under all conditions. The ammunition feed proved to be exceptional, but only when the proper magazines were used. There were several sizes of magazines (holding 10, 20, 30 or 40 rounds) and these were issued together with a loading device. The rounds used on the early Berettas was a special high-velocity 9-mm cartridge but this was later changed to the universal 9-mm Parabellum.

There were several variations on the Model 1938A theme, one of which lacked the bayonet and some of the refinements as it was intended to be a special lightened model for use in desert regions. When Italy entered the war in 1941 some small revision of manufacturing methods was made, but the soldier at the front would be hard

Above: The Model 1938 was a sound and well-balanced weapon that was a joy to handle and use. No expense was spared in its manufacture, and consequently it was very reliable and accurate. This example is fitted with a 10-round magazine. Note the double-trigger arrangement and the well-finished wooden stock.

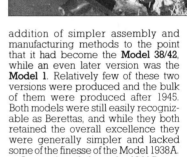

Right: Italian troops in Tunisia, their Beretta Model 1938s ready to hand. The weapon on the left is equipped with a 10-round magazine which was often employed when single-shot fire was required. The Model 1938 was very accurate and could be used in the manner of a rifle at combat ranges up to 300 m (985 ft).

put to recognize them, for the overall finish remained beautiful. Close examination revealed that the barrel jacket was altered to become a stamped and welded part but that was about the only concession to mass-production technology, and the Model 1938A retained its high reputation.

By 1944 the war situation had changed to the extent that Berettas were being produced for the German army, the Italians having surrendered in 1943. By then the basic design of the Model 1938A had been revised by the

addition of simpler assembly and manufacturing methods to the point that it had become the **Model 38/42**, while an even later version was the **Model 1**. Relatively few of these two versions were produced and the bulk of them were produced after 1945. Both models were still easily recognizable as Berettas, and while they both retained the overall excellence they were generally simpler and lacked some of the finesse of the Model 1938A.

As mentioned above, by 1944 Berettas were being produced for the Germans. Earlier in the war the Germans had been happy to use numbers of the Model 1938A and the Romanians had purchased a number (they later purchased the Model 38/42 as well). After the Italian capitulation the Berettas became standard German weapons but were little used outside Italy. The Allies greatly prized the Berettas and used them in place of their own

weapons whenever they could capture sufficient numbers, but their use by the Allies was restricted to a great extent by a shortage of Beretta magazines. Apparently the sub-machine guns were often captured without the vital magazines, which was perhaps just as well for the Italians.

Specification:
Model 1938A
Calibre: 9 mm
Length: 946 mm (37.24 in)
Length of barrel: 315 mm (12.40 in)
Weight loaded: 4.97 kg (10.96 lb)
Magazine: 10-, 20-, 30- or 40-round box
Rate of fire, cyclic: 600 rpm
Muzzle velocity: 420 m (1,380 ft) per second

The nature of the Italian Fascist state was such that by the time any youth entered the Army he was already well trained in the use of most of the weapons they would be issued with. This included the Beretta Model 1938, seen here carried by a Young Fascist being decorated by General Bastico.

The demands of war production meant that Beretta were unable to maintain their pre-war standards of excellence. Even so, the Model 38/42 was a much better weapon design than many of its contemporaries and retained many of the features of the pre-war model.

Modern Sub-Machine Guns

South Africa is one of the many
nations to use the Israeli UZI.
First seeing major service in
the 1956 Arab-Israeli conflict,
the UZI is one of the most
successful post-war sub-
machine gun designs.

*Evolved through necessity in the confined spaces of the
trenches during World War I, the sub-machine gun has found
a useful place in modern armed forces. Small, cheap and
easily concealed, it is an ideal weapon for facing the urban
terrors of the latter half of the 20th century.*

Ever since the assault rifle became a viable weapon during the latter
stages of World War II the pundits have been saying that the sub-
machine gun's day was over. The trouble is that no one seems to have
told the designers of small arms or the men who use sub-machine guns.
Today the numbers of sub-machine guns on the market are as high as
ever, and more seem to appear each year. The modern sub-machine
guns described in this issue are but a few of the more important types
currently in use. There are many more types around, some of them
having been in service since World War II, but most of the types
described are of a much more sophisticated form. All manner of detail
design features have been introduced to differentiate them from the
nasty tube and sheet metal designs of World War II, although the same
basic manufacturing principles are often used. Today there is more time
to apply better finishes and construction methods, but while costs may
have risen somewhat since World War II the modern sub-machine gun
is still a relatively cheap weapon. Perhaps it is this that ensures the
longevity of the type.

But it cannot be cost alone that maintains the sub-machine gun in use
all over the world. Despite the many advantages that the assault rifle has

to offer, it is still a complex and lengthy weapon that is nowhere near as
effective in close-quarter fighting as the sub-machine gun. Despite the
increases in weapon power achieved in recent years, many combats
still take place at close ranges and here the sub-machine gun is still as
effective as it was when it was produced to 'sweep trenches of the
enemy' during World War I. The short and handy sub-machine gun still
reigns supreme in such circumstances.

Today the sub-machine gun is carried by one new operator, the
policeman or the member of a security organization. The growth of
national and international terrorism in recent years has meant that the
agencies set against it have to be armed as effectively as their highly
organized and well-armed opponents. Thus the sub-machine gun has
assumed a new and dangerous era, and it may be many years (if ever)
before the weapon is no longer used in this relatively new and but
dreadfully public cockpit.

*Outside the Washington Hilton, 30 March 1981, President Reagan has just
been shot; his assailant is buried under a swarm of police and secret service
men. Prominent is the Israeli-made UZI sub-machine gun, carried by the
agent in the foreground.*

9-mm PA3-DM

The Argentine **PA3-DM** is a typical example of modern sub-machine gun design in two respects; one is the use of the forward-mounted 'wrap-around' breech block and the other the ability of a relatively unsophisticated engineering industry to produce modern and viable weapons.

The 'wrap-around' bolt is now a virtual fixture on many modern sub-machine guns, for it provides two important functions. One is that the breech block is to a large extent forward of the chamber when the cartridge is fired, so providing extra mass for the recoil to overcome, thereby providing an increase in locking efficiency for what is otherwise a relatively effective but inefficient blowback system. The other advantage is that by placing much of the breech block around the barrel the weapon length can be much reduced, making the overall design shorter and handier for carriage and stowage. Nearly all these 'wrap-around' designs, and the PA3-DM is no exception, use the pistol grip as the magazine housing, and this has the advantage of allowing rapid aiming, for by holding the weapon with the 'master' hand, one-handed firing is possible as though the weapon is a pistol.

The first weapon to use this 'wrap-around' feature was the Czech vz 23 series, and it has appeared on many subsequent weapons. The Argentine

design closely follows the Czech original in overall construction, for it relies on the use of simple stampings and has as its receiver housing nothing more than a section of steel tubing. The PA3-DM has its cocking handle on the left-hand side well forward so that it can be operated by either hand, and a hand grip is provided forward of the metal pistol group assembly. The PA3-DM may be found in two forms: one has a fixed plastic butt, while the other has a wire-form butt which telescopes forward on each side of the receiver. This latter is a direct copy of the wire butt used on the American M3 sub-machine gun. On both versions the barrel screws onto the front of the tubular receiver and the barrel can be adapted to mount a device for launching grenades.

The PA3-DM was used during the Falkland Islands campaign of 1982,

though not in very great numbers. Some 'trophies' were returned to the United Kingdom and may be found in some regimental museums, but otherwise it is not a weapon that is likely to be encountered outside Argentina, where it is issued to the armed forces.

The PA3-DM is manufactured by the Fabrica Militar de Armas 'Domingo Matheu' at Rosario, from which the 'DM' of the designation is derived. It is only the latest model in a long string of sub-machine guns that have been designed and produced in Argentina since the period just after World War II. Many of these sub-machine guns were orthodox designs with little of note to mention, and not all of them reached the full production stage. Some were direct copies of successful designs elsewhere: for example, the **PAM 2** dating from the early 1950s was nothing more than a direct copy of the

Captured by British forces on the Falklands during the South Atlantic conflict, the PA3-DM exemplifies the modern sub-machine gun, being simply designed and easy to manufacture.

US M3A1 calibred in 9 mm (0.354 in). Some of the other designs, such as the **MEMS** series and the **Halcon** gun, were more adventurous designs that made little impact outside Argentina.

Specification
PA3-DM (fixed-butt version)
Calibre: 9 mm (0.354 in) Parabellum
Weight: loaded 3.9 kg (8.6 lb)
Length: 700 mm (27.56 in)
Length of barrel: 290 mm (11.4 in)
Muzzle velocity: 400 m (1,312 ft) per second
Cyclic rate of fire: 650 rpm
Magazine: 25-round box

9-mm L2A3 Sterling

The sub-machine gun that is now almost universally known as the **Sterling** entered British Army use in 1955 although an earlier form, known as the **Patchett**, underwent troop trials during the latter stages of World War II. It was intended that the Patchett would replace the Sten gun, but in the event the Sten lasted until well into the 1960s.

The British army model is designated the **L2A3** and equates to the **Sterling Mk 4** produced commercially by the Sterling Armament Company of Dagenham, Essex. This weapon is one of the major export successes of the post-war years, for to date it has been sold to over 90 countries and it is still in production in several forms. The basic service model is of simple design with the usual tubular receiver and a folding metal butt stock, but where the Sterling differs from many other designs is that it uses a curved box magazine that protrudes to the left. This arrangement has proved to be efficient in use and presents no problems. It has certainly created no problems for the army in India where the type is produced under licence, or in Canada where the design is produced as the **C1** with some slight modifications.

The Sterling is a simple blowback weapon with a heavy bolt, but this bolt incorporates one of the best features of the design in that it has raised and inclined splines that help to remove any internal dust or dirt and push it out of the way. This enables the Sterling to be used under the worst possible conditions. The usual magazine holds 34 rounds, but a 10-round magazine is available along with a string of accessories including a bayonet. The weapon can be fitted with any number of night vision devices or sighting systems, although these are not widely used.

Several variants of the Sterling exist. One is a silenced version known to the British army as the **L34A1**. This uses a fixed silencer system allied to a special barrel that allows the firing gases to leak through the sides of the barrel into a rotary baffle silencer that is remarkably efficient and almost silent in use. There is also a whole range of what are known as paratrooper's pistols that use only the pistol group and the receiver allied to a short magazine and a very short barrel. These are available in single-shot or machine pistol versions. Several types of finish are produced, including what must be that for the most luxurious of sub-

machine guns, for one version is literally gold-plated. These have been produced for various potentates in the Middle East who use them for their personal bodyguards and to impress visitors; both silenced and normal versions have been produced with gold plating. Chromium-plated versions have also been made.

Right: The Sterling saw considerable service in Malaya and Borneo, where the inherent inaccuracy of the sub-machine gun proved no handicap.

Below: The Sterling is seen on exercise in the UK, at Bassingbourn. It is being replaced by the new Enfield Individual Weapon.

Machine Pistols

The virtues of the sub-machine gun in close-quarter combat ...oon led designers to attempt to turn the contemporary self-...ading (or automatic) pistol into a fully automatic weapon.

...most as soon as the automatic pistol was first produced designers were ...mpted into allowing their progeny to fire in fully automatic bursts. The conven-...nal automatic pistol simply fires a round, re-cocks itself and loads another ...und ready to fire on the repeated pull of a trigger. By simply keeping the trigger ...echanism out of the way it was (and is) easy to allow the pistol to produce ...rst fire, but the designers soon learned that this was not a course to be ...dertaken lightly.

The pistol cartridge is weak compared with a rifle cartridge, but can still ...oduce considerable recoil forces. If such cartridges are fired in rapid succes-...n they can soon overcome the mass of a light hand-held pistol and force the ...uzzle to rise or jump about erratically. In either case aimed fire becomes ...most impossible. Moreover, the bolts of most pistols are light, and this allows ...ll automatic fire to be very rapid indeed, to the extent that the limited ammuni-...n capacity of most pistols will be used in less than a second. These two ...nitations have made the machine pistol something of a rarity among combat ...eapons, but the machine pistol has nonetheless turned up throughout small ...ms development.

The first of the machine pistols to be used on any large scale were the ...ausers. Derived from the C/96 pistols, the *Schnellfeuer* (quick fire) pistols ...came very popular at one time. They must be judged as among the more ...uccessful of the type, for the old C/96 'broomhandle' pistols had the bulk and ...eight to overcome, partially at least, some of the recoil forces while the box ...agazines in front of the trigger guard had the space potential to accommodate ...ng magazines. But outside Germany and to a lesser extent Spain these ...auser machine pistols never caught on to any great extent in Europe. In the Far ...st, however, it was a different story. The Chinese took to the Mausers with a ...ll and were soon turning out their own locally-produced copies that varied in ...aterials and manufacturing standards from the excellent to the vile. The ...inese found the machine pistol to be just the sort of weapon that struck fear ...o an opponent, and the war lords who ruled in China between the world wars ...und them ideal for keeping their subjects under control. The Chinese even ...scovered the way to use the machine pistol's muzzle jump to good effect: ...ey simply turned their Mausers onto one side as they fired so that, instead of ...raying bullets at the sky, the machine pistol produced a wide fan of lethal ...ojectiles that could cover a wide horizontal arc. This simple expedient has ...en little used elsewhere, but in the Far East this ploy was standard practice.

During World War II the machine pistol underwent a brief flurry of revival but ...e advantages of the sub-machine gun proved to be too many for the relatively ...pensive machine pistol, and few were made. From time to time interest was ...vived, but it was not until after World War II that service examples were seen ...any numbers. These were intended for use by the crews of armoured or 'B' ...hicles who did not normally require a rifle, or who did not have the space to ...rry one on their normal duties. For such personnel the machine pistol seemed ...tractive and thus the Czech Skorpion, the Polish wz 63 and the Soviet Stechkin ...me upon the scene. The Stechkin may be regarded as an update of the old ...auser pistols. It has even revived the practice of using a wooden holster that ...ubles as a butt stock, and it retains all the old problems of muzzle climb during ...rst fire. At least the Skorpion and the wz 63 have bulk and some degree of ...mpensation built into their designs.

Above: The Heckler und Koch VP-70 is an ingenious modern attempt to produce a controllable machine pistol. Automatic fire is only possible when the holster/stock is fitted, allowing three-round bursts. The burst facility allows reasonable aimed automatic fire.

Below: To convert a blowback pistol to full automatic, all that is required is some means of interrupting the trigger mechanism. This home-made conversion of a Government Model Colt was captured from the IRA in Ulster. Note the extended magazine.

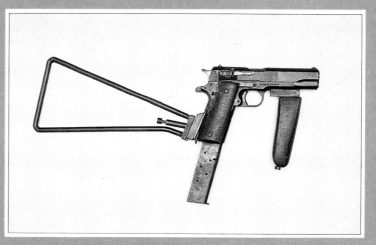

Despite the problems with the machine pistol listed above, it would be as well to list its advantages. The machine pistol can have a considerable shock effect in confined areas where any sudden spray of automatic fire will hit a target. Even the knowledge that a sudden burst of fire might be imminent can be enough for the owner of such a weapon to control local events, and it is this latter fact that makes the machine pistol attractive to many police and security forces. Even so, many sub-machine guns are now small and handy enough to rival the facilities of the machine pistol, the Mini-UZI and the Ingram designs being cases in point. But no doubt the machine pistol will continue to surface in the future.

The Sterling in all its forms has ...oved to be a very reliable and sturdy ...eapon. With many armies, including ...e British army, the weapon is used to ...m second-line personnel who do not ...ve to carry the normal service rifle ...d on vehicles it can easily be folded ...ray to take up very little stowage ...ace. With the British Army the L2A3 ...ll gradually be replaced by the new ...6-mm (0.219-in) Individual Weapon ...V) starting in the near future, but the ...ge numbers of Sterlings still around ...e world mean that it will still be a ...dely used type for many years to ...me.

...ecification
...A3
...libre: 9 mm (0.354 in) Parabellum
...eight: loaded 3.47 kg (7.65 lb)
...ngth: with stock extended 690 mm
...'.16 in) and with stock folded
...3 mm (19 in)
...ngth of barrel: 198 mm (7.8 in)
...uzzle velocity: 390 m (1,280 ft) per
...cond
...clic rate of fire: 550 rpm
...agazine: 10- or 34-round

Replacing the ubiquitous Sten in British Army service, the Sterling L2A3 9-mm sub-machine gun has been sold in over 90 countries, and has proved effective and reliable under the most extreme of weather conditions, ranging from Arctic cold to jungle heat and humidity.

9-mm F1

During World War II a Lieutenant Owen invented the sub-machine gun that still bears his name, and this weapon was used by Australian soldiers during World War II and for many years after it. One of the most recognizable features of the **Owen** sub-machine gun was the vertical magazine, a feature with no particular merit or demerit but one that the Australians found very much to their liking. Thus when the Australian army began searching for a new design to replace the old and worn Owens, it was not averse to choosing a design with an overhead vertical magazine.

Before selecting the design now known as the **F1**, the Australians investigated a number of experimental weapons that rejoiced in such names as 'Kokoda' and the 'MCEM'. Some of these experimental designs had some advanced features but were generally regarded as not being 'soldier-proof' enough to suit Australian conditions. But in 1962 a design known as the **X3** was selected for production, and this became the F1. The predilections of the Australian military were very evident, for the F1 has a vertical magazine but in order to allow a certain amount of interchangeability with other weapons the magazine is now curved and identical to that of the British Sterling and the Canadian C1.

This interchangeability factor is also evident in several other features of the F1. The pistol grip is the same as that used on the L1A1 7.62-mm (0.3-in) NATO rifle, and the bayonet is another Sterling component. In fact it is tempting to regard the F1 as an Australian Sterling but there are too many differences to support such a claim. The F1 uses a simple 'straight-through' design with the butt fixed in line with the tubular receiver, and the pistol group is arranged differently from that of the Sterling. The overhead magazine does produce one difficulty, namely sighting. In action deliberate aiming is not common but has to be taken into account, so a form of offset sighting system had to be introduced. On the F1 this is done simply by using an offset leaf sight (folding down onto the tubular receiver) allied with a fixed offset foresight. The F1 does have one rather unusual safety built into the design

which is not common but yet is simple and effective: on a short-barrelled weapon it is often too easy to place the forward grip over the muzzle or too close to it for safety, but on the F1 a simple sling swivel bracket prevents the hand from getting too close to the muzzle.

The F1 has some other simple but effective design features. One is the cocking handle, which exactly duplicates the position and action of its counterpart on the L1A1 standard service rifle in use with the Australian forces; this handle has a cover which prevents dirt and debris getting into the action, though if enough dirt does get into the action to prevent the bolt closing the cocking handle can be latched to the bolt for the firer to force it closed in an emergency.

For all its many attributes the F1 has yet to be bought outside Australia and some of its associated territories. At one time there was talk of its being replaced by the American M16A1 rifle, but the F1 is still around and seems set for a long service career to come.

Specification
F1
Calibre: 9 mm (0.354 in) Parabellum
Weight: loaded 4.3 kg (9.48 lb) with bayonet
Length: 714 mm (28.1 in)
Length of barrel: 213 mm (8.386 in)
Muzzle velocity: 366 m (1,200 ft) per second
Cyclic rate of fire: 600-640 rpm
Magazine: 34-round curved box

Above: Replacing the extremely popular Owen sub-machine gun in Australian service, the F1 retains the uniquely Australian feature of a vertical top-loading magazine. The F1 is otherwise similar to the Sterling.

Below: Simple and effective, the F1 in its prototype X3 form performed extremely well in the Mekong Delta during the Vietnam War. Modern construction made it almost 1 kg (2.2-lb) lighter than its World War II ancestor.

9-mm Model 45

The 9-mm **Model 45** was produced originally by the Karl Gustav Stads Gevärsfaktori (now part of the FFV consortium) at Eskilstuna, and is thus widely known as the Carl Gustav sub-machine gun. The Model 45 is an entirely orthodox design with no frills, and uses a simple tubular receiver and barrel cover with a simple folding butt hinged onto the pistol grip assembly. The usual blowback operating principle is employed, and overall there is nothing remarkable about the Model 45.

But there is one interesting point regarding the Model 45, and that is the magazine. On many sub-machine guns the magazine is usually one of the most trouble-prone components, for the magazine relies upon simple spring pressure to push the rounds towards the receiver, whence they are fed into the firing system. It is all too easy for rounds to become misaligned or

forced together and the result is then a misfeed or jam, and these can happen at inopportune moments in combat. On the original Model 45 the magazine used was that once used on the prewar Suomi Model 37-39, a 50-round magazine that was then considered to be one of the best in use anywhere. But in 1948 a new magazine was introduced that held 36 rounds in twin rows that were carefully tapered into a single row by the use of a wedge cross-section. This new magazine proved to be remarkably reliable and trouble-free in use, and was soon being widely copied elsewhere. Production Model 45s were soon being offered with a revised magazine housing to accommodate both the Suomi magazine and the new wedge-shaped magazine, and this version was known as the **Model 45/B**. Later production models made provision for the wedge-shaped magazine only.

The Model 45 and Model 45/B became one of Sweden's few major export weapons. Numbers were sold to Denmark and some other nations such as Eire. Egypt produced the Model 45/B as the '**Port Said**' under licence. Copies have also been produced in Indonesia. Perhaps the oddest service use of the Model 45/B was in Vietnam. Numbers of these weapons were obtained by the American CIA and converted in the United States to take a special barrel allied to a silencer. These were used in action in Vietnam by the US Special Forces on undercov-

The 9-mm Model 45 is generally known as the Carl Gustav, after its manufacturer. Conventional in design and operation, it has been in production since 1945 and has been exported widely.

-mm Model 45 (continued)

r missions. According to most reports
e silencers were not particularly
ffective and they were not retained in
se for long.
Numerous accessories have been
roduced for the Model 45, one of the
ddest being a special muzzle attachment that doubles as a blank firing de-
ce or a short-range target training
evice. The attachment is used
ogether with special plastic bullets
hich are shredded into pieces as
ey leave the muzzle for safety. These
ullets generate enough gas pressure
o operate the mechanism and if re-
uired enough pressure is available to
roject a steel ball from the attachment
self. This reusable steel ball can thus
e used for short-range target prac-
ce.

Specification
Model 45/B
Calibre: 9 mm (0.354 in) M39B
Parabellum
Weight: loaded 4.2 kg (9.25 lb)
Length: with stock extended 808 mm
(31.8 in) and with stock folded 551 mm
(21.7 in)
Length of barrel: 213 mm (8.385 in)
Muzzle velocity: 365 m (1,198 ft) per
second
Cyclic rate of fire: 550-600 rpm
Magazine: 36-round box

*Used by many countries, including
Egypt (in the 1967 war with Israel)
and the USA (in a silenced version by
special forces in Vietnam), the Carl
Gustav remains in large-scale
service with the Swedish forces.*

FRANCE
9-mm MAT 49

mmediately after 1945 the French
rmed forces were armed with a varie-
· of sub-machine guns, some of them
ating from before the war and others
ere coming from the United States
nd the United Kingdom. While the
eapons were serviceable enough,
e range of ammunition calibres and
pes was considered to be too wide,
nd after a selection process it was
ecided to standardize on the 9-mm
arabellum round for future develop-
ents. A new sub-machine gun of
rench origins was requested, and
ree arsenals responded with new
esigns. That of the Manufacture
Armes de Tulle (hence MAT) was
elected, and the weapon went into
roduction in 1949.
The **MAT 49** is still in widespread
ervice, for it is a very well made
eapon. Although it uses the now-
ommonplace method of fabricating
arts and assemblies from stampings,
ose in the MAT 49 were made from
eavy-duty steels and are thus very
rong and capable of absorbing a
reat deal of hard use. The design uses
e blowback principle but in place of
hat is now described as a 'wrap-
ound' breech block to reduce the

length of the receiver the MAT 49 has
an arrangement in which a sizable portion of the breech block enters the barrel chamber to have much the same
effect. No other design uses this feature, and there is another aspect of the
MAT 49 which is typically French. This
is the magazine housing, which can be
folded forward with the magazine inserted to reduce the bulk of the
weapon for stowage and transport.
This feature is a carry-over from the
pre-war MAS 38, and was considered
so effective by the French army that it
was retained in the MAT 49: a catch is
depressed and the magazine housing
(with a loaded magazine in place) is
folded forward to lie under the barrel,
while to use the weapon again the
magazine is simply pulled back into
place so that the housing acts as a foregrip. This foregrip is made all the more
important by the fact that the MAT 49
can be fired on automatic only, so a
firm grip is needed to keep the
weapon under control when fired.
Considerable pains are taken on the
MAT 49 to keep out dust and dirt,
which is another historical carry-over
from previous times as the MAT 49 was
intended for use in the deserts of North

Africa. Even when the magazine is in
the forward position a flap moves into
position to keep out foreign matter. If
repairs or cleaning are required the
weapon can be easily stripped without
tools. In action a grip safety locks both
the trigger mechanism and any possible forward movement of the bolt.
Overall the MAT 49 is a sturdy and
foolproof weapon. It is still used by the
French armed forces and by various of
the French police and paramilitary units. It has also been sold abroad to
many of the ex-French colonies and
wherever French interests prevail.
There is a chance that the recent introduction of the 5.56-mm (0.219-in) FA
MAS rifle to the French army may reduce the numbers in service, but there
are enough operators left to ensure
that the MAT 49 will remain around for
a long time to come.

Specification
MAT 49
Calibre: 9 mm (0.354 in) Parabellum
Weight: loaded 4.17 kg (9.19 lb)
Length: with butt extended 720 mm
(28.34 in) and with butt closed 460 mm
(18.1 in)
Length of barrel: 228 mm (8.97 in)
Muzzle velocity: 390 m (1,280 ft) per
second
Cyclic rate of fire: 600 rpm
Magazine: 20- or 32-round box

bove: Entering French service in
949, the 9-mm MAT 49 is an
xtremely rugged design, made
om heavy-gauge steel stampings.
he pistol grip/magazine housing
nges forward for stowage and
ansport.

Right: Designed with colonial service
in mind, the MAT 49 was used
extensively in Indo-China, as well as
with the paratroops so notably
involved in the bloody conflict in
Algeria. It stood such stern tests
successfully.

WEST GERMANY
Heckler und Koch MP5

Since World War II the West German concern of Heckler und Koch has become one of Europe's largest and most important small-arms manufacturers with its success based soundly on the production of its G3 rifle, which has become a standard NATO weapon and is in use all over the world. Working from the G3 and employing its highly efficient breech-locking mechanism, the company has also produced the **Heckler und Koch MP5**, which may thus be regarded as the sub-machine gun version of the G3.

In appearance the MP5 looks very similar to the G3 although it is of course much shorter. It fires the usual 9-mm (0.354-in) × 19 Parabellum cartridge, and although this is relatively low-powered compared with the 7.62-mm (0.3-in) rifle cartridge the MP5 uses the same roller and inclined ramp locking mechanism as the G3. The complexity of this system is more than offset by its increased safety, and by the ability of the MP5 to be fired very accurately as it can fire from a closed bolt, i.e. the breech block is in the forward position when the trigger is pulled so there is no forward-moving mass to disturb the aim as there is with other sub-machine guns. The resemblance to the G3 is maintained by the use of many G3 components on the MP5.

There are six main versions of the MP5. The **MP5A2** has a fixed butt stock while the **MP5A3** has a metal strut stock that can be slid forward to reduce its length. There are no fewer than three differing versions of the **MP5 SD**, which is a silenced version of the basic model for use in special or anti-terrorist warfare. The **MP5 SD1** does not have a butt stock at all; the **MP5 SD2** has a fixed butt as on the MP5A2; and the **MP5 SD3** has the sliding metal butt stock used on the MP5A3. Then there is the **MP5K** which is a very short version of the basic MP5, only 325 mm (12.8 in) long and recognizable by a small foregrip under the almost non-existent muzzle. The **MP5K A1** is a special version of this variant with no protrusions so that it can be carried under clothing or in a special holster.

In all its forms the MP5 has proved to be an excellent and reliable sub-machine gun. It is in use with some of the various West German police agencies and border guards, and numbers have been purchased by Swiss police and the Netherlands armed forces. It is known to be one of the weapons most favoured by the British SAS for close-quarter combat.

Unfortunately some MP5s have fallen into the wrong hands, usually by theft from weapon stores. The MP5 was the main weapon of the Baader-Meinhoff gang and many similar groups are known to have used the MP5 at one time or another. The MP5 has been described by one counter-insurgency authority as 'the most efficient terrorist weapon now in production', and it will no doubt feature in many future terrorist or 'freedom fighter' outrages. This future use might well involve various forms of night sight, for the MP5 has been demonstrated on numerous occasions with such devices, along with other sighting devices such as telescopic sights and other rapid-aiming systems.

Top: The MP5A3 is fitted with a sliding metal strut stock which can allow a considerable reduction in overall length, from 660 mm (26 in) to 490 mm (19.3 in).

Above: The MP5A2 is fitted with fixed plastic butt stock. After 1978 the MP5 was fitted with a curved magazine to improve cartridge feed.

Below: The MP5SD3 is a silenced version of the MP5A3, all parts except barrel and silencer being the same. It is used by several military and police forces around the world.

Right: The extremely short MP5K was introduced for use by special police and anti-terrorist squads, where weapon concealment may be essential.

Specification
MP5A2
Calibre: 9 mm (0.354 in) Parabellum
Weight: loaded 2.97 kg (6.55 lb)
Length: 680 mm (26.77 in)
Length of barrel: 225 mm (8.86 in)
Muzzle velocity: 330 m (1,083 ft) per second
Cyclic rate of fire: 800 rpm
Magazine: 15- or 30-round box

Walther MP-K and MP-L

Walther has for long been in the fore-front of small arms design and development, but the end of World War II saw most of its facilities taken over by the new East German government, so for many years the company was unable to re-enter its chosen market. But by the early 1960s Walther was back in business, and in 1963 introduced its 9-mm (0.354-in) **Walther MP-K** and **MP-L** sub-machine guns.

The MP-K and MP-L (MP standing for *Maschinenpistole*, K for *kurz* or short, and L for *lange* or long) differ only in their barrel length. They are both well-made sub-machine guns constructed in the usual manner from steel stampings, and both use the same blowback operating principle. The butt stock is a skeleton tube arrangement, and when not in use this can be folded along the right-hand side of the receiver. The box magazine is inserted into a housing under the receiver and just forward of the trigger group. This magazine is wedge-shaped in cross-section and contains 32 rounds. As one would expect with Walther products, the overall standard of manufacture is excellent.

From the side both models present a rather deep silhouette. This is because the main mass of the breech block is mounted over the barrel and guided throughout its backward and forward travel on a guide rod. Normally the bolt handle does not move with the breech block, but if required it can be latched into the block in order to clear a stoppage. There are all manner of small detail points on these two weapons. One is that when the stock is folded forward the butt portion can be used as a forward grip. Another is the rear sight, which is normally fixed for use at 100 m (109 yards) using conventional rear and fore sights. But for use in low visibility conditions the upper portion of the sight becomes an open rear sight and is used in conjunction with the top of the fore sight protector. There is a fire selector switch just behind the trigger, allowing rapid and easy selection of 'safe', single shot or full automatic.

The first Walther MP-Ks and MP-Ls were sold to the West German navy and to some German police forces. Since then more have been sold to Brazil, Colombia, the Mexican navy and Venezuela. The types are no longer in production, but both are still being offered for sale by Walther and could be placed back in production within a short time. Some accessories have been offered with these guns. At one point the MP-K was offered with a screw-on silencer, but this was apparently not long developed and there appear to have been few takers. All weapons have provision for sling swivels and these are so arranged that the sling can be used to stabilize the gun when firing bursts.

Specification
MP-K
Calibre: 9 mm (0.354 in)
Weight: loaded 3.425 kg (7.55 lb)
Length: with stock open 653 mm (25.7 in) and with stock folded 368 mm (14.49 in)
Length of barrel: 171 mm (6.73 in)
Muzzle velocity: 356 m (1,168 ft) per second
Cyclic rate of fire: 550 rpm
Magazine: 32-round box

Specification
MP-L
Calibre: 9 mm (0.354 in)
Weight: loaded 3.625 kg (7.99 lb)
Length: with stock open 737 mm (29 in) and with stock folded 455 mm (17.9 in)
Length of barrel: 257 mm (10.12 in)
Muzzle velocity: 396 m (1,299 ft) per second
Cyclic rate of fire: 550 rpm
Magazine: 32-round box

7.62-mm Type 64

The Chinese **Type 64** is one of the most unusual sub-machine guns in service today, for it has been designed and produced from the outset as a silenced weapon. During World War II several types of machine-gun were fitted with various types of suppressor for special missions (such as behind-the-lines and commando-type operations), but no country went to the extent of producing a special weapon for these roles. For reasons best known to themselves the Communist Chinese have done so. The Type 64 fires the standard Soviet 7.62-mm (0.3-in) pistol round, but the use of a Maxim-type silencer arrangement makes this round effective only at short ranges. To make matters more complicated the Chinese use this pistol round fitted with a special bullet known as the Type P, which is slightly heavier than the normal bullet and is thus slightly more effective. As silenced weapons go the Type 64 has been tested to the point where it seems to be effective enough, but the time and trouble involved in the design and production of such a special weapon and cartridge seem wasteful to many Western experts.

The Type 64 is a mixture of various design features mainly lifted from other weapons. The basic overall design and bolt action resemble those of the Soviet PPS-43 of World War II, while the trigger mechanism is taken from the Bren Gun, many of which were used in China during and after World War II. The folding stock also comes from the Soviet PPS-43, while the silencer uses the well-established principles introduced by Hiram Maxim who was at one time as well known for his silencer designs as he was for his machine-guns. The barrel extends along only part of the silencer, and the last part of the barrel is perforated by a

The Type 64 uses a selective fire trigger mechanism derived from that of the Bren gun and a bolt action taken from the Type 43 – the Chinese copy of the Soviet PPS-43.

series of holes; the propellant gases exhaust through these and the muzzle into a series of baffles that continue until the muzzle of the silencer proper. This silencer also acts as a flash suppressor.

The exact operational role of this weapon with the ChiCom forces is not known with exactitude. The few examples seen in the West came mainly from Vietnam and other such Far East origins, and it is doubtful if the Type 64 was kept in production for very long or even if it was produced in any quantity. It remains an enigma.

Specification
Type 64
Calibre: 7.62 mm (0.3 in) × 25 Type P
Weight: empty 3.4 kg (7.495 lb)
Length: with stock extended 843 mm (33.19 in)
Length of barrel: 244 mm (9.6 in)
Muzzle velocity: about 313 m (1,027 ft) per second
Cyclic rate of fire: uncertain
Magazine: 20- or 30-round box

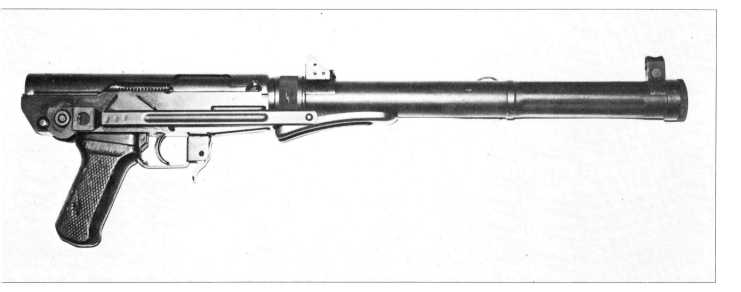

Model 61 Skorpion

The Czech **Model 61 Skorpion** lies in that small-arms no-man's-land where a weapon that is neither a pistol or a true sub-machine gun is described as a 'machine pistol': it is small enough to be carried and fired as a pistol, but it fires fully automatically when required. It has the advantages and disadvantages of both types of weapon and is perhaps below par as both a pistol and a sub-machine gun, but it is now one of the

The Model 61 Skorpion is a favourite weapon of the Palestine Liberation Organization, its small size making for easy concealment.

most feared of all 'underground' weapons, despite the fact that it was originally intended to be a standard service weapon for the Czech armed forces.

The Skorpion was designed for use by tank crews, signallers and other personnel who have no normal need for anything larger than a pistol. But since a pistol is essentially a short-range weapon, the introduction of a fully automatic feature provided this small weapon with a considerable short-range firepower potential. The Skorpion resembles a pistol, though the magazine is not in the butt but forward of the trigger assembly, and a folding wire butt is provided for aimed fire. The overall appearance is short and chunky, and the weapon is small enough to be carried in a rather over-sized belt holster. When fired on full automatic the weapon has a cyclic rate of about 840 rounds per minute, which

Above right: Stock fully extended, the Type 61 can shoot with reasonable accuracy at up to 200 m (220 yards). It uses a simple blowback operation, but the empty case is ejected directly upwards.

makes it a formidable weapon at short ranges, but this benefit is offset by two considerations. One is that using any machine pistol on full automatic makes the weapon almost impossible to aim accurately: the muzzle forces cause the muzzle to climb and judder to such an extent that it is virtually impossible to hold the weapon still for more than an instant. The other consideration is that the Skorpion uses magazines with only 10- or 20-round capacity, and on automatic either would soon be exhausted. But while the Skorpion fires it sprays bullets in an alarming swathe and this makes it a formidable close-quarter weapon.

The Skorpion operates on the blow-back principle. Single shots can be selected, and aiming is assisted by use of the folding wire butt. The basic

Model 61 Skorpion fires the American 0.32-in (actual 7.65-mm) cartridge, making it the only Warsaw Pact weapon to use this round, but the **Model 63** uses the 9-mm short (0.38-in) round and the **Model 68** the 9-mm (0.354-in) Parabellum. A silenced version of the Model 61 is available.

Apart from the Czech armed forces, the Skorpion has also been sold to some African nations, but its main impact has been in the hands of guerrillas and 'freedom fighters'. The firepower impact of the Skorpion is considerable at short ranges, which suits the requirements of assassination and terror squads, so the type is now much favoured by such groups. With them it has turned up in many parts of the world from Central America to the Middle East.

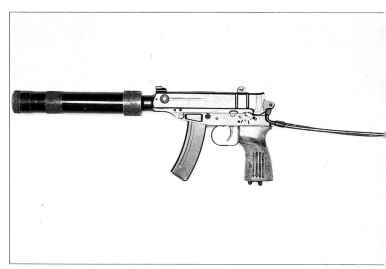

Specification
Model 61 Skorpion
Calibre: 0.32 in (actual 7.65 mm)
Weight: loaded 2 kg (4.4 lb)
Length: with butt extended 513 mm (20.2 in) and with butt folded 269 mm (10.6 in)

Length of barrel: 112 mm (4.4 in)
Muzzle velocity: 317 m (1,040 ft) per second
Cyclic rate of fire: 840 rpm
Magazine: 10- or 20-round box

9-mm wz 63 (PM-63)

The 9-mm **wz 63** (*wzor*, or model) is also known as the **PM-63**, and is one of those weapons that falls into the category of machine pistol. Although only slightly larger than an orthodox pistol, it can be fired fully automatic at a cyclic rate of 600 rounds per minute. It was designed by Piotr Wilniewicz, who led a design team to produce a weapon for those elements of the Polish forces who are unable to carry a conventional weapon during their combat duties. The wz 63 is thus used by Polish tank crews, signallers and other troops such as truck drivers.

The wz 63 is rather long for a conventional pistol and is fitted with a butt that can be folded forward to lie under the barrel. When folded forward the butt either lies under the forward grip, or the butt plate can be folded down to act as a forward grip. This forward grip is essential to hold the weapon steady on automatic fire, for the wz 63 suffers from the usual difficulty of rapid and erratic muzzle movement mainly caused by the cyclic rate of fire. Some of this muzzle movement is compensated for by a simple fixture on the end of

the barrel which is little more than an open trough angled upwards at a slight angle to push the barrel downwards. In practice this device appears to be of marginal value. Accurate single-shot aiming is possible, but even when using the butt any deliberate aim is likely to be disturbed by the bolt moving forward as the trigger is pulled since, like most other blowback-operated weapons, the wz 63 operates from an open bolt. However its effective range using the stock extended into the shoulder is stated to be 200 m (219 yards); on automatic the range is much less.

The wz 63 may be used with either a 25- or a 40-round magazine, although some references also mention a 15-

Although classed as a machine pistol, the wz 63 is more complex than the Skorpion and it would require a firm hand indeed to fire 9-mm × 18 cartridges on full automatic. It is perhaps no accident that the handbook only shows it deployed for two-handed use.

round magazine. It is normally issued together with a special holster and a pouch holding three magazines and a cleaning kit. A sling may also be supplied.

The round fired by the wz 63 is the 9-mm (0.354-in) × 18 Makarov cartridge, which differs in several ways from the usual 9-mm (0.354-in) × 19 Parabellum round. It provides the wz 63 with a considerable striking capa-

bility at short combat ranges but as stated before the ability of any machine pistol to remain on target for more than a fleeting second is unlikely. Instead the wz 63 produces a 'spray' effect which can be of considerable value in combat, but even this effect is reduced by the magazine capacity.

The wz 63 is still used by the Polish troops for which it was designed, and the type is now extensively used by

Polish police and security units. Outside Poland the wz 63 appears to be little used, though numbers of these weapons have turned up in the Middle East and have been observed by several of the organizations involved in the civil war in Lebanon.

Specification
wz 63
Calibre: 9 mm (0.354 in) Makarov

Weight: with empty 32-round magazine 1.8 kg (3.97 lb)
Length: with stock retracted 333 mm (13.1 in)
Length of barrel: 152 mm (6 in)
Muzzle velocity: 323 m (1,060 ft) per second
Cyclic rate of fire: 600 rpm
Magazine: 25- or 40-round box; also references to 15-round box

---

Ingram Model 10

There have been few weapons in recent years that have 'enjoyed' the attentions of the Press and Hollywood to such an extent as that lavished on the Ingram sub-machine guns. Gordon B. Ingram had designed a whole string of sub-machine guns before he produced his **Ingram Model 10**, which was originally intended to be used with the Sionics Company suppressor. First produced during the mid-1960s, the little Ingram Model 10 soon attracted a great deal of public attention because of its rate of fire, supposedly high enough to 'saw a body in half', coupled with the highly efficient sound suppressor. Hollywood and television films added their dramatic commentaries and the Ingram Model 10 soon became as widely known as the old Thompson sub-machine guns of the 1920s.

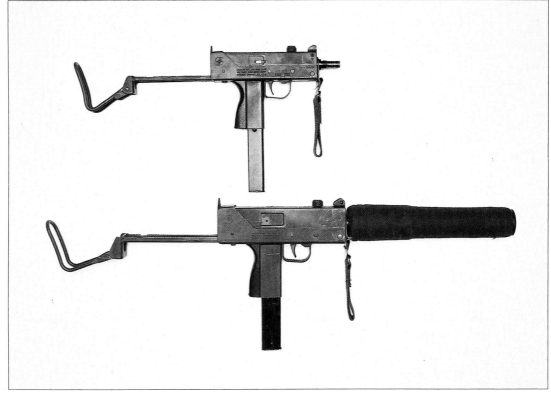

The Ingram Model 11 (top) is chambered for 9-mm Short (.380 ACP), while the Model 10 (below), fitted with a suppressor, can be chambered for either 9-mm Parabellum or .45 ACP. Both are relatively well balanced due to the bolt enveloping the breech.

The Ingram Model 10 is indeed a remarkable little weapon. It is constructed from sheet metal but manufactured to a very high standard and extremely robust. This has to be, for it fires at a cyclic rate of over 1,000 rounds per minute, yet control of the weapon is still relatively easy thanks to the good balance imparted by the centrally-placed pistol group through which the box magazine is inserted. Most versions have a folding metal butt

Its efficient suppressor makes the Ingram a handy weapon for the Special Forces. By reducing the escaping gas to subsonic speed and eliminating flash, the position of the firer can remain a mystery to the target, until hopefully it is too late.

but this may be removed, and many weapons not fitted with the long tubular suppressor use a forward webbing hand-strap as a rudimentary foregrip. The muzzle on most models is threaded to accommodate the suppressor, and when fitted this is covered with a heat-resistant canvas or plastic webbing to allow it to be used as a forward grip. The cocking handle is on top of the slab-sided receiver and when turned through 90° acts as a safety lock. As this handle is slotted for sighting purposes the firer can soon notice if this safety is applied, and there is a normal trigger safety as well.

The Model 10 may be encountered chambered for either the well-known 11.43-mm (0.45-in) cartridge or the more usual 9-mm (0.354-in) Parabellum. The latter round may also be used on the smaller **Model 11** which is normally chambered for the less powerful 9-mm Short (.380 ACP). In all these calibres the Ingram is a dreadfully efficient weapon and not surprisingly it has been sold widely to customers ranging from paramilitary forces to bodyguard and security agencies. Military sales on any large scale have been few but several nations have acquired numbers for 'testing and evaluation'. The British SAS is known to have obtained a small quantity for test-

ing. Sales have not been encouraged by the fact that the ownership and manufacturing rights have changed hands several times, but both the Model 10 and Model 11 are now back in production and selling well. In order to keep sales rolling several variants have been made. Versions firing single-shot only and without the folding butt are available, and at one point a long-barrelled version was produced, though only in limited numbers as the type did not find a ready market.

In the meantime Ingrams will be found in countries as diverse as Yugoslavia, Israel and Argentina. Many have been sold to the Central and South American nations.

Specification
Model 10 (0.45-in model)
Calibre: 11.43 mm (0.45 in)
Weight: loaded with 30-round magazine 3.818 kg (8.4 lb)
Length: with stock extended 548 mm (21.575 in) and with stock folded 269 mm (10.59 in)
Length of barrel: 146 mm (5.75 in)
Length of suppressor: 291 mm (11.46 in)
Muzzle velocity: 280 m (918 ft) per second
Cyclic rate of fire: 1,145 rpm
Magazine: 30-round box

9-mm UZI

Once Israel had fought its War of Independence in 1948 the new nation had some breathing space in which to arm itself for any future conflict. Submachine guns were high on the list of priorities, for the new Israeli army was then equipped with all manner of old weapons varying from Sten guns to Czech weapons. The Czech weapons attracted the close attention of one Lieutenant Uziel Gail, for they had the advantage that their breech blocks or bolts were 'wrapped around' the barrel, so placing the mass of the bolt well forward around the barrel on firing and allowing a short weapon to have a relatively long barrel. The Czech weapons concerned were of the vz 23 series, and using these Gail was able to design and develop his own design that was more suitable to the manufac-

Right: The UZI (with wooden stock) and the Mini-UZI. The Mini-UZI is just 36-cm (14-in) long with its stock folded, making for easy concealment under ordinary clothing. The UZI is a design of great simplicity and is famous for reliability in awkward conditions.

Below: This Israeli carries the UZI fitted with metal folding stock. In addition to a grip safety, the UZI features a ratchet on the cocking handle to prevent accidental firing if the user's hand slips off the handle after the breech block has passed behind a round.

turing methods then available in relatively undeveloped Israel. He came up with a weapon that is now universally known as the **UZI** after its designer.

The UZI is made largely from simple pressings held in place by spot welds or other welding. The main body is made from a single sheet of heavy gauge sheet steel with grooves pressed into the sides to take any dust, dirt or sand that might get into the works. This simple feature makes the UZI capable of operation under even the most arduous conditions, a fact that has been proved on many occasions. The overall cross-section of the main body is rectangular with the barrel secured to the body by a large nut just behind the muzzle. The trigger group is situated centrally, and the box magazine is inserted through the pistol grip, which

makes reloading very easy in the dark for 'hand will naturally find hand'. The normal combat magazine holds 32 rounds, but a common practice is to join two magazines together using a cross-over clip or even tape to allow rapid changing. A grip safety is incorporated into the pistol grip.

The UZI is now virtually one of the symbols of Israeli military prowess, but Israel is not the only nation to use the type. The West Germans also use the UZI, which they know as the **MP2**; this model was produced under licence by FN in Belgium. Numerous other nations also use the UZI. It is part of legend that the President of the United States is always accompanied by bodyguards carrying UZIs in specially fitted brief cases, and many other security agencies and police forces

use the UZI.

The UZI may be encountered wit either a sturdy fixed wooden butt stoc or a metal stock that can be folde forward under the main body with the butt plate still available to assist i steadying automatic fire. The UZI ca be used to fire single-shot by use of change lever just above the pistol but

Specification
UZI (with wooden stock)
Calibre: 9 mm (0.354 in) Parabellum
Weight: loaded with 32-round magazine 4.1 kg (9 lb)
Length: 650 mm (25.59 in)
Length of barrel: 260 mm (10.24 in)
Muzzle velocity: 400 m (1,312 ft) per second
Cyclic rate of fire: 600 rpm
Magazine: 25- or 32-round box

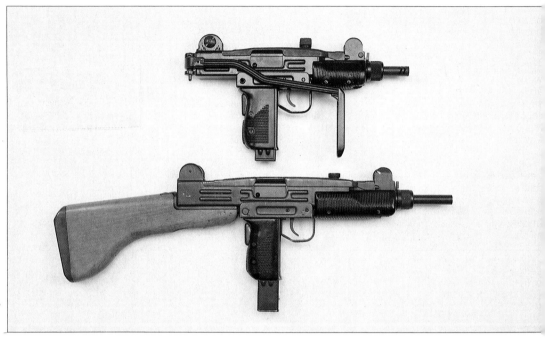

9-mm Mini-UZI

The **Mini-UZI** has been developed by Israel Military Industries from the full-scale UZI and differs from the original only in dimensions and weights. A few modifications have been introduced to the basic design, but these are only superficial while the operating system of the original has been retained unchanged.

The Mini-UZI has been developed as a weapon suitable for concealment by police and security personnel. This prompted an overall decrease in dimensions, and to improve this concealment a smaller 20-round magazine has been introduced, although the Mini-UZI can still use the existing 25- and 32-round magazines if required. The UZI parentage is immediately apparent but one change that can be noted is that the normal folding metal butt has been replaced by a single-strut butt stock that folds along the right-hand side of the body. When folded the butt plate acts as a rudimentary foregrip. but the normal foregrip is a plastic section just forward of the trigger group.

To date the Mini-UZI has been marketed as suitable for police and secur-

ity agencies but it is bound to attract the attentions of various military organizations for special missions. It would make an ideal commando-type weapon where light weight is required, and it must be stressed that although the Mini-UZI is a scaled-down version of the original it still uses the potent 9-mm (0.354-in) × 19 Parabellum round. As the weapon is lighter its breech block is lighter too, and this provides a cyclic rate of fire of 950 rounds per minute, which is much higher than on the original.

The Mini-UZI is being marketed in the United States carried in a specially-fitted brief case together with spare magazines and a small cleaning and spares kit. It has already been suggested that some form of silencer could be fitted to the muzzle.

There are also some UZIs other than the standard version and the Mini-UZI. One is the semi-automatic **Carbine UZI** which has been produced to conform with the legal requirements of some American states that require non-automatic weapons only to be held by their inhabitants. In order to prevent

the rapid conversion of semi-automat versions of automatic weapons the call for such semi-automatic versior to have barrels at least 406 mm (16 i long. Thus the standard UZI may b seen with a long barrel protrudir from the body and this denotes that th weapon can be fired single-shot onl

Another UZI variant that has only re cently been introduced is the UZI pi tol. Although really outside the scop of this survey it is still recognizable an UZI. It can be fired single-shot on and there is no form of butt stock.

Specification
UZI
Calibre: 9 mm (0.354 in) Parabellum
Weight: loaded with 20-round magazine 3.11 kg (6.85 lb)
Length: with stock extended 600 mm (23.62 in) and with stock folded 360 mm (14.17 in)
Length of barrel: 197 mm (7.75 in)
Muzzle velocity: 352 m (1.15 ft) per second
Cyclic rate of fire: 950 rpm
Magazine: 20-, 25- or 32-round box

The UZI in Action

The UZI has proved to be one of the most successful of all the post-war sub-machine gun designs, and it has shown its combat worth on many occasions. It will remain in use for many years to come and is still in production today.

The UZI sub-machine gun was conceived at a time when the new state of Israel had only just come into being. Almost as soon as Israel declared itself to be a state it was involved in a state of war that continues to the present day. In 1948 the neighbouring Arab nations attempted to crush Israel but failed, mainly as a result of the Israelis' determination to exist as a nation, and when the United Nations were at last able to impose a ceasefire the Israelis had established themselves by the simple process of defeating every one of their Arab foes.

All through the fighting of 1948 and 1949 the newly-formed Israeli army was armed with a hotchpotch of weapons. Sub-machine guns included old ex-German weapons and numbers of Sten guns, the latter being the usual weapon of the front-line troops. The Stens worked but were not regarded as being particularly reliable, and a replacement was thus sought. For supply safety it was considered suitable for the replacement to be manufactured locally, but at that time manufacturing facilities in Israel were few so the design had to be easy to make in quantity.

Several designs were put forward at the time. Most of them were 'paper' designs, but that of Lieutenant Uziel Gail was chosen. He had formed his design after careful examination of some Czech designs, notably the vzor (model) 23, 24, 25 and 26. These models were all basically the same, differing only in having a fixed or folding butt or the calibre used, but they all had the same basic mechanism and design feature: the use of a breech block, or bolt, that extended forward around the barrel. This had two main attractions: that at the instant of firing the mass of the bolt was well forward to

ensure a good 'lock', and that as the bolt extended forward the barrel could be placed farther to the rear of the receiver or body to allow a short and handy weapon. Gail had no doubt obtained his study examples from the fighting during the War of Independence, and as at one point Czechoslovakia was happy to provide weapons to the new state, it is possible that the weapons came via a direct route. In any case Gail adopted the 'wrap-around' bolt to so pronounced a degree that his design was very much shorter than any contemporary equivalent. Gail also adopted the method of inserting the magazine through the pistol grip which not only provided a good balance for the weapon but it also made rapid insertion of a magazine

Seen here in South African service, the UZI is one of the most widely used sub-machine guns in the world. With stock extended and in careful hands, the UZI will shoot with reasonable accuracy up to 200 m (220 yards), although it gained its reputation at much closer ranges.

easy using the principle that 'hand finds hand'. The folding metal butt was also taken from the Czech design.

But Gail was no mere plagiarist. He introduced his own ideas, not the least of which was ease of manufacture. The Sten gun and the German MP 38 of World War II had demonstrated that sub-machine guns could be manufactured easily using simple metal stampings and virtually no machining, and Gail simply took this method one stage further: almost the entire body of his design was made from a single sheet steel stamping that was then bent into shape to form a robust body. But Gail went one better. He was aware that much of the terrain over which the resultant weapon was to be used was dusty and arduous to a degree. Any weapon would have to operate with the virtual certainty that dust, dirt and sand would get into the works, so Gail designed two grooves into the initial stamping that could gather up all the debris inside the body and keep it out of the way. Thus the bolt could operate without the friction caused by sand and dirt, and indeed Gail's design can keep working when many other weapons have seized solid.

Gail's design was eagerly adopted and placed into production, initially in a series of small machine shops but eventually using the production facilities of the state-owned Israel Military Industries. By 1953 the weapon was in service, and in deference to its designer was named the UZI. Gail himself went on to a distinguished military career and retired as a lieutenant colonel but his name is still a virtual military fixture.

In its early years, the young Israeli nation was unable to rely on outside help and the need for an indigenous arms industry was paramount. Uziel Gail's UZI design was ideal: simple to manufacture, it entered service in 1953.

The UZI in Action

The UZI had its first major bout of conflict in Israeli hands during the Suez War of 1956. Before then it had been used more on the border patrols and clashes that marked the period, so that by the time it was used on a large scale most of the bugs inherent in any new weapon design had been eliminated. The troops liked the UZI: it was light, handy, and easy to aim and to operate. Versions with solid wooden butts were produced, but the type most favoured by the special forces such as the paratroops was the one with the folding metal butt. Only the special forces used the UZI as a standard weapon. The normal infantry and other units continued to use the standard service rifle of the day, but the UZI was and still is widely carried by second-line troops. It is small and light enough to be carried without any great inconvenience, and can be folded away into any small stowage space or even in a desk drawer.

Right: Two UZI-armed Israelis de-bus from an M3 half track covered by the .30 calibre Brownings of their comrades. The UZI first saw major action in the 1956 Arab-Israeli conflict in the hands of the Israeli airborne forces.

Below: The aftermath of another Arab incursion into Israel: the survivors of a PLO unit are driven away to captivity. Note the magazines clipped together on the UZI; the one out of the gun is empty. When the second magazine is full it projects under the barrel.

This latter point is important, for in Israel any member of the armed services is likely to be called into action at almost any time. Despite Israel's stringent and often irksome security precautions, terrorists are still able to strike at centres of population at any time. Consequently even off-duty personnel frequently carry their personal weapons with them at all times, and even desk-bound personnel keep their weapons close at hand. In many cases this means the UZI, and it is not an uncommon sight in any Israeli town or city to see groups of off-duty personnel enjoying themselves in a sidewalk cafe with UZIs nonchalantly slung from their chairs. Even the women personnel of the Israeli forces have to follow this course of action and the UZI is a common sight in shops and streets all over Israel.

Thus the UZI is now a virtual military badge in Israel, and it may be seen emblazoned on belt buckles and even stamped on T-shirts. It would be safe to say that virtually every Israeli citizen is fully familiar with its workings and knows how to use it properly. Some of this knowledge has no doubt been learned the hard way in battle, for the UZI has been used in every Israeli-Arab conflict since 1956 and in many of the smaller campaigns that have marked the life of Israel. In nearly every newsreel or front-page photograph of Israeli soldiers in action an UZI may be discerned somewhere in the frame.

Typical of the use of the UZI in the hands of the Israeli special forces was the taking of Beaufort Castle on the night of 7 June 1982, during the opening stages of the Lebanese

The UZI remains a favourite weapon of the Israeli special forces, who used it to great effect during the storming of Beaufort Castle on the night of 7 June 1982. Changing magazines in the dark is made easier by having the magazine housed in the pistol grip.

War. Beaufort Castle is situated just to the north of the Litani river inside Lebanese territory, but the Israelis had already advanced to the Litani in what at first appeared to be an anti-PLO campaign. To advance any farther north past the Litani Beaufort Castle had to be taken, for this old crusader fortress is located in a com-

manding position across any advance route to the north.

Needless to say the PLO was as aware of the importance of Beaufort Castle as the Israelis. Despite the age of the fortress the Palestinians had further improved the old fortifications and had manned not only the walls of the fort but the surrounding area. Inside the fortress walls the old underground areas had been further improved and were in use as stores and bomb-proof shelters. Not surprisingly the PLO considered the fortress to be virtually impregnable. It is set on a high and almost inaccessible promentory, and the PLO garrison was ready for an attack. It seemed as though the only way to take the position was by the time-honoured process of siege and a set-piece attack.

The Israelis thought otherwise. They had to take Beaufort Castle quickly in order to press on with advance to Beirut. They decided on a *coup de main* to be carried out by members of their special forces, who approached the castle from the area of the Aqiya Bridge over the deep gorge of the Litani river. The capture of this bridge was itself a major military achievement for it was wired for demolition and was captured before the charges could be fired. As the bulk of the Israeli central sector forces moved north one group moved in their half-tracks and Jeeps towards the castle as the evening of 6 June moved towards darkness. In the failing light they simply drove and fired their way through any PLO positions they encountered and rapidly came to under the walls of the fortress itself. Unfortunately it was not possible to rush the only track leading to the gates, so the steep walls of the point on which the castle stands had first to be scaled before even the walls could be reached. This had to be done by the old way with grappling irons, climbing skills and ropes. Under these combat conditions the UZI proved invaluable. It was easy to sling out of the way when climbing yet easy to get into action when required. In action its high fire rate was devastating at close ranges, and in the dark there was often no time to take deliberate aim. Thus the short UZI came into its own, for the Israelis could get their weapons on target much faster than their opponents armed with AK-47s.

Had he not been close enough to be tackled physically, there can be little doubt that Hinkley's attempt to kill President Reagan would have ended abruptly in a hail of 9-mm fire from the Presidential guards' UZIs.

The UZI in Action

Needless to say the PLO did not stand back and let the Israelis take the castle unopposed. They fought back with a ferocity that surprised the Israelis, and casualties were heavy on both sides. From time to time the Israelis used mortars to fire illumination flares, to allow them to see where they were and where they were going, but much of the fighting was at close quarters and at times (such as when they were still climbing their ropes) the Israeli troops' casualties were heavy. Some of the Israelis had to hang onto their ropes with one hand and fire their UZIs with the other. Some covering fire came from heavy machine-guns mounted on the halftracks far below, but the assault force had to supply most of its own covering fire.

Once the Israelis were over the walls the hand-to-hand fighting continued until just after midnight, when the Israelis took control of the fortress. Even then isolated bands of PLO fighters continued to fight, some to the last, though the castle was under Israeli control. As day broke the Israeli troops were able to appreciate fully the importance of the position they had taken. They were able to observe a wide stretch of terrain that stretched from the Mediterranean far to the west, over the coastal plain and up into the mountains of the interior. They could see the mechanized Israeli columns making their way north without risk of a powerful PLO stronghold in their rear.

Beaufort Castle was an action in which the UZI showed to its best advantage. In any close-quarter combat a short and handy weapon like the UZI provides any combatant with a tactical advantage, and when that advantage is allied to a determination to win such as that displayed by the Israeli soldiers who stormed the castle the result was inevitably a minor military classic.

Right: His UZI by his side, a gunner of No. 4 Battery, 305th Panzer Artillery, pauses by an M113 Armoured Personnel Carrier. The extensive use made of the UZI by West German forces is a great tribute to the design.

An important role fulfilled by the sub-machine gun is that of vehicle crew personal armament. In the confined space of a tank there is obviously no room for a full-size rifle. Here, the crew of a Bundeswehr Leopard pose with their folding-stock UZIs.

9-mm Beretta Model 12s

During World War II the Beretta submachine guns were among the most highly-prized of all war trophies, and many remained for many years after the war in service with both military and paramilitary formations. The last of the 'war-time' Beretta variants was produced in 1949, and in 1958 an entirely new Beretta design was introduced. This owed nothing to previous designs and for the first time Beretta adopted the tubular receiver and stamped component construction that had for long been employed by many other manufacturers. The new design was the **Beretta Model 12**, but although it looked simple it was still a Beretta product, as was revealed by the overall high standard of finish and by its quality manufacture.

The Model 12 had an orthodox construction down to the 'wrap-around' bolt that was by then commonplace. This allowed it to be a short and handy weapon that as usual could be fitted with either a folding metal stock or a fixed wooden stock.

The Model 12 was sold extensively

to such nations as Libya and Saudi Arabia, but only in small numbers to the Italian armed forces, who purchased the type for use only by special units. However, Beretta was able to negotiate licence production of the Model 12 in Indonesia and Brazil for local sales and export.

Beretta then decided to develop the basic design one stage further and produced the **Model 12S**. This is now the current Beretta sub-machine gun and production of the Model 12 has now ceased. Externally the Model 12S looks very like the Model 12 but there are some detail differences. One is the epoxy-resin finish, making the metal resistant to corrosion and wear. The fire selector mechanism on the Model 12 was of the 'push through' type, operated by pushing a button from either side of the receiver just over the pistol grip, but the Type 12S has a conventional single-lever mechanism with a safety that locks both the trigger and the grip safety. The folding butt, when fitted, now has a more positive lock for both the open and the closed positions, and some changes have been made to the sights. One laudable feature that has been carried over from the original Model 12 is the retention of the raised grooves that run along each side of the tubular receiver. These grooves act as catchers for any dirt or debris that find their way into the interior, and enable the Model 12S to operate under really muddy and arduous conditions.

To date the Model 12S has been

purchased by the Italian armed forces in small numbers, and more were sold to Tunisia. Once again Beretta has been able to negotiate licence production and the Model 12S is now

being offered by FN of Herstal, Belgium, as part of its small arms range. Incidentally, the Model 12 is one of the favoured weapons of 'Carlos', the international terrorist.

The men of the Italian Parachute Brigade are mainly equipped with the BM59 rifle, but the Beretta 12S is better suited for close-range work. The 12S is designed to operate in harsh environments, having grooves along the sides of the receiver which catch any debris entering the weapon.

A dramatic break from pre-war Beretta designs, the Model 12 and 12S use heavy sheet metal stampings to form the magazine housing and receiver, but retain the elegant simplicity associated with Beretta.

The 12S can be distinguished from the earlier Model 12 by the single lever fire selector and safety. The white 'S' is for safe, the red 'I' for semi automatic and the 'R' for full automatic.

Specification
Model 12S (metal stock version)
Calibre: 9 mm (0.354 in) Parabellum
Weight: loaded with 32-round magazine 3.81 kg (8.4 lb)
Length: with stock extended 660 mm (26 in) and with stock folded 418 mm (16.45 in)
Length of barrel: 200 mm (7.87 in)
Muzzle velocity: 381 m (1,250 ft) per second
Cyclic rate of fire: 500-550 rpm
Magazine: 20-, 32- or 40-round box

Right: Although widely exported, the Model 12 is only issued to Special Troops of the Italian army, the rest having to content themselves with the MAB 38/49. The Model 12 is a very steady weapon with remarkably low muzzle climb while firing in full automatic.

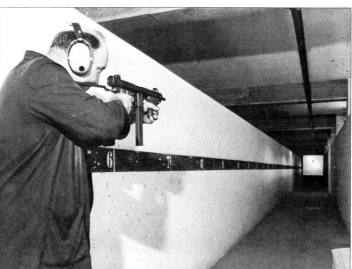

RIFLES

Rifles of the Great War

The introduction of the magazine-loading rifle gave the infantryman more firepower than ever before, but the appearance of quick-fire artillery and machine-guns combined to produce a bloody stalemate.

he years from 1914 to 1918 were very much a period of purgatory for the rdinary foot soldier. He was confined to a miserable life of trench arfare interspersed by periods when attacks were made through arbed wire in the face of massed machine-gun fire. The artillery ruled s existence and his military skills were few.

But every one of the unfortunates who led this odd life had one thing in ommon. He was equipped with a standard service rifle which was upposed to be his main weapon. In the event the individuals rarely got ie chance to use these weapons, apart from the frantic and frenzied eriods when an infantry attack actually reached the enemy's trenches. here the rifle's bayonet could be more useful than its bullet, and if all lse failed the rifle became a very effective club. This close-quarter arfare was far from what the rifle designers had envisaged, namely ccurate fire at long ranges. What the soldiers wanted was something at worked when required, very often at close ranges, and it was this ct that differentiated the true service rifle of World War I from the rget rifles their designers thought they wanted. Under trench condi- ons the rifles that were able to withstand the rough-and-tumble of ervice life were much more favoured than the designers' dreams. Thus fles such as the German Gewehr 98 and the British No. 1 Mk III fared uch better than refined products such as the Canadian Ross or the ritish/American No. 3 Mk I.

The Western Front was not the only battleground of World War I. lsewhere the Austro-Hungarians and Italians fought it out with Mann- :her modello 1895s and Mannlicher-Carcano modello 1891s. The Rus-

Serbian soldiers are seen in April 1916, with the man laden with trophies in the foreground carrying his 7-mm (0.275-in) rifle carefully wrapped against the mud. Part of his booty is a Mannlicher-Carcano carbine. Elaborate decoration of rifles was a Balkan tradition dating back to the 16th century.

sians carried what Mosin-Nagant Model 1891s they could produce through the long series of campaigns against the Germans and Austro-Hungarians, while the French had a variety of weapons, some of them with colonial-warfare origins. Nearly all of these rifles used some form of magazine in which extra rounds could be carried ready to fire, and all of them carried long and wicked bayonets that reduced the rifle to little more than a long-range pike as carried in warfare for hundreds of years.

Nearly all the major types of rifle used by both sides in World War I are mentioned in this study. The men that carried them have now nearly all passed away, all of them remembering every last detail and feel of the weapons that they very often carried to their deaths. They are now part of history, but a surprising number of these rifles survive, not all of them in museums, for many are now collected by enthusiasts who treasure their design and robust construction. If they can fire them the enthusiasts are often agreeably surprised by the high degree of accuracy many are still capable of producing.

he disparity between the length of the Lebel mle 1886/93 in the foreground d the No. 1 Mark III held by the British soldier can be readily appreciated :re. The Lebel was typical of most World War I rifle lengths, while the much iorter No. 1 Mark III was far easier to carry and use in action.

GERMANY
Mauser Gewehr 1898

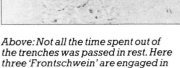

The first Mauser rifle approved for German army service was the **Mauser Modell 1888**. This used a Mauser bolt action that has remained virtually unaltered to this day, but with it a rather dated 8-mm (0.315-in) cartridge. Trials led to the adoption of a new 7.92-mm (0.312-in) cartridge, and a new rifle to fire it became known as the **Gewehr 1898** or **Gew 98** (Rifle Model 1898). This new rifle was destined to be one of the most widely used and successful weapons of its type, and it was produced in large numbers. Many later rifles could trace their origins back to the Gewehr 1898. It was the classic Mauser rifle, handsome and rather long, but well-balanced and with everything excellently designed and in general nicely made. The term 'in general' is used advisedly, for once World War I was into its stride the standards of manufacture had to be relaxed and some comparatively rough specimens were issued to the troops. But most were very well-made with good quality wooden furniture that was emphasized by the use of a pistol-type grip behind the trigger to assist holding and aiming. The original rear-sight was a very elaborate affair with sliding ramps and other niceties that needed experience for effective use, but some larger versions were simpler. The bolt action retained the usual Mauser front-lug locking systems, with the addition of an extra lug to make the number up to three for added safety with the new and more powerful cartridge. The bolt used a straight-pull action which was and still is rather awkward to use quickly and smoothly but in service generated few problems. The integral box magazine held five rounds loaded from a charger clip.

While the Gewehr 1898 was produced primarily for the German armed forces, it was also the starting point for a multitude of rifle designs that spread all over the world. Spain was an early user of the basic Mauser action and versions produced there differed little from the Gewehr 1898. The output of Mauser models from Germany and Spain were soon encountered all over the world in nations as far apart as China and Costa Rica. The Mauser action accrued an enviable reputation for reliability, strength and accuracy, and the arguments rage even today as to whether or not the Gewehr 1898 and its various cousins were the finest service rifles of their time. Many still state that they were but there are many other contenders to the title. What is certain is that during the years 1914 to 1918 the Gewehr 1898 served the German army well. The front-line soldiers had to take care of

them but usually this extended no further than keeping the bolt area covered with a cloth at all times when the rifle was not in use. Some versions such as sniper rifles appeared with special sights, including various forms of optic-

Above: Not all the time spent out of the trenches was passed in rest. Here three 'Frontschwein' are engaged in rifle practice with their Gewehr 1898s.

Left: Years of trench warfare radically altered the appearance of the German soldier. Carrying the Gewehr 1898K, he wears the distinctive 'coal scuttle' helmet. Note the wirecutters tucked into the belt.

al sight, and the weapon still has the claim to fame that it was one of the very first, if not the first, anti-tank weapon. This came about by the chance discovery that the armour of the first British tanks could be penetrated by the simple expedient of reversing the bullets used in the Gewehr 1898 before they were fired: the blunt end simply punched a hole through the armour before the bullet could warp.

The standing figure watches the target and shouts out the score to be marked down by the seated soldier on the right. The date is May 1917.

Specification
Mauser Gewehr 1898
Calibre: 7.92 mm (0.312 in)
Length: overall 1.25 m (49.2 in); barrel 0.74 m (29.1 in)
Weight: 4.2 kg (9.26 lb)
Muzzle velocity: 640 m (2,100 ft) per second
Magazine: 5-round integral box

The German army's Gewehr 1898 was one of the more important Mauser rifles, as it was the standard German service rifle of World War I. It was very well made with a strong bolt action, and fired a 7.92-mm (0.312-in) round using a five-round magazine. It served as the model for many later rifles.

CANADA
Ross Rifles

The first Ross rifle appeared during 1896 and was produced, like the later models, at Sir Charles Ross's own arms factory in Quebec, Canada. Ross was a keen marksman of the old 'Bisley School', and longed for what he considered to be the ideal service rifle: one that would consistently provide accuracy. In pursuit of this ideal he concentrated on items such as barrels and sighting systems as opposed to the more mundane aspects of design that are essential to the true service rifle.

Thus although his products were superb target weapons, they revealed themselves to be less than ideal under the rough-and-tumble of service conditions.

The number of types of Ross rifle runs to well over a dozen. Many of the types produced were often minor modifications of the preceding model and to list them all would be unhelpful. The main service model was known to the Canadian army as the **Rifle, Ross, Mk 3** and may be taken as typical. It

was a long-barrelled rifle to provide accurate long-rifle fire, and used an unusual straight-pull bolt system allied to a box magazine holding five rounds. In common with other Commonwealth armies of the day the Canadian army adopted the British 0.303-in (7.7-mm) cartridge, and this led to the British army taking numbers of Ross rifles in 1914-5.

The Canadian army adopted the Ross after about 1905, and the first Canadian troops to travel to France in

1914 were equipped with them. It was not long before the Ross rifles were found wanting once they encountered the mud of the Western Front trenches, for their bolt actions clogged with remarkable ease once even small amount of debris had entered the system. In his search for accuracy Ross had overlooked that service rifles need to be tolerant of rough conditions, and the Ross rifle required dedicated maintenance and care in handling. The bolt action frequently jammed

98

ned and the resultant clearing revealed another nasty drawback to the design: the bolt had to be put together in a very precise manner, and if it was re-assembled in the wrong way after cleaning or repair it could still fire the rifle even though the locking lugs that held its bolt in place were not engaged. As the Ross used a straight-pull bolt the part could fly back and hit the firer in the face. Thus the Ross soon fell from grace on Salisbury Plain and was replaced by the British No. 1 Mk III. Quite apart from the bolt problems, the length of the Ross rifle was too great for ease of use in the trenches.

The Ross was not completely withdrawn from service use. Fitted with a telescopic sight it was used very suc-

cessfully as a sniping rifle, a role in which its accuracy was most prized. Trained snipers could also provide the weapon with the extra care it required. To this day the Ross is still a much-prized target rifle. Many were used during World War II by various British second-line units, including the Home Guard, but the Ross never overcame the reputation for problems that it gained during its introduction to the trenches during 1914 and 1915.

Specification
Rifle, Ross, Mk 3
Calibre: 7.7 mm (0.303 in)
Length: overall 1.285 m (50.6 in); barrel 0.765 m (30.15 in)
Weight: 4.48 kg (9.875 lb)
Muzzle velocity: 792 m (2,600 ft) per second
Magazine: 5-round box

The Canadian Ross rifle (this is a Mk 2) was an excellent target rifle, but less successful in service, as mud and dirt tended to clog the straight-pull bolt action. Although used in France, the Canadians later exchanged it for the No. 1 Mk III, and the Ross rifles were used for training.

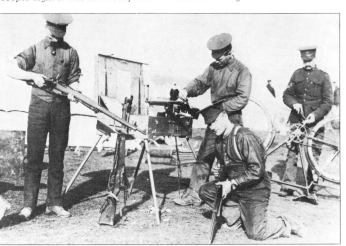

Canadian armourers maintain their Ross rifles on Salisbury Plain in September 1914. The armourers had the job of maintaining bicycles as

well as guns. When well maintained, the Ross was a formidably accurate rifle and remained a prized sniper's weapon.

After the Ross rifle was withdrawn, some were used for training and some were issued to British armed trawler crews to provide them with

some form of defence against German aircraft or even U-boats operating in the North Sea; they were better than nothing.

UK
Rifle No. 3 Mk I

Despite their eventual success, when first introduced the No. 1 Mk III rifles were deemed to lack the features required by some military pundits. In case the new SMLE did not meet requirements a 'back-up' design was put forward, one chambered for a new 7-mm (0.276-in) cartridge and employing a Mauser bolt action. Being only a back-up design at first, this rifle did not appear until 1913 under the general title **P.13**. At the time the design was taken no further and work on the new 7-mm cartridge ceased. Thus things were in abeyance just as the war began in 1914, and by then the P.13 had become the **P.14**.

In 1915 the overall shortage of rifles for the expanding British and Commonwealth armies was such that at one point rifles were being ordered from places as far away as Japan. It was accordingly decided that the P.14 should be ordered from the United States, but chambered for the standard 7-mm (0.303-in) cartridge. Several firms, including Winchester and Remington, became involved in production of the P.14, which was known to the British army as the **Rifle No. 3 Mk I**, and the results were shipped eastwards across the Atlantic.

When they arrived they were hurriedly issued and rushed into combat. They did not fare very well, for the No. rifle was a product of what became

known as the Bisley School of rifle thought. To the Bisley School long-range accuracy was the touchstone of all combat rifle worth. Soldiers were expected to hit man-sized targets at ranges of over 914 m (1,000 yards), and if a rifle could not attain these standards it was reviled. It was exactly this factor that drew so much criticism to the SMLE when it was first issued in 1907, for the SMLE was never a perfect target rifle. With the No. 3 the Bisley School had been given full rein and the result was not unlike the ill-fated Canadian Ross rifles. The No. 3 was quite simply not a good service rifle: it was long and awkward to use under combat conditions, encumbered by a long bayonet it was ill balanced and even less handy, and the bolt action took considerable maintenance. It was withdrawn from service when enough

No. 1 Mk IIIs were to hand.
The No. 3 Mk I did have one saving grace; it was as accurate as the Bisley School had intended. Thus the No. 3 was used mainly for the sniping role, in which it was very successful.

The No. 3 Mk I had one more task to perform in World War I, and that came when the Americans entered the war in 1917. They were even more desperate for service rifles than the British and as the production lines were still producing No. 3s for the British they were changed to manufacture the same rifles chambered for the American 7.62-mm (0.3-in) cartridge. Thus the No. 3 became the **M1917**, known to most Americans as the 'Enfield'. In American hands the M1917 (or **P.17** to some) fared no better than it had with the British, and in 1919 the entire output was placed into store,

only to be dragged out again in 1940 and sold to the United Kingdom to arm the new Home Guard.

Specification
Rifle No. 3 Mk I
Calibre: 7.7 mm (0.303 in)
Length: overall 1.175 m (46.25 in); barrel 0.66 m (26 in)
Weight: 4.35 kg (9.6 lb)
Muzzle velocity: 762 m (2,500 ft) per second
Magazine: 5-round box

The P.14 was a Mauser rifle produced in case the No. 1 Mk III failed to come up to specification. A 0.303-in (7.7-mm) version was ordered from the USA, and this was later adopted by the US Army as the Model 1917. It was an excellent and accurate weapon.

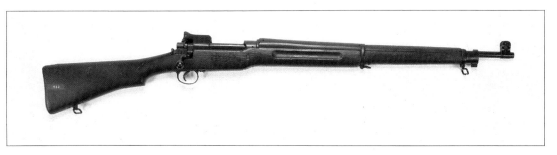

British Rifles

A scene on the Somme, some days after the start of the great battle in July 1916. A British soldier, bayonet fixed on his SMLE, keeps watch while his exhausted companions sleep in their front-line trench.

During the late 19th century the British army adopted the magazine and bolt system developed by the American engineer James Lee, and through a long process of 'in-house' improvements and trials this led to a series of what were known as Lee-Enfield rifles, the Enfield part of the name coming from the Royal Small Arms Factory at Enfield Lock, Middlesex. This series led in 1907 to a new design known as the **Short Magazine Lee-Enfield (SMLE)**, a rifle with a length between those of a normal rifle and a carbine, for the SMLE was another of the weapons intended for use by all arms from infantry to cavalry. At first SMLE had a rough introduction into service, but improvements and some modifications overcame these and in 1914 the SMLE was taken to France with the BEF; by then it had been re-designated the **Rifle No. 1 Mk III**.

The No. 1 Mk III is another of the candidates for the accolade 'best service rifle of the time'. It was a fully-stocked weapon with a snub-shaped

The onset of winter in 1914 led to the appearance of an astonishing variety of improvised fur coats. In spite of all the vagaries of life in the trenches, some Scottish regiments retained the kilt until the end of the war.

fitting at the muzzle to accommodate a long knife bayonet. The bolt action was of the turn-bolt variety and used rear locking lugs as opposed to the front-locking lugs of the Mauser system. In theory this meant that the Lee system was less safe than that of the Mauser, but in service it caused no problems at all, and the smooth action of the Lee-Enfield mechanism made the British rifle easy and extremely fast. The detachable box magazine in front of the trigger group held 10 rounds, which was twice the capacity of many of its contemporaries. There was also a cut-out device that held all the rounds in the magazine while single rounds were fed into the chamber by hand; this arrangement was supposed to retain the magazine rounds for use only when really needed. The main sights were of the ramp type and calibrated to well over 1,000 yards (914 m), and on the left-hand side of the rifle stock was a peculiar long-range sight that was used to provide really long-range area fire to cover an area; it was used only under careful control when volley fire would be employed.

The No. 1 Mk III rifle was often known as the SMLE (Short Magazine Lee-Enfield) and was one of the best service rifles of World War I. It could

Australian troops move up into the line near Fricourt in October 1918, carrying the No. 1 Mk IIIs that their descendants were to carry

Above: Two well-laden British soldiers are seen in action holding the south bank of the River Aisne during the battle of May 1918, in the aftermath of the series of German breakthroughs that started during March of that year. The rifle is a No. 1 Mk III.*

Below: A cosy scene indicates the Entente Cordiale that was in being in March 1918. The picture was taken well behind the lines, for the No. 1 Mk III lacks the usual wrappings that would have kept it clean in the dirt and mud of the trenches.*

be fired at a rapid rate of over 15 shots a minute as the bolt action was easy to operate, and the magazine could be quickly loaded.

throughout World War II; Australian production of this rifle did not end until 1955 at the Lithgow arsenal. Note the mixture of headgear worn.

While the No. 1 Mk III was an excellent service rifle, it was expensive and time-consuming to make, for virtually everything had to be machined or made by hand. Consequently when trench warfare set in and an ever increasing number of rifles was needed, some production short cuts were made, including the removal of the magazine cut-out and the long-range sights. The result was the **Rifle No. 1 Mk III***, and this may be regarded as the standard British rifle of World War I. It was produced in tens of thousands, not only in the United Kingdom but also in India and Australia (where it remained in production until 1955). It was a sturdy and sound rifle that was well able to withstand the rigours of trench fighting. All manner of devices were invented to increase its usefulness, these ranging from periscopic sights to grenade-launcher devices. In the hands of a fully-trained soldier it was capable of high rates of fire: a rate of 15 rounds per minute was accepted as the norm and trained soldiers could produce far more. At Mons in 1914 the German forces involved thought they were up against machine-guns at some stages. They were not; it was simply the massed rapid fire produced by the superbly-trained soldiers of the BEF using their No. 1 Mk IIIs to full advantage.

Specification
Rifle No. 1 Mk III*
Calibre: 7.7 mm (0.303 in)
Length: overall 1.133 m (44.6 in); barrel 0.64 m (25.2 in)
Weight: 3.93 kg (8.656 lb)
Muzzle velocity: 634 m (2,080 ft) per second
Magazine: 10-round box

Lebel mle 1886

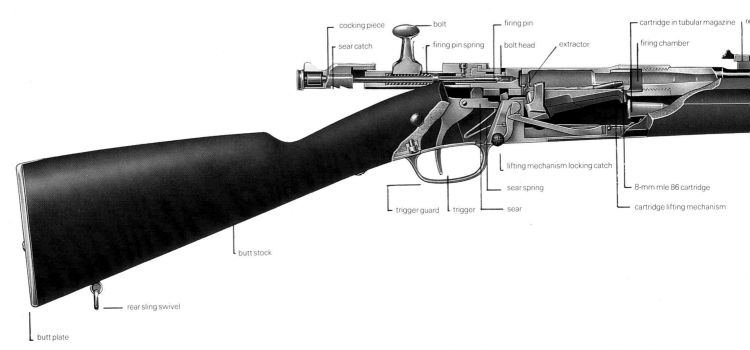

cocking piece — bolt — firing pin — cartridge in tubular magazine

sear catch — firing pin spring — bolt head — extractor — firing chamber

lifting mechanism locking catch

sear spring — 8-mm mle 86 cartridge

trigger guard — trigger — sear — cartridge lifting mechanism

butt stock

rear sling swivel

butt plate

A section of French infantry guards a canal bank for the benefit of the camera in September 1914. Note the Berthier carbine beside the officer, its longer bol handle contrasting with those of the Lebel used by the others.

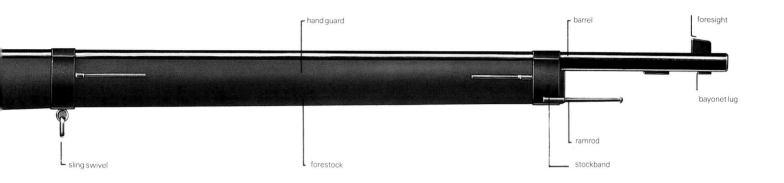

hand guard

barrel

foresight

bayonet lug

ramrod

sling swivel

forestock

stockband

...ater in the war, Poilus of the French army march towards the front. As usual ...ith the infantryman, his rifle (in this case the Lebel) forms only a small part of ...is burden.

Fusil Lebel mle 1886

By 1886 the French army was in a position to introduce a new 'small' cartridge with a calibre of 8 mm (0.315 in) to fire the new completely smokeless propellant developed by Paul Vielle. With the new cartridge came a new rifle, the **Fusil mle 1886**, usually known as the **Lebel** after the name of the officer who led the commission that recommended the adoption of the new rifle and round.

The Lebel was for its time only a tentative improvement of the existing Gras mle 1874. The new rifle did indeed have the ability to fire the new 8-mm cartridge, but the bolt action of the Gras design was retained and, in place of the by-then acceptable box magazine, the Lebel used a tubular magazine in which the rounds were loaded nose-to-tail. This magazine was located under the fore-stock and contained eight rounds. It was still possible to load single rounds directly into the chamber and, as loading the tubular magazine was a somewhat slow process, the full loading was usually kept for use only when large amounts of fire were required.

The original mle 1886 underwent a major modification programme in 1893 and the designation was accordingly changed to **mle 1886/93**. Another revision came in 1898 when the ammunition was updated, but the designation remained unaltered.

The original mle 1896 has one major claim to fame, for it was the first service rifle to fire smokeless propellant cartridges. For a short while the French army was thus ahead of all its contemporaries, but this advantage did not last long once the 'secrets' of the propellant became widely known. Within a few years all other major nations had converted to the new propellant and had also adopted the new 'small-calibre' type of cartridge, so the Lebel soon lost its early lead. In fact it assumed something of a back place in rifle development as a result of its anachronistic tubular magazine. One of the major disadvantages of such a magazine was the relatively long loading time that had already been mentioned; another was the safety aspect, for as the rounds lay nose-to-tail in the magazine there was always the chance that a sudden jolt would cause the nose of one round to hit the primer of the round in front with dire results. Thus there was a gradual move away from the Lebel towards the Berthier rifles, but in 1914 the Lebel remained in service in large numbers, and it was still standard issue to most front-line units. It served throughout World War I and was still in large-scale use in World War II.

The Lebel could mount a long cruciform bayonet, and was by all accounts a pleasant rifle to handle and aim. However, the loading was awkward and there was always the chance of magazine explosion when it was least expected. Another drawback was the two-piece bolt which took a degree of maintenance and was prone to clogging with dirt and dust at the earliest opportunity. A special 5.5-mm (0.216 in) training version was produced in small numbers.

Specification
Fusil Lebel mle 1886/93
Calibre: 8 mm (0.315 in)
Length: overall 1.303 m (51.3 in); barrel 0.798 m (31.4 in)
Weight: 4.245 kg (9.35 lb)
Muzzle velocity: 725 m (2,379 ft) per second
Magazine: 8-round tubular

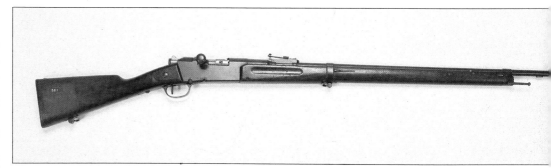

Above: The long mle 1886/93 was basically an 1874 Gras rifle modernized by the use of an eight-round tubular magazine, and was one of the standard French rifles of World War I. It used a straight-action bolt system and fired an 8-mm (0.315-in) cartridge.

Left: Taken on manoeuvres in July 1914, this photograph gives an indication of the French attacking tactics at the Battle of the Frontiers. These massed rushes were supposed to carry all before them, but in the event the soldiers were mown down in heaps.

Above: A French Zouave is seen at Vincennes, 1917, standing guard with a mle 1886/93 fitted with the spike-like Epée-bajonette mle 1886. This converted the rifle into a pike for close combat, where it was to prove very effective, but it lacked the general usefulness of the blade-type bayonet.

French troops are shown in action a short distance from the Turkish lines at Gallipoli. The rifle in the foreground can be recognized as a mle 1886/93 by the inline bolt; if it was a Berthier the bolt handle would be turned down. The hardness of the ground has made trench-building impossible; hence the barricades.

French carbines

During World War I the carbine was a widely-used weapon with most armies other than those of the British and the Americans who never favoured the type. As a general rule these carbines were cut-down versions of the standard service rifles of the day and were originally intended for use by cavalry. However, between 1914 and 1918 the carbine was used by many more types of unit, usually in the second line, by signallers, drivers, military police and many others who required some form of weapon but not the long and awkward service rifle.

The carbines used by the French army can be taken as typical of the types in use elsewhere. While the French front-line troops were equipped with the normal service rifle, many other French soldiers carried carbines. At the top of this list inevitably came the cavalry, but after 1914 the French cavalry had little to do and many were used as infantry and were thus given the normal service rifles. Other second-line troops used a variety of weapon types. The oldest of them was the **Mousqueton Gras mle 1874**, like its longer relation a single-shot weapon with no magazine. Surprisingly the mle 1886 Lebel and its derivatives were not produced in carbine form (other than trials models) and most French carbines were based on the Berthier.

The first Berthier carbine was the **Mousqueton Berthier mle 1890** produced for the cavalry. The later **mle 1892** was for use by artillery units, and there was also a slightly different version for the Gendarmerie, a branch of the French armed forces. The mle 1892 was probably produced in greater numbers than the mle 1890, and was provided with such accessories such as a bayonet and cleaning rod. From the mle 1892 evolved the mle 1907 rifle. By 1914 the mle 1892 was in service with many arms other than the artillery for which it was originally intended, and the mles 1890 and 1892 met most of the carbine requirements of the French armed forces during World War I. In 1916 they were joined by the **mle 1916** (a carbine version of the Berthier mle 1916 rifle with its five-round box magazine), but relatively few of these were produced.

While carriage of these various carbines was certainly easier than that of the long service rifles, firing them was an unpleasant experience. All the carbine versions of standard rifles had two

nasty drawbacks when fired: excessive flash combined with blast, and heavy recoil giving a pronounced 'kick' as the bullet left the muzzle. Both were produced by the fact that the cartridges were designed for barrels of conventional length. In the carbine some of the firing gases were still unexpended as the bullet left the muzzle, producing the flash and blast that in turn produced the recoil. The carbines were thus not much liked as weapons but were simply carried in lieu of the more awkward rifles. When they were used in action it was very much as a last resort and their performance was at best indifferent when compared with rifles of orthodox size and length.

Specification
Mousqueton Berthier mle 1892
Calibre: 8 mm (0.315 in)
Length: overall 0.945 m (37.2 in); barrel 0.45 m (17.7 in)
Weight: 3.1 kg (6.83 lb)
Muzzle velocity: 634 m (2,080 ft) per second
Magazine: 3-round box

French cavalrymen carrying Berthier carbines pass elements of the 58th (London) Division during April 1918. At that stage of the war the cavalry were still held in reserve in case of the breakthrough that never came, for by then their place had been taken by the tank.

Above: The Mousqueton Berthier 1890 et 1892 was the forerunner of the Berthier rifles, and is seen here with the Sabre-Bajonette mle 92/16 used during World War I. The magazine held only three rounds, but the carbine handled well, retaining, however, the violent recoil 'kick' of all carbines.

A French soldier in the Dardenelles during 1915 is seen here with a Berthier mle 1892 carbine fitted with a long knife bayonet. The use of such a carbine would indicate that he is not a foot soldier but possibly some form of specialist such as a signaller.

Fusil Berthier mle 1907

Soon after the Lebel had been adopted for service it was appreciated that the design had several drawbacks, the most important being the use of a tubular magazine. By the time this had been realized the Lebel was in large-scale production so there was little chance of any immediate change-over to a new design. Instead there began a slow and gradual process of introducing a new rifle design known generally as the **Berthier**. This began in 1890 with the introduction of a cavalry carbine and gradually as new requirements arose new Berthier weapons were introduced.

This culminated in 1907 with the adoption of a **Fusil mle 1907** for use in the various French colonies (Indo-

China in particular). The Berthier rifle was typical of the Berthier series for it was a long, slender weapon that used a box magazine and a bolt action based on that already in use on the Lebel. While the change-over to the box magazine was a belated but good move, the Berthier magazine could hold only three rounds, a poor capacity in comparison with those of rifles already in use elsewhere, and therefore something of a disadvantage to the firer.

The mle 1907 was widely used by French troops serving in the colonies, and more were issued to colonial levies. Some were even issued to troops on the mainland of France, but in 1914 the Lebel was still the standard

rifle. The situation was changed by 1915, for by then the French forces were expanding rapidly in numbers and weapons were in short supply. Accordingly the Berthier was rushed into mass production, the mle 1907 being used as the baseline model. Some changes had to be made to the finer design points (especially to the bolt and sights) and the resultant weapon became the **mle 1907/15**. It was soon in service alongside the Lebel, and was used by the French armed forces throughout World War I, and was still in widespread use in 1939.

The mle 1907/15 still retained the three-round box magazine, however, and this was clearly insufficient for the requirements of 1915. Accordingly the

basic design was altered so that a five-round box could be used, and this variant was later placed into production as the **mle 1916**; it could be distinguished by the box magazine protruding from under the fore-stock, whereas on the mle 1907/15 the magazine was flush with the woodwork. The mle 1916 even had the facility to use a charging clip for loading the five rounds, a feature lacking on the mle 1907/15 in which each round had to be loaded individually.

The mle 1907/15 and mle 1916 soon became popular rifles. They certainly had a very attractive appearance for even under wartime production conditions the graceful shape of the long fore-stock was retained. In service the

Fusil Berthier mle 1907 (continued)

Berthiers were rather long for the conditions of trench warfare, but they were easy to handle when firing and were usually preferred to the Lebel. The mle 1907/15 was manufactured in large quantities, and at one point was even placed in production by Remington in the United States, but only for French use as the US Army never used the type. The final development of the type occurred in 1934, when mle 1907/15 weapons were modified to fire the 7.5-mm (0.295-in) round developed for light machine-guns. The revised designation was **mle 1907/15 M34**, and the type had a five-round magazine.

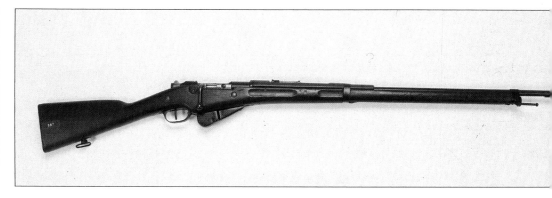

Specification
Fusil Berthier mle 1907/15
Calibre: 8 mm (0.315 in)
Length: overall 1.306 m (51.4 in); barrel 0.797 m (31.4 in)

Weight: 3.8 kg (8.38 lb)
Muzzle velocity: 725 m (2,379 ft) per second
Magazine: 3-round box

Usually known as the Berthier rifle, the mle 1907 was a rifle version of the mle 1890 et 1892 carbine. This example is a mle 1916 modified from

the original to take a five-round box magazine. This version was used by many armies after 1918, and was still in widespread use in 1939.

Fusil FN-Mauser mle 1889

The Belgian **Fusil FN-Mauser mle 1889** is something of an international weapon, for although it was designed in Belgium the action was a direct copy of the Mauser bolt action. It was accepted as the standard Belgian service rifle in 1889 and although some of them came from the Belgian state arsenal, most were produced by an entirely new concern established specifically to manufacture the Model 1889, the Fabrique Nationale, now more commonly known as FN and one of the largest arms manufacturing establishments in the world.

As was then usual the mle 1889 was accompanied in production by a carbine variant, the **Carabine FN-Mauser mle 1889**, some of which were intended to be used in conjunction with a sword-like bayonet known as a 'Yatagan'; most of these were issued to fortress troops and some Gendarmerie units. In its rifle form the mle 1889 was a very well-made weapon with some unusual features. One was that over its entire length the barrel was encased in a metal tube. This was intended to ensure that the barrel would not come into contact with any of the woodwork, which was prone to warping and could thus impair accuracy. While this feature had some advantages, such as the ability to mount the sights on the tube and not on the barrel, it was rather expensive to manufacture and under some conditions rust could accumulate between the barrel and the tube. But this was a long-term condition and during World War I caused few problems.

When it entered service, the mle 1889 was set for a long life, for it remained in use until 1940, and even after that date the type was taken in German garrison use. Some examples were manufactured for export to Abyssinia and a few nations in South America, but generally speaking the mle 1889 was kept in production for the Belgian army only. When the Germans overran much of Belgium in 1914 the requirements of the remaining Belgian forces

The Belgian mle 1889 was a Mauser design built under licence, and had a distinctive muzzle surround and a pronounced curve to the front of the five-round magazine. It was produced at the FN plant at Herstal and remained the standard Belgian service rifle until World War II.

were met by switching production to Hopkins & Allen in the United States. For much of the war the small Belgian army was stationed on the far left of the Allied trench lines along the River Lys, when conditions were not suitable for large-scale troop movements, and

accordingly the Belgian positions remained static for much of World War II.

The mle 1889 may be distinguished from other Mauser weapons by the magazine, which had a distinctive bulge on its forward edge. This bulge accommodated the hinge of the magazine platform that fed the rounds upwards into the bolt mechanism under the control of a leaf spring. The box magazine held five rounds fed into the box from a charger clip, and unlike the practice in later Mauser magazines the rounds were held in a vertical stack. (The later versions used a 'staggered'

arrangement.) Another recognitio[n] point is the barrel jacket, which ex[tends] to some way behind the muzzle[.] The usual Mauser cleaning rod wa[s] present and a long bayonet could b[e] fitted.

Specification
Fusil FN-Mauser mle 1889
Calibre: 7.65 mm (0.301 in)
Length: overall 1.295 m (51.0 in); barre[l] 0.78 m (30.6 in)
Weight: 4.01 kg (8.8 lb)
Muzzle velocity: 610 m (2,001 ft) per second
Magazine: 5-round box

Belgian troops armed with mle 1889 Mauser rifles set up a roadblock outside Louvain in a vain attempt to arrest the onrush of the German armies through Belgium during August 1914.

Into the Unknown

Before the war it was assumed that the great increases in firepower produced by the magazine rifle and quick-fire artillery would make battles more bloody but no less decisive. But the new firepower simply drove the armies into the earth, and machine-guns kept them there.

The first shot of this ciné film sequence taken during the Battle of the Somme in 1916 shows an officer leading a section of British infantry out of a trench. The officer wears jodphurs and carries a cane, making him an obvious target; later in the war they carried rifles and wore battledress.

When war broke out in 1914 there were few tacticians on either side who could envisage the manner in which the machine-gun was to dominate infantry tactics in the years to come. That with the better appreciation was the German side, for the Germans alone had taken the care to invest in numbers of these weapons adequate to equip their infantry units, and in 1914 the effect of these weapons was profound. A single machine-gun is sufficient to arrest the movement of an entire infantry or cavalry battalion at times, but in 1914 this simple fact was a novelty and the tacticians of the time could think of nothing other than getting behind some form of protection until a set-piece attack could be mounted. In practice this meant the digging of trenches, but it was to be four years before the infantry could get out of them.

In 1914 armies on all sides were prepared for a war with the usual manœuvres and marching warfare that would bring the two sides to battle. Accordingly the infantry trained to march over long distances and when the time came for action the idea was for whole battalions to advance to positions where fire fights would dictate the eventual result. This era did not last long, coming to an abrupt halt with the Battle of the Frontiers for the French, and with Mons and Ypres for the small British Expeditionary Force (BEF). Away in the east the Russian steamroller was annihilated in the vast wheeling battles of Tannenberg and all the others, for on the Eastern Front the static conditions of trench warfare never became fully established and a form of mobile warfare prevailed right until 1917, when the Russians withdrew from the unequal contest.

Once the trench lines were set up on the Western Front, infantry tactics became moribund for some years. And when the 'Old Contemptibles' of the BEF had vanished in the holocaust of Loos in 1915, the greater part of the British army was made up of barely-trained conscripts led by junior officers who were only marginally better trained. The French too had lost their best soldiers in the early stages of the war and were content to base themselves on their trench lines for what were essentially local offensives. For much of the war these operations were confined to local trench raids at night and perhaps the odd company action against limited objectives.

In all these actions apart from the raids the infantry tactics were much the same. A prearranged artillery bombardment was directed against known enemy positions, and at a pre-set time the infantry clambered out of the trenches and walked towards the enemy lines. In the years since 1918 these simple tactics have come in for much criticism, but the fact remains that given the state of manning and training in most armies the protagonists had little alternative. The standard of training and understanding of military basics was such that conscripts had to be used en masse, with little finesse in the way of advancing with mutual fire support between units or the use of flanking support moves. It was quite simply a case of massing enough men, attempting to destroy the enemy's positions and weapons with artillery, and then advancing in a straight line towards the enemy trenches where (if they arrived) the soldiers could engage in hand-to-hand fighting.

Above: The unfortunate man on the right appears to have become one of the many dead, and did not even make it out of the start trench.

Below: His comrades are already on their way through the machine-gun fire, but as so often in 1916 few will actually reach their objective across no-man's land.

The tactics were for many years as crude as that, and as the world now knows in many cases the unfortunate infantry never even made it beyond the middle of the 'no-man's land' that divided the trench lines. Some of the enemy's machine-guns always managed to survive the artillery fire and pop out of the dugouts and bunkers in time to halt the advancing infantry.

However, for much of 1915 the German army was on the defensive while tacticians pondered on how to break the trench-warfare deadlock. In 1916 they came up with the dreadful philosophy of the 'killing ground', which they put into action at Verdun. This philosophy was meant to make the French army defend an area chosen by the Germans in such a manner that the German war machine would simply grind away the strength of its foe. But in order to make the French defend Verdun the Germans had first to attack and this they did in a more sophisticated manner. Instead of the extended lines of walking infantry, the Germans attacked with small sections of infantry supported by light machine-guns, moving forward not in an extended line but in short unco-ordinated rushes that diverted the defenders and dispersed defensive fire. The attack was still preceded by the usual massive artillery action that tore up the ground, but in the main this favoured the attackers. Although the Verdun battles were eventually lost by the Germans, in that their original objectives were not achieved, the novel tactics were noted for future use.

They were certainly not adopted by the British in 1916 when the Somme offensives went ahead in exactly the same manner as those of 1915. Lines of infantry rose out of their trenches at the appointed time and walked forward in extended lines. The only changes from 1915 was that the preliminary artillery barrage was much heavier and that more use was made of chemical warfare. In the latter stages of the offensive the tank appeared on the scene, but only in small numbers that did not make a material contribution.

The tank was nevertheless to have the greatest effect on infantry tactics of the time, but 1918 started with the Germans once more refining their Verdun

This is the type of terrain over which the infantry of both sides had to advance during the many battles of the war. The open, pock-marked landscape was dominated by artillery and the machine-gun, and men could only survive underground or behind protection such as that supplied by tank armour.

If the German machine-guns were not enough of an obstacle in no-man's land the barbed wire could always be relied on to slow down a rushed attack to a slow walk. The standing infantry made ideal targets for enemy machine-gunners and riflemen, in their relatively safe trenches.

tactics for use during the last major German offensives, arranged to crush the Allies before the Americans could arrive on the scene in vast numbers. In series of set-piece battles the German infantry were used in small squads that moved forward, taking advantage of cover and ground where possible, to sweep past rather than into the Allied trenches to create mayhem in the rear areas. These new tactics worked wonderfully. Allied formations, conditioned by years of static trench warfare, were suddenly faced with swarms of small infantry squads moving through their lines while gas, artillery and even tanks kept them occupied and seeking what cover there might be to hand. These German tactics created great holes in the Allied lines, and the Germans were halted only when final reserves had been brought up from the rear areas. But it had been a near-run thing, especially for the British forces in front of Amiens.

Eventually the German offensive petered out. By the middle of the year the Allies were ready for their final offensive, and this time it was to be different. The years since 1914 had not all been spent in carrying out the same mistakes over and over again, and with the advent of the tank new tactics could be used. The early conscript armies had grown not only in numbers but in skills, and the long series of attacks that finally defeated the Germans on their own terms were made not by the old set-piece attacks but by tactics based on a high degree of inter-arm co-operation. No longer did the artillery simply blast a way through the trench lines: instead it provided a lifting barrage of defensive fire as the infantry and tank advanced in mutual support. Overhead the new Royal Air Force corrected artillery fire and flew ground-attack sorties. Some units were even supplied at times from the air using parachuted stores and ammunition. No one arm moved forward by itself. It was a balanced and co-operative effort using tactics that were to see their full fruition in World War II. No longer was the foot soldier simply a rifle-carrier. Instead he moved forward with fire support from tanks and artillery to occupy territory and winkle out the enemy from his positions. It was a very long way from the early days of August 1914.

Rifles of the Great War

he Second Naval Brigade practise an attack on Imbros, June 1915. The dense rush of men provided an excellent rget for those Turks who had survived the British barrage. On the Western Front fluid small-unit tactics were radually introduced, and contributed greatly to the German breakthrough in March 1918.

Above: After its disastrous performance in the Balkan wars of 1912-3, the Turkish army was once again written off as an effective force. But to the surprise of their enemies, the Turks fought with dogged tenacity when the British and French attacked at Gallipoli. This Turk carries a Mauser rifle and a packed cartridge belt. The cloth hat shaped like a solar topee but without a peak replaced the traditional fez in 1908.

bove: The tactics that were to be used by the German stormtroopers of arch 1918 were formulated during 1917 when small squads of infantry tacked using hand grenades as their main weapons. This picture was taken the German training area at Sedan. Note how rifles were carried slung.

Below: Taken from the German trench lines, this photograph shows troops advancing across open terrain. The troops in the foreground still have their rifles slung, perhaps indicating that they are about to move forward to a support position that cannot be seen from the camera position used.

Mosin-Nagant Model 1891

By the late 1880s the Russian army was in the process of converting its massive forces away from the use of the obsolete Berdan rifles. The army carried out a series of investigations, in the course of which it was attracted by a number of rifles produced by the Belgian Nagant brothers, but it also had on its doorstep a design produced by a tsarist officer known as Sergei Mosin. The planners decided to amalgamate the best features of the two designs and the result was the **Mosin-Nagant** rifle which was introduced into service in 1891; its full Russian title was **Russkaya 3-lineinaye vintovka obrazets 1891g** (Russian 3-line rifle model 1891).

The term '3-line' in the designation denotes that the calibre was gauged in an old Russian linear measurement known as a line, equal to 2.54-mm (0.1 in). This was later changed in 1908 when a new cartridge was introduced and the calibre became 7.62 mm (0.3 in). The original sights were calibrated in the equally old arshins (1 arshin = 0.71 m = 27.95 in), but these too were changed to metres after 1908. Overall the Model 1891 was a sound and rugged rifle design but it did have a few unusual features. One was found in the five-cartridge magazine, for with the system employed the top cartridge was always kept free of magazine spring pressure for the actual bolt-loading process, which had the advantage that feeding jams were less frequent than they might otherwise have been. But this was balanced by the introduction of some complexity in the mechanism. The two-piece bolt was also generally judged to be more complicated than was really necessary, though it gave little enough trouble in use. One other unusual feature was that the rifle was issued with a long bayonet with a screwdriver point that could be used to dismantle parts of the rifle. This bayonet was of the socket type, and during World War 1 it was a virtual fixture on the rifle at all times.

Overall the Model 1891 was a rugged weapon that could take hard knocks and was generally undemanding of care and attention. A **Dragoon Rifle Model 1891** carbine version was produced for use by cavalry and the ubiquitous Russian mounted infantry, but this variant was only slightly shorter than the rifle and much longer than other carbines produced at the time; a genuine **Carbine Model 1910** variant was produced in 1910.

The main problem for the Russians was that they had selected a good service rifle, but there were never enough of them and production facili-

Above: These Russian troops are armed with Mosin-Nagant Model 1891 rifles, all with the long spike bayonets that were such a fixture that the sights were usually adjusted permanently to compensate for their weight. The bayonets used the ancient socket method of fixing.

Above: The Russian army went to war in the Slavic uniforms adopted after 1877 and armed with the rugged Mosin-Nagant series of rifles. Lack of competent commanders rather than a shortage of modern equipment was to lead to the heavy defeats of 1914.

Part of the Russian contingent is seen at Salonika in July 1916. This was the last year in which the Russian army could adequately sustain combat; the Herculean offensive launched by General Brusilov dealt a savage blow to Austria-Hungary but could not save the tottering Tsarist empire.

ties were overstretched. Those that existed had to make the rifles virtually by hand as the concept of mass production was far from Russian thoughts before 1914. Consequently, when extra Russian army units were formed from the reserves in 1914 there were very often no rifles with which to arm them.

The Model 1891 played its part in the revolutions of 1917 and was again in action during the civil war that followed in 1918. Between the wars the Model 1891 was replaced in production by the shorter **Model 1891/30**, and it was with this that the Red Army was armed in World War II, though some Model 1891s survived after 1941.

Specification
Mosin-Nagant Model 1891
Calibre: 7.62 mm (0.3 in)
Length: overall 1.305 m (51.38 in); barrel 0.802 m (31.6 in)
Weight: 4.37 kg (9.62 lb)
Muzzle velocity: 810 m (2,657 ft) per second
Magazine: 5-round box

Fucile modello 91

The Italian service rifle of World War I was the **Fucile modello 91**, and was of a type known as the **Mannlicher-Carcano**. This was developed at Turin Arsenal between 1890 and 1891 and was an overall amalgamation of a Mauser bolt action taken from the Belgian/German mle 1889, the box magazine arrangement of the Mannlicher system and a new bolt-sleeve safety device produced by one Salvatore Carcano. The Italians thought highly of the resultant weapon and adopted it in 1892; it remained the standard Italian service rifle until World War II.

Unfortunately no else seemed to share their enthusiasm, for the only sales made outside Italy before World War I were to Japan, and this batch was made to accommodate the Japanese 6.5-mm (0.256-in) round which differed in dimensions from that in Italian use. In service the modello

91s proved sound enough, but the amalgamation of diverse features in the bolt and magazine areas resulted in a design that was rather more complicated than it might have been, and in the field the modello 91 required considerable attention, especially in

This Mannlicher-Carcano carbine is the 6.5-mm (0.256-in) Moschetto modello 91 per cavalleria. As it was meant for use by cavalry troops it had a fixed folding bayonet and the magazine held six rounds, but many were used with other special troops such as gunners and signallers.

he colonial territories in Africa; in particular, the straight-pull bolt action was prone to jamming when dirty.

The modello 91 spawned a whole group of carbine types that were produced in variants for use by cavalry, special troops (including gunners and engineers) and others. While these carbines were handy and easy to carry they suffered from the usual shortcomings inherent on firing short-barrelled weapons, even though the cartridge used was less powerful than many others then in use elsewhere. Some of these carbines were provided with spiked bayonets; the modello 91 rifle used a knife-type bayonet.

As the modello 91 was used only by the Italians during World War I their service use was confined to the border campaigns against Austro-Hungarian troops, coming to a climax with the battle of Caporetto in 1917. During this action the Italians lost heavily and the resultant withdrawals led to some British divisions being diverted from the Western Front in an attempt to stabilize matters. The outcome of Caporetto was not due entirely to the performance of the modello 91, which was much the same as that of many of its contemporaries, but even at the time it was generally accepted that the Italian 6.5-mm cartridge was rather underpowered and the bullet it fired generally lacked striking power. But these points were marginal, for the modello 91 handled and fired quite well. The small cartridge produced less recoil than was usual among other designs (though the carbine versions kicked as nastily as other types) and the general lack of protrusions and items that could catch on things made the modello 91 a good weapon to use when moving across rough country. But even now the overall impression left by the modello 91 is that it was a rather more complicated weapon than others of the time, and despite the Italians' under-

Troops of the 35th Italian Division march through Salonika during August 1916, carrying their Mannlicher-Carcano modello 91

standable enthusiasm for a national product it was among the 'also rans' in the World War I rifle stakes.

Specification
Fucile modello 91
Calibre: 6.5 mm (0.256 in)

rifles at the trail. Known as the Fucile modello 91, this rifle was still in service in 1940. It differed from the normal Mannlicher rifles only in detail.

Length: overall 1.285 m (50.6 in); barrel 0.78 m (30.7 in)
Weight: 3.8 kg (8.4 lb)
Muzzle veclocity: 630 m (2,067 ft) per second
Magazine: 6-round box

Mannlicher Modell 1895

By the early 1890s the Austro-Hungarian army had in service a number of types of rifle based on the bolt action designed by Ferdinand von Mannlicher. This employed a straight-pull bolt action of two-piece construction, and the first of the type was taken into service as early as 1884. There followed a number of models with various modifications, all of them firing the old black-powder propellant, and it was 1890 before the first 'smokeless' model appeared. It was not until 1895 that the design was finally 'frozen' and it was thus that the **Mannlicher Modell 1895**, also known as the **8-mm Repetier Gewehr Modell 1895** (8-mm repeating rifle model 1895) became the standard rifle of the Austro-Hungarian army.

The Modell 1895 was a sound and straightforward weapon that proved reliable in service. Like so many other rifles of the period the Modell 1895 was rather long but the straight-pull bolt action appears to have produced few problems. It fired the 8-mm (0.315-in) Modell 1890 round-nosed cartridge that was the first Austro-Hungarian round with smokeless propellant, and these were introduced into the five-round integral box magazine by using a cartridge clip and a charger guide on the receiver, in itself something of an innovation for the time.

It was the Modell 1895 that the Auro-Hungarian armies carried when they went to war in 1914. By then the rifles had been joined by a carbine variant known as the **Modell 1895 8-mm Repetier-Stutzen-Gewehr** and issued to troops such as engineers, drivers, signallers and gunners. For once the usual proliferation of carbine types did not occur in the Austro-Hungarian armies and the Stutzen became a familiar sight throughout Central Europe, during World War I and after it, for the Modell 1895 rifle and carbine became virtual fixtures for many armies. One of the first to adopt the Modell 1895 was Bulgaria. After 1918 the type was taken over by Italy as war reparations and the rifle became one of the standard Italian weapons. Others ended up in Greece and Yugoslavia, and of course once the Austro-Hungarian Empire had been split up after 1918 both Austria and Hungary

Above: The Mannlicher Modell 1895 was the standard service rifle of the Austro-Hungarian army and fired a 6.5-mm (0.256-in) cartridge. It was a sound and strong weapon with a five-round box magazine and a straight-pull bolt action. The projection under the muzzle is a cleaning rod.

Below: Austro-Hungarian troops outside Jaroslav carry their Mannlicher Modell 1895s. This rifle used a straight-pull bolt action and was known as the Repetier-Gewehr from its use of a five-round box magazine compared with earlier Mannlicher rifles, such as the Modell 1890.

retained their familiar weapons.

Both the Modell 1895 and the Stutzen are now collector's pieces but for a very long period they were the standard service weapons for much of Central Europe. They were sound if unspectacular weapons that provided good service for over half a century.

Specification
Repetier-Gewehr Modell 1895
Calibre: 8 mm (0.315 in)
Length: overall 1.27 m (50 in); barrel 0.765 m (30.1 in)

Weight: 3.78 kg (8.3 lb)
Muzzle velocity: 619 m (2,031 ft) per second
Magazine: 5-round box

Recruited from a bewildering variety of nationalities, the Austro-Hungarian army proved to be a deceptively fragile instrument. As the war dragged on the Empire was forced to rely on the sort of hapless conscripts epitomized by the Good Soldier Svějk.

Model 1903 Springfield

At the turn of the century the US Army was equipped with a rifle known as the Krag-Jorgensen which had been adopted in 1892. It was not long before the Americans realized that in the rapid developments of the late 1800s the Krag-Jorgensen left a lot to be desired and accordingly decided to adopt a better rifle. They cast around for ideas and were soon impressed sufficiently with the basic Mauser system to negotiate a licence to manufacture Mauser-based rifles in the USA.

The Mauser system was modified to produce a rifle built around a new American cartridge known as the Cartridge, Ball, Caliber .30 in M1903. This had a blunt nose but when the Germans introduced their 'spitzer' sharp-nosed bullet with better all-round performance the Americans were quick to follow suit and the rifle was accordingly modified to what was to be its classic form. In fact the rifle was ready in 1903, and was first manufactured at the Springfield Arsenal in Illinois, whence it took its generally-accepted name of the **Springfield** rifle. In appearance it was obviously a Mauser but the length was something new.

The new rifle was officially the **Magazine Rifle, Caliber .30, Model of 1903**, but this was usually abbreviated to **Model 1903** or simply **M1903**. It differed from most of its contemporares by being an interim length between a full-length rifle and a carbine, for it was intended to be the service rifle for all arms from cavalry to infantry. This compromise between lengths resulted in an extremely attractive and well-balanced rifle that was and still is a joy to handle. The bolt action was of the turn-down design with a well-placed bolt handle that was easy to operate rapidly when required; the overall fine standard of finish and detail design made the weapon extremely accurate, and the M1903 and its later versions are still much prized as target rifles. The original Model 1903 was the rifle

Above: The American M1903 Springfield was a Mauser-based rifle first introduced in 1903 and still in service during the Korean War. It was an excellent weapon and this is the original version, shown with a bayonet from the earlier Krag-Jorgensen Model 1896 service rifle.

the US Army took to France in 1917 but it was soon overtaken on the production lines by later variants including the **M1903 Mk 1**. This was basically a model 1903 adapted to accommodate the ill-fated Pedersen Device, a gadget that was supposed to turn the bolt action rifle into a form of automatic assault rifle by removing the bolt and replacing it with a new receiver firing special 7.62-mm (0.3-in) pistol ammunition fed from an overhead magazine; the rounds were fired using the normal rifle barrel. Although this device was issued, it was produced too late for widespread issue and was held in reserve for the expected offensives of 1919. After the war it was withdrawn from use altogether, the Mk 1 rifles being converted back to normal Model 1903 standards.

After 1918 the Model 1903 was furth-

The first contingent of American troops that arrived in England in 1917 are seen here with M1903 Springfields piled. They are probably men from the famous

er modified into various forms, usually with a view to easier production, and it was still in US Army service as a sniper rifle as late as the Korean War. By any standards it is still regarded as one of the best service rifles of its period, and quite apart from its continuing use as a target rifle, the type is now retained as a collector's item.

'Rainbow Division' formed from all the states of the Union and the first t« be sent to Europe, where their fresh numbers would have ensured an eventual Allied victory.

Specification
M1903
Calibre: 7.62 mm (0.3 in)
Length: overall 1.097 m (43.2 in); barr 0.61 m (24 in)
Weight: 3.94 kg (8.69 lb)
Muzzle velocity: 853 m (2,800 ft) per second
Magazine: 5-round integral box

Winchester Model 1895

It may seem rather odd to have a rifle more usually regarded as being part of the plains warfare of the American West included in a study of the rifles of World War I, but the fact remains that the **Winchester Model 1895** was for one nation an important part of its World War I inventory. That nation was Russia, which entered the war with a will in 1914 only to suffer a series of catastrophic defeats of which the Battle of Tannenburg was but one. The basic problem for the Russian military planners was that although they had almost bottomless reserves of men they lacked the industrial base to equip them. The Russian economy before 1914 was indeed getting itself on an industrial footing, but it was as yet insufficient to sustain wartime production. Matters got to the point where soldiers were sent into battle without rifles but were expected to obtain them from among the fallen. Things clearly could not continue for long like that.

The easy way out was to purchase weapons from abroad. The Americans duly obliged and in particular the Winchester Repeating Arms Company of New Haven, Connecticut, took the opportunity to use the assembly line

for its well-known range of manually-loaded rifles that used the loading lever beneath the trigger. This was operated by the fingers that gripped the stock; a rapid downwards movement loaded a new round from the tubular magazine under the barrel. By World War I this type of rifle was militarily obsolescent but it suited the Russian requirement and accordingly a 'militarized' version was churned out especially for the Russian army.

This was the Model 1895, which was chambered for the Russians 7.62-mm (0.3-in) cartridge and had sights calibrated in arshins, then the usual method of range measurement used in Russia (1 arshin = 0.71 m = 27.95 in). The resultant rifle could still be recognized as a descendant of the famous Winchester 75 of plains fame, but overall it was longer, heavier and more rugged. It needed to be, for all that

made it to Russia (some were lost as a result of U-boat attacks) were sent straight to the front, and into the hands of rapidly-trained recruits who had little time for maintenance and cleaning. In all 293,816 were actually delivered to Russia and those that survived the rigours of the fighting against German and Austro-Hungarian armies later played their part in the revolutions of 1917 and in the civil war that followed. Moreover, some were captured by the Germans in World War II. It was noticed that some of these 'later' examples had their sights marked in metres, but when this was carried out is uncertain.

By any standard the appearance of the Winchester Model 1895 on the Battlefields of World War I was odd, but it happened nevertheless. Few records actually survive of how the Model 1895 fared in action but no doubt it gave a

good account of itself. It was almc certainly the only lever-action rifle be used during World War I and c that score alone it is worthy of mentio

Specification
Winchester Model 1895
Calibre: 7.62 mm (0.3 in)
Length: overall 1.175 m (46.25 in); barrel 0.71 m (28 in)
Weight: 4.2 kg (9.26 lb)
Muzzle velocity: not known
Magazine: 5-round tubular

One of the oddest rifles of World W. I was the Winchester Model 1895 th still used the Winchester lever actic made famous on the American Plains. They were ordered by Russi in 1914 to arm the expanding Tsaris armies. 293,816 were produced anc sent to Russia, all in 7.62-mm (0.3-in calibre.

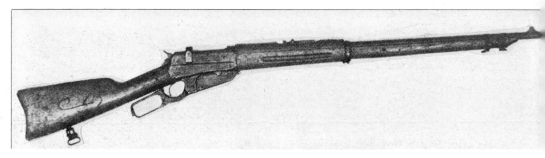

Rifles of World War II

World War II saw the decline in importance of the infantryman as marksman and the first appearance of his replacement, the infantryman as firepower component. After an uncharacteristically tentative start, it was Germany who, as so often, led the way.

Manufactured in enormous numbers, the American M1 carbine was designed for rear echelon and vehicle-mounted troops. Its light and easy handling, however, made it preferable to the heavy full-sized rifle issued to many front-line troops.

In any army the new soldier is always trained in the use of one basic form of service rifle, whatever his eventual trade may be. During World War II this was as true as it is now, but the rifle with which the individual soldier might be trained varied a great deal. Depending on the particular nation, the soldier might have been issued with a venerable antique while in others he might have received a shiny new model embodying all the latest technology, for the rifles used in World War II varied greatly.

At one end of the scale there were the old bolt-action rifles that had been in use since long before World War I; and at the other were the new self-loading or automatic rifles that eventually led to the first of what are now known as assault rifles. There were none of the latter in service when the war started in 1939, but as the war progressed the first operational models of such weapons appeared in service. These gave the infantryman a greatly increased firepower potential, but it was not until the true assault rifles (with their lower-powered cartridges) arrived from about 1943 onwards that the full quantum jump from the slow and steady single shots of the bolt-action rifle to the full automatic fire of the assault rifle was fully appreciated. The bolt-action rifles were usually sound and reliable weapons, but they lacked the shock effect of an assault rifle fired in the fully automatic mode.

Thus World War II was a war of transition for the basic infantryman. When the war started, usually all he had to hand was a bolt-action rifle of a well-tried but frequently elderly pattern. By the time the war was over every soldier had at least a foretaste of what the future had in store in the form of the assault rifle. There were some odd digressions along the way, such as the underpowered US Carbine M1 and the ingenious but complex German FG 42. Some nations, such as the United Kingdom, did not make the transition and relied upon the Lee-Enfield bolt-action rifles throughout, but the move towards the self-loading or assault rifle was still there.

This analysis does not contain all the rifles used during World War II, but the weapons discussed are typical of the period. Millions of soldiers used them under all manner of conditions, and the survivors will remember them until their last days.

The Gewehr 98 was the standard rifle for the bulk of the German army throughout the war. While not as advanced as many models introduced after 1939, the Mauser design, dating from the late 1880s, provided sterling service throughout two world wars and was a sound, reliable weapon.

Gewehr 98 and Karabiner 98k

The 7.92-mm (0.312-in) **Gewehr 98** was the rifle with which the German army fought through World War I. It was a Mauser rifle first produced in 1898, but was based on a design dating back to 1888. In service the Mauser action proved sturdy and reliable, but in the years following 1918 the German army carried out a great deal of operational analysis that demonstrated that the Gewehr 98 was really too long and bulky for front-line use. As an immediate result the surviving Gewehr 98s underwent a modification programme that changed their designation to **Karabiner 98b**. *Karabiner* is the German for carbine, but there was nothing of the carbine in the Karabiner 98b, whose length was unchanged from that of the original Gewehr 98. The only changes were to the bolt handle, the sling swivels and the ability to use improved ammunition. To confuse matters further the original Gewehr 98 markings were retained.

The Karabiner 98b was still in service with the German army in 1939 (and remained so throughout the war), but by then the standard rifle was a slightly shorter version of the basic Mauser known as the **Karabiner 98k**. This was slightly shorter than the original Gewehr 98 but was still long for a carbine, despite the letter suffix 'k' standing for *kurz*, or short. This rifle was based on a commercial Mauser model known as the **Standard** and widely produced throughout the inter-war years in countries such as Czechoslovakia, Belgium and even China. The German version was placed in production in 1935 and thereafter made in very large numbers. At first the standard of production was excellent, but once World War II had started the overall finish and standards fell to the extent that by the end of the war the wooden furniture was often laminated or of an inferior material, and such items as bayonet lugs were omitted. All manner of extras were evolved by the gadget-minded Germans for the Karabiner 98k, including grenade-launching devices, periscopic sights and folding butts for weapons used by airborne troops. There were also variations for sniper use, some with small telescopic sights mounted half way along the forestock and others with larger telescopes mounted over the bolt action.

Despite all the innovations by the Germans during World War II, the Karabiner 98k was still in production as the war ended, looking not all that different overall from the original

Gewehr 98, other than in the rough finish resulting from wartime shortages of labour and materials. By that time the Germans had to hand a whole array of Mauser rifles drawn from nearly all the armies of Europe, and most of them were used to equip one arm or another of the services by 1945. Some of these Mausers, most of which were very similar to the Gewehr 98 or Karabiner 98k, were kept in production on Czech and Belgian lines for German use after 1939-40. Away to the east the Chinese armies were mainly equipped with the Mauser Standard rifles that were virtually identical to the Karabiner 98k.

There will always be arguments as to whether or not the Mauser rifles were better service rifles than the Lee-Enfield, M1903 Springfield or the M1 Garand, but although the Mausers lacked some of the overall appeal of the Allied rifles they provided the German forces with long and reliable service. Few remain in use, but many are still prized as collector's pieces and many are retained for match rifle use.

Specification
Gewehr 98
Calibre: 7.92 mm (0.312 in)
Length: 1.25 m (49.2 in)
Length of barrel: 740 mm (29.1 in)
Weight: 4.2 kg (9.26 lb)
Muzzle velocity: 640 m (2,100 ft) per second
Magazine: 5-round box

Specification
Karabiner 98k
Calibre: 7.92 mm (0.312 in)
Length: 1.1075 m (43.6 in)
Length of barrel: 600 mm (23.6 in)
Weight: 3.9 kg (8.6 lb)
Muzzle velocity: 755 m (2,477 ft) per second
Magazine: 5-round box

An officer of the SS aims his Gewehr 98 on the Eastern Front in the winter of 1942. This sturdy weapon, dating from the end of the 19th century, served Germany for nearly 50 years.

Wehrmacht soldiers train for combat, armed with Karabiner 98k rifles. The photograph was probably taken between the wars, as indicate by the old and new pattern helmets being worn at the same time.

Left: Digging in during the early stages of the war. The length of the Mauser-designed 98k is obvious, making it difficult to handle in confined spaces. Given the short combat ranges typical of World Wa II, the long-range performance of th 98k was largely superfluous.

Gewehr 41(W) and Gewehr 43

The German army maintained an overall 'quality control' section that constantly sought ways in which the German forces could increase their efficiency, and by 1940 this section had discovered a need for some form of self-loading rifle to improve combat efficiency. A specification was duly issued to industry, and Walther and Mauser each put forward designs that proved to be remarkably similar. Both used a method of operation known as the 'Bang' system (after its Danish designer), in which gases trapped around the muzzle are used to drive back a piston to carry out the reloading cycle. Troop trials soon proved that the

Mauser design was unsuitable for service use and it was withdrawn, leaving the field free for the Walther design which became the 7.92-mm (0.312-in) **Gewehr 41(W)**.

Unfortunately for the Germans, once the Gewehr 41(W) reached front-line service, mainly on the Eastern Front, it proved to be somewhat less than a success. The Bang system proved to be too complex for reliable operation under service conditions and it was really too heavy for comfortable use, making the weapon generally unhandy. The Gewehr 41(W) also proved to be difficult to manufacture and, as if all this was not enough, in action the

weapon proved to be difficult and time-consuming to load. But for a while it was the only self-loading rifle the Germans had and it was kept in production to the extent of tens of thousands

Most of the Gewehr 41(W)s were used on the Eastern Front, and it was there that the Germans encountered the Soviet Tokarev automatic rifles. These used a gas-operated system that tapped off gases from the barrel to operate the mechanism, and once this system was investigated the Germans realized that they could adapt it to suit the Gewehr 41(W). The result was the **Gewehr 43**, which used the Tokarev

system virtually unchanged. Once t Gewehr 43 was in production, man facture of the Gewehr 41(W) promp ceased. The Gewehr 43 was muc easier to make and it was soon bei churned out in large numbers. Fro line troops greatly appreciated th ease with which it could be loade compared with the earlier rifle and was a popular weapon. All manner production short-cuts were introduc into the design, including the use wood laminates and even plastics f the furniture, and in 1944 an even si pler design known as the **Karabiner** was introduced, the *Karabiner* d signation being adopted although th

verall length was reduced by only
me 50 mm (2 in).

Both the Gewehr 41(W) and the later
ewehr 43 used the standard German
92-mm (0.312-in) cartridge, and were
no way related to the assault rifle
rogramme that involved the 7.92-mm
urz cartridge. The retention of the
le cartridge enabled the Gewehr 43
be used as a very effective sniper
le, and all examples had a telescopic
ght mount fitted as standard. The
ewehr 43 was so good in the sniper
le that many were retained in Czech
my service for many years after the
ar.

pecification
ewehr 41(W)
alibre: 7.92 mm (0.312 in)
ngth: 1.124 m (44.25 in)
ngth of barrel: 546 mm (21.5 in)
eight: 5.03 kg (11.09 lb)
uzzle velocity: 776 m (2,546 ft) per
cond

Magazine: 10-round box

Specification
Gewehr 43
Calibre: 7.92 mm (0.312 in)
Length: 1.117 m (44 in)

Length of barrel: 549 mm (21.61 in)
Weight: 4.4 kg (9.7 lb)
Muzzle velocity: 776 m (2,546 ft) per
second
Magazine: 10-round box

*Developed from the Gewehr 41(W)
and influenced by the Tokarev, the
Gewehr 43 was fitted with telescopic
sights as standard, and was an
excellent sniper's rifle.*

GERMANY
Fallschirmjägergewehr 42

*Above: A drill book photograph of
the FG 42 being fired in the prone
position wth bipod folded. The FG 42
was a precursor of the modern-
concept assault rifle.*

the strange world of Nazi Germany
ternal strife and rivalry flourished
vas even fostered), and in no sphere
as this internal feuding more rife than
etween the German army and the
uftwaffe. By 1942 the Luftwaffe were
ncroaching on the preserves of the
my to an alarming extent for no other
ason than petty wrangling, and when
e army decided to adopt a self-
ading rifle the Luftwaffe decided that
too had to have such a weapon. In-
ead of following the path followed by
e army with its adoption of the *kurz*
und, the Lufwaffe decided instead to
tain the standard 7.92-mm (0.312-in)
le cartridge and asked Rheinmetall
design a weapon to arm the Luftwaf-
parachute troops, the *Fallschirm-
ger*.

Rheinmetall accordingly designed
d produced one of the more remark-
le small-arms designs of World War
This was the 7.92-mm (0.312-in) **Fall-
hirmjägergewehr 42** or **FG 42**, a
eapon that somehow managed to
mpress the action required to pro-
ce automatic fire into a volume little
ger than that of a conventional bolt
tion. The FG 42 was certainly an
e-catching weapon, for the first ex-
ples had a sloping pistol grip, an
ples plastic butt and a prom-
ent bipod on the forestock. To cap it
. there was a large muzzle attach-
ent and provision for mounting a
ike bayonet. The ammunition feed
is from a side-mounted box maga-

*The FG 42, an early model of which is
seen here, was an attempt to arm the
German parachute forces with a rifle
capable of providing full-power MG
performance.*

zine on the left, and the mechanism
was gas-operated. All in all the FG 42
was a complex weapon, but was not
innovative as it was an amalgam of
several existing systems.

Needless to say the Luftwaffe took to
the FG 42 avidly and asked for more.
They did not get them, for it soon trans-
pired that the novelties of the FG 42
had to be paid for in a very complex
manufacturing process that consumed
an inordinate amount of time and production facilities. Thus supply was
slow and erratic, and in an attempt to
speed production some simplifications
were added. A simpler wooden butt
was introduced and the pistol grip was
replaced by a more orthodox component. The bipod was moved forward to
the muzzle and other short-cuts were
introduced. It was to no avail, for by the
time the war ended only about 7,000
had been made. But it was after the
war that the FG 42 made its biggest
mark, for many of its design features
were incorporated into later designs.
Perhaps the most important of these
was the gas-operated mechanism
which could fire from a closed bolt
position for single-shot fire and from an
open bolt for automatic fire, all compressed into a relatively small space.

One thing that was not copied was the
side-mounted magazine. This proved
to be less than a success in action for
not only did it snag on clothing or other
items but it tended to unbalance the
weapon when fired.

The FG 42 was a highly advanced
design for its day and it incorporated
many of the features now used on many
modern assault rifles. Typical of these
was the use of a 'straight line' layout
from butt to muzzle and the gas-
operated mechanism already mentioned. But for all this the FG 42 was too
difficult to produce, and even by 1945
there were still some bugs that remained to be ironed out before the
weapon was really problem-free. But
for all that it was a truly remarkable
design achievement.

Specification
FG 42
Calibre: 7.92 mm (0.312 in)
Length: 940 mm (37 in)
Length of barrel: 502 mm (19.76 in)
Weight: 4.53 kg (9.99 lb)
Muzzle velocity: 761 m (2,500 ft) per
second
Magazine: 20-round box
Cyclic rate of fire: 750-800 rpm

*First operational use of the FG 42 was
in Skorzeny's daring commando raid
to free Mussolini. Special camouflage
smocks were worn for the raid, and
the usual* Fallschirmjäger *helmets
were worn.*

German Rifles

Left: A section of Wehrmacht infantry armed with the venerable Gewehr 98K is seen on the first day of the German invasion of the Soviet Union.

Above: An Obergefreiter (Corporal) trumpeter sounds a call during the 1940 invasion of France. Cradled under his arm is his Gewehr 98.

Below: In complete contrast, one of the defenders of the Reich is seen with a Gewehr 43 self-loading rifle in the east in February 1945.

Maschinenpistole 43 and Sturmgewehr 44

Despite the orders of Hitler, the German army was so determined to develop and use the assault rifle that had been developed by Louis Schmeisser to fire the new Polte *kurz* (short) 7.92-mm (0.312-in) cartridge that it hid the experimental work under a new name. Originally the new rifle/cartridge combination had been known as the **Maschinenkarabiner 42(H)** (the H was for Haenel), but to distract attention once Hitler had issued his ill-advised order it was changed to **Maschinenpistole 43**, or **MP 43**. With the weapon in this form, the army went ahead from the development to the production stage, and the first examples were rushed to the Eastern Front where they soon proved to be invaluable.

The full development story of the MP 43 is provided elsewhere, but it must be stressed that the MP 43 was the first of what are today termed assault rifles. It could fire single shots for selective fire in defence, and yet was capable of producing automatic fire for shock effect in the attack or for close-quarter combat. It was able to do this by firing a relatively low-powered round that was adequate for most combat ranges but which could still be handled comfortably when the weapon was producing automatic fire. Tactically this had a tremendous effect on the way the infantry could fight, as they were no longer dependent on supporting fire from machine-guns, being able to take their own personal support fire with them. This enabled the German infantry to become a far more powerful force because of the quantum increase in firepower that units could produce compared with those equipped with conventional bolt-action rifles.

Once the importance of this firepower increase had been fully realized, the MP 43 became a priority weapon and urgent requests for more and more were made by the front-line troops. Initial supplies went mainly to elite units, but most went to the Eastern Front where they were most needed. Unusually for wartime Germany, prior-

The SS were among the first units to acquire the MP 43, and many were used in the battle of the Ardennes. First combat use was probably on the Eastern Front, however, where the weapon was an immediate success.

ity was given to production rather than development, and the only major change to the design was the **MP 43/1** which had fittings for a grenade-launching cup on the muzzle. In 1944 Hitler rescinded his opposition to the MP 43 and bestowed the more accurate designation of **Sturmgewehr 44 (StG 44)** upon the weapon, but there were few if any production alterations to the basic design.

Some accessories were produced for the MP 43 series. One was an infra-red night sight known as *Vampir*, but one of the oddest items ever to be produced for any weapon was the *Krummlauf* curved barrel that could direct bullets around corners. Apparently this device was developed to clear tank-killing infantry squads from armoured vehicles, but it was a bizarre device that never worked properly and yet managed to absorb a great deal of development potential at a time when that potential could have been directed towards more rewarding things. The curved barrels were intended to direct fire at angles of between 30° and 45°, and special periscopic mirror sights were devised to aim

Developed to fire the lower-powered Kurz (short) 7.92-mm round, the MP 43 was the first of the modern assault rifles. The lower-powered round followed German combat analyses, which found that battles were usually fought at ranges which did not require high-power bullets.

their fire. Few were actually produced and even fewer were used operationally.

After the war large numbers of MP 43s were used by several nations such as Czechoslovakia, and were also used during some of the early Arab-Israeli conflicts. A few still turn up in the hands of 'freedom fighters' in Africa and elsewhere.

Specification
StG 44
Calibre: 7.92 mm (0.312 in)
Length: 940 mm (37 in)
Length of barrel: 419 mm (16.5 in)
Weight: 5.22 kg (11.5 lb)
Muzzle velocity: 650 m (2,132 ft) per second
Magazine: 30-round box
Cyclic rate of fire: 500 rpm

Tokarev rifles

The Soviets have developed over the years a considerable talent for small arms innovations, and accordingly they were early in the move towards self-loading rifles. The first of these was the **Avtomaticheskaia Vintovka Simonova** introduced in 1936 (and thus known also as the **AVS36**) and designed by one S. G. Simonov. Although many were made and issued for service, the AVS was not a great success for it produced a prodigious muzzle blast and recoil, and it was all too easy for dust and dirt to get into the rather complex mechanism. The AVS thus had but a short service life before it was replaced.

The **SVT38 (Samozariadnyia Vintovka Tokareva)** that in 1938 replaced the AVS was designed by F. V. Tokarev, and it was initially not much of an improvement on the AVS. It was a gas-operated weapon, like the AVS, but in order to keep the rifle as light as possible the mechanism was far too light for the stresses and strains of prolonged use. While the combination of a gas-operated system and a locking block cammed downwards into a recess in the receiver base proved basically sound, it gave rise to frequent troubles mainly because parts broke. Thus the SVT38 was removed from production during 1940 to be replaced by the **Continued on page 1286**

Above: The SVT 40 was an early Soviet self-loading rifle, usually issued to NCOs or marksmen. A most influential weapon, it was to lend features to the German MP 43, and was the start of a chain leading to the modern AK range.

Right: Marines of the Soviet Northern Fleet in defensive positions, probably on exercise near Murmansk. The nearest marine has a PPSh 41 sub-machine gun, the remainder being armed with SVT40 Tokarevs.

Development of the German Assault Rifle

World War II saw a revolutionary development in the type of personal weapon carried by private soldiers. Self-loading rifles had become familiar in the 1930s, but it was German wartime experience that was to spearhead future design of the rifle.

For a nation usually in the vanguard of military innovation the Germans were surprisingly slow in the development of automatic or self-loading rifles. A few tentative attempts to produce an automatic rifle had been made by the Germans during World War I, but the results were hardly a great success and the designs were dropped in the inter-war years. However, out of the mass of operational analysis carried out by various sections of the German General Staff came the realization that most infantry combat took place at ranges well under 400m (437 yards) but that the infantry were carrying rifles firing cartridges intended for use at ranges well over 1000m (1,095 yards). If the infantry had weapons firing lower-powered cartridges, not only would they be able to carry more ammunition, but the prospect of automatic fire also seemed possible.

Not much was done as the result of this research until 1934, when a new cartridge began a programme of development. By late 1940 the new round was ready, and this became generally known as the *kurz* or short cartridge for it resembled a conventional 7.92-mm (0.312-in) cartridge shortened and containing less propellant; it lacked the range of the full-size round, but at most expected combat ranges was more than effective.

Even before the cartridge development was complete specifications for a new 'machine carbine' to fire the new round had been issued to industry. Two designs resulted, one from Walther and the other from Haenel, where the chief designer was Louis Schmeisser. These were the 7.92-mm (0.312-in) Maschinenkarabiner 42(W) and Maschinenkarabiner 42(H) respectively. Troop trials soon demonstrated that the Haenel weapon was the better of the two and the go-ahead for full production was given. According to legend the Haenel design showed its promise when a batch was dropped by parachute to an isolated unit of German soldiers who had been surrounded by the Soviets. Using the new weapon they fought their way out and in the aftermath the German army became enthusiastic about the assault rifle.

But at this point the heavy hand of Hitler descended, the Führer forbidding any further development of the new rifle and its short round. No doubt he had an eye to ammunition supply as not only were there millions of conventional 7.92-mm (0.312-in) rounds stockpiled ready for use, but the production facilities for yet more was ready and to hand; introduction of a new cartridge would impose considerable logistic and production burdens. Not to be outdone, the staff planners simply ignored the order and initiated production of the new rifle under the designation Maschinenpistole 43 (machine pistol model 1943) and the type went into full-scale production. The front line troops waxed lyrical regarding the new rifle as it provided them with a vast increase in potential firepower, and the rifle itself proved sound and easy to use. Using mainly simple metal stampings for its construction, the MP 43 could be produced relatively quickly and cheaply, and it seemed to be the ideal weapon for the conditions on the Eastern Front where most of the MP 43s were sent.

After a while the army was making so many demands for the new rifle that Hitler came to hear of it once more. Despite his initial order he overlooked the disobedience of the staff planners, and even bestowed the rifle with a new name. It became the Sturmgewehr 44 (assault rifle model 1944), but there was no real change from the original design which was produced by Haenel at Suhl,

December 1944, and in the misty Ardennes an SS soldier waves others forward. The lighter weight of bullet for the StG 44 he carries enables him to carry more rounds, and the automatic fire capability gives any size unit great firepower.

Walther at Zella-Mehlis, the Steyr Group and the Sauer-Gruppe at Suhl. Demand always outstripped supply.

Meanwhile the Luftwaffe watched all these developments with some trepidation: if the army was getting an assault rifle, the Luftwaffe field troops had to have one as well. But there was little chance of the Luftwaffe ever getting any of the *kurz* rounds for their formations, so any design produced for them had to use the normal rifle cartridge. Rheinmetall duly settled to the task in its usual innovative fashion, and eventually came up with the Fallschirmjägergewehr 42, one of the more remarkable weapons of World War II. The FG 42 proved to work very well indeed (and its ingenious gas-operated mechanism was destined to be used in many post-war weapon designs), but the weapon itself could make little impact on the events of World War II. The FG 42 proved to be expensive and slow to produce, and by the time the war ended only about 7,000 had been issued. In contrast the MP 43 and the later StG 44 were churned out in the tens of thousands and made an impact out of all proportion to the numbers involved in many infantry scraps.

German Gebirgsjäger (mountain trooper) adjusts his skis with his StG 44 assault rifle across his back. The StG 44 gave such troops extra firepower, but was almost 25 per cent heavier than a bolt action rifle.

Such was the demand for assault rifles that suitable captured weapons were employed if available in sufficient numbers. The US M1 carbine proved popular with the Germans, mainly for its ease of handling.

SVT40 in which the same basic mechanism was retained, but everything was made much more robust and the result was a much better weapon. However, the SVT40 suffered from the same problems as the AVS and the SVT38 in that the weapon had a fierce recoil and considerable muzzle blast. To off-set these effects at least partially, the SVT40 was fitted with a muzzle brake, initially with six ports but eventually with two. These muzzle brakes were of doubtful efficiency.

In order to get the best from the SVT40 the weapon was usually issued only to NCOs or carefully trained soldiers who could use their rapid fire potential to good effect. Some were fitted with telescopic sights for sniper use. A few weapons were converted to produce fully-automatic fire as the **AVT40**, but this conversion was not a great success and few were made. According to some accounts there was also a carbine version but this probably suffered excessively from the heavy recoil problem and again only a few were made.

When the Germans invaded the Soviet Union in 1941 they soon encountered the SVT38 and the SVT40. Any they could capture they promptly used

under the designation **Selbst-ladegewehr 258(r)** and **Selbst-ladegewehr 259(r)**, but once the basic gas-operated mechanism was examined it was promptly copied and incorporated into the Gewehr 43.

Soviet production of the SVT40 continued almost until the end of the war. Although there were never enough produced to meet demands, the SVT40 had a considerable influence on future Soviet small-arms development for it initiated a series of automatic rifles that eventually culminated in the AK-47 series. It also made a considerable impact on Soviet infantry tactics for the SVT40 demonstrated the importance of increased firepower for the infantry, a factor later emphasized by the introduction of the German MP 43 on the Eastern Front.

Specification
SVT40
Calibre: 7.62 mm (0.3 in)
Length: 1.222 m (48.1 in)
Length of barrel 625 mm (24.6 in)
Weight: 3.89 kg (8.58 lb)
Muzzle velocity: 830 m (2,723 ft) per second
Magazine: 10-round box

Soviet Marines of the Baltic Fleet prepare for one of their many amphibious assaults on German positions along the Baltic coast. Armament includes PPSh 41s, SVT40s and a Degtyayrov LMG.

 USSR
Mosin-Nagant rifles

A Red Army private at about the time of the Winter War with Finland in the winter of 1940. He is armed with the 1930 model of the Mosin-Nagant, a dragoon-length version of the rifle.

When the Russian army decided to adopt a magazine rifle to replace its Berdan rifles during the late 1880s, it opted for a weapon combining the best features of two designs, one by the Belgian Nagant brothers and the other a Russian design from a Captain Mosin. The result was the **Mosin-Nagant Model 1891** with which the Tsarist army fought its last battles up to 1917. The Model 1891 was then adopted by the new Red Army following the 1918 upsets, and it remained in use for many years thereafter.

The Model 1891 fired a 7.62-mm (0.3-in) cartridge and it was a sound but generally unremarkable design. The bolt action was rather complicated and the ammunition feed used a holding device that offered only one round under spring tension to the bolt for reloading. But for all this it was a sound enough weapon, although rather long. This was mainly to increase the reach of the rifle when fitted with the long socket bayonet, which was almost a permanent fixture once the user was in action. The bayonet had a cruciform point that was used to dismantle the weapon.

The original Model 1891s had their sights marked in arshins, an archaic Russian measurement equivalent to

0.71 m (27.95 in), but after 1918 these sights were metricated. In 1930 there began a programme to modernize the old rifles, and all new rifles were produced in a new form. This new form was the **Model 1891/30**, which was slightly shorter than the original and had several design points introduced to ease production. It was the Model 1891/30 that was the main Red Army service rifle of World War II and the one used with telescopic sights as a sniper's rifle. Other 'extras' included a grenade-launching cup and a silencer.

The Mosin-Nagant weapons were also produced in carbine form for cavalry and other uses. The first of these was the **Model 1910**, followed much later by the **Model 1938** (the Model 1891/30 equivalent). In 1944 the **Model 1944** was introduced, but this was only a Model 1938 with a permanently fixed folding bayonet alongside the forestock.

The Mosin-Nagant rifles were also used by the Finns (**m/27** shortened Model 1891, **m/28/30** with altered sights, and re-stocked **m/39**), the Poles (**karabin wz 91/98/25**) and also by the Germans. The Germans captured piles of ex-Soviet rifles during 1941 and 1942, and many were issued by the Germans to their own second-line garrison and militia units. Most of these were Model 1891/30s redesignated **Gewehr 254(r)**, but by 1945 even Model 1891s were being issued to the hapless Volkssturm units under the designation **Gewehr 252(r)**. Many units

A Model 1938 Mosin-Nagant carbine. This model, like the 1930, was simplified for ease of manufacture, and was issued to the cavalry. A great many were captured by Germany in the early war years.

along the Atlantic Wall were issued with the Model 1891/30.

With the introduction of the automatic rifle in the post-war years the old Mosin-Nagant rifles were swiftly removed from Red Army use. Some were sold on the open market but most appear to have been stockpiled. Only the short and handy carbines now remain in service today, many in China and the Far East. Many still turn up in the hands of 'freedom fighters'.

Specification
Model 1891/30
Calibre: 7.62 mm (0.3 in)
Length: 1.232 m (48.5 in)
Length of barrel: 729 mm (28.7 in)
Weight: 4 kg (8.8 lb)
Muzzle velocity: 811 m (2,660 ft) per second
Magazine: 5-round box

Specification
Model 1938 carbine
Calibre: 7.62 mm (0.3 in)
Length: 1.016 m (40 in)
Length of barrel: 508 mm (20 in)
Weight: 3.47 kg (7.6 lb)
Muzzle velocity: 766 m (2,514 ft) per second
Magazine: 5-round box

Above: A pair of Soviet snipers are armed with Moisin-Nagant M1891/30 rifles fitted with telescopic sights. Although an old design, it was a rugged and accurate weapon.

Below: On the Second Ukrainian Front in 1944, Hero of the Soviet Union Nikolai Ilyin aims his SVT 40 Tokarev sniping rifle. The Tokarev was usually issued to NCOs and sharpshooters.

British Rifles

Above: British troops of the 5th Hampshires squat ready behind a M4 Sherman tank during the Salern operation near Naples. They are armed with SMLE Mk 1 rifles, soon be replaced by the Lee-Enfield No.

Left: A British sniper takes aim through a shell hole in the roof of a house in Gennep, to the south of Nijmegen. He is armed with a Lee-Enfield No. 4 Mk 1(T), a specially-adapted version of the standard n

The Lee-Enfield Story

Dating from the last years of the 19th century, the Lee-Enfield has had a longer service career than most of its contemporaries, having seen action in the Boer War and, in largely unaltered form, more than 80 years later in the hands of Afghan tribesmen. Its tough, rugged reliability and ease of maintenance will ensure the Lee-Enfield's survival for many years to come.

The first Lee-Enfield rifle was approved for production during late 1895. It was almost identical to the Lee-Metford that it replaced, but the main difference was that the new rifle incorporated a new and more effective form of barrel rifling. The change was made possible by the introduction of a new smokeless propellant that burned much more cleanly than the old form of cordite, allowing a more efficient rifling profile to be adopted. This rifling was developed at the Royal Small Arms Factory at Enfield Lock to the north of London.

The name Lee in the new rifle's designation came from one James Paris Lee, an American with a penchant for introducing new small arms and principles. One of his greatest successes was the bolt action that was embodied in the Lee-Enfield rifles and the form of box magazine that was for many years used on them. His basic designs had been adopted by the Royal Small Arms Factory and were developed over the years to a high degree of efficiency. Many small arms experts believe that the Lee-Enfields were the best bolt-action service rifles ever made.

The first combination of the Lee rifle with the Enfield rifling was known as the Lee-Enfield Mark I. In common with many other designs of the period it was a long weapon capable of use at ranges of up to 1645m (1,800 yards). It was also thought to be capable of effective employment at ranges well over this by the use of a form of auxiliary sight on the side of the forestock. This sight was not meant for use by an individual but for controlled firing by sections or even platoons in order to cover an area with fire. This method of fire was not effective unless the users were both highly trained and drilled, but it was a method that was retained in the drill books until the 1930s, although by then the practice was hardly used.

In common with well-established then current practice, a short carbine version of the Lee-Enfield Mark I was produced for cavalry use, and there was even a special variant for use by the police in Ireland.

It was the Lee-Enfield with which the British Army fought throughout the Boer War, and many hard lessons were learned during the prolonged period of guerrilla warfare that followed the early pitched battles. The hardy Boers were able to inflict many lessons in musketry on the conventionally drilled British soldiers, and after the war some of these lessons were put to a practical application. One lesson learned was that the provision of a special rifle for infantry and a special rifle for cavalry was an unnecessary luxury. It was clearly far better to have a slightly shorter rifle for use by all arms, and that included the Royal Navy as well. In 1902 a new shorter version of the Lee-Enfield was ready and this was put through various troop trials.

This new design was the Short, Magazine Lee-Enfield Mark I, soon known as the SMLE. But the weapon had a very rough ride during its early days. Needless to say neither the infantry or the cavalry liked the weapon at all: it was widely felt by the infantry that the shorter barrel would mean a loss in long-range accuracy, and the cavalry felt that the SMLE was too long for its requirements. But the design stuck. Over the period up to 1907 all manner of detail changes were incorporated until the point was reached where the Mark III emerged. This was the classic Lee-Enfield and, despite all the unpleasant things said about it at the time of its introduction, it went on to be a world-beater which was used throughout two world wars and many other more minor conflicts and skirmishes.

A brief description of the Mark III will suffice for all the later marks. Starting at the muzzle, this was surrounded by a metal cap with a boss

The SMLE (Short, Magazine, Lee-Enfield) was still in service at the start of the war, when it was known as the No. 1 Rifle. Troops are seen house-clearing, possibly on exercise.

Canadian troops in Italy in 1944. The rifle is the No. 4 which was introduced as a replacement for the original SMLE. Street fighting was a dangerous pastime, and it was wise to deposit a calling card such as a grenade before entering a building.

The Lee-Enfield Story

and lug for mounting a long blade bayonet. Two 'ears' on top of this cap protected the foresight, while the whole length of the barrel was surrounded by the wooden forestock. Halfway along the barrel was a band carrying the forward sling swivel, and farther back along the barrel were the rear sights, set on top of the forestock. The rear sights were calibrated in 200-yard (183-m) intervals from 200 yards (183m) up to 2,000 yards (1830m). The long range fire sight was mounted to the left of these rear sights. Behind the barrel was the bolt action, which by the time the Mark III was ready had been developed to a high degree of efficiency: as the firer lifted the bolt handle and pulled it to the rear the spent cartridge case was pulled from the chamber and ejected as it struck a fixed post; as he pushed it forward, the

Left: In the ruins of Caen, Allied troops had to take particular care as the rubble provided excellent cover for snipers. This corporal, armed with a No. 4, is using a drawbridge as a vantage point while keeping watch.

Below: Normandy, July 1944; the Allies have been ashore for a month and a half, and in the Odon Valley British troops have dug in. Seasoned campaigners by now, when given a chance to sleep, they sleep!

bolt picked up the next cartridge and propelled it forward into the chamber while recocking the firing spring at the same time. The rifle was then ready to fire if the safety catch (to the left of the bolt) was forward. It was easy to see if the rifle was loaded and ready to fire by a glance at the bolt catch, which would be to the rear if it was cocked. The 10-round box magazine was under the bolt action and worked together with a device known as a 'cut-out'. With the cut-out in place the loaded magazine was separated from the bolt action: the idea was that to conserve ammunition only single rounds would be loaded into the bolt action by hand, leaving the full magazine to be used when some form of emergency arose, whereupon the cut-out would be withdrawn to allow the magazine to be used. The rounds were loaded into the magazine using clips each holding five rounds. This clip was placed in a charger bridge guide over the bolt action, after which a quick push from the thumb would load all five rounds in one move. If required the magazine could be easily removed for loading by hand. The wooden butt had a metal butt trap containing an oil bottle and a cord 'pull-through' for cleaning and maintaining the rifle), and the rear sling swivel was under the butt.

Most of the features mentioned above were common to all later Lee-Enfields, but once World War I got under way some short cuts had to be introduced to speed production. One

of the first features to go was the long-range sight, although the mounting plate was often retained. On some examples the magazine cut-out was removed, and several production expedients were introduced to more minor components. This made the rifle the SMLE Mark III*, and this version was produced not only by several British factories but also by arsenals in India and Australia. The Australian factory continued production of the Mark III right up to 1957 as the Australians never adopted later versions.

Three members of the 8th Rifle Brigade make their way forward somewhere in north west Europe in 1944. The riflemen have fixed bayonets, and the Bren gunner in the centre is ready for immediate action.

It was during the years from 1914 to 1918 that the Lee-Enfields revealed themselves as the excellent service rifles they were. During 1914 the highly-trained British Expeditionary Force (BEF) was able to use aimed rapid fire to such an extent that at times the advancing German

Rifle No. 4 Mark I

Although the old Lee-Enfield No. 1 Mark III rifle performed sterling service throughout World War I, it was an expensive and time-consuming weapon to produce as every example had virtually to be made by hand. In the years after 1919 consideration was given to a version of the basic design that could be mass-produced, and in 1931 a trial series of rifles known as the No. 1 Mark VI was produced. These were accepted as suitable for service, but at the time there were no funds to launch production, so it was not until November 1939 that the go-ahead was given for what was then redesignated the **Rifle No. 4 Mark I**.

The No. 4 Mark I was designed from the outset for mass-production, and differed from the original No. 1 Mark III in several respects: the No. 4 Mark I had a much heavier barrel that improved overall accuracy; the muzzle protruded from the forestock by an easily recognizable amount and provided the No. 4 Mark I with a definite recognition point; and the sights were moved back to a position over the receiver, which made them easier to use and also provide a longer sighting base, again an aid to accuracy. There were numerous other small changes, most of them introduced to assist production, but for the soldier the biggest change was to the muzzle, where a different fitting was introduced for a new bayonet, which was a light and simple spike with no grip or anything like it, so depriving the soldier of one of his favourite front-line tools. The spike bayonet was not liked, but being simple and easy to produce it was retained in use for many years.

The first No. 4 Mark Is were issued

for service during late 1940, and thereafter the type supplemented the old No. 1 Mark IIIs. But during the war years the No. 1 Mark III was never entirely replaced. This was not for lack of production effort, for the No. 4 Mark I was churned out in hundreds of thousands by numerous small arms production facilities all over the UK and even in the USA. These 'American' rifles were produced at the Stevens-Savage plant at Long Branch and were known as the **No. 4 Mark I*** as they differed in the manner in which the bolt could be removed for cleaning. These American examples also differed in various other small details, most of which were introduced to assist production using American methods.

In service the No. 4 Mark I proved itself an excellent weapon, to the extent that many now regard the design as one of the finest of all service rifles of the bolt-action era. It was capable of withstanding even the roughest handling, and could deliver accurate fire for prolonged periods. It was relatively easy to strip and keep clean using the 'pull-through' carried inside the butt trap along with an oil bottle and a few pieces of the famous 'four by two' cleaning rag.

Special sniper's versions of the No. 4 were also produced. These used various types of telescopic sight over the receiver along with a special butt plate. These rifles were usually selected from production examples and were virtually rebuilt and restocked before issue. They were designated **Rifle No. 4 Mark I(T)**.

The No. 4 Mark I is still in widespread service around the world.

A No. 4 Mk 1 rifle dating from 1941 (top). The No. 4 was a simplified version of the No. 1, or SMLE (below). Major differences include deletion of the nose cap, relocation of the rear sight and redesign of the foresight.

Many current service examples have been rebarreled with new 7.62-mm (0.3-in) barrels, and more have been converted to match or hunting rifles.

Specification
Rifle No. 4 Mark I
Calibre: 0.303 in (7.7 mm)
Length: 1.129 m (44.43 in)
Length of barrel: 640 mm (25.2 in)
Weight: 4.14 kg (9.125 lb)
Muzzle velocity: 751 m (2,465 ft) per second
Magazine: 10-round box

The Lee-Enfield Story

As in many inspired designs, the operation of the bolt-action Lee-Enfield is as simple as possible. A minimum of working parts ensures strength and trouble-free operation, which are necessities in a successful infantry rifle.

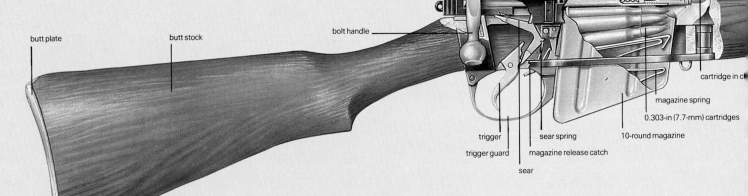

rear sight · charger guide · firing pin spring · bolt · firing pin · bolt head · extractor · breech · cocking piece · bolt handle · cartridge in chamber · magazine spring · 0.303-in (7.7-mm) cartridges · trigger · sear spring · 10-round magazine · trigger guard · magazine release catch · sear · butt plate · butt stock · sling swivel

formations thought they were under massed machine-gun fire, but by late 1915 the BEF was no longer in existence. Instead the war settled down to a long period of trench warfare in the most appalling conditions. The SMLE was able to keep firing through even the most hostile weather and mud conditions the trenches could inflict. Soldiers of many nations learned to keep the bolt action free of mud by wrapping it in a piece of cloth, and the muzzle was kept free of dirt at all times. Many sniper and periscopic sights were used with the SMLE, and even worn or old rifles were kept in use by converting them to launch rifle grenades.

Once World War I was over it was realized that good as the SMLE proved, in any future conflict ease of production would be of paramount importance. For all its attributes the Mark III and Mark III* were expensive and time-consuming weapons to make as every one had to be made virtually by hand with every component carefully machined and finished to suit a set of sealed gauges and tools. In order to speed any future production a new Lee-Enfield design was proposed and in 1926 and after a new type of weapon was introduced.

Design frozen

During the 1920s the old SMLE Mark III and Mark III* had become the Rifle No.1 Mark III and Mark III*. The new design became the Rifle No.1 Mark VI, and later the No.4 Mark I once all the details had been settled. The final design was frozen in 1931, but at that time there was no prospect of any procurement so it was set aside ready for the time when a need might arise.

That need duly came in 1939. The 'new' design was put into production and it turned out to be even better than the original. In the changes introduced to assist production were several new features. One was a heavier barrel which greatly enhanced accuracy, and the relocation of the sights to a position back to over the bolt action also provided a longer sighting base and added to this improved accuracy. Some features such as the long-range sights and the cut-out were removed altogether as they were deemed no longer necessary, and in place of the old blade bayonet a new and short spike

Bolt action cycle of operation

1 Full withdrawal of the bolt assembly allows the spring-loaded magazine to feed a cartridge into line with the bolt.

2 Forward pressure on the bolt engages the cartridge, and feeds it into the breech.

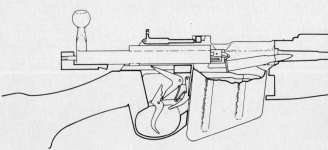

3 In the last fraction of travel forward, the bolt engages the trigger sear, cocking the weapon. Rotating the bolt locks the cartridge into the breech. Pressure on the trigger will now fire the rifle.

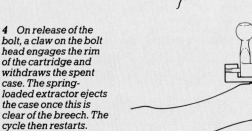

4 On release of the bolt, a claw on the bolt head engages the rim of the cartridge and withdraws the spent case. The spring-loaded extractor ejects the case once this is clear of the breech. The cycle then restarts.

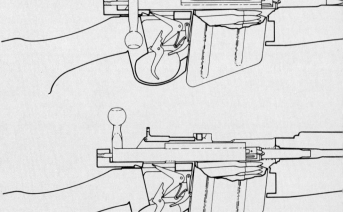

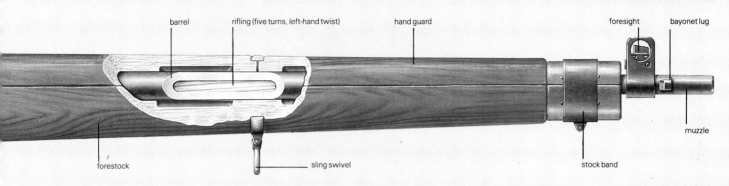

barrel · rifling (five turns, left-hand twist) · hand guard · foresight · bayonet lug · muzzle · forestock · sling swivel · stock band

yonet was introduced to fit over the length of rrel that now protruded from the forestock. As the war progressed the new No.4 gra-ally replaced the old No.1s though even by e time the war was over in 1945 the No.1 was ll around. It is still around in very large num-rs in such countries as India, for the Indian senal at Ishapore churned out the No.1 roughout the two world wars. Even in the ited Kingdom the BSA works continued to oduce No.1 right up until 1944. It was, and still an excellent service rifle by any account.

The No.4 was also an excellent service rifle, d by service rifle it must be understood that it a rifle that is handled by soldiers, not by ghly trained marksmen. The average soldier n usually manage to hit an obvious target at rvice ranges, but is rarely called upon to oduce expert fire at the extreme ranges ce considered essential by marksmen of the d Bisley school. A service rifle has to be very

hardy, easy to clean and to maintain, easy to load, and rapid in action. The Lee-Enfields were all of these things, and they continue to function even under the direst of physical conditions.

They continue to give good service to this day. Even when the British army started to turn to automatic self-loading rifles in the 1950s, the Lee-Enfields did not vanish from the scene. Instead many were reworked to accommodate the new semi-rimmed 7.62-mm (0.3-in) NATO cartridge in place of the old 7.7-mm (0.303-in) round. There are several forms of rifle in this new calibre. One is the L8, a straightforward conversion of the No.4; another is the L39A1, used for match-and target-firing; and another is the L42A1, a special sniper's version.

All Lee-Enfield rifles have been used for sniping at some time or another, usually with a telescopic sight. Over the years there have been several versions, but the current L42A1

with its improved cartridge is probably better than any of them.

This account of the Lee-Enfield cannot mention every separate variant that has seen service, for that would fill a book and there are already several on the market that accomplish the task very well. No mention of the various 5.56-mm (0.22-in) training rifles has been made and reference to the No.5 'jungle carbine' will be found elsewhere. But one thing that must be repeated is that the Lee-Enfield has long been an excellent service rifle, and so long as it remains in widespread service all over the world it will continue to demonstrate its sterling qualities for many years to come. It will probably be around well into the next century.

ove: 14 January 1945, and a reconnaissance trol of the 6th Airborne Division pauses in the w of the Ardennes. The rifleman is equipped h telescopic sights for his No. 4, but the leading dier is using an improved Sten sub-machine n, the Mk V.

Right: Fighting in the jungles of Burma, the XIV Army often felt like forgotten men. By 1945, however, modern equipment was getting through for the final victorious stages of the Burma campaign, and No. 4 rifles were replacing SMLEs.

Rifle No. 5 Mark I

By 1943 the British and Commonwealth armies were heavily involved in jungle warfare in Burma and other areas of the Far East, and for the conditions the existing No. 1 and No. 4 Lee-Enfield rifles proved to be too long and awkward in use. Some form of shortened No. 4 was requested, and by September 1944 approval was given for such a rifle to be introduced as the **Rifle No. 5 Mark I.** This was virtually a normal No. 4 Mark I with a much shortened barrel. The forestock was modified to accommodate the new shortened barrel, and the sights were modified to reflect the decreased range performance of the new barrel. There were two other modifications introduced as well, both of them associated with the short barrel: these were a conical muzzle attachment that was meant to act as a flash hider, and a rubber pad on the butt. Both had to be introduced as the shortening of the barrel gave rise to two unwanted side effects: the prodigious muzzle flash produced by firing a normal rifle cartridge in a short barrel, and the ferocious recoil produced by the same source.

In a normal long rifle barrel most of the flash produced on firing is contained within the barrel and so are some of the recoil forces. In a shortened barrel a good proportion of the propellant gases are still 'unused' as the bullet leaves the muzzle, hence the added recoil. The soldiers did not like it one bit but they had to admit that in jungle warfare the No. 5 Mark I was a much handier weapon to carry and use. They also welcomed the reintroduction of a blade-type bayonet that fitted onto a lug under the muzzle attachment. In fact, following on from the first production order for 100,000

rifles made in 1944 it was thought that the No. 5 Mark I would become the standard service rifle of the post-war years, despite all the recoil and flash problems. But this did not happen.

The No. 5 Mark I had one built-in problem, quite apart from the flash and recoil, and that problem was never eradicated. For a reason that was never discovered the weapon was inaccurate. Even after a long period of 'zeroing' the accuracy would gradually 'wander' and be lost. All manner of modifications to the stocking of the weapon was tried, but the inaccuracy was never eliminated and the true cause was never discovered. Thus the No. 5 was not accepted as the standard service rifle, the No. 4 Mark I being retained until the Belgian FN was adopted in the 1950s. Most of the No. 5s were retained for use by specialist units such as those operating in the Far East and Africa, and many are still in use in those areas by various armies.

Specification
Rifle No. 5 Mark I
Calibre: 0.303 in (7.7 mm)
Length: 1.003 m (39.5 in)
Length of barrel: 476 mm (18.75 in)
Weight: 3.25 kg (7.15 lb)
Muzzle velocity: about 730 m (2,400 ft) per second
Magazine: 10-round box

Developed specifically for jungle operations, the No. 5 rifle was not an unqualified success, having a vicious recoil. It saw action in Kenya and Malaya (shown here), as well as at the end of World War II.

De Lisle carbine

The **De Lisle** carbine was one of the more unusual weapons of World War II but very little has ever been written on the subject. The weapon was designed by one William Godfray De Lisle who was, in 1943, an engineer in the Ministry of Aircraft Production. During that period he patented a silencer for a 5.59-mm (0.22-in) rifle, and this attracted the attention of persons interested in producing silent weapons for use during the commando raids which were then being conducted around the coasts of occupied Europe.

Further development of the basic De Lisle silencer resulted in a drastic modification of a Lee-Enfield No. 1 Mark III rifle to accommodate the firing of an 0.45-in (11.43-mm) pistol cartridge. The basic bolt action was retained, but in place of the large box magazine a small magazine casing was substituted. Forward of the bolt action was the silencer itself, and this comprised a series of discs held within a tubular housing that allowed the gases produced on firing to 'swirl' around before they were discharged from ports around the muzzle. Firing the subsonic 0.45-in (11.43-mm) pistol cartridge with this silencer system produced very little noise at all, and even this sounded quite unlike a firearm being discharged. There was also no flash.

The first De Lisle carbines were produced in one of the tool rooms of the Ford works at Dagenham. From

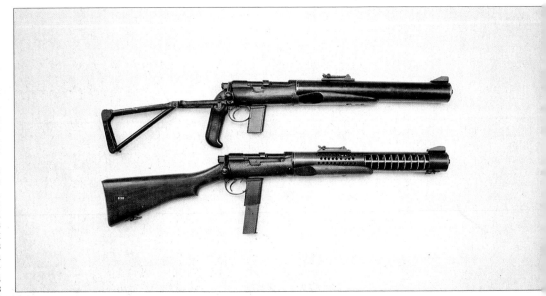

there the early prototypes were taken for field testing in commando raids along the north French coast. They proved themselves remarkably successful, and even these early weapons were used in what was to be their main operational role, a form of silent sniping to pick off sentries or other personnel during the early stages of a raid. As the De Lisle carbine fired a pistol car-

tridge its maximum effective range was limited to 250 m (275 yards), but this was usually more than enough for raids carried out on dark nights.

With trials successfully completed, a production order for 500 carbines was placed and this was later increased to 600. The 'production' programme of modifying the Lee-Enfield rifles was carried out by the Sterling Armament

Some folding stocked De Lisles (to were used in the Far East, having been designed for paratroops. Th early model (below) has been cut away to show the silencer mechan

Works, also in Dagenham, but wh the programme got under way thi had changed.

By the time the De Lisle carbi

were being produced it was mid-1944 and the invasion of Europe had taken place. With the Allies safely ashore there was far less need for a silenced commando weapon and the order was cancelled. By then about 130 had been completed and issued, but as they lacked a role in Europe most were sent to the Far East, where they were used by specialist units in Burma and elsewhere. Many were retained in the area after the war to see action once more during the Malayan Emergency. Some of these weapons did not have the solid butt of the earlier weapons, having instead a metal butt that folded under the weapon. This version had originally been produced for parachute troops, but only a small number was ever made.

Very few De Lisle carbines now exist, even in the most comprehensive small-arms collections. Most of them appear to have been destroyed during the post-war years, probably as the result of their potential as assassination weapons.

Specification
De Lisle carbine
Calibre: 11.43 mm (0.45 in)
Length: 895 mm(35.25 in)
Length of barrel: 184 mm (7.25 in)
Weight: 3.74 kg (8.25 lb)
Muzzle velocity: 253 m (830 ft) per second
Magazine: 7-round box

JAPAN
Rifle Type 38

The **Rifle Type 38** was adopted for Imperial Japanese service in 1905 and was a development of two earlier rifles selected by a commission headed by one Colonel Arisaka, who gave his name to a whole family of Japanese service rifles. The Type 38 used a mixture of design points and principles taken from contemporary Mauser and Mannlicher designs, mixed with a few Japanese innovations. The result was a sound enough rifle that had a calibre of 6.5 mm (0.256 in). This relatively small calibre, coupled with a rather low-powered cartridge, produced a rifle with a small recoil that exactly suited the slight Japanese stature.

This fact was further aided by the Type 38 being a rather long rifle. When the rifle was used with a bayonet, as it usually was in action, this gave the Japanese soldier a considerable reach advantage for close-in warfare, but it also made the Type 38 a rather awkward rifle to handle. As well as being used by all the Japanese armed forces, the Type 38 was exported to such nations as Thailand, and was also used by several of the warring factions then prevalent in China. At one point during World War I the Type 38 was even purchased as a training weapon by the British army.

A shorter version, the **Carbine Type 38** was widely used, and there was a version with a folding butt for use by airborne troops. There was also a version of the Type 38 known as the **Sniper's Rifle Type 97** which, apart from provision for a telescopic sight, had a revised bolt handle.

During the 1930s the Japanese gradually adopted a new service cartridge of 7.7-mm (0.303-in) calibre, and the Type 38 was revised as the **Rifle Type 99**. The Type 99 had several new features, including a sight that was supposed to be effective for firing at aircraft, and a folding monopod to assist accuracy. A special paratroop model that could be broken down into two halves was devised but proved to be unreliable so it was replaced by a 'broken down' version known as the **Parachutist's Rifle Type 2**. Not many of these were made.

Once the Pacific war was under way in 1942 the production standards of Japanese rifles and carbines deteriorated rapidly; any items that could be left off were so, and simplifications were introduced onto the lines. But overall standards went down to the point where some of the late production examples were virtually lethal to the user, many of them being constructed from very low-quality raw materials, both wood and metal, for the simple reason that the Allied blockade and air raids prevented the use of anything better. By the end the arsenals were reduced to producing very simple single-shot weapons firing 8-mm (0.315-in) pistol cartridges, or even

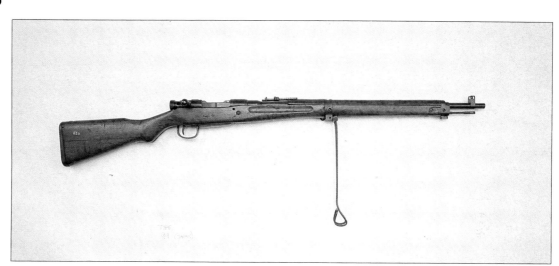

black-powder weapons. There was even a proposal to use long bows and crossbows firing explosive arrows. It was all a long way from the days when the Type 38 was one of the most widely used service rifles in the Orient.

Specification
Rifle Type 38
Calibre: 6.5 mm (0.256 in)
Length: 1.275 m (50.2 in)
Length of barrel: 797.5 mm (31.4 in)
Weight: 4.2 kg (9.25 lb)
Muzzle velocity: 731 m (2,400 ft) per second
Magazine: 5-round box

The Type 99 was a monopod fitted version of the Type 38 employing the new 7.7-mm (0.303-in) calibre cartridge. The Japanese design utilized contemporary Mauser and Mannlicher features, and first appeared in 1905.

Japanese infantry assault the Yenanyaung oilfields in Burma. The great length of the Arisaka type rifle, especially with bayonet attached, is obvious. This made the weapon awkward to handle but gave the generally short-statured Japanese soldier an effective reach in close combat.

Lebel and Berthier rifles

In 1939 the French army was equipped with an almost bewildering array of rifles, for the French appear to have adopted a policy of never throwing anything away. Some of them could trace their origins back to the mle 1866 Chassepot rifle. One of them, the **Fusil Gras mle 1874**, was still only a single-shot weapon, but was still in use with some French second-line and colonial units in 1940 when the Germans invaded.

The original Lebel rifle, the **Fusil d'infanterie mle 1886**, was updated in 1893 to produce the **mle 1886/93**. It was with this Lebel rifle that the French army fought World War I, but another weapon also in use at that time was a Berthier carbine, the **Mousqueton mle 1890** (and similar **mle 1892**), a version of the original mle 1886 allied to a new Mannlicher magazine system. On the Berthier the magazine was of the ortho-dox box type loaded from a clip, but the Lebel system used a tubular maga-zine holding more rounds loaded one at a time. The first Berthier rifle was the **Fusil mle 1907**, but in 1915 this colonial-troop weapon was largely replaced by the **Fusil d'infanterie mle 07/15**. With the introduction of the mle 07/15 the older Lebel rifles gradually faded in importance as production concen-trated on the Berthiers, but the Lebels were never replaced in service. They just soldiered on, and were still avail-able in 1939.

A Muslim Spahi of the 1st Moroccan Spahi regiment of the Vichy colonial army is armed with the old Lebel rifle. Note the long bayonet in his belt.

The original Berthier magazine sys-tem held only three rounds, but it was soon realized that this was not enough and the **Fusil d'infanterie mle 1916** had a 5-round magazine. To complicate matters further there were carbine or other short versions of all the models mentioned above, and to complicate matters still further the French sold or gave away masses of all of these weapons in the inter-war years to many nations who promptly applied their own designations. Thus Lebel and Berthier rifles turned up not only in all the French colonies but in nations such as Greece, Yugoslavia, Romania and other Balkan states.

In 1934 the French decided to attempt to make some sense out of their varied rifle and carbine arsenal by adopting a new calibre. Up till then the normal French calibre had been 8 mm (0.315 in), but in 1934 they adopted a smaller calibre of 7.5 mm (0.295 in). That same year they started to modify the old Berthier rifles to the new calibre and at the same time fitted a new magazine (still holding only five rounds) and several other changes along with the new barrel. This 'new' version was the **Fusil d'infanterie mle 07/15 M34**, but the change-over prog-ramme went so slowly that in 1939 only a small proportion of the available stocks had been converted, ensuring that all the other models were still in use.

After the events of May and June 1940 the Germans found masses of all the various French rifles on their hands. Some they could use as they were, and many were issued to garri-son and second-line formations. But

Breton resistance fighters gather in a village outside Brest. Their mixed collection of weapons include captured Mausers and old French Lebels and Berthiers.

many others were stockpiled, to be dragged out in 1945 to arm Volkssturm and other such units. No doubt the Ger-mans found that the array and variety of French rifle and carbine types were too much, even for their assorted stocks, but as they never had enough rifles to arm their ever-growing forces the French weapons were no doubt handy.

Few of the old French rifles are to be encountered today other than in the hands of museums and collectors. Most of them were museum pieces even in 1939 and only the general unpre-paredness of France for war ensured that the relics were retained.

Specification
mle 1886/93
Calibre: 8 mm (0.315 in)
Length: 1.303 m (51.3 in)
Length of barrel: 798 mm (31.4 in)
Weight: 4.245 kg (9.35 lb)
Muzzle velocity: 725 m (2,380 ft) per second
Magazine capacity: 8-round tube

Specification
mle 1907/15 M34
Calibre; 7.5 mm (0.295 in)
Length: 1.084 m (42.7 in)
Length of barrel: 579 mm (22.8 in)
Weight: 3.56 kg (7.85 lb)
Muzzle velocity: 823 m (2,700 ft) per second
Magazine capacity: 5-round box

Fusil MAS36

In the period following World War I the French army decided to adopt a new standard service cartridge with a calibre of 7.5 mm (0.295 in). The new cartridge was adopted in 1924, but fol-lowing some low-priority and there-fore lengthy trials, it was found that the new cartridge was unsafe under cer-tain circumstances and thus had to be modified in 1929. In that year the French decided to adopt a new rifle to fire the new round, but it was not until 1932 that a prototype was ready. Then followed a series of further trials that went on at a slow pace until 1936, when the new rifle was accepted for service.

The new rifle was the **Fusil MAS36** (MAS for Manufacture d'Armes de Saint-Etienne). This used a much-modified Mauser action which was so arranged that the bolt handle had to be angled forward quite sharply. The box magazine held only five rounds. The MAS36 had the odd distinction of being the last bolt-action service rifle to be adopted for military service any-where (all later new weapons using some form of self-loading action) and in some other ways the MAS36 fea-tured other anachronisms. In typical French style the weapon had no safety catch, and the overall appearance of the design belied its year of introduc-tion, for it looked a much older design than it was.

Production of the new rifle was so slow that a modification programme to convert some of the old rifles for the new cartridge had to be undertaken. This lack of urgency was typical of the period for the nation seemed to suffer from an internal lethargy that could be traced back to the nation's exertions of World War I. Thus by 1939 only a re-latively few French army units were equipped with the MAS36, and these were mainly front-line troops. The MAS36 could have had little effect on the events of May and June 1940, but many of the troops who left France at that time took their MAS36s with them and for a while it remained the favoured weapon of the Free French

forces in exile. The Germans also took over numbers of MAS36s and used them under the designation **Gewehr 242(f)** for their own garrison units based in occupied France.

One odd variation of the basic MAS36 was a version known as the **MAS36 CR39**. This was a short-barrelled version intended for para-troop use, and had an aluminium butt that could swivel forward alongside the butt to save stowage space. Only a relative few were ever made, and even fewer appear to have been issued for service use.

When the war ended the new French army once more took the MAS36 into use and retained it for many years, using it in action in North Africa and Indo-China. Many are still

The MAS 36 was the last bolt action rifle adopted by a major army anywhere. It was a fair weapon, but few saw service before 1939.

retained for use as ceremonial parade weapons and the type is still used by the forces and police authorities of many colonial or ex-colonial states.

Specification
MAS36
Calibre: 7.5 mm (0.295 in)
Length: 1.019 m (40.13 in)
Length of barrel: 574 mm (22.6 in)
Weight: 3.67 kg (8.09 lb)
Muzzle velocity: 823 m (2,700 ft) per second
Magazine: 5-round box

Above: A Foreign Legionnaire of the 13th Brigade uses his MAS 36 rifle as an improvised flagstaff to raise the colours at Bir Hacheim.

Below: A member of the 26e Cie de Meharistes is seen with his Berthier carbine in one of the great sandy wastes of the central Sahara.

Rifle, Caliber .30, Model 1903

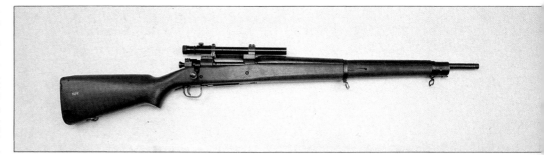

In 1903 the US Army decided to replace its existing Krag-Jorgensen rifles and adopted a rifle based on the Mauser system. This rifle, officially known as the **US Magazine Rifle, Caliber .30, Model of 1903** (or **M1903**) was first produced at the famous Springfield Arsenal and has thus become almost exclusively known as the **Springfield**. It was produced to be a form of universal weapon that could be used by both infantry and cavalry, and was thus much shorter than most contemporary rifles, but it was a well-balanced and attractive rifle that soon proved itself to be a fine service weapon with an accuracy that makes it a prized target rifle.

Almost as soon as the M1903 was placed in production the original blunt-nosed ammunition was replaced by newer 'pointed' ammunition that is now generally known as the .30-06 (thirty-ought six) as it was an 0.3-in (7.62-mm) round introduced in 1906. This remained the standard US service cartridge for many years and is still widely produced. The original M1903 served throughout World War I in US Army hands, and in 1929 the design was modified slightly by the introduction of a form of pistol grip to assist aiming, and this became the **M1903A1**. The **M1903A2** was produced as a sub-calibre weapon for inserting into the barrels of coastal guns and was used for low-cost training on these guns.

When the USA entered World War II in 1941 the new M1 Garand rifle was not available in the numbers required, so the M1903 was placed back into large-scale production, this time as the **M1903A3**. This version was modified to suit modern mass-production methods, but it was still a well-made rifle. Some parts were formed by using stampings instead of machined parts, but the main change was to the sights which were moved back from over the barrel to a position over the bolt action.

Above: A Mauser patterned rifle, the M1903 Springfield proved a fine weapon, serving into the Korean war. The sniper version had a Weaver telescopic sight, and the conventional 'iron' sights have been removed entirely.

Right: The accuracy of the M1903 made it a popular weapon with sharpshooters, and in positions where a single well-aimed shot can be decisive the small box magazine of five rounds was no handicap.

The only other version of the M1903 (apart from some special match rifle models) was the **M1903A4**. This was a special sniper's version fitted with a Weaver telescopic sight, and was specialized to the point where no conventional 'iron' sights were fitted. Numbers of the M1903A4 were still in service during the Korean War of the 1950s.

The M1903 was used by several Allied armies during World War II. Many of the US troops who landed in Normandy on D-Day in June 1944 were still equipped with the Springfields, but by then many had been passed on to various resistance units in France and elsewhere, and the M1903 was a virtual standard issue to the various 'island watchers' among the Pacific islands. In 1940 some were sent to the UK to equip Home Guard units, and the type was even placed back into production to a British order, only for the order to be taken over for the use of US forces.

The M1903 and its variants may still be encountered today with a few small armed forces around the world. But many are also retained as target or hunting rifles, for the M1903 Springfield is still regarded as one of the classic rifles of all time. It is still a rifle that a delight to handle and fire, and mar are now owned by weapon collecto for those reasons alone.

Specification
M1903A1
Calibre: 7.62 mm(0.3 in)
Length: 1.105 m (43.5 in)
Length of barrel: 610 mm (24 in)
Weight: 4.1 kg (9 lb)
Muzzle velocity: 855 m (2,805 ft) per second
Magazine: 5-round box

Rifle, Caliber .30, M1 (the Garand)

One of the main distinctions of the **Rifle, Caliber .30, M1**, almost universally known as the **Garand**, is that it was the first self-loading rifle to be accepted for military service. That acceptance happened during 1932, but there followed a distinct gap before the rifle entered service as it took some time to tool up for the complex production processes demanded by the design. The rifle was created by John C. Garand, who spent a great deal of time developing the design to the point that once in production it required very few alterations. Thus the last M1 looked very much like the first.

As already mentioned, the M1 was a complicated and expensive weapon to manufacture, and required a large number of machining operations on many of the components. But it was a strong design and proved to be sturdy in action, although this was balanced in part by the weapon being rather heavier than comparable bolt-action designs. The M1 was a gas-operated weapon.

When the USA entered World War II at the end of 1941, most of her regular forces were equipped with the M1, but the rapid increase of numbers of men in uniform meant that the old M1903 Springfield rifle had to be placed back

into production as a quick increase in the flow of M1s from the lines was virtually impossible, as a result largely of the tooling problems already mentioned. But gradually M1 production built up, and some 5,500,000 had been churned out by the end of the war; production was resumed during the Korean War of the early 1950s.

For the American forces the M1 Garand was a war-winner, whose strong construction earned the gratitude of many. But it did have one operational fault, namely its ammunition feed. Ammunition was fed into the rifle in eight-round clips, and the loading system was so arranged that it was possible to load only the full eight rounds or nothing. There was a further operational problem encountered when the last of the eight rounds was fired, for the empty clip was ejected from the receiver with a definite and pronounced sound that advertized to any nearby enemy that the firer's rifle was empty, sometimes with unfortunate results to the M1 user. This problem was not eliminated from the M1 until 1957, when the US Army introduced the M14 rifle which was virtually a reworked M1 Garand with an increased ammunition capacity.

Many sub-variants of the M1 were produced but few actually saw service

The Garand was the first self-loadir rifle accepted as a standard militar weapon. Strong and sturdy, the gas operated M1 was rather heavier tha the bolt action M1903 Springfield.

as the basic M1 proved to be mo than adequate for most purpose There were two special sniper ve sions, the **M1C** and the **M1D**, both pr duced during 1944 but never in a great numbers. Each had such extr as a muzzle flash cone and butt plate

The M1 attracted the attention of t

A US Marine flattens out after landing on Eniwetok in February 1944. He is armed with the M1 Garand rifle, which was the first self-loader to be adopted as a standard weapon by any army.

USA's enemies to the extent that the Germans used as many as they could capture, with the designation **Selbstladegewehr 251(a)**, and the Japanese produced their own copy, the 7.7-mm (0.303-in) **Rifle Type 5**, but only prototypes had been completed by the time the war ended.

Post-war the M1 went on for many years as the standard US service rifle, and some are still issued to National Guard and other such units. Several nations continue to use the M1, and many designers have used the basic action as the basis for their own products: many of the modern Italian Beretta rifles use the Garand system as does the American 5.56-mm (0.22-in) Ruger Mini-14.

Specification
Rifle M1
Calibre: 7.62 mm (0.3 in)
Length: 1.107 m (43.6 in)
Length of barrel: 609 mm (24 in)
Weight: 4.313 kg (9.5 lb)
Muzzle velocity: 855 m (2,805 ft) per second
Magazine: 8-round box

Garand-armed infantrymen of the US 4th Armored Division are seen in action in the Ardennes during the drive to relieve Bastogne and the trapped 101st Airborne Division.

 USA

Carbine, Caliber .30, M1, M1A1, M2 and M3

The traditional weapon for second-line troops and such specialists as machine-gunners has generally been the pistol, but when the US Army considered the equipment of such soldiers during 1940 they made a request for some form of carbine that could be easily stowed and handled. The result was a competition in which several manufacturers submitted their proposals, and the winner was a Winchester design that was adopted for service as the **Carbine, Caliber .30, M1**. The M1 used an unusual gas-operated system and was designed for use with a special cartridge that was intermediate between a pistol cartridge and a rifle cartridge in power.

From the start the Carbine M1 was an immediate success. It was light and easy to handle, to the extent that its use soon spread from the second-echelon troops who were supposed to be issued with the weapon to front-line troops such as officers and weapon teams. In order to speed its introduction into service the M1 was a single-shot weapon only, but there was a special variant with a folding stock known as the **M1A1**. This was produced for use by airborne units. When time

allowed later during the war the automatic fire feature was added. This version was known as the **M2**, and had a cyclic rate of fire of about 750 to 775 rounds per minute; the weapon used a curved box magazine holding 30 rounds that could also be used on the M1. The **M3** was a special night-fighting version with a large infra-red night sight, but only about 2,100 of these were made. The M3 proved to be the one version of the Carbine M1 series that was not produced in quantity, for by the time the war ended the production total had reached 6,332,000 of all versions, making the weapon the most prolific personal weapon of World War II.

For all its handiness, the Carbine M1 series had one major drawback, and that was the cartridge used. Being an intermediate-power cartridge it generally lacked power, even at close ranges. Being a carbine the M1 also lacked range, and was effective only to 100 m (110 yards) or so. But these drawbacks were more than countered by the overall handiness of the weapon. It was easy to stow in vehicles or aircraft, and the M1A1 with its folding butt was even smaller. It handled

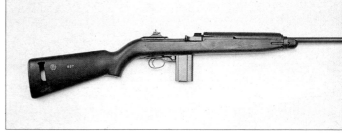

well in action and was deemed good enough for German Army use as the **Selbstladekarabiner 455a** after enough had been captured during the latter stages of the war in Europe.

But for all its mass production and war-time success, the M1 is now little used by armed forces anywhere. Many police forces retain the type, mainly because of the low-power cartridge fired which is safer in police situations than more powerful rounds. Typical of these is the Royal Ulster Constabulary, which uses the Carbine M1 as a counter to the far more powerful Armalites of the IRA. Another part of the M1 story is the current lack of adoption of the M1's intermediate-power cartridge. During the war years these cartridges were churned out in millions but now the cartridge is little used and has not been adopted for any other major weapon system.

Originally produced by Winchester the lightweight M1 carbine was eventually manufactured by more than 10 companies in numbers exceeding six million.

Specification
Carbine M1
Calibre: 7.62 mm (0.3 in)
Length: 904 mm (35.6 in)
Length of barrel: 457 mm (18 in)
Weight: 2.36 kg (5.2 lb)
Muzzle velocity: 600 m (1,970 ft) per second
Magazine: 15- or 30-round box

A Marine, member of a machine-gun crew, clutches his M1 carbine and the ammo for a Browning machine-gun while waiting for his partner to hurl a grenade.

Left: Front-line troops soon found that the easy handling M1 carbine was much less of a burden than a rifle when slogging through the surf or the jungle, and it began appearing with front-line Marine Corps units.

The Role of the Sniper

was an uneventful patrol. The enemy had gone from the sector, and the reconnaissance unit could afford to take it easy. Suddenly there was a shot, and the officer collapsed. Leaderless, the patrol fell back, and the well-concealed sniper relaxed. He had done his job.

During two world wars the sniper has managed to gain a reputation out of all proportion to the numbers involved, for the sniper is an individual who delivers deliberately aimed fire from positions that are hidden from the unfortunate target. Usually firing only a single shot and then moving on, the sniper can have an effect on an enemy where a single man can prevent movement, demoralize whole units and cause havoc by picking off officers and NCOs.

In order that he can use his personal rifle to best effect, the sniper almost invariably uses some form of telescopic sight, and the rifle with a telescope has become his trademark. But the use of a telescopic sight does not make a poor shot into a good one: all that the optical sight achieves is to make the target that much clearer for the sniper to take an accurate aim. But this does not mean that every sniper has to be a crack shot. Many snipers in both wars would be forced to admit that their marksmanship was only average. Where they differed from the normal infantryman was they were prepared to go to great lengths to make sure that when they fired they hit their target. This meant all manner of things other than sheer accuracy of fire. It also meant careful maintenance and handling of the rifle involved, a very high standard of fieldcraft and personal concealment, thorough and careful reconnaissance of an area before going into action, accurate map-reading, and personal discipline and conduct of a high degree.

Again contrary to expectation the sniper is not usually a loner. Instead he often worked as a member of a team. In some armies the sniper could (and often did) work alone, but more often snipers worked in teams of two men. One of them used the rifle and made the required shot but the other man acted as an extra pair of eyes, usually using a powerful telescope or binoculars and often selecting the target. In order to keep both men on their toes mentally the roles were frequently exchanged.

The sniper's weapon was usually a version of the standard service rifle of the nation concerned. Sniper's rifles were usually carefully selected examples of production models, but some were built for the role from scratch. Any weapon selected was normally carefully re-stocked and fitted with the mountings for the telescopic sight, and was then subjected to a long and careful process of calibration and zeroing, hopefully by the individual who would use the rifle in action. Once ready for use the rifle was kept in a special strong case to prevent hard knocks and was at all times carefully handled and kept clean. Ammunition was also carefully selected from special production batches giving consistent performance.

By the end of World War II many snipers were already using a self-loading rifle. The self-loading function prevented unnecessary movement by the sniper and allowed bursts of rapid fire in the event of an emergency. Many nations did, however, stick to their well-tried bolt action rifles when a choice was possible. National characteristics came out very noticeably among the various nations. The Germans approached sniping in a thorough and methodical way that often brought very good results. The Japanese made much use of their talent for novelty and personal concealment, but they often worked as individuals which would put them at a disadvantage. The Soviets made much of the results achieved by their numerous snipers, some of whom were claimed to have gained remarkable personal tallies, but later analysis has placed some of these claims in doubt. Some Red Army claims would, if true, have wiped out half the

Well concealed in the rubble of a partially destroyed house, a British sniper aims his telescopically sighted No. 4 rifle. The modern British army rifle is a development of the same weapon.

US Marines on Tarawa are pinned down behind a sand dune, while a single Japanese sniper is operational. The value of snipers lies in the fact that a single man can hold down much larger units of the enemy.

German army. The Americans made much good use of their national talent for accurate musketry, but they appear to have made only slight use of snipers on many fronts although after a period into the war they did produce some remarkable sniping teams. In contrast the British and many of the Commonwealth armies relied upon sheer hard work and thorough application to the sniper's task. The British tendency was to careful training of selected personnel rather than to the use of an individual's flair that was more prevalent in many other armies. Wherever the British infantry went sniping schools were established and the skills were developed. All too often the good sniper turned out to be not a marksman of the Bisley type, but a gamekeeper turned poacher who could make good use not only of his rifle but of the surroundings and the approach to a target; typically he was a man who put preparation before everything else. It was the careful man who made a good sniper, not a cowboy.

Adequate camouflage is essential for the sniper, as his value can be lost if his position is too easily located. This Soviet sniper, armed with a Mosin-Nagant Model 1930, has just begun to move up a hill into position, being very careful not to skyline himself.

The sniper's version of the Lee-Enfield No. 4 rifle differs from the standard only in the addition of a cheek pad and telescopic sights. By the end of the war, however, many armies preferred self-loading rifles for their snipers, rather than bolt actions such as the No. 4.

135

A Marine sits inside the mouth of a cave on Okinawa, his M1 Carbine at the ready. Probably made in larger numbers than any other wartime US firearm, the M1 Carbine was popular for its ease of handling.

Post-War Infantry Weapons

The 1950s were a significant era in the design of infantry weapons as gun designers absorbed, or in some cases ignored, the lessons of World War II. Some weapons introduced during this period anticipated those in service today, while others turned out to be unsatisfactory compromises between old and new.

The small arms of the 1950s were an interesting interim between the weapons of World War II and the sleek, efficient designs of today. In part they were produced as a result of the combat lessons learned the hard way during World War II, whilst at the same time the conservative streak inherent in nearly all military structures ensured that in many ways little was changed. Some weapons even ignored the tactical and manufacturing innovations of World War II and thus went back to the days before 1939, while other weapons demonstrated the way ahead to the extent that they (or their influence) are with us still.

Thus this study is a collection of dinosaurs as well as of the modern. Dinosaurs such as the odd Soviet Stechkin (APS) machine pistol can be found, while the AR-10 and Stoner 63 System were on hand to indicate what was to follow. Weapons such as the SIG sub-machine guns ignored the cheap and rapid production methods used during World War II and suffered sales losses accordingly, though their Danish Madsen equivalents, with simplicity and cheapness built in, surprisingly did little better. Gun makers did their best to ignore these 'stamped steel' weapon designs but in the end they were overcome by the requirements of low-cost mass production.

Although little-mentioned in the main text, the main small arms design trend of the 1950s was the conflict between the conservatives and the requirements of modern combat. During the 1950s the conservatives won, but only for a while. This was particularly true in the case of NATO ammunition standardization which made such an impact that, even now,

The guard at Lenin's mausoleum retain SKS rifles to this day; modern rifles might be superior weapons, but have not been popular with drill instructors from Moscow to London. The SKS was designed during World War II to fire an intermediate power cartridge.

it will be felt for years to come, yet as will be outlined, that decision resulted in a wrong choice at a time when the Soviets were making a very good one with their 7.62-mm×39 cartridge. The results of those decisions and designs are with us still, so this study has more than passing interest to all who study small arms.

During the Vietnam War the Long Range Reconnaissance Patrols or LRRPs (pronounced 'Lurps') used an incredible mixture of kit, weaponry often being a matter of personal choice. Here LRRPs examine a Soviet AK-47 and a Carl Gustav SMG.

CETME Modelo 58 assault rifle

The **CETME Modelo 58** has a long history stretching back to the German Sturmgewehr 45 (StG 45) of World War II. This was an attempt by Mauser designers to produce a low-cost assault rifle that incorporated a novel system using a system of rollers and cams to lock the bolt at the instant of firing. After the Allied victory the nucleus of the StG 45 design team moved to Spain, via France, and established a new design team under the aegis of the Centro de Estudios Tecnicos de Materiales Especiales (CETME), just outside Madrid.

With CETME the roller locking system was gradually perfected at a leisurely pace. The resultant assault rifle looked nothing like the StG 45 starting point but the original low-cost manufacturing target was met. The assault rifle produced by CETME was made from low-grade steels and much of it was stamped and shaped using sheet steel. An automatic-fire capability was featured, and in overall terms the weapon was simple and basic.

It was 1956 before the first sales were made, to West Germany. This involved a batch of only 400 rifles, but the Germans decided that some modifications to the rifles were required to meet their requirements and by a series of licence agreements (between a CETME licence production offshoot in the Netherlands and Heckler & Koch) the CETME rifle ended as the Heckler & Koch G3, though the Spanish appear to have gained little from the deal.

In 1958 the Spanish army decided to adopt the CETME rifle in a form known as the **Modelo B**, and this became the Modelo 58. The Modelo 58 fired a special cartridge outwardly identical to the standard NATO 7.62-mm (0.30-in)

Above: The core of the Mauser team which designed the German Sturmgewehr 45 decamped to Spain after the war and developed a new assault rifle based on its layout. It is made of low-grade steel and is built with the emphasis on cheapness and reliability rather than looks.

cartridge but using a lighter bullet and propellant charge. This made the rifle much easier to fire (as a result of reduced recoil) but also made the cartridge non-standard as far as other NATO cartridge users were concerned. In 1964 the Spanish adopted the NATO cartridge in place of their own less powerful product and rifles adapted or produced to fire the NATO round became the **Modelo C**.

The Modelo 58 has since been produced in a number of versions, some with bipods, some with semi-automatic mechanisms and others with folding butts, and there has even been a sniper version fitted with a telescopic sight. The latest version is the **Modelo L** chambered in 5.56 mm (0.219 in), but the basic Model 58 is still available from CETME.

Specification
Modelo C
Calibre: 7.62 mm (0.30 in)
Weight: 4.49 kg (9.9 lb)
Lengths: overall 1.016 m (40 in); barrel 450 mm (17.7 in)
Muzzle velocity: 780 m (2,559 ft) per second
Rate of fire: (cyclic) 600 rpm
Feed: 20-round box

The Spanish army adopted the CETME as its standard rifle in 1958, initially buying the Modelo B, chambered for a unique, light, 7.62-mm round. In 1964 Spain decided to adopt the more powerf[ul] 7.62-mm NATO cartridge, and CETME modified their design accordingly to make the Modelo 58 C.

SIG sub-machine guns

The sub-machine guns produced by the Schweizerische Industrie-Gesellschaft (SIG) in the period after 1945 were scarcely among the most successful of that company's products. The first of these designs was the **SIG MP48**, a weapon that was the first truly all-Swiss sub-machine gun to reach production, and although it was made in the usual SIG way (i.e. with great attention to detail, superb finish and high-quality materials throughout), the MP48 was a commercial flop.

SIG had noted the World War II production trends towards cutting corners in manufacturing weapons of all types, but instead of making use of stampings and welds for mass assembly the Swiss decided to make use of precision castings which would require a minimum of machining. Further savings were made in omitting any form of safety mechanism. Instead the magazine was made to fold forward when the weapon was not in use – this saved space while at the same time removing the ammunition feed from the gun. Otherwise there was little remarkable about the MP48 and the world was not impressed. The MP48 did not sell in a market already sated with vast stockpiles of cheap World War II weapons. One small batch was sold to Chile.

The SIG designers returned to their drawing board and came up with the **MP310** in 1958. In many ways this was similar in overall concept to the MP48

and featured the same folding magazine system. However, the MP310 was made to be sold at a much lower price than the MP48. More use was made of cheaper plastics and other low-cost materials, and a two-stage trigger mechanism was introduced: a slight squeeze of the trigger produced single shots, while more pressure produced fully-automatic fire. The MP310 used the same telescoping butt arrangement as the MP48.

The MP310 was slightly more successful than the MP48, but even so only about 1,000 were produced. Small batches were sold, mainly in South America and the Far East, but all the time the MP310 suffered from the same factor that had affected the MP48: the potential markets were still working their way through the stockpiles of World War II surplus weapons.

Specification
MP48
Calibre: 9 mm (0.354 in)
Weight: empty 2.92 kg (6.44 lb)
Length: stock extended 711 mm (28 in); stock folded 570 mm (22.5 in); barrel 196 mm (7.75 in)
Muzzle velocity: 381 m (1,250 ft) per second
Rate of fire: 700 rpm
Feed: 40-round box

Specification
MP310
Calibre: 9 mm (0.354 in)
Weight: 3.15 kg (6.94 lb)
Length: stock extended 735 mm (28.95 in); stock folded 610 mm (24 in[?]) barrel 200 mm (7.83 in)
Muzzle velocity: 365 m (1,198 ft) per second
Rate of fire: 900 rpm
Feed: 40-round box

The MP310 was another new design which suffered from the effects of the post-war surplus of small arms, despite the use of plastics and precision castings, instead of expensive machined components, to keep the costs down.

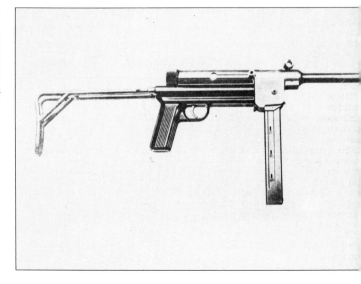

Fusil Automatique modèle 49

The Belgian **Fusil Automatique modèle 49** was known by several other names: to some it was the **Saive**, to others the **SAFN (Saive Automatique, FN)** and to more as the **ABL (Arme Belgique Legère)**. The weapon was actually designed before World War II but the arrival of the war shelved the project, ready for it to be revived once peace arrived again. The weapon was designed by one D. J. Saive who moved to the UK when the Germans arrived in Belgium in 1940 and spent the war working on small arms designs for the British. In 1945 he offered his pre-war design to the British army, which tested it and turned down the offer. Once back in Belgium the rifle was actually produced by FN (Fabrique Nationale d'Armes de Guerre) at Herstal, near Liège. The company made a lot of money out of it.

By whatever name it was called, the modèle 49 was in basic design a gas-operated self-loading rifle. The bolt locking was achieved by using cams in the sides of the receiver causing the bolt to tilt at the correct instant. This action was thus strong and could

absorb a great deal of hard use, but it meant that the entire rifle mechanism had to be very carefully machined out of high-quality materials. This made the weapon rather expensive to produce, but when the modèle 49 was placed on the open market in 1949 it sold surprisingly well. This was partly due to the fact that the modèle 49 was offered in a variety of calibres, ranging from 7 mm (0.275 in) and 7.65 mm (0.301 in), both established Continental calibres, to the then widely used 7.92 mm (0.312 in) and the American 0.30 in (7.62 mm). All these calibres were for the well established full-power rifle cartridges.

The modèle 49 was sold not only in Europe but to Venezuela, Colombia and Indonesia. One of the largest sales batches went to Egypt, where the modèle 49 remained in use for some time (and may still be encountered). But perhaps the most important impact made by the ABL was that it was used as the design starting point for the FN FAL, the Fusil Automatique Legère, destined to be one of the most important rifles within NATO and elsewhere

for the following decades.

Specification
modèle 49
Calibres: 7 mm (0.275 in), 7.65 mm (0.301 in), 7.92 mm (0.312 in) and 0.30 in (7.62 mm)
Weight: 4.31 kg (9.5 lb)
Lengths: overall 1.116 m (43.94 in); barrel 590 mm (23.23 in)
Muzzle velocity: dependent on calibre
Feed: 10-round box

Right: Weapons produced to a high standard often lose sales to cheaper weapons, but FN managed to sell their mle 49 to several different armies, offering it in many calibres. This Egyptian soldier carries the 7.92 mm model.

Below: The FN mle 49 is the ancestor of the FN FAL, designed before the war by Dieudonné Saive, who escaped to Britain when the Germans overran Belgium. While in England he continued to develop his designs, and after the war the mle 49 was sold to Egypt and Latin America.

EM-2 assault rifle

The **EM-2** story is one of political considerations taking precedence over military requirements, for although the EM-2 was an excellent weapon it was never accepted for service.

The British army learned some hard lessons during World War II, one being that its time-honoured 0.303-in (7.7-mm) cartridge was well outdated. It was too powerful and used cordite, which had been overtaken by more efficient propellants. Thus after 1945 the army initiated a series of trials to find something better and came up with a short-cased cartridge known as the 0.280-in (actually 7-mm/0.276-in) type. A rifle was devised to fire the new round though the first attempt, known as the **EM-1**, was not fully developed as it was deemed too complicated.

Then a new design team came up with the EM-2. For its day the EM-2 (Enfield Model 2) was a novelty, for it used a 'bullpup' layout with the magazine behind the trigger group. This made the weapon short and handy without making the barrel shorter, the receiver being in the butt. Gas operation was used and the weapon fired from a closed breech. A selective-fire mechanism was introduced and there was something then completely new, a permanently-fixed optical sight.

The EM-2 proved to be extremely reliable during trials, and in 1951 it was announced that the EM-2 would be adopted by the army as the **Rifle, Auto-**

matic, 7 mm No. 9 Mk 1. All seemed well until politics intruded. The Americans announced that they did not consider the British round powerful enough, and since the newly-formed NATO alliance was supposed to introduce ruthless standardization a conference was held to determine that all new weapon and ammunition development should cease until a new NATO round was determined. This duly emerged as the American-based 7.62-mm (0.30-in) cartridge still in use today. There was no way the EM-2 could be usefully engineered to accommodate this more powerful round, so the decision to adopt the EM-2 was reversed and the British army

got the Belgian FN FAL instead.

For a short while the EM-2 was retained as a research tool to determine an 'optimum' cartridge, despite the NATO decision, but that project was eventually terminated. A few rifles were rechambered to accommodate some odd rounds (one was even chambered for the American M1 Carbine 0.30-in/7.62-mm cartridge) but gradually the EM-2s were relegated to museums where some still remain today, examples of yet another intriguing small arms 'might have been'.

Specification
EM-2
Calibre: 0.276 in (7 mm)

Weight: loaded with sling 4.78 kg (10.54 lb)
Lengths: overall 889 mm (35 in); overall with bayonet 1.092 m (43 in); barrel 622 mm (24.49 in)
Muzzle velocity: 771 m (2,530 ft) per second
Rate of fire: (cyclic) 600-650 rpm
Feed: 20-round box

By the end of World War II the British Army needed a new rifle and the EM-2 automatic rifle would have been an excellent choice, but its 'bullpup' layout was regarded with suspicion and the Americans opposed the small calibre (they have since been forced to eat their words).

M14 rifle

USA

The rifle that was eventually to be the standard American service rifle for most of the late 1950s and 1960s had a simple origin but a most convoluted development period. When the American military planners virtually imposed their 7.62-mm (0.30-in) cartridge upon their NATO partners, they had to find their own rifle to fire it, and quickly. For various reasons it was decided simply to update the existing M1 Garand rifle design to fire the new ammunition and to add a selective-fire mechanism. Unfortunately these innovations proved to be less than simple to achieve, for the development period from M1 had to progress through a number of intermediate 'T' trials models. Eventually, in 1957, it was announced that a model known as the **T44** had been approved for production as the **M14** (a planned heavy-barrel version, the **M15**, did not materialize) and the assembly lines began to hum, involving four different manufacturing centres at one time.

The M14 was basically an M1 Garand updated to take a new 20-round box magazine and a selective-fire mechanism. The M14 was a long and rather heavy weapon that was very well made, involving a great deal of machining and handling during manufacture at a time when other weapon designers were moving away from such methods. But the Americans could afford it and the soldiers liked the weapon. In service there were few problems, but the selective-fire system that had caused so much development time was usually altered so that automatic fire could not be produced: the US Army had soon discovered that prolonged bursts overheated the barrel and that ammunition was in any event wasted firing non-productive bursts.

Production of the basic M14 ceased in 1964, by which time 1,380,346 had been made. In 1968 a new version, the **M14A1**, was introduced. This had a pistol grip, a bipod and some other changes and it was designed for use as a squad fire-support weapon producing automatic bursts, but the bursts had to be short as the barrel could not be changed when hot. Also produced as variants were experimental folding-butt versions and a sniper model, the **M21**.

The M14 is still in use with the US armed forces, although by now most are with units such as the National Guard and other reserve formations. As the M14s were replaced by M16s many were passed to nations such as Israel where they remained in combat service until replaced by Galils. Even now many civilian guards carrying M14s can be seen around Israel, guarding schools and bus stations.

Specification
M14
Calibre: 7.62 mm (0.30 in)

Weight: 3.88 kg (8.55 lb)
Length: overall 1.12 m (44 in); barrel 559 mm (22 in)
Muzzle velocity: 853 m (2,798 ft) per second
Rate of fire: (cyclic, M14A1) 700-750 rpm
Feed: 20-round box

Above: The M14A1 is the only variant of the M14 to be adopted in any numbers. The rifle is fitted with a straight-line stock, pistol- and fore-grips and mounted on a bipod. It looks and feels like a light machine-gun but is hardly suited to the role, as it has no facility for barrel change.

Below: Once NATO had decided to adopt a standard rifle cartridge, the USA needed a weapon to fire it. Most other nations opted for the versions of the Belgian FN, but the 'not invented here' syndrome reared its head and the US Army received the M14 – basically a modernized M1.

Rebel Philippine soldiers open fire on government forces defending a TV station during the last days of the Marcos regime. Note the spent case ejecting from the M14; this weapon has been supplied to other American allies in the Far East, including Taiwan and South Korea.

USA
Stoner 63 System

Eugene Stoner was one of the most influential and innovative weapon designers of the 1950s and 1960s, and his hand can still be discerned in many weapons in use today. His innovation was such that at one point he was involved in developing a modular weapon system that not surprisingly became known as the **Stoner 63 System**.

Produced not long after Stoner left Armalite Inc. in the late 1950s, the Stoner 63 System was formed from 17 modular units that could be assembled and arranged to produce a whole series of weapons. The basis for the system was the rotary lock mechanism first used on the AR-10 and later on the AR-15/M16 rifles. However, the Stoner 63 System used a different method of gas operation based on a long-travel piston. The only components common to all weapons in the system were the receiver, the bolt and piston, the return spring and the trigger mechanism. To these could be added butts, feed devices, various barrels and such items as bipods or tripods to produce weapons as tactical situations or requirements changed.

Originally the Stoner System was developed to use the 7.62-mm (0.30-in) NATO cartridge, but when it became clear that the 5.56-mm (0.219-mm) calibre was the future favourite the system was revised to accommodate the lighter round. This made many of the components much lighter, and as a result the weapons too were lighter.

The basic weapon was a carbine with a folding butt, and then came an assault rifle. Magazine- and belt-fed light machine-guns using bipods were next, while the addition of a heavy barrel, belt feed and tripod produced a medium machine-gun. It was even possible to produce a fixed solenoid-fired machine-gun for co-axial use in armoured vehicles.

The Stoner 63 System attracted a great deal of attention. The system was placed into small-scale production by Cadillac Gage, under whose aegis Stoner had developed the project. Plans were made with a Dutch firm for licence production, but military interest was not so forthcoming. The US Marines carried out a series of trials and more were carried out in Israel. The system performed well throughout all these trials but nothing resulted. Exactly why this was the result is not easy to determine, but perhaps the main reason was that for a set of components to be produced to perform so many roles a number of the parts had to be something of a compromise and thus less successful than a purpose-built design. The Stoner System gradually faded from the scene and is now no longer offered.

Specification
Stoner 63 (assault rifle)
Calibre: 5.56 mm (0.219 in)
Weight: loaded 4.39 kg (9.68 lb)
Length: overall 1.022 m (40.23 in); barrel 508 mm (20 in)
Muzzle velocity: about 1000 m (3,280 ft) per second
Rate of fire: (cyclic) 660 rpm
Feed: 30-round box

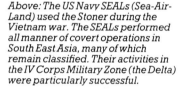

Above: The US Navy SEALs (Sea-Air-Land) used the Stoner during the Vietnam war. The SEALs performed all manner of covert operations in South East Asia, many of which remain classified. Their activities in the IV Corps Military Zone (the Delta) were particularly successful.

Above: A Stoner is shown mounted on its tripod. The US Marine Corps conducted exhaustive testing of the Stoner system, which led to some improvements being made. Several armies acquired the weapon for trials purposes, but in the event no production orders materialized.

Right: Eugene Stoner produced several innovative designs during the late 1950s; the Stoner system, manufactured by Cadillac-Gage, consisted of 15 assemblies and a tripod, from which a whole range of small arms could be constructed. This is the M63A1 rifle.

US Weapons

Above: The M14 replaced the Garand in US service, and was the main weapon in the hands of the first American troops into Vietnam. Here a member of the 1st Infantry Division is seen on a search and destroy mission in 1965.

Right: The Stoner system was an ingenious attempt to be all things to all men, but like all such things did not prove entirely satisfactory. A Seal is seen with the LMG version of the Stoner in the Mekong Delta.

NATO's Lost Chance

In 1944 the Germans introduced a rifle chambered for a new, lower-powered cartridge, capable of fully automatic fire. This 'assault rifle' soon proved superior to the pre-World War I designs which equipped most armies, and after the war the British and Soviets produced assault rifles of their own. The Soviet AK-47 entered service in 1957 and has since been judged the most successful post-war rifle, while the British weapon was sacrificed to American prejudice.

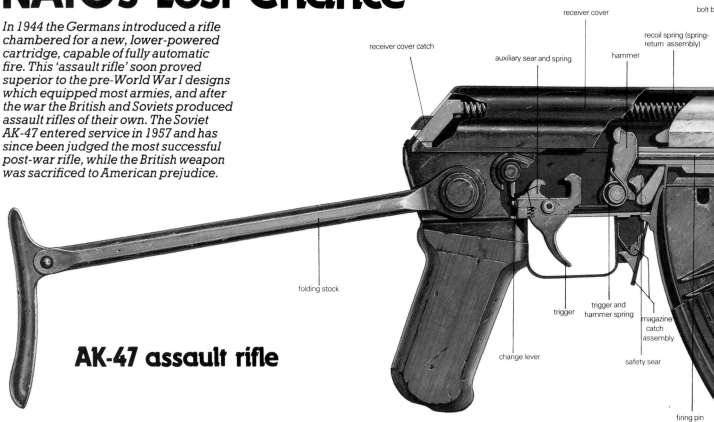

receiver cover catch · auxiliary sear and spring · receiver cover · hammer · bolt b · recoil spring (spring-return assembly)

folding stock · trigger · trigger and hammer spring · magazine catch assembly · change lever · safety sear · firing pin

AK-47 assault rifle

Combat analysis of World War II infantry engagements revealed the fact that the majority of tactical fire-fights took place at ranges far less than 400 m (437 yards), yet most soldiers on both sides were issued with rifles and ammunition having range potentials of 2000 m (2,187 yards) or more. The Germans were first to see that if lighter, less powerful ammunition was developed to be effective only up to actual combat ranges, not only could a soldier carry more ready-to-use rounds but his firepower potential could also be vastly increased by the introduction of selective-fire weapons as the associated recoil forces would be much reduced. The German army took these lesson to heart and introduced the Sturmgewehr assault rifles and their innovative 7.92-mm×33 *kurz*

(short) cartridge. The first figure denotes the calibre, in this case 7.92 mm (0.312 in), and the second the length of the cartridge case, i.e. 33 mm (1.3 in). The combination of less powerful ammunition and assault rifle gave the German infantry a vast increase in combat firepower by the introduction of automatic fire for every man. Once again the Germans had shown the way ahead in small arms developments, but they lost the war.

They had, however, taught the Allies an important lesson. Nearly every one of them was using rifle ammunition that dated back decades, and it was abundantly clear that such ammunition would have to be replaced. For a while the Allies were saddled with their existing *matériel* for the simple reason that they

already had the manufacturing facilities to tu them out by the million, and also huge stoc piles that must first be consumed. To take on new type of ammunition would involve v outlays of money and materials, and few tions were willing or able to envisage suc programme. The development of ne ammunition also took time, so it was not surpr ing that the major conflict of the 1950s, t Korean War, was fought mainly with Wo War II weapons and ammunition.

There was little prospect of the German *k* cartridge being adopted by any of the Alli but the Soviets were most impressed by having been on the receiving end on ma occasions. From the *kurz* cartridge they c veloped their own 7.62-mm×39 round a evolved the SKS and AK-47 rifles to fire it. T 7.62-mm×39 round has proved to be one of best military cartridges of all time and certain one of the most used, for it is still in widespre use to this day and seems set fair to remain for ages to come. It combines good letha and hitting power at combat ranges, yet is co pact and contains a load light enough to enab it to be fired from portable selective-f weapons.

The Soviets were not alone in developin

The Soviets lost no time in adopting an intermediate cartridge, but US insistence prevented NATO following suit, forcing Britain t cancel the EM-2. Work continued with bullpup designs such as this prototype Individual Weap but only in 1985 has the IW entered service.

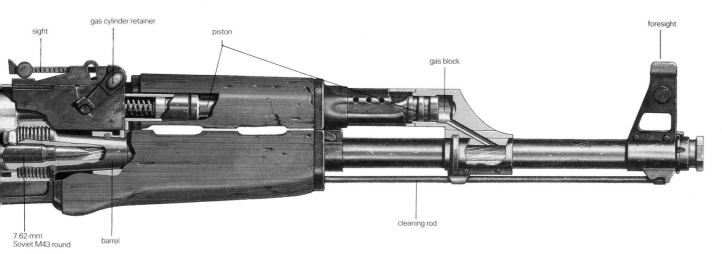

sight | gas cylinder retainer | piston | gas block | foresight

7.62-mm Soviet M43 round | barrel | cleaning rod

magazine spring and platform

w light cartridge. The British used the years er World War II to investigate new combat munition to replace their elderly 0.303-in 7-mm) rifle round, a type loaded with inicient cordite propellant and rimmed as ll, making it awkward to use in automatic eapons. After a series of trials a new rimless nd known as the 0.280-in (actually 7-n×44) was produced, along with the EM-1 d EM-2 experimental rifles for potential serre introduction. The 0.280-in proved to be an cellent cartridge, having a good combat rformance combined with light weight and e. All seemed set therefore for the introduc-n of the 0.280-in cartridge to the British army.

eapons standardization

Then international politics intruded. The 80-in cartridge arrived on the scene about e time the NATO agreement was signed 49) and the participant nations were bound the terms of the treaty to adopt a program-e of weapons standardization as far as possi-e, with small-arms ammunition high on the list priorities. The idea of using a common car-lge throughout the NATO made good sense t it also led to a wrong choice for one basic ison: the Americans were not impressed by

Navy SEALs seen in Vietnam, 1970, carry their ual mixture of hardware including (on the left) a ner 63. This system proved another blind alley small arms design, originally developed for the TO 7.62-mm round but revised because the A adopted 5.56-mm calibre with the M16.

the need for any change to less powerful ammunition, and they certainly did not approve of the British 0.280-in which they casti-gated as lacking power at long ranges (ignor-ing the fact that the round had been deliberate-ly designed to give of its best at short combat ranges).

Exactly why this lack of appreciation of tac-tical lessons arose is difficult to determine with exactitude, but it no doubt stemmed in general from the in-bred independence and frontier lore that seems to colour so much American behaviour and thought. Perhaps many soldiers had been put off by the introduction of the odd .30 Carbine cartridge (based on a pistol round) for the M1 Carbine that had proved so ineffec-tive during World War II. The US Army, im-pressed by the German Sturmgewehr, called for similar light automatic weapons but firing powerful 'full-strength' ammunition. The two requirements were incompatible, but Amer-ican small arms designers did their consider-able best to comply. It should be noted that many American designers were as anxious as any to introduce lightweight ammunition, but with no prospect of the US Army adopting any such round the designers had to produce what the customer wanted.

The then-current American rifle cartridge, known as the .30-06 (actually 7.62-mm×63), was considered ripe for replacement as it dated from 1906, but it was taken as the starting point for a new American round. By cutting the case down to 51 mm (2 in) the designers appeared to go part-way to producing a shor-ter cartridge, but the bullet remained much the

same weight as before and the propellant load meant that overall performance was only mar-ginally less than that of the .30-06.

The US Army adopted the new 7.62-mm×51 cartridge in 1952. This meant in effect that the rest of NATO had to do the same for most of the new NATO allies were in such a poor state financially from the effects of World War II that they had to accept that the USA would be foot-ing many of Europe's defence bills for years to come. This meant that in their turn the Euro-peans had in their turn to accept the American 7.62-mm×51 round.

The 7.62-mm×51 cartridge has been the NATO standard ever since and, despite the recent introduction of the 5.56-mm×45 SS109 cartridge, it will be around for decades to come. It was not a happy choice. Assault weapons produced to fire the new round tended to be heavy and expensive, and were often limited to single-shot fire to keep within manageable proportions the recoil developed by the power of the propellant load. And on the other side of the coin the NATO round remains an indifferent cartridge for use in longer-rang-ing machine-guns. Soldiers found themselves still limited to carrying only as many rounds (usually about 200) as their World War II coun-terparts. Only the introduction of the 5.56-mm×45 ammunition has permitted a return to the type of weapons and firepower potential the German *Frontschwein* ('grunts') were using at the end of World War II. Thus the adoption of the 7.62-mm×51 cartridge was a lost opportun-ity of great significance.

Armalite AR-10 assault rifle

USA

During 1954 the newly-formed Armalite Division of the Fairchild Engine & Airplane Company started the development of an assault rifle firing the World War II 0.30-in (7.62-mm) rifle cartridge. By 1955 Eugene Stoner had joined the company and development had switched towards using the new NATO 7.62-mm cartridge though the Armalite team, greatly influenced by Stoner, was not restricted to using established small-arms design conventions. The team thus evolved an innovative 'all-in-line' layout with sights above the weapon, but perhaps the most important contribution to small arms design was the reintroduction of the rotary bolt locking system that has now become virtually a standard on subsequent assault rifle designs throughout the world.

The rifle emerged during 1955 as the **Armalite AR-10**. This made great use of aluminium in construction and steel was used only on the barrel, bolt and bolt carrier. This made the weapon light, too light really as its tendency to 'rear' when fired automatically meant that a muzzle compensator had to be fitted to overcome this failing. The cocking lever was on top of the receiver protected by a carrying handle that also carried the rear sights. Originally it was planned that there would be sub-machine gun and light machine-gun variants of the basic AR-10, but only prototypes were produced.

The Armalite team found that marketing its product was rather more difficult than designing it. Tooling up for production was slow and sales were not helped by the fact that the NATO nations had already made their various new rifle decisions by the time the AR-10 appeared. The Dutch

seemed to offer hope of sales and arrangements were made with a Dutch company known as NWM for licence production of AR-10s but that project all came to naught, despite a great deal of preparatory work.

All this was a pity, for the AR-10 was really far better than any weapon then in NATO use and far more advanced than most. It was simple, easy to handle and had plenty of potential. Some sales were made, by far the largest being to the Sudan. The Portuguese purchased

1,500 and other batches went to Burma and Nicaragua, some via the Dutch NWM. Perhaps the greatest importance of the AR-10 was that it paved the way for the later AR-15/M-16 rifles. Production ceased in 1961.

Specification
AR-10
Calibre: 7.62 mm (0.30 in)
Weight: loaded 4.82 kg (10.63 lb)
Lengths: overall 1.029 m (40.5 in); barrel 508 mm (20 in)

The ancestor of the M-16, the AR-10 was a good rifle, better than most of its competitors, and it deserved a better fate. It appeared too late to compete in the struggle for a NATO 7.62-mm rifle and so had little hope of major sales. Production ceased in 1961.

Muzzle velocity: 845 m (2,772 ft) per second
Rate of fire: (cyclic) 700 rpm
Feed: 20-round box

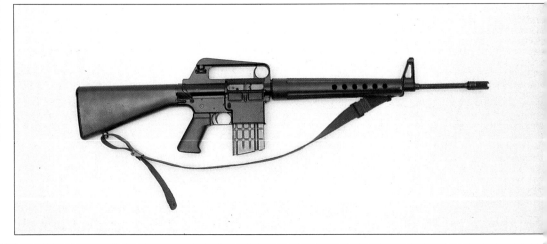

The innovative AR-10 used aluminium for most of its metal parts, steel being used only for the barrel, bolt and bolt carrier. It was a very light weapon which suffered from pronounced muzzle climb when fired fully automatic.

Valmet m/60 and m/62 assault rifles

FINLAND

Although not a member of the Warsaw Pact, because of its proximity to the USSR Finland inevitably has to go along with the Soviet way of doing things in some matters. So it was when the Finnish army decided to adopt a new service rifle in the late 1950s: not surprisingly it opted for the Soviet AK-47 assault rifle and its ammunition, and the country negotiated a manufacturing licence for both. Once the AK-47 design was in their hands, the ever-active Finnish small-arms designers at Valmet decided to make a few changes and the result was the **Valmet m/60**.

The AK-47 origins can be discerned in the m/60, but the energetic re-working by the Finns resulted in a much

The m/62 has different sights to those fitted on the AK-47 and introduced a three-pronged flash eliminator, but the selector lever and safety catch are exactly the same as on the Soviet weapon. In addition to serving with the Finnish army, the m/62 has been bought by Qatar.

etter all-round weapon. For a start
he m/60 used no wood whatever in its
onstruction, the wooden furniture of
he AK-47 being replaced by plastics
r metal tubing. The tubular butt of the
/60 was not only easier to produce, it
as also more robust and it carried the
leaning tools and equipment. The pis-
l grip and forestock were cast from
ard plastic, while the trigger was left
rtually unguarded to allow gloves to
e worn when firing, an important
oint considering Finnish winter con-
itions.

Other changes from the AK-47 in-
luded slightly altered sights, a three-
ronged flash hider at the muzzle and
revised bayonet mounting bracket to
ccommodate the Finnish bayonet,
hich could also be used as a fighting
nife. Internally the AK-47 mechanism
as left virtually unchanged apart from
few manufacturing expedients, and
e curved magazine and its housing
ere also left untouched to allow AK-
7 magazines to be used.

A later model, the m/62, was virtually
e same as the m/60 apart from a few

extra cooling holes in the forestock and
the introduction of a vestigial trigger
guard.

The m/60 and m/62 are still used by
the Finnish armed forces today. They
are excellent weapons that are ideally
suited to the tough conditions that the
local climate imposes. In design terms
they are rated to be much better
weapons than the AK-47 from which
they were derived, but in ease of production they have been partially overtaken by the introduction of the Soviet
AKM.

Specification
m/62
Calibre: 7.62 mm (0.30 in)
Weights: empty 3.5 kg (7.7 lb); loaded
4.7 kg (10.36 lb)
Lengths: overall 914 mm (36 in); barrel
420 mm (16.54 in)
Muzzle velocity: 719 m (2,359 ft) per
second
Rate of fire: (cyclic) 650 rpm
Feed: 30-round box

*The m/62 is the Finnish variant of the Soviet AK-47. It uses no wood in its
construction and has a tubular butt which, apart from being easy to
manufacture, has the added bonus of being able to carry the cleaning tools
and equipment.*

DENMARK

Madsen sub-machine guns

lmost as soon as the last Germans left
openhagen in 1945 the Danish Mad-
en concern returned to its pre-war
ctivities of designing automatic
eapons. After a brief excursion into
n unremarkable sub-machine gun
esign known as the **m/45**, the comany produced a more successful
odel known as the **Madsen m/46**.
his sub-machine gun used the pro-
uction techniques pioneered by
eapons such as the British Sten and
e American M3 'Grease Gun', but
lied them to a thorough rethinking of
asic design concepts. Thus the m/46
ade much use of steel stampings, and
ese were formed into a remarkably
mple and sound design.

For all its innovations the m/46 re-

mained a straightforward blowback
weapon. The butt was a simple rect-
angular-shaped piece of steel tubing
that could be folded about a hinge to
rest against the side of the receiver; a
piece of leather was wrapped around
the butt itself to provide some vestige
of comfort for the firer. The receiver
was square in cross-section as was the
bolt, but the main item of note about the
weapon body was its construction. The
entire receiver was produced in two
longitudinal halves, held together by a
larger barrel nut. When this barrel nut
was undone the short barrel could be
removed to allow the two halves to
open up (around the butt hinge) to expose the workings. This made the
working parts extremely easy to clean

and repair, which no doubt added to
the weapons' reputation for reliability,
a feature further aided by there being
no single-shot facility, the m/46 thus
being capable of automatic fire only.

The m/46 was not a great sales success, mainly because it was produced
at a time when the world small-arms
markets were still awash with the residue of World War II. The successor
to the m/46 was the **m/50**, and this was
rather more successful though differing from the m/46 only in detail. An
even later version, the **m/53**, differed
mainly in using a curved box magazine
instead of the earlier straight versions,
and the m/53 could be fitted with an
optional barrel jacket that could carry
a bayonet.

The main markets for the Madsen
sub-machine guns were South America and Asian nations such as Thailand.
As a result of their extremely sound
design and construction the Madsens
may still be encountered today.

Specification
m/50
Calibre: 9 mm (0.354 in)
Weight: 3.17 kg (6.99 lb)
Lengths: stock extended 794 mm
(31.26 in); stock retracted 523 mm
(20.6 in); barrel 198 mm (7.8 in)
Muzzle velocity: 390 m (1,280 ft) per
second
Rate of fire: (cyclic) 550 rpm
Feed: 32-round box

*Left: The Madsen endeavoured to
make use of wartime mass
production techniques without
suffering the usual problems of
hastily-put together weapons.*

*Right: The Madsen was used in
Vietnam by Special Forces, and it is
seen here in the hands of a Laotian
mercenary.*

*Below: The Madsen's receiver was
hinged, and once the barrel nut was
removed the two halves could be
swung apart, exposing the
mechanism. This made the weapon
very easy to maintain.*

Samozaryadnyi Karabin Simonova (SKS)

The semi-automatic rifle known as the **SKS** was actually devised during World War II, but was not placed in production until some time afterwards. The designer was Sergei Simonov, who was responsible for many important Soviet small arms, but with the SKS Simonov decided to play things safe and stick to a relatively uninspired design.

The SKS was the first weapon designed to use the new Soviet 7.62-mm (0.30-in) cartridge derived from the German 7.92-mm (0.312-in) *kurz* round. The SKS used a gas-operated mechanism with a simple tipping bolt locking system. So conservative was the overall design that the SKS even outwardly resembled a conventional bolt-action rifle, complete with extensive wooden furniture. A fixed folding bayonet was fitted under the muzzle and the box magazine could hardly be seen: it held only 10 rounds and was fixed to the receiver. Loading was by chargers or insertion of single rounds; to unload, the magazine was hinged downwards, allowing the rounds to fall free. In typical Soviet fashion the SKS was very strongly built, so strong that many Western observers derided it as being far too heavy for the relatively light cartridge it fired. Despite this the SKS was well able to withstand the many knocks and rough treatment likely to be encountered during service use, and the SKS was the standard

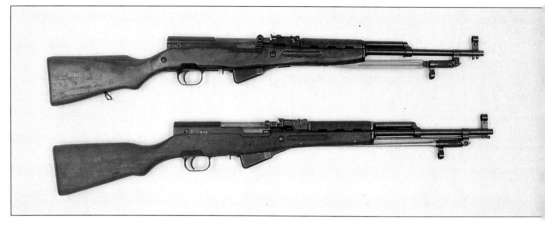

rifle of the Warsaw Pact nations for years until the AK-47 and AKM arrived in sufficient numbers.

The SKS is no longer in Warsaw Pact service other than as a ceremonial weapon for parades or 'honour guards'. However, it may still be encountered elsewhere as enormous numbers were produced, not only in the USSR but in East Germany and Yugoslavia where it was known as the **m/59**. The communist Chinese still produce a slightly revised version of the SKS known as the **Type 56**, and they are currently offering this version for export. Exactly what success they are

having is difficult to determine in an arms market where the AK-47 and its derivatives are all the vogue.

With so many SKS rifles produced it is not surprising that many remain in use throughout the Middle and Far East. Many were encountered by US and South Vietnamese forces during the Vietnam conflict, and from there many have passed into irregular hands. Being simple and robust weapons they are easy to use after a minimum of training and the SKS will be around for many years to come.

The SKS carbine was designed during World War II and produced in vast numbers after the war. The top rifle is a Chinese copy, the Type 56.

Specification
SKS
Calibre: 7.62 mm (0.30 in)
Weight: empty 3.85 kg (8.49 lb)
Lengths: overall 1.021 m (40.2 in); barrel 521 mm (20.5 in)
Muzzle velocity: 735 m (2,411 ft) per second
Feed: 20-round box

Ruchnoy Pulemyot Degtyarev (RPD)

Soviet designers have always been conservative in machine-gun design and when the **RPD** arrived on the scene in the early 1950s the continuation of a line through the DP, DPM and RP46 light machine-guns was very evident. However the RPD did have some innovations of its own and it has proved to be such a successful weapon that many remain in widespread use to this day.

The RPD may be regarded as the squad support weapon equivalent to the AK-47 assault rifle. It fired the same 7.62-mm (0.30-in) short cartridge and used a gas-operated mechanism that had much in common with that of the AK-47. Over the years many modifications have been made to the RPD and its mechanism to improve component life and overall accuracy, but it has always remained a typical Soviet design in that it is robust, simple and efficient.

The RPD uses a belt feed but the problem of ammunition belts flapping around to pick up dirt or snag on anything nearby has been overcome by the introduction of a drum holding a belt of 100 rounds ready to feed. The belt is held at the centre of gravity to assist carrying, but the gas-operated mechanism has a bit of a task to lift and feed a fully-loaded belt and if the belt or mechanism is dirty or even slightly damaged malfunctions can occur. Another potential problem carried over from earlier designs is that the barrel is not removable for changing when hot, and the barrel can become overheated after only a few prolonged bursts. RPD gunners therefore have to be trained to keep bursts short and not too frequent to prevent jamming. The RPD can fire on automatic only.

Although no longer in production in

the USSR, the RPD was (and still is) widely issued throughout the Warsaw Pact armed forces, although no longer as a front-line weapon as it has largely been replaced by the later RPK. Elsewhere it is still in the front line and may be encountered in armies as diverse as those of Pakistan, Egypt and Angola. In China the RPD is still being produced as the **Type 56** and is being offered for export to all who will buy. There have been some takers, for the RPD is now likely to be encountered

throughout the Middle East, usually in irregular hands. It has been observed in action in Lebanon and is one of the weapons used by the PLO.

Specification
RPD
Calibre: 7.62 mm (0.30 in)
Weight: gun only 7.1 kg (15.65 lb)
Length: overall 1.036 m (40.78 in); barrel 521 mm (20.5 in)
Muzzle velocity: about 700 m (2,297 ft) per second

Rate of fire: (cyclic) 700 rpm
Feed: 100-round belt

Designed in 1943 to take the new 7.62-mm × 39 cartridge, the RPD was introduced in the 1950s as the squad support weapon to complement the AK-47. The Soviets have no illusions about the standard of conscripts' rifle shooting, and have always relied on their machine-guns.

Avtomaticheskiy Pistolet Stechkina (APS)

he pistol known to the West as the echkin and to the Soviet bloc as the PS fell into the category known as achine pistols. Although it resem-ed a conventional automatic pistol it d a fire-selection mechanism that lowed it to fire fully automatically, i.e. bursts. Machine pistols were much vogue in the year before World War but operational experience soon owed them to be somewhat less than fect other than at extremely short nges: they were also very wasteful of munition. This waste was caused by e fact that as soon as the trigger was lled the recoil forces forced up the uzzle away from the target.

It was therefore something of a sur-ise when the Soviets produced the PS during the decade after World 'ar II. It seems that the APS was in-nded more as a police than a military eapon, but many were used by War-w Pact front-line forces. The APS d a magazine holding only 20 unds, a factor which limited any urst that might be fired. The round ed was the then-standard Soviet 9-m (0.354-in) automatic type used with viet sub-machine guns. These were ally too powerful for the APS's blow-ck system and made the violent re-il of the weapon even more pro-unced. In an attempt to control the coil the Soviet designers intended e pistol to be used with a bulky

wooden holster acting as a shoulder butt. This holster was almost identical to the old 'broomhandle' Mauser com-ponent, which no doubt acted as the starting point for the whole APS de-sign, but the butt was bulky and awk-ward to use, even if it did allow aimed fire up to 200 m (219 yards) and contain the pistol's cleaning tools and equip-ment.

The APS had a relatively short career in Soviet terms. It was issued throughout the Warsaw Pact armed forces, but it was never liked and was gradually relegated from front-line use to second-line duties. Today it is still around, but usually in the hands of bor-der guards and other such paramilit-ary forces. Many have found their way into the hands of terrorists/freedom-fighters who are often attracted by the APS's volume of fire rather than its combat efficiency.

Specification
APS
Calibre: 9 mm (0.354 in)
Weights: empty 1.03 kg (2.27 lb); empty with stock 1.58 kg (3.48 lb)
Lengths: overall 225 mm (8.86 in); barrel 127 mm (5 in)
Muzzle velocity: 340 m (1,115 ft) per second
Rate of fire: (cyclic) 750 rpm
Feed: 20-round box

A Soviet tank commander takes aim with an APS machine pistol. This was another attempt to produce a pistol capable of fully automatic fire; a shoulder stock like that of the Mauser Military Model was provided to give at least a hope of accuracy on automatic.

Fusil Mitrailleur Modèle 49 (MAS 49)

e **Fusil Mitrailleur Modèle 49 (MAS**) was one of the first semi-automatic les to enter service, and although sembling the bolt-action MAS 36, d indeed using the same two-piece ock, it was not merely an automatic rsion of the MAS 36 but a completely w design. At over 4.5 kg (10 lb) it is lightweight, but its strength proved valuable in the campaigns in Indo-ina and Algeria.

The MAS 49 is a gas-operated eapon, but uses no cylinder or piston; stead, some of the propellant gas is flected into a tube and conducted to e bolt carrier where it expands, forc-g the carrier back. This type of sys-m is generally eschewed by gun de-ners because it can produce exces-e fouling, but the MAS 49 has not ffered unduly. The breech is locked the same simple manner as on the mle 49, namely by tilting the breech ock. Unusually, the MAS 49 has an tegral grenade launcher, with a sight ed on the left hand side.

The MAS 49 was modified in 1956 to oduce the **MAS 49/56** which is still in rvice with units of the French army hough it will eventually be com-etely replaced by the FA MAS. The AS 49/56 is easily distinguished from e earlier weapon; the wooden fore-ock is much shorter and the barrel s a combined muzzle-brake/gre-de-launcher with raised foresight. e length of the whole weapon was duced by 90 mm and that of the bar-by 60 mm. The French obstinately ick with the 7.5 mm ×54 M 1929 car-dge, although a few MAS 49/56s re experimentally modified to fire ndard NATO 7.62 mm. Armour-ercing ammunition was produced, t has proved very unkind to barrels.

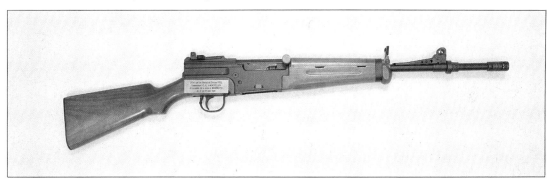

Above: This MAS 49/56 was presented to the Weapons Museum at the School of Infantry, Warminster. The MAS 49/56 gas-operated self-loading rifle has served the French army for nearly 30 years, although it is now being replaced by the FA MAS.

Right: Legionnaires of the 2nd REP are seen armed with (left) a MAT-49 sub-machine gun and (right) a MAS-49/56 self-loading rifle, which can be used as a grenade launcher. The MAS 49/56 fires the French 7.5-mm ×54 cartridge. An armour-piercing round is available as well as standard ball and tracer.

Specification
Fusil Mitrailleur Modèle 49
Calibre: 7.5 mm (0.295 in)
Weights: (without magazine) 3.9 kg (8.6 lb); (loaded) 4.34 kg (9.52 lb)
Lengths: overall 1010 mm (39.76); barrel 521 mm (20.51 in)
Muzzle velocity: 817 m (2,680 ft) per second
Feed: 10-round box

CZECHOSLOVAKIA

Samonabiject Puska vz 52

For a few years after the end of World War II Czechoslovakia was a completely independent nation and for a while returned to the importance of the pre-war days when its armament industry was one of the leaders in Europe. One of the small-arms results of this post-war period was a 7.62-mm (0.30-in) self-loading rifle known as the **Samonabiject Puska vz 52** (vz for *vzor*, or model) that followed many of the design trends indicated by the World War II German automatic rifles. The Czechs also developed a new short assault rifle cartridge (also known as the vz 52) based on German *kurz* cartridge experience for use in the new rifle.

As always the Czechs followed their own design paths and the vz 52 rifle had some unusual features, not the least of which was a method of tipping the bolt to lock the mechanism. There was also a permanently-fixed bayonet, and the 10-round box magazine was filled using chargers. The gas-operated mechanism used a gas piston system wrapped around the barrel. Hard-

ly innovative was the trigger mechanism which was a direct lift of that used on the American M1 (Garand) rifle. Overall the vz 52 was rather heavy but this made it easy to fire as recoil was limited. Even so the vz 52 took up quite a lot of manufacturing potential, and was really too complex a weapon for the period. Only the Czech army took the vz 52 into service for a while, and when other better weapons came along (such as the vz 58 assault rifle) the vz 52s were withdrawn and sold on the international arms markets, so some may still turn up in terrorist/freedom-fighter use.

By the time the vz 52s were deleted Czechoslovakia had been drawn into the Soviet sphere of influence. The Czech 7.62-mm vz 52 cartridge had nothing in common with the Soviet equivalent, although both had been designed from the same starting point. The Soviet military authorities were very strict regarding standardization throughout the armies under their control, and the Czechs were thus forced to abandon their cartridge and convert to the Soviet equivalent. Since the Czech and Soviet short cartridges were far from interchangeable this meant the vz 52 rifles had to be mod-

ified accordingly and late vz 52s using the Soviet ammunition were known a the **vz 52/57**.

Specification
vz 52
Calibre: 7.62 mm (0.30 in)
Weights: empty 4.281 kg (9.44 lb); loaded 4.5 kg (9.92 lb)
Lengths: overall, bayonet folded 1.003 m (39.49 in); overall, bayonet extended 1.204 m (47.4 in); barrel 523 mm (20.6 in)
Muzzle velocity: about 744 m (2,441 ft) per second
Feed: 10-round box

In the brief interlude between liberation from the Germans and take-over by the Russians, Czechoslavakia resumed production of indigenously designed small arms. The vz 52 fired a 7.62 mm×45 cartridge.

CZECHOSLOVAKIA

Lehky Kulomet vz 52 and Kulomet vz 59

The Czech ZB 26 light machine-gun was one of the major small-arm design successes of the years between the world wars (it led to the Bren Gun and its present-day derivatives), so it was no surprise that once the Czech small-arms industry re-established itself after World War II the design was used again as the basis for a new weapon. This emerged in time as the **Lehky Kulomet vz 52** (light machine-gun model 52) that carried over many features of the pre-war ZB 26 with the addition of a rather complicated belt or box magazine feed system. The new weapon retained many of the pre-war manufacturing methods of 'machining from the solid' so that although the weapon was reliable and robust it was also difficult to make and correspondingly expensive. The vz 52 was produced to fire the Czech short 7.62-mm (0.30-in) cartridge, but this had to be changed to the Soviet equivalent once the Soviets took over Czechoslovakia. Weapons chambered for the Soviet cartridge were known as the **Lehky Kulomet vz 52/57**.

By 1959 the Czechs had learned that the complex belt/magazine feed system was more trouble than it was worth and engineered it out of the design to produce the **Kulomet vz 59**. The opportunity was also taken to convert the design from that of a light machine-gun to a general-purpose machine-gun. This was done by the adoption of interchangeable light and heavy barrels and the introduction of a heavy tripod for the sustained-fire role. Another difference was the change from the short cartridge to the more powerful Soviet standard 7.62-mm rifle cartridge. Some alterations were also made to manufacturing techniques.

All these changes made the vz 59 into a more flexible and powerful

weapon. It is still in service today with the Czech armed forces and is produced in a special co-axial tank version. It has even been produced in export form to chamber NATO 7.62-mm ammunition. Fitted with a light bipod it is used in the light machine-gun role; fitted to a heavy tripod it becomes a heavy machine-gun; the same tripod can be adapted for the anti-aircraft role. Various optical sights have been produced for use with the vz 59.

Specification
vz 59
Calibre: 7.62 mm (0.30 in)
Weights: on bipod 8.67 kg (19.1 lb); on tripod 19.24 kg (42.4 lb)
Lengths: with heavy barrel 1.215 m (47.8 in); with light barrel 1.116 m (43.94 in); heavy barrel 693 mm (27.28 in); light barrel 593 mm (23.35 in)
Muzzle velocity: heavy barrel 830 m (2,723 ft) per second; light barrel 810 m (2,657 ft) per second
Rate of fire: (cyclic) 700-800 rpm
Feed: 50-round belt

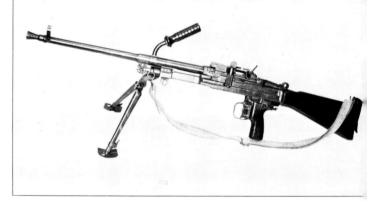

Above: The vz 52 light machine-gun was the last Czech development of the pre-war ZB 26, which was developed into the British Bren gun. It was a complicated gun to produce, and after the Soviet take-over it had to be converted to fire Soviet ammunition.

Below: The vz 59 replaced the vz 52. was a true general purpose machine gun, with different barrels for the squad support and sustained fire roles. It is a simpler design than its predecessor and is considerably easier to manufacture.

SIG assault rifles

he Swiss were rather slow to work
ieir way round to designing an assault
fle, but when they did produce one it
rned out to be one of the best of its
me. It had its origins in a weapon
nown as the **Sturmgewehr Modell 57**
 (StuG57) that took advantage of the
elayed-blowback roller breech-
cking system pioneered by the
panish CETME rifles. This rifle was
roduced by SIG for the Swiss army
alibred for the national 7.5-mm (0.295-
) rifle cartridge, and even carried
ver the fluted chamber of the CETME
fle.

At first sight the StuG57 looked odd
id awkward. In use it was quite the
pposite. As always the high standard
 SIG manufacture made it a good
eapon to handle and the Swiss sol-
ers liked the integral bipod and gre-
ide-launcher. However, the use of
e Swiss cartridge limited sales so
G went one stage further and de-
eloped the **SIG SG510** series of rifles,
esigned to fire more internationally
ccepted rounds. In many ways the
3510 was identical to the StuG57 and
urried over the extremely high stan-
ards of workmanship which, in their
rn, meant that although the weapon
as a soldier's dream it was very ex-
ensive. Consequently international
les were few. The Swiss army purch-
ed the larger batches but some went
 some African and South American
itions.

This was not for want of trying on the
irt of the SIG designers. They pro-
iced several versions; the first was
e SG510-1 chambered for the 7.62-

mm (0.30-in) NATO cartridge. The
SG510-2 was a lighter version of the
SG510-1. The **SG510-3** was produced
to fire the Soviet 7.62-mm short cartridge used on the AK-47. The **SG510-4**
was another 7.62-mm NATO round
model, and there was also a single-
shot only sporting version known as
the **SG-AMT** which was sold in large
numbers to Swiss target-shooters.

The SG510-3 and SG510-4 had some
extra features. One was an indicator on
the magazine to show how many
rounds were left and another was a

folding winter trigger. The bipod (folding up over the barrel) was retained
and both had provision for fitting optical sights for night vision or sniping.

The StuG57 and SG510 can still be
found hanging on the walls of many
Swiss army reservists, and numbers of
the SG510 are still in use in Bolivia and
Chile.

Specification
SG510-4
Calibre: 7.62 mm (0.30 in)
Weight: 4.45 kg (9.81 lb)

*SIG produced one of the most
unusual post-war rifles, the AK 53,
which used a stationary bolt and a
moving barrel, reducing the overall
length of the gun. The disadvantages
of this operation include potential
cook-off and a tendency to jam.*

Lengths: overall 1.016 m (40 in); barrel
505 mm (19.8 in)
Muzzle velocity: 790 m (2,592 ft) per
second
Rate of fire: cyclic 600 rpm
Feed: 20-round box

Beretta BM59 rifle

1945 Beretta started the licence pro-
iction of the American M1 Garand
le for the Italian armed forces, and
 1961 about 100,000 had been made,
me for export to Denmark and In-
onesia. The introduction of the NATO
32-mm (0.30-in) cartridge meant that
ese rifles would have to be replaced
 they fired the American World War
 0.30-in round, for a simple
chambering of the Italian Garands
ould have meant that the Italian
med forces were saddled with an
tdated rifle design for years to come.

The Beretta designers had for some
ne before 1961 been contemplating
revision of the basic Garand design
 produce a selective-fire automatic
eapon using the existing mechanism
 as great an extent as possible. The
sult was the **Beretta BM59**, which was
 Garand at heart but modified to
ovide the required automatic-fire fe-
ıre. It fired the NATO standard 7.62-
m cartridge. A 20-round detachable
x magazine replaced the old eight-
und magazine and some other slight
erations were introduced, but basi-
lly tho BM59 was (and still is) a
eathed-on' Garand.

Almost as as soon as the BM59 was
aced in production for the Italian
med forces a number of variants be-
n to appear. The base model was
 BM59 Mark 1, issued to most of the
lian army. Then came the **BM59
ark 2** with a pistol grip and a light
pod. The next two variants were vir-
ally identical: the **BM59 Mark 3 Para-
disti** for use by airborne units had a
movable grenade-launcher at the
uzzle, while the **BM59 Mark 3 Alpini**

model for mountain troops had a fixed
grenade-launcher. These two versions
both had folding skeleton butts and
light bipods. On the **BM59 Mark 4** the
bipod was a much more robust piece
of equipment for this version was intended for use as a squad fire-support
weapon. The Mark 4 also had a heavier
barrel and a butt strap to allow it to be
used for its fire-support role.

The BM59 proved to be an excellent
modification of an existing design and
it is still in use by the Italian armed
forces. It was built at one time under
licence in Morocco and Indonesia, and

Nigeria planned to produce the BM59
as well, though the Biafran War put
paid to that project. The one drawback
to the BM59 compared with many contemporary designs was (and still is) its
weight, and the need for extensive
machining during manufacture. For all
that the BM59 is a very robust and reliable weapon that still has some service
life left to run.

Specification
BM59 Mark 1 Ital
Calibre: 7.62 mm (0.30 in)
Weight: unloaded 4.6 kg (10.14 lb)

*The BM59 is based on the US M1
Garand self-loading rifle, which
Beretta was producing under licence
when NATO adopted the 7.62-
mm×51 cartridge. Beretta modified
the M1 design to accept the new
round.*

Lengths: overall 1.095 m (43.1 in);
barrel 490 mm (19.29 in)
Muzzle velocity: 823 m (2,700 ft) per
second
Rate of fire: (cyclic) 750 rpm
Feed: 20-round box

Two generations of personal weapons are visible in this picture of US troops running for a helicopter in a 'hot' LZ. The lightweight M16 embodies an entirely different technology compared to the earlier M14.

Modern Assault Rifles

A typical Vietnam situation, with the soldier in the foreground keeping his M16A1 well clear of the water. He is wearing bandoliers of 7.62-mm ammunition for the section M60 machine-gun. In such conditions the light weight and handiness of the modern assault rifle came to the fore.

Since the turn of the century, and largely as a result of experience gained during colonial wars, conventional military thinking held that the infantry rifle must be accurate at long range. Strangely, the relatively short-range fighting in the trenches of World War I made little impact upon prevailing opinion. As a result of the lessons of the first years of World War II, however, a radical re-appraisal of infantry doctrine was required.

The modern assault rifle had its roots in the novel art of combat analysis carried out by the German army after 1939) coupled with ammunition development carried out by the German concern of Polte. The combat analysis revealed that most infantry combats took place at ranges well below 400 m (435 yards), yet the standard infantry rifle of the day was designed to perform at ranges up to over 1000 m (1,095 yards). The short-range combat did not need such a powerful cartridge as the existing rifles so the Polte ammunition developments were studied to reveal a potential cartridge that would be efficient at the short range. The resultant cartridge produced such low recoil forces that automatic fire from a hand-held rifle was possible, and from this the modern assault rifle was born.

The modern assault rifle uses a cartridge that is adequate for infantry combat at ranges up to about 400 m (435 yards) but no more. Most of these cartridges are smaller and lighter than conventional rifle cartridges, and can thus be fired in fully automatic bursts to provide a considerable increase in fire power over single-shot weapons but yet can be used for aimed single-shot fire when required. Since the recoil forces are usually relatively low the construction of the assault rifle need not be very robust, with consequent benefits in light weight and simple mass production methods. For all that some modern assault rifles are very well manufactured and are very robust, though others follow the sheet steel and stampings approach adopted by many of the later sub-machine gun designs.

Tactically the assault rifle has had a considerable impact. A single infantry fire section can now produce fire power that would have been inconceivable only a few years ago and this had led to the fire saturation tactics often employed to neutralize enemy positions and movement. Thus the early promise of lighter ammunition loads for the laden foot soldier has been replaced by extra numerical loads of cartridge carried on the person. But now a relatively small number of men can lay down defensive fire to halt an attack yet advance rapidly firing bursts of automatic fire to overcome opposition; in both cases the expenditure of ammunition can be considerable. In irregular or guerrilla hands the assault rifle is a formidable weapon capable of spraying fire over a lethal radius in a very short time and then vanishing, for the assault rifle is a relatively small weapon.

The assault rifle has largely replaced the sub-machine gun, for the two provide the same product (automatic fire at short ranges for close-quarter combat) yet the assault rifle can also provide useful fire at ranges up to 400 m (435 yards).

British infantry with their L1A1s 'de-bus' from their FV432 armoured personnel carrier. They usually 'de-bus' about 400 m from the enemy position.

Steyr 5.56-mm AUG

The **Steyr AUG** (Armee Universal Gewehr, or army universal rifle or gun) is one of the most striking in appearance of all the modern assault rifles and it may almost be said to have a 'Star Wars' look about it. It is a 'bull-pup' design weapon, with the trigger group forward of the magazine, which makes it a short and compact weapon. The thoroughly modern appearance is enhanced by the liberal use of nylonite and other non-metallic materials in the construction. The only metal parts are the barrel and the receiver with the internal mechanism; even the receiver is an aluminium casting. All the materials are very high quality of their kind but the non-use of metal has been carried even as far as the magazine which is clear plastic so that the soldier can see at a glance how many rounds the magazine contains.

The Steyr AUG has been designed to be not only an assault rifle, for by varying the barrel length and the fittings on top of the receiver it can be easily produced as a carbine, or a specialist sniper, or a night-action rifle, or even a form of light machine-gun. By changing the fittings on the receiver the AUG can be fitted with a wide range of night sights or sighting telescopes, but the usual sight is a simple optical telescope with a graticule calibrated for normal combat ranges. Stripping the AUG for cleaning is rapid and simple, and cleaning is facilitated by the use of a chromed barrel interior. The AUG has been designed on a modular system so repairs can be easily effected by changing an entire module such as the trigger group, bolt group etc.

Production of the AUG began in 1978, and since that date the Steyr production line has been kept busy supplying the Austrian army, various Middle East states and some South American armed forces. Production is still well under way with no signs of the market weakening, and the AUG seems set for a long future.

Specification
Steyr AUG (assault rifle version)
Calibre: 5.56 mm (0.22 in)
Length: 790 mm (31.1 in)
Length of barrel: 508 mm (20.0 in)
Weight loaded: 4.09 kg (9.02 lb)
Magazine: 30-round box
Rate of fire, cyclic: 650 rpm

Above: The standard Steyr 5.56-mm AUG showing the overall 'bull-pup' layout and the optical sight over the receiver. The weapon has a 40-mm MECAR rifle grenade over the muzzle, which can be fired using normal ammunition to a range of about 100 m; HE, smoke and other grenades can be used.

Right: A Steyr 5.56-mm AUG in use by an Austrian soldier. Note the slender barrel with the flash-suppressor/grenade launcher, and how the folding foregrip is easy to hold and use to 'point' the weapon. The ×1 optical sight can be replaced by night sights or image intensifiers for use in poor light.

FA MAS

For some years before and just after World War II the French armaments industry lagged behind the rest of the world in small-arms design, but with the **FA MAS** assault rifle it has made up that leeway with a vengeance. The FA MAS is a thoroughly modern and effective little rifle, and yet another example of the overall compactness that can be achieved by using the unorthodox 'bull-pup' layout with the trigger group in front of the magazine. Even using this design the FA MAS is very short and handy, and must be one of the smallest in-service assault rifle designs of all.

The FA MAS has now been accepted as the standard service rifle for the French armed forces and this alone will keep the weapon coming off the production lines at St Etienne for at least the next 10 years. The first have

already been issued to some paratroop and specialist units, and the type was used by French troops in Chad and the Lebanon in 1983. The FA MAS is easy to spot, for in appearance it is quite unlike any other assault rifle. It fires the American M193 5.56-mm cartridge and has over the top of the receiver a long handle that doubles as the rear- and fore-sight base. The butt is prominent and chunky, and from the front protrudes a short length of barrel with a grenade-launching attachment.

The French 5.56-mm FA MAS rifle, one of the smallest and most compact of the modern assault rifles. The magazine has been removed, but note that the carrying handle contains the sights and that the cocking lever is just underneath; note also the folded bipod legs.

here is provision for a small bayonet nd bipod legs are provided as standard. The fire selector has three positions: single-shot, automatic and three-ound burst. The mechanism to control his last feature is housed in the butt ong with the rest of the rather complex trigger mechanism. The operaon is a delayed blow-back system. se is made of plastics where possible nd no particular attention is paid to etail finish: for instance, the steel barel is not chromed.

Despite its unusual appearance the A MAS is comfortable to handle and e, and presents no particular problems in use. Attention has been given such features as grenade sights and enerally easy sighting. In service the eapon has proved to be easy to hand-, and training costs have been re-

duced by the introduction of a version that uses a small sparklet gas cylinder to propel inert pellets for target training; this version is identical to the full service version in every other respect.

The French have offered the FA MAS for export at various defence exhibitions but the production programme for the French armed forces is such that it may be some years before significant numbers appear in service with other nations. Expected to be in the queue are the various ex-French colonies who still look to France for equipment and training.

Specification
Calibre: 5.56 mm (0.22 in)
Length: 757 mm (29.80 in)
Length of barrel: 488 mm (19.21 in)
Weight loaded: 4.025 kg (8.87 lb)

Magazine: 25-round box
Rate of fire, cyclic: 900-1,000 rpm
Muzzle velocity: 960 m (3,150 ft) per second

An FA MAS fitted with a TN$_2$1 night sighting infra-red spotlight under the muzzle. This equipment has a useful range of 150 m, and the soldier picks up the infra-red reflections in the night vision binoculars held over his eyes. This equipment is in service with the French army.

FN FAL and L1A1

oduced by the Belgian concern of abrique Nationale, or FN, the rifle w known as the **Fusil Automatique égère** (FAL, or light automatic rifle) as originally produced in 1948. At at time the prototypes fired the Geran 7.92-mm×33 *kurz* (short) cardge but later attempts at NATO nmunition standardization meant that e FAL was eventually chambered for e standard 7.62-mm×51 cartridge. such it has since been widely opted, not only throughout NATO it in many other nations, and has en been licence-produced by nans as diverse as South Africa and exico. Many of these overseas proction models differ in detail from the iginal FAL but the overall appearce is the same.

The FAL is a sturdy weapon which es many of the manufacturing ethods of a bygone era. High-grade aterials are used throughout, and exnsive use is made of machining and e tolerances. The action is gaserated, using a gas regulation sysn that taps off propellant gases from ove the barrel to operate a piston at pushes back the bolt action for locking the breech. The unlocking stem has a delay action built in for creased safety. Automatic fire is ssible on most models by use of a lector mechanism located near the gger group.

FAL models are many and various. st have solid wooden or nylonite tts and other furniture but some dels, usually issued to airborne ces, have folding butts that are far rdier than many other folding butts use. Overall, sturdiness is a feature the FAL, for the high manufacturing ndards have resulted in a weapon ll able to withstand the rigours of rvice life.

One production version of the FAL t deserves further mention is the tish version, known by its service signation **L1A1**. The L1A1 was opted by the British armed forces ly after a lengthy series of trials and difications that resulted in the elination of the automatic fire feature, e L1A1 thus firing single-shot only. ere are some other differences as ll, but the L1A1 itself has been opted by many other nations, inding India where the type is still in oduction. The Australians also opted the type and even produced a

Top: A British L1A1, the standard British infantry weapon; centre: the FN FAL with a shortened barrel; bottom: an Argentinian FN FAL with folding butt. Note the overall similarity of all these weapons; the bottom two can fire on full automatic, unlike the L1A1.

shorter version, the **L1A1-F1**, to suit the stature of the New Guinea troops.

Both the FAL and the L1A1 are equipped to fire rifle grenades, but these grenades are now little used Bayonets can also be fitted and some versions of the FAL have heavy barrels and bipods to enable them to be used as light machine-guns. Night sights are another optional fitting.

Although the 7.62-mm FAL is still in production, the trend is now towards a 5.56-mm version and a new model in this calibre is now in production as the **FNC**.

Specification
Calibre: 7.62 mm (0.3 in)

Length: 1143 mm (45.0 in)
Length of barrel: 554 mm (21.81 in)
Weight loaded: 5 kg (11.0 lb)
Magazine: 20-round box
Rate of fire: 30-40 rpm (single shot) or 650-700 rpm (FAL, cyclic)
Muzzle velocity: 838 m (2,750 ft) per second

Australian infantrymen with their locally-produced version of the British L1A1; these rifles were produced at Lithgow in New South Wales. The Australians also produced a short version called the L1A1-F1 for use by local troops in New Guinea. They also use the M16A1.

Royal Marines exercise aboard HMS Hermes on their way to the Falklands. Their L1A1 rifles are versions of the Belgian FN FAL, probably the most successful Western rifle of the post-war years.

he British army has been trying on nd off to adopt a new small-calibre fle cartridge since before 1914. For arious reasons, both military and poli-cal, it has been unable to do so until omparatively recently. In the years fter 1945 it did attempt to adopt a rifle nown as the EM-2 which used a 7.11-um (0.280-in) cartridge, but the adop-on by NATO of the 7.62-mm×51 cart-dge scotched that idea.

During the early 1970s another ttempt to produce a new calibre was ade. This time various researches in-icated that a 4.85-mm projectile allied the case of the American 5.56-mm und would be an ideal choice and a ew weapon, the **Individual Weapon L65E5**, was produced and demons-ated.

The Individual Weapon (IW) eemed to be an ideal rifle for the Brit-h army, but once again the British ere foiled in their project. NATO de-ded that any new cartridge would ave to be the standard round for all e NATO nations, and each nation had s 'pet' cartridge and weapon project. he result was one of the most exhaus-ve series of small-arms trials ever arried out over a series of years. lthough the 4.85-mm round and the V performed very well it soon be-ame obvious that the extensive pro-uction facilities already set up to urn out the M193 5.56-mm round ould be the final factor in the choice 'winner'. The outcome was the election of a Belgian round, the 5.56-m SS109, and this marked the end of e 4.85-mm IW.

But all was not lost for the IW. De-oite the choice of a new NATO stan-ard round every nation involved de-ded to stick to its own choice of eapon design. The UK thus went lead with the IW rechambered to ke the new SS109 cartridge. The re-lt is the **IW XL70E3**, now undergoing final troop trials before production ets under way some time during 1984.

The IW is a compact weapon of the ull-pup' type. It is only one compo-ent of a new British Army small-arms mily known as 'Small Arms 1980', or 80, the other component being the ght Support Weapon XL73E2. This tter weapon is almost identical to the V but has a heavier barrel and a pod to act as a section support eapon. The IW itself has undergone me external changes in appearance nce the time of the 4.85-mm IW, but ese alterations have been made urely for production reasons. Basical-the IW is still an 'in-line' bull-pup esign with a prominent optical sight er the body and a receiver and stock nstructed from steel pressings. The restock is tough nylon, and the muz-e has provision for a small bayonet d a built-in rifle grenade launcher. simplify logistics to some extent the agazine now used is the same as that ed on the American 5.56-mm 16A1. Night sights can be fitted if quired.

When it enters service the IW will e a compact and easy-to-use weapon

Above: This is the original 4.85-mm XL65E3 Individual Weapon, from which the present 5.56-mm XL70E3 has been developed. It differs from the current model in several ways, especially the shape of the forestock, and the magazine is now a slightly curved M16A1 item. Note the large optical sight, known as a SUSAT.

Right: The Light Support Weapon is the section support weapon version of the Individual Weapon. This model is the original version, the XL65E5, which has now been replaced by a 5.56-mm model: the XL73E2, with a revised forestock shape and other modifications.

for it handles well and is easy to aim and fire: there is no firing recoil to mention and the optical sight makes aiming very simple. One thing that will cause problems for the British army is that a new form of rifle drill will have to

be developed!

Specification
XL70E3
Calibre: 5.56 mm (0.22 in)
Length: 770 mm (30.31 in)

Length of barrel: 518 mm (20.39 in)
Weight loaded: 4.6 kg (10.14 lb)
Magazine: 30-round box
Rate of fire, cyclic: 700-850 rpm
Muzzle velocity: 900 m (2,955 ft) per second

e soldier on the right is holding the test form of the 5.56-mm XL70E3 dividual Weapon (IW), while the her holds the 5.56-mm Light pport Weapon (LSW) XL73E2. any components of the two eapons are interchangeable and th are entering British Army rvice.

M16 and M16A1

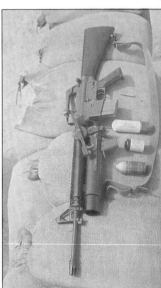

USA

Unlike so many rifles of its type, the rifle that is now the **M16A1** was a commercial design. It was a product of the prolific designer Eugene Stoner and first emerged as a product of the Armalite concern as its **AR-10** during the mid-1950s. The AR-10 used 7.62-mm ammunition, and with the advent of the 5.56-mm Fireball cartridge the AR-10 was redesigned to suit the new calibre. The result was the **Armalite AR-15.**

The AR-15 was submitted for a competition to decide the new standard rifle for the US armed forces. But before the competition was decided, commercial sales had already started: the British army took a batch of 10,000, making it one of the first customers to purchase significant quantities of the new design, and the US Air Force made another purchase soon afterwards. That was in 1961, and soon after this the AR-15 was selected by the US Army to become its new standard rifle as the **M16.** Production was then switched to the Colt Firearms Company, which took out a production and sales contract with Armalite. Since then Colt has kept its production contract, but somehow the name 'Armalite' still clings to the rifle that is now the M16A1.

The M16 became the M16A1 in 1966 with the addition of a bolt closure device fitted as the result of experiences in Vietnam. Since then the M16A1 can perhaps be regarded as the AK-47 of the Western world, for it has been produced in hundreds of thousands and has been widely issued and sold to nations all around the world. Numerous developments have been produced and tried, ranging from the usual light machine-gun variant with a heavy barrel and a bipod, down to short-barrel versions for special forces; there has even been a submachine gun variant. For all these changes the current M16A1 looks much like the first AR-15. Over the years there have been some changes as the rifling has been modified and more use is now made of internal chroming to aid cleaning. A recent introduction has been the **M16A2** which

has a heavier barrel that can be used with the new NATO 5.56-mm SS109 cartridge, demanding yet another change in rifling.

The M16A1 is a gas-operated weapon that uses the almost universally adopted locking system of the rotary bolt. A carrying handle over the receiver also acts as the rear-sight base, and nylonite is used for all the furniture. Although lending itself to mass production the M16A1 does not have the tinny appearance of many of its contemporaries, and has all the feel and finish of a high-quality weapon. In service it has become the carrier for a number of accessories which range from a blank adaptor to a special 40-mm grenade launcher mounted under the forestock (the M203).

The M16A1 and its variants seem set to remain in production for many years to come. Already licence production is under way in South Korea, the Philippines and Singapore, and more nations may well adopt the type in addition to the 12 or more who have already done so. The M16A1 is also widely used as a police weapon and the type can even be purchased commercially in many countries. It is already a favoured guerrilla weapon.

Above: Top: the original M16, recognized by the absence of the bolt-assist plunger of the M16A1 which is located above the trigger group. Below: the Colt Commando, a carbine version of the M16 and used in trials in Vietnam, where it was not a great success.

Right: M16A1 fitted with a 40-mm M203 grenade launcher under the barrel. This launcher can propel small spin-stabilized grenades to a range of about 350 m. Some of these grenades can be seen alongside the launcher and can be produced in a wide range of offensive loads, including HE and CS.

Despite the universal adoption of the L1A1 and the forthcoming IW, the British army still uses its examples in Belize and elsewhere, usually for issue to the Special Forces.

Specification
M16A1
Calibre: 5.56 mm (0.22 in)
Length: 990 mm (38.98 in)
Length of barrel: 508 mm (20.00 in)
Weight loaded: 3.64 kg (8.02 lb)
Magazine: 30-round box

Rate of fire, cyclic: 700-950 rpm
Muzzle velocity: 1000 m (3,280 ft) per second

Armalite AR-18

USA

Once the Armalite concern had cleared its design desks of the AR-15 with production under way by Colt Firearms of the M16/M16A1 series, it decided to look to the future for new products. With the 5.56-mm round well established, Armalite decided that what was needed was a simple weapon that could fire the cartridge. While the AR-15 was a sound weapon it was not easy to produce without sophisticated machine tools, and throughout much of the world these machine tools were not available. Thus the need for a weapon which could be simply produced by Third World nations was recognized, and a drastic revision of the AR-15 design was undertaken.

The result was the **AR-18**, which is very basically an AR-15 adapted for manufacture by the now-familiar production expedients of pressed steel, plastics and castings. For all these expedients the AR-18 is a sound design that is easy to produce, maintain and use. In general appearance and layout

it is similar to the AR-15 but the stamped steel receiver gives it a bulkier outline. The plastic butt is designed to fold alongside the receiver for stowage or firing from the hip.

Once the AR-18 design was complete Armalite attempted to find purchasers, but with the AK-47 and the M16A1 flooding the world markets there were few takers. An arrangement to produce the AR-18 in Japan fell through and for some years the design was in abeyance. Then the Sterling Armaments Company of the United Kingdom took out a licence, undertak-

ing some production and at one time moving production to Singapore. Some sales were then made locally but what was more important was that the local defence industry took the design as the basis for its own weapon designs, the AR-18 now living on disguised in many forms and under various labels.

Specification
Calibre: 5.56 mm (0.22 in)
Length: 940 mm (37.00 in) with stock extended or 737 mm (29.00 in) with stock folded

This AR-18 was originally manufactured in Japan but was captured from the IRA in Belfast. It the standard production model wit a butt that can be folded along the right-hand side of the receiver. The cocking handle can be seen poking upwards above the magazine.

Weight loaded: 3.48 kg (7.67 lb) w 20-round magazine
Magazine: 20-, 30- and 40-round bo
Rate of fire, cyclic: 800 rpm
Muzzle velocity: 1000 m (3,280 ft) p second

he M16 in Action

he M16 was first produced to an Armalite design in the late 1950s. Light, and firing
lightweight high velocity bullet, it was handy and effective at most combat ranges.
nce that time it has become the standard US Army rifle and has sold in millions
roughout the world. Not without problems in early operational use, the M16 has
roved itself in action time and time again.

uring the late 1950s the standard US Army
rvice rifle was the M14, a bulky and heavy
1 kg/11.24 lb loaded) weapon that fired the
2-mm×51 cartridge. It was a sound enough
eapon that used the basic operating mechan-
n of the Garand M1 rifle of World War II.
hile this rifle was perfectly adequate for ser-
:e in Europe and many other places, it was
t the preferred weapon for the close cones of jungle fighting and it was with jungle
hting that the Americans were beginning to
d themselves involved.

When the French and British withdrew from
Far East it left a power void that many local
litical activists were anxious to fill. China and
Soviet Union were only too happy to assist
eir endeavours and the United States de-
ded that it was in the national interest to take a
nd in the affairs of the region. Usually this
eant some form or another of economic aid or
idance, but in the wake of these early prog-
mmes came the need for military aid as well.
any of the small nations in the Far East were
ll using weapons left over from World War II,
d the Americans usually offered to replace
relics in use with modern weaponry. In the
e department they were not too well placed
meet the requirements. The peoples of the

Far East are usually of slight stature and rifles
such as the M14 were too large for them to
handle with comfort. Even the older M1 was
really too bulky a load so the Americans cast
about for a suitable new rifle.

They soon found the weapon required in the
Armalite AR-15, a thoroughly modern weapon
that was light, not too large and had virtually no
recoil when fired. A large quantity was procured and handed out to various nations, American military advisers carrying out the necessary training. It was during this period that the
advisers, who were highly-qualified weapon
technicians quite apart from their advisory
capacity, noted the attributes of the AR-15 and
wondered why they were handing out to all
and sundry a rifle that was in many ways better
than their own service equivalent. Their views
soon reached the ears of the higher US Army
echelons, who set about running their own
trials.

That was in 1958. The recommendation at the
time was that the AR-15 should replace the
M14, but that meant a drastic change-over in
ammunition supply and, as time was to show, it
was the ammunition change-over that was to be
crucial. But the US Army was pushed into action
when in 1961 the US Air Force procured a

batch of AR-15s under the designation M16.
Later the same year the US Army also purchased a batch and the M16 gradually started to
filter through the US Army supply system. At
first issues were made only to Special Forces
units, and it was these units which were mainly
involved in the American activities in South
East Asia.

For the Americans, East Asia became increasingly to mean the protracted internal
struggles of Vietnam. More and more American troops were sent to the area until a size-
able proportion of the US Army was involved.
These troops were usually given a priority
issue of the M16 and it was not long before
large-scale actions involving American forces
were taking place. Soon the first intimations
that the M16 rifle was not behaving as it should
filtered through the US Army network.

All manner of alarming stories were then told
of the M16 breaking down in action. Analysis of
these reports gradually showed that the M16s
were jamming solid as a result of excessive
fouling. These reports grew in volume and reg-
ularity to the extent that a special investigation
board was established by the US Army, and the
House of Congress set up its own special inves-
tigatory board. This latter board went into its
task with great application and it was this
board's final report that set out the whole sorry
tale.

Airborne cavalry of the US Army leap from a Bell
UH-1D 'Huey' in Vietnam in one of many anti-Viet
Cong sweeps. The troops have their M16s at the
ready. It was under such conditions that the early
M16s began to show signs of trouble due to the 'no
need to clean' claim.

The M16 in Action

Foresight *The foresight is a fixed post protected by a prominent guard.*

Flash hider *The flash hider on the muzzle can be used as a rifle grenade launcher.*

Gas tube *The extracted gas impinges directly upon the bolt carrier, via a gas tube. Weight is thus saved on the need for a gas piston.*

Gas action *Firing gases are tapped off from the barrel just above the bayonet lug, and heat is vented through holes above the forestock. It was at the gas port that the Vietnam fouling troubles started and then spread through the gas system to the bolt.*

Hammer *The M16A1 uses a rotary lug bolt action which operates alon[g] cams in the receiver wall. If this is n[ot] cleaned the bolt will seize.*

It now seems almost impossible to comprehend how a nation as rich and powerful as the USA could make the kind of blunders that led to the M16 débacle. When the US Army carried out its initial tests on the rifle all went well, to the extent that when the rifle was issued to the troops it was handed out with the message that the rifle was so efficient that it would never require cleaning. Exactly where this odd message originated is now impossible to determine, but needless to say the troops were happy to accept such statements and they never did clean their rifles. This was one of the major factors that led to the numerous breakdowns that started to occur, but there was another reason also.

This unsuspected factor was that the ammunition specification had been changed without anyone being told. When the initial AR-15 trials were being carried out commercial ammunition was used. This commercial ammunition was based on a propellant known as IMR (improved military rifle), which had been in use for many years. When fired in the 5.56-mm cartridge it presented no problems, burning cleanly and reliably. Most of the early trials ammunition and early batches of service ammunition used this type of propellant which tended to hide the problems that were to come in later batches based on an entirely different propellant. This new propellant was known as ball powder, and was introduced for general service use during 1954. Later it was introduced for filling the cases of 5.56-mm ammuni-

tion and when these reached the troops th[e] troubles began.

It has already been mentioned that th[e] troops had been told they did not need to clea[n] their M16s. When this lack of cleaning w[as] combined with the residue left by the new ba[ll] powder-filled cartridges a sticky residue w[as] formed. When hot this residue formed a stic[ky] paste, but once cooled the carbon elements [in] the residue became solid and jammed the M[16] mechanism, especially the bolt head. For th[is]

M16-armed troops disembark from a Bell UH-1D [in] Vietnam. The helicopter is armed with a 7.62-mm Minigun, a rifle-calibre version of the Gatling, which is here partly hidden under a canvas cove[r] for weather protection.

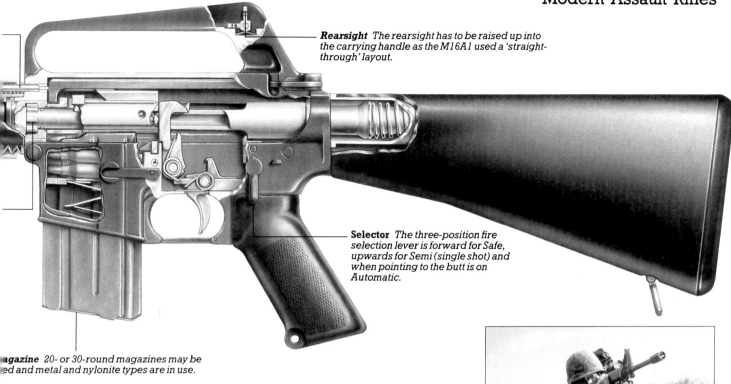

Rearsight The rearsight has to be raised up into the carrying handle as the M16A1 used a 'straight-through' layout.

Selector The three-position fire selection lever is forward for Safe, upwards for Semi (single shot) and when pointing to the butt is on Automatic.

Magazine 20- or 30-round magazines may be ...ed and metal and nylonite types are in use.

...low: Near Duc Pho City, Vietnam, June 1967. ...merican soldiers patrol to find North Vietnamese ...its and both are carrying M16s. The soldier in ...foreground has 7.62-mm ammunition belts for ...section M60.

On the ranges with an M16A1. This photograph clearly shows the early type of flash hider, which has now been replaced by a revised design with a cruciform notch along the centre to improve its performance.

This M16A1 is fitted with an AN/PVS-2 Starlight night-sighting telescope, which uses an internal image intensifier to amplify available light so that the user can aim at targets in what appears to be complete darkness to the naked eye.

A M203 40-mm grenade launcher is fitted onto the forestock of a M16A1. The M203 uses its own sleeve to clip over the forestock, and once in place the launcher uses its own trigger system separate from that of the M16A1.

The M16 in Action

soldier in the field there was no way of clearing this problem for the M16 has no bolt handle, only a cocking piece. The only way the guns could be unjammed was by shoving a cleaning rod or something similar down the bore of the barrel. Stories of soldiers leaping around firing parapets and jamming cleaning rods down the barrels of their comrades' rifles became legion and many casualties resulted from this undesirable practice. It was also noted that quite apart from the jamming, components were breaking long before they should.

By this time, the mid-1960s, the US government had taken the whole affair out of the hands of the military, which continued its own investigations and set up its own enquiry board. Many of the civilians involved were ex-military men who were horrified at what they discovered. They were shown M16 rifles that were covered in dirt and rust and they were shown

The new US Army Kevlar helmet was in operational service for the first time in Grenada during October 1983. The troops are from the 82nd Airborne Division and are carrying M16A1s, the one on the right fitted with a M203 launcher.

examples of M16s clogged solid with fouling. It was not long before the ammunition change was discovered. What had happened was quite simply that the demands of an ever-growing Vietnam involvement had outstripped the abilities of the American ammunition suppliers to keep filling the 5.56-mm cartridges with the satisfctory IMR propellant. Ball powder had been substituted, but somewhere along the line the information had been 'lost'. Full trials had not been carried out on the effects of the new ball powder and the troops in the field had to discover the hard way that not only did the ball powder burn leaving carbon and other deposits, but also that it burned at a rate which increased the rate of fire of the M16 beyond a safe limit; hence the breakages.

Under normal circumstances the fouling would have been serious enough. When combined with the lack of cleaning it was a disaster. Immediately the facts became clear a crash training programme was introduced and cleaning kits and lubricants were issued. Troops started to clean their M16s and things immediately improved. Changes were introduced on the M16 production lines; one was the introduction of a revised buffer arrangement inside the receiver to slow down the rate of fire using the ball powder propellant. Another change was the introduction of a thumb-operated bolt closure device on the right-hand side of the weapon above the trigger group. If a round did jam or the bolt seized, the soldier could at least force the offending round into the chamber to free things by firing. These changes altered the designation from M16 to M16A1.

Another outcome of the Congress report was an investigation into the methods of weapon and propellant procurement by the US Army,

A vision of the future as US Army troops leave a M Bradley ICV. They are carrying the M16A1 and ar wearing the new pattern helmet, which is made c Kevlar resin and nylon-based material in place o steel.

which no doubt caused a few upsets. But t immediate outcome was that the M16A1 b came a perfectly satisfactory service rifle ar the fouling days were over. This has now led yet another problem, for the daily cleaning ar lubrication of the M16 now means that the M jams when used in dust and sand conditio such as those encountered in the Middle Ea. The formation of the Rapid Deployment For (RDF) has meant extensive exercises in tl Egyptian deserts and elsewhere in the regic It now looks as though another course of rem dial action will have to be taken.

Despite these difficulties the M16A1 h turned out to be an excellent service rifle. T one reservation of many military observers the ammunition; in general terms it lacks po er. In many cases the bullet is so small that i strikes a target the impact is so slight that tl effect is far less than that of an equivalent bul of larger calibre. However, if the bullet 'tu bles', as it sometimes will, the shock effect frc the resultant large wound is severe. To sor extent these ammunition drawbacks have n been largely overcome by the introduction the new SS109 round.

But to return to the original reason for issui the M16, or the AR-15 as it then was: the pe ples of the Far East and South East Asia ha taken to the weapon with alacrity. It is now tl standard weapon for many armed forces in t region and some nations even produce the own for re-sale throughout the region.

Ruger Mini-14

USA

hen it was first produced in 1973, the uger Mini-14 marked a significant rn away from the mass production ethods introduced during World ar II towards the fine finish and tention to detail that was formerly the allmark of the gunsmith's art. The ini-14 is an unashamed example of w guns used to be made before the eel stamping and the die-cast alloy ame upon the scene.

From a design viewpoint the Ruger ini-14 is a 5.56-mm version of the 62-mm (0.30-in) Garand M1 service fle of World War II. By adopting the arand action Ruger has managed to mbine a sound and well-engineered esign with the ammunition of a new chnology. When this is allied to aftsmanship and a deliberate appeal those who look for that something xtra in a weapon the result is a re-arkable little rifle.

In appearance the Mini-14 has the aracteristics of a previous age. The aterials used are all high quality and an age where plastics have now ken over the furniture is all manufac-red from high-grade walnut. But sual appeal has not been allowed to ke precedence over functional safe-for the Mini-14 has been carefully igineered to prevent dust and debris atering the action. But some degree eye appeal has been allowed to ect the finish, for the weapon has een carefully blued all over, and ere is even a stainless steel version at sells very well in the Middle East.

The Mini-14 has not yet been adopted by any major armed forces but it has been sold to such establish-ments as police forces, personal body-guard units and to many special forces who prefer a well-engineered and ba-lanced weapon to the usual 'tinny' modern products. To suit the require-ments of some armed forces Ruger has now developed a special version that should appeal to many soldiers. This is the **Mini-14/20GB**. Police forces have been catered for by the introduction of the **Ruger AC-556** with glassfibre furni-ture, and another innovation is the **AC-556F** with a folding stock and a shorter barrel. The two AC-556 designs can be used to fire on full automatic for bursts, whereas the normal Mini-14 is a single-shot weapon only.

Specification
Mini-14
Calibre: 5.56 mm (0.22 in)
Length: 946 mm (37.24 in)
Length of barrel: 470 mm (18.50 in)
Weight loaded: 3.1 kg (6.83 lb) with 20-round magazine

Top: The attractive lines of the Ruger Mini-14 seen fitted with a 10-round box magazine. The bottom weapon is the Ruger AC-556F, which is intended for service as a purely military assault carbine. It has a folding metal butt and is seen here fitted with a 30-round box magazine.

Magazine: 10-, 20- or 30-round box
Rate of fire, cyclic: 40 rpm
Muzzle velocity: 1005 m (3,300 ft) per second

Vz.58

CZECHOSLOVAKIA

first sight the Czech **vz.58** assault le looks very like the Soviet AK-47, t this resemblance is deceptive for e two designs are different mechani-lly. The vz.58 is a gas-operated eapon but the unlocking mechanism es a pivoted locking piece in place the rotating bolt of the AK-47 family. e trigger mechanism is also diffe-nt and employs flat springs rather an coil springs. The overall result is entirely different mechanism. Ex-tly why the Czechs felt it necessary produce their own design in view of e availability of the AK-47 adopted all other Warsaw Pact nations is certain, but one fact that has re-lted from this 'go it alone' stance has en that the vz.58 has been sold on e open arms market with a facility at would not have been possible with e AK-47.

The vz.58 is very well made, with the ceiver machined from solid metal.

Early versions used a wooden butt, with plastic for such items as the pistol grip and the forestock. More recent versions have used a form of plastic into which wooden chips and shavings have been compressed resulting in a characteristic appearance. Three basic models have been produced, one with a conventional butt, one with a folding butt and a version with the re-ceiver fitted to take a variety of night sights. The last version may also be fitted with a light bipod and a promin-ent flash hider over the muzzle.

The facility with which the Czechs can market the vz.58 is such that the type can be purchased commercially 'over the counter' in many countries, but has still been used by armed forces as disparate as the Viet Cong and the IRA. One great attraction of the vz.58 is the price. Although this varies according to the quantity involved it is still relatively low compared with many other weapons. The Czechs are very willing to supply the 7.62 mm×39 ammunition as well, again at a very attractive price.

Specification
Calibre: 7.62 mm (0.3 in)
Length: 820 mm (32.28 in)
Length of barrel: 401 mm (15.79 in)
Weight loaded: 3.28 kg (8.42 lb)
Magazine: 30-round box
Rate of fire, cyclic: 800 rpm
Muzzle velocity: 710 m (2,330 ft) per second

Seen here carried by a young Czech tank crewman, the Vz.58, also shown below, differs internally from the otherwise ubiquitous Kalashnikov. Also different is the compressed plastic/woodchip mixture which forms the butt and foregrip.

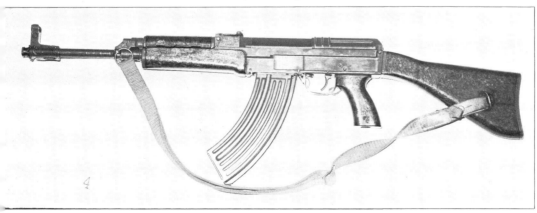

AK-47 and AKM

The **AK-47** must be rated as one of the most successful and widely-used of any type of small arm ever produced. Both it and its successor, the **AKM**, are now used all over the world by forces regular and irregular, and both types are still in production in one form or another in many countries.

The first AK-47 was designed around a short 7.62-mm calibre cartridge that owed much to the introduction of the German 7.92-mm *kurz* round. The Red Army was often on the receiving end of the German assault rifle family (the MP 43, MP 44 and StuG 44) and asked for their own counter. The result was the 7.62-mm×39 cartridge and the AK-47. The designer was Mikhail Kalashnikov and his design is often referred to by his surname. The first examples were issued for service during 1946 and the weapon gradually became the standard weapon of the Warsaw Pact forces. The production lines were huge and the numbers that rolled off them were vast, but such was the demand that most Warsaw Pact nations set up their own production facilities. From this sprang the large numbers of AK-47 sub-variants that continue to delight the gun research buff to this day.

The basic AK-47 is a sound and well-made weapon that carried over few of the mass production expedients employed by its German wartime equivalents. The AK-47 receiver is machined and good-quality steel is used throughout with wooden furniture as standard; the result is a weapon that can absorb any amount of hard use and mishandling. As there are few moving parts and stripping is very simple, maintenance is also simple and can be accomplished with even a minimum of training.

Before long different production versions of the basic AK-47 emerged, even within the Soviet Union, and a version with a folding steel butt was produced. All these different versions used the same mechanism, a simple rotary bolt that was cammed into corresponding grooves in the receiver by bolt cams. Operation is by gas tapped from the barrel via a gas port.

AK-47s were produced in China, Poland and East Germany and the basic design was copied by several designers abroad, including those of the Finnish **Valmet M60** and **M62**.

For all its huge success and accept-ance, it was finally admitted during the late 1950s that production of the AK-47 was too involved in manufacturing facilities. A redesign produced the AKM, which outwardly resembles the earlier design but is generally revised to facilitate production. The most obvious external change is to the receiver, which is formed from a steel stamping in place of the former machined equivalent, but internally the locking system has been revised to make it more simple. There are numerous other differences but the overall changes are in manufacturing methods.

The AKM did not immediately take the place of the AK-47 but acted more as a supplement to numbers. The other Warsaw Pact production lines gradually switched to the AKM, some nations (such as Hungary) even going so far as to modify the basic design to produce their own version, which often differs in many ways from the original (the Hungarian **AKM-63** even looks different but retains the basic mechanism of the AKM). A version with a folding steel butt is known as the **AKMS.**

The AKM is still being produced, and the AK-47 and AKM will remain in service until well into the next century, if not beyond. This longevity must be partially attributed to widespread availability and the numbers produced but the basic fact is that the AK-47 and AKM are both sound and tough weapons that are easy to use and simple to maintain.

Specification
AK-47
Calibre: 7.62 mm (0.3 in)
Length: 869 mm (34.21 in)
Length of barrel: 414 mm (16.30 in)
Weight loaded: 5.13 kg (11.31 lb)
Magazine: 30-round box
Rate of fire, cyclic: 600 rpm
Muzzle velocity: 710 m (2,330 ft) per second

Top: AK-47 with folding metal butt; centre: AKM identifiable by muzzle brake attachment and hand-grip on forestock, and bottom: Chinese Type 56 from Zimbabwe, the Chinese version of the AK-47 with its own integral bayonet seen folded under the forestock.

Specification
AKM
Calibre: 7.62 mm (0.3 in)
Length: 876 mm (34.49 in)
Length of barrel: 414 mm (16.30 in)
Weight loaded: 3.98 kg (8.77 lb)
Magazine: 30-round box
Rate of fire, cyclic: 600 rpm
Muzzle velocity: 710 m (2,330 ft) per second

Egyptian troops during the Yom Kippur War of 1973. Their weapons are AKMs with the characteristic angled muzzle attachments and the handgrip grooved into the forestock. The AKM is now the standard Egyptian service rifle.

The AK-47 has been manufactured throughout the Warsaw Pact countries, and this East German infantryman would be armed with the MPiKM version, made in the DDR.

Above: North Vietnamese troops are seen in one of their early actions with the Americans in 1965. They are armed with Chinese Type 56 weapons, the SKS copy being in front of the AK 47 copy.

Below: KGB border guards patrol the Soviet frontier. The rifle is an AK-47, identifiable by its lack of a muzzle brake. The AK series has been made in greater numbers than any other firearm in history.

The Assault Rifle in Guerrilla Hands

Above: Tamil guerrillas on Sri Lank: practise with an assortment of weapons, including an M16 with grenade launcher and several FN FALs. The pistol is an FN Browning High-power.

Left: The troubles in Central Americ: have seen rich pickings for the sellers of weapons. This M16-armec guerrilla was seen in the early 1980s after a convoy ambush in El Salvado:

The Assault Rifle in Guerrilla Hands

While the major powers have maintained a sometimes uneasy peace, the 40 years since the end of World War II have been far from quiet for the rest of the world. Freedom fighters, revolutionaries, terrorists and dictators have all turned to the gun as arbiter of any dispute; demand for modern weapons is ever-increasing, and the primary requirement is for individual weaponry.

Members of a PLO guerrilla group, with a typical mix of Soviet-supplied weaponry. Visible are AK-47s and AKMs and two RPG-7 anti-tank rocket launchers. Just visible on the extreme left is an RPD, a machine-gun version of the AK-47.

In the shady war that seems to be taking place in all too many nations, the guerrilla has to use whatever weapons he can acquire. Although the urban or rural guerrilla will use whatever weapon he (or she) can lay his hands on, he will always try to adopt some form of 'standard' weapon. The advantages of such a course of action are several. One advantage is that training can be simplified, as few guerrilla organizations have time or facilities for proper training, yet modern rifles need the care and attention that cannot be ignored. Thus if one weapon type is the norm, more people can pass on the words relating to its use. Another advantage is supplies. If even a tentative supply route can be established, so can a supply of ammunition and spare parts. If several calibres are in use by any one organization the ammunition supply alone becomes complicated and uncertain. Yet another advantage of a 'standard' weapon is that it can be picked up, used and hidden by any member of the organization without the need for familiarization before every mission.

Many guerrilla movements have now virtually standardized on two types of rifle, the AK-47 (and the essentially similar AKM) and the AR-15 (the M16 or M16A1) together with its descendant the AR-18. The latter two weapons are usually lumped together as 'Armalites'. Of the two the AK-47 must be the more numerous, for it appears in locations as far separated as Belfast and Malaysia.

Exactly where all the AK-47s originate is not easy to establish. AK-47s and their many derivatives are now produced in many countries including, Poland, China, Hungary, North Korea, Yugoslavia, Romania and the many copies produced in such odd corners as Afghanistan. Of all these nations China is perhaps the most liberal in handing out the AK-47, in the version known as the Type 56, but this is an exact copy of the normal AK-47. Examples of these Chinese weapons have even turned up in Europe. But it must not be thought that all these AK-47s turn up as the result of ideological support for the guerrilla. Most appear to end up in

guerrilla hands by the simple expedient of commercial transactions carried out through the armaments trade, both overt and clandestine. One nation that is known to have unloaded masses of AK-47s onto the open market is Israel; as the result of the various Middle East conflicts Israel has amassed stockpiles of captured AK-47s and these have been sold off to obtain much-needed hard currency. While

Another guerrilla group, this time in Afghanistan, displays captured weapons. The central figure holds a 5.45-mm AK-74; on the left and right are AKMs. The machine-gun is a DP and the heads of two RPG-7s can be seen.

The Assault Rifle in Guerrilla Hands

Above: Young guerrillas in El Salvador. The boy in front is holding a Heckler und Koch G3, the secon has an M16A1.

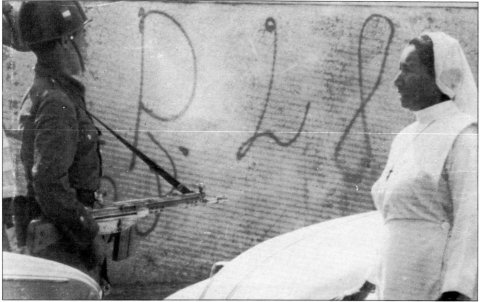

Left: During the tension following the assassination of Archbishop Romero of San Salvador in 1980, confrontation between the Church and the gun became more frequent.

many of these captured weapons have been purchased legally enough, many have now found their way into guerrilla hands by underground purchases with money obtained through the usual guerrilla methods of robbery and protection rackets.

Once in guerrilla hands the AK-47 is an ideal weapon. It is robust, easy to use and at close ranges can produce lethal volumes of fire. It is also relatively easy to conceal, especially the versions with folding steel butts which can be folded down to a length of only some 700 mm (25.76 in). This length can easily be hidden under a coat or under a baby in a pram. Ammunition supply is relatively easy, for so many nations now use the AK-47 or its derivatives that some sort of supply route can be readily established; the same route could also be used for weapon supply.

With the AR-15, the usual supply route is through normal commercial supply methods.

In some of the states of the USA AR-15s can be purchased quite openly with no legal restraints and the same applies to many other nations. Thus small arsenals can be built up without difficulty. Many countries have insisted on these open purchases being restricted to single-shot versions only, but any gunsmith or mechanic with a minimum of skill can usually convert such weapons to full automatic fire. Again, ammunition supply is no problem, for the 5.56-mm×45 cartridge design is based on that of a commercial hunting cartridge. Theft from arsenals is another source of Armalites, for not all armed forces treat their weapon stocks with the degree of security they require and many European guerrilla movements obtain their arms from just such sources.

While the AK-47s and the Armalites are widely used by guerrilla forces, they are not ideal for the purpose. They are far bulkier than sub-machine guns or pistols and in confined

spaces less destructive than grenades o bombs. But they have great effect as moral weapons. The very sight of a guerrilla arme with an assault rifle is enough to produce pani in many situations, which is just what the gue rilla wants. The rifle is also a very effectiv assassination weapon at ranges far greate than those obtained by normal hand weapon such as pistols, and the urban sniper is now well-established feature of terrorism. Th Armalites have the edge over the AK-47s in th respect but both are lethal enough in traine hands.

One weapon type seems likely to supple ment the AK-47s and the Armalites in guerril hands, and that is the Heckler und Koch G During the Iranian revolution huge numbers G3s were handed out to all and sundry, and fe of them were ever handed back. Numbers them are now appearing all over the world an no doubt more will appear in the future.

bove: An El Salvador guerrilla armed with a eckler und Koch G3, probably captured from a overnment soldier as it is the standard El alvador rifle.

ght: An armed Shi'ite grandmother holding an 16 for the camera, Lebanon, 1983. While this icture is probably posed, the struggle in Lebanon as seen all age groups actively fighting.

AK-74

The Soviet Union was surprisingly slow in following the Western adoption of small-calibre cartridges for its future weapon designs. Perhaps the huge numbers of AK-47s and AKMs already in service made such a change a low priority, so it was not until the early 1970s that any intimation of a new Warsaw Pact cartridge was given. In time it emerged that the new cartridge had a calibre of 5.45-mm×39 and the first examples of a new weapon to fire it were noted. In time the weapon emerged as the **AK-74**, which is now in full-scale production to meet the requirements of the Red Army; in time it can be expected that the AK-74 will be issued to other Warsaw Pact armed forces.

The AK-74 is nothing more than an AKM revised to suit the new cartridge. It is almost identical to the AKM in appearance, weight and overall dimensions. Some changes, such as a plastic magazine, have been introduced and there is a prominent muzzle brake. There are versions with the usual wooden stock and with a folding metal stock.

One matter relating to the AK-74 that deserves special mention is the bullet used. To gain maximum effect from the 5.45-mm calibre bullet the designers have adopted a design that is very effective but outlawed by international convention, for the steel-cored projectile has a hollow tip and the centre of gravity far to the rear. This has the effect that when the nose strikes a target the nose deforms, allowing the weight towards the rear to maintain the forward impetus and so tumble the bullet. In this way the small-calibre bullet can have an effect on a target far in excess of its cross-sectional area. Some high-velocity projectiles can display this nasty effect, but on some, such as the M193 5.56-mm cartridge, it is an unintended by-product. On the Soviet 5.45-mm the effect has been deliberately designed into the projectile. International conventions have for many years outlawed such 'Dum-Dum' bullets and its various progeny, but to date no corresponding strictures appear to have been forthcoming regarding the 5.45-mm bullet.

Specification (provisional)
Calibre: 5.45 mm (0.215 in)
Length: 930 mm (36.61 in)
Length of barrel: 400 mm (15.75 in)
Weight unloaded: 3.6 kg (7.94 lb)
Magazine: 30-round box
Rate of fire: 650 rpm
Muzzle velocity: 900 m (2,955 ft) per second

Right: An AK-74 (top), with an AKM for comparison beneath. The AK-74 has a skeleton butt, but note the prominent muzzle brake and the brown plastic magazine. Note also the size difference between the 5.45-mm cartridges (top) and the 7.62-mm×39 cartridges.

The AK-74 is now in wide use in the Soviet armies, and has seen service in Afghanistan, where this example was captured. It is to all intents and purposes a small calibre AKM, with many parts seeming identical.

Galil and R4

The exact provenance of the **Galil** assault rifle is a trifle clouded, for although it is claimed that the design is an indigenous Israeli effort, there are some obvious likenesses to the Finnish Valmet assault rifles that were produced in a variety of models and calibres. Things are made more confused by the fact that the Valmet rifles were modelled on the Soviet AK-47. Though it would be an oversimplification to state that the Galil is an AK-47 derivative, there are some resemblances in operation (the usual rotating bolt) and general layout, but these are now common to many designs.

The Galil assault rifle has been produced in both 5.56-mm and 7.62-mm calibres, and is now one of the most widely used weapons issued to the various Israeli armed forces. It is produced in three forms: one is known as the **Galil ARM**, which has a bipod and a carrying handle and is the all-purpose weapon; another is the **Galil AR**, which lacks the bipod and handle; and the third is the **Galil SAR**, which has a shorter barrel and no bipod or carrying handle. All three have folding stocks. The bipod on the ARM can be used as a barbed wire cutter, and all three versions have a bottle cap opener fitted as standard to prevent soldiers using other parts of the weapon as bottle openers (eg the magazine lips). A fixture over the muzzle acts as a rifle grenade launcher.

In its full ARM version the Galil can be used as a form of light machine-gun and 35- and 50-round magazines are produced; there is also a special 10-round magazine used to contain the special cartridges for launching rifle grenades. As usual a bayonet can be fitted.

The Galil has proved to be very effective in action and has attracted a great deal of overseas attention. Some

The Israeli Galil ARM assault rifle with the metal stock folded forward to reduce the length. This version cannot be used to fire rifle grenades and does not have the bipod fitted to the longer models. It can be found calibrated for 5.56-mm and 7.62-mm ammunition.

ave been exported and the design as also been copied – the Swedish .56-mm **FFV 890C** is obviously based n the Galil. One nation that negotiated cence production was South Africa, nd its version is the **R4**, now the standard rifle for the front-line units of the outh African defence forces. The R4 s produced in 5.56-mm calibre and iffers in some details from the original, the changes resulting mainly from perational experience in the South frican and Namibian bush. The R4 as also been exported to some unspecified countries.

Specification
Galil 5.56-mm ARM
Calibre: 5.56 mm (0.22 in)
Length: 979 mm (38.54 in)
Length of barrel: 460 mm (18.1 in)
Weight loaded: 4.62 kg (10.19 lb) with 5-round magazine
Magazine: 35- or 50-round boxes

Rate of fire, cyclic: 650 rpm
Muzzle velocity: 980 m (3,215 ft) per second

Specification
Galil 7.62-mm ARM
Calibre: 7.62 mm (0.3 in)
Length: 1050 mm (41.34 in)
Length of barrel: 533 mm (20.98 in)
Weight loaded: 4.67 kg (10.30 lb)
Magazine: 20-round box
Rate of fire, cyclic: 650 rpm
Muzzle velocity: 850 m (2,790 ft) per second

South Africa has adopted a modified form of the Galil as the new standard weapon of the Defence Forces: the R4 has been strengthened to withstand the rigours of the bush. The bipod is fitted as standard.

ITALY
Beretta AR70

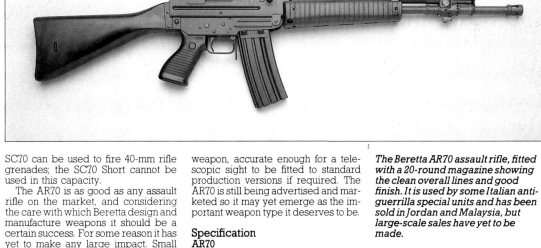

he **Beretta AR70** was developed following a series of manufacturer's in-ouse trials involving several types of ssault rifle designs, and from these volved a gas-operated design using ne rotary bolt locking principle but in very simple form. For increased safey Beretta decided to strengthen the ocking system with extra metal round the chamber area. The result is functional and well-made weapon hat can be stripped down into its few perating parts with ease.

There are three production versions f the AR70: one is the AR70 proper, /hich has a nylonite stock and furni-ure; another is the **SC70**, which has a olding butt constructed from shaped teel tubing; and the **SC70 Short** is a ersion of the SC70 with a shorter bar-el for special troops. The AR70 and

he AR70 has several equipment ptions, including the fitting of night ights, a bayonet or a MECAR rifle renade. The butt is relatively easy to emove and replace with a skeleton utt to convert the rifle to SC70 tandard.

SC70 can be used to fire 40-mm rifle grenades; the SC70 Short cannot be used in this capacity.

The AR70 is as good as any assault rifle on the market, and considering the care with which Beretta design and manufacture weapons it should be a certain success. For some reason it has yet to make any large impact. Small numbers have been adopted by the Italian special forces and some have been exported to Jordan and Malaysia, but the numbers involved have not been large. This is rendered even more odd when it is realized that the care in design and construction is such that the AR70 is a very accurate

weapon, accurate enough for a telescopic sight to be fitted to standard production versions if required. The AR70 is still being advertised and marketed so it may yet emerge as the important weapon type it deserves to be.

Specification
AR70
Calibre: 5.56 mm (0.22 in)
Length: 955 mm (37.60 in)
Length of barrel: 450 mm (17.72 in)
Weight loaded: 4.15 kg (9.15 lb)
Magazine: 30-round box
Rate of fire, cyclic: 650 rpm
Muzzle velocity: 950 m (3,115 ft) per second

The Beretta AR70 assault rifle, fitted with a 20-round magazine showing the clean overall lines and good finish. It is used by some Italian anti-guerrilla special units and has been sold in Jordan and Malaysia, but large-scale sales have yet to be made.

The Beretta AR70 in service in the Malaysian jungles; note the applied camouflage paint scheme. The AR70 weighs only 4.15 kg loaded with 30 rounds and is thus a fairly handy weapon for the small-statured Asian races to handle, but they have begun to use the M16.

Heckler und Koch G3

The **Heckler und Koch G3** assault rifle is a development of the CETME design and was adopted by the West German Bundeswehr during 1959. In many ways it has proved to be one of the most successful of all the post-war German weapon designs and it is still in production not only in West Germany but in numerous other countries which have produced their own weapons under licence.

Although the makers would not like it to be said, the Heckler und Koch G3 is the nearest that designers have come to the use-and-throw-away rifle. Despite the cost the G3 is a weapon designed from the outset for mass production using as much simple machinery as is possible. On the basis of the CETME design Heckler und Koch have developed the design so that plastics and pressed steel are used wherever possible. The ex-CETME locking roller system is retained to provide a form of delayed blow-back when firing.

There is a general resemblance to the FN FAL in the G3 but there are many differences. The G3 is a whole generation ahead of the FN FAL, and this is reflected not only in the general construction and materials but also in the development of a whole family of variants based on the basic G3. There are carbine versions, some with barrels so short they could qualify as sub-machine guns, sniper variants, light machine-gun versions with bipods and heavy barrels and so on. There is also a version for use with airborne or other such troops: this is the **G3A4**, which has a butt that telescopes onto either side of the receiver.

For all its overall simplicity the G3 has some unusual features. One is the bolt, which is so designed that it locks with the bulk of its mass forward and over the chamber to act as an extra mass to move when unlocking. Stripping is very simple and there are only a very few moving parts. With very few changes the basic G3 can be produced with a calibre of 5.56 mm and this version is already in production as the **Heckler und Koch HK 33**.

The success of the G3 can be seen in the number of nations that have

adopted the type. There are to date no fewer than 48, and of these 13 produce their own weapons under licence. The G3 was prominent in the overthrow of the Shah in Iran and was one of the weapons obtained despite sanctions by Rhodesia when defying the world before the establishment of Zimbabwe. Some nations find it profitable to produce the G3 under licence for further export sales. Into this category have come France and the United Kingdom. In many ways the G3 can be regarded as one of the most important of all modern assault rifles, but it uses the over-powerful NATO 7.62-mm×51 cartridge, in common with other de-

signs such as the FN FAL. Despite this it remains a popular assault rifle and one that will remain in production and service for years to come.

Specification
Heckler und Koch G3A3
Calibre: 7.62 mm (0.3 in)
Length: 1025 mm (40.35 in)
Length of barrel: 450 mm (17.72 in)
Weight loaded: 5.025 kg (11.08 lb)
Magazine: 20-round box
Rate of fire, cyclic: 500-600 rpm
Muzzle velocity: 780-800 m (2,560-2,625 ft) per second

The Heckler und Koch HK 21, a 7.62-mm light machine-gun version of the basic G3. This version uses a belt feed which can be altered to take a 20-round box magazine if required. This model is produced in Portugal and has been widely sold in Africa.

Using the same basic layout as the G3, this 5.56-mm version is known as the HK 33. It can take 20- or 40-round magazines and exists in several versions, including a special sniper's rifle and a version with a telescopic folding butt. Most versions can fire rifle grenades.

Heckler und Koch G11

With the **Heckler und Koch G11** the way ahead in small-arms design can be seen. Although it is still not yet fully developed, the G11 has taken a great step forward in the concepts of small-arms design to such an extent that it might even be described as revolutionary.

The G11 is unusual in many ways but at the heart of it all there is the ammunition, which is caseless. Caseless ammunition has been tried in the past but Heckler und Koch appear to have been able to make it work. It took much development before the new round emerged as a rectangular block of propellant with the 4.7-mm calibre bullet projecting from one end. When fired, all the propellant is consumed within the chamber, leaving no case to eject. The propellant in its final form is sensitive enough to fire but not so sensitive that it will 'cook-off' from the chamber temperature after a period of firing.

Having developed the caseless ammunition Heckler und Koch have now developed a rifle to use it. This is the G11, a very unusual weapon indeed. In appearance it is quite unlike anything else of its kind. The entire rifle, including the barrel, is enclosed in a smooth outer casing with a combination optical sight/carrying handle above and a pistol grip and trigger beneath. There are no projections or apparent holes through which dirt and debris can enter (other than the muzzle) and the only control is a rotary disc set into the butt. This disc, or knob, is the only clue to the G11's mechanism, which is unique. Very basically, the caseless rounds are fed vertically downwards into a rotary device which turns in line with the barrel for firing and then rotates back for the next round. The rounds are packed inside sealed magazines each holding 50 rounds. These magazines are slipped into the rifle over the barrel so there is

no way debris can get into them, and once their contents have been fired they are simply removed and discarded. In this way the G11 gets over the disadvantages of the reusable magazine, and another possible cause of feed problems is removed. If a round fails to fire the misfire is cleared by rotating the rotary disc by hand. This opens an ejection port which is closed again once the clearing operation is complete.

A simple switch by the trigger can be used to select either single-shot, automatic or three-round bursts. Using the last, the G11 can fire up to 2,000 rpm (cyclic) and the rate of the burst is such that it sounds like a single round being fired.

There are still many features of the G11 about which details have yet to be released. The exact method of operating the rotating ammunition feed/bolt has yet to be fully explained and many of the composition details of the prop-

ellant are being maintained as commercial secrets. Development is still continuing and it may be some time before the G11 emerges as a full operational weapon, but the West German armed forces are watching progress closely and may even delay the adoption of the new NATO 5.56-mm SS109 round in favour of the new concept.

Specification
Calibre: 4.7 mm (0.185 in)
Length: 750 mm (29.53 in)
Length of barrel: 540 mm (21.26 in)
Weight loaded with 100 rounds: 4.5 kg (9.92 lb)
Magazine: 50-round sealed strip
Rate of fire: 600 rpm (cyclic, automatic) or 2,000 rpm (cyclic, three-round bursts)
Muzzle velocity: (estimated) 930 m (3,050 ft) per second

Modern Sniping Rifles

Since the introduction of accurate long-range firearms to the battlefield, the sniper, or sharpshooter as he used to be called, has had an influence upon the conduct of war out of all proportion to the numbers involved in his deadly trade. In that time his weapon has evolved enormously.

The modern sniping rifle is a remarkable piece of equipment that embodies all the finer points of the gun designer's, gun maker's and ammunition specialist's skills. Although it is very often based on an existing design it is usually manufactured to high degrees of precision to ensure that its user, the sniper, secures the all-important first-round hit on the target every time.

Sniping rifles fall into two general categories. The first has already been mentioned: the conversion of the existing weapon, usually a standard service rifle. These very often do not look all that different from the originals and can often be handled and used in much the same manner. The second category is very different, for its members are the specially designed rifles that often appear not to be rifles at all but some form of 'space-age' weaponry. There are several examples of the latter in this study and they will be easily discerned. They seem to be (and often are) marvels of the gun maker's art, but they are rarely weapons that the sniper will want to use on the battlefield. All sniper's rifles require

The Yugoslav M76 semi-automatic rifle, seen here fitted with a passive optical night sight, has obvious design similarities to the Soviet Dragunov SVD. It uses a 10-round magazine and is in service with the Yugoslav armed forces.

special care and handling, but some of the more recent examples show every mark of being laboratory test tools rather than practical weapons.

Most of the current crop of sniper's rifles are included in this study. They include stalwarts such as the Soviet SVD and British L42A1, magnificient tools for the job such as the US Marines' M40A1 and the superlative Mauser SP 66. No doubt less readily acceptable to the sniper in the front line are designs such as the Walther WA2000 and the decidedly odd-looking Iver Johnson rifles. But one thing all these rifles have in common is that they are extremely accurate, and in the hands of the right man they are lethal.

The Israelis have eschewed the radical design approach which has produced such over-complex and unreliable weapons as the Walther WA 2000 in favour of the studied development of their existing service rifle into the Galil sniper.

7.62-mm SSG 69

With this Austrian rifle the designation **SSG 69** stands for **Scharfschützengewehr 69** (sharp-shooter rifle 69), 1969 being the year of the weapon's acceptance for service by the Austrian army. It is manufactured by the Steyr-Daimler-Puch AG concern at Steyr and was, in 1969, the latest in a long line of rifles produced by the concern.

The 7.62-mm (0.3-in) SSG 69 has some unusual design features, one of them being the use of a Männlicher bolt action with a form of rear locking instead of the far more common Mauser forward-lug locking. The bolt action is now uncommon, although it has been used on other recent Steyr rifles, and is so arranged that the entire action is very strong and the chamber is well

The Steyr SSG 69 rifle is the standard Austrian army sniper's rifle, and is used by mountain troops as it is possible for a single sniper to virtually seal a mountain pass against advancing troops for long periods. The SSG 69 is robust enough to survive in such conditions and retain its accuracy.

within the receiver for added rigidity. A safety catch locks both the bolt and firing pin when engaged. The barrel is cold-forged using a machine hammering process in which the barrel rifling is hammered into the bore using a mandrel. Another odd feature is the use of the Männlicher rotary magazine, a design feature that dates back to well before World War I. This rotary magazine holds five rounds, but a more orthodox 10-round box magazine can be fitted.

The rifle stock is made of a synthetic material and is adjustable in length to suit the firer. The firer can also adjust the double-pull trigger pressure. It is also possible to make various adjustments to the standard Kahles ZF69 telescopic sight which has a magnification of ×6. Other forms of sight (including night sights) can be used on the SSG 69, the receiver having an overhead longitudinal rib that can accommodate a wide range of vision devices. 'Iron' sights are provided for emergency use only.

The SSG 69 is very accurate. Trials have shown that it is possible to fire 10-round groups no larger than 400 mm (15.75 in) at 800 m (875 yards), which is the maximum graduated range of the ZF69 sight; at shorter

ranges the groupings get much tighter.

Since the introduction of the SSG 6 Steyr has developed some more adv anced sniper rifle models, but the SSC 69 remains in service with the Au strians for the simple reason that it is a excellent military sniper's rifle and fa more practical than some of the mor modern technical marvels now avai able. A target shooting version of th SSG 69 with a heavier barrel an match sights has been produced.

Specification
SSG 69
Calibre: 7.62 mm (0.3 in)
Lengths: overall 1140 mm (44.9 in); barrel 650 mm (25.6 in)
Weight: empty, with sight 4.6 kg (10.14 lb)
Muzzle velocity: 860 m (2,821 ft) per second
Magazine capacity: 5-round rotary or 10-round box

The Steyr SSG 69 rifle uses a Kahles ZF69 telescopic sight graduated up to 800 m (875 yards) – this example i not fitted with the usual 'iron' sights. The SSG 69 uses an unusual five-round rotary magazine, but can also be fitted with a 10-round box magazine.

Beretta Sniper

When the market for high-precision sniper's rifles expanded in the 1970s, virtually every major small-arms manufacturer in Europe and elsewhere started to design weapons they thought would meet international requirements. Some of these designs have fared better than others on the market, but one that does appear to have been overlooked by many is the **Beretta Sniper** 7.62-mm (0.3-in) sniping rifle. This design appears to have been given no numerical designation and it has only recently appeared on the scene, two factors that would normally indicate that the rifle is only just out of the development stage. But there are reports that it is already in use with some Italian paramilitary police units

for internal security duties.

Compared with many of the latest 'space-age' sniper rifle designs, the Beretta offering is almost completely orthodox but well up to the usual high standards of Beretta design and finish. The Sniper uses a manual rotary bolt action allied to the usual heavy barrel, and one of its most prominent features is the large and unusually-shaped hole carved into the high-quality wooden stock that forms a prominent pistol grip for the trigger.

Despite the overall conventional design there are one or two advanced features on the Sniper. The wooden forestock conceals a forward-pointing counterweight under the free-floating barrel that acts as a damper to reduce

the barrel vibrations produced on firing. At the front end of the forestock is a location point for securing a light adjustable bipod to assist aiming. The underside of the forestock contains a slot for an adjustable forward hand stop for the firer, and this forestop can also be used as the attachment point for a firing sling if one is required. The butt and cheek pads are adjustable and the muzzle has a flash hider.

Unlike many of its modern counterparts the Beretta Sniper is fully provided with a set of all-adjustable precision match sights, even though these would not normally be used for the sniping role. Over the receiver is a standard NATO optical or night sight mounting attachment to accommodate

virtually any military sighting syster The normal telescopic sight is th widely-used Zeiss Divari Z with a zoo capability from ×1.5 to ×6, but othe types can be fitted.

Specification
Beretta Sniper
Calibre: 7.62 mm (0.3 in)
Lengths: overall 1165 mm (45.87 in); barrel 586 mm (23 in)
Weights: empty 5.55 kg (12.23 lb); complete 7.2 kg (15.87 lb)
Muzzle velocity: about 865 m (2,838 ft) per second
Magazine capacity: 5 rounds

FRANCE
FR-F1 and FR-F2

When the French army required a sniper's rifle to replace the varied selection of weapons which it had used since World War II, it decided that the easiest design course to follow was to modify its existing service rifle, the 7.5-mm (0.295-in) modèle 1936. This rifle had the dubious distinction of being one of the very last bolt-action rifles to be accepted as a standard service weapon by any of the major European powers, but it was not regarded as a very good design, even at the time, and was used mainly because of its French origins. Using this weapon as a starting point the resultant sniper's rifle, the **mle FR-F1**, emerged as not particularly brilliant.

The number of modifications involved in converting the modèle 1936 into the FR-F1 meant that very little of the original remained; it was just about discernible that the modèle 1936 had been used as the origin, but that was all. The main change was the introduction of a bipod, the addition of a pistol grip for the trigger, a longer barrel with a long flash hider, and a telescopic sight. The butt was provided with a

In this photograph the French sniper is using the telescopic sight of his FR-F1 as an observation aid, resting the barrel on a tree branch. He would never fire the weapon from such a stance, for accuracy would be minimal.

cheek rest and the bolt action considerably altered.

Even with all these alterations the mle FR-F1 was not an immediate international success. For a start, the rifle fired the old French 7.5-mm standard cartridge at a time when other nations were changing to the new 7.62-mm (0.3-in) NATO round. This change to the new cartridge was so pronounced that eventually the French had to convert to it as well, and later-production mle FR-F1s were chambered for 7.62-mm ammunition; many of the older 7.5-mm rifles are still in use, however. The modèle 1936 bolt action was also retained, albeit in a much altered form. This action was regarded as an awkward one to use, and even in its revised form was little improved. The bipod was also rather flimsy and dif-

ficult to adjust. Also the weapon was considered by many to be too heavy.

The mle FR-F1 has now been replaced by the **mle FR-F2**. Basically this is much the same as the earlier weapon, but the long barrel is now encased in a thick black nylonite sleeve to reduce the heat haze from the barrel that might interfere with the performance of some night sights. The bipod has also been altered and relocated so that it is now secured directly to the barrel. The forestock has been changed from all-wood to all-metal, covered in a plastic coating. The mle

FR-F2 has only been in production for a limited period so it is still too early to determine how it will fare in international esteem.

Specification
FR-F1
Calibre: 7.5 mm (0.295 in) or 7.62 mm (0.3 in)
Lengths: overall 1138 mm (44.8 in); barrel 552 mm (21.73 in)
Weight: empty 5.42 kg (11.95 kg)
Muzzle velocity: 852 m (2,795 ft) per second
Magazine capacity: 10 rounds

UK
Rifle 7.62-mm L42A1

The Lee-Enfield rifle has had a long career with the British army reaching back to the 1890s, and throughout that time the basic Lee-Enfield manual bolt mechanism has remained little changed. It is still in service with the army to this day in the form of the **Rifle 7.62-mm L42A1**. These weapons are used only for sniping, and are conversions of 0.303-in (7.7-mm) No. 4 Mk 1(T) and Mk 1*(T) rifles, as used during World War II. The conversions involved new barrels, a new magazine, some changes to the trigger mechanism and fixed sights, and alterations to the forestock. The World War II No. 32 or 3 telescopic sight (renamed the L1A1) and its mounting over the receiver have been retained, and the result has for long been a good, rugged and serviceable sniping rifle, used not only by the army but also by the Royal Marines.

In modern terms the L42A1 is very much the product of a previous generation, but it can still give excellent first-shot results at ranges over 800 m

(875 yards), although this depends very much on the skill of the firer and the type of ammunition used. Normally the ammunition is selected from special 'Green Spot' high-accuracy ammunition produced at the Royal Ordnance facility at Radway Green. The rifle itself is also the subject of a great deal of care, calibration and attention. When not in use it is stowed (and transported) in a special wooden chest that contains not only the rifle but the optical sight, cleaning gear, firing sling and perhaps a few spares such as extra magazines: the L42A1 retains the 10-round magazine of the 0.303-in version but with a revised outline to

accommodate the new rimless ammunition. The often-overlooked weapon record books are also kept in the chest.

The L42A1 is not the only 7.62-mm Lee-Enfield rifle still around. A special match-shooting version known as the **L39A1** is still retained for competitive use, and there are two other models, the **Envoy** and the **Enforcer**. The former may be regarded as a civilian match version of the L39A1, while the Enforcer is a custom-built variant of the L42A1 with a heavier barrel and revised butt outline, produced specifically for police use. The L39A1 and Envoy are not normally fitted with

optical sights but the basic information relating to the L42A1 applies to the three variants.

The L42A1 is now due to be replaced by a new sniper's rifle, a 7.62-mm design from Accuracy International.

Specification
L42A1
Calibre: 7.62 mm (0.3 in)
Lengths: overall 1181 mm (46.5 in); barrel 699 mm (27.5 in)
Weight: 4.43 kg (9.76 lb)
Muzzle velocity: 838 m (2,750 ft) per second
Magazine capacity: 10 rounds

Below: The L42A1 rifle is a 7.62-mm (0.30-in) conversion of an earlier .303-in (7.70-mm) Lee-Enfield rifle, and it has served the British Army well over the years. It was used by the Army and the Royal Marines during the Falklands war, usually in the form shown here with the weapon covered in camouflage scrim netting.

Changes to the old No. 4 Lee-Enfield rifle for the 7.62-mm (0.30-in) sniping role involved a new heavy barrel, a new 10-round box magazine, and cutting back the forestock over the barrel. A cheek rest was added to the butt and the rifle was virtually rebuilt. Changes were also made to the trigger, and a scope mount was added.

Parker-Hale Model 82

The Parker Hale Model 82 was selected by the Canadian Armed Forces as their sniper rifle, and is seen here in winter camouflage. It uses a Mauser-type bolt action and is fitted with a four-round box magazine.

Parker-Hale Limited of Birmingham has for many years been manufacturing match rifles and their associated sights, and also produces sniping rifles. The company's best-known product to date is the 7.62-mm (0.3-in) **Parker-Hale Model 82**, also known as the **Parker-Hale 1200TX**. The Model 82 has been accepted for military and police service by several nations.

In appearance and design terms the Model 82 is an entirely conventional sniping weapon. It uses a manual bolt action very similar to that used on the classic Mauser 98 rifle, allied to a heavy free-floating barrel; the barrel weighs 1.98 kg (4.365 lb) and is manufactured from chrome molybdenum steel. An integral four-round magazine is provided. The trigger mechanism is an entirely self-contained unit that can be adjusted as required.

The Model 82 is available in a number of forms to suit any particular customer requirements. Thus an adjustable cheek pad may be provided if wanted, and the butt lengths can be altered by adding or taking away butt pads of various thicknesses. The sights too are subject to several variations, but the Model 82 is one weapon that is normally supplied with 'iron' match-type sights. If an optical sight is fitted the rear-sights have to be removed to allow the same mounting block to be used. The forward mounting block is machined into the receiver. Various types of 'iron' foresight or optical night sights can be fitted.

The Australian army uses the Model 82 fitted with a Kahles Helia ZF 69 telescopic sight. The Canadian army uses a version of the Model 82/1200TX altered to meet local requirements; this service knows the Model 82 as the **Rifle 7.62-mm C3**. New Zealand also uses the Model 82.

Parker-Hale produces a special training version of the Model 82 known as the **Model 83**. This single-shot rifle is fitted with match sights only and the is no provision for a telescopic sight has been accepted by the Briti Ministry of Defence as the **Cad Training Rifle L81A1**.

The Model 82 has now been u dated to the **Model 85**. This has a vised butt outline compared with t Model 82, a 10-round box magazi and a bipod (optional on the Model 8 is fitted as standard. This weapon w one of the rifles competitively test by the British army to determine new sniper rifle, a competition won Accuracy International.

Specification
Model 82
Calibre: 7.62 mm (0.3 in)
Lengths: 1162 mm (45.75 in); barrel 660 mm (25.98 in)
Weight: unloaded 4.8 kg (10.58 lb)
Muzzle velocity: about 840 m (2,756 f per second
Magazine capacity: 4 rounds

Below: In service with the armed forces of Australia, New Zealand ar Canada, the Parker Hale Model 82 intended to hit point targets at up t 400 m in good light, or up to the maximum range of any sights fitted

Mauser SP 66 and SP 86

The Mauser-Werke at Oberndorf in West Germany can lay claim to a long and distinguished design and production background for its manual bolt-action rifles that are now known under the blanket name of Mauser. The company's forward-locking bolt action is still widely used by designers who require maximum locking with accuracy, but the masters of its use are now undoubtedly the Mauser-Werke. The company has even introduced its own variations to the action, one of them being the relocation of the bolt handle from the rear of the bolt to the front.

On most rifles this would be of little account, but on a specialist sniper rifle it means that the firer can operate the bolt action without having to move his head out of the way as the bolt itself can be made relatively short; it also means the barrel can be made correspon-

dingly longer for enhanced accuracy. This has been done on a custom-built Mauser-Werke sniper's rifle known as the **Mauser SP 66**. The revised bolt action is but one instance of the care lavished on this weapon, for it also has a heavy barrel, a butt with a carefully contoured thumb aperture, provision for adjustable cheek and butt pads, and a special muzzle attachment. This last is so designed that on firing the great bulk of the resultant flash is directed out of the firer's vision, and it also acts as a muzzle brake to reduce recoil. Reducing both these factors enables a user to fire second and subsequent shots more rapidly.

The standard of finish and careful design throughout the production of the SP 66 is very high. Even such details as roughening all surfaces likely to be handled to prevent slipping have been carried out with meticulous care, and the trigger is extra wide to allow it to be used when gloves have to worn.

The sights have been selected w equal attention. There are no fix sights and the standard telesco sight is a Zeiss-Divari ZA with zo capability of from ×1.5 to ×6. Ni sights can be fitted, though it is reco mended that the manufacturer sele and calibrates them to an exact ma for the rifle on which they are used. is usual with such rifles the ammunit

This version of the SP 66, known as the Model 86 SR, is equipped with a set of target sights and a bipod for super-accurate competition shooting; the service version is basically the same weapon fitted with a telescopic sight but without the bipod.

red from the SP 66 is taken from care-
lly-selected batches of 7.62-mm (0.3-
.) NATO rounds produced specifical-
y for use by snipers.

The SP 66 has been a considerable
iccess even though it is manufac-
red virtually to order only. It is in
ervice with the West German armed
rces and more have been sold to a
rther 12 or so nations, most of which
re unwilling to divulge their names for
ecurity reasons.

pecification
P 66
alibre: 7.62 mm (0.3 in)
engths: overall not divulged; barrel
30 mm (26.77 in)
Veight: not divulged
Muzzle velocity: about 860 m (2,821 ft)
er second
Magazine capacity: 3 rounds

*This Mauser SP 86 is fitted with a
night vision device. It is
recommended that the manufacturer
selects and calibrates the sights of
each individual weapon.*

*Long-range accuracy depends on
good ammunition, and Mauser select
theirs from batches of NATO 7.62-
mm cartridges. This Mauser is fitted
with a laser rangefinder.*

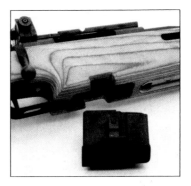

*A close-up of the double-row,
detachable nine-round magazine of
the Mauser SP 86, one of the
improvements incorporated into this
development of the SP 66.*

WEST GERMANY

Walther WA2000

'ith the **Walther WA2000** it would
ppear that small-arms design is
ready in the 'Star Wars' era, for this
eapon has an appearance all of its
vn. The rifle was designed from the
itset for the sniping role and the
'alther approach has been to put
iide all known small-arms design
recepts and start from scratch after
alysing the requirements.

The most important part of any rifle
esign is the barrel, for it alone imparts
e required degree of accuracy.
alther decided to clamp the barrel
the front and rear to ensure that the
rque imparted by a bullet passing
rough the bore would not lift the bar-
l away from the intended point of
m. The barrel is also fluted longitudi-

nally over its entire length. This not
only provides more cooling area but
also reduces the vibrations imparted
on firing, vibrations that can also cause
a bullet to stray. The designers also
decided to go for a gas-operated
mechanism to reduce the need for bolt
manipulation between shots, and to reduce recoil effects to a minimum the
barrel is in direct line with the shoulder so that the muzzle will not be
thrown upwards after every shot.

Thus the strange outline of the
WA2000 begins to make sense, but
there is more to come for the WA2000
is a 'bullpup' design with the gas-operated bolt mechanism behind the trigger group. Such an arrangement
makes the overall design that much

shorter and easier to handle without
reducing the barrel length. It does
mean that the ejection port is close to
the firer, so special left- and right-hand
versions have to be produced.

The overall standard of finish of the
WA2000 is all that one would expect.
The butt pad and cheek rests are
adjustable, and there is a carefully-
shaped pistol grip for added aiming
stability. The normal telescopic sight is
a Schmidt und Bender ×2.5 to ×10
zoom, but other types can be fitted.

Walther has decided that the best
round for the sniping role is now the
.300 (7.62-mm) Winchester Magnum
cartridge, but while the WA2000 is
chambered for this round others such
as the 7.62-mm (0.3-in) NATO or much-

favoured 7.5-mm (0.295-in) Swiss cartridge can be accommodated with the
required alterations to the bolt and rifling.

Specification
WA2000
Calibre: see text
Lengths: overall 905 mm (35.63 in);
barrel 650 mm (25.59 in)
Weights: empty, no sights 6.95 kg
(15.32 lb); loaded, with sight, 8.31 kg
(18.32 lb)
Magazine capacity: 6 rounds

*Supplied with a Schmidt & Bender
telescopic sight, the remarkable
Walther WA2000 fires the 0.30-in
Winchester magnum cartridge.*

Heckler & Koch G3 SG/1 Rifle

front sight
flash suppressor
operating handle
operating handle support
barrel
lockin
bipod (closed)
7.62-mm round

The range of Heckler & Koch rifles has now become so large that a weapon suitable for just about any application can apparently be selected from the array. Sniper's rifles have not been neglected but generally speaking most of these specialized weapons are little more than standard designs produced with a little extra care, a few accessories and a mounting for a telescopic sight. This does not detract from their serviceability or efficiency, many of them being more suitable for field conditions than other designs that have been produced with emphasis on supreme accuracy rather than serviceability. Typical of these Heckler & Koch sniper weapons are the 7.62-mm (0.3-in) **H&K G3 A3ZF** and **G3 SG/1** pro-

duced for the West German police. The latter model has a light bipod.

Good as these weapons are they are basically only 'breathed on' versions of standard weapons originally designed with mass production rather than specialization in mind. Accordingly Heckler & Koch has turned its attentions to production of a special design known as the **PSG 1** that continues to use the basic Heckler & Koch rotary lock mechanism but allied to a semi-automatic system and a precision heavy barrel with a polygonal-rifled bore. G3 influence can still be seen in the outlines of the receiver and in the 5- or 20-round magazine housing (it is also possible to load single rounds manually), but the rest is all-new. Forward of

the magazine housing is a new fore-stock and the long barrel, while the butt has been reconfigured to the widely-used all-adjustable form.

The PSG 1 uses a ×6 telescopic sight adjustable up to 600 m (656 yards). It has been stated that the weapon is extremely accurate. These claims are difficult to confirm independently as the weapon is still in the development stage with the military and paramilitary police market in mind. It is even possible that the final form of the PSG 1 will alter, the stamped receiver body perhaps being replaced with something purpose-built to ensure that the sight mounting is more rigid. For special purposes there has been mention of a precision aiming tripod for this

weapon, but its form is still u announced. It may well emerge th this tripod will be an adaptation of or of the Heckler & Koch machine-g mountings; the butt used on the PSG is a much-modified HK 21 machine gun component.

Specification
PSG 1
Calibre: 7.62 mm (0.3 in)
Lengths: overall 1208 mm (47.56 in); barrel 650 mm (25.59 in)
Weight: less magazine 8.1 kg (17.85 l
Muzzle velocity: about 860 m (2,821 ft per second
Magazine capacity: 5 or 20 rounds

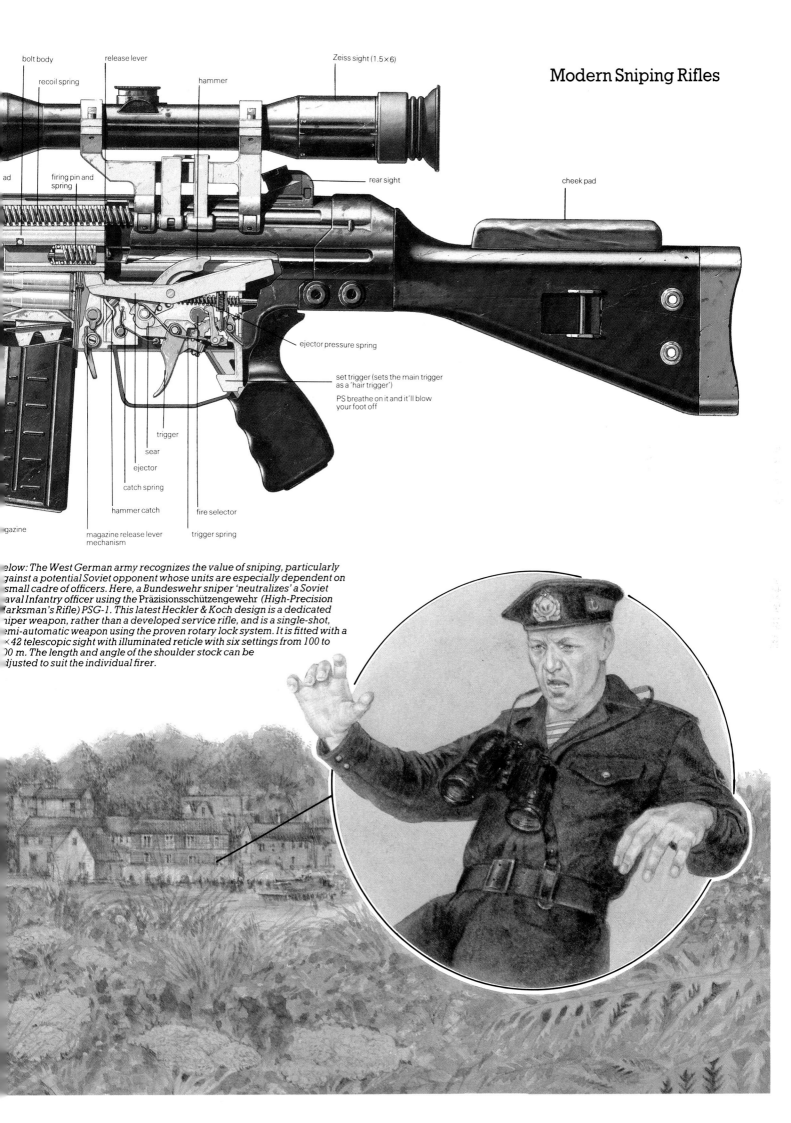

Modern Sniping Rifles

bolt body

release lever

recoil spring

hammer

Zeiss sight (1.5×6)

firing pin and spring

rear sight

cheek pad

ejector pressure spring

set trigger (sets the main trigger as a 'hair trigger')

PS breathe on it and it'll blow your foot off

trigger

sear

ejector

catch spring

hammer catch

fire selector

magazine

magazine release lever mechanism

trigger spring

Below: The West German army recognizes the value of sniping, particularly against a potential Soviet opponent whose units are especially dependent on a small cadre of officers. Here, a Bundeswehr sniper 'neutralizes' a Soviet Naval Infantry officer using the Präzisionsschützengewehr *(High-Precision Marksman's Rifle) PSG-1. This latest Heckler & Koch design is a dedicated sniper weapon, rather than a developed service rifle, and is a single-shot, semi-automatic weapon using the proven rotary lock system. It is fitted with a ×42 telescopic sight with illuminated reticle with six settings from 100 to 00 m. The length and angle of the shoulder stock can be adjusted to suit the individual firer.*

Snipers in Action:
The Tangling Machine

Clausewitz once described the many natural factors affecting the movement of armies as 'friction'. To the normal military headaches such as river crossings, mountains and the weather, the sniper can add such problems as dead commanders, increasing the normal friction to the point where the whole delicately-balanced army machine seizes up.

The popular image of a sniper is one man firing at a distant enemy from a carefully-concealed position. This may have been true in past conflicts, but it is anticipated that any major war of the future will be a series of mobile battles in which the sniper will have little chance to exercise such traditional skills. What role, therefore, is there for the sniper in such a war, and why is a great deal of thought and money going into providing him with highly sophisticated equipment?

An FR-F1 sniper's rifle is shown in use somewhere in the French Alps. This rifle is based on a service weapon first used in 1936, although only a few parts from the original are retained. Normally the sniper would use the bipod, but in snow this is not always possible. Note the unorthodox holding method employed here.

The short answer is that even in this era of highly-mechanized warfare there will be times when battles will settle down to allow both sides to regroup and supply themselves in preparation for the next round: tanks and all the other associated machines of mobile warfare will have to be resupplied with fuel and ammunition, and casualties replaced. This takes time, and during this time the sniper can return to his task, which is little changed from that of old, i.e. being the big game hunter of the battlefield.

The sniper is not just a killer who can pick off his targets at long ranges. He is also a highly-trained observer who can move across country in such a way as to avoid notice by an enemy and thus reach areas in which he is not expected. Once there he does not simply fire at will. He has to save his all-important fire for the

The Steyr AUG assault rifle can be produced in a sniper version fitted with a heavy barrel, a folding bipod and the usual telescopic sight. However, the 5.56-mm (0.219-in) cartridge fired is designed for relatively close ranges and lacks the power of the heavier 7.62-mm round, so its effectiveness is limited.

Right: The Galil sniper rifle is a first-rate weapon, externally similar to the standard assault rifle from which it was developed but in fact a very different gun; each part is manufactured to a very high standard and is capable of impressive accuracy.

Snipers in Action

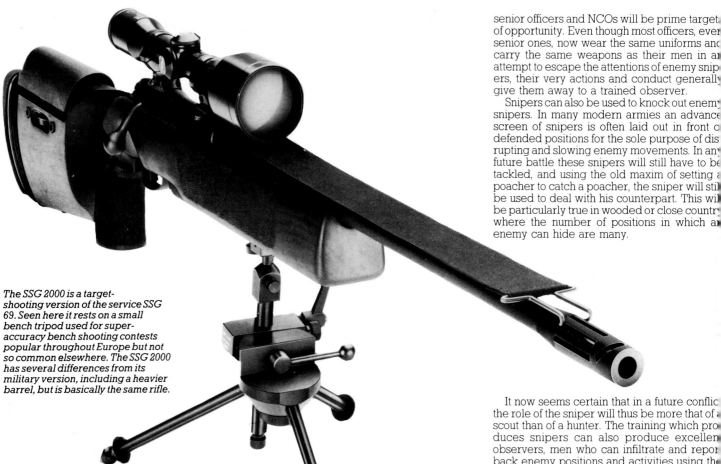

The SSG 2000 is a target-shooting version of the service SSG 69. Seen here it rests on a small bench tripod used for super-accuracy bench shooting contests popular throughout Europe but not so common elsewhere. The SSG 2000 has several differences from its military version, including a heavier barrel, but is basically the same rifle.

important target. For this to happen he acts not as an independent agent but under strict control after careful preparation and planning.

In any future conflict the sniper will rarely operate alone. In general, each infantry battalion in any army has a team of about eight snipers (sometimes more), and these often operate in pairs. The idea is that one man concentrates on observation and location of targets, using a telescope or binoculars, while the other man sticks to the shooting. This is not a hard and fast rule, for there will be many occasions when the snipers will be operating primarily as observers and will use their weapons only if absolutely necessary or if a target of importance is detected. At other times the sniper may work alone.

Interval in warfare

In the static conditions produced by the intervals in mobile warfare there is much the sniper can do. He can infiltrate enemy positions to observe movements and strengths, and he can disrupt and unsettle an enemy attempting to recuperate or carry out maintenance tasks. And if he remains within his own defended area the sniper can keep watch for an enemy carrying out exactly the same infiltration tactics in return. He can also prevent enemy reconnaissance patrols from getting too close by skilful anticipation of the enemy's likely approach paths and the establishment of an appropriate ambush point.

In more mobile conditions the sniper can still have an important battlefield role. Infantry do not constantly operate from the armoured confines of personnel carriers: to close with an enemy they have to leave their 'battle taxis' and fight on foot. They then become prone to all the

battlefield hazards encountered by the foot soldiers of the past: machine-gun or other weapon fire can then pin them down, often from undetected fire positions.

Under such circumstances the sniper may infiltrate enemy positions before an advance gets under way. Using camouflage and stealth, small teams of snipers can possible work their way through the enemy lines to lie in wait until their colleagues make their move. They can then smooth the advance by detecting and knocking out weapon positions from the rear, probably with the old ploy of knocking out the weapon rather than its team. In past conflicts a heavy weapon such as a machine-gun or mortar was often taken out of action far more effectively by a single well-placed armour-piercing bullet than by the slower and more uncertain method of knocking out every member of the weapon team: the same no doubt applies to modern weapons such as missile-launchers, and some sniper teams will no doubt be detailed to infiltrate as far into the enemy rear as the artillery lines to create mayhem and general disruption. Weapons will not be the only targets to be engaged. As always the enemy

senior officers and NCOs will be prime targets of opportunity. Even though most officers, even senior ones, now wear the same uniforms and carry the same weapons as their men in an attempt to escape the attentions of enemy snipers, their very actions and conduct generally give them away to a trained observer.

Snipers can also be used to knock out enemy snipers. In many modern armies an advance screen of snipers is often laid out in front of defended positions for the sole purpose of disrupting and slowing enemy movements. In any future battle these snipers will still have to be tackled, and using the old maxim of setting a poacher to catch a poacher, the sniper will still be used to deal with his counterpart. This will be particularly true in wooded or close country where the number of positions in which an enemy can hide are many.

It now seems certain that in a future conflict the role of the sniper will thus be more that of a scout than of a hunter. The training which produces snipers can also produce excellent observers, men who can infiltrate and report back enemy positions and activities using the latest miniature radios that transmit information in short 'bursts' of coded data. Such information is in general invaluable to a commander who also knows that his observer has the capability to knock out important enemy weapons and men. Exactly how secondary this offensive capability will be to the observing function is almost impossible to predict, but one thing that does seem certain is that the trained sniper will rarely use his rifle to take out targets at ranges greater than 800 m (875 yards): there are usually too many imponderables involved and the sniper is always loth to give away his position.

Why then, one might ask, is so much effort directed towards designing and producing the super-accurate weapons that are featured in this study? The short answer is that they are intended more for internal security and terrorist/hostage situations than overt military conflict. Weapons such as the Iver Johnson Model 300 and Walther WA2000 would not last long on any battlefield. They are too demanding of care and are generally too flimsy to withstand the unavoidable knocks and bumps of standard military service, even though they can theoretically ensure a hit at 1000 m (1,094 yards). The military sniper is far more likely to be carrying a weapon resembling the SVD, the Galil sniping rifle, or the US Marines' M49A1, a weapon that would not have looked too much out of place on a World War II battlefield. Whatever weapon he carries, the military sniper of any future conflict will still have to know that when he sees a target he will be able to hit it, first time and effectively. Even if the battle moves to and fro around him the sniper will still be there watching and waiting, still carefully concealed and with a definite objective in mind: to use his observation skills and his skill-at-arms for the maximum possible results.

SVD

nyone who reads accounts of the
reat Patriotic War (World War II to
e rest of the world) cannot but help
te the emphasis given to sniping by
e Soviet army. That emphasis re-
ains undiminished, and to carry out
e sniping role the Soviets have de-
eloped what is widely regarded as
e of the best sniper's rifles around
day; this is the **SVD**, sometimes
own as the **Dragunov**.

The SVD (Samozariyadnyia Vintokv-
a Dragunova) first appeared in 1963,
d ever since has been one of the
ost prized of infantry trophies. It is a
mi-automatic weapon that uses the
me operating principles as the AK-
assault rifle but allied to a revised
s-operated system. Unlike the AK-
, which uses the short 7.62-mm (0.3-
)×39 cartridge, the SVD fires the old-
r 7.62-mm×54R rimmed cartridge
iginally introduced during the 1890s
r the Mosin-Nagant rifles. This re-
ains a good round for the sniping
le, and as it is still used on some
viet machine-guns availability is no
oblem.

The SVD has a long barrel, but the
eapon is so balanced that it handles
ell and recoil is not excessive. If the
ng barrel is not a decisive recogni-
n point then the cut-away butt cer-
nly is. The weapon is normally fired
ing a sling rather than the bipod
voured elsewhere, and to assist aim-
g a PSO-1 telescopic sight is pro-
ded. This is secured to the left-hand
de of the receiver and has a mag-
fication of ×4. The PSO-1 has an un-
ual feature in that it incorporates an
fra-red detector element to enable it
be used as a passive night sight,
thought it is normally used in con-
nction with an independent infra-red
rget-illumination source. Basic com-

bat sights are fitted for use if the optical
sight becomes defective.

Perhaps the oddest feature for a
sniper rifle is that the SVD is provided
with a bayonet, the rationale for this
remaining uncertain. A 10-round box
magazine is fitted.

Tests have demonstrated that the
SVD can fire accurately to ranges of
well over 800 m (875 yards). It is a
pleasant weapon to handle and fire,
despite the lengthy barrel. SVDs have
been provided to many Warsaw Pact
and other nations and it has been used
in Afghanistan, some ending in the
hands of the guerrillas, who are certainly no newcomers to sniping. The
Chinese produce a direct copy of the
SVD and offer this version for export,
quoting an effective range of 1000 m
(1,094 yards).

Specification
SVD
Calibre: 7.62 mm (0.3 in)
Lengths: overall less bayonet 1225 mm
(48.23 in); barrel 547 mm (21.53 in)
Weight: complete, unloaded 4.385 kg
(9.667 lb)
Muzzle velocity: 830 m (2,723 ft) per
second
Magazine capacity: 10 rounds

*The Soviets have always given
snipers a great deal of prominence in
the field and have always provided
them with good weapons. The
current Dragunov SVD, although
long and bulky, is a reliable weapon
although not as accurate as, say, the
L42. It uses a modified AK-47 gas-
operated semi-automatic action
allied to a large magazine.*

*ght: The Dragunov uses a bolt
stem similar to that of the AK-47
nd its derivatives, but it is modified
suit the different characteristics of
e rimmed 7.62 mm ×54 cartridge
iginally produced in 1908 for the
oisin-Nagant rifle.*

*e Dragunov has an excellent sight which displays a graduated range-finding scale, based on the
eight of the average man. By fitting the target into the grid, the firer gets an accurate idea of the
nge and aims accordingly. Simple, but effective.*

*China produces a direct copy of the SVD and is now
offering it for export with various extras including
this bayonet/wire-cutter.*

Galil Sniping Rifle

Ever since Israel was formed in 1948 the role of the sniper within the Israeli armed forces has been an important one, but over the years snipers have usually been equipped with an array of weapons from all around the world. At one point attempts were made to produce sniper rifles locally, so for a period Israeli army snipers used an indigenous 7.62-mm (0.3-in) design known as the **M26**. This was virtually a hand-made weapon using design features from both the Soviet AKM and Belgian FAL rifles. But for various reasons the M26 was deemed not fully satisfactory, so work began on a sniping rifle based on the Israel Military Industries 7.62-mm Galil assault rifle, the standard Israeli service rifle.

The resultant **Galil Sniping Rifle** bears a resemblance to the original but it is virtually a new weapon. Almost every component has been redesigned and manufactured to very close tolerances. A new heavy barrel is fitted, as is an adjustable bipod. The solid butt (which can be folded forward to reduce carrying and stowage bulk) has an adjustable butt pad and cheek rest, while a Nimrod ×6 telescopic sight is mounted on a bracket offset to the left of the receiver. The mechanism is now single-shot only, the original Galil 20-round magazine being retained. The barrel is fitted with a muzzle brake/compensator to reduce recoil and barrel jump on firing. A silencer can be fitted to the muzzle, but subsonic ammunition must then be used. As would be expected, various night sights can be fitted.

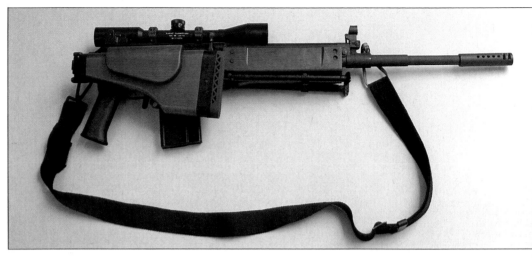

The Galil Sniping Rifle is now in production and has been offered for export. It is a very serviceable weapon that is far more suitable for the rigours of military life than many of the current crop of super-accuracy models. Despite its basic design approach it can still place groupings of less than 300 mm (11.8 in) at a range of 600 m (656 yards), which is more than adequate for most sniping purposes. Careful selection of the ammunition and use of the bipod ensures even better performances.

The Galil Sniping Rifle retains its 'iron' combat sights. When not in use the rifle is kept in a special case together with the telescopic sight, optical filters to reduce sun glare when using optical sights, a carrying and firing sling, two magazines and the all-important cleaning kit.

Specification
Galil Sniping Rifle
Calibre: 7.62 mm (0.3 in)
Lengths: overall 1115 mm (43.9 in); barrel 508 mm (20 in)
Weights: rifle only 6.4 kg (14.1 lb); complete 8.02 kg (17.68 lb)
Muzzle velocity: 815 m (2,674 ft) per second
Magazine capacity: 20 rounds

The design of the Galil sniper rifle was shaped by the IDF's extensive battlefield experience, and it is perhaps not surprising that the gun is built more for reliability in combat than exceptional accuracy in ideal conditions.

The semi-automatic Galil is a gas-operated weapon with a rotating bolt and a 20-round magazine. It fires standard NATO 7.62 mm ×51 and is built to hit the head at 300 m, half-body at 600 m and full figure at 800-900 m.

FN Model 30-11

Fabrique Nationale (FN) has for long kept an astute eye on the arms market from its Herstal headquarters, so when it noted an increased demand over recent years for highly accurate rifles for use against point targets the company came up with the **FN Model 30-11**. At first sight the Model 30-11 appears to be a highly conventional design. And so it is, though in order to make the weapon as accurate as possible it has been designed and manufactured with great care to obtain the best possible results.

The Model 30-11 fires carefully selected 7.62-mm (0.3-in) NATO ammunition. The manual bolt action is the frequently used Mauser forward-locking action but manufactured using a very high standard of craftsmanship. The same can be said of the heavy barrel which is connected to the receiver with great care. A five-round

The Belgian FN Model 30-11 rifle was originally produced for police and para-military use, but many are in military hands. The example seen here is fitted with target sights. The odd butt shape is due to the degree of individual adjustment that can be incorporated.

ox magazine is used, but normally ingle rounds only are loaded by hand irect into the chamber. The butt is djustable in two planes (up and down/ orward and back) to suit the individual ser's comfort. Swivels are provided or a shooting sling, and there is provi-ion for mounting a bipod under the orestock; the same bipod is used on ne FN MAG machine-gun.

This bipod is recommended for use vhen the Model 30-11 is employed vith any of the larger sighting devices nat can be fitted. Unlike many other niper rifles the Model 30-11 can be sed with precision-adjustable match-ype 'iron' sights, but there is also a vide range of telescopic sights avail-ble. For use at night or in poor visibil-y conditions image intensifier or ther-al imaging sights can be used. The ights selected are normally kept in a pecial protective carrying case ogether with the rifle when they are eing transported or stored.

The Model 30-11 is used by the Bel-ian army, although most have been sued to Belgian paramilitary police nits. Some sales have been made to ther nations, but only in small num-ers, for the degree of care lavished

on producing the Model 30-11 means that the weapon is not cheap. This has apparently prevented the usual appearance of high-class target-shoot-ing versions for commercial sales, although anyone fortunate enough to obtain a standard Model 30-11 with 'iron' sights will find themselves the owner of a superlative match rifle.

Specification
Model 30-11
Calibre: 7.62 mm (0.3 in)
Lengths: overall 1117 mm (43.97 in); barrel 502 mm (19.76 in)
Weight: rifle only 4.85 kg (10.69 lb)
Muzzle velocity: 850 m (2,788 ft) per second
Magazine capacity: 5 rounds

The FN Model 30-11 can be fitted with a wide range of accessories. The large sight seen here is a standard NATO infra-red night vision sight, and the bipod fitted is that used on the FN MAG machine-gun. A range of other such items can be used with this weapon, which is supplied with a special carrying case.

USA
Rifle M21

Vhen the US armed forces made the 1ove from the 7.62-mm (0.3-in) NATO artridge to the smaller 5.56-mm 0.223-in) round during the late 1960s 1ey not surprisingly decided to retain 1e larger calibre for the sniping role. 'his was for the simple reason that the maller round had been designed om the outset to impart its best per-rmance at ranges much shorter than 1e usual sniping distances. This meant 1e retention of the then-current snip-1g rifle, at the time known as the **Rifle 62-mm M14 National Match (Accu-sed)**, but now known as the **Rifle M21**.

The M21 is a special version of the 62-mm M14, for many years the stan-ard US service rifle. It retains the asic appearance and mechanism of 1e original, but some changes were 1troduced at the manufacturing stage. or a start the barrels were selected so 1at only those with the closest manu-.cturing tolerances were used. These arrels were left without their usual 1romium plating inside the bore, gain to reduce the possibility of 1anufacturing inaccuracies. A new 1uzzle supressor was fitted and eamed to the barrel to ensure correct lignment. The trigger mechanism 1as assembled by hand and adjusted provide a crisp release action, and a 1ew walnut stock was fitted, this latter eing impregnated with an epoxy re-1n. The gas-operated mechanism was so the subject of attention to ensure mooth operation. The fully-automatic re mode is retained on the M21 but 1rmally the weapon is fired on semi-1tomatic (single shot) only.

The main change on assembly was 1e fitting of a ×3 magnification tele-copic sight. As well as the usual aim-g cross-hairs, this uses a system of raticules that allows the user to judge ccurately the range of a man-sized rget and automatically set the angle elevation. Using this sight the M21 1n place 10 rounds within a 152-mm -in) circle at 300 m (329 yards).

One piece of equipment that can be

fitted to the M21 is a sound suppressor. This is not a silencer in the usually accepted sense of the word, but a series of baffles that reduces the veloc-ity of the gases produced on firing to below the speed of sound. This pro-duces a muffled report with none of the usual firing signatures, and its use makes the source of the sound (and the firer) difficult to detect.

Specification
M21
Calibre: 7.62 mm (0.3 in)
Lengths: overall 1120 mm (44.09 in); barrel 559 mm (22 in)
Weight: loaded 5.55 kg (12.24 lb)
Muzzle velocity: 853 m (2,798 ft) per second
Magazine capacity: 20 rounds

This M14 is from the collection of the Weapons Museum at the School of Infantry, Warminster. The M21 is a special version of the M14, with all parts manufactured to the closest tolerances and with a muzzle suppressor and × 3 scope fitted.

Although many Israeli snipers use the Galil sniping rifle some still retain the American M21, the accurized version of the M14 rifle. They were observed in use during the early stages of the invasion of Lebanon, and many were used against the PLO in Beirut in August 1982.

Sniping Rifle M40A

USA

The US Marine Corps has always been allowed its own equipment procurement system as it has long been accepted that its particular amphibious role requires equipment to match. Thus when the selection of a new sniping rifle to replace the M1C and M1D weapons based on the M1 Garand rifles came about, this service went its own way.

For the US Marines the sniper has always had a special role, often operating in advance of other supporting units to gain information as well as acting as a long-range killer. So when they contemplated weapons such as the

When the US Marine Corps decided to select their own sniping rifle they ordered numbers of commercial Remington Model 700 rifles, some still with 'iron' sights, as seen here. These became the M40 sniping rifle and many are still in use, despite the introduction of the later M40A1, but they are used only by the Marines.

M14/M21 sniper rifles they decided they wanted something better. They could not find exactly what they wanted on the open market but the design that came closest to their requirements was a commercial rifle known as the **Remington Model 700**. This became the **M40** in 1966.

The M40 has a Mauser-type manual bolt action and a heavy barrel. It is normally fitted with a Redfield telesopic sight with a zoom magnification of from ×3 to ×9. A five-round magazine is fitted, and the M40 is an entirely conventional but high-quality design. In service with the US Marines the M40 proved to be perfectly satisfactory, but experience gained with the basic design showed them that something better could be produced. They accordingly asked the Remington Arms Company to introduce a few modifications. These included the replacement of the barrel by a new stainless steel component, the replacement of the wooden furniture by fibreglass and the introduction of a new sight. This new telescopic sight has been produced entirely to demanding US Marine specifications and employs a fixed ×10 magnification. No iron sights are fitted in addition to this optical sight.

With all these changes embodied the M40 is now the **M40A1**, and it is produced by Remington only for the US Marines. By all accounts it is one of the most accurate sniping rifles ever

The Marines adopted the Remington 700 in 1966 and have had the weapon modified to meet their requirement. The M40A1 rifle differs from the M40 in having a heavy stainless steel barrel, a fibreglass stock and a powerful telescopic sight.

produced, although exact figures are not available to confirm this assertion. The main reasons for this are the heavy stainless steel barrel and the superb optical sight. The magnification of the sight is much more than usual on such devices, but it produces a bright and clear image for the firer. All the usual windage and other adjustments can be introduced to the sight.

As always with a weapon of this type, the degree of accuracy is dependent on the skill of the user (the US Marines spend a great deal of time training their snipers) and the performance of the ammunition selected, but by all accounts the M40A1 is the rifle 'everyone else wants'.

Specification
M40A1
Calibre: 7.62 mm (0.3 in)
Lengths: overall 1117 mm (43.97 in); barrel 610 mm (24 in)
Weight: 6.57 kg (14.48 lb)
Muzzle velocity: 777 m (2,549 ft) per second
Magazine capacity: 5 rounds

USA

Iver Johnson Model 300 Multi-Caliber Rifle

This weapon has undergone a few changes in name since it first emerged some years back from the drawing boards of the Research Armament Industries concern in Rogers, Arizona. Its full current title is the **Iver Johnson Model 300 Multi-Caliber Long-Range Rifle**, and it is marketed by Napco International Inc.

The Model 300 is another of the attempts to produce the perfect sniping rifle capable of being effective at ranges up to 1500 m (1,640 yards). On the Model 300 everything that can eliminate technical error has been incorporated, these features ranging from a fluted barrel with a counterweight beneath, to reduce vibrations and whip in the free-floating barrel, to an all-adjustable butt with a cheek pad. A ×9 Leupold telescopic sight is the only means of aiming the weapon and a bipod is provided for maximum aiming stability. A manual bolt action is used.

The designers also decided to provide what they regard as the optimum cartridge for long-range sniping. This was developed from an existing Rigby hunting cartridge by Research Arma-

ment Industries and has a calibre of 8.58 mm (0.338 in). Tables supplied to demonstrate the efficiency of this cartridge show that it has a much higher muzzle velocity than most comparable rounds and a considerably higher muzzle energy, giving the bullet a flatter ballistic path over longer ranges. However, the designers also realized that the acceptance of this new cartridge might be an uphill task, so they have also produced barrel and bolt head to enable existing 7.62-mm (0.3-in) NATO cartridges to be used; the calibres can be switched from one to the other as required. This provides the Model 300 with its 'Multi-Caliber' designation.

To date the Model 300 has had a mixed reception. It has attracted much attention by its very appearance but apparently hard orders have been slow in coming. Unconfirmed reports speak of some being used by US Special Forces, but that is all. The US Marines have procured trial numbers of the **Model 500**, a much larger and heavier version of the Model 300 that fires the 12.7-mm (0.5-in) machine-gun cartridge. The ballistic limitations of

this cartridge apparently ensured that the Model 500 was not a great success with the US Marines, and one feature of the Model 500 they did not accept is the fact that on this larger version the bolt has to be removed to load every round. After a few rounds the bolt often jammed and could not be removed without force, i.e. kicking it out.

Specification
Model 300
Calibre: 8.58 mm (0.338 in) or 7.62 mm (0.3 in)

Length: barrel only, both calibres 610 mm (24 in)
Weight: 5.67 kg (12.5 lb)
Muzzle velocity: 8.58-mm 915 m (3,002 ft) per second; 7.62-mm 800 m (2,625 ft) per second
Magazine capacity: 8.58-mm 4 rounds; 7.62-mm 5 rounds

The 'space age' Iver Johnson rifles are intended for super-long range use. The Model 300 (foreground) can fire either a 7.62-mm (0.30-in) or a special 8.58-mm cartridge.

Yugoslavia is not one of the nations that automatically springs to mind when the international arms market is considered, but it is currently one of the nations most involved in the selling of arms to the Third World. Its small-arms industry is not particularly innovative, preferring to adapt or develop existing designs rather than branch out into startling new ventures. Thus when a requirement came to replace all the elderly World War II sniping weapons still in use by the Yugoslav armed forces it was again decided to adapt an existing design, in this case the M70B1 assault rifle, the Yugoslav derivative of the Soviet AKM.

Not surprisingly the resultant weapon, the **M76** semi-automatic sniping rifle, has much in common with the Soviet SVD. The main difference is the choice of cartridge, which on the M76 is a 7.92-mm (0.312-in) type, a left-over from the German World War II standard rifle calibre. Yugoslavia still uses this cartridge for some machine-guns, so its retention for the sniping role is understandable. For marketing purposes the Yugoslavs also offer the M76 chambered for the 7.62-mm (0.3-in) NATO cartridge and the elderly Soviet 7.62-mm (0.3-in) rimmed cartridge.

Having said that, the M76 resembles the original AKM design much more than does the Soviet SVD. The M76 is a semi-automatic weapon with a long barrel but much of the original M70B1/M4 outline survives, including the solid wooden butt. The M76 uses a 10-round box magazine, and a telescopic sight with a ×4 magnification mounted over the receiver. This sight has much in common with the Soviet

PSO-1, including the rubber eyepiece, and is stated to make the M76 effective at ranges of 800 m (875 yards) or more. A variety of night vision devices, usually passive infra-red sights, can be fitted in its place. The normal combat sights of the M70B1 are retained, but the bayonet feature of the SVD is not.

Although the M76 may be regarded as a derivative of a Soviet design there is nothing derivative in its production standards. In common with most other Yugoslav weapons, the M76 is well-made and rugged enough to withstand the hard knocks of service life. From this point of view it is a far more prac-

tical weapon than many of the 'super-accuracy' designs now likely to be encountered. The M76 is already in service with the Yugoslav armed forces, but it is difficult to determine exactly how export sales have fared.

Specification
M76
Calibre: 7.92 mm (0.312 in)
Lengths: overall 1135 mm (44.69 in); barrel 550 mm (21.65 in)
Weight: empty, complete 5.08 kg (11.2 lb)
Muzzle velocity: 720 m (2,362 ft) per second
Magazine capacity: 10 rounds

The Yugoslav M76 sniping rifle can be found chambered for 7.92-mm (0.312-in) and both Soviet and NATO 7.62-mm (0.30-in) ammunition. It is basically a specially produced variant of the Yugoslav M70 assault rifle based on the AKM and fitted with a longer barrel and an optical sight mounting.

The concealing face netting used by this Yugoslav army sniper is standard equipment for most snipers. In use here is an M76 rifle, noticeable by its long barrel, fitted with a standard × 4 magnification telescopic sight.

MACHINE GUNS

Machine-Guns of World War 1

World War I differed in kind and degree from any previous human conflict. It was the first true industrial war, in which more men were killed in battle than ever before. The two paramount weapons were artillery and – the scourge of no-man's land – the machine-gun.

Indian Army soldiers in France fire a Hotchkiss Mk 1 from a position very like the sangars of the North West Frontier. The strip feed used on the Hotchkiss machine-gun can be clearly seen, as can the cooling fins around the barrel.

During World War I the machine-gun dominated the battlefields in a manner that is now difficult to comprehend. In fact it would be safe to say that the machine-gun dictated the very way in which World War I was fought, and this dominance of a tactical situation by a single weapon spurned the development of novel weapons to counter that same machine-gun.

Throughout World War I military planners sought desperately to overcome the power of the machine-gun. Time and time again prolonged artillery bombardments battered an enemy defensive system until it seemed that nothing could survive, but every time the hapless infantry moved forward from their trenches there seemed always to be a machine-gun that could prevent further progress. Thus it was that the artillery destroyed while the machine-gun killed. But in tactical terms many of these machine-guns were large and heavy weapons that could not be moved easily or rapidly, and a new family of lighter machine-guns was devised even as the war continued. It was these light machine-guns that were partly able to break the pattern of static emplacements and massed frontal assaults, by allowing the evaluation of a new tactical situation in which relatively mobile infantry could supply a fair proportion of their own fire support where and when it was most needed. Even so, it should not be forgotten that despite all the dreadful success of the machine-gun it was the arrival of the tank that finally did away with the mincing-machine apparatus of trench warfare on the Western Front.

Included in this study are some superb examples of machine-gun design, ranging from the magnificent Vickers machine-gun and the sturdy PM1910 to the dreadful Chauchat. All the weapons included here used some mechanical devices that tested the skills of designers and metallurgists alike, and the results were often technical marvels of their day. Many of the weapons mentioned here would still be viable in any form of combat were it not for the fact that they have been replaced by new and yet more powerful generations of weapons.

French and British soldiers operate together, with a Hotchkiss mle 1900 ready to provide fire support. This 1918 scene reflects the return to mobile warfare which preceded the end of the war and at last brought the machine-gun out of the trenches. It would have been inconceivable only six months before.

Hotchkiss mle 1909

In the years up to 1914 the French army was trained in the tenet that the attack (or the offensive) was the key to victory in any future war. The infantry and cavalry were trained to attack at all times, overcoming any opposition by the force of their onslaught and by their determination. In this optimistic scenario the machine-gun hardly featured, but at one point in the early 1900s it was thought that some form of light Hotchkiss machine-gun would be useful for cavalry units, and might also be portable enough for attacking infantrymen to carry.

The result of this suggestion was the **Fusil-mitrailleur Hotchkiss mle 1909**, which used the basic gas-operated mechanism of the larger Hotchkiss machine-guns, though for some reason the ammunition feed was complicated further by inversion of the ammunition feed strip mechanism. When it was introduced the cavalry units did not take to the weapon at all and it proved to be too heavy for infantry use, so the numbers produced were either relegated to use in fortifications or stockpiled. However, export sales of the mle 1909 were more encouraging for the weapon was adopted by the US Army who knew it as the **Benét-Mercié Machine Rifle Model 1909**; it was used mainly by cavalry units.

When World War I began the mle 1909 was once more taken from the stockpiles, and it was even adopted by the British army as the **0.303-in Gun, Machine, Hotchkiss, Mk 1** in an attempt to get more machine-guns into service. The mle 1909 was produced in the United Kingdom chambered for the British 7.7-mm (0.303-in) cartridge and in British use many were fitted with a butt and a bipod in place of the original small tripod located under the centre of the gun body.

However the mle 1909 was not destined to be used very much in the trenches: the ammunition feed was a constant source of troubles and gradually the Hotchkiss was diverted to other uses. The mle 1909 in its several forms became an aircraft gun and it formed the main armament of many of the ear-

ly tanks such as the British 'Female' tanks with their all-machine-gun armament, and the little Renault FT17. On the tanks the ammunition feed strips sometimes limited the traverse available inside the close confines of the tank mountings, so many guns, especially those of the British, were converted to use the three-round linked strips intended for use on the larger Hotchkiss mle 1914. Some of these guns were still in British army use in 1939, and more were later taken from the stockpiles for use as airfield defence weapons and for arming merchant shipping.

The mle 1909 was one of the first light machine-guns, but it had little impact at the time, although it was used in quite large numbers. Its main disadvantage was not so much a technical difficulty as a tactical problem, for the tactics involved in trench warfare of the period and the lack of appreciation of the potential of the weapon never gave the mle 1909 a chance to shine. As a tank weapon it made its mark on history, but it was less successful as an aircraft gun, the feed strip mechanism proving a definite drawback in an open aircraft cockpit.

Above: The Hotchkiss mle 1909 was used by the French, the British (as the Hotchkiss Mk 1) and also by the US Army, who knew it as the Benét-Mercié.

Below: A drummer of the 1/7th Lancashire Fusiliers demonstrates Hotchkiss Mk 1 to newly-arrived U. Army soldiers in France in May 19

Specification
Fusil-mitrailleur Hotchkiss mle 1909
Calibre: 8 mm (0.315 in)

Lengths: overall 1.19 m (46.85 in); barrel 600 mm (23.62 in)
Weight: 11.7 kg (25.8 lb)
Muzzle velocity: 740 m (2,428 ft) per

second
Rate of fire: (cyclic) 500 rpm
Feed: 30-round metal strip

Hotchkiss medium machine-guns

In the 1890s the only viable machine-guns were those produced by Maxim and Browning, both of whom wrapped their products in a tight wall of patents to prevent others enjoying the fruits of their invention. Many armament concerns were desperate to find some way of getting around the patent wall, and one of these was the French Hotchkiss company. Thus when it was approached by an Austrian inventor who described to them a novel method of gas operation to power a machine-gun, the invention was quickly purchased and developed by Hotchkiss.

The first Hotchkiss machine-gun was the **Mitrailleuse Hotchkiss mle 1897**, and although this model was hardly a viable service weapon it was the first gas-operated machine-gun. This was followed by the **mle 1900** and later by the **mle 1914**, the latter being the model mainly used in World War I. These models all had air-cooled barrels, but as these tended to overheat the company very quickly introduced a feature that was to remain as a virtual 'trademark' of the Hotchkiss machine

gun: this consisted of five prominent 'doughnut' collars around the end of the barrel closer to the receiver. These rings (sometimes brass and sometimes steel) enlarged the surface area of the barrel at the point where it became hottest and thus provided greater cooling.

For operating, gas was tapped off from the barrel and used to push back a piston to carry out all the various extracting and reloading operations. It was a system that worked well and reliably, and was soon to be used in one form or another by many other machine-gun designers. The weapon had its first exposure to action during the Russo-Japanese War of 1904-5, in

French and British infantry at the Battle of the Aisne in 1918 in the follow-up to the Allied advance. The gun is a Hotchkiss mle 1900 mounted on the mle 1916 tripod, with ammunition boxes close to hand behind the gunner. To the left of the gun are two ammunition handlers ready to assist.

easily recognized by the large doughnut cooling rings around the barrel, the Hotchkiss mle 1914 became the standard French heavy machine-gun of World War I. Although heavy, it was well made and generally reliable, but the strip feed sometimes gave trouble. It fired an 8-mm (0.315-in) round.

which it performed well enough though one feature did cause trouble. This was the ammunition feed, the Hotchkiss using a method whereby the rounds were fed into the gun mounted in metal strips; originally brass strips were used, but these were later replaced by steel strips. These strips carried only 24 or 30 rounds, which severely limited the amount of sustained fire that could be produced. On the mle 1914 this was partly overcome by redesigning the strip system to give three-round strips linked together to form a 249-round 'belt'. Even in this form the strips were prone to damage and any dirt on them tended to cause jams. The feed mechanism was thus the weakest point in an otherwise reliable and serviceable design.

There were some variations on the basic design. Versions for use in fortifications had a downwards 'V'-shaped muzzle attachment that was supposed to act as a flash hider, and several types of tripod were in use during World War I, including a mle 1897 mounting that had no provision for traverse or elevation.

The Hotchkiss machine-guns were used mainly by the French army during World War I, but in 1917 large numbers were handed over to the American Expeditionary Force when it arrived in France. The Americans continued to use them until the war ended.

Specification
Mitrailleuse Hotchkiss mle 1914
Calibre: 8 mm (0.315 in)
Lengths: overall 1.27 m (50 in); barrel 775 mm (30.51 in)
Weight: gun 23.6 kg (52.0 lb)
Muzzle velocity: 725 m (2,379 ft) per second
Rate of fire: (cyclic) 400-600 rpm
Feed: 24- or 30-round strip, or 249-round strip in 3-round links

---

FRANCE

Chauchat

Officially known as the **Fusil-trailleur mle 1915**, the **Chauchat** or **CSRG** is one of the more unpleasant weapon production stories of World War I. It was intended as a light machine-gun, and was created by a commission of designers in 1914, the result being a long and awkward weapon using a mechanism known as 'long recoil' in which the barrel and breech block moved to the rear after firing, the barrel then being allowed to move forward while the bolt is held and released to feed the next round. This mechanism works, but is rather complicated and the movement inside the gun makes aiming difficult. The Chauchat was apparently intended for ease of manufacture, but when the design was rushed into production in 1915 its manufacture was farmed out to a large number of firms, some of whom had virtually no weapon-manufacturing experience. The result was a horror, for many manufacturers used the Chauchat simply as a means of making maximum profit and so used cheap and unsuitable materials that either wore out quickly or broke in action. Even when the materials were suitable the service versions of the Chauchat were still bad: the weapon handled badly and tended to jam at the slightest excuse. The half-moon magazine under the body did little to make the weapon easier to carry, and the light bipod was so flimsy that it bent very easily. The French soldiers hated the weapon, many later proclaiming that the manufacturers' greed for profits had caused the deaths of many French soldiers, as they no doubt had.

Unfortunately, the manufacturers were not alone in their search for weapon production profits. When the Americans entered the war some French politicians prevailed upon the Army to adopt the Chauchat, and the unsuspecting Americans agreed. They accepted over 16,000 Chauchats and a further 19,000 were ordered of a version chambered for the American

The Fusil-Mitrailleur mle 1915 or 'Chauchat' was one of the worst machine-guns ever built and was reviled by the soldiers who had to use it in action. It was poorly made,

7.62-mm (0.3-in) cartridge; this model had a vertical box magazine instead of the French half-moon magazine. Neither of these versions proved to be any better in American hands than they were in French hands. The Americans often simply cleared jams by throwing the jammed weapon away and taking up a rifle, especially when the rechambered weapons reached their ranks. The American cartridge was more powerful than the French 8-mm (0.315-in) round and made the gun components break even more rapidly.

In the end existing production contracts were allowed to run their course, but the resultant weapons were usually stockpiled to be dragged out and later dumped upon unsuspecting post-war markets. In France some parliamentary investigations were made into the Chauchat affair in an attempt to determine exactly how the production contracts were placed and where the profits ended, but by then

unreliable and awkward to handle.

so many parliamentarians and industrialists were involved that the whole affair gradually fizzled out.

Most references state that the Chauchat in all its forms was one of the worst machine-guns of World War I in all aspects. From basic design to manufacture and the materials used, it was a disaster, but what now appears worse is the fact that the whole programme was not controlled at all. The result was that many soldiers suffered from having to use the weapon while others pocketed the profits their greed had generated.

Specification
Chauchat
Calibre: 8 mm (0.315 in)
Lengths: gun 1.143 m (45.0 in); barrel 470 mm (18.5 in)
Weight: 9.2 kg (20.3 lb)
Muzzle velocity: 700 m (2,297 ft) per second
Rate of fire: 250-300 rpm
Feed: 20-round curved box magazine

Below: A French soldier fully attired in his horizon bleu uniform and greatcoat holds his Chauchat in the prescribed drill book manner for use in the assault.

Light Machine-Gun Tactics 1915-1918

The first machine-guns were not the most mobile of weapons, being emplaced in battle rather like pieces of artillery. It did not take long for the troops on the Western Front to appreciate how effective a machine-gun could be, advancing with them into battle, and so the light machine-gun was born.

When World War I started the light machine-gun was virtually unknown. Belgian troops did carry into action a number of Lewis Guns, but these were used at that time in exactly the same way as conventional heavy machine-guns, i.e. they were carefully emplaced before an action and used to provide supporting or covering fire. As the troops moved forward into an attack the machine-guns stayed where they were, being considered too heavy to be carried forward.

This was unfortunate, for in the Lewis Gun the Belgians had an excellent infantry weapon that was quite capable of taking on a new role. This new role was indicated during 1915 when the first of the setpiece attacks along the German lines began, with their massive artillery overtures and the subsequent confusion and carnage when the planned infantry attacks stalled either on the barbed wire or in front of emplaced heavy machine-guns. At times like these there was no way in which the infantry could get themselves out of their predicament. Using their rifles alone they could rarely produce enough firepower to make an enemy machine-gunner keep his head down, and there was no way that artillery or machine-gun support could be called upon, for radio was in its infancy and telephone wires were soon cut. For this reason all artillery and machine-gun fire plan support had to be prepared beforehand using rigid fire plans on a timetable basis. If an enemy machine-gun intervened there was no way any supporting fire could be diverted from the fire plan, and the 'poor bloody infantry' thus had to suffer.

Fire support

But by the end of 1915 the first inklings of how supporting machine-gun fire could be produced to counter this problem had been suggested by a few forward-looking officers. It was 1916 before their ideas came to the hardware stage: the overall solution to the crossing of no man's land was of course the tank, but an interim solution was found with the service introduction of the Lewis Gun. This had been adopted by the British army for economic rather than tactical reasons: the expanding British armies clearly had to be equipped with machine-guns, and it was found that five or six Lewis Guns could be churned out in the time that it took to produce one of the heavier and more complex Vickers machine-guns. Initially there were four Lewis Guns to a battalion, to replace the Vickers machine-guns that had been passed to the newly-formed Machine Gun Corps. By mid-1916 this allotment had been increased to eight, and a month later a further four were added. By the end of 1916 there was one Lewis Gun to every four platoons, and by the end of the war every two platoons shared one Lewis Gun. By that time there were even four Lewis Guns in every battalion dedicated to the anti-aircraft defence role. This rapid growth in numbers was pushed through by a realization that in the Lewis Gun the long-suffering infantry battalions could have their own local fire support weapons. No longer did the infantry have to rely upon Vickers machine-guns emplaced away to the rear for local fire support. If a target presented itself the Lewis gunners operating right up in the front lines with the first waves of infantry were on the spot to throw themselves down and open fire right away. In this way isolated pockets of resistance left behind by the artillery bombardment could be overcome as quickly as possible. Some units even devised a drill whereby the Lewis Guns were moved forward by two men in the first wave of attackers. One man held the Lewis Gun by looping his arms around the barrel. The other man fired the gun at anything that presented itself. In this manner the gun could be fired without the gunner having to adopt the prone position and fire could also be opened up all the more rapidly.

But these tactics were not universal. Despite the firepower potential of the Lewis Gun, the men that used it were just as vulnerable to enemy fire as the rest, and all too often the Lewis gunners were among the first to be picked off by the carefully-emplaced defenders. In time the infantry tactics changed: they had to, for men were simply not able to walk through a hail of enemy fire to carry out an attack. Instead of proceeding forward in a sedate manner, the infantry instead adopted a method whereby small sections of men rushed forward one after the other. As each section moved forward the other sections provided covering fire over the trench system being attacked. The French adopted this method after suffering from its effects when it was used by the Germans at Verdun in 1916.

French infantry operate in the Vosges mountains, with the unfortunate soul i the foreground carrying a Hotchkiss mle 1900 on his back; others would hav to carry the tripod and the boxes of ammunition strips. Note that all have rifl or carbines to carry as well while most carry their packs.

Above: This Indian cavalryman is seen as he would have been on the Western Front during 1914-5. The Lewis Gun was ideal for use with cavalry as it was relatively light.

Left: The German MG 08/15 was an air-cooled machine-gun develope from experience gained during World War I. Designed by Rheinmetall, it had an 'all-in-line' layout and a novel form of locking mechanism.

Above: Any enemy aircraft flying within range of this array of Lewis Guns would have been in for a nasty shock. These Indian Army guns are shown somewhere in Mesopotamia and are fitted with 47-round magazines. Some have slings for ease in carrying their 11.8 kg (26 lb) bulk.

Above: A section of the Gordon Highlanders is seen in action during March 1918 near the Somme, with their Lewis Gun being used in the classic supporting fire role. The figure in the tree is probably spotting for targets for the Lewis team and shouting down fire corrections.

The British were reluctant to assume this form of tactics mainly because of the overall poor standard of training they were able to provide for their mass armies, but gradually the soldiers themselves devised methods for the mutual support of sections by other sections. It was here that the Lewis Gun came into its own, for the firepower potential of the weapon was such that a single Lewis Gun could assume the support role of a whole section of riflemen. Thus infantry sections reached the point where a single Lewis Gun team of two men could cover the forward progress of almost an entire platoon.

As ever, by this time the Germans were already one stage ahead. They had seen the requirements for a portable machine-gun as early as 1915 and had devised the MG 08/15 Maxim gun for a new array of infantry tactics. Using experience gained on the Eastern Front, the Germans had already designed a new system of infantry warfare employing the same balanced mutual fire support role that had been tentatively evolved by the Allies. However, the Germans took it one stage further. Realizing that infantry alone could not hope to take control of a Western Front trench system, they did not even attempt to take a trench by storm. Instead the German infantry were divided up into small assault teams that were trained simply to pass around any strongpoints they might encounter: so rather than attempting to attack any defensive emplacements that might be in their path, they moved away to the flanks and filtered round into the rear areas. Once there they could disrupt the movement of men and supplies to the forward trenches, attack command posts and generally disrupt the enemy's rear areas. If necessary, troublesome strongpoints could be attacked from the rear.

In this type of combat the light machine-gun had many roles to play. The most important was still that of providing supporting fire while the other sections moved, but the Germans' activities were hampered by a shortage of MG 08/15s. Supply of this weapon could not meet demand, so captured Lewis Guns were pressed into German use. Stretcher bearers became involved in this process of obtaining enemy weapons, some units ordering their stretcher bearers to carry back to the rear as many Lewis Guns as they could find on the battlefield, each one carried on a stretcher along with a casualty.

By 1918 light machine-guns were being used in defence as well as attack. As the German army fell back during the later months of 1918 it worked out a method whereby small light machine-gun teams were used to cover the withdrawal of much larger bodies of men. At times a single MG 08/15 would be used to hold up a whole battalion advancing across open ground, the gun team simply picking up and carrying its gun away to the rear, ready for another holding action, as soon as the Allied assault forces came uncomfortably close to their position.

Above: The MG 08/15 was converted from its aircraft role for the ground role during World War II, again a carry-over from World War I when many weapons were similarly converted. This conversion involved the fitting of a light bipod and a rudimentary butt, but the end result was not very successful.

Right: A Schütztruppen NCO holds an ammunition box for his MG 08. A critical shortage of artillery made the machine-guns of the German army in East Africa doubly important.

Saint-Etienne

The Hotchkiss was a commercial design, and the French military authorities wanted to have their own design of machine-gun to match. Unfortunately their efforts were not a success, and indeed were not helped by the fact that the gas-operated mechanism devised by Hotchkiss was protected by a long list of patents that were almost impossible to circumvent. Not deterred, the French, attempted to produce a model known as the **mle 1905** or **Puteaux**. It was so unsuccessful that it was withdrawn from use within two years, the basic design being used for another attempt that was known as the **Mitrailleuse mle 1907** or **Saint-Etienne**, after the arsenal at which it was manufactured.

The French military designers decided to use a gas mechanism based on the Hotchkiss, but to reverse the overall process. Instead of gases in the barrel pushing back a piston, the Saint-Etienne used a system whereby the gases were tapped forward where the piston compressed a spring. The compressed spring was then released to power the rest of the operation. This system worked, but only at the expense of complication and of the use of more pieces that could break or go wrong, so in practice the whole idea was simply not worth the trouble involved. The mle 1907 had an inherent source of ammunition and other jams, and the return spring that was supposed to do all the work got so hot that it either lost its tempering and ceased to operate or else simply broke. In the end the designers could do nothing more than leave the spring exposed to the elements, which aided cooling but also allowed dust and dirt to enter the workings and so produce more jams.

Despite all these inherent troubles, the mle 1907 Saint-Etiennes were used during World War I for the simple reason that the French army became so desperate for weapons that it used

Above: The French mle 1907 was a state-produced machine-gun intended to improve upon the basic Hotchkiss designs. It was less successful, many being sent to the colonies or relegated to fortress use.

anything it could obtain. The tribulations of the mle 1907 simply had to be borne, and as late as 1916 attempts were made to eradicate some of the more obvious faults. None of the modifications was of any use, and gradually the mle 1907s were phased out in favour of the far more reliable Hotchkiss guns. The mle 1907s were shunted off to the French colonies, where they were used to arm local levies and police units. Others were issued to fortress units.

All in all the Saint-Etienne was not a success; indeed, it even carried over the failings from other models. The mle 1905 Puteaux had already indicated the impracticality of some of the mle 1907's features, and the troublesome ammunition feed strip method of the Hotchkiss guns was adopted even when it was known that it should have been phased out in favour of a better method. The result was that in the dreadful conditions of the Western Front trenches the Saint-Etienne often failed.

A mle 1907 St Etienne machine-gun team poses for a publicity photograph on one of the levels of the Eiffel Tower in an attempt to prove that Paris was able to defend itself against German air raids. The mle 1907 was no more successful in this role than it was in any other.

Specification
Mitrailleuse Saint-Etienne mle 1907
Calibre: 8 mm (0.315 in)
Lengths: gun 1.18 m (46.46 in); barrel 710 mm (27.95 in)
Weight: 25.4 kg (56.0 lb)
Muzzle velocity: 700 m (2,297 ft) per second
Rate of fire: 400-600 rpm
Feed: 24- or 30-round metal strip

Browning M1917

Almost as soon as the Colt-Browning Model 1895 was in production, Browning was already at work on a recoil-operated weapon. Unfortunately for Browning, at that time the American military authorities had no interest in any more machine-guns: they considered they had enough already, and anyway funds to purchase more were few. Thus virtually nothing happened until 1917 when the USA found itself at war with few modern weapons and even fewer serviceable machine-guns. In a very short space of time the 'new' Browning machine-gun was ordered into production in large numbers as the **Machine-Gun, Caliber .30, M1917**.

Externally the M1917 resembled other machine-guns of the time, especially the Vickers Gun. In fact the M1917 was quite different: it used a mechanism known as the short recoil system, in which the recoil force produced on firing the cartridge pushes back the barrel and breech block to

The Colt Model 1917 was the first of many successful Browning-designed machine-guns that are in use to this day. Chambered for the American 0.30-in (7.62-mm) cartridge, they were used by the US Army in France.

ie rear of the gun; after the barrel and olt have travelled back together for a hort distance, the two components art and the barrel movement is alted; a swinging lever known as an ccelerator then throws the bolt to the ear, and as it travels a series of cams nove the belt feed mechanism to insert another round; a return spring nen pushes forward the bolt to the arrel and the whole assembly is then eturned for the cycle to start again. This basic mechanism was retained for ll future Browning machine-gun designs, from the air-cooled 7.62-mm).3-in) to the large 12.7-mm (0.5-in) M2 reapons.

One component that differentiated ie M1917 from the Vickers machinein (apart from the internal workings) as the firing grip: the Vickers used vo spade grips, but the M1917 used a istol grip and a conventional trigger. lose inspection between the two rpes will soon reveal many other difrences, but the pistol grip is easily oticed.

The M1917 was rushed into production at several manufacturing centres and was churned out in such numbers that by the time the war ended no less than 68,000 had been made. Not all of these reached the troops in France, but after 1918 the M1917 became one of the standard American heavy machine-guns and remained in service until well after World War II. Also after 1918 some slight alterations were introduced as the result of combat experience, but these changes were slight. More drastic changes came after 1918 when the water cooling jacket was removed altogether to produce the **M1919**.

In service the M1917 proved to be relatively trouble free, and despite the rush with which it was placed in service few problems appear to have been recorded. Relatively few M1917s actually reached France before the Armistice, but many were on their way. Those which did arrive were extensively used, for the M1917s were among the few purely-American

weapons that were issued to the American troops: up until then all they had from home were their Springfield rifles and a few other sundry items. It was just as well that the M1917 turned out to be an excellent weapon design.

Specification
M1917
Calibre: 7.62 mm (0.3 in)
Lengths: gun 0.981 m (38.64 in); barrel 607 mm (23.9 in)
Weights: gun less water 14.79 kg (32.6 lb); tripod 24.1 kg (53.15 lb)
Muzzle velocity: 853 m (2,800 ft) per second
Rate of fire: 450-600 rpm
Feed: 250-round belt

Completely unprepared for a major conflict, the US Army was compelled to rely on Britain and France for much of the equipment for its Expeditionary Force. One honourable exception was the Browning M1917, a fine weapon destined to enjoy a long career.

Colt-Browning Model 1895

.hn Moses Browning started design ork on a machine-gun as early as 389, at a time when the American rmed forces were still heavily involved with the hand-operated Gatling un and when Maxim had already itented his recoil-operated machinein. Browning was thus directed towards a gas-operated mechanism, hich he gradually refined until it ached the point where the Colt Pant Firearms Manufacturing Comany built some prototypes, one of hich was demonstrated to the US avy. It was 1895 before the US Navy ecided to purchase a batch chamered for the Krag-Jorgensen 7.62-mm .3-in) cartridge, but later this was tered to the .30-06 cartridge that was remain in use for two world wars.

The **Colt-Browning Model 1895** was gas-operated weapon that used ases tapped off from the barrel to ush down a piston. This in turn ished down a long lever that swung elow the gun body to operate the gun .echanism. It was this lever that gave e weapon the nickname of 'potato gger', for if the gun was mounted ose to the ground a small pit had to e dug into which the lever could .ove, otherwise it would hit the round and cause stoppages. This rawback was partially offset by the ct that being based on a mechanical peration the movements were very efinite and precise, and so able to rovide a smooth and trouble-free acon. Ammunition was fed into the eapon in 300-round belts.

The Model 1895 first went into action ith the US Marine Corps during the uban campaign of 1898. The US Army ok over a few, and some sales were .ade to Belgium and Russia. By the ne that World War I came around the odel 1895 was already regarded as osolete, but since by that time the US rmy was largely starved of funds to rocure more modern weapons the odel 1895s were all that were availle and were retained for training. ome did make the journey to France 1917 and 1918 but few were used in ction; instead the Americans took er numbers of French and British

machine-guns. The Model 1895 did remain in production for a while during World War I: production was switched to the Marlin-Rockwell Corporation, which modified the weapon by designing out the lever action and replacing it by a more orthodox gas piston system. The result was known as the **Marlin Gun.** It resembled the Model 1895 but was much lighter and was a better weapon overall. Many were produced for the US Army air service as aircraft weapons, and some were produced to become the standard machine-gun for tanks produced in America. In the event the war ended before many of the Marlin Guns could reach the front in sizable numbers, and the bulk of the production run was stockpiled, only to be sold to the United Kingdom for home defence in 1940.

Despite its awkward underbody lever that swung down during firing, the Colt Model 1895 was selected for use as a weapon for early combat aircraft such as this Voisin. This was mainly due to its relatively light weight and air-cooled barrel, though it was not used as such for long.

The Belgian and Tsarist Russian armies used the Model 1895 throughout World War I, some of the Russian weapons being prominent during the political upheavals of 1917. A few of the Russian Model 1895s were still being used as late as 1941.

Specification
Colt-Browning Model 1895
Calibre: 7.62 mm (0.3 in)
Lengths: gun 1.20 m (47.25 in); barrel 720 mm (28.35 in)

The Colt Model 1895 was known to the troops as the 'potato digger' because of the arm that swung down under the body when the gun was firing. This weapon was still in use when the Americans entered the war in 1917 and was used in France.

Weights: gun 16.78 kg (37 lb); tripod 29.0 kg (64 lb)
Muzzle velocity: 838 m (2,750 ft) per second
Rate of fire: 400-500 rpm
Feed: 300-round belt

Browning Automatic Rifle

USA

In 1917 Browning demonstrated two new automatic weapon designs to the Congress in Washington: one was the heavy machine-gun that was to become the M1917, and the other a weapon that is still regarded by many as a hybrid and which became known to all as the **Browning Automatic Rifle**, or **BAR**. The BAR was in an odd category, for to many the weapon was a light machine-gun but to the US Army it was an automatic rifle, in some ways an early assault rifle. It was a light and portable weapon that could fire single shot or automatic, and it could be carried and used by one man.

By early 1918 the BAR was in production at several centres, but as Colt held the Browning patents at that time it produced the drawings and gauges that the other centres were to use. It was September 1918 before the BAR actually reached the stage where it was used in action, but it made a tremendous impact on the American soldiers who soon grew to value the weapon highly, so highly in fact that they were still using the BAR during the Korean War of the 1950s. Exactly why the Americans went so overboard regarding the BAR was (and still is) rather difficult to determine. The first BARs, as used in World War I, were simply hand-held weapons. There was no bipod or any form of support for use when the weapon was fired on automatic in the prone position, and as the box magazine held only 20 rounds the

length of bursts was strictly limited. As a light machine-gun the BAR was really too light, and as an automatic rifle it was too large and heavy.

But the American soldiers took to the BAR very well, no doubt as a relief from having to deal with the dreadful Chauchat. Apart from the Springfield rifles, the BAR was one of the first 'all-American' weapons to reach them, and no doubt they wanted to demonstrate the quality of American small arms. The BAR was certainly an impressive-looking weapon. It was excellently made, was provided with well-finished wooden furniture, and was capable of taking hard knocks. The mechanism was gas operated and so arranged that at the instant of firing the mechanism was locked in place by the bolt engaging in a notch in the top of the receiver. This notch was the

source of the 'hump' on top of the gun just in front of the rear sights. For maintenance and repairs the BAR could be rapidly and easily stripped down to its 70 component parts and reassembled just as easily.

In the field the US Army devised some combat drills for the BAR. One that did not last long was a drill whereby attacking infantry would fire one shot every time the left foot touched the ground. In fact most of the tactical drills involving the BAR were formulated after 1918, when the lessons of the few months of combat that the US Army had to endure were analysed. Along with the drills the BAR itself changed by the addition of a bipod and a shoulder strap for carrying, and the BAR became more of a section support weapon that could deliver automatic fire in support of riflemen rather than

The Browning Automatic Rifle, or BAR, was a cross between a heavy machine rifle and a light machine-gun. Its magazine held only 20 rounds and there was no bipod on the first models. The US Army found it a very useful weapon and used it in large numbers.

the assault-type weapon role it had been used for in the trenches.

Specification
BAR
Calibre: 7.62 mm (0.3 in)
Lengths: overall 1.194 m (47 in); barrel 610 mm (24 in)
Weight: 7.26 kg (16 lb)
Muzzle velocity: 853 m (2,800 ft) per second
Rate of fire: (cyclic) 550 rpm
Feed: 20-round box magazine

Vickers Gun

UK

The UK was among the first to adopt the Maxim gun following demonstrations held in the country as early as 1887. A manufacturing line for various models was set up at Crayford in Kent by a company that came to be known as Vickers' Sons & Maxim Limited, and from this factory Maxim guns went to the British armed forces and to many other countries. The Vickers engineers realized the virtues of the Maxim gun but considered that some weight savings could be made by a redesign, and by careful stress studies much of the mechanism was gradually lightened and the basic action inverted so that the toggle lock invented by Maxim could be made lighter.

The result came to be known as the **Vickers Gun**. In relative terms it was not all that much lighter than a comparable Maxim machine-gun, but the operating principles were much refined making the weapon more efficient. It was approved for British army service in November 1912 as the **Gun, Machine, Vickers, 0.303-in, Mk 1**, and all production initially went to the British Army, where the machine-gun was still regarded with such suspicion that the rate of issue was only two per infantry battalion.

Once World War I started that allotment changed drastically. New production centres were soon opened, some of them located in Royal Ordnance Factories, but the basic design remained unchanged throughout its long production life. The last Vickers machine-gun was very like the first and changes were confined to details. Like most machine-guns of its period, the Vickers was subject to jams, most of them induced by the ammunition, and a series of drills were devised to

clear the weapon rapidly. These drills took a bit of learning so in time a new Machine Gun Corps was formed within the British Army so that experience and skills could be confined within a relatively small body and not spread throughout all the regiments of the expanding armies. The Machine Gun Corps also raised its own esprit de corps, and that enabled the machine-gunners to use their weapons with a little extra spirit; their cap badge was two crossed Vickers machine-guns.

In action a Vickers could be kept firing for as long as ammunition could be fed into it. The water in the cooling jacket had to be kept topped up, and after early experiences where steam from the jacket gave way the gun's position a special condenser system

(using a hose fed into a water can) was introduced to conceal the steam. After a while the water could be replaced in the jacket.

The Vickers machine-gun was usually mounted on a heavy tripod. Variations on the basic gun included air-cooled versions for use on aircraft, usually on fixed installations only. Many more variations were produced between the two world wars, and the Vickers is still in service with some armed forces to this day; it did not pass from British service until the 1970s. The Vickers machine-gun was, in the opinion of many authorities, one of the best of all the World War I machine-guns, and would still be a very useful weapon today.

Specification
Vickers Gun
Calibre: 7.7 mm (0.303 in)
Lengths: gun 1.156 m (45.5 in); barrel 721 mm (28.4 in)
Weights: gun 18.14 kg (40 lb); tripod 22.0 kg (48.5 lb)
Muzzle velocity: 744 m (2,440 ft) per second
Rate of fire: 450-500 rpm
Feed: 250-round fabric belt

This Vickers is an American-built version mounted on the British Mk 4 tripod. It was the standard British machine-gun and was even used as the badge of the Machine-Gun Corps, a formation whose very creation underscores the importance of the machine-gun during World War I.

The Vickers in Action

Hiram Maxim produced one of the most successful of early machine-guns, variants equipping many of the armies taking part in World War I. The modified Maxim produced by Vickers, still in service today, became one of the finest machine-guns of the 20th century.

When the first Vickers machine-guns entered service in 1907, few British army officers knew exactly what to do with their new charges. Few appreciated the potential power of the weapon, and those few who did were regarded as eccentrics.

The initial rate of issue of the Vickers machine-gun was two to an infantry battalion; few cavalry battalions took to the weapon and only a few carried them across to France in 1914. Once there they soon learned that the machine-gun was a powerful weapon and the first to suffer were the cavalry units. A single machine-gun hidden away on a distant horizon could keep an entire cavalry battalion immobile for as long as it kept firing. The Battle of Loos further reinforced the lesson for the British, and they began to look at the Vickers weapon in a different light.

The Vickers machine-gun was developed from the earlier Maxim Gun. Vickers had manufactured the Maxim Gun at its Crayford factory in Kent, and although the Maxim had sold very well to many customers, the Vickers design engineers thought that they could improve upon the basic concept to produce a lighter and more efficient weapon. This they did by reversing the Maxim toggle lock device so that it opened upwards instead of downwards. This can perhaps be better explained by going through the sequence of operations involved in the Vickers short recoil mechanism.

At the moment a cartridge was fired the toggle mechanism, formed from two levers, was in an all-in-line position with the central hinge in line with both levers. This gave the mechanism a very positive and strong lock, for the only way to break the toggle joint was by an upward movement. This was not imparted at the moment of firing, for the recoil forces tended to push the breech block (the lock) backwards in a straight line. As the bullet left the muzzle the gases expanded in a small muzzle chamber and forced back the barrel which in turn provided more impetus for the breech block. Together they moved to the rear, but as they did so the rear of the two toggle levers struck a fixed post, the lever being so arranged that it was then pushed upwards. This broke the positive lock and the breech could then move separately to the rear, taking with it the spent case from the chamber. At the same time the reloading operation could start: as the breech block moved to the rear it placed a load on a spring known as the fuzee spring, which would eventually return the breech block back to the original position. This operation would continue for as long as the trigger in front of the firer's spade grips was pressed.

Prolonged firing made the barrel very hot, so it was cooled by water contained in a metal jacket around the barrel. This jacket held 3.98 litres (7 pints) of water, which would boil after three minutes of sustained fire at the rate of 200 rounds per minute. At first this boiling assisted the cooling process as minute air bubbles helped to carry the heat away from the barrel, but soon the heat caused the water to evaporate as steam. In the early days this was allowed to escape from the top of the jacket, but it was soon noticed that the cloud of steam gave away the gun position and invited retaliatory fire, so an easy solution was found by diverting it via a flexible pipe into a can of water where it could condense harmlessly back to water and eventually be returned to the jacket. This last was important in areas where water was scarce.

Seated in front of his Vickers machine-gun, with the tripod reversed to allow the barrel to be elevated for anti-aircraft use, this Anzac soldier is taking a quick break. Using the Vickers in this role could be successful – Australian soldiers claimed responsibility for shooting down von Richtofen's Fokker triplane.

Despite the water cooling system the barrel had to be changed every 10,000 rounds. As it was possible to fire 10,000 rounds in an hour it often became a drill that in action a barrel was replaced every hour on the hour. A well trained crew could accomplish this in about two minutes with no loss of water other than that which entered the barrel as it was pushed in from the rear. In fact it was this type of operation that led to the use only of specialists on the Vickers machine-gun. At first men from ordinary battalions were assigned to the weapons, but the need

An Australian soldier demonstrates the drill-book method of packing a Vickers machine-gun onto a packhorse or mule. The special harness carried a complete machine-gun and tripod along with ammunition, water, spares and sighting equipment, even including spare barrels.

Vickers machine-gunners keep their gun in action during the aftermath of a chemical attack in July 1916. The primitive respirators of the time caused severe restriction on vision but were just adequate. Note the strap around the barrel that was used for rapid movement in an emergency.

The Vickers Gun Mk 1*

Rearsight adjusting wheel
This allowed the gunner to alter the range up to 1000 m (1,094 yards), but this varied on some marks, as did the size of the adjusting wheel

Spade grips Not used to hold the gun steady for firing, but merely made a comfortable grip for the gunner; the tripod held the gun steady

Firing lever Connected to the internal trigger by a linkage. It was pressed by the gunner's thumbs as they held the two spade grips

External tail of cocking lever outside the breech casing. If a stoppage occurred the exact position of this tail, and thus the lever, indicated to the gunner the cause of the stoppage (e.g. a misfed cartridge)

Hinge of toggle mechanism This broke upwards to allow the lock to move backwards under the influence of the muzzle gases

Cocking lever handle The gunner pulled this back to manually load a cartridge from the belt into the system ready to fire the first round. Its position after a stoppage, combined with the lever tail, could indicate the stoppage cause

Tumbler Part of the actual firing mechanism; when the trigger was moved by a linkage from the firing, the tumbler moved upward to allow the firing pin to move forward and strike the cartridge primer

Extractor This clipped over the rim of the cartridge case ready to extract it after firing as the lock moved to the rear

Barrel chamber, seen here with a round in place ready for firing. The thickened barrel section covering the chamber impinged on the breech block or lock to actuate the mechanism

Crosshead arm holding the elevating wheel and elevating gear

Elevating wheel This raised and lowered the angle of elevation of the gun on the tripod

Socket allowing some slight degree of traverse for the gun, usually effected by the gunner striking the side of the breech casing with his hand to move the gun a precise amount in order to spread the arc of fire to one side or the other

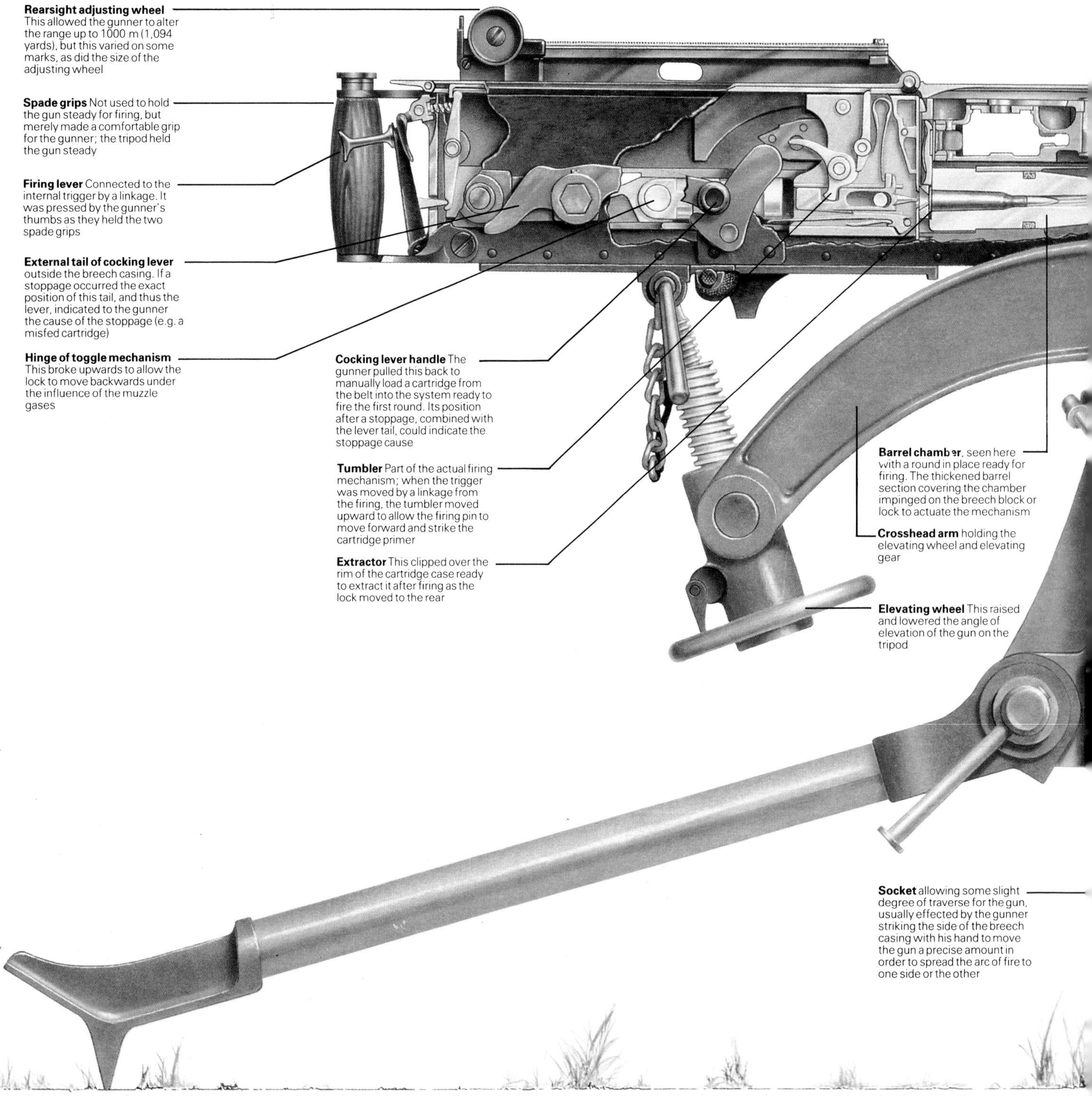

for experience (not only in the actual servicing of the weapon but its tactical use and resupply over prolonged periods) led to formation of the Machine Gun Corps in October 1915. Gradually the heavy machine-guns assigned to divisions were reallocated as companies of this new corps, and its ultimate importance can be seen in the fact that when World War I ended it contained 6,432 officers and 124,920 other ranks. These men gradually improved the art of using machine-guns in battle by formulating procedures whereby they were fired not in isolation but as part of a mutually-supporting fire plan. Steadily they improved these fire plans so that at times the machine-gun fire plans resembled those of the artillery. Indeed, on occasions machine-guns were used to harass the enemy in much the same way as artillery.

However, it was soon discovered that if machine-guns were given the task of providing prolonged fire support, they required not only highly trained crews but also a highly organized supply system. The Vickers machine-gun could devour ammunition at a prodigious rate, and considerable ammunition supplies had therefore to be kept in the supply line at all times. One snag soon encountered was that of transport: there were few places in the front lines of 1914-8 where supply vehicles could get anywhere close to the forward trenches, so the

ammunition had to be carried over considerable distances by manpower alon[e]. Once on site the ammunition could not be simply loaded into the gun. T[he] rounds were supplied in metal cases that often held the ammunition in the for[m] of small cardboard cartons each containing 100 rounds, as being intended [for] use by many types of weapon (Lee-Enfield rifles, Lewis Guns and so on) and [it] was not possible to provide the rounds already loaded into their fabric belts, a[nd] this had to be done before they could be fed into the gun. This was often done [by] hand, which was a time-consuming process, though later a special loadi[ng] machine was devised and issued.

So there was more to using the Vickers machine-gun in action than simp[ly] pressing a trigger and watching the enemy tumble. In time the members of t[he] Machine Gun Corps became every bit as proficient as their German count[er] parts when it came to using machine-guns in action, and were sometimes mu[ch] more imaginative in the tactical use of their weapons.

An example of this can be found in the instance when 10 Vickers machi[ne] guns of the 100th Machine Gun Company played their part in the battle to secu[re] High Wood on 24 August 1916, as part of the battle now known as the Battle [of] the Somme. This was a dour slogging match that lasted months under the mo[st]

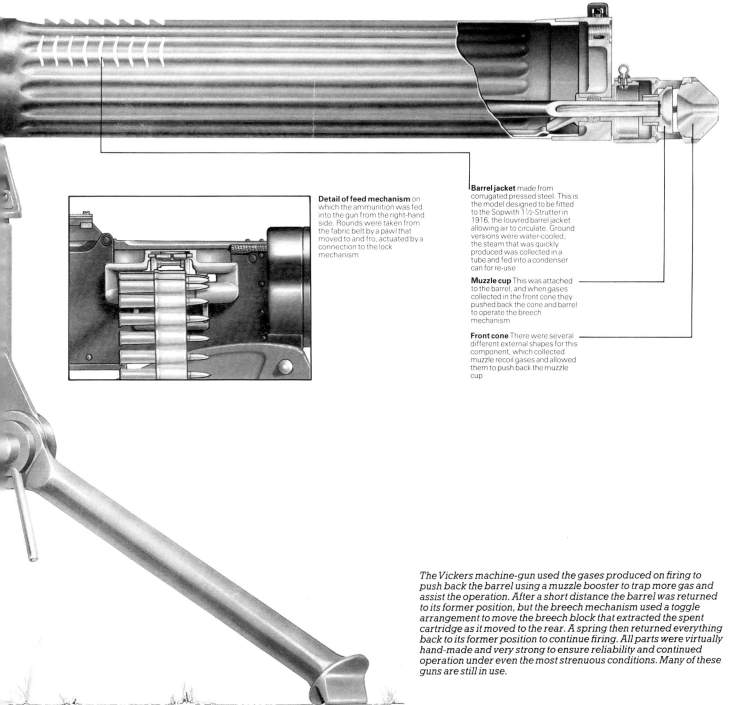

Detail of feed mechanism on which the ammunition was fed into the gun from the right-hand side. Rounds were taken from the fabric belt by a pawl that moved to and fro, actuated by a connection to the lock mechanism

Barrel jacket made from corrugated pressed steel. This is the model designed to be fitted to the Sopwith 1½-Strutter in 1916, the louvred barrel jacket allowing air to circulate. Ground versions were water-cooled; the steam that was quickly produced was collected in a tube and fed into a condenser can for re-use

Muzzle cup This was attached to the barrel, and when gases collected in the front cone they pushed back the cone and barrel to operate the breech mechanism

Front cone There were several different external shapes for this component, which collected muzzle recoil gases and allowed them to push back the muzzle cup

The Vickers machine-gun used the gases produced on firing to push back the barrel using a muzzle booster to trap more gas and assist the operation. After a short distance the barrel was returned to its former position, but the breech mechanism used a toggle arrangement to move the breech block that extracted the spent cartridge as it moved to the rear. A spring then returned everything back to its former position to continue firing. All parts were virtually hand-made and very strong to ensure reliability and continued operation under even the most strenuous conditions. Many of these guns are still in use.

eadful conditions, with the British attacking most of the time. After an attack in e High Wood area it was noted that an earthwork known as Savoy Trench 'fered a good fire position that commanded the German front line about 330 m (2,000 yards) distant. It was decided that the next foray on the German nt line would be supported by the machine-guns of the 100th Company; once iis had been completed the inevitable German counterattack would be halted / keeping the area behind the front-line trenches covered by machine-gun fire sting 12 hours.

Such a formidable fire plan called for considerable preparation. The night fore the attack two infantry companies were needed to move forward the nmunition and the water for the guns. The guns were carefully emplaced and mouflaged under netting and made ready for the battle ahead.

As the attack went in the machine-guns opened fire and kept firing for the next 2 hours. At intervals the gunners were changed, along with the faithful nmunition numbers who were responsible for guiding the ammunition belts to the gun to prevent them from twisting or dragging along the ground and so cking up dirt. The firer had little to do other than keep down the trigger etween the two spade grips; he could feel little of the firing recoil, which was

mostly absorbed by the heavy tripod. From time to time he gave the side of the gun a sharp tap to move the barrel slightly to cover a wider area and a few moments later another tap would move the barrel again.

When necessary the water in the cooling jackets was topped up with some of that so carefully stockpiled during the previous night. Barrels were changed every hour. All through the 12-hour period a party of men was kept busy moving ammunition from the dump built the previous night to two men who kept a loading machine in constant action. From the loading machine another party took the full belts to the guns. By the time the action ended the 10 guns had managed to fire just 250 less than one million rounds. Throughout that period only two guns gave any trouble, one with a broken extractor pawl and another that had something wrong with its lock mechanism and so suffered random jams. All the stockpiled water had been consumed, and the guns had only been kept going by use of the company water bottles and the crews' personal resources. But in the end it all worked. The enemy front-line trenches had been taken and the anticipated counterattack had not taken place, for the simple reason that no German soldier could cross the area of ground beaten by the fire of the 10 Vickers machine-guns of the 100th Machine Gun Company.

Above: An Australian Army Vickers machine-gun team engages a low-flying enemy aircraft. This usually involved reversing the tripod head to provide the required barrel elevation and some care with the ammunition feed, but this anti-aircraft method could be highly effective against the German ground attack aircraft which appeared in large numbers in 1918.

Right: A Vickers machine-gun is hidden in farm buildings near Haverskerque during the period of relatively fluid warfare that followed the German offensives of early 1918. As always, one man directs the gunner's fire and another guides the ammunition belt into the gun. The condenser hose is fitted to the jacket.

Left: A sergeant of the Machine Gun Corps uses his Vickers machine-gun at close range (note the rearsight in the 'down' position). He is personally armed with a revolver, and on his arm can be seen the machine-gun proficiency badge, awarded only to the most skilful machine-gunner who knew the Vickers backwards.

Below: Vickers machine-gun teams operate from specially-prepared positions somewhere among the Flanders battlefields. This photograph provides an indication of the field conditions the Vickers had to operate in during World War I, but the guns could absorb all manner of hard and mud-infested u

DENMARK
Madsen machine-guns

he first Madsen machine-gun was roduced in Denmark by the Dansk ndustri Syndikat in 1904 and the last in 950. The Madsen series was really a ong string of near-identical models roduced in a very wide array of alibres to suit the requirements of nany export customers all around the world.

Although it was not fully realized at ne time that the first were produced, ne **Madsen 8-mm Rekytgevaer M1903** nachine-gun was one of the very first f the light machine-guns, and even eatured the world's first overhead box nagazine of its type. The weapon used unique operating principle that has een used in no other design and vhich even for its time was expensive, omplex and difficult to manufacture. his was a system that used the Pea-ody-Martini hinged block action, an ction familiar on small-calibre match fles. What Madsen did was to convert iis essentially manually-operated ac-on to a fully automatic. By using a ombination of the recoil plus the novement of a plate moving on cams nd levers, the action opened and osed the hinged block, but as this lock had no integral bolt action (as ith a normal breech block) a sepa-ate rammer and extractor mechanism ad to be used. It sounds and was com-icated, but the system had one major ttribute and that was that it worked ery reliably under a wide range of onditions and with all sorts of am-unition, although rimmed ammu-tion such as the British 7.7 mm .303 in) was not so successful.

As well as being produced in many alibres for customers as far away as nailand, the Madsen was also manu-ctured in a wide variety of forms. aving an air-cooled barrel the Mad-n was not ideally suited for the sus-

tained-fire role, but various types of heavy tripod were produced. The more usual mounting was a bipod se-cured just under the muzzle though some models, including those for the Danish armed forces, had a short pedestal under the barrel for resting the barrel on parapets in houses or fortifications. A carrying handle was often fitted. One feature that promoted the Madsen's reliability was the type's excellent manufacture using the best materials available, which no doubt added to the overall costs.

During World War I the Madsen was not an official weapon used by any of the major protagonists, but all the same many Madsens appeared in nearly every continental army. The Madsen was one of the first weapons

used by both sides for early experi-ments in aircraft armament, although it was soon passed over in favour of other weapons. It was also used in small numbers by German troops ex-perimenting on the Eastern Front with their *Sturmtruppen* tactics, and more were used by some of the Central European armies, again in small num-bers only. When the light machine-gun concept became more widely accepted the Madsen was investi-gated by many nations, and the British even attempted to use it in 7.7-mm calibre. Unfortunately this cartridge was rimmed and it was one that did not work well in the Madsen mechanism; the guns were thus put by only to be issued again in 1940, this time to the new Home Guard.

The Madsen machine-gun was one of the first light machine-guns, and used a complex falling block locking system. It was produced in many calibres and models and was widely used throughout World War I. This version was used for a while by the British Army chambered for 0.303-in (7.7-mm) ammunition.

Specification
Rekytgevaer M1903
Calibre: 8 mm (0.315 in)
Lengths: overall 1.145 m (45.0.8 in); barrel 596 mm (23.46 in)
Weight: 10 kg (22.05 lb)
Muzzle velocity: 825 m (2,707 ft) per second
Rate of fire: (cyclic) 450 rpm
Feed: 20-round box magazine

RUSSIA
Pulemet Maksima obrazets 1910

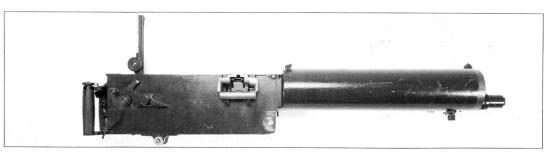

he first Maxim machine-guns for Rus-an service were ordered direct from ckers in the early 1900s, but it was t long before the Russians were pro-cing their own models at the state senal at Tula. The first 'Russian' mod-was the **Pulemet Maksima obrazets 05** (Maxim gun model 1905), which as a direct copy of the original Maxim n but produced with a typical Rus-n flourish in the bronze water jacket.

1910 this bronze jacket was re-aced by a sheet steel jacket and this as known either as the **obr 1910** or the M1910.

The PM1910 was destined to be the ngest-produced version of all the ny Maxim gun variants, for it re-ained in full-scale production until 43. Although there were several riants over the years, the basic M1910 was a solid piece of equip-ent that served very well under even most drastic conditions and all ex-mes of climate, a fact which suited Russians very well considering eir far-flung empire. This reliability d to be purchased at a cost, and that st was weight. The PM1910 and any-ng to do with it was very heavy, so avy in fact that the usual carriage sembled a small artillery field car-ge. On this carriage, known as the kolov mounting, the gun was usually otected by a removable shield. The n rested on a large turntable for

traversing and was elevated by a large wheel-operated screw. The turntable was carried on two spoked steel wheels and the whole arrangement could be towed by hand using a U-shaped handle. On many of these early Sokolov mounts there were two side legs that could be extended forward to raise the entire weapon and carriage for firing over parapets; on later mod-els these legs were omitted.

The weight of the PM1910 complete with the mounting was no less than 74 kg (163.1 lb). This meant that at least two men were required to drag the weapon (more across rough ground, for which drag ropes were provided). A special sledge mounting was avail-able for use during the winter months, and the weapon could also be carried on the widely-available peasant carts used all over Russia. To offset this

weight penalty, the PM1910 could be kept firing for as long as belts were fed into the mechanism. It required next to no maintenance, which was just as well for the state of training in the Tsarist armies usually meant that no servicing (other than rudimentary cleaning) was provided.

PM1910s were produced in vast numbers until 1917, by which time pro-duction had spread to centres other than Tula. The only change made dur-ing World War I was that the original smooth water-cooling jackets were re-placed by corrugated jackets to in-crease the surface area slightly and thus increase cooling. At times the heavy shields were left off to decrease the weight slightly. During World War I the amount of rough handling the PM1910 could absorb became legen-dary, so much so that the Germans

Originally built by Vickers for the Russian army, the Maxim gun was soon being manufactured in the Imperial Arsenal at Tula, outside Moscow. It was to remain in quantity production until 1943.

used as many as they could capture, though only on the Eastern Front.

Specification
PM1910
Calibre: 7.62 mm (0.3 in)
Lengths: overall 1.107 m (43.58 in); barrel 720 mm (28.35 in)
Weights: gun 23.8 kg (52.47 lb); mounting with shield 45.2 kg (99.65 lb)
Muzzle velocity: 863 m (2,831 ft) per second
Rate of fire: (cyclic) 520-600 rpm
Feed: 250-round fabric belt

Lewis Gun

The **Lewis Gun** is put into an international category for although its origins were American it was first produced and manufactured in Europe. Its inventor was an American, one Samuel Maclean, but the basic concept was developed further and 'sold' by Colonel Isaac Lewis, another American. The American military authorities were unenthusiastic about the new gun, so Lewis took the design to Belgium where it was accepted and put into production for the Belgian army. That was in 1913, and in the following year production was switched to the UK where Birmingham Small Arms (BSA) took over the programme.

The Lewis Gun was put into production at BSA as the **Lewis Gun Mk 1** for the British Army for the simple reason that five or six Lewis Guns could be produced in the time it took to produce a single Vickers machine-gun. The fact that the Lewis was light and portable was secondary at that time, but once in service the Lewis proved to be a very popular front-line weapon with a host of mobile tactical uses. The Lewis Gun was one of the first of the true light machine-guns and with its distinctive overhead drum magazine it was soon a common sight on the Western Front. The Lewis Gun was a gas-operated weapon, gas being tapped off from the barrel on firing to push a piston to the rear; the piston pushed back the breech block and mechanism and also wound up a coil spring under the gun which was used to return everything to the start position. The mechanism was rather complex and took careful maintenance, but even then was still prone to an alarming number of jams and stoppages, some of them introduced by the overhead drum magazine, which was a constant cause of trouble especially when only slightly damaged. The barrel was enclosed in a special air cooling jacket that was supposed to use a forced draught system of cooling, but experience showed that the jacket's efficiency had been over-rated and the gun worked quite well without it. Versions of the Lewis Gun intended for use on aircraft did not have this complex cooling jacket.

Only after the Lewis Gun had been produced in thousands in Europe did the American military authorities finally realize the potential of the weapon, and it went into production for the US Army (and air corps) chambered in the American 7.62-mm (0.3-in) calibre. Thus the Lewis Gun became truly international, especially as the Germans were in the habit of using as many captured examples as they could to bolster their own machine-gun totals. Some Lewis Guns were used on the early tanks and more were used by naval vessels. A similar role cropped up again in World War II when stockpiled Lewis Guns were distributed for the defence of merchant shipping and for Home Defence in the hands of the Home Guard and Royal Air Force airfield defence units.

The Lewis Gun was a complex

Above: The Lewis Gun was widely used by the British Army but it was originally produced in Belgium. It was easily recognizable from its bulky air-cooling jacket and the flat pan magazine, here holding 47 rounds.

weapon, but in service it made quite an impression in a way that was not possible using the heavy machine-guns. The Lewis Gun was the first of the true light machine-guns in more ways than one.

Specification
Lewis Gun Mk 1
Calibre: 7.7 mm (0.303 in)
Lengths: gun 1.25 m (49.2 in); barrel 661 mm (26.02 in)
Weights: 12.25 kg (27 lb)
Muzzle velocity: 744 m (2,441 ft) per second
Rate of fire: 450-500 rpm
Feed: 47- or 97-round overhead drum magazine

A British Lewis Gun team in action shows the ready-filled ammunition pans still in their box. The fins of the air-cooling jacket can be seen under the ammunition pan on the gun; these fins were supposed to force air along the barrel, but were superfluous.

A British Army Lewis gunner firing his Lewis Gun as if it were a rifle, no doubt at some hastily-presented target. Firing the Lewis Gun in this fashion was usually inaccurate, for the weight of the gun was too high for prolonged firing and the recoil soon shook the aim off the target.

Contrary to general belief, the German army was not an avid proponent of the machine-gun when Hiram Maxim started to demonstrate his product around the European capitals in the 1890s. His gun aroused some interest but few sales, and the first made to the German army were actually paid for out of the private funds of Kaiser Wilhelm II. Thereafter things began to look up and gradually a licensing agreement was made between Maxim and the German army. From this agreement Maxim machine-guns were soon being produced by both commercial concerns and the Deutsche Waffen und Munitionsfabriken at Spandau, near Berlin. Several models were produced before the 'standard' weapon appeared in 1908 as the **schwere Maschinengewehr 08**, or **sMG 08**. It fired the standard 7.92-mm (0.312-in) rifle cartridge of the day.

As a machine-gun the sMG 08 differed little from many other Maxim guns, and the Maxim recoil-operated mechanism was used unchanged. Construction was very solid, and once in service the **'Spandau'** proved to be very reliable under the most demanding battlefield conditions. Where the sMG 08 did differ from other machine-guns of the time was the mounting.

The schwere Maschinengewehr 08 (sMG 08) was the standard German machine-gun of World War I and used the basic Maxim system unchanged. It was a very heavy weapon capable of a prodigious amount of fire. Emplaced in well-constructed dugouts protected by dense thickets of barbed wire, it took a fearful toll of Allied troops.

Even the early German Maxims used a type of mounting known as a *Schlitten* (sledge) that was intended to be dragged across country when folded with the gun on top. As an alternative this mounting could be carried by two men as if it was a stretcher. The mounting, known as the Schlitten 08, provided a stable firing platform but was very heavy, to the extent that in 1916 an alternative tripod mounting known as the Dreifuss 16 was introduced.

During World War I the sMG 08 took a fearful toll of the Allies' manpower strengths. It was usually the sMG 08 that was responsible for mowing down the massed infantry attacks of 1914 to 1917, for after 1914 the numbers of machine-guns used by the German army increased greatly and (probably more important) the Germans learned to use them widely. Instead of simply placing a machine-gun to face directly across no man's land, the Germans learned to set them up firing to a flank so that one gun could enfilade and break up an infantry attack to much better effect, while at the same time providing more cover for the gun crew. The German machine-gunners were picked men who often maintained their guns in action to the last, and they were highly trained in all aspects of their task. They knew the sMG 08 backwards and could carry out repairs in the front line if need arose.

At times two or three men using a single sMG 08 could break up entire Allied infantry battalions once the latter had left the shelter of their trenches. The slaughter of Neuve Chapelle, Loos, the Somme and all the other costly infantry carnages can be traced to sMG 08s and their determined crews.

After 1918 the sMG 08 was maintained in German service, and many were still in use when 1939 came around, but by by then they had been relegated to second-line duties.

Specification
sMG 08
Calibre: 7.92 mm (0.312 in)
Lengths: gun 1.175 m (46.26 in); barrel 719 mm (28.3 in)
Weights: gun complete with spares 62 kg (136.7 lb); sledge mount 37.65 kg (83.0 lb)
Muzzle velocity: 900 m (2,953 ft) per second
Rate of fire: 300-450 rpm
Feed: 250-round fabric belt

Bulgarian machine-gun teams in action use Maxim Model 1908 machine-guns purchased from Vickers in the United Kingdom. These guns fire an 8-mm (0.315-in) cartridge and were very similar to the German sMG 08.

Above: The heavy tripod-mounted guns in service in 1914 had to be broken down into several loads for prolonged marching. Here a Jäger (light infantryman) in 1914 service kit shoulders the burden of the sMG 08.

Maschinengewehr 08/15

By 1915 the German army had come to appreciate that there was a need for some form of light machine-gun for front-line use. While the sMG 08 was an excellent heavy machine-gun, it was too heavy for rapid tactical moves and trials were held to determine what type of weapon would suffice. Among weapons tested was the Danish Madsen, and light Bergmann and Dreyse machine-guns, but the choice fell upon a lightened form of the sMG 08. This emerged as the **MG 08/15** and the first examples of the type were issued in 1916.

The MG 08/15 retained the basic mechanism of the sMG 08 and the water cooling system, but the water jacket was smaller; the receiver walls were thinner, some detail parts were eliminated, a bipod replaced the heavy sled mounting, and a pistol grip and butt were added; some changes were also made to the sights. By no stretch of the imagination could the MG 08/15 be called light, for it still weighed a hefty 18 kg (39.7 lb), but it was portable and could even be fired from a standing position with the weight taken by a sling. A shorter fabric belt was introduced to make handling easier, or a belt drum could be fitted to the side of the weapon to prevent feed belts dragging in the mud.

The choice of the basic sMG 08 mechanism meant that no additional training was required to use the lighter weapon, and there was a fair degree of spares interchangeability. Late in the

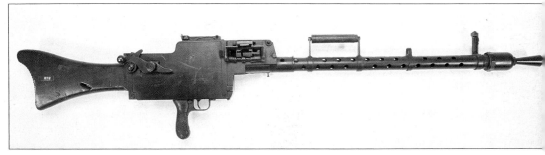

war the designers went one stage further and did away with the water-cooling jacket altogether to produce the **MG 08/18**. The war ended before this version could be widely used, the few that were produced being issued to the more mobile units of the German army; few actually reached the front-line infantry.

There was one further variant of the MG 08/15 known as the **LMG 08/15**, where the L denoted *Luft* (air). This version was one of several air-cooled machine-guns used in fixed mountings by the new German air arm and was basically an MG 08/15 with a perforated water jacket to allow air-cooling of the barrel. The guns were fired via a cable and were synchronized so as not to shoot through the aircraft propeller. Ammunition was fed into the gun from a drum and another spring-loaded drum was often used to prevent the used fabric belt flapping around in the

slipstream. Some of the early Maxim aircraft guns had been lightened sMG 08 models known as the **LMG 08**, but these passed out of use once the LMG 08/15 was established.

The ground-used MG 08/15 equipped front-line troops at company level and below, while the heavier sMG 08 was retained at battalion level or even deployed in special heavy machine-gun companies. The portability of the MG 08/15 enabled it to be used by the *Sturmtruppen* of 1917 and 1918, but it was never a handy weapon to use in action: in comparison with other light machine-guns of the period it was much larger and bulkier. But it remained every bit as reliable in action as its large counterpart and the German troops were well trained in its use. Perhaps the most effective use was made of the MG 08/15 during the latter stages of the 1918 campaign, when the retreating German army used small

The MG 08/18 was the last of the World War I versions of the sMG 08 to see service. It used an air-cooled barrel without the usual large casing and was an attempt to provide German troops with a light machine gun.

MG 08/15 teams to cover its withdrawals, single weapons sometimes holding up whole battalions and preventing the Allied cavalry from taking part in any action.

Specification
MG 08/15
Calibre: 7.92 mm (0.312 in)
Lengths: overall 1.398 m (55.0 in); barrel 719 mm (28.3 in)
Weight: complete 18 kg (39.7 lb)
Muzzle velocity: 900 m (2,953 ft) per second
Rate of fire: 450 rpm
Feed: 50-, 100- or 250-round fabric be

Schwarzlose machine-guns

The first indigenous Austro-Hungarian machine-gun was invented by one Andreas Schwarzlose in 1902, and was later manufactured at the Waffenfabrik Steyr. The first model was the **Schwarzlose Maschinengewehr Modell 07**, soon followed by the **MG Modell 08** and the full standard model, the **MG Modell 12**, to which standard the two earlier models were later converted by the Austro-Hungarian armed forces. There was little of note to mention between all these various models, for they all used an identical method of construction and the same operating principle.

The Schwarzlose machine-guns were all heavy belt-fed and water-cooled weapons working on an unusual principle, namely that known as delayed blow-back, in which the recoil forces impinge to the rear upon a heavy breech-block held in position (with the spent case still in the chamber) by a levered mechanism. Only after a short period of time has elapsed do these levers move sufficiently for the breech block to travel to the rear; this time is just long enough for the bullet to leave the muzzle and for the pressure in the barrel to fall to a safe limit. But the system means that the barrel length is limited: too long a barrel and the breech opens before the bullet has left the muzzle. So the operating system is a compromise between cartridge propellant strength, barrel length and the delayed-action lever timing.

In practice the Schwarzlose machine-guns worked well enough, but the barrel used was really too short for the standard Austro-Hungarian 8-mm (0.315-in) cartridge of the period,

and this resulted in excessive muzzle flash. As a result a long tapering flash hider had to be fitted, and this became one of the distinguishing features of the Schwarzlose. Another design feature of the series was the feed, which was amongst the first to use a drive sprocket to carry a cartridge into the system in a very precise manner. This added to the overall reliability of the Schwarzlose weapons.

Between 1914 and 1918 the main operators of the Schwarzlose were the Austro-Hungarian armies, but later in the war Italy had also become a major user, mainly by means of captured weapons. The Netherlands was another major buyer, but was a neutral during World War I. By 1914 nearly all the versions in use were the 07/12, 08/

12 and 12 models. The original Modells 07 and 08 used lubricated ammunition, but on the Modell 12 this feature was eradicated and the earlier models were modified up to Modell 12 standards. There was also a **Modell 07/16** intended for use on aircraft and featuring a rudimentary system of air-cooling, but it was not a great success and not many were produced.

All the Schwarzlose machine-guns were large and heavy weapons notable for the excellence of their manufacture. Indeed, they were so heavy and well made that few appear to have worn out, so that many were still in service during 1945 in Italy and Hungary. The delayed action blow-back system has not been widely copied, and is now regarded as an oddity.

The Austro-Hungarian armies used the heavy Schwarlose machine-gun in several forms, most of them looking very like this M 07/12. It used the blow-back principle for operation and was very reliable even though early models used an oil pump to lubricate the ammunition.

Specification
Modell 07/12
Calibre: 8 mm (0.315 in)
Lengths: gun 1.066 m (41.97 in); barrel 526 mm (20.71 in)
Weights: gun 19.9 kg (43.87 lb); tripod 19.8 kg (43.65 lb)
Muzzle velocity: 620 m (2,034 ft) per second
Rate of fire: (cyclic) 400 rpm
Feed: 250-round fabric belt

Above: A sergeant of the British Machine Gun Corps comes out of the line with a captured German MG 08/15. As can be seen, it was not a small piece of equipment, weighing in at some 18 kg (almost 40 lb).

Below: Austrian machine-gunners prepare a pair of Schwarzlose MGs in an anti-aircraft position. Machine-gun fire from the ground was one of the perils most feared by trench-strafing pilots.

A Browning 0.50 gunner scans the skies at Remagen, a Browning automatic rifle at his side. Both these very different products of the fertile brain of J.M. Browning served the US Army for decades.

Machine-Guns of World War II

A German MG 34 gunner in the USSR. The MG 34 was the first successful general-purpose machine-gun, combining the direct firepower of the heavy machine-gun with the relative ease of handling of the light machine-gun.

he machine-gun stood out amongst the new weapons troduced on a large scale during World War I. In fixed sitions, providing direct and indirect fire in support of assed infantry, it largely dictated infantry tactics. Towards e end of the conflict, however, a new, more mobile kind of arfare emerged. The introduction of armoured vehicles, d the German infiltration tactics, meant that any future attles would be very different.

uring World War II the machine-gun never quite succeeded in regain-g the influence over the battlefield that it managed to acquire during orld War I. Generally speaking tactics were more fluid and mobility as the key concept, but this did not mean that the machine-gun had no fluence on tactics: it remained a dreadful man-killer, it could still mmand ground, and it had been developed to still higher levels of chnical perfection than the equivalent weapons of World War I.

The machine-guns of 1939 to 1945 were still similar to those of World ar I, but among the remaining relics of the earlier conflict there were any new designs. There was even a new type of machine-gun that had own out of the analysed results of World War I. In that conflict there d been two machine-gun types, the light machine-gun and the heavy achine-gun: the light machine-gun could be carried by one man, was cated on a small bipod for aiming and firing, and usually carried the nmunition in some form of magazine; the heavy machine-gun was a am or squad weapon capable of high and prolonged fire rates and ually mounted on a heavy tripod; it was so heavy it was virtually static. om these two types of weapon the inter-war designers produced the

general-purpose machine-gun, a machine-gun light enough to be car-ried by one man and used as an assault weapon but still capable of being mounted on a tripod and used to produce the fire power of a heavy machine-gun. The first design to combine these two possibly opposing requirements successfully was the German MG 34, but this was only the forerunner of many designs to come.

Apart from the MG 34 there were many other superb designs of machine-gun in use (and some very poor ones to balance them, the Breda modello 1930 perhaps being one of the worst); it remains as ever a paradox that the peak of human ingenuity should be devoted to the mechanized destruction of fellow humans. Thus the years 1939 to 1945 suffered from the excellence of the Bren Gun, the American M1919 series and the power of the 12.7-mm (0.5-in) Browning. But from the design viewpoint perhaps the best design of all was the MG 34's succes-sor, the magnificent MG 42.

November 1943, near Rome. A typical light machine-gun position. Note the spare barrel for the Bren gun kept ready to hand above the spotter; prolonged fire heated the barrel and affected accuracy, necessitating a quick change.

Lehky Kulomet ZB vz.26 and vz.30 light machine-guns

When Czechoslovakia was established as a state after 1919 it contained within its borders a wide range of skills and talents, and among them was small arms expertise. In the early 1920s a company was established at Brno under the name of Ceskoslovenska Zbrojovka for the design and production of all types of small arms. An early product was a machine-gun known as the **Lehky Kulomet ZB vz.24** using a box magazine feed, but it remained a prototype only for an even better design was on the stocks. Using some details from the vz.24 the new design was designated the **Lehky Kulomet ZB vz.26**.

This light machine-gun was an immediate success and has remained one of the most inspirational of all such weapons ever since. The vz.26 was a gas-operated weapon with a long gas piston under the barrel and fed from an adjustable gas vent about half-way down the finned barrel. Gas operating on the piston pushed it to the rear and a simple arrangement of a hinged breech block on a ramp formed the locking and firing basis. Ammunition was fed downwards from a simple incline box magazine, and the overall design emphasized the virtues of easy stripping, maintenance and use in action. Barrel cooling was assisted by the use of prominent fins all along the barrel but a simple and rapid barrel change method was incorporated.

The vz.26 was adopted by the Czech army and soon became a great export success, being used by a whole string of nations that included China, Yugoslavia and Spain. The vz.26 was followed in production by a slightly improved model, the **Lehky Kulomet ZB vz.30**, but to the layman the two models were identical, the vz.30 differing only in the way it was manufactured and in some of the internal details. Like the vz.26, the vz.30 was also an export success, being sold to such countries as Iran and Romania. Many nations set up their own production lines under licence from ZB, and by 1939 the two designs were among the most numerous light machine-gun types in the world. When Germany started to take over most of Europe, starting with Czechoslovakia, the vz.26 and vz.30 became German weapons (**MG 26(t)** and **MG 30(t)**) and even remained in production at Brno for a while to satisfy the demands of the German forces. They were used all over the world and were even issued as standard German civil and military police machine-guns. Of all the nations involved in World War II none took to the type more avidly than China where production facilities were established. Perhaps the

Above: The Czech ZB vz.26, one of the most influential designs of its day and the forerunner of the British Bren gun; this example has its straight 20- or 30-round box magazine missing.

Right: Chinese Nationalist troops fighting under General Chian Kai Shek training with a ZB vz.26 light machine-gun.

most lasting influence the vz.26 and vz.30 had was on other designs; the Japanese copied them and so did the Spanish who produced a machine-gun known as the **FAO**. As is related elsewhere the vz.26 was the starting point for the British Bren, and the Yugoslavs produced their own variants.

If the Czech light machine-guns had any faults it was not in performance or handling but in production, for they were very expensive to make as many of the subassemblies had virtually to be machined and milled from solid metal. But this merely made them more robust and less prone to damage. They were, and still are, excellent light machine-guns.

Specification
ZB vz.26
Calibre: 7.92 mm (0.31 in)
Length: 1161 mm (45.71 in)
Length of barrel: 672 mm (26.46 in)
Weight: 9.65 kg (21.3 lb)
Muzzle velocity: 762 m (2,500 ft) per second
Rate of fire, cyclic: 500 rpm
Feed: 20- or 30-round box

Specification
ZB vz.30
Calibre: 7.92 mm (0.31 in)
Length: 1161 mm (45.71 in)

Length of barrel: 672 mm (26.46 in)
Weight: 10.04 kg (22.13 lb)
Muzzle velocity: 762 m (2,500 ft) per second
Rate of fire, cyclic: 500 rpm
Feed: 30-round box

Waffen SS troops firing a Czech ZB vz.30, a development of the ZB vz.26 the Germans knew this gun as the MG 30(t) and used it widely.

Breda machine-guns

During World War I the standard Italian machine-gun was the water-cooled Fiat modello 1914 and post-war this was modernized as the air-cooled Mitragliice Fiat modello 1914/35. But it was still a heavy weapon, even in its new air-cooled form, and a newer design of light machine-gun was initiated. The new design was produced by Breda who used the experience gained by the production of earlier models in 1924, 1928 and 1929 to produce the **Fucile Mitragliatori Breda modello 30**. This became the standard Italian army light machine-gun of World War II.

The modello 30 was one of those machine-gun designs that could at best be deemed unsatisfactory. In appearance it looked to be all odd shapes and projections and this was no doubt a hindrance to anyone who had to carry it, for these projections snagged on clothing and other equipment. But this was not all, for the Breda designers had tried to introduce a novel feed system using 20-round chargers which were rather flimsy and gave frequent trouble. These chargers were fed into a folding magazine that had a delicate hinge, and if this magazine or

the fitting was damaged the gun could not be used. To compound this problem, the extraction of the used cartridge cases was the weakest part of the whole gas-operated mechanism, and to make the gun work an internal oil pump was used to lubricate the used cases and thus assist extra extraction. While this system worked in theory the added oil soon picked up dust and other debris to clog the mechanism, and in North Africa sand was an ever-present threat. And as if this were not enough, the barrel-change method, although operable,

was rendered awkward by the fa that there was no barrel handle (a thus no carrying handle), so the ope ator had to use gloves. With no oth type in production the modello 30 h to be tolerated, and there was eve later **modello 38** version in 7.35-m (0.29-in) calibre.

The other two Breda machine-gu were at least better than the mode 30. One was the **Mitragliera Breda R modello 31**, produced for mounting the light tanks operated by the Itali army. This had a calibre of 12.7 m (0.5-in) and used a large curved vert

box magazine that must have res-
cted the weapon's use in AFV in-
riors.
As a heavy machine-gun the com-
ny produced the **Mitragliace Breda
odello 37**, and while this was overall
satisfactory weapon it did have an
usual feed feature: a flat 20-round
ed tray which worked its way
rough the receiver to accept the
ent cartridge cases. Exactly why this
mplex and quite unnecessary sys-
n was adopted is now impossible to
certain, for the spent cases had to be
moved from the tray before it could
e reloaded with fresh rounds. The
-pump extraction method was also
ed, rendering the modello 37 prone
the same debris clogging as the
hter modello 30. Thus the modello
was no more than adequate, even
ough the type became the standard
lian heavy machine-gun.
A version of the modello 37 for
ounting in tanks was produced under
e designation **Mitragliace Breda
odello 38**.

ecification
odello 30
alibre: 6.5 mm (0.256 in)
ngth: 1232 mm (48.5 in)
ngth of barrel: 520 mm (20.47 in)

Weight: 10.32 kg (22.75 lb)
Muzzle velocity: 629 m (2,065 ft) per
second
Rate of fire, cyclic: 450-500 rpm
Feed: 20-round charger

Specification
modello 37
Calibre: 8 mm (0.315 in)

Length: 1270 mm (50.0 in)
Length of barrel: 740 mm (29.13 in)
Weight: 19.3 kg (42.8 lb)
Weight of tripod: 18.7 kg (41.2 lb)
Muzzle velocity: 790 m (2,590 ft) per
second
Rate of fire, cyclic: 450-500 rpm
Feed: 20-round tray

*A Breda modello 30 6.5-mm (0.256-
in) light machine-gun, one of the
least successful machine-guns ever
designed. For all its faults it served
the Italians throughout the war.*

JAPAN

Type 11 and Type 96 light machine-guns

e Japanese heavy machine-guns
ed between 1941 and 1945 were
th derivations of the French Hotch-
ss machine-gun with only a few local
anges. When it came to the lighter
achine-guns the Japanese designed
eir own, the first of which was based
the same operating principles as
e Hotchkiss but with the usual local
riations.
The first of these was the 6.5-mm
256-in) **Light Machine-Gun Type 11**,
hich entered service in 1922 and re-
ained in service until 1945. Its Hotch-
ss origins were readily apparent in
e heavily ribbed barrel and less
viously in the internal mechanisms.
e design was credited to one
eneral Kijiro Nambu and it was by
e name of 'Nambu' that the type was
own to the Allies. It was in its
mmunition feed system that the Type
was unique, for it used a hopper
stem employed by no other
achine-gun. The idea was that a
all hopper on the left of the receiver
uld be kept filled with the rounds

fired by the rest of the Japanese infantry squad. The rounds could be fed into
the hopper still in their five-round
clips, thus rendering special magazines or ammunition belts unnecessary. But in practice this advantage
was negated by the fact that the internal mechanism was so delicate and
complex that firing the standard rifle
round caused endless troubles. Thus
special low-powered rounds had to be
used and things were made no better
by having to use a cartridge-
lubrication system that attracted the
usual dust and other debris to clog the
works. The Type 11 was capable of
automatic fire only, and when the
weapon was fired the ammunition hopper tended to make the whole system
unbalanced and awkward to fire. A
special version, the **Tank Machine-
Gun Type 91**, was produced for use in
tanks, with a 50-round hopper.
The bad points of the Type 11 became very apparent after early combat experience in China during the
1930s, and in 1936 the first examples of

*Above: The Japanese 6.5-mm
(0.256-in) Type 96 light
machine-gun was one of the
few machine-guns ever
equipped with a bayonet, and
was a combination of Czech
and French designs.*

*Right: Much of the fighting of the
Pacific island war was between the
Marines of the combatants. This
Japanese Leading Seaman is a
marine, and is carrying a Type 96
light machine-gun.*

a new design known as **Light Machine-Gun Type 96** started to reach the troops. While the Type 96 was a definite improvement on the Type 11, it did not replace the earlier model in service, mainly as a result of the fact that Japanese industry could never produce enough weapons of any type to meet the demands of the armed forces. Overall the Type 96 used a mixture of the old Hotchkiss principles and some of the features of the Czech ZB vz.26 that the Japanese had encountered in China. One of these ex-Czech features was the overhead box magazine that replaced the hopper of the Type 11, but internally the cartridge-oiling system had to be retained along with the attendant clogging. But the Type 96 did have a quick barrel-change system and there was a choice of drum or telescopic rear sights. Once in production the telescopic sights soon became the exception, but a handy magazine-filling device was retained. One accessory that was unique to the Type 96 among all other machine-gun designs was that it had a muzzle attachment to take a bayonet.

Specification
Light Machine-Gun Type 11
Calibre: 6.5 mm (0.256 in)
Length: 1105 mm (43.5 in)
Length of barrel: 483 mm (19.0 in)
Weight: 10.2 kg (22.5 lb)
Muzzle velocity: 700 m (2,295 ft) per second
Rate of fire, cyclic: 500 rpm
Feed: 30-round hopper

Specification
Light Machine-Gun Type 96
Calibre: 6.5 mm (0.256 in)
Length: 1054 mm (41.5 in)
Length of barrel: 552 mm (21.75in)
Weight: 9.07 kg (20 lb)
Muzzle velocity: 730 m (2,395 ft) per second
Rate of fire, cyclic: 550 rpm
Feed: 30-round box

The Japanese Type 99 light machine-gun was a development of the earlier Type 96 calibred for a 7.7-mm (0.303-in) cartridge, but it retained a bayonet lug under the bipod hinge.

 USA
Browning Automatic Rifle

The Browning Automatic Rifle M1918A2. The last production variant of this light machine-gun/automatic assault rifle used a 20-round box magazine and lacked the rapid barrel change of other more modern light machine-guns. It is shown below carried by a US soldier in 1944.

The **Browning Automatic Rifle**, or **BAR** as it is usually known, is one of those odd weapons that falls into no precise category. It may be regarded as a rather light machine-gun or as a rather heavy assault rifle, but in practice it was used as a form of light machine-gun.

As its name implies, the BAR was a product of John M. Browning's inventive mind, and Browning produced the first prototypes in 1917. When demonstrated they were immediately adopted for US Army service and were thus taken to France for active use during 1918. But the numbers involved at that time were not large, and the few used were employed as heavy rifles. This was not surprising as the first models, the **BAR M1918**, had no bipod and could only be fired from the hip or shoulder. A bipod was not introduced until 1937 with the **BAR M1918A1** and the full and final production version, the **BAR M1918A2**, had a revised bipod and the facility for a stock rest to be added for added stability. It was the M1918A1 and M1918A2 that were to become the main American operational models, and they were issued to bolster squad fire power rather than as a squad support weapon.

The original M1918 did have a role to play in World War II, for it was sent over to the United Kingdom in 1940 to provide some form of weapon for the British Home Guard and some found their way into other second-line use. The later models were produced in thousands in the USA and once in service in large numbers they became the sort of weapon upon which soldiers came to rely. This is not to say that the BAR did not have faults, for the box magazine had a capacity of only 20 rounds, which was far too few for most infantry operations. Being something of an interim weapon type it had few tactical adherents in the theoretical field but the soldier swore by the BAR and always wanted more that could be produced. After 1945 the BAR was used again in Korea and was not finally replaced until 1957 by the US Army. Even today new versions intended to arm police forces are still available under the name **Monitor**.

One little-known facet of BAR production is the pre-1939 output of variant designated **modèle 30** from Fabrique Nationale (FN) plant at Liège in Belgium. From this factory emerged a string of BAR models in various calibres for the armies of Belgium itself, Sweden, some Baltic states and some Central and South American states, including Honduras. Many found their way to the Chinese army. Poland set up a national assembly line for the BAR but their calibre was 7.92 mm (0.31 in), whereas the bulk of the FN output was in 7.65 mm (0.301 in) to suit the domestic preferred calibre. Many of these Polish BARs ended up in Soviet army hands after 1939, and even the German army used the BAR after capture from a variety of sources. The Poles thought very highly of the BAR and went to the extent of mounting the weapon on specially produced and very complex and heavy tripods; there was also a special anti-aircraft version.

Specification
BAR M1918A2
Calibre: 7.62 mm (0.3 in)
Length: 1214 mm (47.8 in)
Length of barrel: 610 mm (24.0 in)
Weight: 8.8 kg (19.4 lb)
Muzzle velocity: 808 m (2,650 ft) per second
Rate of fire, cyclic: 500-600 rpm (fast rate) or 300-450 rpm (slow rate)
Feed: 20-round box

USA
Browning M1919 machine-guns

e **Browning M1919** series differed
m the earlier M1917 series in that
e original water-cooled barrel was
placed by an air-cooled barrel. This
-cooled model was originally in-
ded for use in the many tanks the
ited States was going to produce,
t the end of World War I led to the
k contracts being cancelled along
th those for the original M1919. But
e air-cooled Browning was de-
loped into the **M1919A1**, the
919A2 (for use by the US Cavalry)
d then the **M1919A3**. The production
als for these early models were nev-
very high, but with the **M1919A4** the
als soared. By 1945 the production
al stood at 438,971 and more have
en produced since then.
The M1919A4 was produced mainly
infantry use and it proved to be a
st-class heavy machine-gun capable
pouring out masses of fire and
sorbing all manner of abuse and
nishment. As a partner for this infan-
version, a special model for use on
ks was produced as the **M1919A5**.
ere was also a special US Air Force
del, the **M2**, for use on both fixed
ng and flexible installations, and the
Navy had its own range based on
 M1919A4 and known as the **AN-
:**.
Among all these types and in such a
ng production run there were
nerous minor and major modifica-
ns and production alterations, but
 basic M1919 design was retained
oughout. The basic M1919 used a
ric or metal-link belt feed. The nor-
l mount was a tripod, and of these
re were many designs ranging from
mal infantry tripods to large and
mplex anti-aircraft mountings.
ere were ring- and gallows-type
untings for use on all sorts of trucks
m jeeps to fuel tankers, and there
re numerous special mountings for
manner of small craft.
Perhaps the strangest of the M1919
iants was the **M1919A6**. This was
duced as a form of light machine-
1 to bolster infantry squad power,
ich until the introduction of the
919A6 had to depend on the fire-
wer of the BAR and the rifle. The
919A6 was a 1943 innovation: it was
sically the M1919A4 fitted with an
kward-looking shoulder stock, a
od, a carrying handle and a lighter

*Above: A Browning M1919A4
machine-gun on its normal tripod
and clearly showing the perforated
barrel cooling jacket and the square
receiver; it was produced in huge
numbers and the type is still in use all
over the world.*

*A Long Range Desert Group Jeep
armed with Vickers-Berthier G.O.
machine-guns and with a Browning
M1919A4 mounted at the front; this
gun has every appearance of being
adapted from an aircraft mounting.*

barrel. The result was a rather heavy
light machine-gun that at least had the
advantage that it could be produced
quickly on existing production lines.
Disadvantages were the general
awkwardness of the weapon and the
need to wear a mitten to change the
barrel when it got hot. For all that the
M1919A6 was churned out in large
numbers (43,479 by the time production ended), and the troops had to put
up with it, for it was better in its role
than the BAR.
If there was one overall asset that
was enjoyed by all the versions of the
M1919 series of machine-guns it was
reliability, for the types would carry on
working even in conditions in which
other designs (other than perhaps the
Vickers) would have given up. They all
used the same basic recoil method:
muzzle gases push back the entire barrel and breech mechanism until a bolt
accelerator continues the rearward
movement to a point at which springs

return the whole mechanism to restart
the process.
The M1919 series (including the unlovely M1919A6) is still in widespread
use, although the M1919A6 is now used
by only a few South American states.

Specification
M1919A4
Calibre: 7.62 mm (0.3 in)
Length: 1041 mm (41.0 in)
Length of barrel: 610 mm (24.0 in)
Weight: 14.06 kg (31 lb)
Muzzle velocity: 854 m (2,800 ft) per
second
Rate of fire, cyclic: 400-500 rpm
Feed: 250-round belt

Specification
M1919A6
Calibre: 7.62 mm (0.3 in)
Length: 1346 mm (53.0 in)
Length of barrel: 610 mm (24.0 in)
Weight: 14.74 kg (32.5 lb)
Muzzle velocity: 854 m (2,800 ft) per
second
Rate of fire, cyclic: 400-500 rpm
Feed: 250-round belt

USA
Browning 12.7-mm (0.5-in) heavy machine-guns

er since the first Browning 12.7-mm
-in) heavy machine-gun was pro-
:ed in 1921 the type has been one of
 most fearsome anti-personnel
apons likely to be encountered.
 projectile fired by the type is a
digious man-stopper, and the
:hine-gun can also be used as an
our-defeating weapon, especially
en firing armour-piercing rounds.
 round is really the heart of the gun,
d early attempts by Browning to pro-
:e a heavy machine-gun all found-
d on the lack of a suitable cartridge.

*e classic Browning machine-gun
its usual tripod. It was first placed
roduction in 1921 and remains
as it is one of the best anti-
sonnel weapons ever developed;
so has a very useful anti-armour
ability.*

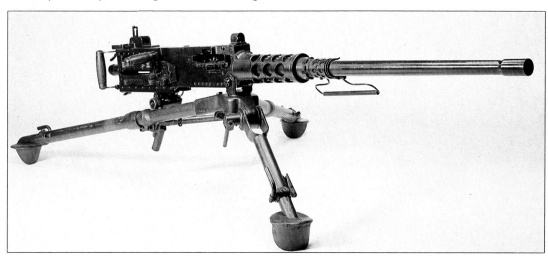

It was not until the examination of a captured German 13-mm (0.51-in) round (used in the Mauser T-Gewehr anti-tank rifle) that the solution was found, and thereafter all was well. The basic cartridge has remained essentially unchanged, although there have been numerous alternative propellants and types of projectile.

From the original **Browning M1921** heavy machine-gun evolved a whole string of variants based on what was to become known as the **M2**. On all these variants the gun mechanism remained the same, being very similar to that used on the smaller M1917 machine-gun. Where the variants differed from each other was in the type of barrel fitted and the fixtures used for mounting the gun.

One of the most numerous of the M2s has been the **M2 HB**, the suffix denoting the use of a Heavy Barrel. The HB version can be used in all manner of installations and in the past has been employed as an infantry gun, as an anti-aircraft gun and even as a fixed or trainable aircraft gun. For infantry use the M2 HB is usually mounted on a heavy tripod, but it can also be used mounted on vehicle pintles, ring mountings and pivots. Other M2 types include versions with water-cooled barrels, which were usually employed

as anti-aircraft weapons, especially on US Navy vessels where during World War II they were often fixed in multiple mountings for use against low-flying attack aircraft. Single water-cooled mountings were often used to provide anti-aircraft defence for shore installations. The main change between ground-based and aircraft versions was that the aircraft model had a barrel 914 mm (36 in) long whereas the ground version had a barrel 1143 mm (45 in) long. Apart from the barrel and some mounting fixtures, any part of the M1921 and M2 machine-guns can be interchanged.

More 12.7-mm (0.5-in) Browning machine-guns have been produced in the United States than any other design. To date the figures run into millions and the production run is still not complete, for during the late 1970s two American companies found it worthwhile to put the type back into production, and the same applied to the Belgian FN concern. Many more companies throughout the world find it profitable to provide spares and other such backing for the M2 series, and almost every year another ammunition producer introduces yet another type of cartridge for use with the weapon. Many dealers find it profitable just to sell or purchase such weapons alone,

so there is no sign yet that demand for the gun is weakening in any way.

The M2 will be around for decades to come, and there is no sign of any replacement. It must rank as one of the most successful machine-gun designs ever produced.

Specification
M2 HB
Calibre: 12.7 mm (0.5 in)
Length: 1654 mm (65.1 in)

This anti-aircraft mounting, known as the M45 Maxson Mount, used for heavy barrelled Browning M2s.

Length of barrel: 1143 mm (45.0 in)
Weight: 38.1 kg (84 lb)
Weight of tripod: 19.96 kg (44 lb) for M3 type
Muzzle velocity: 884 m (2,900 ft) per second
Rate of fire, cyclic: 450-575 rpm
Feed: 110-round metal-link belt

Fusil Mitrailleur modèles 1924/29 and Mitrailleuse 1931 machine-guns

The French army was not slow to realize the impact of the light machine-gun on tactics during World War I, and soon after the Armistice spent considerable time and effort developing a national design suitable for extensive French deployment. Despite all the effort, the eventual result was a weapon with a mechanism based on that of the American Browning Automatic Rifle but altered in several ways to suit a new cartridge with a calibre of 7.5 mm (0.295 in). The first production model was the **Fusil Mitrailleur modèle 1924** (Automatic Rifle M1924), which was manufactured at the large arsenal at Saint-Etienne. The design was clean and modern-looking, and used an overhead box magazine holding 25 or 26 rounds. A dual-trigger system was provided for single shots or full automatic fire.

Unfortunately neither the gun nor the cartridge was fully developed before the type was introduced into service, resulting in a series of internal barrel explosions and other shortcomings. The solution was to redesign the cartridge to make it slightly less powerful (becoming shorter in the process) and to beef up some of the weapon's parts. The result was the **Fusil Mitrailleur modèle 1924/29**, and it was this type that eventually became the standard French light machine-gun for much of the army in 1939. A range of mountings was devised for the weapon, and there was even a small monopod for mounting under the butt to make prolonged fire more accurate.

A special variant of the mle 1924/29 was produced, initially for use in the Maginot Line defences but eventually also for tanks and other AFVs. This was the **Mitrailleuse modèle 1931**, and at first sight it had little in common with the earlier model. The mle 1931 had a peculiarly-shaped butt and a prominent side-mounted drum magazine

holding no less than 150 rounds. Despite appearances the internal arrangements were the same as those of the mle 1924/29, even if the overall length and barrel length were increased. In static defences the increased weight was no handicap and the mle 1931 was produced in large numbers. In fact so many were produced that ultimately the model was used outside the concrete defences as an anti-aircraft weapon, often arranged in pairs on special or even improvised anti-aircraft mountings.

With the events of 1940 the mle 1924/29 and mle 1931 passed into German hands as the **Leichte MG 116(f)** and **Kpfw MG 331(f)** respectively. Only a relatively few remained in French hands in the Middle East and North Africa, and there they were used until 1945. After 1945 the type was once more put into production and it remained in service for many years,

some examples ending up in the hands of the Viet Cong in the Far East. Post-war production involved only the mle 1924/29.

The German booty of 1940 meant that many mle 1924/29s and mle 1931 machine-guns were later incorporated into the defences of the Atlantic Wall, and the mle 1931 was especially favoured by the Germans as an anti-aircraft weapon. But for all this widespread use the mle 1924/29 and mle 1931 were never entirely trouble-free, and the cartridge they fired was generally deemed underpowered and lacking in range: maximum useful range was only 500 to 550 m (550 to 600 yards) instead of the 600+ m (655+ yards) of many contemporary designs.

Specification
Fusil Mitrailleur mle 1924/29
Calibre: 7.5 mm (0.295 in)
Length: 1007 mm (39.65 in)

A Chatellerault modèle 1924/29 light machine-gun, the standard French light machine-gun of 1940; it had a calibre of 7.5 mm (0.295 in) and used two triggers, one for automatic fire and the other for single shots.

Length of barrel: 500 mm (19.69 in)
Weight: 8.93 kg (19.7 lb)
Muzzle velocity: 820 m (2,690 ft) per second
Rate of fire, cyclic: 450-600 rpm
Feed: 25-round box

Specification
Mitrailleuse mle 1931
Calibre: 7.5 mm (0.295 in)
Length: 1030 mm (40.55 in)
Length of barrel: 600 mm (23.62 in)
Weight: 11.8 kg (26.0 lb)
Muzzle velocity: 850 m (2,790 ft) per second
Rate of fire, cyclic: 750 rpm
Feed: 150-round drum

bove: An airborne trooper fires his BAR after parachuting onto Corregidor in
ebruary 1945. US forces used the weapon for squad support, and it proved
ery popular with the ordinary GI.

Below: Similar in appearance to the Vickers and Maxim designs, the Browning
0.30 in was introduced in 1917. It is seen here in action with men of the 331st
Infantry Regiment street fighting in St Malo in August 1944.

US Machine-Guns

Above: A US Navy PT Boat attacks the Schouten Islands, off the north coast of New Guinea. The twin M2 Browning 0.50-in in the bows have been supplemented by an Oerlikon 20-mm cannon.

Below: An American tank destroyer pressing into the Reich in 1945 sports an impressive array of weaponry, the main armament being supplemented by a pair of M2HB Browning 0.50-in and an 0.30-in M1919 Browning.

During the Eighth Army's capture of Tavoleto in Italy during September 1944, a Gurkha Bren gunner takes up a position in a window backed by a companion with a Thompson sub-machine gun.

How machine-guns work

The very first machine-guns operated on what was basically a recoil principle. The very simplest operated on the blow-back principle, in which the recoil forces attendant on firing a rifle-power cartridge impinge directly on a breech block and force it back, only the mass of the block and perhaps some springs preventing the block from moving back while the internal pressures in the barrel remain at a dangerously high level. The simplicity of this system is overcome by the weights and masses involved, so the blow-back principle is not widely used in machine-guns, especially where powerful cartridges such as those in the 12.7-mm (0.5-in) calibre category are concerned.

What is required is some form of system that can operate by using the considerable energy released when a cartridge is fired without any danger of these forces endangering the weapon or the firer. Thus the breech block and the barrel have to remain 'locked' during the short period that the projectile is pushed down the barrel by the rapid gas expansion of the detonated propellant charge. This locking is usually carried out by mechanical means, and until recently the number of principles employed was legion. Only in recent years has the modern rotary lock become established to the point of virtual exclusion of other systems. But during World War II the rotary lock was well in the future and several other locking systems were thus employed.

It would be difficult to mention all these locking systems in a few lines, but suffice to say they all operated using two methods of overall propulsion. One was the recoil system and the other the gas-operated system. The recoil system usually operates by using the gases produced at the muzzle to propel the entire barrel and the locked-on breech mechanism to the rear; at some point during this rearwards progress the barrel is held by a fixed stop, leaving the breech block to move even farther backwards, taking with it the spent cartridge case until a point is reached where compressed springs push the whole arrangement back to the start position, loading a new round on the way ready for the next firing cycle. On many designs once the barrel and breech were unlocked a mechanical device known as an accelerator ensured that the breech block (or bolt) moved to the rear at an increased rate. The recoil system could even be divided into short or long recoil systems.

The gas-operated system is generally much lighter than the recoil system and the individual parts are not so highly stressed as those on the recoil system and can thus be made smaller and simpler. Thus the gas-operated system was most usually found in World War II light machine-guns. The principle uses propellant gases tapped off from a point along the barrel through which they are diverted even while the projectile is still in the barrel. This is safe as the gases have to overcome the inertia of a gas piston, which eventually moves to the rear taking the breech block away from the fixed barrel. Again, accelerators may be used but the gas pressure usually provides all the propulsion required until a point is reached where the breech is far enough to the rear for the gases to be vented through open ports in the receiver. Springs then return the piston and the breech block to the start position, loading a new round on the way. Needless to say there are several variations on this principle but they all operate along the same general lines.

The locking devices involved in both recoil and gas-operated mechanisms were many and varied. Most relied on some form of ramp or roller to form an obstacle with sufficient mechanical advantage (at the precise point when the round was fired and pressures were at their highest) to prevent the breech from moving. Some, usually involving rollers and lugs, actually used the rearward forcing gas pressures of the cartridge case to form the 'lock' at the instant of firing, while others used a simple wedge system. Some were very complex and some were simple to the point of absurdity, but generally speaking the simpler the system the more reliable it was in operation.

Gas tube and piston
The gas piston was made from high quality metals, as it had to bear the brunt of the gas operating system. As the firing gases came through the regulator they impinged directly onto the piston face, driving it to the rear. When the piston had been pushed back to the correct distance the gases were allowed to escape through vents in the side of the piston wall.

Quick release lever
The barrel was easy to change, by releasing the lever and drawing off by the carrying handle.

Gas regulator
The gas regulator has four positions, which allow the firing gases to escape through holes of four varying sizes into the gas piston cylinder.

Flash hider
At the end of the barrel the flash hider minimizes the amount of flame issuing from the weapon.

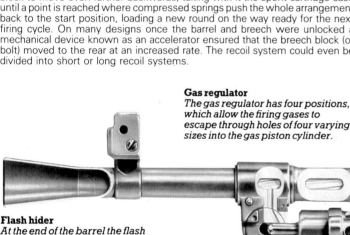

Propellant gases are drawn off through the regulator to act on a piston. This forces back the working parts, against the pressure of the return spring in the butt.

The hammer and bolt assembly, while withdrawing, extracts the empty cartridge case from the breech. Once clear it is ejected.

A fresh cartridge is fed from the magazine. The working parts are then moved back into position by the return spring in the butt.

The Bren gun is seen here in its original production form with a drum rearsight and adjustable bipod legs – later versions had these removed and replaced by simpler components.

Magazine *The magazine was curved to accommodate the rimmed 0.303-in cartridge and could hold up to 20 rounds.*

Hammer *The hammer actuator was a fixed post which struck the rear of the firing pin to allow it to strike the cartridge primer. The pin could not strike the primer until the round was properly chambered.*

Sights
Early models used drum sights with the rearsight on an arm, but later models used the simpler leaf sight.

Recoil spring
The main recoil spring was contained within the butt and was connected to the main moving parts by a steel rod which protruded into the receiver, so normally the recoil spring was neither touched nor seen when stripping. The rod was flexibly mounted to allow the piston group to be withdrawn for stripping.

Trigger *A fire selector lever close to the trigger had three positions; single shot, safe and automatic.*

UK
Bren light machine-gun

The **Bren Gun** was a development of the original Czech ZB vz.26 light machine-gun, but the development path was one that involved as much British as Czech expertise. During the 1920s the British army sought far and wide for a new type of light machine-gun to replace the generally unsatisfactory Lewis Gun, trying all manner of designs, most of which were found wanting in some way or other. By 1930 a series of trials commenced involving several designs, among them the vz.26 in the form of a slightly revised model, the ZB vz.27. The ZB vz.27 emerged as a clear winner from these trials but it was made in 7.92-mm (0.31-in) calibre only, and the British army wanted to retain its 7.7 mm (0.303-in) cartridge with its outdated cordite propellant and its awkward rimmed case.

Thus started a series of development models that involved the vz.27, the later vz.30 and eventually an interim model, the ZB vz.32. Then came the vz.33 and it was from this that the Royal Small Arms Factory at Enfield Lock evolved the prototype of what became the Bren Gun (Bren from the

BR of Brno, the place of origin, and EN from Enfield Lock). Tooling up at Enfield Lock resulted in the first production **Bren Gun Mk 1** being turned out in 1937, and thereafter the type remained in production at Enfield and elsewhere until well after 1945. By 1940 well over 30,000 Bren Guns had been produced and the type was well established in service, but the result of Dunkirk not only supplied the Germans with a useful stock of Bren Guns (**Leichte MG 138(e)**) and ammunition but also led to a great demand to re-equip the British army.

The original design was thus much modified to speed up production, and new lines were established. The original gas-operated mechanism of the

ZB design was retained and so was the breech locking system and the general appearance, but out went the rather complicated drum sights and extras such as the under-butt handle in the **Bren Gun Mk 2**. The bipod became much simpler but the curved box magazine of the 7.7-mm (0.303-in) Bren was carried over. In time more simplifications were made (**Bren Gun Mk 3** with a shorter barrel and **Bren Gun Mk 4** with a modified butt assembly), and there was even a reversion to the 7.92-mm (0.31-in) calibre when Brens were manufactured in Canada for the Chinese army.

The Bren Gun turned out to be a superb light machine-gun. It was robust, reliable, easy to handle and to maintain, and it was not too heavy for its role. It was also very accurate. In time a whole range of mountings and accessories was introduced, including some rather complex anti-aircraft mountings that included the Motley and the Gallows mountings. A 200-round drum was developed but little used, and various vehicle mountings were designed and introduced. The Bren Gun

outlived all these accessories, for after 1945 the type remained in service and the wartime 'extras' were phased out.

The Bren Gun on its basic bipod did linger on, however, and is still in British Army service as the **Bren Gun L4A2**. It now boasts a calibre of the standard NATO 7.62 mm (0.3 in) and the barrel is chrome-plated to reduce wear and the need to change barrels during prolonged fire using the simple barrel-change device. Today the type is still in army service with second-line and support arms and also with the Royal Navy, and there seems to be no replacement for the type in sight. It was and still is an excellent light machine-gun.

Specification
Bren Light Machine-Gun Mk 1
Calibre: 7.7 mm (0.303 in)
Length: 1156 mm (45.5 in)
Length of barrel: 635 mm (25.0 in)
Weight: 10.03 kg (22.12 lb)
Muzzle velocity: 744 m (2,440 ft) per second
Rate of fire, cyclic: 500 rpm
Feed: 20-round box magazine

Vickers machine-guns

The **Vickers machine-gun** range had its origins in the Maxim gun of the late 19th century, and was little changed from the original other than that the Maxim locking toggle design was inverted in the Vickers product. The **Vickers Machine-Gun Mk 1** had performed well in World War I, outperforming in many ways nearly all of its contemporaries. Consequently after 1918 the Vickers remained the standard heavy machine-gun of both the British army and many of the Commonwealth forces as well. Many were exported all over the world but many of these were ex-stock weapons as production was kept at a very low ebb at Vickers' main production plant at Crayford in Kent.

However, some innovations were introduced before 1939; the introduction of the tank in all its various forms had led to the design of Vickers machineguns to arm the new fighting machines, and by 1939 Vickers had in production two types of special tank machine-gun. These were in two calibres: the **Vickers Machine-Gun Mks 4B, 6, 6* and 7** being of 7.7-mm (0.303-in) calibre and the **Vickers Machine-Gun Mks 4 and 5** of the 12.7-mm (0.5-in) type firing a special cartridge. Both were produced for all types of tank initially, but the introduction of the air-cooled Besa machine-guns for the bulk of the heavier tanks meant that most of the Vickers tank machine-guns ended up either in the light tank series or in the infantry tank types, the Matilda 1 and 2. The 12.7-mm (0.5-in) machine-guns were also produced in a variety of forms for the Royal Navy as the **Vickers Machine-Gun Mk 3** with all manner of mountings for anti-aircraft defence of ships and shore installations. The ship installations included quadruple mountings, but the cartridge produced for the weapon was not a success and proved underpowered. Nevertheless, in the absence of an alternative the weapon was produced in some numbers, only later being replaced by 20-mm cannon and other such weapons.

Thus 1939 found the Vickers machine-gun in service still and in some numbers. By 1940 all manner of ancient models from stock were being used in all roles including emergency anti-aircraft mountings to bolster home defences and production was soon under way again in large quantities. Demand was so heavy (most of the British army's machine-gun stocks were lost before and during the Dunkirk episode) that production short-cuts were introduced, the most noticeable of which was the replacement of the corrugated barrel water jacket by a

simple smooth jacket. Later a new muzzle booster design was introduced and by 1943 the new Mark 8Z boat-tailed bullet was in widespread use to provide a useful effective range of no less than 4100 m (4,500 yards). This enabled the Vickers machine-gun to be used for the indirect fire role and a mortar sight was adapted for the role.

After the war the Vickers served on (and still does) with armies such as

those of India and Pakistan. The British army ceased to use the type in 1968 but the Royal Marines continued to use theirs until well into the 1970s.

Specification
Vickers Machine-Gun Mk 1
Calibre: 7.7 mm (0.303 in)
Length: 1156 mm (45.5 in)
Length of barrel: 721 mm (28.4 in)
Weight of gun: 18.1 kg (40 lb) with water
Weight of tripod: 22 kg (48.5 lb)
Muzzle velocity: 744 m (2,440 ft) per second
Rate of fire, cyclic: 450-500 rpm
Feed: 250-round belt

A Vickers machine-gun in its late production form with no corrugations on the barrel jacket, the final form of the muzzle attachment and the indirect-fire sight in position

The machine-gun seen here is not the usual 7.7-mm (0.303-in) version but a heavier 12.7-mm (0.5-in) version which was originally produced for use on light tanks; it is seen here in use on a Chevrolet truck belonging to the Long Range Desert Group.

Men of the Cheshire Regiment using their Vickers machine-guns on a range, in about 1940; note the water cans to retain evaporated steam from the barrel jacket.

Vickers-Berthier light machine-guns

Above: The Vickers-Berthier Mk 3B produced for the Indian Army, showing the overall clean lines and general resemblance to the Bren Gun; the 30-round box magazine is not fitted.

Right: A patrol of the newly-formed SAS in North Africa in 1943; their jeeps are liberally armed with Vickers-Berthier G.O. guns and they have 96-round drum magazines.

The **Vickers-Berthier** series of light machine-guns originally evolved from a French design produced just before World War I. Despite some promising features the design was not adopted in useful numbers by any nation, but in 1925 the British Vickers company purchased licence rights on the type, mainly to keep its Crayford production lines in being with a new model to replace the Vickers machine-gun. After a series of British army trials the type was adopted by the Indian army as its standard light machine-gun and eventually a production line for this **Vickers-Berthier Light Machine-Gun Mk 3** was established at Ishapore.

In general appearance and design the Vickers-Berthier light machine-gun was similar to the Bren Gun, but internally and in detail there were many differences. Thus at times the Vickers-Berthier was often referred to by observers as the Bren. Apart from the large Indian Army contract the only other sales were to a few Baltic and South American states, and today the Vickers-Berthier is one of the least known of all World War II machine-guns. This is not because there was anything wrong with the type (it was a sound and reliable design) but because it had poor 'press' coverage and numerically was well outnumbered by the Bren Gun. But even today it remains in reserve use in India.

There was one Vickers-Berthier gun derivative that did, however, obtain a much better showing. This was a much-modified version of the basic design with a large drum magazine mounted above the receiver and a

spade grip fixed to the rear where the butt would normally have been. This was a special design intended for open cockpit aircraft, and was intended for use on a Scarff ring by the observer. Large numbers of this design were produced for the Royal Air Force, by whom it was known as the **Vickers G.O** (G.O. for gas operated) or **Vickers K** gun, but almost as soon as the type was introduced into service the open cockpit era came to a sudden close with the introduction of higher speed aircraft. The Vickers G.O. proved difficult to use in the close confines of aircraft turrets and impossible to use in wing installations, so it was placed almost immediately into store; some were used by the Fleet Air Arm on such aircraft as the Swordfish and thus remained in use until 1945 but their numbers were relatively few.

In 1940 many Vickers G.O. guns were taken out of store and widely used on various emergency mountings for anti-aircrft defences on airfields and other such installations. In North Africa the Vickers G.O. was avidly seized upon by the various irregular forces that sprang up for behind-the-lines operations, and the Vickers G.O. was thus used by such units as 'Popski's Private Army' on their heavily armed jeeps and trucks. The weapon proved ideal in the role and gave a good indication of how the original Vickers-Berthier machine-guns would have stood up under such conditions if they had been given the chance. The Vickers G.O. guns were used right until the end of the war in Italy and a few other theatres and they then passed right out of use, once more outnumbered by the more generally available Bren Guns.

This sepoy, carrying a Vickers-Berthier Mk 3, is dressed in standard issue khaki drill, with two large pouches for spare magazines. The Indian Army was the major user of the Vickers-Berthier gun.

Specification
Vickers-Berthier Light Machine-Gun Mk 3
Calibre: 7.7 mm (0.303 in)
Length: 1156 mm (45.5 in)
Length of barrel: 600 mm (23.6 in)
Weight: 11.1 kg (24.4 lb)
Muzzle velocity: 745 m (2,450 ft) per second
Rate of fire, cyclic: 450-600 rpm
Feed: 30-round box

Specification
Vickers G.O. Gun
Calibre: 7.7 mm (0.303 in)
Length: 1016 mm (40.0 in)
Length of barrel: 529 mm (20.83 in)
Weight: 9.5 kg (21 lb)
Muzzle velocity: 745 m (2,450 ft) per second
Rate of fire, cyclic: 1,000 rpm
Feed: 96-round drum

Maschinengewehr 34 general-purpose machine-gun

The terms of the Versailles Treaty of 1919 specifically prohibited (by means of a special clause) the development of any form of sustained-fire weapon by Germany, but this provision was circumvented by the arms concern

Rheinmetall-Borsig by the simple expedient of setting up a 'shadow' concern under its control over the border at Solothurn in Switzerland during the early 1920s. Research carried out into air-cooled machine-gun designs re-

sulted in a weapon that evolved into the **Solothurn Modell 1930**, an advanced design that introduced many of the features that were incorporated in later weapons. A few production orders were received, but it was felt

by the Germans that something better was required and thus the Modell 1929 had only a short production run before being used as the starting point for an aircraft machine-gun, the **Rheinmetall MG 15**. This long remained in production for the Luftwaffe.

From the Rheinmetall designs came what is still considered as one of the finest machine-gun designs ever produced, the **Maschinengewehr 34** or **MG 34**. Mauser designers at the Obendorff plant used the Modell 1929 and the MG 15 as starting points for what was to be a new breed of machine-gun, the general-purpose machine-gun. This new type could be carried by an infantry squad and fired from a bipod or mounted on a heavier tripod for sustained fire over long periods. The mechanism was of the all-in-line type and the barrel had a quick-change facility for cooling. The feed was of two types, using either the saddle-drum magazine holding 75 rounds inherited from the MG 15 or a belt feed. To add to all this technical innovation the MG 34 had a high rate of fire and could thus be effective against low-flying aircraft.

The MG 34 was an immediate success and went straight into production for all the various arms and auxiliaries of the German armed forces (and even the police). Demand for the MG 34 remained high right until 1945, and consistently outstripped supply. The supply situation was not aided by the number of mounts and gadgets that were introduced to go with the weapon. These varied from heavy tripods and twin mountings to expensive and complex fortress and tank mountings. There was even a periscopic gadget to enable the weapon to fire from trenches. These accessories consumed a great deal of production potential to the detriment of gun production proper, but production of the MG 34 was in any case not aided by one fact and that was that the design was really too good for military use. It took too long to manufacture and involved too many complex and expensive machining processes. The result was a superb weapon, but actually using it was rather like using a Rolls-Royce car for ploughing a field – it was too good for the task. Thus the German forces found themselves using a weapon they could not afford in terms of production potential, while demands meant they had to keep production going until the end.

Variants of the basic model were the **MG 34m** with a heavier barrel jacket for use in AFVs, and the shorter **MG**

An MG 34 mounted for the heavy machine-gun role on a Lafette 34 tripod and complete with the indirect-fire sight; the pads on the front leg rested against the carrier's back when folded for transport.

34s and **MG 34/41** intended for use in the AA role and capable of automatic fire only. The overall length and barrel length of the two latter were about 1170 mm (46 in) and 560 mm (22 in) respectively.

Specification
MG 34
Calibre: 7.92 mm (0.31 in)
Length: 1219 mm (48.0 in)
Length of barrel: 627 mm (24.69 in)
Weight: 11.5 kg (25.4 lb) with bipod
Muzzle velocity: 755 m (2,475 ft) per second
Rate of fire, cyclic: 800-900 rpm
Feed: 50 round belt (five belt lengths), or 75-round saddle drum

An MG 34 advancing through the USSR with the man on the right carrying the folded Lafette 34, the man in the centre the MG 34 and the one on the right with a spare barrel slung across his back; the other man by the MG 34 carrier has an ammunition case.

Two Afrika Korps soldiers with an MG 34 in the heavy machine-gun role on a Lafette 34. By removing the indirect fire sights and trigger, the MG 34 quickly converts to an LMG.

Maschinengewehr 42 general-purpose machine-gun

espite the overall excellence of the
G 34 it was really too good for its task
terms of cost and production re-
irements, so despite the establish-
ent of a full production facility and
nstant demand, by 1940 the Mauser
signers were looking for something
npler. With the production example
the 9-mm MP 40 sub-machine gun as
example in production simplicity
d low cost, they decided to adopt
w production methods using as few
pensive machining processes as
ssible allied with new operating
echanisms. The new mechanisms
me from a wide range of sources.
perience with the MG 34 had indi-
ed how the feed could be revised,
d designs captured when Poland
s overrun appeared to promise a
w and radical breech locking sys-
n. Other ideas came from Czecho-
vakia, and the Mauser team also induced its own ideas. From this
alth of innovation came a new de-
n, the **MG 39/41**, and from a series of
als carried out with this design came
e **Maschinengewehr 42** or **MG 42**, a
sign that must rank among the finest
ts kind.

The MG 42 introduced mass-
duction techniques to the machine-
n on a large scale. Earlier designs
d used some simple sheet metal
mpings and production short-cuts
e example being the little-known
nch Darne light machine-gun), but
harsh environment that the
chine-gun has to endure meant that
had any success. On the MG 42
success was immediate. Sheet
tal stampings were extensively
d for the receiver and for the barrel
sing which incorporated an inge-
us barrel-change system. The latter
very necessary for the MG 42 had
rodigious rate of fire that sounded
tearing linoleum. This was pro-
ed by the locking mechanism em-
yed, a mechanism that was de-
oped from several sources and was
h simple and reliable. The system
olved the use of two locking rollers
ning up and down an internal ramp:
he forward position they locked the
ech very effectively by mechanical
antage and then allowed the ramp
elease the locking. On the ammuni-
feed an arm on the bolt was used to
the ammunition belts across into
receiver in a simple and very
ctive fashion. Only the 50-round
was used with the MG 42.

hese design details merged to
n a very effective general-purpose
chine-gun and as is related else-
ere the type was attached to a wide
ge of mounts and other accessories.
MG 42's operational debut came
942, when it appeared in both the
R and North Africa. Thereafter it
used on every front and in gener-
ssue was made to front-line troops
, for though the MG 42 was in-
ded to supplant the MG 34 it in fact
supplemented the earlier type.

ot content with producing one of
finest machine-gun designs ever
duced, the Mauser design team
d to go one better and came up
the **MG 45** with an even higher
of fire. The end of the war put paid
hat design for the time being, but
MG 42 lives on with many armies.

*MG 42 for use in the light
chine-gun role, with a bipod.*

*Above: An MG 42 mounted on the
Lafette 42 for the heavy machine-gun
role; this heavy tripod could be
quickly adapted for the anti-aircraft
fire role.*

*Right: MG 42 awaiting invasion as
part of a fortified position on the
Atlantic Wall, complete with
ammunition belt loaded and spare
barrel at the ready by the
ammunition case.*

Specification
MG 42
Calibre: 7.92 mm (0.31 in)
Length: 1220 mm (48.03 in)
Length of barrel: 533 mm (20.98 in)
Weight: 11.5 kg (25.4 lb) with bipod
Muzzle velocity: 755 m (2,475 ft) per
second
Rate of fire, cyclic: up to 1,550 rpm
Feed: 50-round belt

The MG 42 in Action

Produced out of the need to simplify the manufacture of the MG 34, the MG 42 was soon to become a weapon respected and feared by anyone who faced it. When the time came for West Germany to re-arm, the MG 42 was the natural machine-gun choice, and the weapon is in use in modernized form to this day.

The MG 42 had its origins in the fact that the existing MG 34 was too expensive to manufacture and too costly in materials and time for extensive war-time production. While the MG 34 was an excellent weapon the ever-expanding German forces and the increasing amounts of territory they had to cover after 1940 meant that new machine-guns were constantly in great demand at rates that German industry could not meet. From this situation the MG 42 emerged.

The MG 42 had its origins in 1937, when a project to produce a new and cheap form of machine-gun was initiated by the German Army weapons department, the *Heereswaffenamt*, which wanted a relatively cheap machine-gun that would be reliable under all conditions and one that could use the accessories and ammunition feed systems of the existing MG 34. In general the expensive close tolerances of the MG 34 were to be avoided to ease manufacture and assist operations in the field. From this requirement came one design with a novel breech-locking system that offered much, but none of these early submissions appeared to warrant further development. It was not until 1940 that the real impetus came and by that time the Mauser design team had been able to examine some Czech and Polish 'paper' designs of considerable promise. By that time the principle of using mass-production techniques for weapon manufacture was fully accepted and in employment for several types of small arm, including the revolutionary MP 38 and MP 40 sub-machine guns.

A trials weapon, known as the MG 39/41, was produced in 1941 using a new locking device that had small steel rollers set into the sides of a

breech block. As the breech block was pushed into the locking position by a spring the rollers were pushed outwards into grooves in the receiver walls where they formed a mechanical advantage for the critical instant of firing. The system operated smoothly and reliably, and had the advantage of a high operating speed providing a high rate of fire (almost double that of existing machine-gun designs). The overall system was of the recoil type aided by a muzzle device to trap the muzzle gas pressures.

With some slight alterations to this system the type was soon in production as the MG 42. Quick introduction onto the production lines was aided by the intended fact that many existing machine tools could be easily adapted to the task and that the need for special machine tools was kept to a minimum. Great use was made of simple steel pressings, and welds were employed where pins and screws would normally have been employed. For all this ease of manufacture the MG 42 worked even better than the MG 34 and had a very high rate of fire. This was about 1,500 rpm, and the accompanying noise was not dissimilar to that of a band saw. Thus small-capacity magazines, although they could be fitted, were of limited use and reliance was generally placed on 50-round belts that could be linked together for prolonged fire. Such prolonged fire and the high fire rate made necessary some form of barrel-change mechanism, and the system used was very simple and rapid: as the lever on the side of the barrel jacket was pulled outwards a rotary device turned the barrel to release the locking lug, at the same time freeing it to be pulled out readily to the rear.

The MG 42 followed the MG 34 in that it was

American troops firing a captured MG 42; the Americans were so impressed by the MG 42 that they tried to produce a copy, which was a failure.

designed as a general-purpose machine-gu For infantry use a simple bipod was fitted, b in the heavier roles some very complex d vices were introduced. The basic trip turned out to be a special one for the MG alone and a great chance was missed to enab many of the MG 34 accessories to be used w the new design despite the earlier intentio In fact almost every accessory produced w for the MG 42 alone and only a few of t existing MG 34 items proved to be usable w the later weapon. Some of the MG 42 mountin turned out to be very complex affairs, especi ly the very expensive ball mountings produc for use in fortifications and other similar b mountings produced for mounting in the fr hulls of heavy tanks such as the Tiger and Panther. Rather less expensive but no le complex were the various *Zwillingslafett* (twin mountings) produced for anti-aircraft d fence and often carried on small towed ha carts.

The MG 42 was in service by the end of 19 both in North Africa and the Soviet Union soon proved to be a formidable weapon a was feared by all who encountered it. So Allied troops tried to capture as many as pos

Above: An abandoned MG 42 in an excellent infantry position overlooking a road in Italy. No the Stielgranate (stick grenades) lying ready for use.

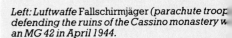

Left: Luftwaffe Fallschirmjäger (parachute troop defending the ruins of the Cassino monastery w an MG 42 in April 1944.

le for their own use, surely one of the best accolades for any weapon design, and the US army examined the design (and built prototypes in 7.62-mm/0.3-in calibre) for possible future adoption. Until 1945 the MG 42 was usually reserved for front-line units only, the MG 34 being gradually switched to rear support echelons; but the MG 42 had not fully replaced the MG 34 before 1945.

After 1945 large numbers of MG 42s were issued to several European armies, including the French army which used the MG 42 during their Indo-China campaigns. One nation took over large numbers of captured MG 42s and completely re-equipped its front-line army units. That nation was Yugoslavia, and so impressed was it with the MG 42 that it even established a national production line. The Yugoslavs even retained the 7.92-mm (0.31-in) calibre, and to this day maintain the type in production for possible export sales. They now the MG 42 as the M53 and their product is exactly the same as the original MG 42, right down to accessories such as the tripod.

Germany re-arms

By 1957 the Federal Republic of Germany was established as a full member of NATO and some thought was given to the rearming of the West German forces. When it came to machine guns the MG 42 was the immediate choice, but as Mauser (being in East Germany) was no longer on the side of the NATO allies the production base was switched to Rheinmetall GmbH. Using an actual example as a starting point, Rheinmetall restarted production once again in 1959, but this time in the standard NATO calibre of 7.62 mm (0.3 in). The product was known at first as the MG 42/59, but in time this was changed to MG 1 to aid the export image. There are several sub-variants of the MG 1, including one in which the butt can be removed to aid anti-aircraft use from vehicle ring mountings. When sufficient old war stocks of MG 42s were released from warehouses they too were converted to the NATO 7.62-mm (0.3-in) calibre and these became the MG 2. Then came the MG 3 with a number of minor Rheinmetall-inspired improvements including a version with several light alloy components to reduce weight. Even this fully modernized variant is immediately recognizable as an MG 42.

Today the West German Bundeswehr continues to use the MG 1 and MG 3 in exactly the same manner as its predecessor used the MG 42. It is still employed either mounted on its own bipod or mounted on a heavier tripod for the sustained-fire role. Leopard tanks mount MG 3s where Panthers once mounted MG 42s, and a number of new types of vehicle mounting have been designed and produced. On the infantry side the MG 3 is still used on occasion in the anti-aircraft manner when emergency targets appear. One man of the squad acts as a temporary firing stand while another aims and fires, using his partner's back as a stand for the gun. Infantry squad tactics remain much the same, in that a section of up to eight infantrymen depends on its section MG 3 for the bulk of its own supporting firepower. The squad moves only under covering fire from the MG 3, and once emplaced the section then supplies the machine-gun team with covering fire as it moves forward. The section also carries the bulk of the machine-gun's ammunition either hand-carried in boxes or in belts slung about their persons.

German Gebirgsjäger (mountain troops) with an MG 42 in use in the light machine-gun role; note the stamped receiver and components, which made the gun easier to manufacture.

In defence the MG 3 is usually mounted on a heavy tripod, carefully emplaced to provide a good field of fire. At night the machine-gun is emplaced to provide fire along special fixed lines of approach, and for this (and for indirect fire) the machine-gunners use a special indirect foresight very similar to that used on light mortars. Mechanized infantry often mount their machine-guns on top of the vehicle in the same manner as that employed on World War II half-tracks, but these days more often than not the MG 3 is protected by some form of turret cover. For anti-aircraft defence the *Zwillingslafette* has been revived.

Today the MG 1 (or MG 3) is in licence production in several locations in such countries as Italy, Spain, Turkey, Portugal and Pakistan. Every year it appears that more nations adopt the type and the market is still far from sated. It seems that the basic MG 42 design will still be in widespread service after the turn of the century. The reasons for this are not difficult to discover. The MG 42 and its later derivatives are easy to manufacture, to maintain, to clean and to use in action, and have been developed to the point where no bugs remain. Add to this the ready availability of numerous accessories to suit almost any application and the ability to obtain spares from a number of easily-accessible sources, and the popularity of the type becomes clear. But these alone are not the full answer. That must lie somewhere in the overall appearance and feel of the weapon. The MG 42 and its descendants all have that look of a thoroughbred design that can be relied upon. Many other weapon designs quite simply do not have this asset, but the military mind is not so simple as to rely on appearances alone. The military mind wants quality that can be relied upon under all circumstances, and the MG 42 series can provide that quality.

DShK 1938, SG43 and other Soviet machine-guns

If there has ever been one factor differentiating Russian and Soviet machine-gun designs from those of other nations it was the simple factor of weight. For many years these machine-guns were built to such a standard of robustness that weight alone was used as a means of incorporating strength, the ultimate example being the old M1910 Maxim guns that almost resembled small artillery pieces with their wheeled and shielded carriages. Eventually this avoidable trait was recognized by the Red Army when mobility made its way into long-term planning and by the mid-1930s, when a new heavy machine-gun was required, emphasis being placed more on design than sheer mass for strength.

The new heavy machine-gun was intended to be in the same class as the 12.7-mm (0.5-in) Browning, but the Soviet equivalent turned out to be slightly lighter. It used a 12.7-mm (0.5-in) cartridge and was intended for a variety of roles. To the credit of the new design, the **DShK1938** (in full the *Krasnoi Pulemet Degtyereva-Shpagina obrazets 1938g*), has proved to be almost as successful as the Browning, for it is still in production, albeit in a post-war modified form as the **DShK1938/46**, and is still in widespread service.

If the DShK1938 was lighter as a gun than the Browning the same could not be said of the mount, for as an infantry gun the DshK1938 retained the old wheeled carriage of the M1910, but a special anti-aircraft tripod was introduced and is still in use. The type became a virtual fixture on most Soviet tanks from the JS-2 heavy tanks onwards, and the Czechs have produced a quadruple mounting with DShK1938s for anti-aircraft use. There was even a special version for use on armoured trains.

The smaller **SG43** was introduced during 1943 to replace earlier 7.62-mm (0.3-in) machine-guns, including the venerable M1910. During the initial phases of the German invasion of the USSR the Soviet forces lost huge amounts of material, including machine-guns, and if their new production facilities were to replace these losses they might as well be modern designs. Thus the *Stankovii Pulemet Goryunova obrazets 1943g* came into being. It was a gas-operated and air-cooled design that combined several operating principles (including the well-established Browning principles), but overall the design was original and soon proved to be sound. As the SG43 the design was issued in very large numbers and even today the basic weapon is still in widespread use, albeit in a much modified and upgraded form as the **SGM.**

Both the SG43 and the larger DShK1938 have the same basic operational: simplicity. Working parts have been kept to a minimum and very little routine maintenance apart from simple cleaning is required. Both designs can operate under extremes of temperature and they are most forgiving of dirt and dust in the works. In other words both suit exactly the type of environment in which they will be used.

Right: Similar in performance to the 12.7-mm (0.5-in) Browning, the DShK 38/46 is still in production and service.

Specification
DShK1938
Calibre: 12.7 mm (0.5 in)
Length: 1602 mm (63.1 in)
Length of barrel: 1002 mm (39.45 in)
Weight: 33.3 kg (73.5 lb)
Muzzle velocity: 843 m (2,765 ft) per second
Rate of fire, cyclic: 550-600 rpm
Feed: 50-round metal-link belt (five belts joined)

Specification
SG43
Calibre: 7.62 mm (0.3 in)
Length: 1120 mm (44.1 in)
Length of barrel: 719 mm (28.3 in)
Weight: 13.8 kg (30.4 lb)
Muzzle velocity: 863 m (2,830 ft) per second
Rate of fire, cyclic: 500-640 rpm
Feed: 50-round metal-link belt

The SG 43 was designed by P.M. Goryunov in 1942 to provide a wartime replacement for the elderly Maxim Model 1910, and even used the old Maxim's wheeled carriage.

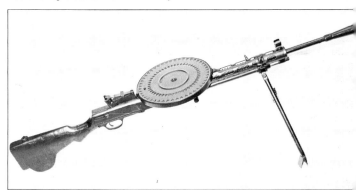

Above: The Degtyerev DP Model 1928 was a major Soviet light machine-gun during World War II. Simple and robust, the DP could stand rough treatment and extreme of weather. It can still be found in th hands of guerrilla groups all over t world.

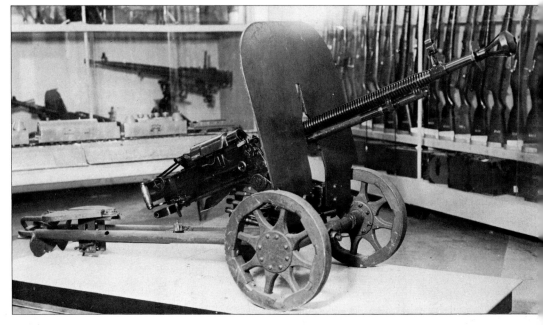

Modern Machine-Guns

An American soldier in Vietnam uses an M60 from an emplaced position, with plenty of ammunition belts ready to hand. In such belts about one round in six is tracer.

The use of automatic weapons steadily increased during World War II, and today most infantrymen carry weapons capable of burst fire. But the machine-gun remains the prime firepower component of the infantry squad, and classic designs like the Bren have lost none of their effectiveness.

The modern machine-gun is still one of the foot soldier's most powerful weapons, but it has changed much since World War I, when the machine-gun dominated the battlefields of France and elsewhere. Today's machine-gun is much lighter, more reliable and in general more flexible in its tactical applications. Most of the machine-guns here discussed are portable enough to be used in locations where it was once unthinkable that such weapons could even be carried, but they are still as lethal and efficient as they ever were.

The machine-gun is now in its second generation of development since World War II. The first generation weapons are still very much in evidence with virtually every armed force in the world, and are the post-war general-purpose machine-guns, or GPMGs. In the years after 1945 the GPMG was embraced by many as the way ahead in machine-gun design, but the soldiers in the front line discovered the hard way that the all-purpose machine-gun is as much a myth as the all-purpose truck. Thus the second generation of machine-guns is now entering service.

The second-generation weapons are more specialized than the GPMGs. The light machine-gun has made a come-back as the squad support weapon, while the heavy machine-gun has returned in the form of the post-war GPMGs retained for the heavy fire-support role. They are now in the position of either being retained indefinitely, or are slowly being replaced by the larger-calibre weapons such as the really heavy machine-guns (of 12.7/0.5-in calibre and upwards) or the machine weapons now generally known as cannon. It is the machine-guns that are covered in this study.

At first sight the variety of modern machine-guns looks somewhat bewildering, and the types mentioned here are but a selection of what is available. More types than can be covered in these pages are around or in the wings, for machine-gun development is still very progressive. Nearly all the major nations are either attempting to gild the lily by using the existing types, or alternatively chasing the myth of the perfect design. Some of the designs mentioned here do appear to have achieved near-perfection, for how otherwise can one contemplate the longevity of the MG3 and L4A4 Bren Gun designs? Others, such as the M60, make one wonder how they have lasted so long.

The most widely-used present-day version of the World War II Bren gun is the British L4A4, a conversion to standard NATO calibre. Seen here in action with the South African Army, it is also used by the British and many of the ex-Commonwealth armies, including India.

7.62-mm FN MAG

World War II established the general-purpose machine-gun (GPMG) as a viable weapon with its ability to be fired from a light bipod in the assault role and from a heavy tripod in the defensive or sustained role. After 1945 many designers tried to produce their own version of the GPMG concept, and one of the best was produced in Belgium during the early 1950s. The company concerned was Fabrique Nationale or FN, based at Herstal, and its design became known as the **FN Mitrailleuse d'Appui Général** or **MAG**. It was not long before the MAG was adopted by many nations, and today it is one of the most widely-used of all modern machine-gun designs.

The MAG fires the standard NATO 7.62-mm (0.3-in) cartridge and uses a conventional gas-operated mechanism, in which gases tapped off from the barrel are used to drive the breech block and other components to the rear once a round has been fired. Where the FN MAG scores over many comparable designs is that the tapping-off point under the barrel incorporates a regulator device that allows the firer to control the amount of gas used and thus vary the fire rate to suit the ammunition and other variables. For the sustained-fire role the barrel can be changed easily and quickly.

In construction the MAG is very sturdy. Some use is made of steel pressings riveted together, but many components are machined from solid metal, making the weapon somewhat heavy for easy transport. But this structural strength enables the weapon to absorb all manner of rough use, and it can be used for long periods without maintenance other than changing the barrels when they get too hot. The ammunition is belt-fed, which can be awkward when the weapon has to be carried with lengths of ammunition belt left hanging from the feed and snagging on just about everything.

When used as an LMG the MAG uses a butt and simple bipod. When used as a sustained-fire weapon the butt is usually removed and the weapon is placed on a heavy tripod, usually with some form of buffering to absorb part of the recoil. However, the MAG can be adapted to a number of other mountings, and is often used as a co-axial weapon on armoured vehicles

or as a vehicle defence weapon in a ball mounting, and as an anti-aircraft weapon on a tripod or vehicle-hatch mounting. It is also used on many light naval vessels.

The MAG has been widely produced under licence. One of the better-known nations is the UK, where the MAG is known as the **L7A2**. The British introduced some modifications of their own, (and have produced the weapon for export), and there is no sign of it being replaced in the foreseeable future as far as the British armed forces are concerned. Other nations that produce the MAG for their own use in-

clude Israel, South Africa, Singapore and Argentina, and there are others. Even longer is the list of MAG users: a brief summary includes Sweden, Ireland, Greece, Canada, New Zealand, the Netherlands and so on. There is little chance of the MAG falling out of fashion, and production continues all over the world.

Specification
FN MAG
Calibre: 7.62 mm (0.3 in)
Weights: gun only 10.1 kg (22.27 lb); tripod 10.5 kg (23.15 lb); barrel 3 kg (6.6 lb)

The Belgian FN MAG is one of the most widely used of the post-World War II general-purpose machine-guns. Well made from what are usually solid metal billets machined to spec, the MAG is a very sturdy but heavy weapon that is still in production worldwide.

Lengths: gun 1260 mm (49.61 in); barrel 545 mm (21.46 in)
Muzzle velocity: 840 m (2,756 ft) per second
Rate of fire: (cyclic) 600-1000 rpm
Type of feed: 50-round belt

Below: The FN MAG is licence-produced in Israel by Israel Military Industries and is used by all branches of the Israeli armed forces

Above: During the Falkland Islands campaign L7A1s were hastily pressed into use on improvised anti-aircraft mountings to provide some measure of defence against Argentine attacks on the shipping in San Carlos harbour.

Below: The FN MAG is fitted to the turrets of the German Leopard 2 tanks in service with the Dutch army. Pictured here in September 1984 on Exercise 'Lionheart', the MAG has been fitted with a blank firing adaptor.

FN 5.56-mm Minimi

ith the turn away from the heavy ATO 7.62-mm (0.3-in) cartridge to- ards the smaller 5.56-mm (0.219-in) und for use by the standard rifles of ost of the NATO nations (and many ners), it followed that there was a ed for a light machine-gun to use the w calibre. FN accordingly drew up e design of a new weapon that even- ally became known as the **FN Minimi** d was first shown in 1974. The Mini- is intended for use only as a squad pport weapon as there is no way that e light 5.56-mm cartridge can be ed effectively for the heavy support sustained-fire role, for it simply cks the power to be effective at nges much beyond 400 m (437 rds). Thus heavier-calibre weapons ch as the FN MAG will still be re- ned for this role in the future.

The Minimi uses some design fea- res from the earlier FN MAG, includ- g the quick-change barrel and the s regulator, but a new rotary locking vice is used for the breech block ich is guided inside the receiver by o guide rails to ensure a smooth vel. These latter innovations have ade the Minimi into a remarkably liable weapon, and further reliability s been introduced into the ammuni- n feed. This is one of the Minimi's ajor contributions to modern light achine-gun design as it does away th the long and awkward flapping mmunition belts used on many de- gns and which snag on everything en carried. The Minimi uses a sim- e box (under the gun body) which ntains the neatly-folded belt. When e weapon is fired from a bipod, the x is so arranged that it will not inter- re with normal use and on the move it out of the way of the carrier. But the inimi goes one step further: if re-

quired, the belt feed can be replaced by a magazine feed. FN has shrewdly guessed that the American M16A1 rifle would quickly become the standard weapon in its class, and has thus made provision for the Minimi to use the M16A1's 30-round magazine. This can clip into the receiver just under the belt feed guides after the belt has been removed.

The association with the American M16A1 rifle has turned out well for FN, for the Minimi has been adopted as the US Army's squad fire-support weapon, and is now known there as the **M249 Squad Automatic Weapon**, or **SAW**. This version will fire the new standard NATO SS109 5.56-mm cartridge rather than the earlier M193 cartridge. The SS109 has a longer and heavier bullet than the earlier cartridge and uses a

different rifling in the barrel, but is otherwise similar to the American car- tridge.

Two possible variants of the Minimi are a 'para' version which uses a shor- ter barrel and a sliding butt to make the weapon shorter overall, and a vehi- cle model with no butt at all for mount- ing in armoured vehicles. The Minimi itself has many ingenious detail points as well: the trigger guard may be re- moved to allow operation by a man wearing winter or NBC warfare gloves, the front handguard contains a cleaning kit, the ammunition feed box has a simple indicator to show how many rounds are left, and so on.

Overall the Minimi may be re- garded as one of the best of the new family of 5.56-mm light machine-guns. It will be around for a very long time.

The FN Minimi has been adopted by the US Army for the Squad Automatic Weapon (SAW) as the M249. It is now entering service with the airborne divisions of the Rapid Deployment Joint Task Force (RDJTF).

Specification
FN Minimi
Calibre: 5.56 mm (0.219 in)
Weights: with bipod 6.5 kg (14.33 lb); with 200 rounds 9.7 kg (21.38 lb)
Lengths: weapon 1050 mm (41.34 in); barrel 465 mm (18.31 in)
Muzzle velocity: (SS 109) 915 m (3,002 ft) per second
Rate of fire: (cyclic) 750-1000 rpm
Type of feed: 100- or 200-round belt, or 30-round box magazine

---

7.62-mm vz 59

ech machine-gun designers can ce their progeny back to the range highly successful machine-guns rted with the vz (*vzor*, or model) 26 1926 and which resulted in the nous Bren Guns. As successor to ese designs the Czechs produced a w model during the early 1950s as e **vz 52**, which may be regarded as e old design updated to use an mmunition belt-feed system. This was t the success of the earlier weapons, d is now rarely encountered other an in the hands of 'freedom fighters' d the like, and the vz 52 has now en superseded by the **vz 59**. The vz 59 is much simpler than the rlier vz 52 but follows the same neral lines in appearance and op- ation. In fact many of the operating inciples of the vz 52 have been car- d over, including the gas-operated

mechanism. The ammunition feed sys- tem is also a carry-over from the vz 52, in which it was regarded by many as being the only successful feature. In this feed system the belt is carried into the receiver by guides where a cam system takes over and pushes the car- tridge forward through the belt link into the weapon. This system was copied on the Soviet PK series, but on the vz 59 the belts are fed from metal boxes; for the light machine-gun role with the light barrel and designation **vz 59L**, one of these boxes can be hung from the right-hand side of the gun in a rather unbalanced fashion. The weapon may be used in the LMG role with bipod or tripod mountings.

For the heavy machine-gun role the vz 59 is fitted with a heavy barrel. In this form it is known merely as the vz 59. When fitted with a solenoid for

firing in armoured vehicles on a co- axial or similar mount it is known as the **vz 59T**. This does not exhaust the varia- tions of the vz 59 series for, no doubt with an eye to possible sales outside Czechoslovakia, there is a version that fires standard NATO 7.62-mm (0.3-in) ammunition and known as the **vz 59N**; the vz 59 series usually fires the Soviet 7.62-mm cartridge.

One rather unusual feature of the vz 59 is the telescopic sight, which can be used with the bipod and the tripod. This optical sight may be illuminated internally for use at night and is also used for anti-aircraft fire, for which role the vz 59 is placed on top of a tubular extension to the normal tripod.

To date the vz 59 is known to have been adopted only by the Czech army, although other nations may by now have the type in use. In the past Czech

weapons have appeared wherever there is a market for small arms, and Czech weapons have thus recently turned up in the Middle East, and especially in Lebanon; some vz 52s have certainly been seen there. To date there is no record of any nation purchasing the NATO-ammunition version, but no doubt that version will turn up in some unexpected trouble spot one day.

Specification
vz 59
Calibre: 7.62 mm (0.3 in)
Weights: with bipod and light barrel 8.67 kg (19.1 lb); with tripod and heavy barrel 19.24 kg (42.42 lb)
Lengths: with light barrel 1116 mm (43.94 in); with heavy barrel 1215 mm (47.84 in); light barrel 593 mm (23.35 in); heavy barrel 693 mm (27.28 in)
Muzzle velocity: with light barrel 810 m (2,657 ft) per second, and with heavy barrel 830 m (2,723 ft) per second
Rate of fire: (cyclic) 700-800 rpm
Type of feed: 50- or 250-round belts

The Czech 7.62-mm (0.30-in) vz 59 is a development of the earlier vz 52/57, but much easier to produce. Developed with an eye to the international export market, the vz 59 has been adopted by the Czech armed forces but others crop up in various corners of the world.

Machine-Gun Tactics

The conflicting requirement for machine-guns to be portable yet capable of sustained fire led to the concept of the general-purpose machine-gun. However, in recent years the emphasis has been on specialization, heavy-barrel versions of rifles being introduced at squad level and sustained fire entrusted to such stalwarts as the Browning 0.50-calibre machine-gun.

During World War I the machine-gun was a weapon that could dominate the battlefield in a manner that made movement virtually impossible, and at times during that dreadful war machine-guns were often massed in batteries which rendered whole tracts of territory impassable to men and animals. Such a dominance was not to arise again, for in the wars that followed the static conditions of the Western Front arose only infrequently. The main dominance of the battlefield passed to the artillery and tanks, and only rarely were machine-guns able to reassert their former role. Instead the machine-gun took on a new role, that of fire support for troops in attack and defence. As warfare took on a more mobile and fluid form, the machine-gun was often able to pour such volumes of fire on attacking infantry or onto a position that the enemy's tactical movement or intention became temporarily difficult or impossible.

In these mobile and fluid conditions the machine-gun often became the pivot around which an infantry unit or squad could act. By moving to a flank, a machine-gun could keep an enemy's head down while the rest of the squad moved into a favourable position or made an attack. These tactics are still widely used, though the form of the machine-gun has changed.

By the end of World War I there were two types of machine-gun. The more widely used was the heavy machine-gun (HMG), which sat on a tripod and poured out volumes of fire. Then there was the lighter and more portable light machine-gun (LMG), which could be used at lower command levels than the ponderous heavy weapon. But by the end of World War II these two types had been joined by a third, the general-purpose machine-gun (GPMG). This was a German notion that caught on fast. Very basically the idea was that one weapon could be used for both the light and the heavy roles. The GPMG was air-cooled, and thus much lighter than the water-cooled, heavy machine-guns, and when used in the HMG role the GPMG simply overcame the problem of barrel heating (produced by large volumes of fire) by means of a rapid-barrel-change capability. Spare barrels could be held close at hand and fitted in a few seconds. The same weapon could be fitted with a light bipod for producing rapid aimed fire, and was thus capable of LMG use.

The first GPMGs were the German MG34 and MG42, the latter having the greater long-term influence to the extent that it is still in production. In the post-war period these two designs were soon joined by many others, and for a period it was GPMGs all the way. Economically the idea made good sense: only one weapon type would be needed, and with luck that basic type could be adapted for other roles outside the GPMG range, such as co-axial mountings for tank guns, helicopter guns and so on. Many of the post-war generation could

The British-produced version of the Belgian FN MAG is known as the L7A1 or L7A2, and is seen here with its butt removed for the sustained fire role and mounted on a buffered tripod. No feed belt is visible as it is fed in from the left-hand side of the gun from a belt box.

indeed carry out these ancilliary roles (and do so quite happily to this day), but th soldiers soon learned that the GPMG concept has its limits.

The problem for the soldier was that while a GPMG could make a satisfactor heavy machine-gun it was less successful as a light machine-gun or squa weapon. Most GPMGs use belt-fed ammunition, and when a flapping ammuni tion belt is dragged through ditches and across country it creates problems fo the feed, to say nothing of the task faced by the hapless carrier, who ha constantly to free the thing from undergrowth and projections. The GPMG als errs on the weighty side for the squad role, and many in-service GPMGs are fa heavier and more awkward to handle than they should be for such use. A simpl example of this is deployment of the L7A2 (the British army's version of the F MAG) in the squad role compared with the lighter and handier Bren Gun which replaced: many soldiers were not happy at that transition, and remain unhapp to this day.

The L7A1 and L7A2 have been adapted for mountings firing out of the sides o Army Air Corps Lynx helicopters for providing fire support during an airborne landing. A special version for carrying in helicopter pods is known as the L20A1. Although effective, these guns are really too light for this role.

Royal Marine Commandos are seen clearing the whaling station on South Georgia during the Falkland campaign. The guns are a 7.62-mm L4A4 Bren in the foreground with an L7A2 GPMG behind.

Machine-Gun Tactics

Above: An M60 team from the Secon Marines is seen on a search-and-clear operation about 27 km (17 miles) south west of Da Nang, at the height of the US involvement in Sout East Asia.

Left: Viet Cong fighters lie in ambus! for a South Vietnamese patrol in the mid-1960s. The weapon is a Soviet-designed RPD light machine-gun, possible the Chinese-built type 56 model.

Thus there has been a move back towards the specialist LMG, and with the adoption of the new 5.56-mm (0.219-in) cartridge such LMGs can be really light yet capable of producing appreciable amounts of automatic fire. Today the LMG has returned to its original role of producing automatic fire support for the infantry squad. As these modern squads move they can produce firepower out of all proportion to their numbers from their assault rifles and squad support weapon, but it is the latter that produces the volume of accurately-aimed fire that is tactically so useful.

This move back to the LMG has not done away with the role of the HMG. There is still a place on the modern battlefield for the centrally-controlled volume fire of the heavy weapon. This is still important, for most LMGs are capable of accurate fire only to about 600 m (655 yards) at best, and HMGs often have to tackle targets or target areas at ranges well over 1000 m (1,100 yards). The current 5.56-mm rounds quite simply cannot do this, for their propellant loads are tailored to much shorter ranges. It is true that the recent Belgian SS 109 cartridge has more power at longer ranges than the American M193, but it still cannot match the power of the larger 7.62-mm (0.3-in) round in either its NATO form or the far more ancient (but still good) Soviet equivalent.

Thus the GPMG appears to be fading away as a concept, even if many of the GPMG generation live on in a support role. They will be maintained at company or battalion level and distributed as required, while the lighter weapons will be distributed at squad level. Some observers have remarked that many current light machine-guns are little more than machine rifles, i.e. rifles fitted with heavier barrels and a light bipod, and for some of the designs mentioned in this study this is true; the examples of the Soviet RPK and some of the Heckler & Koch rifles are obvious. But ideally a squad weapon has to be more than a machine rifle, especially if the squad is expected to operate in rough or difficult terrain. Under such conditions it is likely that the LMG will be the only fire support the squad can expect, and it thus has to be capable of more than short bursts of fire.

There is one factor that is now often overlooked when dealing with modern infantry tactics. Modern infantry is usually carried into action on some sort of vehicle (usually an armoured personnel carrier). Frequently the squad weapons, including the machine-guns, have to be fired from inside the vehicle, especially in patrolling and policing situations. Thus special consideration has to be given to the types of mounting the machine-gun will use, and thus to the cost of the basic weapon has to be added the expense of special mountings, be they simple pedestal mounts in Jeeps or more complex ball mountings in armoured vehicles.

But for many armed forces the image of the machine-gunner is usually that of an overloaded individual lugging about a heavy weapon and festooned with ammunition belts. Not far away is his equally loaded assistant carrying more

No GPMG can equal the range and stopping power of the heavy-calibre machine-guns. Many countries use the Browning 0.50-calibre in the sustained-fire role. This is the M2 HB version produced by FN, which features a quick barrel change.

belts, spare barrels and all his own gear. Contrast this with the future ideal of a heavy support weapon carried on an armoured vehicle, with the squad equivalent carrying a weapon weighing only a little more than the squad's standard rifles. For some armies this is already becoming a reality. The example of the Enfield Weapon System, with the IW and the LSW working closely together and swapping ammunition magazines when required, is to be seen in the British army in the near future. They will not be alone, for the Red Army has been using the AKM/RPK combination for years and the US Army will soon have the M249 Minimi/M16A1 mix. When that happens the M60s, FN MAGs, L7A2s and all the other cumbersome weapons will go back to the heavy support role, and the front-line soldier will be happy at the prospect.

Spent cases are seen in flight as they are ejected from the M60's feed mechanism. The M60 uses a mechanism based on the German World War II MG42 allied with some other features derived from the German FG42, also of the war period. The M60 is gas-operated and is the first of its kind to be used by the US armed forces.

✚ 7.62-mm SIG 710-3

The Swiss 7.62-mm (0.3-in) **SIG 710-3** is a weapon that on paper appears to be one of the finest of its class. The overall design, construction and reliability of the SIG design is such that it would appear to be a world leader. In fact nothing of the kind has occurred, for this most promising of machine-gun designs has now been taken out of production, and around the world it can be found in service with nations such as Brunei, Bolivia and Chile.

The reason for this strange state of affairs can perhaps be seen in the fact that when the Swiss produce any weapon design they do so in a manner that can only attract superlatives. The Swiss produce weapons with a magnificent degree of care and attention to finish, and while people may be willing to pay heavily for similarly-engineered Swiss watches, they are not willing to pay on the same scale for machine-guns. The SIG products tend to be expensive, and in a world where machine-guns can be produced on simple machine tools and metal stamping jigs the finely machined weapon has little chance of commercial success.

The SIG 710-3 is actually the third in a series of machine-guns, the first of which were produced during the early post-war years. In simple terms the first SIG 710 models were machine-gun versions of the Swiss Sturmgewehr Modell 57 (assault rifle model 1957), and the machine-gun employs the same delayed roller and block locking system as the CETME and the Heckler & Koch rifles. On the Swiss weapons

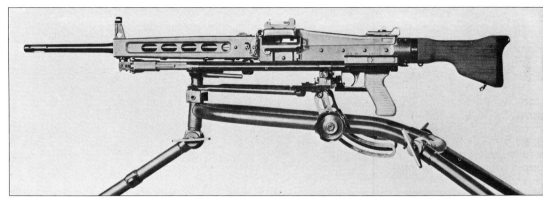

the system constitutes a form of delayed blowback, with the chamber fluted to prevent spent cases 'sticking'. The first SIG 710s were virtually handmade weapons that attracted much attention (but few orders), so an increasing number of production expedients was incorporated into the design, to the point where the SIG 710-3 makes use of some stampings; needless to say, these are of very high quality. The machine-gun sports some features from German weapons. The Swiss were very influenced by the MG42 and in the years after the war produced several designs based on features of the model. The SIG 710-3 trigger mechanism is the same as that of the MG42, and so is the ammunition feed which is so efficient that it accommodates both American and German belt linkings without trouble.

The locking system is identical with that employed on the Sturmgewehr 45 which failed to reach service with the German army before the surrender of May 1945.

But the SIG 710-3 does have many original Swiss features, not the least of which is the type of rapid barrel change. Many extras were developed for these machine-guns, including one buffered tripod for sustained fire. Special features such as dial sights and telescopic sights were also produced, and in the end the SIG 710-3 could be regarded as one of the most advanced machine-guns available anywhere. But it was all for nothing as far as SIG was concerned, high development and production costs (combined with the strict rules of the Swiss government regarding arms sales) leading to an early exit from production.

The 7.62-mm (0.30-in) SIG 710-3 general-purpose machine-gun was based on German wartime design experience and should have emerged as one of the finest machine-gun designs ever, but in the event only small numbers were produced.

Specification
SIG 710-3
Calibre: 7.62 mm (0.3 in)
Weights: gun 9.25 kg (20.39 lb); heavy barrel 2.5 kg (5.51 lb); light barrel 2.04 kg (4.5 lb)
Lengths: gun 1143 mm (45 in); barrel 559 mm (22 in)
Muzzle velocity: 790 m (2,592 ft) per second
Rate of fire: (cyclic) 800-950 rpm
Type of feed: belt

USA

7.62-mm M60

The **M60** is a general-purpose machine-gun that can trace its origins back to the latter period of World War II, when it was known as the **T44**. The design was greatly influenced by the new German machine-gun designs: the ammunition feed is a direct lift from the MG42, and the piston and bolt assembly was copied from the revolutionary 7.92-mm (0.312-in) Fallschirmjägergewehr 42 (FG42). The T44 and its production version, the M60, made extensive use of steel stampings and plastics, and the first examples were issued for service with the US Army during the late 1950s.

These first examples were not a success. They handled badly and some of the detail design was such that changing a barrel involved taking half the weapon apart. These early difficulties were gradually eliminated, and the M60 is now as efficient a weapon as any, but many serving soldiers still profess not to like the weapon for its generally awkward handling properties. But the M60 is the US Army's first general-purpose machine-gun, and it now serves in a host of roles.

In its basic form as a squad support weapon, the M60 is fitted with a stamped steel bipod mounted just behind the muzzle. For this purpose it is carried by a small handle which is rather flimsy for the loads placed on it; moreover the point of balance of the handle is entirely wrong. Instead many soldiers prefer to use a sling, and the weapon is often fired on the move while being steadied by the sling. For the light machine-gun role the M60 is a bit hefty, but it will be replaced in the

near future by the 5.56-mm (0.219-in) M249 Minimi for the US Army. For heavier use the M60 can be mounted on a tripod or on a vehicle pedestal mount.

Some special versions of the M60 have been produced. The **M60C** is a remotely-fired version for external mounting on helicopters. The **M60D** is a pintle-mounted version with no butt for mounting in helicopter gunships and some vehicles. The **M60E2** is a much-altered variant for use as a co-axial gun on armoured vehicles.

Throughout much of its production life the M60 has been manufactured by the Saco Defense Systems Division of the Maremount Corporation, which was always aware of the shortcomings of the M60's design, especially in the light machine-gun role. Accordingly the company has now produced what

it calls the **Maremount Lightweight Machine-Gun**, which is the M60 much modified to reduce weight and improve handling. The bipod has been moved back under the receiver and a foregrip has been added. The gas-operated mechanism has been simplified, and there is now provision for a winter trigger. The result is a much lighter and handier weapon than the original, although it can now be used only for the light machine-gun role. The new weapon is currently undergoing evaluation trials by several armies.

The M60 is now in service with several armies other than the US Army. Taiwan not only uses the M60 but produces it as well. South Korea is another Asian operator, while farther south the Australian army also has the M60 in service.

The American M60 is a rather bulky and heavy weapon that is awkward to handle. First produced in the late 1940s, it underwent a protracted development programme before it entered service in the late 1950s, and has been widely used ever since. It is now a reliable and efficient weapon used by several armies.

Specification
M60
Calibre: 7.62 mm (0.3 in)
Weights: gun 10.51 kg (23.17 lb); barrel 3.74 kg (8.245 lb)
Lengths: gun overall 1105 mm (43.5 in); barrel 559 mm (22 in)
Muzzle velocity: 855 m (2,805 ft) per second
Rate of fire: (cyclic) 550 rpm
Type of feed: 50-round belt

'Busting Caps'- The M60 in Vietnam

In the desperate close-range actions against the Viet Cong, the M60 machine-gun teams had to achieve fire superiority over a well-armed and skilful enemy – no easy task with a complicated and sometimes temperamental weapon.

In 1884, the prototype Maxim machine-gun (water-cooled) weighed 27.2 kg (60 lb) and fired an 11.43-mm (0.45-in) bullet at the rate of 600 rounds per minute. In 1984, the M60 machine-gun (air-cooled) weighs 10.4 kg (23 lb) and fires a 7.62-mm (0.3-in) bullet also at the rate of 600 rounds per minute. Add the tripod, and you have a total weight of 23.6 kg (52 lb).

The main difference between the two are, of course, accuracy and reliability; but the tactical use (particularly in the US Army) remains the same: the machine-gun is primarily a static defensive weapon, only offensively used to provide fire-support for advancing infantry. In the case of the M60, this has as much to do with the United States' strategic doctrine as to tactics: the USA is perceived only as fighting a defensive war (as in the instance of NATO forces facing a Warsaw Pact advance), and overall, the USA relies on firepower over flexibility and manoeuvrability.

As the US Army re-equips with a new Kevlar helmet and new body armour, the 7.62-mm (0.30-in) M60 machine-gun soldiers on until the new M279 Minimi replaces it in the light machine-gun role.

If nothing else, Vietnam showed that the best defence can often be attack, and that flexibility can be as important as firepower. Nonetheless it is best to forget the idea of the M60 being fired from the hip as film-makers would have it: even though the M60 is exceptionally well balanced, after only four rounds on automatic it will pull high and to the right.

As in all weapon systems, there is a distinct gap between the theory and practice of firing the M60. Instructors may (often do) wax lyrical about Dangerous Space (the distance a round or burst remains at a man's height above the ground); Cones of Fire (shot dispersal around lines of fire); and the Beaten Zone (pattern of descending shots). But the M60 machine-gunner in the US Army (or any machine-gunner, for that matter) is interested in accuracy, reliability, maintenance, how easy it is to fire and how easy it is to carry. For its size, the M60 scores well on all points, as well it might, because it owes much of its design to the famous German World War II machine-gun, the MG42, an updated version of which is still in service with the West German army as the MG3. So, remembering that no comparisons with British Bren, LMG or possibly even the GPMG should be made, we should now take a look at the M60 in action. And where else to look but the M60 in Vietnam.

A rifle company has harboured up for the night. With two M60s per platoon (three or four platoons per company) plus at least a couple more M60s belonging to company HQ, plus the 12.7-mm (0.5-in) machine-guns that have been dismounted from the personnel carriers, plus mortars, plus rockets, you can begin to under-stand why a modern rifle company is said to have a fire power equal to a World War I infantry brigade. If you are the M60 gunner, you will have made sure that your weapon is firmly positioned; that means either using the tripod or resting the barrel on tree trunks or sandbags. If you are firing through a ground-level embrasure, you may be using the attached bipod; but you would prefer not to, because that means you have to use your left hand to hold the butt into the ground when firing on automatic, and that increases the risk of getting your shoulder into too close contact with the butt end, which could mean at best a very nasty bruising, at worst a dislocated shoulder. More to the point, unless you are a 'natural' machine-gunner, it will play all sorts of hell with your accuracy when you are firing on automatic. And as you do not expect to fire on single shot, you will definitely need to be well planted. You have loaded with ball ammunition, with tracer in reserve. In the daytime you might have both incendiary and spotter ammunition in reserve, but you certainly would not need armour-piercing: if the enemy do have any AFVs, they keep them well hidden.

As an M60 gunner, you have an E4 specialist rating. It is not a command rank, but it does put you firmly in charge of (i.e. responsible for) the gun; you are the head man of the three-man crew the M60 requires. In fact, you are not expecting to be called tonight; there are no heavy enemy troop concentrations in the area, so the most you can expect is a sniper, or a few rounds of mortar fire or possibly an artillery barrage. And there will not be very much that you can do about those, at least in your present position.

M60s are still encountered in South East Asia; many were handed over to pro-American local forces, while many more were captured by various guerrilla and other forces. This example was photographed in North Vietnam in 1975.

Like soldiers the world over, you have man
aged to make yourself reasonably comfortabl
. . . until your sergeant walks over to tell yo
that your squad is going out on ambush tonigh
and would you (please) be ready to move out i
20 minutes.

The first thing you do is check your weapor
Never mind that you checked it only that afte
noon; if it breaks down in a company strong
point, at least there are a minimum of seve
other M60s (not to mention the 12.7-mm/0.5-i
M2s) to take up the slack while you site a ne
weapon. On this ambush there will only be on
M60 because at night, in the jungle, two M60
will get in each other's way, probably end u
shooting their own troops. Your number tw
carries the spare parts and cleaning kit, an
although everything checks out OK, you de
cide to change the barrel. It only takes tw
seconds (you once did it in 1.5 in training) and
is not as if you are being wasteful, because you
number two always has at least three spar
barrels with him. Twenty minutes later, an
you are ready to move out.

Your M60 (or 'pig' as you have come to call i
is slung around your neck and shoulders. Spar

*Below: The M60 was known as 'the Pig' to the men
who had to lug it through the jungle, but it
provided the squad with tremendous firepower.
Shooting in combat was dubbed 'busting caps', a
derisive reference to playing with cap guns as
children.*

*Above: A Vietnam M60 is seen in action with an
improvised addition to the ammunition feed to
ensure a trouble-free entry of the belt into the
weapon. Snagged or twisted belts could often*
*cause jams at the most difficult moments, and it
was normal for one man to watch the feed at all
times to avoid troubles.*

ands of ammunition also criss-cross your shoulders, and you are carrying a box of ammunition in your left hand. Your number two (a private first class) is carrying a box in each hand, plus one on his shoulders, plus spare parts and the cleaning kit. Your number three (a private) is carrying the tripod (it weighs kg/6.7 lb) and even more ammunition than your number two. Tonight the sergeant has decreed that all other squad members will also carry spare ammunition for the M60 (no wonder they call it a 'pig') and it will be our number three's job to make sure the spare ammunition centralized and available when you need it.

Moving through the night, the two places you not walk are point and rear. As far as possible, your squad will provide a shield for you until you are in position; you carry the major firepower, and are thus the most vulnerable to a sniper's bullet. The track your squad is following runs through dense primary jungle. It is supposedly clear of mines and booby traps, because the enemy uses it for a courier and supply route; even so, possibly you reflect that one of the good points about being high on a sniper's target list is that someone else is liable step on a mine before you do. So long as you keep in single file, that is, and make sure to follow the steps of the man in front ... not always easy to do at night in the jungle.

Your sergeant signals that you have reached the ambush point, and indicates to you where to set up. The team swings into action. Normally, it takes less than one minute to be ready to fire from the moment the tripod hits the ground. But tonight, as you will be firing down the track, towards the approaching enemy (no point in firing from the side of the track because you would be too close to get in a proper burst), your weapon has to be clamped on a fixed line of fire otherwise you might end up spraying your own squad. Now, with your weapon fixed, ammunition stacked around you, your number two beside you, everyone and everything camouflaged up, you sit behind your 'pig' and wait. And wait. And wait. And you are probably still waiting when dawn breaks ... unless, just for once, intelligence was 100 per cent accurate and the enemy did appear.

Right: During the Vietnam War the M60 became a virtual symbol of the American presence in the conflict, as cameramen tended to become attracted by the military and aggressive appearance of the weapon. It was widely used in Vietnam, as its high rate of fire was used as a counter to the elusive guerrilla targets.

'Busting Caps' – The M60 in Vietnam

Assuming they did, the firefight would probably have been over very quickly. First, your weapon has an effective range of up to 1000 m (1,100 yards, which means that at 100 m (110 yards) it is one of the most effective weapons available, with a stopping power that is close to being awesome; and second, no one stays around for too long when they are facing the wrong end of an M60. While most armies teach an Immediate Action drill on being ambushed that entails charging through the ambushing enemy, it is a very brave, lucky or foolhardy soldier that manages to charge any machine-gun . . . and lives to tell the tale.

So, if intelligence has been correct, the firefight has probably lasted less than a minute before the enemy have been killed, captured or have simply melted away into the surrounding darkness. And if that has happened, you wonder (not for the first time) why so much spare ammunition is always carried. The answer is simple. Your weapon is the principal, indeed the only, weapon capable of providing fire support for your squad. Your role is not simply to kill the enemy but to save the lives of your fellow soldiers. That means covering fire, when you try to make the enemy keep their heads down and think twice about chasing after you or even firing back. And covering f expends an enormous amount of ammuniti because often you do not have a firm targe

So, whether successful or not, your squ makes its way back to base. This has probal been the last ambush you will go on, becau you are due for a transfer to helicopter gunne Probably 'someone' has noticed how accura you are, and firing an M60 from a Huey nee accuracy. In fact, when the M60 was first us on 'choppers', it was attached to the ski which meant it could only fire in the directi the chopper was pointing. But now it mounted on a pintle by the door that allows y three-way movement; you will soon learn training school how to use that movement compensate for the movement of the Huey

Whatever happens, you seem destined stay an M60 gunner, unless you are promot away from it. You might call it a 'pig', but i more accurate and more comforting than M16. In fact, it is as accurate as the old M1 rif old soldiers in the US army talk about th weapon in the same way as their British cou terparts talk about the Lee Enfield.

Left: The machine-guns carried on these Bell UH 1Ds were special versions of the M60, known as M60D. The M60D was mounted on a pintle and h no butt, and used a special accessory on the fee mechanism. It was widely used in Vietnam for a suppression fire and many M60Ds were mounte on the exterior of vehicles.

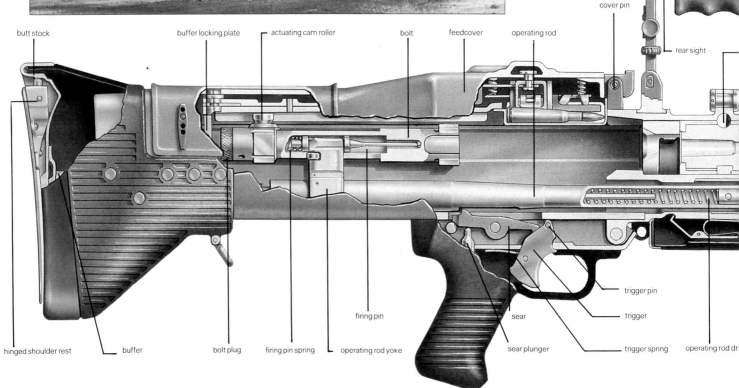

Above: An M60 light machine-gun team in action during troop exercises in South Korea, where the M60 is used not only by the US Army and Marine Corps but also by the Republic of Korea (ROK) troops. Other nations that use the M60 include Australia and Taiwan, and some have passed into guerrilla hands, including the IRA.

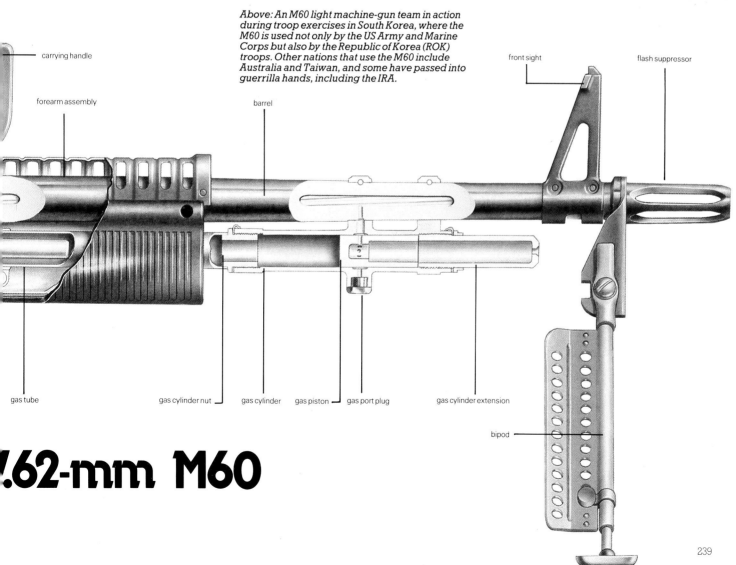

carrying handle

forearm assembly

barrel

front sight

flash suppressor

gas tube

gas cylinder nut

gas cylinder

gas piston

gas port plug

gas cylinder extension

bipod

7.62-mm M60

5.56-mm CIS Ultimax 100

The relatively small nation of Singapore has in recent years become a major member of the international defence matériel market. Starting from virtually nothing, Singapore has rapidly built up a defence manufacturing industry and among recent products has been a light machine-gun called the **CIS Ultimax 100** or 3U-100.

The Ultimax 100 can trace its origins back to 1978. To provide a framework in which to work, the newly-formed Chartered Industries of Singapore (CIS) had obtained a licence to produce the 5.56-mm (0.219-in) Armalite AR-18 and also the Colt M16A1 rifles. Using these two weapons as a basis, CIS decided to build in some ideas of their own and the Ultimax 100 was the result. Some of the early prototypes were less than successful, but diligence and the application of some sound engineering removed the early problems, and the Ultimax 100 is now regarded as one of the best weapons in its class.

The Ultimax 100 fires the M193 5.56-mm cartridge, although there is no reason why it could not be converted to fire the new SS 109. It is a light machine-gun that is really light, for CIS was understandably keen to produce a weapon suited to the relatively light-statured personnel found in the Asian world. The result is that the Ultimax 100 handles very like an assault rifle. CIS has taken great pains to reduce recoil forces to a minimum, and has even introduced a feature it calls 'constant recoil'. With this feature the breech block does not use the back-plate of the receiver as a buffer, as is normal in many similar designs: instead a system of springs absorbs the forces and the result is a weapon that can be handled with ease and smoothness. The Ultimax 100 can be fired from the shoulder with no problems at all.

The likeness to an assault rifle is carried over to the ammunition feed. The Ultimax 100 uses a 100-round drum magazine under the body that can be changed with the same facility as a conventional box magazine. The drum magazines can be carried in a special webbing carrier. For firing on the move a forward grip is provided, and to make the weapon even handier the butt may be removed. For more accurate firing a bipod is a fixture and the barrel change is rapid and easy. If required normal M16A1 20- or 30-round

box magazines can be used in place of the drum.

Already accessories for the Ultimax 100 abound. Perhaps the most unusual of them is a silencer which is used in conjunction with a special barrel. More orthodox items include a special twin mounting in which two weapons are secured on their sides with the drum magazines pointing outwards. One very unusual extra is a bayonet, a feature which few similar weapons possess. Rifle grenades can be fired from the muzzle without preparation.

To date the Ultimax 100 is available in two versions; the **Ultimax 100 Mk 2** with a fixed barrel and the **Ultimax 100 Mk 3** with the easily-changed barrel. More versions are certain, for the Ultimax 100 has a most promising future. It is already in service with the Singapore armed forces and many more nations are showing a great interest in the weapon. It is certainly one of the handiest and most attractive of the 5.56-mm light machine-guns.

The Ultimax 100 Mark 3 light machine-gun is a small and light weapon that is ideally suited for many South East Asian armed forces. It is light and easy to handle and after a period of development is now a reliable and efficient weapon. It is now in full-scale production in Singapore.

Specification
Ultimax 100
Calibre: 5.56 mm (0.219 in)
Weights: gun empty 4.7 kg (10.36 lb) loaded with 100-round drum 6.5 kg (14.33 lb)
Lengths: overall 1030 mm (40.55 in); barrel 508 mm (20 in)
Muzzle velocity: (M193) 990 m (3,248 per second
Rate of fire: (cyclic) 400-600 rpm
Type of feed: 100-round drum, or 20-30-round box magazine

Below: The Ultimax 100 uses a drum magazine holding 100 5.56-mm (0.219-in) rounds. It can also use 20 or 30-round box magazines. The full 100-round drum can be fitted in on 11.6 seconds, but more drums can carried in the special carrier show here. A bayonet can be fitted and a silencer is available.

7.62-mm PK

One very noticeable feature in Soviet small-arms design is the strange mixture of innovation and conservatism that seems to beset every generation of weapons. Despite the impact made by the then-novel 7.62-mm (0.3-in)×39 cartridge used in the AK-47 assault rifle family, Soviet machine-guns have continued to use the much more powerful 7.62-mm×54R cartridge, which retains a distinct rim at its base. This rim was originally used for extraction from the old Mosin-Nagant rifles that can be traced back to 1895, if not before, but the same round is used for the Red Army's current general-purpose machine-gun known as the **PK** series.

There are several members of the PK range. The PK is the basic gun with a heavy barrel marked by flutes along

its exterior. This was first seen in 1946, and since then the **IKM** has arrived on the scene; this is an improved version of the PK that is lighter and simpler in construction. The **PKS** is a PK mounted on a tripod which can be used for anti-aircraft as well as ground fire. The **PKT** is a version for use on armoured vehicles, while the **PKM** is a PK mounted on a bipod. When the PKM is mounted on a tripod it becomes the **PKMS**. The **PKB** has the usual butt and trigger mechanism replaced by spade grips and a 'butterfly' trigger arrangement.

The PK appears to be all things to all men, and as far as the Red Army is concerned it is a true multi-role type: the PK is used in roles ranging from infantry squad support to AFV use in special mountings. All the PK machine-guns operate on the same

principle, based on the Kalashnikov rotary-bolt system used in many other current Soviet weapons. The interior of the PK is populated by surprisingly few parts: there are just the bolt/breech block, a piston and a few springs. The ammunition feed makes up a few more parts, and that is about it. Thus the PK has few parts to break or jam and it is very reliable. When used in the light machine-gun role the ammunition is normally carried in a metal box slung under the gun. For tripod operation variable lengths of belt are used. In the sustained-fire role the barrel has to be changed at regular intervals even though it is chromium-plated to reduce wear (a common Soviet practice).

These PK weapons must rank among the most numerous of all mod-

ern machine-guns. They are used only throughout the Red Army but a by many members of the Wars Pact. The Chinese produce a cc known as the Type 80. Both the PK the Type 80 have been passed on many nations in the third world a some are now in the hands of 'freed fighters'.

The one odd thing regarding the series is the retention of the old r med 7.62-mm cartridge. Even the c servative British discarded their loved 7.7-mm (0.303-in) cartridge cades ago, but the Soviets appea be more conservative still. Thus the originated the odd alliance of the perb PK machine-gun with all its ma fine points and a cartridge that v developed during the 1890s.

K
alibre: 7.62 mm (0.3 in)
eights: gun empty 9 kg (19.84 lb);
pod 7.5 kg (16.53 lb); 100-round belt
14 kg (5.38 lb)
ngths: gun 1160 mm (45.67 in);
rrel 658 mm (25.91 in)
uzzle velocity: 825 m (2,707 ft) per
cond
ate of fire: (cyclic) 690-720 rpm
rpe of feed: 100-, 200- and 250-round
elts

ie Soviet 7.62-mm (0.30-in) PK
achine-gun is seen here in its light
achine-gun form as the PKM. It is a
mple and sturdy weapon with few
oving parts, and is widely used by
any Warsaw Pact armed forces and
her forces around the world.

USSR
7.62-mm RPK

fires exactly the same 7.62-mm×39 ammunition as the assault rifle, but the commonality goes further. Some spare parts can be interchanged between the two weapons, and any soldier who can use the AKM (and that means all of them) can pick up and fire the RPK with equal facility. If the special 75-round drum magazine of the RPK is not available any magazine from an AKM can be fitted in its place. One thing the Soviet soldier will miss if he ever has to use the RPK in close action is that it

Seen here in the hands of a Bulgarian paratrooper, the RPK is used by many Warsaw Pact armies as a squad fire support weapon. Developed from the AKM, it fires the same 7.62-mm (0.30-in) ammunition as the rifle but uses a larger 40-round box magazine. The barrel cannot be changed.

does not have a mounting bracket for a bayonet.

Considering that the weapon is intended as a light machine-gun, it is surprising that the RPK does not have provision for changing the barrel when it gets hot. In order to ensure the barrel does not overheat, recruits are trained to limit burst-firing to about 80 shots per minute. For most tactical purposes this will be more than adequate, but there must be times when this fire rate will have its disadvantages. Apart from the 75-round drum already mentioned, there are curved box magazines holding 30 or 40 rounds. Some RPKs have been seen with infra-red night sights. A copy produced by the Chinese is known as the **Type 74**.

In recent years the Red Army has changed its standard rifle calibre to the new 5.45-mm (0.2146-in)×18 cartridge. For this round the AK-74 rifle was developed, and it follows that a new version of the RPK would follow. It has now appeared as the **RPK-74**. Apart from the scaling down of some parts to suit the smaller calibre, the RPK-74 is in overall terms identical with the RPK.

The RPK appears to be a popular weapon with the Red Army and the many Warsaw Pact nations to which it has been delivered. The type appears to be produced in East Germany and as far as can be determined the RPK is still in production in the Soviet Union (and China). It has been handed out to

some nations sympathetic to the Soviet way of thinking, and needless to say the RPK has found its way into the hands of many 'freedom fighters'. RPKs were observed during the recent fighting in Lebanon and more have been seen in action in Angola. Despite its rate-of-fire limitations, the RPK will no doubt be around for many years to come, and the Red Army still retains huge numbers of the type despite the introduction of the RPK-74.

Specification
RPK
Calibre: 7.62 mm (0.3 in)
Weights: gun 5 kg (11.02 lb); 75-round drum 2.1 kg (4.63 lb)
Lengths: gun 1035 mm (40.75 in); barrel 591 mm (23.27 in)
Muzzle velocity: 732 m (2,402 ft) per second
Rate of fire: (cyclic) 660 rpm and (practical) 80 rpm
Type of feed: 75-round drum, or 30- and 40-round box magazines

The Soviet RPK is the standard Warsaw Pact squad fire support weapon. It does not have an interchangeable barrel and so is not capable of sustained fire. The design may be regarded as a development of the AKM assault rifle, and it fires the same 7.62-mm (0.30-in) ammunition. A Chinese version is known as the Type 74.

hereas the Red Army uses the PK ries as a general-purpose machine-n, the 7.62-mm (0.3-in) **RPK** is very ich a light machine-gun used for uad support. The RPK was first ed in 1966 and it may be regarded an enlarged version of the AKM sault rifle. It has a longer and heavier rrel than the AKM, plus a light od, but otherwise the RPK is the ne weapon as the AKM.

This commonality of weapons kes a great deal of sense. The AKM

Automatic Firepower

Machine-guns are at the forefront of all current infantry actions, whether silencing guerrilla ambushes or halting movement in a battle area with sustained fire. In many combat zones, the latest modern weapons serve side by side with guns whose designs pre-date World War II.

When one considers recent conflicts, a factor readily appreciated is that the modern machine-gun has had considerably less effect on the modern battle scene than might have been expected. In the last few years not many wars have settled down to a hefty war of attrition, the main exception being, of course, the prolonged and bitter war between Iran and Iraq. There the old conditions of trench warfare have been re-established and there the machine-gun still retains the malign dominance that it had during World War I. Both sides use a mixture of weapon types. The Iraqis rely mainly on Soviet-supplied machine-guns, while the Iranians also use Soviet weapons leavened by an assortment of types culled from the international weapons market. In this relatively static campaign the conditions are often very like the protracted days of trench warfare in World War I, long periods of inactivity being dramatically interspersed with short periods of horror when the Iranians attempt to use their manpower in human wave attacks. All too often these massed attacks are easily broken up by machine-gun fire before they can even get close to their target trenches.

Happily these scenes are not being repeated anywhere else in the world at the moment.

On most flashpoint fronts a more fluid and mobile warfare has been apparent, even when a carefully sheltered enemy is attacked by an equally prepared force. Such conditions occurred on several occasions in the Falkland Islands campaign of 1982. There both sides used the machine-gun to equal effect, but one oddity of that campaign was that both sides were using the same weapon. The Argentines had the Belgian FN MAG, while the British forces used the British-made equivalent, the L7A2. At times during that short conflict there were occasions when the machine-guns pinned down one side or the other: at Goose Green, for example, FN MAGs equipped with night-vision sights pinned down the attackers from the Parachute Regiment for long periods during the nocturnal operation. But for most of the time the machine-guns were used mainly in the light machine-gun role, and at the end of it all heaps of Argentine FN MAGs were captured intact. Unhappily they proved to be of little benefit to the victors. In the transition from Belgian to British manufacturing methods and standards so many changes were introduced into the L7 that few parts of the Belgian and British versions can be interchanged. Thus the war booty was of little use to the British army, though the ammunition was and still is.

Away from the South Atlantic, few people outside the surrounding areas are aware that a nasty little war has been conducted along the borders of South Africa and her neighbouring states. In this theatre the South African defence forces have been conducting a constant counter-terrorist campaign against infiltrating 'freedom fighter' groups, which have constantly made limited and small raids into South African territory.

In such wars the machine-gun is rarely more than limited value, for ranges are usua short and the terrain often prevents vision any direction for more than a few yards. T South African defence forces have discovere however, that the machine-gun is a power anti-ambush weapon. At any sign of an ambu quick bursts of fire from the ubiquitous F MAG would soon break up any intende attack. In order to provide themselves wi superior mobility the South Africans oft moved on trucks or light armoured vehicl such as the Buffel (Buffalo), and the best cou ter to them was soon discovered by the guerr las to be the land mine, to which machine-gu do little.

But the guerrillas (and especially the SW PO guerrillas operating out of Angola) did the best to provide themselves with machine-gu While their Cuban comrades kept themselv and their Soviet-supplied weapons out of t way as much as possible, the SWAPO guerr las were left to use whatever they could muste captured weapon displays show some ve odd relics, ranging from MG34 to Czech ZB 26 weapons. The fact that so many of the machine-guns have been captured by t South Africans is in itself an indication of he little effect they have had on that confli Although sporadic outbreaks still occur, th little war now seems likely to be terminated the very near future although no doubt t South Africans will remain on their guard some time to come.

Farther north in Africa, unhappy Eritrea another location of protracted guerrilla warfa carried out with merciless thoroughness both sides while around them hordes of peop starve to death. This is yet another campai where the machine-gun can do little more th boost the morale of one side or another. T simple fact is that wherever it is fought, guer la warfare rarely has much use for machin guns, although it is conceivable that the ne light machine-guns might find a place for the combination of light weight and firepower. course the sudden appearance of a dete mined man in the middle of a civilian commu ity when he is carrying a machine-gun w every show of using it can have a numbi effect on the onlookers. The mere thought bursts of machine-gun fire in an enclosed ar is usually enough to make anyone obey a te rorist's bidding. But for the guerrilla su opportunities are few and far betwee although IRA terrorists have killed British s diers in Northern Ireland with M60s stolen fr arsenals in the USA. Machine-guns are handy things to carry or to hide, and as t emotional and/or propaganda importance the machine-gun to an underground organi: tion often appears to be greater than its act worth, the possession of such a weapon fr quently imposes a degree of inflexibility a immobility on the group concerned. This al has happened in Northern Ireland, when I terrorists have opted to stand and fight in ord to buy time for others to get the precious M6 a safe house. In some cases this has resulted the capture of the M60 by the British army a the death or imprisonment of the IRA membe concerned.

An L4A4, the 7.62-mm version of the Bren, is seer a South African position on the border of South West Africa. In the struggle against SWAPO the main aim is to prevent the guerrillas entering the country from their sanctuaries in Angola.

ove: A roof mounting for an MG3 is carried on a
ndeswehr truck. This form of mounting can be
ed against ground targets, but is primarily
tended for use as an anti-aircraft defence
ounting. 7.62-mm (0.30-in) machine-guns are
ally too light for anti-aircraft use, but have an
portant morale role.

American troops from the US Army's component of
the Allied Mobile Force (Land) (AMF(L)) alight
from a Bell UH-1 helicopter and immediately take
up a defensive position with an M60. The gunner is
festooned with a spare ammunition belt, while his
Number 2 ensures the belt in use is fed cleanly.

Left: The uniform of the Bundeswehr Gebirgsjäger
and the retention of the MG3 for current use, many
years after its World War II predecessor the MG42
first appeared, gives the mountain warfare
division of the West German army a definite
wartime air; but it is simply a case of using the best
uniform and weapon for the job.

To many observers, the major shooting war in progress today is that being fought daily in Afghanistan, despite the far more massive conflict in progress not far away on the Iran-Iraq borders. Again, this is a war where the machine-gun cannot have much effect on the actual fighting, but where it can have a fearful nuisance effect when handled properly. This is particularly true in the steep mountain valleys where one carefully emplaced machine-gun can hold up a Soviet supply convoy for hours while the hapless Red Army soldiers and Afghan conscripts attempt to find the source of the fire. Fortunately for the Red Army this does not happen often, for the Afghans rely more on their rifles for this sort of ambush. In return the Soviet soldiers can do little more than rake the surrounding hillsides in the hope that some of their rounds find a billet.

The Afghan campaign has seen one return to an old machine-gun tactic, and that is firing upon fixed lines. During World War I machine-guns were often set up to fire on locations where an enemy was likely to be, rather than to undertake aimed fire at a definite target. This ploy was often used at night (when the target was in any case invisible) and at least it had the advantage that it was likely to deny an easy exit or access point to the enemy. In Afghanistan this practice has once more been found useful. The Afghan guerrillas often creep up to an Afghan army or Soviet outpost and open fire with rockets or rifles in order to harass or demoralize rather than destroy anything important. These missions are usually carried out at night, when the defenders cannot readily see the attackers, so here a few pre-laid machine-guns covering likely approach routes or defiles are simply fired off. The machine-guns are emplaced on tripods with their barrels elevated to the correct degree and with their muzzles kept on target by the use of stakes on each side of

the barrel. All the firer has to do is pull the trigger and keep the ammunition feed topped up. As the weapon fires the spread of fire is such that there is a good chance of hitting anything in the chosen field of fire.

In NATO there is at present a state of transition as far as machine-guns are concerned. Many nations, including the USA and the UK, have now chosen to discard the general-purpose machine-gun (GPMG) concept and are reverting to the old ways of using a light machine-gun designed for the job of squad fire support. This will have the advantage of providing the machine-gunner with a far more manageable load and enable the squad to car-

The American M60 machine-gun is used here in
the light machine-gun role by a trooper of the 82nd
Airborne Division. The ammunition feed belt can
be clearly seen, and both in action and on the move
it can be something of a nuisance as it tends to
snag anything nearby; the belts can cause jams
when twisted.

ry just one type of ammunition. At present a squad going into action has to carry ammunition packed into magazines or into belts, which means two logistic loads instead of one. In future the squad fire-support weapon and the standard weapon will use the same box magazines, with all the logistic advantages that this entails. All this is nothing new to the Red Army, which was well to the fore in its post-war tactical analysis and many years ago decided not only to adopt the GPMG concept but also develop a special machine rifle for squad fire support. Thus the Red Army has for long used a mix of APK assault rifles and RPK machine rifles, the latter being used as rather light LMGs. The term light is used advisedly, for the RPK cannot deliver heavy bursts of fire. The Red Army relies upon the PK for this role, which perhaps defeats the object at times, for the PK uses a different ammunition and is also a much heavier weapon. But already the RPK is in the process of being replaced in the Red Army's front-line units by the RPK-74 firing the new 5.45-mm (0.2146-in) round.

An L7A1 is seen on its buffered tripod for the sustained fire role. The tripod uses a spring mounting to absorb the gun's recoil forces to keep the gun on its selected firing line for long periods without having to constantly re-sight the weapon.

The MG3 and its predecessor, the World War II MG42, are widely used outside NATO and some have turned up in guerrilla hands all over the world. The bulk of these are old MG42s from various stocks, but without looking at markings and detail points they are difficult to differentiate from the modern MG3s.

7.62-mm Bren Gun

'hen considering modern machine-
ins, it seems something of a surprise
at a weapon as old as the **Bren Gun**
iould be included, especially as this
eapon can be traced back as far as
e early 1930s. But the original Bren
uns were chambered for the 7.7-mm
.303-in) rimmed cartridge, and when
e decision was made to convert to
e new standard NATO 7.62-mm (0.3-
) cartridge the British armed forces
ll had large stockpiles of the Bren
un to hand. It made sound commer-
al sense to convert them for the new
alibre, and such a programme was
on put into effect at the Royal Small
rms Factory at Enfield Lock in Mid-
esex.

The conversion to the new calibre
itailed a complete overhaul, but the
sk was made easier by the fact that
iring World War II a Canadian com-
iny produced numbers of Bren Guns
7.92-mm (0.312-in) calibre for China.
s this round was rimless, it was found
at the breechblocks intended for the
hina contract' were equally suitable
r the new 7.62-mm cartridge and
iese were used in place of the origin-
s. A new barrel was produced with a
iromium-plated interior. This not
ily diminished wear on the barrel but
so reduced the need for the frequent
irrel-changes required on World
ar II versions. Thus the new gun was
sued with only the one barrel.

The current version of the Bren Gun
ed by the British Army is the **L4A4**.
iis is not used as a front-line infantry
eapon, but instead is issued to the
any other arms of the service who
quire a machine-gun. Thus the L4A4
used by the Royal Artillery for anti-
rcraft and ground-defence of its bat-

teries, by the Royal Signals for the defence of its installations in the field, by
units assigned for home defence, and
so on. The L4A4 is also used by the
Royal Air Force, and a version known
as the **L4A5** is used by the Royal Navy.
There is also a version known as the
L4A3 that is not often encountered as it
is a conversion of the old Bren Mk 2
gun; the L4A4 is a conversion of the
improved Bren Mk 3.

In all these versions the gas-
operated mechanism of the original
Bren Gun remains unchanged. So few
are the changes involved in the
change of calibre that the only points of
note are that the 7 62-mm version uses
a nearly-vertical magazine in place of
the old curved equivalent, and the
muzzle lacks the pronounced cone-

shape of the old weapon.

For the anti-aircraft role the L4A4
has been fitted with some fairly sophisticated sighting arrangements. The
L4A4 does not use a tripod as did the
old Bren Guns, but instead it can be
mounted on the roof hatches of self-
propelled guns and howitzers as well
as on other armoured vehicles.

So the old Bren Gun soldiers on in a
new form, and there seems to be no
sign of its passing from use in the foreseeable future. Many of the Commonwealth nations still use the Bren, some
in its original 7.7-mm form, so although
the original design may be old the
weapon is still regarded as effective
and in its L4A4 form the old Bren Gun is
as good as many far more modern designs.

*The latest version of the venerable
wartime Bren gun is the British L4A4,
chambered for the NATO 7.62-mm
(0.30-in) round. It has a new barrel,
breech block and a new vertical 30-
round box magazine and is now used
by support and second-line British
Army units.*

Specification
L4A4
Calibre: 7.62 mm (0.3 in)
Weights: gun only 9.53 kg (21 lb);
barrel 2.72 kg (6 lb)
Lengths: gun 1133 mm (44.6 in); barrel
536 mm (21.1 in)
Muzzle velocity: 823 m (2,700 ft) per
second
Rate of fire: (cyclic) 500 rpm
Type of feed: 30-round box

5.56-mm Light Support Weapon (LSW)

ir many years the standard squad
iht machine-gun for the British army
s been a version of the FN MAG
ed with a bipod and known as the
'A2. While this is a fine weapon, it is
iher a cumbersome load and it fires a
rtridge that is now generally consi-
ired too powerful for the squad-
oport role. With the imminent arrival
the Enfield Weapon System (or
iall Arms 80, otherwise SA 80), the
'A2 is due to be replaced in the
uad support role by a new weapon
rrently known as the **XL73E2 Light
pport Weapon** or **LSW**; the L7A2 will
retained for the sustained-fire func-
n for some years to come.

The LSW is one half of the Enfield
eapon System, the other component
ing the Individual Weapon or IW,
uch will be the standard rifle while
e LSW will become the squad-
pport weapon. The two new
iapons have many things in common
d can be easily recognized as com-
j from the same stable, but the LSW
s a heavier barrel and a light bipod
unted well forward under the bar-
. There is also a rear grip under
iat might be regarded as the butt to
ovide the firer with a better hold for
stained firing.

The term butt is rather misleading as
e LSW is based on a 'bullpup' layout
which the trigger group is placed
ward of the magazine. This arrange-
ent makes the LSW more compact
in a conventional weapon. Much of
e LSW is steel, but the foregrip and

*With the FN rifle about to be
replaced by the 5.56-mm Individual
Weapon, the British Army is
adopting a squad support weapon of*

the pistol grip for the trigger are tough
nylonite. The LSW uses the same
magazine as the IW, namely a standard M16A1 30-round box.

The LSW has undergone several
changes of calibre since it was first
mooted. Originally it was calibred for
the British experimental 4.85-mm
(0.19-in) cartridge, but this was over-
ruled in favour of the American M193

*the same calibre to replace the FN
MAG general purpose machine-gun.
The latter will be retained for the
sustained fire role.*

cartridge, which in turn was superseded yet again in favour of the new
NATO standard 5.56-mm (0.219-in) SS
109. The first production versions will
be for the SS 109 round, and will also
have an optical sight known as the
Sight Unit Small Arms Trilux or SUSAT
mounted on a bracket over the receiver. It will be possible to change this
sight for some form of night sight.

*Seen here in front of the GPMG is the
4.85-mm version of the Light Support
Weapon, produced to complement
the proposed 4.85-mm rifle. When
NATO adopted the Belgian 5.56-mm
round as standard, the 4.85-mm
designs were abandoned despite
their superior performance.*

The Light Support Weapon shares many components with the 5.56-mm rifle; obvious differences are the heavy barrel, the bipod and the rear grip. The LSW uses the same magazine as the Individual Weapon – the 30-round M16A1 box.

Various accessories will be available for the LSW once it gets into service, which should be some time during 1985 if the current trials go well. A training adapter firing low-powered ammunition will be available, as will a blank-firing attachment. A multipurpose tool is already in use for stripping and first-line repairs, and it will be possible to fit a sling for carrying. The muzzle attachment is so arranged that it is possible for rifle grenades to be fired from the muzzle, although it is not envisaged that the LSW will be used extensively for this purpose.

The LSW has undergone a protracted development period, some of the period being elongated by the change of NATO standard calibre and

other considerations. By the time it reaches the hands of the troops in the near future the LSW should be an excellent weapon with no bugs left to iron out.

Specification
LSW
Calibre: 5.56 mm (0.219 in)
Weights: gun complete and loaded 6.88 kg (15.17 lb); gun less magazine and sight 5.6 kg (12.346 lb)
Lengths: overall 900 mm (35.43 in); barrel 646 mm (25.43 in)
Muzzle velocity: 970 m (3,182 ft) per second
Rate of fire: (cyclic) 700-850 rpm
Type of feed: 30-round box magazine

FRANCE

7.5-mm AA 52

Above: The French Foreign Legion use exactly the same weapons as the rest of the French army and so the AA 52 machine-gun, seen here in its light machine-gun form, is a familiar sight wherever the legion operates.

The machine-gun now known as the **AA 52** was designed and developed directly as a result of the Indo-China campaigns of the early 1950s. At that

time the French army was equipped with a wide array of American, British and ex-German weapons, and the furnishing of support and spares for this array was too much for the army, which decided to adopt one standard general-purpose machine-gun. The result was the 7.5-mm (0.295-in) AA 52, a weapon designed from the outset for ease of production, and thus making much use of stampings and welded components.

The AA 52 is unusual among modern machine-guns in relying on a form of delayed-blowback operation, in which the force of the cartridge firing is employed to force back the breech block to the starting position, and also to power the feed mechanism. This system works very well with pistol cartridges in sub-machine guns, but using rifle cartridges in machine-guns demands something more positive if safety is to be regarded. On the AA 52 a two-part block is used: a lever device is so arranged that it holds the forward part of the block in position while the rear half starts to move to the rear; only when the lever has moved a predetermined distance does it allow the forward part of the block to move back. In order to make the spent cartridge easier to extract the chamber has

grooves that allow gas to enter between the chamber wall and the fired cartridge to prevent 'sticking', and a cartridge fired from an AA 52 can always be recognized by the fluted grooves around the case neck.

The AA 52 can be fired from a bipod or a tripod, but when a tripod is used for the sustained fire role a heavy barrel is fitted to the weapon. When used in the light machine-gun role the AA 52 is a rather clumsy weapon to carry, especially if a 50-round ammunition box is carried on the left-hand side. For this reason the box is often left off and the ammunition belt allowed to hang free. One unusual feature of the AA 52 is that for the light machine-gun role a monopod is fitted under the butt. This can be awkward at times, and another awkward point is the barrel change: the barrel can be removed readily enough, but the bipod is permanently attached to the barrel and in the light machine-gun role this can make barrel-changing very difficult, especially as the AA 52 barrels have no form of barrel plating that might reduce the temperature of the gun and barrel.

The AA 52 was originally intended to fire a 7.5-mm (0.295-in) cartridge first developed for use by the mle 1929 light machine-gun. This cartridge is powerful enough, but the switch to the NATO 7.62-mm (0.3 in) cartridge left the French army using a non-standard cartridge, and export prospects for the AA 52 were thus reduced. The basic

design has therefore been adapted to fire the NATO cartridge in a version known as the **NF-1**. Some of these have been issued to French army units, but exports have not materialized.

Overall the AA 52 is an adequate machine-gun, but it has many features (some of them regarded by some nations as inherently unsafe) that are best undesirable. The weapon is no longer in production but is still offered for export.

Specification
AA 52
Calibre: 7.5 mm (0.295 in)
Weights: with bipod and light barrel 9.97 kg (21.98 lb); with bipod and heavy barrel 11.37 kg (25.07 lb); tripod 10.6 kg (23.37 lb)
Lengths: with butt extended (light barrel) 1145 mm (45.08 in) or (heavy barrel) 1245 mm (49.02 in); light barrel only 500 mm (19.69 in); heavy barrel only 600 mm (23.62 in)
Muzzle velocity: 840 m (2,756 ft) per second
Rate of fire: (cyclic) 700 rpm
Type of feed: 50-round belt

The French AA 52 uses a delayed blowback mechanism with a fluted chamber to ease extraction. A 7.62-mm (0.30-in) version known as the AA 7.62 NF-1 may also be encountered, but neither model is now in production. Bipod and tripod versions are in use, as are vehicle-mounted models.

Heckler & Koch machine-guns

The West German concern Heckler & Koch, based at Oberndorf-Neckar, is among the most prolific of all modern small-arms designers, and in addition to its successful range of assault rifles and sub-machine guns it also produces a wide variety of machine-guns. It may be an oversimplification, but Heckler & Koch machine-guns are basically modified versions of the company's G-3 and associated assault rifles. They all use the same delay-roller mechanism in their breech blocks, and some of the light machine-guns are simply rifles with heavier barrels and a bipod. To confuse the issue, Heckler & Koch produce virtually every model in belt-and magazine-fed versions, and some are produced in 7.62-mm (0.3-in) NATO or 5.56-mm (0.219-in) calibres, with the added variation in the latter for the new SS 109 cartridge or the older American M193.

One of the 'base' models in the range is the 7.62-mm **HK 21A1**, a development of the earlier **HK 21** which is no longer in production. The HK 21A1 uses a belt feed and may be used as a light machine-gun on a bipod or in the sustained-fire role on a tripod. For the latter, barrel changing is incorporated. Even in this version of the Heckler & Koch range the outline of the G-3 is apparent, and this is carried over to the latest versions of the HK 21, the **HK 21E**, which has a longer sight radius and a three-round burst selection feature. The barrel is longer, and changes have been made to the ammunition used. There is also a 5.57-mm counterpart to this variant, and this is known as the **HK 23E**.

All the variants mentioned above are belt-fed weapons. There is also a magazine-fed version for every one of them: the **HK 11A1** is the magazine counterpart of the HK 21A1, while the **HK 11E** and **HK 13E** are the magazine counterparts of the HK 21E and HK 23E.

All this may sound rather confusing, but the basic factor that emerges is the ability of Heckler & Koch to produce a machine-gun suited to virtually any requirement. The belt-fed versions may be regarded as general-purpose machine-guns (although the 5.56-mm versions may really be too light for the sustained-fire role), and the magazine-fed versions as true light machine-guns. They offer a surprising amount of interchangeability of spare parts, and the magazines are usually the same as those used on their equivalent assault rifles, making the use of the automatic guns as squad support weapons even easier.

Specification
HK 21A1
Calibre: 7.62 mm (0.3 in)
Weights: gun with bipod 8.3 kg (18.3 lb); barrel 1.7 kg (3.75 lb); 100-round ammunition box 3.6 kg (7.94 lb)
Lengths: overall 1030 m (40.55 in); barrel 450 mm (17.72 in)
Muzzle velocity: 800 m (2,625 ft) per second
Rate of fire: (cyclic) 900 rpm
Type of feed: 100-round belt

The HK 21A1 is a development of the earlier HK 21. It uses a belt feed only, but the belt can be contained in a box slung under the receiver.

The Heckler & Koch HK 11 is the box magazine feed variant of the HK 21 and is a 7.62-mm (0.30-in) weapon.

The Heckler & Koch HK 13 is produced in several versions. This model accommodates a 40-round box magazine.

The Heckler & Koch HK 13E has a three-round burst capability as well as full automatic fire.

The Heckler & Koch HK 21 is no longer produced, but is still in use with nations such as Portugal.

7.62 mm MG3

One of the outstanding machine-gun designs of World War II was the MG42, a weapon that introduced the advantages of mass production to an area of weapon design that had for long clung to traditional methods of construction. With the MG42, the new era of steel pressings, welds and the elimination of many machining processes was allied to an excellent design that attracted widespread respect and attention. Thus, when the Federal Republic of Germany became a member of NATO and was once more allowed a measure of weapon production for rearmament, the MG42 was one of the first designs to be resurrected.

The original MG42 had a calibre of 7.92 mm (0.312 in), but with the adoption of the standard NATO 7.62-mm (0.3-in) round the old design was reworked to accommodate the new calibre. At first stockpiled MG42s were simply modified to this calibre with the designation **MG2**, but in parallel with this activity a production programme was under way by Rheinmetall to produce new weapons in 7.62-mm calibre. There were several variants of this production version, all having the designation **MG1**, although there were some minor changes to suit ammunition feed and so on. The current production version is the **MG3**, still manufactured by Rheinmetall.

In appearance, the war-time MG42 and the MG3 are identical apart from some minor details, few of which can be detected by the untrained eye, and there are more changes between the MG1 and MG3. Overall, however, the modern MG3 retains all the attributes of the original, and many of the mountings used with the MG3 are just adaptations or modifications of the World War II originals. Thus the MG3 can be used on a tripod that is virtually identical to the original, and the twin mounting for anti-aircraft use could still accommodate the MG42 without trouble. There are now available many mountings for the MG3.

The original MG42 was designed for ease of mass production, and this same feature makes the MG3 very suitable for manufacture in some of the less well-equipped arsenals that now abound in 'third-world' nations. The MG3 has proved to be relatively easy for such facilities and it is now licence-produced in nations such as Pakistan, Chile, Spain and Turkey; some of these nations fabricate versions of the MG1 rather than the MG3 proper. Yugoslavia also produces a version of this weapon, but the Yugoslav model is a direct copy of the MG42, still in 7.92-mm calibre and designated **SARAC M1953**.

Within NATO the MG3, or one of other of its variants, are used by th Bundeswehr, by the Italian arme forces, and by nations such as De mark and Norway. Portugal makes th MG3 for use by the Portuguese arme forces, and is now offering the type f export. Thus from many sources th old MG42 design soldiers on. There even talk of further development produce a lighter version, but this proceeding at a low priority, for th basic design of the MG3 is still a sound as it ever was, and any attem to improve or modify the origin appears to many to be an exercise a out as fruitful as redesigning the whee

Specification
MG3
Calibre: 7.62 mm (0.3 in)
Weights: basic gun 10.5 kg (23.15 lb); bipod 0.55 kg (1.213 lb); barrel 1.8 kg (3.97 lb)
Lengths: gun with butt 1225 mm (48.23 in); gun less butt 1097 mm (43.19 in); barrel 531 mm (20.91 in)
Muzzle velocity: 820 m (2,690 ft) per second
Rate of fire: (cyclic) 700-1,300 rpm
Type of feed: 50-round belt

The West German MG3 is the modern version of the wartime MG42, and is currently rated as one of the best machine-guns of its type used by NATO. It has a high rate of fire and an easy and rapid barrel change, and can be fired from the bipod shown or from a heavy tripod for the sustained fire support role.

7.62-mm Uirapuru Mekanika

Over recent decades Brazil has changed from being a defence-equipment importer to a nation that exports over 95 per cent of its defence industry's produce. The nation has undoubted talent for the defence-based industries, and in an effort to harness some of this talent to producing small arms a design team was established in the early 1960s to develop a general-purpose machine-gun. This first design team was led by a team of three experts, but while its initial designs worked they had many inherent problems. These were too numerous for the possibility of acceptance by the Brazilian army, who turned the design problem over to a private concern. This fared no better than the original team, so one of the original triumvirate took over the project on his own.

Using the facilities of a design and research establishment, this individual approach worked. Thus there emerged a design now known as the **Uirapuru Mekanika** after a Brazilian jungle bird. The Uirapuru is a general-purpose machine-gun firing standard NATO 7.62-mm (0.3-in) ammunition. It can be used as a light machine-gun with a butt and bipod, or it can be fired from a heavy tripod for the heavy machine-gun role. It can also be fitted with a solenoid for use as a co-axial weapon on armoured vehicles, and it can be adapted to firing from a number of other mounts.

In appearance the Uirapuru is a rather long, ungainly-looking weapon, especially when fitted with a butt for the light machine-gun role. It uses a conventional gas-operated mechanism with an orthodox belt feed for the ammunition, and the barrel can be changed rapidly using a handle that also acts as a carrying handle for the weapon. The receiver of the weapon is very simple, being little more than a length of tube containing the breech block and its return spring. What appears to be a rectangular receiver is in fact the ammunition feed mechanism. The method of tapping off gas from the barrel is also simple. No gas regulating block or valve is used, the gas impingeing directly onto the return mechanism. No provision appears to have been made for firing single shots.

The barrel of the Uirapuru has a large pepperpot-type muzzle brake and it is recommended that the barrel is changed after every 400 rounds have been fired. Most of the parts appear to require some machining, which should ensure a rugged construction. The Brazilian army gave its approval to the Uirapuru after lengthy trials, and the type is now being prepared for full production at a factory near Rio de Janeiro. If past Brazilian salesmanship is any guide, it will not be long before the first examples are seen outside Brazil, for if the Uirapuru can withstand the varied combat conditions that can be encountered in Brazil it will put up with virtually anything, and the simple construction certainly should keep the price of a weapon down.

Specification
Uirapuru Mekanika
Calibre: 7.62 mm (0.3 in)

The Brazilian 7.62-mm (0.30-in) Uirapuru Mekanika is the first locally-produced machine-gun design to enter production, and although it appears at first sight to be rather long it is an efficient and basically simple weapon.

Weight: with butt and bipod 13 kg (28.66 lb)
Lengths: with butt 1300 mm (51.2 in); barrel 600 mm (23.62 in)
Muzzle velocity: 850 m (2,789 ft) per second
Rate of fire: (cyclic) 650-700 rpm
Type of feed: 50-round belt

Pakistani troops high in the Himalayas man an MG3 post. The weapon, modified from the classic MG 42 of World War II, is manufactured under licence in Pakistan.

SHOTGUNS
AND
RIOT CONTROL
EQUIPMENT

Combat Shotguns

***hotguns are unrivalled as close combat weapons, but
lthough they saw service in the trenches during World War I
* was not until British troops used them in Malaya during the
950s that their true military value began to be appreciated.
'oday their potential is at last being developed, and purpose-
uilt combat shotguns are entering service.***

*The Pancor Jackhammer may well point the way to future combat shotguns,
borrowing from current assault rifle technology to provide a more
battleworthy weapon. The 10-round, quick-change magazine is also more
practical than previous methods of charging one's piece.*

he shotgun has for long been regarded as an 'unmilitary' weapon that
·r ill-defined reasons should have no place in military activities. That
titude has been proved wrong many times over the last century, and
ungs have finally reached the state where a properly conceived and
esigned combat shotgun is in the offing. This change of thought has
een produced by experiences gained over two world wars, numerous
mall wars' and a great deal of guerrilla activity, but it is still a change not
eadily accepted by some military minds.

For many forms of combat the shotgun is a weapon beyond compari-
on. Jungle and trench warfare (and other such fighting where ranges
·e short and targets fleeting) require a personal weapon that can fire
umerous effective projectiles over an area, and this the shotgun does to
erfection. At longer ranges the shotgun becomes less efficient, but
·chnology has now reached the stage where shotgun projectiles such
; the flechette have much greater useful ranges than simple round shot.
s infantry combat ranges seemingly become shorter, the shotgun type
· weapon becomes all the more attractive and at long last it has been
:cepted that in action most soldiers cannot aim their weapons with any

great accuracy. Thus their weapons have to do their own aiming by
spreading multiple projectiles over an area.

We are witnessing a stage of transition in small-arms design. More
and more military planners are realizing that the combat shotgun is
necessary, and in this study are contained some of the weapons that
point the way ahead. Also included are the many sporting weapons that
have indicated the trends that true combat shotguns must inevitably
follow. Even a short perusal of the weapons included here will make one
wonder why it has taken the shotgun so long to be an accepted weapon
of war.

*While shotguns have long been used in combat (and are likely to become ever
more useful in that role now that the attention of small-arms designers has
been fixed on them), it is in police and paramilitary hands that they have seen
most action, as here in Miami in the early 1980s.*

Browning Automatic series

Left: A British soldier of the 18th Independent Brigade on patrol in the jungle during the Malayan Emergency carries a Browning A5, which provided formidable short-range firepower.

Any description of the Browning automatic shotguns as combat weapons is beset by the difficulty that there has never been a purpose-produced military version of these designs. The first **Browning Automatic** (actually semi-automatic or self-loading) shotgun was conceived as early as 1898, but it was left to the Belgian Fabrique Nationale (FN) to start production and many guns still in use are Belgian-produced. They were all primarily sporting weapons but it was not long before many ended in military hands, often as security guard weapons or for similar duties. John M. Browning also negotiated a production licence with the American Remington concern and many Remington guns used by the US Army and others during World War II were in fact Browning Automatics (typical being the **Remington Model 11A** and **Model 12**).

After World War II sporting Brownings were widely used as military weapons in such localities as Central and South America, but it took the Malayan Emergency of 1948 to 1960 to

make the Browning Automatic established military weapon. The Br ish army used Greener GP guns a Browning Automatics throughout th long campaign, often (but not alway with the long sporting barrel cut ba to as short a length as possible. Mc guns used by the British were gauge weapons with five-round mac zines and fired commercial heavy sl cartridges.

It was not long before the Briti relearned the old lesson that the au matic shotgun is an almost-perfe weapon for the close-quarter comb of jungle warfare. As an ambush counter-ambush gun the Browni Automatic was ideal and could used to fire off five rounds in as few three seconds. At the time little publ ity was given to the combat use these shotguns (Remington Moc 870Rs were also employed) but ma soldiers who served in Malaya duri the Emergency probably carrie Browning Automatic at some time another.

After 1960 the British army set asi its Brownings for more convention weapons, but doubtless some are s retained for 'special purposes'. L spite the type's Malayan popular soldiers found that the weapon w slow to reload and took some looki after, especially when shortened b rels imposed excessive firing loads the self-loading components.

Brownings popped up again duri the Rhodesian anti-guerrilla/freedo fighter campaigns, and the gun is sti widely used 'small campaign' weapc But there is still no sign of a comb version of the Browning Automatic, c spite a brief flurry of design activ during the 1960s. 'Military' Browni Automatics continue to be primar sporting weapons.

Specification
Browning Automatic (standard mode
Calibre: 12 gauge
Weight: loaded 4.1 kg (9 lb)
Length: barrel 711 mm (28 in)
Feed: 5-round tubular magazine

The Browning Automatic shotguns were not produced as dedicated military weapons, but proved toug enough for the rigours of service lif They were useful weapons in terra which favoured the ambusher; in a emergency they could fire five rounds in three seconds.

FN Riot Shotgun

As its name implies, the **Fabrique Nationale Riot Shotgun** is primarily a police and paramilitary weapon. In design terms it is a relatively unremarkable design: a manual pump-action shotgun with a tubular magazine holding five rounds. FN is no stranger to shotgun design, for it was among the first to produce the many John M. Browning automatic shotgun designs in the 1920s, and ever since that time the company has been in the forefront of world manufacture of these weapons. Many of FN's designs are intended for sporting purposes, but it takes little to transform a sporting shotgun into a law-enforcement weapon and FN has never been slow to undertake the transformation.

The Riot Shotgun first appeared in

1970 and was based on the widely-used FN automatic sporting gun of the period. It was at one time available in three interchangeable barrel lengths. The first models had rear and fore sights, but on later production models these have been removed and the standard barrel length is now 500 mm (19.7 in). Rubber butt pads and sling swivels are fitted as standard.

The main difference between the Riot Shotgun and the FN sporting models is that the riot version is much more rugged than the civilian shotguns. For instance there is a bolt that runs right through the stock to strengthen the component and all metalwork has been 'beefed up' to withstand the rigours of hard use. The metal surfaces have also been specially plated so that

they require only a minimum of care and maintenance.

FN even decided to retain the original five-round tubular magazine and has thus never introduced the extension magazines used on many other contemporary paramilitary shotguns, mainly to maintain an overall high degree of reliability. Instead FN decided to retain the simple manual action, each 'pump' ejecting a spent case and

Right: Shotgun ammunition comes in a bewildering variety of forms, which different countries unhelpfully divide into different categories. On the left is a conventional birdshot round for the FN shotgun; in the centre a flechette round; and on the right a brenecke rifled slug.

N Riot Shotgun (continued)

ading another. At one time there was
ı attempt to introduce a fully-automa-
ɔ version of the Riot Shotgun, but this
odel was produced as a prototype
ıly and had a six-round magazine.
FN has produced its Riot Shotgun in
form suitable for firing full-calibre
ugs, but the majority of guns in use
e used to fire 12-gauge shot only: in
ct there has never been a Riot Shot-
ın in any other calibre. The type is
ed by the Belgian police and some
aramilitary units, and it has been sold
some overseas police forces. It is a
ery reliable and rugged weapon and
more than adequate for its intended
ıramilitary role.

ɔecification
N Riot Shotgun
alibre: 12 gauge
eight: 2.95 kg (6.5 lb)
ɪngths: overall 970 mm (38.19 in);
ırrel 500 mm (19.7 in)
ɪed: 5-round tubular magazine

ump-action shotguns like the FN
e used by police forces all over the
orld. They are reliable weapons
ith high short-range hit probability,
ıd do not produce stray bullets
hich are still lethal to bystanders
ındreds of yards away.

Beretta RS200 and RS202P

mi Beretta SpA is one of the most
ɪspected names in small-arms design
d manufacture, and is no stranger to
otgun production. The company fol-
ᴠed the move towards manufactur-
ɡ robust shotguns for police and pa-
military purposes and introduced its
-gauge **Beretta RS200 (Police Model)**
ınual pump-action shotgun. As with
other Beretta weapons, this is a
ɪll-designed and superbly-finished
ɪapon that has been suitably streng-
ɪned for the rough handling it can
pect.

Beretta introduced no innovations
th the RS200 other than a special
ˈety sliding-block breech locking
ᴠice that prevents firing before
:king is complete. The hammer also
s a special safety lug feature and
ɪre is a bolt catch that enables a
ɪrtridge to be safely removed from
ɪ chamber without having to fire it.
.other feature of the RS200 is that it
n be used to fire small tear gas car-
ɪges (to a range of about 100 m/109
ırds) as well as the usual shot or slug
ɪdings.

Though now out of production, the
200 is used by many police and
ɪer forces. It was replaced by the
202P, which differs mainly in the
ɪding procedure, which was made
ɪch easier, and in slight variations to
ɪ bolt mechanism. With the introduc-
ɪ of the RS202P came two variants.
ɪe first was introduced to reduce the
ɪerall length of the weapon for stow-
ɪ and handling: this **RS202-M1** has a
ɪleton-type folding butt that can be
ᴠed alongside the left-hand side of
ɪ body. The second variant carries
ɪr this folding butt but in addition
ɪ a variable choke device over the
ɪzzle (to vary the spread of shot) and
ɪerforated barrel jacket to make
ɪdling easier: it is impossible to hold
ɪ barrel once it gets hot. To assist
ɪid aiming special sights have been
ɪd to this second variant, which is

*Right: The RS202-M1 is the folding
stock version of the successful RS
202P 12-gauge shotgun. Loading is
marginally easier than on the
original weapon and the bolt
mechanism has been altered.*

*Below: This RS202-M2 has a
perforated barrel jacket, which
makes for easier handling of a gun
with a hot barrel from repeated
firing. Beretta provide a variable
choke unit to give a choice of spread
patterns.*

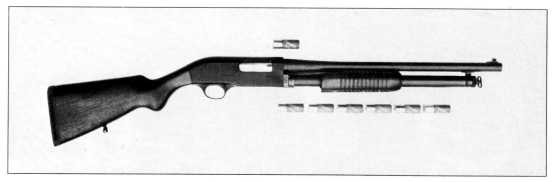

*The original RS200 has six 12-gauge shells which it carries in the magazine, plus a seventh which can be
chambered. The inertia-operated firing pin on the RS200 prevents the gun from firing unless the bolt is fully locked.*

known as the **RS202P-M2**.

The RS202P shotguns have followed the overall acceptance of the RS200 but sales have not been remarkable, mainly because they seem to lack the aesthetic appeal of some of the more modern designs. The RS200 has for some time been out of production and the RS202P is apparently being produced to order only. For all this they are both reliable and well-made guns that seem set to remain in use for many years to come.

Specification
RS200
Calibre: 12 gauge
Weight: about 3 kg (6.6 lb)
Lengths: overall 1030 mm (40.55 in); barrel 520 mm (20.47 in)
Feed: 5- to 6-round magazine

This close-up of the receiver of the Beretta RS200 shows its loading gate (bottom) and shiny ejection port. The Beretta has several safety devices.

ITALY
SPAS Model 12

The **SPAS Model 12** (SPAS standing for Special-Purpose Automatic Shotgun) is one of the most interesting and influential shotgun designs to appear for a long time. It was designed, and is produced by, Luigi Franchi SpA, a firm which has produced sporting shotguns for many years. When the demand for a combat shot-firing weapon became apparent, the Franchi team decided to design a new weapon using a novel approach: it decided to build a true combat weapon, not a conversion of an existing sporting model, and the result is the **SPAS Model 11**.

Like its later version, the Model 12, the Model 11 is a formidable piece of kit. It is a long and heavy weapon that is so robust it can be used as a club. It has a distinctive appearance: there is no orthodox butt, but rather a fixed skeleton metal butt (Model 11) or a folding stock (Model 12). The mechanism at first sight appears to be a bulky manual pump action, but is in fact a semi-automatic or fully automatic system; the firing mode can be selected by sliding the fore-grip backwards and forwards. The tubular magazine under the short barrel can accommodate up to seven rounds. These rounds can vary from light bird shot to heavy metal slugs that can penetrate steel plate.

The rest of the SPAS is well provided with novel features. The variant most likely to be encountered is the Model 12, which has a bulky front handguard and a folding stock. The stock has a piece of curved metal under the 'butt plate' that loops around the forearm and allows the weapon to be held and fired in one hand although anyone firing the weapon in such a way will soon learn what a handful the

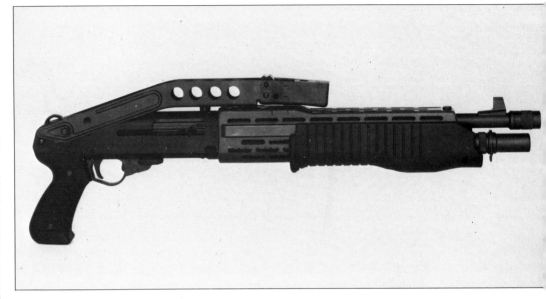

Model 12 can be. There is a pistol grip, the muzzle can be fitted with a shot-spreading choke device and another muzzle attachment is a grenade launcher. Small tear gas and CS projectiles can also be fired. Sights are provided but the spread of shot from a normal 12-gauge cartridge is such that at 40 m (47 yards) the shot pellets cover a circle with a diameter of 900 mm (35.4 in), so aiming is not terribly important at such ranges.

The SPAS is a true combat shotgun and in the hands of a fully-trained operative can be a formidable weapon. The Model 12 has been sold to several military and paramilitary armed forces, and some have appeared on the civil market. Many of these have been snapped up by shotgun enthusiasts, but in many countries the short barrel breaks legal regulations and so needs a barrel extension.

Specification
SPAS Model 12
Calibre: 12 gauge
Weight: 4.2 kg (9.26 lb)
Lengths: overall (butt extended) 930 mm (36.6 in) or (butt folded) 710 mm (27.95 in); barrel 460 mm (18.11 in)
Feed: 7-round tubular magazine
Rate of fire: automatic, cyclic 240 rpm

Many military and police shotguns are modified sporting weapons, bu Luigi Franchi SpA have designed tl SPAS 11 and 12 as combat weapons from the outset. This formidable semi-automatic shotgun can even l set to full automatic, firing four rounds a second.

With its phosphated black externa. metal parts and skeleton butt, the Franchi looks every inch a combat weapon while retaining the aesthe appeal of Italian gun designs. At 40 m the spread of shot reaches a diameter of 0.9 m.

Combat Scatterguns in Action

Shotguns first saw military service in the Philippine jungle at the turn of the century, and it is in such terrain that shotguns have been most widely used. The advantages are obvious: massive short-range firepower can be directed without careful aiming to hit a target obscured by tropical vegetation.

The first use of the shotgun in 20th century counter-insurgency campaigns in Asia occurred during the Moro Insurrection in the Philippines, starting in 1900. The US Army found itself fighting tough Moslem guerrillas, frequently so rugged that they did not even feel the impact of the soldier's Krag-Jorgensen rifles. The fighting on the trails of Samar and Mindanao was a series of fleeting encounters, and the US Army needed a weapon that allowed quick reaction: the shotgun was the obvious answer.

The US military adopted the 12-gauge five-shot Winchester M1897 slide (pump) action shotgun, with its single barrel shortened to 50.8 cm (20 in) to make it handier in close terrain and to keep it from catching on vines and branches. The shotgun proved a popular and effective weapon and a useful supplement to the service rifles.

Given the shotgun's success in the Philippines, it was not surprising that the US Army again re-adopted the weapon when the USA entered World War I. The M1897 Winchester was adopted as the standard 'trench broom' modified so that it could mount a bayonet. It was supplemented by the 12-gauge five-shot Remington M10. About 40,000 shotguns were procured, many seeing action in France.

World War II again brought the US Army back to the jungle, this time in the Pacific. Again the service reached for the Winchester M1897. It was further modified, with a take-down feature, a Parkerized finish, and a stronger stock. Supplemented by more recent Win-

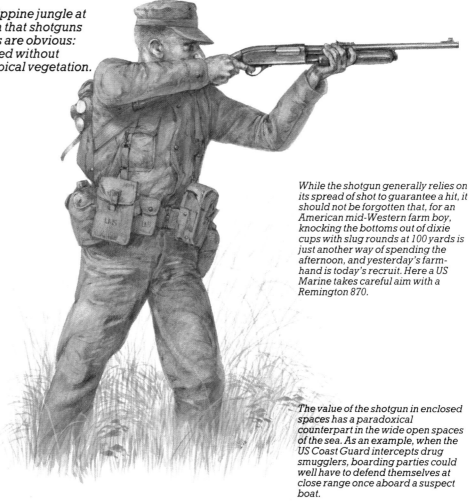

While the shotgun generally relies on its spread of shot to guarantee a hit, it should not be forgotten that, for an American mid-Western farm boy, knocking the bottoms out of dixie cups with slug rounds at 100 yards is just another way of spending the afternoon, and yesterday's farm-hand is today's recruit. Here a US Marine takes careful aim with a Remington 870.

The value of the shotgun in enclosed spaces has a paradoxical counterpart in the wide open spaces of the sea. As an example, when the US Coast Guard intercepts drug smugglers, boarding parties could well have to defend themselves at close range once aboard a suspect boat.

Combat Scatterguns in Action

chester, Remington, Stevens and Ithaca models (the Remington M11 'riot gun' also saw widespread use), US Army shotguns were used for jungle fighting, guarding prisoners, and clearing out strongpoints. These same weapons were also used in Korea.

The use of the shotgun then spread to the British army and its Commonwealth allies. The British army had used shotguns in Burma during World War II and in other campaigns, although never in the same numbers as the US Army. In 1948, when the Communist insurgency started in Malaya, the British found that the most troublesome guerrillas were those who

US forces used shotguns in small numbers during the Pacific campaign. The density of this jungle on Guadalcanal gives an idea of why weapons with a range of under 100 yards were used effectively.

used not the British-made Lee Enfield rifle and Sten sub-machine guns that had been i

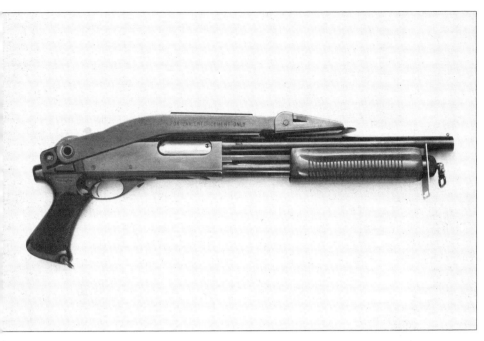

Shotguns, when suitably modified, make fine VIP protection weapons. The Presidential protection unit of the US secret service uses these modified 12-gauge Remington Model 870s.

serted into Malaya for use against the Japanese, but those who used shotguns. The same advantages that led the Americans to adopt the shotgun in the Philippines (plus the fact that, as a local weapon, many guerrillas were familiar with its use) brought home to the British that the shotgun would be an effective weapon to adopt in the jungle.

The Special Air Service, re-formed as specialized counter-insurgency infantry in Malaya, became the foremost users of shotguns in the British forces. A 1952 British study showed that in the conditions of jungle war, a shotgun had a greater chance of hitting a fleeting target than any other infantry weapon. After a great deal of experimentation and use of field expedients, the British standardized the Browning A5 semi-automatic shotgun. The British preferred a semi-automatic design because it offered a rapid second-shot capability.

The instant-reaction capability of the shotgun appealed to the SAS. Sergeant Bob Turnbull of the SAS tracked down Ah Tuck, a guerrilla leader who always kept his Sten gun cocked and loaded. Hunter and hunted finally met in a 'quick draw' situation that was more Wild West than Far East. At a range of some 18 m (20 yards) Ah Tuck never got a round off in his last showdown. Turnbull showed the effectiveness of the shotgun in another encounter on a jungle

Green Beret Ambush

A staff sergeant of the Green Berets opens fire on Viet Cong ambushers with an Ithaca 37 12-gauge shotgun while leading a Montagnard patrol in the Central Highlands of South Vietnam, 1964. His captain holds an M14 rifle and the tribal soldiers following sport M1 carbines which are better suited to their stature. Note the wrist bands worn by the Special Forces, which were ceremonially presented by Montagnard sorcerers to bind these American advisers to the tribe. US experience revealed No. 4 shot to have the right balance of spread and penetration for close combat in tropical jungle.

Winchester Model 12 12-gauge

The Winchester Model 12 is an improved version of the grandfather of all fighting shotguns, the Winchester Model 1897. In almost 90 years of combat use, the 'Combat Trombone' has changed very little in its basic design, improvements being confined to materials used in manufacture and to details of the mechanism. The main external change has been the loss of a visible hammer.

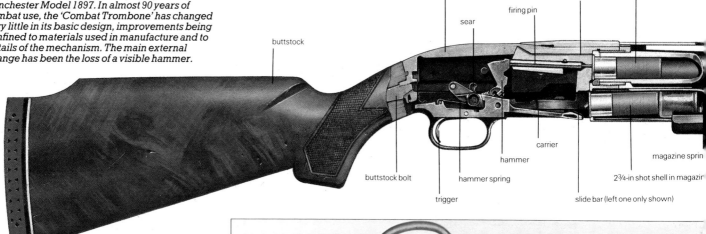

buttstock

heat-treated steel receiver

2¾-in shot shell in chamber

bolt assembly

firing pin

sear

buttstock bolt

trigger

hammer spring

hammer

carrier

magazine sprin

2¾-in shot shell in magazir

slide bar (left one only shown)

track, dropping a guerrilla with his shotgun while the officer next to him was still slipping his safety catch.

The British 12-gauge rounds used in Malaya were loaded with nine buckshot. The British found that although the full force of a shell was extremely effective, guerrillas hit by just one shot were incapacitated. He would then have to be carried by his comrades, leaving a trail that could be followed and making the group abandon its mission.

The American involvement in Vietnam saw the most widespread use of shotguns in any modern conflict. The US Marines started issuing them in 1965. Unlike the British, who

Above: In complete contrast to the old Winchester, the Italian-made Franchi SPAS 12 is as up-to-date as they come. The hook on the folding butt is designed to wrap round the forearm while firing the gun one-handed (although even with this support it is quite a handful!).

Below: First used in combat against Moro tribesmen in the Philippines, the Winchester Model 1897 soon found adherents world-wide. This particular weapon was acquired by the Roya. Irish Constabulary, and may well have been in use during the 1916 Easter Rising.

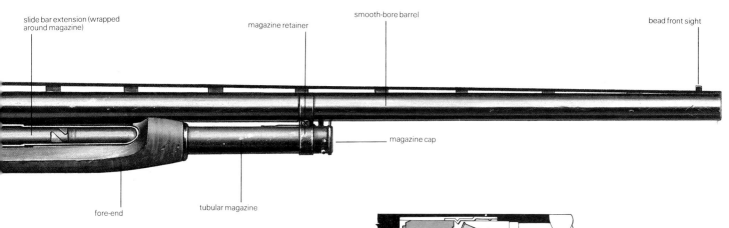

slide bar extension (wrapped around magazine)

magazine retainer

smooth-bore barrel

bead front sight

magazine cap

fore-end

tubular magazine

preferred semi-automatic shotguns, the Americans stayed with the pump-action types they had used since 1900. While this was reportedly because they were considered more reliable when dirty than semi-automatic weapons, the fact that Americans were used to pump-action shotguns and that the military had always used them certainly played a role. The favourite military shotgun was the Ithaca M37. If the trigger was held back, it would fire as fast as you could work the pump action. The other standard military shotgun, the Remington 870, lacked this feature. the Remington M10 shotgun and M11 'riot gun' were also used, along with the Winchester M1897 and M1912. While excellent weapons, the older Winchester designs were considered too delicate for Vietnam conditions.

Ammunition shortcomings

The ammunition of choice, as in Malaya, was buckshot. However, the terrain in the area of South Vietnam where the US Marines were deployed was not jungle. Where there were few engagements at longer than 69-m (75-yard) range in Malaya, the US Marines found themselves firing at targets farther away than those the British would have had to hit in Malaya. While the buckshot shells could easily kill at 27 m (30 yards) and wound at 55 m (60 yards), the spread pattern made it possible to miss a man-size target at anything more than point-blank range.

One attempt to make US shotguns more lethal was the flechette load for shotgun shells. Finned 25.4-mm (1-in) flechette (penetrating projectiles with a low mass, but high velocity) were introduced to Vietnam as fillings for the 'beehive' artillery shells intended for self-defence use by howitzers in danger of being overrun by massed infantry attacks. Flechettes, packed into shotgun shells, had a velocity of 610 m (2,000 ft) per second and could penetrate a flak jacket at 437 m (400 yards). What they could not penetrate was undergrowth, so dense bush would shield a target from a flechette shell.

Shotguns were also useful for irregular

Modern combat shotguns have until recently been conversions of sporting or police weapons. As such they are usually available in a variety of styles, and the Mossberg 500 family shown here is fairly typical. Variations include finish, magazine size and sights (rifle sights indicating choked barrels).

1 Pumping the slide disengages the bolt, which also claws out the cartridge in the chamber. Winchester have utilized the force of the recoil to make this a particularly smooth action.

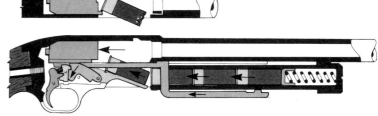

2 When the slide is fully back, the shell carrier drops, unblocking the mouth of the tubular magazine. A shell is fed into the carrier, while the old shell is ejected from the ejection port.

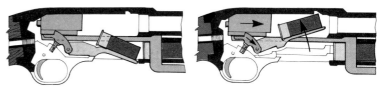

3 Pushing the slide forwards raises the shell carrier, simultaneously closing the magazine and feeding the fresh shell into the chamber. When fully forward, the bolt rotates, locking in place with four lugs.

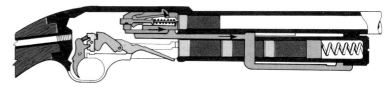

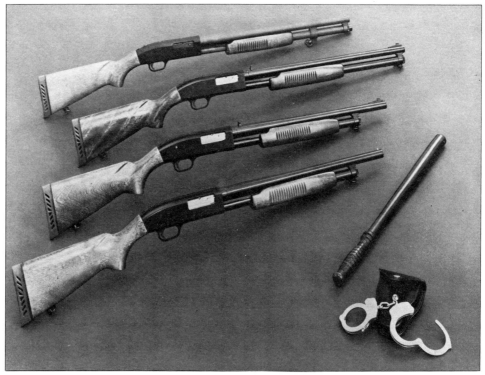

Combat Scatterguns in Action

troops. Even those without much marksmanship training or fire discipline can at least point a shotgun at the enemy and fire. At the range of most jungle encounters, something should hit. Most Asian farmers are likely to know how to use shotguns. The British used aboriginal trackers in Malaya and Iban tribal trackers in Borneo, and these were mainly armed with shotguns. The British-formed Home Guard units in Malaya (a key element in the ultimate victory as it involved the populace in defeating the guerrillas) made heavy use of shotguns. This British experience led to the widespread adoption of the shotgun by village defence forces, South Vietnamese army regional forces and irregular units in Vietnam. Later in the war, it was proposed to equip the village defence forces with riot-type shotguns. Over 100,000 Savage, Ithaca, Remington and Winchester weapons were delivered but the uncrated weapons, stored in Saigon, were captured at the end of the war.

The 'Bloop gun'

The most widespread 'shotgun' used in Vietnam was not a shotgun at all, but rather the US M79 40-mm grenade-launcher. Found in each US Army rifle squad, the 'Bloop gun' replaced the rifle grenade, firing a high explosive grenade up to 274 m (300 yards). Because of the fragmentation radius of the grenade, it had a minimum range under which it would not explode to avoid killing the gunner himself. Therefore, for close range use, two shells, one containing 27 buckshot and the other containing 45 flechettes, were developed for the M79. when close-range action was anticipated, as when clearing buildings or bunkers, the M79 gunner would quickly load a shotgun round. The Vietnam tableau in the Imperial War Museum in London shows this taking place.

The US military shotguns were used for the traditional tasks of patrolling, guard, and trench-clearing. They were also used for self-protection. Helicopter pilots liked to use shotguns because they were more effective than a pistol and could be fired from a hovering helicopter or moving vehicle.

One occasion when the shotgun's rapid rate of fire and quick reaction saved a helicocpter full of wounded was during the bitter close-range fighting around Hiep Duc during Operation 'Frederick Hill' on 18 August 1969. Wounded troopers of the Americal Division were being loaded onto a 'dust-off' medical evacuation Bell UH-1 helicopter flown by Warrant Officer 2 Steven Hill of the 176th Aviation Company. Out of the smoke and dust emerged a North Vietnamese regular, armed with an AK-47 and grenades. He raised his Kalashnikov at the same time as Hill grabbed for his shotgun, and he got the first round off through the cockpit window. The North Vietnamese was decapitated by the blast.

Since Vietnam, the US Army still retains an interest in shotguns. The 12-gauge Mossberg M500 pump shotgun is currently being procured. A current project is the Heckler & Koch Close Assault Weapon (CAW) which would automatically fire 19.5-mm belted shotshells. This design was based on the lessons of Malaya and Vietnam and emphasizes reliability, rapidity of fire, fast reloadability, large magazine capacity, maximum hit probability, and high single-round lethality. While this remarkable weapon is still under development, the day of the shotgun in counter-insurgency conflict is by no means over.

Above: The modern shotgun can fire a very wide range of ammunition. The varieties shown include birdshot, buckshot, solid rifled slugs (which can stop an elephant or a car at close range), solid shot, and a special penetrator CS gas shell.

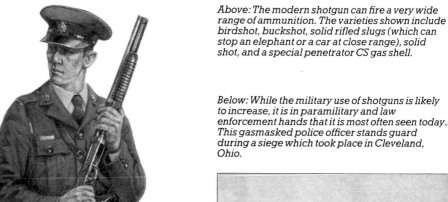

Below: While the military use of shotguns is likely to increase, it is in paramilitary and law enforcement hands that it is most often seen today. This gasmasked police officer stands guard during a siege which took place in Cleveland, Ohio.

Above: The South African police have been seen using shotguns more often than most of late. Whatever the rights and wrongs of a political case, the shotgun allows small numbers of security men to control large crowds on the edge of riot. Used injudiciously, however, such weapons can exacerbate disturbances.

Webley Greener GP

The **Webley Greener GP** shotgun is hardly a modern weapon, for the first of the type appeared around the turn of the century. The series is still in use and is included here as an example of shotgun designs from an earlier era, although many of them have been replaced by more modern designs with semi-automatic mechanisms and multi-round magazines.

The Greener GP is a single-shot weapon that has to be hand-loaded for every shot. In place of the usual break-open shotgun mechanism the Greener uses a variation of the Martini falling block action that was in use before the Lee-Enfield bolt-action rifle was accepted for British service in the 1890s. On this action a lever behind the trigger is pulled down to open the falling block. This ejects any spent cartridge and a fresh cartridge is inserted along a groove to guide it into the magazine. Lifting the lever closes the block and cocks the weapon ready to fire. This action is simple to use and can be operated quite rapidly for ejection and loading, but its main attributes are its strength, simplicity and safety. It rarely wears out and keeps working reliably. When allied to a weapon as strong as the Greener, this operating system produces a shotgun that is ideal for general police and other such uses, and this goes a long way to explain why Greeners can still be encountered.

There have been three main marks of Greener GP. Two, the **GP Mk I** and **GP Mk III**, are now rarely encountered or they were chambered for specially-loaded police cartridges that are now rarely found except in collector's

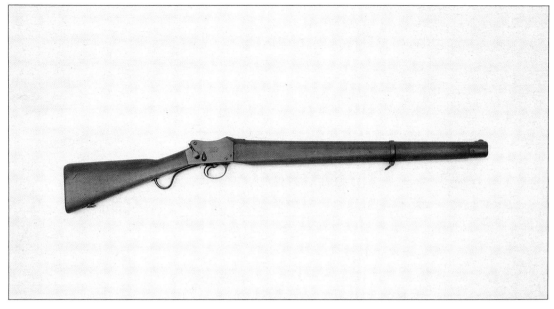

hands. The **GP Mk II** was (and still is) chambered for the orthodox 12-gauge cartridge. The Greener GP may be found with barrels of varying lengths, including 710 mm (27.95 in), 760 mm (29.9 in), 810 mm (31.89 in) and 860 mm (33.86 in). These make the Greener GP acceptable for police use but in the past the overall length has proved too long for combat use. Thus when combat shotguns have been required in a hurry, as happened during the Malayan Emergency of the late 1940s, Greeners were seized in vices to have

their barrels considerably shortened by hacksaws. In this form they were used for some time, but these sawn-off weapons are no longer official (nor were they at the time) and will not be found in police or other official hands.

Greener GPs are still used by some overseas police and paramilitary forces and there is no sign yet that they will wear out in the near future.

Specification
Webley Greener GP Mk II (710-mm barrel)

Chambering a round into the Webley Greener reminds one of Rorkes Drift; it is a single-shot weapon employing a falling block mechanism similar to that on the Martini-Henry. In police and paramilitary hands since the turn of the century, it is a sturdy if cumbersome weapon.

Calibre: 12 gauge
Weight: 2.95 kg
Lengths: overall 1130 mm (44.48 in); barrel 710 mm (27.95 in)
Feed: single shot

Viking Arms SOS

The pace of small arms design in recent years has been such that the relatively recent 'all-in-line' assault rifle design has become so established that a whole generation of recruits has been trained with them and many have never fired a conventionally-stocked rifle or shotgun. Thus when many soldiers are introduced to orthodox weapons such as the usual run of combat shotguns they are somewhat at a loss as to how to aim and handle them. With this in mind Viking Arms Limited of Harrogate has devised the **Viking Arms SOS** shotgun which is so arranged that it has the now accepted 'in-line' layout: the butt, action and barrel are all in one straight line with the rear sights raised above the receiver and the fore sight raised on a post over the muzzle.

The SOS is in fact a conventional manual pump-action 12-gauge shotgun stocked to produce the in-line configuration. It has a wooden butt and a pistol grip in exactly the same way as a modern assault rifle, and the simple sights are raised above the receiver in such a manner that the rear sight housing can be used as a carrying handle for the weapon, again exactly as on an established service rifle such as the American M16 series. Thus a newly-trained soldier encountering the SOS for the first time will be quite familiar with its general handling. His reaction to the firing recoil after handling a virtually recoilless 5.56-mm (0.219-in) rifle is another matter, even though the in-line configuration helps to keep recoil

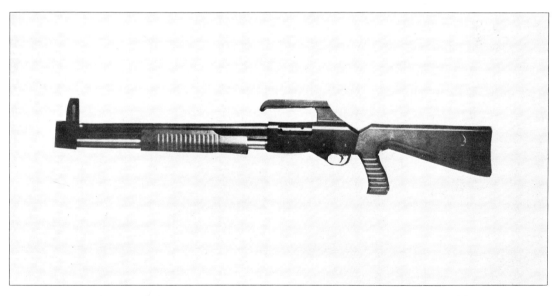

forces under control and muzzle 'jump' is minimized.

The SOS uses a manual slide pump action allied to a tubular magazine holding seven rounds. These may be of the shot or slug variety.

Where the SOS appears to have the edge on many of its contemporaries is that although it is well made and robust it is relatively inexpensive. It is also easy to maintain. The SOS has therefore appealed to many police forces who have to operate on limited

budgets and some sales have been made to forces in Europe and elsewhere. Other sales have been made to civilian shotgun enthusiasts and to satisfy their more orthodox shooting requirements it is possible that a butt stock of more conventional form may be produced for the SOS.

Specification
SOS
Calibre: 12 gauge
Weight: 3.37 kg (7.43 lb)

The Viking Arms SOS shotgun is representative of the trend towards militarization which has swept through the shotgun world in the wake of the Franchi. Apart from the M16-style carrying handle-cum-sight housing, it is otherwise a conventional 12-gauge shotgun.

Length: barrel 616 mm (24.25 in)
Feed: 7-round tubular magazine

Smith and Wesson Shotguns

Smith and Wesson is well-known for its range of pistols, but the company has also produced shotguns for many years, mainly for the police market. Typical of such police weapons are the pump-action **Smith and Wesson Model 912** and **Model 3000** (the latter is still in production). In recent years Smith and Wesson has been researching the future shotgun market, and has as a result designed the **Smith and Wesson AS** (Assault Shotgun) series of combat shotguns.

The AS shotguns are similar in concept to the weapons of the US Army's CAWS programme. Although still in the development stage the AS is to be available in three versions. The **AS-1** is a semi-automatic weapon, the **AS-2** is also a semi-automatic version with a three-round burst capability, and the **AS-3** is a fully automatic weapon capable of multiple-round burst firing. In overall appearance the three versions are similar, and all resemble an assault rifle of the M16 variety. Thus they all have all-in-line configurations and all use detachable 10-round box magazines located in front of the trigger position, which is complete with a pistol grip. As always with such weapons, the sights are raised above the receiver, this time on a long rib.

The AS series can all fire 12-gauge shot or slug cartridges, but the new CAWS ammunition is an option. The mechanism has a rotary locking bolt with no fewer than 12 locking lugs. Aluminium forgings are used for the receiver housing, and high-impact plastics are used for much of the furniture. The weapon can be easily stripped for cleaning or maintenance, and the barrel can also be changed quickly when necessary. The muzzle is fitted with a compensator to reduce barrel 'jump' on firing and also to reduce firing flash.

It would appear that with the AS series Smith and Wesson are setting its cap at the military rather than police market. In American service terms the AS arrives on the scene during the CAWS programme, for which the candidates appear to have already been selected, so it remains to be seen how Smith and Wesson fares. One thing is for sure: by the time the CAWS programme is completed the result (if any) will be expensive and by then the AS series will probably be in production at a more attractive price than most competitors.

Specification
AS
Calibre: 12 gauge
Weights: empty 4.42 kg (9.74 lb); loaded 5.69 kg (12.54 lb)

The Smith and Wesson Model 3000 series was designed specifically for police and military security work. The AS series, a prototype of which is seen here, are combat weapons pure and simple.

Lengths: (overall) 1054 mm (41.5 in); barrel 476 mm (18.74 in)
Feed: 10-round box magazine
Rate of fire: AS-3, cyclic 375 rpm

Mossberg 500 series

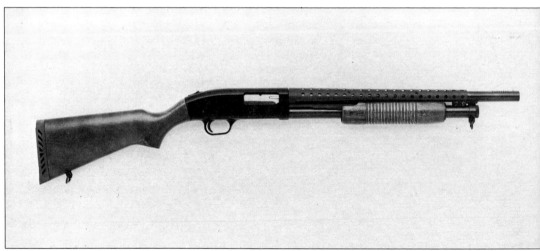

O.F. Mossberg and Sons Inc. is a relative newcomer to combat as opposed to sporting shotguns, for its first such weapon, the **Mossberg Model 500**, appeared in 1961. This was an attempt to break into the police shotgun market, then dominated by the many established 'big names'. After a while Mossbergs made their market breakthrough and the Model 500 is still the company's 'base' product.

The Model 500 is a manual slide-action 12-gauge weapon. The receiver body is forged from high-grade aluminium and the steel bolt locks into a barrel extension to take the firing loads off the receiver. Most components such as the extractors and action slides are 'doubled' to produce strength and reliability, and this makes the Model 500 a very robust weapon despite its low overall price. These points have made the Model 500 and its derivatives widely-used police weapons, but Mossberg has also produced combat versions.

One is the **Model ATP-8SP**. This is basically a police Model 500 with a non-reflective finish and extra attention given to the protective finish of every component. A bayonet mount is provided and there is even provision for mounting a telescopic sight for use when firing slugs, although this feature would appear to be little used. A perforated handguard may be fitted over the barrel and, as with most of the Model 500 range, an up-and-over folding metal stock may be used in place of the normal hardwood fixed component. The Model 500 ATP-8SP has sold well but is now due to be replaced by an updated combat model.

This is the **Model 500 Bullpup 12**. As its name implies, this is a 'bullpup' design with a pistol grip assembly placed forward of the receiver. This makes the weapon considerably shorter than its conventional equivalent, and thus much easier to handle and stow in confined spaces, a considerable selling point for many police and military authorities. On the Bullpup 12 the receiver and much of the weapon body is entirely enclosed in a strong thermoplastic material so there are few components to catch on clothing or anything else. This is partly negated by the all-in-line bullpup layout that dictates that the rear and fore sights have to stick up on posts, but these can be folded down when not required.

The Bullpup 12 can be manufactured 'from new', but Mossberg produces a kit to convert existing Model 500s to the revised configuration.

Although produced by a much younger company than many of its competitors, the Mossberg 500 series soon found success. Latest models appear very different, but the gun mechanism itself is hardly altered.

Specification
Bullpup 12
Calibre: 12 gauge
Weight: 3.85 kg (8.49 lb)
Lengths: (overall) 784 mm (30.87 in); barrel 508 mm (20 in)
Feed: 6- or 8-round tubular magazine

n the USA the shotgun is a well-estab-
ished police and penal establishment
weapon, to the extent that many shotgun manufacturers find it well worth
their while to produce weapons tai-
ored to individual police department
pecifications. Some of these police
weapons come very close to military
pecifications, and such a weapon is
he Ithaca LAPD shotgun, a weapon
ased on the Ithaca DS. In its turn the
Model DS is based on a very well-
stablished design known as the Itha-
a 37 M and P, very robust and well-
nade weapons that have been pro-
uced with policing requirements in
nind.

The Model 37 series has been
round for some time: during World
War II it was one of the shotguns
elected by the US Army for military
se. It was used during that period for
eneral shotgun purposes, including
ot control, guard duties and even
keet and sport shooting for officer re-
reation, and was then available in
ree barrel lengths. The current Mod-
l M and P models are not dissimilar to
e World War II versions, but are now
nade that much more rugged.

The current Model 37 M and P 12-
auge shotguns are produced with a
ange of options available. They may
e fitted with a five- or eight-round
ibular magazine, and the two barrel
engths are 470 mm (18.5 in) and
08 mm (20 in). Both are used to fire the
sual range of 12-gauge shot car-
idges using a cylinder choke barrel
hereas the Model DS (DeerSlayer,
om the Ithaca trademark) has a preci-
on-bored cylindrical barrel that can
e used to fire heavy slugs. The Model
S has a 508-mm (20-in) barrel only,
nd sights are provided. The option of
five- or eight-round magazine is car-
ed over.

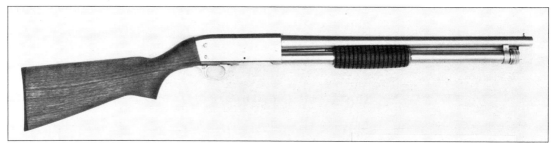

Developed from a lightweight design dating from World War I, the Ithaca 37 was one of the standard military shotguns of World War II. The M and P (Military and Police) model is available with both five- and eight-round magazines.

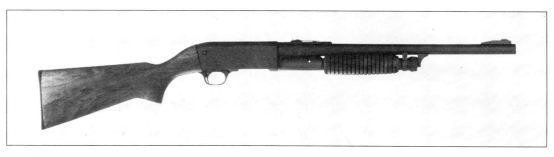

The eight-shot Model 37 M and P is available only with a 508-mm (20-in) barrel, although a shorter barrel can be fitted to the five-shot version. The DS (Deer Slayer) is an especially accurate model, fitted with rifle-type sights.

With the Model LAPD the Model DS
is taken one stage further. Produced
for the Los Angeles Police Department
(hence LAPD) this model has a rubber
butt pad, special sights, sling swivels
and a carrying strap. It has a 470-mm
(18.5-in) barrel, a five-round tubular
magazine and, like all the other models
in the Model 37 M and P range, uses a
robust manual slide pump action.
Some of these weapons are used by
the 'special forces' of several nations as
they are ideal combat shotguns. Some

reports mention their use by the British
SAS.

All the weapons in the Model 37 M
and P range have Parkerized finishes
to reduce wear and the need for constant cleaning.

Specification
Model P and M
Calibre: 12 gauge
Weight: 2.94 kg (6.48 lb) or 3.06 kg
(6.745 lb)
Lengths: overall (508-mm barrel)

1016 mm (40 in); barrel 470 or 508 mm
(18.5 or 20 in)
Feed: 5- or 8-round tubular magazine

*The more highly finished
appearance of this Ithaca 37 DS
Police Special attests to its original
role as a civilian hunting weapon.
Nevertheless, its light weight,
accuracy and reliable action make it
effective as a paramilitary and law
enforcement arm.*

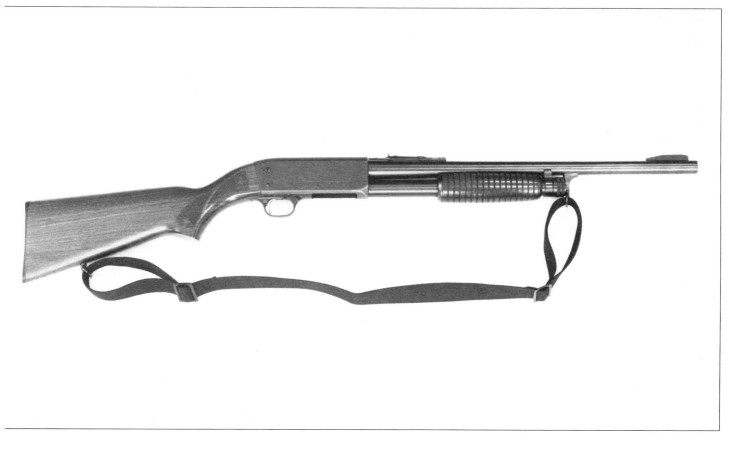

Ithaca Mag-10 Roadblocker

USA

For the Americans the motor car has become such a feature of everyday life that it now appears that even crime cannot be committed without the assistance of the internal combustion engine. To counter this use of automobiles most American police forces employ various methods of preventing car occupants from continuing their unlawful activities, methods that vary from Teflon-coated bullets to crack engine cylinder blocks to heavy shotgun projectiles that can penetrate vehicle bodies and hit occupants. One such heavy shotgun is the **Ithaca Mag-10 Roadblocker**.

The Roadblocker is a 10-gauge shotgun. Normally this heavy cartridge, which is as much as half as powerful again as the 12-gauge type, is used only by the most ardent of big game hunters. It produces a powerful recoil, but when heavy cartridge loadings or solid slugs are used the 10-gauge shotgun becomes a truly formidable piece of short-range weaponry, ideal for countering criminals in speeding motor cars. The heavy shot or slug projectiles can easily pass through most ordinary vehicle bodies or windscreens and still retain enough power to wreak havoc to the interior.

The Roadblocker is a semi-automatic shotgun that partially overcomes the heavy recoil problem by incorporating a patented 'Countercoil' compensator that absorbs some of the recoil forces and prolongs them over a short interval to make the recoil felt by the firer more acceptable; there is also a rubber butt pad. Even so firing the

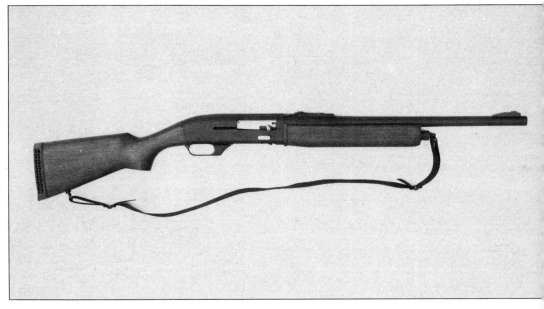

Roadblocker is not a comfortable task. A tubular magazine holds only three cartridges. The barrel may be left in a plain form or it may be covered by a ventilated rib. In both cases all metalwork is Parkerized to reduce the need for constant cleaning.

Weapons such as the roadblocker may be an extreme method of apprehending criminals but they can also have a combat role. In jungle warfare counter-ambush situations the heavy load of a 10-gauge cartridge could cut through heavy foliage far more effectively than even a heavy 12-gauge load, and the effect on a human target can be left to the imagination. A weapon like the Roadblocker could also be used to disable the light military vehicles in special forces operations. The main drawback would appear to be the weight of the weapon.

In tests, solid rifled slugs from a 10-gauge fired at cars from 25 m (27 yards) to the rear have passed through the whole vehicle and cracked the engine block.

Specification
Roadblocker
Calibre: 10 gauge
Weight: 4.87 kg (10.74 lb)
Length: barrel 558 mm (21.97 in)
Feed: 3-round tubular magazine

Ithaca Stakeout

USA

In the USA the police term stakeout is usually employed to denote an undercover or clandestine operation, usually in plain clothes. In such operations the shotgun has found a niche as a powerful close-range weapon for offensive and defensive purposes, and some manufacturers have seen fit to develop special models for this undercover role. Such a model is the **Ithaca Stakeout**, a weapon unlikely to be encountered in a military combat role but very suitable for civil and military police use.

The Ithaca Stakeout is a short weapon without a stock, even a folding one. It has been designed to be as short as possible to enable it to be concealed under clothing or in a briefcase or similar innocuous container. To hold the weapon a pistol grip is provided, and the usual pump-action foregrip is retained, a small strap being provided to make the foregrip more positive. The Stakeout is based on the Model 37 M and P but is produced in two calibres. One is the usual 12 gauge, but since it is felt that this could prove to be a bit of a handful in some

circumstances there is a more manageable 20-gauge version. At the close ranges envisaged for the Stakeout a 20-gauge cartridge can be just as effective as the 12-gauge type. Only shot-loading cartridges are fired from the Stakeout as the recoil from firing heavy slugs would make the gun too difficult to handle.

The 20-gauge Stakeout has a blued finish, but the 12-gauge version may be obtained in either a Parkerized or a spectacular chrome-plated finish, placing the latter well out of most military specifications. Even so many military as well as civil police forces have added the Stakeout to their armouries.

There is another Ithaca model similar in concept and employment to the Stakeout but known as the **Handgrip**. This is in effect a standard Model 37 with the butt stock replaced by a pist[ol] grip similar to that of the Stakeout. In [all] other respects the Handgrip is exact[ly] the same as the Model 37 M and [P] shotguns and carries over the sam[e] magazine capacity and barrel leng[th] options. The overall length of th[e] Handgrip makes it generally unsu[it]able for the clandestine role of th[e] Stakeout but it can be easily carrie[d] and stowed within the confines [of] police vehicles. The Handgrip is use[d] to fire shot cartridges only.

Specification
Stakeout
Calibre: 12 or 20 gauge
Weight: (12 gauge) 2.26 kg (4.98 lb) o[r]
(20 gauge) 1.58 kg (3.48 lb)
Length: barrel 336 mm (13.23 in)
Feed: 5-round tubular magazine

Left: Notably compact and light, the Ithaca Stakeout gives the security agent or bodyguard enormous firepower, being a derivative of the Model 37 M and P which retains the five-shot magazine. It is available in both 12- or 20-gauge and in a number of finishes. Solid slugs are not recommended for use in these weapons, as the recoil could make handling a little tricky.

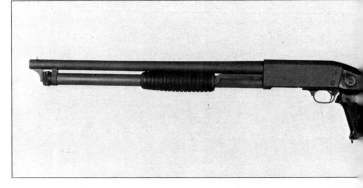

Unlike the Stakeout, the Handgrip Model 37 is basically a standard Model 37 M and P with a pistol grip. It is designed for use within vehicles.

Winchester shotguns

The US Repeating Arms Company, usually known as Winchester, is best known for its rifles, but also produces shotguns for the sporting market and also for police and paramilitary use. In the past Winchester shotguns were produced in a wide variety of models, including the **Winchester Model 12** used during World War II and some of the few box-magazine combat shotguns ever produced, but current models are limited to a few manual slide-action models.

The basic Winchester shotgun model is a 12-gauge design known as the **Defender** and produced primarily for police employment, although it has been found in military hands. Overall the Defender is a conventional design but the action is compact and as always with Winchester weapons the standard of manufacture and finish is first-class. Operating the slide action opens and closes a rotary bolt that provides a very positive and safe lock, and the unlocking is recoil-assisted to speed the overall action considerably, placing the weapon almost into the semi-automatic class. The tubular magazine extends to just under the muzzle and can hold six or seven cartridges, depending on whether they are normal shot cartridges or the longer heavy slug type. The finish is usually blued or parkerized, but there is a version produced specially for police use, all the metalwork being stainless steel. This version may be fitted with rifle-type sights for firing slugs, and the magazine is slightly shorter than that of the standard Defender. Sling swivels are also provided.

Perhaps the most unusual of the current Winchester shotguns is one produced specially for use by naval or marine forces. This is based on the Defender but is more akin to the stainless steel police model for it has been designed to be corrosion-resistant. All weapons in a naval environment are subject to the effects of corrosive salts and stainless steel is proof against many of them. To ensure virtually complete protection the 'marine' Winches-

Right and below: Winchester has produced the Defender in three plated versions, all available in butted or pistol grip form. The police model is built from stainless steel, and has a smaller magazine capacity than the standard Defender.

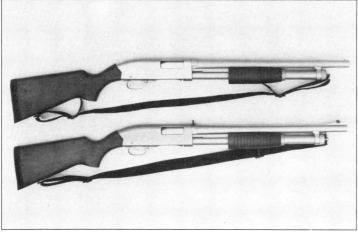

US Repeating Arms Company (otherwise known as Winchester) Model 1200 slide-action shotguns have 457-mm (18-in) barrels and are finished in a satinized chrome which minimizes reflected light and resists corrosion.

ter also has all its external metal parts chrome-plated. The result is a striking-looking weapon but one which would seem to have some eye-catching drawbacks in combat situations. However, this model has been sold, usually to paramilitary forces such as coastguards who use shotguns to arm boarding parties.

Specification
Defender
Calibre: 12 gauge
Weight: 3.06 kg (6.74 lb) or (stainless steel models) 3.17 kg (6.99 lb)
Length: barrel 457 mm (18 in)
Feed: 6- or 7-round tubular magazine or (stainless steel models) 5- or 6-round tubular magazine

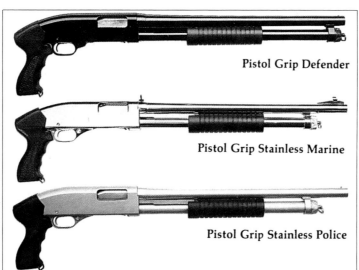

Pistol Grip Defender

Pistol Grip Stainless Marine

Pistol Grip Stainless Police

Above: In future, British police may well follow this Winchester armed American model, with fireproof overalls, bulletproof vest and visored helmet. Shotgun-armed policemen are now seen on the streets of London when Scotland Yard's specialist weapons officers are on duty.

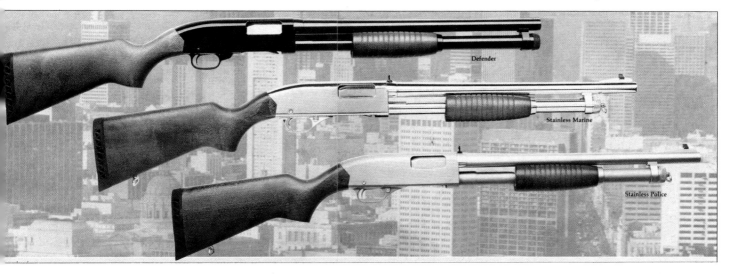

Defender

Stainless Marine

Stainless Police

Remington Model 870 Mark 1

USA

It is very probable that over the years more Remington shotguns have been used for combat purposes than any other make. The list of Remington guns is such that even a listing would probably cover a page, so only one combat model will be considered. This is the **Remington Model 870** modified for use by the US Marines and known as the **Shotgun, 12-gauge, Remington, Model 870, Mark 1**.

The Model 870 has been one of the most widely-used of all shotguns for some time. It has been produced in basic models such as the **Model 870R** (Riot) and **Model 870P** (Police), but there have been many other types and an equally large number of conversions and adaptations. The Model 870 is a slide-action weapon, and when the US Marine Corps conducted prospective combat shotgun trials during 1966 it decided that, for reasons of reliability in combat, such a weapon would be preferable to one of the many semi-automatic actions available, and the Model 870 was the USMC's main choice. After a few modifications to suit the USMC's requirements exactly, the Model 870 Mark 1 was placed in production and has remained in USMC service ever since.

The Model 870 Mark 1 has a seven-round tubular magazine and is used to fire a wide range of ammunition from light shot to flechettes. The gun has many 'extras' to suit the US Marines (such as sling swivels) and the magazine extension holding bracket has a lug to mount a bayonet (of the same type as that used on the M16A1 rifle). The ventilated hand-guard over the barrel and the rubber butt pads found on many 'civilian' Model 870s are not fitted to the Mark 1 as they were not deemed necessary for combat use.

The US Marines have used their Model 870 Mark 1s quite often since they were introduced. The weapon is not one that is usually carried during large-scale amphibious operations, but the US Marines have many other combat tasks including forming boarding parties during actions such as that carried out during the almost-forgotten 'Mayaguez incident' of May 1975. The guns were used widely during the Vietnam War (often by SEAL teams) and there is no reason to suppose that the US Marines have now forgotten how to use shotguns.

At one point there was a project to convert the Model 870 Mark 1 to accommodate a 10- or 20-round box

Remington shotguns have a long history of combat usage, but the Model 870 was not officially adopted until the mid-1960s, when the United States Marine Corps took the weapon to war in the jungles of Vietnam. It has also been widely adopted as a police weapon.

magazine but the end of the Vietnam War terminated the scheme at the advanced development stage.

Specification
Model 870 Mark 1
Calibre: 12 gauge
Weight: 3.6 kg (7.94 lb)
Lengths: (overall) 1060 mm (41.73 in); barrel 533 mm (21 in)
Feed: 7-round tubular magazine

Below: Such is the usefulness of the shotgun in the jungle, that the British Army made extensive use of the weapon in counter-terrorist operations in Malaya, both against Communists and during the Indonesian confrontation. The fully-stocked Remington 870 is one actually used in the Far East; the other is a folding stocked riot gun with extended magazine.

Pancor Jackhammer

USA

The **Pancor Jackhammer** is a very recent arrival on the combat shotgun scene but it uses an operating mechanism that has been around for some time. The weapon has many original features, not the least of which being that it can fire on full automatic and it also uses a pre-loaded rotary magazine.

The Jackhammer possesses an unusual appearance and has a 'bullpup' configuration with the rotary magazine placed behind the trigger. The pre-loaded plastic magazine holds 10 rounds and is clipped into the weapon before the fore-end of the stock is moved to and fro to cock the weapon. On firing the barrel moves forward. As it does so a gas-operated stud moves in

an angled groove on the magazine to start the rotation to the next round. Once forward, the barrel is pushed back by a spring and the magazine rotation is completed. (This system was used on the World War I Webley-Fosbery revolver.) Once the barrel has returned the weapon is ready for the next shot. On full automatic the cyclic rate of fire is 240 rounds per minute and barrel jump is partially offset by a downward-angled muzzle compensator that doubles as a flash eliminator.

The Jackhammer makes much use of tough plastics throughout its construction. In fact only the barrel, return spring, magazine rotation mechanism and muzzle flash eliminator are steel. The magazines, known as 'ammo cas-

settes', are delivered pre-loaded and sealed in plastic film colour-coded to signify the type of cartridge enclosed. This sealing film has to be removed before loading. It is not possible to load single cartridges, although single-round fire can be selected.

The sights are contained in a channel on the assembly that acts as a carrying handle. This extends for almost the entire length. Firing the Jackhammer is not the problem for left-handed firers that bullpup layout weapons usually are, for no spent cartridge cases are ejected: they remain in the rotary magazine that can be discarded once all rounds have been fired. When the magazine is empty a retaining catch opens and allows the component

to fall free.

The Pancor Jackhammer is still the advanced development stage, and it is very possible that some alteration to the mechanism and/or appearance may be made before full production gets under way. In the meantime the Jackhammer appears to be a very interesting and promising design.

Specification
Jackhammer
Calibre: 12 gauge
Weight: loaded 4.57 kg (10 lb)
Lengths: (overall) 762 mm (30 in); barrel 457 mm (18 in)
Feed: 10-round rotary magazine
Rate of fire: cyclic 240 rpm

Close-Assault Weapon Systems

The efficacy of the shotgun in close-quarter combat has led to the US Joint Services Small Arms Program issuing a specification for a Close Assault Weapon System. Many authorities see this as a viable small-arm system for the future.

the late 1970s the US Army had been forced accept the fact that no matter how good the training of the average soldier before he goes to action, combat stresses render him unable to fire a service rifle accurately. This simple fact was no revelation to most military authorities although few were able to do anything about it (other than impose yet more training), but in 1979 the US Army determined to see what could be done to rectify the matter.

The US Army's approach was to develop a weapon that does not require accurate aiming to hit a combat-type target. This form of weapon did not require much development for it has been around for years: it is called the shotgun. However, the US Army wanted something slightly more certain of effective target engagement at combat ranges than a simple scattergun. Thus the **Close-Assault Weapon System (CAWS)** was born, the latest in a long line of similar projects.

CAWS is not just a weapon programme but more of an ammunition approach as the combat shotgun is now well established. What has been done by the US Army Joint Small Arms Program (JSSAP), sponsors for CAWS, is to approach two commercial organizations and got them to develop the ammunition and weapons. These organizations are the AAI Corporation of Baltimore and a consortium of the American Olin Industries and the West German Heckler und Koch.

With both the approach has been to develop flechette ammunition. The flechette is one of a cluster of small arrow-like finned projectiles

The Olin/Heckler & Koch entrant into the Close Assault Weapon System competition is fired. The CAWS is more akin to modern assault rifles than to current shotgun designs, which is not really surprising in a weapon designed for the front line.

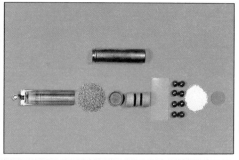

A CAWS buckshot shell is broken down into its constituent parts. One of the results of British analysis of shotgun performance in Malaya was the realization that a hit by a single shot, out of the eight or so per shell, could incapacitate a man.

fired from a single cartridge at high velocity, and is no newcomer to warfare. Flechettes were fired from shotguns in Vietnam, and they have been a recurrent feature of American ammunition development since World War II. For the CAWS programme flechettes are fired from 12-gauge brass or plastic cartridge cases 76.2 mm (3 in) long. AAI uses eight flechettes to a loading; the Olin cartridge uses 20. Both loadings have to be effective up to 150 m (164 yards). Standard 12-gauge shot cartridges are also fired from the CAWS weapons and other ammunition (such as armour-piercing, high explosive and riot-control munitions) are under development.

With both types of flechette ammunition the propellant pushes forward a plastic piston to eject a pusher plate supporting the flechette tails, each having a small plastic drag cone. The pusher plate soon falls away to allow the drag cones to stabilize the flechettes in flight. Accuracy is such that a CAWS cartridge can put its entire flechette load into a 914-mm (36-in) circle at 50 m (55 yards). The effect of this on

the human frame is best left undescribed.

The AAI CAWS weapon is a fairly conventional gas-operated design that can be fired on fully automatic yet is contractually obliged to have no more recoil than a normal shotgun. It has a 12-round detachable box magazine, an optical sight and uses some M16 components.

In contrast the Olin/Heckler und Koch submission resembles a 'space age' weapon, for it is an adaptation of the Heckler und Koch G11 rifle, originally designed to fire caseless ammunition. Unlike the rifle much of the body is steel, but the fore end is high-impact plastic with a small optical sight set over the body. The 10-round magazine is located behind the trigger. The West German military authorities are taking great interest in CAWS with a view to possible adoption of the resultant weapon and ammunition.

The Olin/Heckler & Koch Close Assault Weapon System displays a family resemblance to the revolutionary G11 rifle, although the outer case is steel rather than plastic.

The unusual Pancor Jackhammer uses an action similar to that of the Webley-Fosbery self-loading revolver of World War I. When firing, the recoil forces the action back, engaging a groove in the cylinder which turns it and presents a new shell for firing. Because the used shells remain in the cylinder, the Jackhammer avoids the problems associated with bullpup designs, in particular the ejection of cartridges close to a shooter's face. On full automatic, the 10-shell magazine can be emptied in 2⅓ seconds. The Cutts-style compensator on the muzzle brake holds the weapon down when firing at that rate.

 USA

Savage Model 77E

The **Savage Model 77E** is another shotgun with a long history. It was originally known as the **Model 520** and was in production during World War I, when it was acquired by the US Army for trench fighting. Later produced for sporting uses in a form known as the **Model 620**, it went out of production entirely in 1932 and was then resurrected during World War II as a standard US Army 'riot gun', complete with bayonet and sling.

After 1945 most of the Model 520/620s went back into storage, only to be dragged out again when the Vietnam conflict flared. They were then issued to local armed forces for general guard and other duties and the demand was such that a revised version with a short stock and rubber butt pad to suit the stature of South East Asian users was placed back into production. This was the Model 77E.

The 12-gauge Model 77E is finished to military specifications but is otherwise similar to the earlier sporting Model 520. It is an orthodox and sturdy manual pump-action weapon with a tubular magazine holding five rounds, and it can be easily broken down into two basic halves for stowage and carriage. Although originally intended for Vietnamese forces Model 77Es were soon in use with the US Army and US Marines, who used them to such good effect that subsequent combat analyses showed that more casualties were inflicted by the Model 77E than the then-controversial M16A1 rifle. Experience showed that in order to be fully effective at close quarters the Model 77E had to be fired as rapidly as possible every time it was used. This gave rise to the battle phenomenon known as 'rolling burst'. However, the restricted capacity of the magazine limited this tactic and troops carrying the Model 77E took every opportunity to keep the magazine fully topped up. Standard shot and flechettes were the usual combat loads.

The Model 77E proved the efficiency of the shotgun in modern warfare to the extent that shotguns are once more a firmly established part of the American armed forces' armoury. However, the Model 77E is now no longer part of this armoury for although the weapon worked well in South East Asia American troops disliked the short stock and the limited magazine capacity. The Model 77Es were handed over to local friendly forces or placed back in store. Many are still to be found here and there in the hands of various armed forces, both regular and irregular.

Specification
Model 77E
Calibre: 12 gauge
Weight: 3.08 kg (6.8 lb)
Lengths: (overall) 978 mm (38.5 in); barrel 505 mm (19.9 in)
Feed: 5-round tubular magazine

SOUTH AFRICA

Armsel Striker

The **Armsel Striker** is a semi-automatic 12-gauge shotgun that has only recently appeared on the market, so recently that few specifications are available. It is an indigenous South African design (now being made by Reunert Technology Systems near Johannesburg but originally created by Armsel), intended for uses ranging from civilian self-protection to full military combat applications.

The Striker's main feature is its 12-round rotary magazine. This is a spring-wound design loaded with cartridges through a trap on the right rear of the drum; the magazine spring is tensioned by a key at the front of the magazine. Once the weapon is loaded, one pull of the trigger fires a round and rotates the next round into line with the firing pin, it being impossible to fire the weapon until the firing pin is exactly in line with the next cartridge. The recoil is claimed to be less than that of a normal shotgun, although exactly why this should be is not clear for the barrel is certainly shorter than those of most other similar weapons. It is possible that the recoil is masked by the fact that the Striker has a foregrip under the barrel and a pistol grip; there is also a metal stock that can be folded up and over the barrel. The barrel has a perforated metal sleeve to dissipate heat produced by prolonged firing and to prevent the hot barrel being touched by the firer's hand, for the rapid firing of the full 12 rounds would certainly produce a very hot barrel.

The Striker can fire a wide range of 12-gauge ammunition ranging from bird shot (often used in South Africa to disperse crowds) to heavy metal slugs. The weapon may be fired with the butt folded, although firing the heavier loads without using the butt could prove somewhat too lively for comfort. The sights are very simple, for the Striker is obviously not meant as anything other than a very short-range weapon for clearing crowds or perhaps in close-quarter combat in built-up areas. It could also prove to be very useful in bush warfare where infantry engagements and ambushes are often at very close ranges as a consequence of the overall lack of visibility resulting from the prevalent short scrub vegetation.

Development of the Striker is said to be complete and the weapon is now in production. As yet there is no indication that it has been accepted for police or military use, but considering the circumstances that trouble South African society it will be very surprising if it does not find some form of official acceptance in the very near future.

Specification: not available

It would be surprising if a nation in arms like South Africa did not come up with some interesting small arms developments. The semi-automatic Armsel striker is a case in point, its 12-shot rotary magazine giving considerably more firepower than conventional guns.

Riot Control Weapons

After the introduction of police forces the management of civil disorder ceased to be the responsibility of the military, but in recent years many armies have found themselves back in the front line against their own countrymen. Armies and paramilitary forces need special weapons for this unenviable task, since only the most extreme circumstances justify the use of lethal force.

We live in difficult times. Even the most orderly and established societies now find themselves subject to all manner of disorderly and riotous behaviour or assembly which, if left unchecked, could topple the very establishment of written and unwritten laws by which modern societies exist. Many of these disorders are instigated by particular sections of society for their own ends, while others are the result of extreme or imagined injustices, or of deprivation. Many other causes can be adduced, but the result is outbursts that the established forces of law and authority have to contain as best they can.

To maintain order most modern police and internal security forces now have access to a wide range of equipment. Much of it is very specialized and designed to produce a specific end, i.e. the rapid re-establishment of an ordered and lawful situation with a minimum of force and casualties. Many modern anti-riot munitions are therefore non-lethal in their effects: they are meant only to disable temporarily or to persuade wrongdoers to act otherwise. Lethal weapons are maintained in the anti-riot weapons arsenal, but usually only for use as a last resort.

A US Police Officer armed with Smith and Wesson Shoulder Gas Gun ventures into the Overtown district of Miami during the 1982 riots. This rugged weapon fires a wide variety of 37-mm projectiles.

The arsenal is now quite extensive, ranging from disabling agents to baton rounds. Contained in the arsenal are some odd 'weapons' such as water cannon and impact weapons. There are even specialized vehicles that are produced with little more than internal security and riot- or crowd-control in mind. Several of them are included in this study, but the contents cannot cover the entire internal security- and riot-control scene. This is now a very large area that comprises not only the police and associated paramilitary forces, but also the military who are often drafted in to help out when a populace gets troublesome.

Hotspur Armoured Products offer a useful internal security vehicle based on the chassis of a Land Rover. Vehicles designed for this role must provide protection against weapons from petrol bombs and crowbars to grenades and mines.

Smith and Wesson No. 210 Shoulder Gas Gun

USA

In addition to its well known hand gun activities Smith and Wesson has also made considerable inroads into the international riot-control munitions market. It has produced a wide range of munitions filled with everything from irritant agents to smoke, and has also built the weapons to launch them. One of the most widely used of these launchers is the **Smith and Wesson No. 210 Shoulder Gas Gun**.

The No. 210 has a calibre of 37 mm (1.456 in), a riot-control munition calibre established in the USA (mainly by the efforts of Smith and Wesson) and now universally accepted as the calibre for the role. The basis of the weapon is the frame of the Smith and Wesson 'N frame' revolver, but instead of using revolving chambers the No. 210 is a single-shot weapon. The barrel breaks down in shotgun fashion, using the frame as a pivot. The outline of the pistol butt can still be discerned and in its place there is now a wooden butt fitted with a much-needed rubber recoil pad. The firing mechanism can be either single- or double-action, and there is an external hammer. The barrel can be removed for carrying or storage, and the weapon is usually issued with a shoulder sling. Fixed sights are used for aiming.

The No. 210 can fire a wide range of munitions. Some of these are rather unusual, such as the No. 14 Goliath projectile which is a CS-carrying baton projectile that can be fired through thin barricades. There are two types of No. 17 baton round, both thin metal cased, the longer-ranged version being fired to about 137 m (150 yards). The No. 18 baton round is similar to the No. 17 but uses a rubber slug with no metal casing. The No. 21 is intended for closer-range situations and fires a dense cloud of CS to a range of about 11 m (35 ft). Some of these rounds can be produced in a 'Tru-Flite' form with tail

The 37-mm (1.45-in) Smith and Wesson Shoulder Gas Gun is based on the 'N frame' revolver, but is a single-shot weapon which breaks open like a shotgun. Possible loadings include the No. 14 'Goliath' barricade-piercing baton/CS gas round.

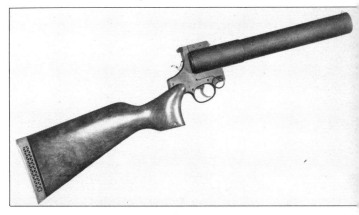

fins that impart better directional stability; these rounds also use a slightly heavier propellant charge. The heavier charge means that 'Tru-Flite' rounds cannot be fired from the No. 210 shoulder gun's stable-mate, the **No. 209 Gas Pistol**. This has a much shorter barrel than the No. 210, and has a standard revolver butt and frame.

The No. 210 has been in production for some years and is still in demand. It cannot be said that it is an easy launcher to fire for some rounds produce considerable recoil, and like many weapons of its kind it is not particularly accurate other than at very close ranges. The British army has used the type in Northern Ireland but has now

moved over to the L1A1, though many British police forces retain the No. 210.

Smith and Wesson has recently decided to leave the riot-control munitions market and has offered this side of its business for sale as a going concern.

Specification
No. 210 Shoulder Gas Gun
Calibre: 37 mm (1.456 in)
Length: 736.6 mm (29 in)
Weight: about 2.7 kg (5.95 lb)
Maximum range: long-range baton round 137 m (150 yards)

No longer in production, the No. 210 was one of the first generation of riot control weapons, able to fire many different rounds but inaccurate except at point blank range.

PPS-50 Bingham Carbine

USA

The **PPS-50 Bingham Carbine** is the latest model in a series of what are essentially sub-machine guns chambered for the 5.56-mm (0.22-in) Long Rifle cartridge. The use of this relatively low-powered cartridge allows the weapon to be fired fully automatically without the heavy recoil that a more powerful round produces: this enables the firer to maintain a high degree of accuracy when it is required (e.g. in urban warfare or in guarding high-security prisons) to ensure hitting a point target.

The Bingham carbine is a conventional blowback weapon designed along the lines of the Soviet PPSh-41 sub-machine gun, hence the PPS in the

Resembling the Soviet PPSh SMG of World War II, the Bingham carbine is a semi-automatic weapon firing .22 Long Rifle. The gun is intended for use in circumstances when full power rounds might endanger innocent lives.

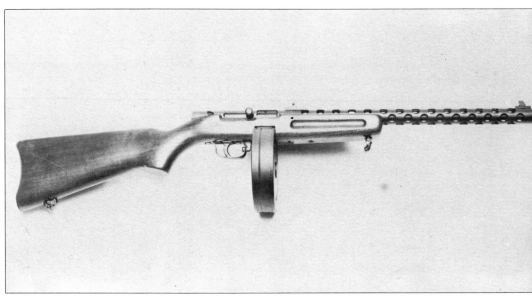

esignation. The Bingham design has much longer barrel than the original, ut retains the drum magazine that ow holds 50 rounds. Also available re curved or straight box magazines ach holding 30 rounds. A silenced ersion is under development, for use y Special Forces.

The Bingham carbine concept is artially based on an earlier and simi- r design known as the **American 180 1-2**. This also used the 5.56-mm Long ifle cartridge and was basically a ub-machine gun with an unusual

drum magazine over the receiver. It was not a great success and appears to have passed from the scene, but at the time attracted a great deal of attention because of its futuristic sighting system. This was a laser projector under the barrel that projected a circle of pink light calibrated to be directly in the line of fire: so all a user had to do was place the laser circle on the target and the barrel was aligned. Quite apart from the aiming purpose, the idea was that the target would also see the circle of pink light and give up

without further ado if the circle came to rest on him. The laser projector was known as a Laser Lok and it would appear that the Bingham carbine would be an ideal weapon to carry a modern equivalent. It could then be used in internal security or prison riot situations to great advantage and considerable saving of life. However the Laser Lok, despite the great interest shown in it during the early 1970s when it first appeared, did not catch on, and these days it lives on only in Hollywood epics.

Specification
PPS-50
Calibre: 5.56 mm (0.22 in) Long Rifle
Lengths: overall 844 mm (33.23 in); barrel 408.9 mm (19.09 in)
Weight: empty 2.94 kg (6.48 lb)
Muzzle velocity: about 330 m (1,083 ft) per second
Magazine capacity: 50-round drum or 30-round box (curved or straight)

USA
Federal Riot Gun

he **Federal Riot Gun** is now one of the ost widely-used riot guns ever pro- uced, and is in service with armies, aramilitary and security forces all round the world. It was originally de- eloped by Federal Laboratories Inc. Saltsburg, Pennsylvania, to fire the xtensive range of anti-riot munitions roduced by Federal. At first most of ese products were used by Amer- an penal institutions, but over the ears their use has spread to many her organizations.

The Federal gun is a simple single- ot weapon with few frills. It is ex- emely robust and is manufactured sing various non-rusting alloys. The test version is the **Model 203A** which as an in-line barrel and butt arrange-

ment and a very strong barrel and frame locking mechanism just forward of the large pistol grip. The firing mechanism is double-action only, and there is no external hammer to snag in clothing or other equipment. There is a foregrip with a connection for a sling, attached at the other end to the high-quality wooden butt. The sights are fixed at 45.7 m (50 yards). Most other models of the Federal riot gun are basically similar to the Model 203A.

One of the reasons for the Federal gun's widespread use is that it often comes as part of a package deal associated with Federal anti-riot munitions. These come in the standard 37-mm (1.456-in) calibre and can be fired by other types of riot gun. As usual

there are many types of munition, but two deserve special mention. One is the Federal 'Spedeheat' CS round that can be fired to a range of about 100 m (109 yards): the round has a thin aluminium bullet-shaped casing and can emit CS fumes for up to 30 seconds, and can also double as a baton round. Another CS round is the Federal SKAT round that fires five small CS grenades at the same time: these are designed to land in front of a crowd and bounce in an erratic fashion. They usually bounce outwards in a fan-shaped arc to disperse their CS contents in an intense cloud. As they emit fumes for only about 15 seconds it is difficult for any rioter to pick up the grenades and throw them back.

The Federal riot gun was one of the weapons obtained by the British army at the start of the Northern Ireland troubles. It was found to be a serviceable weapon but difficult to fire accurately, especially as it has quite a powerful recoil. It has now been replaced by the L1A1 grenade-launcher, but many British police forces use the Federal riot gun.

Specification
Federal Riot Gun
Calibre: 37 mm (1.456 in)
Length: 737 mm (29 in)
Weight: not recorded
Range: up to 100 m (109 yards)

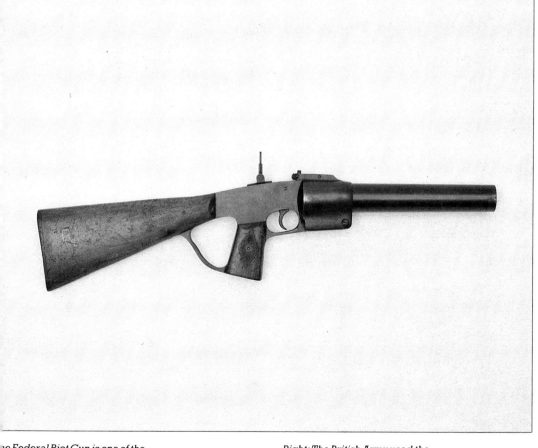

e Federal Riot Gun is one of the ost widely used weapons of its pe, and serves with armies and lice throughout the world. anufactured in non-rusting alloys, s a double-action, single-shot gun th no exposed hammer.

Right: The British Army used the Federal Riot Gun in Northern Ireland, finding it to be a reliable weapon, but its monstrous recoil and inherent lack of accuracy did not endear it to the troops. It has been superseded by the L1A1.

Riot Control Grenades

A depressingly large number of regimes have little compunction in using the full force of the military to stamp out civil disorder, but democratic governments seek other alternatives. The use of gas and plastic bullets remains subject to controversy, but it must be accepted that non-lethal weapons are preferable to appalling incidents like 'Bloody Sunday' and Kent State.

Riot-control grenades take two forms, chemical and kinetic. Chemical grenades are designed to emit fumes that irritate or disable to the extent that they prevent persons from carrying out a chosen course of action, i.e. they quell rioters. The main requirement of such agents is that they irritate or disable but do not permanently harm. For many years the chosen irritant agent was tear gas, a relatively harmless substance that does little more than bring tears to the eyes and impart a general feeling of choking and helplessness. Tear gas is now generally known as CN, but its proper chemical name is alpha-chloroaceto-phenone.

The main disadvantage to tear gas was found to be that in open areas its vapour cloud generally dispersed in such a manner that it easily lost its disabling properties. It was also relatively easy to get used to, and many fit young people could carry on their disorderly activities after exposure to CN with only a minimum of inconvenience. Inside a building it was often another matter, but in the open tear gas was soon seen to be relatively inefficient as an anti-riot weapon. During the early 1950s the search for a new agent was made and a new chemical, ortho-chloro-benzalmalono-nitrile, was put forward as an alternative and efficient disabling agent. It was not long before this new substance was given the handy appellation CS.

CS is normally a solid substance, but on contact with air it forms a white or light grey vapour cloud with a general odour of pepper (CS is thus sometimes known as pepper gas). The vapour can induce the usual tears, but with the addition of a general choking sensation and difficulty in breathing. The effect is distinctly unpleasant and high CS concentrations may cause nausea and vomiting. To add to its effects it can be persistent, especially if vapour droplets adhere to clothing. However, CS is not totally disabling and there are no long-term effects.

Left: The unacceptable face of law enforcement? A police officer in Washington, 1970, with CS gas rounds for his Riot Gun ready to hand. Early gas rounds could be picked up and thrown back, leading to the development of multiple gas pellets for rapid dispersal.

Below: Theoretically, baton rounds are not to be fired at individuals at close range but the new generation of riot control weapons are accurate enough to do so should it be necessary.

Above: The US Marines provide security for US Embassies around the world, and must be able to defend them against hostile crowds without immediate recourse to firearms. Seen here in Manila, this Marine has a tear gas grenade projector attached to his Remington 870 shotgun.

CS was first used during the late 1950s and was soon found to be a remarkably efficient method of breaking up mobs. At first it was usually delivered in hand grenades that were exactly the same as the tear gas and smoke grenades used previously. While these were eay to use and manufacture they suffered from the same drawbacks as the earlier grenades: it took time for the vapour cloud to build up, range was limited by the strength of the thrower (who thereby came well into missile range of the offending crowd) and the grenades could be picked up by an adventurous rioter and thrown back. A redesign of the basic CS grenade has therefore taken place.

New grenade design

Modern CS grenades nearly all contain small multiple containers or pellets to emit the CS fumes. As the grenade body lands it scatters these small containers or pellets (the British L11A1 grenade releases 23) over a wide area, and the emission period is usually short to prevent any possibility of their being returned. The other design point is that CS grenades are now rarely thrown, but rather projected using a small propellant charge from a launcher to a range of 100 m (109 yards) or more, the launcher usually being some form of riot gun. When riot guns are used the usual diameter of the grenade is 37 mm (1.456 in), but this is now generally regarded as being too small and the British army has opted for a grenade diameter of 66 mm (2.6 in) and uses a specialized grenade-launcher rather than riot guns.

CS is not the only modern form of irritant agent, but it is the most widely used. Other irritant agents are mild hallucinogenic agents that impart a temporary feeling of panic or fear, but the use of such agents is disliked by many on humanitarian grounds, and they may thus be a double-edged weapon. Some of the 'mind' agents have a nasty habit of being just as effective on their users as on their intended targets, even when respirators are used. Most police and paramilitary respirators are limited in their effectiveness to protection against CS and CN only and some powerful modern agents could overcome their protective properties.

Humanitarian considerations also come to the fore when kinetic grenades are considered. These are usually the baton rounds or the infamous 'rubber bullets' that are used to disable by stunning. These kinetic projectiles were first mooted during the 1950s, when some authorities considered their use in riot situations in which guns could not be used but something more powerful than irritant agents was required. At first disabling missiles of several types were considered, ranging from lead shot in thick bags to heavy rubber rings. These were usually fired from ordinary riot guns and it was not long before the baton round in its present form appeared. At first wooden projectiles were used, but these were soon discarded as they were prone to splintering and causing nasty wounds. Then rubber was used for some time before it was discovered that under certain circumstances rubber was also likely to be too injurious. The current baton rounds are flat-ended PVC slugs that are not as heavy as rubber but are still likely to impart a powerful blow.

Baton rounds can cause serious injuries if used at very close ranges, and they have caused deaths. They are also very inaccurate and often have to be used more as area weapons than as point target weapons. But they can break up hostile crowds and when used with extreme care can even disable riot ringleaders or troublesome individuals. They can certainly keep crowds out of hand-thrown missile range. Despite this, the use of baton rounds has often resulted in great public outcry against their employment. But in the absence of anything better the baton round is an established anti-riot munition.

The L67A1 produced by the Royal Ordnance Factory at Enfield is in service with the British Army. It fires the L18A1 CS gas round, which holds four gas pellets designed to burst 6 m above the ground so the crowd cannot pick up the gas canister and throw it back.

Fabrique National have produced this grenade-launcher to fit on to the FNC 5.56-mm light assault rifle; or, fitted with a stock, it can be used as a weapon in its own right.

Above: The Hilton multi-purpose gun is an anti-riot gun which can fire an impressive variety of projectiles from gas shells to single and multiple baton rounds. It is a far cry from the simple, almost crude, riot guns initially produced.

Below: British troops take cover from a hail of missiles while one soldier returns fire with a plastic bullet. The British Army adopted flat-nosed PVC slugs in place of rubber baton rounds, which produced too many fatalities. In experienced hands these can be surprisingly accurate.

USA

MM-1 Multi-Round Projectile-Launcher

The **MM-1** is one of a new breed of anti-riot weapons that uses a rotary magazine to hold a number of anti-riot rounds ready to fire; in the case of MM-1 this magazine holds 12 rounds. The MM-1 has been designed for situations where a single anti-riot round would be of limited use: most current anti-riot weapons are single-shot only and have to be reloaded manually after every firing. In the face of a mob rushing directly at a firer that single round is often insufficient to deter everyone in the mob, and the firer can easily be overwhelmed.

With the MM-1 this is far less likely to happen. Using the MM-1 it is possible to fire 12 rounds in as few as six seconds, something that might make even the most determined mob have second thoughts. The rounds are held in 12 chambers on a rotating plate: as each round is fired a spring mechanism brings the next chamber into line with the barrel ready for another pull of the trigger. The MM-1 has no butt, being held by the firer by a foregrip and a pistol grip behind the large and bulky magazine. After each loading the chamber plate is wound up by turning it in a counter-clockwise direction to tension the spring mechanism.

The MM-1 can fire either 37-mm (1.456-in) or 40-mm (1.575-in) anti-riot munitions of all kinds, and adaptors can be used to fire conventional shotgun cartridges. Flares can also be fired. The maximum range is about 120 m (131 yards), but this capability is less important to most users than the shock effect of a number of rounds being fired in rapid succession. This is not the only advantage of the MM-1, for with it one man can lay down a wide CS or smoke screen from a range of over 100 m (109 yards). This fact has been rapidly appreciated by many police and special forces in the Middle East,

the USA, Europe and Africa, and the MM-1 is now a widely-used weapon. The only problem that arises is that it is a bulky weapon and it takes some time to reload. The MM-1 is produced by Hawk Engineering Inc. of Northfield, Illinois.

Above: The basic design of a rotary magazine grenade-launcher dates from before World War II. Most anti-riot guns are single-shot weapons which obviously render the firer temporarily vulnerable while he reloads.

Specification
MM-1
Calibre: 37 or 40 mm (1.456 or 1.575 in)
Length: 546 mm (21.5 in)
Weight: loaded 9 kg (19.84 lb)
Range: up to 120 m (131 yards)
Magazine capacity: 12 rounds.

Above: Pace Hollywood, the MM-1 i not a light piece of kit but offers a number of advantages over more conventional designs. One man car lay a large smokescreen or generat a big cloud of CS gas amongst a crowd from outside the range of hand-thrown missiles.

 USA

Power-Staf/KA-1 Impact Weapon

The **Power-Staf/KA-1** impact weapon comes into that unpleasant category of devices that have been labelled by the media as 'cattle prods'. It is true that in the past genuine cattle prods (imparting powerful but short electric shocks on contact) have been used as riot- or crowd-control devices, but the usual public reaction to the employment of them is one of such outrage that their use is actually counterproductive. The Power-Staf/KA-1 does not deliver an electric shock: instead it imparts a power kinetic blow.

The Power-Staf resembles a long baton with a very large handle. The handle contains a piston on a rod with an impact tip and a high-pressure air regulation system. When the Power-Staf is held horizontally and the operating trigger is pressed, the air-pressure system forces out the piston from the baton shaft at a speed of about 7.62 m (25 ft) per second. As it reaches its maximum extension the piston retracts immediately. The whole operation takes about 82 milliseconds. It takes little imagination to realize that any person in the path of the piston rod will receive a very nasty blow from its impact tip.

The air container in the device has enough pressure for about 30 piston actuations. After that the refillable air container has to be changed, this tak-

ing about 15 seconds. Ordinary compressors or air cylinders can be used for the refill process. It is possible to use the Power-Staf with a backpack carrying three air cylinders and enough air for 300 piston actuations. A special form of Power-Staf used with this backpack arrangement is known as the KA-1, and the entire backpack system is known as a **Riot Pac**.

When in use the Power-Staf has an effective strike range of between 1.68 and 1.98 m (5.5 and 6.5 ft). The blow is said to be powerful enough to ensure that anyone receiving it will involuntarily move away, so under riot conditions the Power-Staf and devices like it may well have their uses. Unfortunately they are also used within some of the stricter types of penal institution in many countries to ensure order and obedience of orders, something that does little to enhance the extreme dislike of such devices by many sensible people.

Specification
Power-Staf
Weight: 3.17 kg (6.99 lb)
Lengths: 787 mm (31 in); rod extension 610 mm (24 in)
Effective strike range: 1.68 to 1.98 m (5.5 to 6.5 ft)
Rod velocity: 7.62 m (25 ft) per second

ITALY

MOD-T-22 CS Rocket-Launcher

The **MOD-T-22 CS** is a novel approach to the dispensing of anti-riot agents (in this case CS) for it uses a rocket grenade fired from a barrel. The rocket grenade resembles a mortar bomb, complete with tail fins, while the projector at first sight appears to be a simple tube. These first impressions are deceptive, especially with regard to the projector, for the design is rather more complex than it appears.

The projector looks like a simple barrel but it is in fact two concentric barrels. The inner barrel is used to fire the rocket grenade while the outer barrel is used to direct the rocket exhaust gases forward around the muzzle. This enables the launcher to be fired from within an enclosed area, making it possible (for example) to fire grenades through a window from within a room. The launcher barrel has a hinged breech to allow loading from behind or from within an armoured vehicle, and the barrel can be elevated within limits in a simple steel frame.

The rocket grenades are entirely plastic and are designed to break up on impact to release their CS contents. The nose of the grenade is made from a flexible material that is designed to prevent injury if it strikes a person during its flight, although it seems likely that some wounding could result as the

grenade weighs 0.62 kg (1.37 lb). T grenades are fired electrically, a their rocket motors are contained wi in the tails. The grenades have a bo diameter of 75 mm (2.95 in) and can fired to ranges between 100 and 250 (109 and 273 yards), considerab more than most comparable proje tors.

The MOD-T-22 CS rocket-launch may be used from static or mob positions. With the static positio launchers may be placed arou vulnerable areas, i.e. buildings like to attract the attention of rioters duri periods of civil unrest, or around stallation perimeters. They can th be fired from a central control positi as and when required. Mobile lau chers are usually mounted on police special anti-riot vehicles, and usua located close to a hatch so that they c be easily reloaded.

Specification
MOD-T-22 CS launcher
Internal calibre: 75 mm (2.95 in)
Length: 550 mm (21.65 in)
Weight: 4.5 kg (9.92 lb)

MOD-T-CS grenade
Calibre: 75 mm (2.95 in)
Length: 350 mm (13.78 in)
Weight: 0.62 kg (1.37 lb)
Range: 100 to 250 m (109 to 273 yards)

276

Schermuly Multi-purpose Gun

The Schermuly multi-purpose gun has a calibre of 37 mm (1.456 in) to enable it to fire a wide range of anti-riot and other munitions, thereby warranting its multi-purpose designation. It can fire all manner of baton, smoke, irritant agent and other rounds.

The Schermuly gun is produced by Webley and Scott but marketed by Schermuly. The basis of the weapon is a signal pistol, a much-updated version of a World War II design that now makes use of high-tensile aluminium alloys. The gun may be regarded as an enlarged version of the signal pistol, having a butt, a long smooth-bored barrel and a foregrip. Loading uses the conventional shotgun break-open system, and there is a large interlock device over the chamber to ensure the barrel is securely locked for firing; thus the weapon cannot fire unless properly closed. The double-action trigger demands a long and firm pull to ensure it does not go off accidentally and there is also an automatic rebound device in the striker mechanism to prevent a loaded gun from firing if dropped.

The Schermuly gun makes much use of aluminium and high-grade aluminium castings to keep down weight, but the result is a quality weapon that has been deliberately designed to have the 'feel' of an expensive shotgun, though the shotgun analogy is spoiled somewhat by the fact that leaf sights are fitted and a foregrip is provided under the barrel. Various barrel lengths can be produced, but one special feature of the Schermuly is that it can be fitted on the machine-gun weapon mounts of many armoured vehicles used in the internal security role, such as the Saracen armoured personnel carrier and the Shorland armoured car. Very often anti-riot guns can be of much more use than machine-guns in internal security operations so this provides the Schermuly gun with a valuable 'extra'.

As mentioned above, the Schermuly gun can fire a wide range of munition types. It fires not only the usual 'official' rounds produced for the British Army but also many commercial products manufactured for a wider market. Schermuly is also known as Pains-Wessex, so it is not surprising to learn that the company also makes various anti-riot munitions to go with its gun. Available are irritant agent and other rounds, some of which are used by the British army, which has also used the gun.

Specification
Schermuly gun
Calibre: 37 mm (1.456 in)
Length: 828 mm (32.6 in)
Weight: 3.18 kg (7 lb)
Range: up to 150 m (164 yards)

Left: The Schermuly is made of light alloy, and different barrels, calibres and chamber configurations are all possible. The foregrip helps achieve accuracy as well as keeping the firer's hand away from a hot barrel, and is adjustable to suit the firer.

Above: The Schermuly riot gun is produced by Webley and Scott. It fires 37-mm (1.45-in) projectiles to a maximum range of 150 m and can be fitted to the machine-gun mounts on vehicles such as the Saracen APC.

Above: Riot guns tend to be fired like shotguns, i.e. from a standing posture, and the Schermuly has been deliberately designed to handle like a shotgun for this reason. The hardwood butt attached to the pistol grip assembly also mounts the back sight.

Grenade Discharger L1A1

UK

When the current outbreak of troubles in Northern Ireland began in 1969 the British army was ill-equipped to carry out many of its internal security duties. For a while it was forced to make purchases of often-unsuitable riot munitions launchers from the USA or to rush into use hasty conversions of old signal pistols. Typical of the latter was the **L67A1** riot gun, a conversion of an old World War II signal pistol to take a rifled barrel, simple sights and a rudimentary butt. The L67A1 may still be encountered, mainly in training roles, but it was an awkward weapon to use, not very accurate and prone to damage.

Something better was required, and came in the form of the **Grenade Discharger L1A1**. This was designed specifically to fire CS grenades, and at first sight seems to be a very simple weapon. Simple it is, but with a number of important safety and handling design features.

The L1A1 is muzzle-loaded, and after the grenade is inserted into the launcher cup a safety sequence of operations has to be followed to ensure that the grenade is fired only when it is required and not at any other time. First, a cocking plunger located at the fore end of the pistol grip has to be pressed. The safety catch must then be pressed and only then does pressure

on the trigger, while the safety is still held down, fire the grenade. The firing pulse comes from two ordinary U2 batteries behind the butt plate.

The L1A1 can launch grenades to a range of about 100 m (109 yards) and the type of grenade fired is one that cannot be picked up and returned; however, the L1A1 is not just a riot gun, for it can also fire smoke and marker grenades for battlefield operations, although it is not often so used.

The design sophistication of the L1A1 is such that it can be easily stripped for maintenance and cleaning, and its simple construction also makes it very robust. It is also easy to handle in action, although it cannot be said that it is an accurate weapon. Having been designed to fire mainly CS grenades it is an area weapon and there is little chance that it will ever hit a point target. It cannot fire baton rounds.

The L1A1 was produced at the old Royal Small Arms Factory at Enfield Lock in Middlesex, now Royal Ordnance, Small Arms Division. It is no longer in production.

Specification
Grenade Discharger L1A1
Calibre: 66 mm (2.6 in)
Length: overall 695 mm (27.36 in)
Weight: 2.7 kg (5.95 lb)
Range: 100 m (109 yards)

The L1A1 replaced the various grenade launchers acquired by the British Army when troops were sent to Northern Ireland in 1969. It is a single-shot muzzle loader which fires its grenade electrically, current being provided by a pair of standard U2 dry cells.

The L1A1 is designed to fire 550-g CS gas grenades into a crowd from outside the range of hand-thrown missiles. Its grenades are so designed as to make it impossible for rioters to smother them or throw them back.

Arwen

UK

The **Arwen** (Anti-Riot Weapon ENfield) is something of an innovation and certainly an advanced design in comparison with many contemporaries. It is a very sophisticated piece of engineering that can perhaps be called a weapon system, as it is a riot munition launcher allied to a novel range of ammunition. The Arwen is produced by Royal Ordnance, Small Arms Division, at Enfield Lock, Middlesex.

Arwen has a calibre of 37 mm (1.456 in) and may be considered as two tubes joined together by a rotary magazine. The rear tube holds a butt plate and can be adjusted telescopically to suit the firer. The rear tube is joined to a firing mechanism, complete

This automatic 37-mm weapon was one of three prototype designs built and tested at the Royal Ordnance Factory at Enfield.

GUN RIOT 37 mm XL77E1-N¹

278

with pistol grip, while the forward tube is the barrel with its corrugated cooling profile. The barrel is fitted with a foregrip, also adjustable in position to suit the firer. Between these sections is the rotary magazine that holds five rounds. The firing mechanism is simple and controlled by the trigger. Pulling the trigger rotates the magazine until a round is in line with the chamber. Further trigger pressure fires the round. Leaf sights are provided, for Arwen is more accurate than most similar weapons.

Five types of round are fired from Arwen, although not all may be encountered operationally. The main anti-riot munition is a baton round with a mushroom-shaped head that provides the PVC projectile with a good ballistic trajectory, allowing deliberate aim at point targets to be made. The others include a CS round, a screening smoke round, a baton round with a CS element and a round that fires a projectile to penetrate thin barricades while carrying some form of irritant agent. It is possible that this last round will not be placed in production. The main design point regarding all these rounds is that their aluminium cases act as their own firing chambers. At the instant of firing each round has it own internal charge and is fired with support provided by sprockets at the front and rear of the rotary magazine – the rest of the case is quite unsupported as only relatively small propellant charges are used.

Arwen can be fired with a good degree or accuracy up to a range of about 100 m (109 yards) using the baton round. The usual rate of fire, including ejecting spent cases and reloading through a rim on the right-hand side of the magazine, is about 12 rounds per minute. These two factors make Arwen a formidable anti-riot weapon, and the weapon has already been purchased by many police and security forces, especially in the USA, where it is now a favoured weapon for guards in maximum security penal establishments.

Specification
Arwen
Calibre: 37 mm (1.456 in)
Length: adjustable from 760 to 840 mm (29.9 to 33 in)
Weights: empty 3.1 kg (6.83 lb); loaded 3.8 kg (8.36 lb)
Magazine capacity: 5 rounds
Range: baton round 100 m (109 yards)

Above: The production model of the Arwen has a 5-round rotary magazine adapted from the revolver principle. After firing it ejects the spent cartridge case and rotates a new round in line with the barrel.

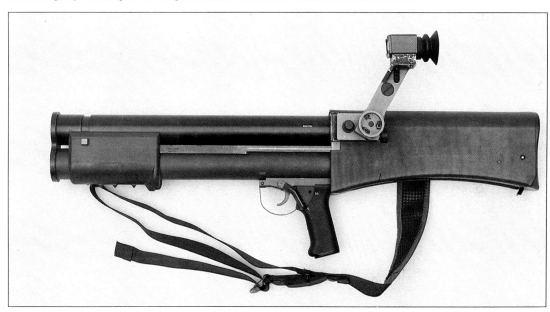

Anyone who thinks a pump action shotgun makes a menacing sound when the action is operated should hear the awesome mechanism of this pump action Arwen prototype, which is a deterrent in itself.

WEST GERMANY
TRGG Portable Irritant Agent Projector

At first sight the West German **TRGG** portable irritant agent projector resembles a flamethrower: it is carried in a backpack bearing flamethrower-type tanks, and the user aims and fires the irritant agent using a hand-held projector that looks very like a flamethrower gun. In fact the analogy is quite close, but the TRGG is designed to project an irritant agent instead of a flame jet.

The backpack of the TRGG has two tanks: one contains the agent and the other a pressurizing gas, usually carbon dioxide. When the user pulls a trigger on the projector the pressurized gas forces out the agent from its tanks and along a flexible tube leading to the projector. The agent concerned can be any one of a number from tear gas to CS. The weapon can also project powerful dyes to mark rioters for later apprehension.

The TRGG has a maximum operational range of 20 m (21.9 yards). The contents of the tanks are sufficient for about 80 jets of agent, and each jet is usually automatically monitored to prevent waste or excessive concentrations of agent. When refills are required the tanks can be quickly and easily changed (within a few seconds) without recourse to tools. This is usually done by a person other than the user who would otherwise have to remove the carrying frame for reloading.

Riot-control devices such as the TRGG are not favoured by some police and paramilitary forces. The very apearance of the TRGG is distinctive and makes it and its user a target for possible retaliation, while the weight of the equipment is such that the user is unable to move very rapidly if circumstances demand it. The device also has a relatively restricted range. The 20 m (21.9 yards) mentioned above may not be achieved against even a slight headwind and at longer ranges the irritant agent can be dispersed to such an extent that it may have little effect on determined rioters. At closer ranges, however, it is a formidable deterrent. But again, at these short ranges the TRGG requires a considerable degree of protective support and many police or paramilitary forces might not think that it deserves such an outlay of manpower. To date the TRGG has seen little use outside West Germany although organizations elsewhere have investigated its possibilities.

The TRGG is produced by Heckler & Koch GmbH at Oberndorf-Neckar.

Specification
TRGG
Weights: empty 10.5 kg (23.15 lb); full 20.5 kg (45.2 lb)
Maximum range: about 20 m (21.9 yards)
Number of jets: about 80

279

BAT Riot Munitions

Sweden is not normally reckoned as a nation where riots are a major problem, but the Swedish authorities take no chances and keep a close eye on riot-control equipment used elsewhere. During the 1970s their observers noted that many current anti-riot grenades were not very efficient as most could be picked up and returned to their previous owners. Grenade-launchers, if used, were also very inaccurate. The Swedes decided that if they were to have such munitions they would design their own, and invited a private concern to produce something suitable.

The result was a device known as the **BAT grenade**. This is a 40-mm (1.575-in) diameter can-type grenade with a filling of CS (Swedish law prohibits the use of any other agents within Sweden) fired from a muzzle-mounted launcher on an in-service weapon. As the grenade strikes the ground a protruding glass tip is broken which then releases the CS but with the added feature that the CS is driven out by internally generated gas pressure. This internal pressure is sufficient for the contents to act as a form of rocket motor, making the grenade streak about erratically, emitting CS all the while. The effect is that the grenade is almost impossible to grasp and its path is difficult to predict. The CS cloud is emitted for up to three seconds.

The accuracy requirement was met by fitting a detachable 40-mm (1.575-in) launcher onto the muzzle of a 9-mm (0.354-in) Carl Gustav sub-machine gun, although other similar weapons do equally well. The grenades are fired using ordinary blank cartridges and adequate accuracy at ranges up to 200 m (219 yards) can be obtained. Up to 10 grenades a minute can be fired using the semi-automatic mode of the Carl Gustav sub-machine gun. The Swedish police have purchased the BAT grenade and its launcher, and more have been sold to Denmark and Norway. Many other organizations, some including special forces, have evaluated the BAT grenade and its associated launcher.

A by-product of the research that led to the BAT grenade is the **BAT aerosol generator** that can be used with virtually any irritant agent. This device is portable, weighing about 5 kg (11 lb), and can be carried on a backpack or under an arm. A pressure bottle is used with a container of the irritant agent, and by careful use of the system controls various densities of aerosol cloud can be produced. This system has been purchased by police forces in Sweden, Norway and Denmark and has aroused interest elsewhere, usually with CS in mind.

Specification
BAT grenade
Calibre: 40 mm (1.575 in)
Length: 120 mm (4.72 in)
Weight: 150 grams (0.33 lb)
Maximum operational range: 200 m (219 yards)

Above: The BAT grenade can be fired from grenade launchers, thrown by hand or used for close-range personal defence by striking the impact fuse against a hard surface, which makes it discharge the gas in a powerful jet aerosol.

To deal with point targets, for example to shoot gas grenades through a window to flush out a sniper, stabilizers can be fitted.

If an area covering is needed, for instance when dealing with crowds, the projectile is also provided with an impact absorber/stabilizer.

Stopper

Recent events in South Africa have tended to hide the fact that civil unrest has long been a feature of South Africa's mixed racial society, and the police forces there have always been well schooled in anti-riot tactics and equipment. One of their latest items of equipment that has been prominent in newsreels is a riot control weapon known as **Stopper**.

Stopper is an orthodox design with a smooth-bored barrel having a calibre of 37 mm (1.457 in). It is used to fire a variety of projectiles including baton rounds, irritant agent rounds and even paramilitary rounds such as smoke and illuminating. The weapon itself is very simple, being little more than an oversized break-open shotgun with a body made from metal stampings. The twin pistol grips are interchangeable and the butt is a simple assembly that retracts into the body when not required. Rudimentary sights set at 50 m (55 yards) are provided. Stopper is very easy to use as little more is required of the user other than knowing how to load it (just like a shotgun) and pulling the trigger after pulling back the external hammer. Stopper has been produced with the realization that it will get very little care in use or storage.

The matt black finish is covered with a thin film of dry lubricant that prevents rust and other corrosion over the entire service life of the weapon. Stopper is usually issued fitted with a shoulder sling.

The main anti-riot rounds used with Stopper are CS and the usual baton rounds. The baton rounds are simple flat-nosed PVC or rubber slugs with no design finesse, while the CS round is also a straightforward design that starts to emit fumes following a 1.5-second delay after firing. Both rounds use aluminium cartridge cases. The CS round continues to emit gas for between six and 25 seconds depending on the local conditions. It has been demonstrated that it can be grasped and thrown while still emitting its CS fumes.

Stopper can be fired from the shoulder or hip and its effective range is limited to a maximum of about 100 m (109 yards). It can be fired to a maximum of approximately 300 m (328 yards), but at that range it is very inaccurate and baton rounds will have virtually no stopping power. It is also not very accurate even at its operational ranges and can only be used effectively as an area weapon unless the target is very close.

Specification
Stopper
Calibre: 37 mm (1.457 in)
Lengths: butt extended 700 mm (27.56 in); butt retracted 506 mm (19.92 in); barrel 390 mm (15.35 in)
Weight: with sling 3.7 kg (8.157 lb)
Range: operational 50 to 100 m (55 to 109 yards); maximum 300 m (328 yards)

The Stopper is a brutally simple 37-mm smooth-bore riot gun firing either CS gas shells or baton rounds. The twin pistol grips are interchangeable, and the butt can retract into the body of the weapon. Its matt black finish is covered with dry lubricant to protect it from corrosion.

Water Cannon

One of the most effective anti-riot weapons is water, and when fired from a water cannon it becomes even more effective. For many years the water cannon has been used to disperse crowds and mobs for the simple reason that it works very well. Few rioters will stand in the path of a water jet without taking protective action, which usually takes the form of running away. If high-pressure hoses are used the sheer effort of simply standing upright becomes difficult and any ideas of riotous behaviour usually vanish.

Water cannon have many other advantages to their users. High on the list is that such devices rarely cause serious casualties to produce the martyrs so beloved of many causes. Water jets may cause bruises by knocking people over, but it is uncommon for them to cause anything worse. Another advantage is that water is cheap and usually plentiful. All that is required to make water into an anti-riot weapon is to pass it through a water pump. These are usually easy to find, often in a mobile form.

Water cannon rarely cause much damage to buildings and installations. They may cause temporary flooding and associated nuisance, but rarely more. There is also a simple way that water can cause rioters to be singled out for later apprehension: mixing a dye with the water marks rioters in a manner they cannot easily remove.

Specialized types of water cannon have been produced. One still kept in reserve in Northern Ireland is known as the **Special Water Dispenser**. This is mounted on an old Saracen armoured carrier and is designed to deliver short 'slugs' of water at point targets up to 40 m (43.7 yards) distant. The effect of one of these slugs has been likened to receiving a heavy blow from a fist, and anyone hit by, such a slug is likely to lose interest in the local proceedings for some time but is not likely to be permanently harmed. The SWD has not yet been used 'operationally'.

Water cannon have their limitations, however. In many urban centres they might not be able to get near their intended targets as they cannot get past parked vehicles or barricades. They are also limited in range. Other than on a few of the more specialized designs the useful range is limited to about 30 m (33 yards), well within thrown-missile range. Unless they are ready prepared they take some time to get operational, and once their tanks are empty they may take even longer to refill. In some situations the mere sight of water cannon vehicles can inflame tensions or passions to a dangerous level.

But for all these drawbacks water cannon are still very useful anti-riot weapons. Even the most determined rioter cannot remain long in the path of a powerful water jet, and it should also be noted that the dislike of water by crowds is so intense that few riots take place in the rain.

Water Cannon, seen here in action in West Germany, have proved useful anti-riot weapons especially in chilly weather, although they do not deter the really hard-core rioter.

Model 02 LAPA Carabina Automatica

The **Model 02 LAPA Carabina Automatica** is designed to fire the relatively low-powered 5.56-mm (0.22-in) Long Rifle cartridge and is intended for use by police, prison guards and similar paramilitary personnel. The design is an offshoot from the Model 03 LAPA (Laboratorio de Pesquisa de Armamento Automatico Ltda) assault rifle, and uses a very similar operating mechanism. Both weapons are currently under development in the LAPA workshops in Rio de Janeiro.

The Model 02 is a fully automatic weapon that bears some resemblance to the LAPA assault rifle but has been made much lighter (and thus easier to handle and to carry) than the full military version. It is still under development and to date two versions have appeared. One uses an 18-round box magazine inserted into the pistol grip, while the other has a curved 30-round magazine inserted into a housing just forward of the pistol grip. The final form has apparently yet to be decided. Both versions have an M16-type carrying handle over the in-line receiver, which also houses the rear sights, and the cocking lever is under this handle. As with other weapons of this type the low-powered round used produces very little recoil, enabling accurate fire even on fully-automatic bursts.

The Model 02 is intended to deliver automatic fire with accuracy in urban warfare conditions, usually in internal security situations. As a result of its design it can fire at cyclic rates of up to 2,400 rpm, although this depends on the ammunition being used, for some makes of cartridge generate much lower rates of fire.

The **Carabina Esportiva** is a semi-automatic version of the Model 02 using a 10-round magazine in the grip. It is intended for civilian use, hopefully as a sporting weapon, but it could also be used for paramilitary purposes.

The Model 02 makes full use of modern materials in its design, the entire body being made of a strong plastic material. Its smooth outlines certainly make it an easy weapon to carry in the close confines of a police vehicle, and its all-in-line configuration makes the weapon easy to aim and to control. The overall design is reported to be still under development but it seems very likely that orders will be placed by Brazilian police and paramilitary units in the near future.

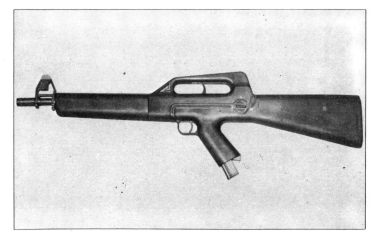

Specification
Mode 02 LAPA Carabina Automatica
Calibre: 5.56 mm (0.22 in) Long Rifle
Lengths: overall 775 mm (30.5 in); barrel 370 mm (14.57 in)
Weight: unloaded 2.1 kg (4.63 lb)
Muzzle velocity: about 330 m (1,082 ft) per second
Magazine capacity: 18 or 30 rounds

Intended for use by paramilitary personnel, the LAPA carbine fires .22 Long Rifle cartridge which has low lethality (although it tends to produce infectious wounds). The use of such a low-powered cartridge reduces recoil and muzzle climb, making automatic fire more accurate.

INDEX

Note: Page numbers in **bold** indicate an illustration.
An asterisk signifies a reference to a detailed directory entry.
Introductory and feature article entries are in **bold**.

0.303-in Gun, Machine, Hotchkiss, Mk 1 (see Hotchkiss mle 1909)
37 M and P shotgun (see Ithaca)
94 Skiki Kenju pistol: 39*, **39**
500 series shotgun (see Mossberg)
1200TX (see Parker-Hale Model 82)

A

A5 (see Browning)
AA 52 machine-gun: 246*, **246**
AC-556 (see Ruger Mini-14)
Afghanistan
   Army: 243
Aisne, battle of the: 9, 192
AK-47 (see Kalashnikov)
AK-53 (see SIG)
AK-74 (see Kalashnikov)
AKM (see Kalashnikov)
AKM-63 (see Kalashnikov AKM)
AKMS (see Kalashnikov AKM)
Alexander II, King: 20
American 180 M-2 (see Bingham PPS-50 Carbine)
American Expeditionary Force: 193, 197
AN-M2 (see Browning M1919)
AN/PVS-2 Starlight night sight: 161
APS (see Avtomaticheskiy Pistolet Stechkina)
AR-10 (see Armalite)
AR-15 (see Armalite)
AR-18 (see Armalite)
AR70 (see Beretta)
Ardennes, battle of the: 118, 134
Arisaka, Colonel: 129
Armalite
   AR-10: 137, 141, 146*, **146**, 158
   AR-15: 141, 146, 158, 159, 160, 162, 167, 168
   AR-18: 158*, **158**, 167, 240
Armee Pistole (AP) 28
Armsel Striker shotgun: 270*, **270**
Arnhem operation: 65
Arwen anti-riot weapon: 278*, **278**, 279*, **279**
Assault Rifle in Guerrilla Hands, The: 167-171
AS shotgun (see Smith & Wesson)
Atlantic Wall: 120, 214, 223
AUG (see Steyr)
Australia
   Army: 62, 82, 202, 234
Austria
   Army: 67, 154, 174
Austria-Hungary
   Army: 111, 206
Austro-Hungarian pistols: 15*
Automatic Choice, The: 43-46
Automatic Firepower: 242-244
Automaticky Pistole vz. 38 (CZ 38) 39*, **39**
Automatic series (see Browning)
AVT40 (see Tokarev rifles)
Avtomaticheskaia Vintovka Simonova (see Tokarev rifles)
Avtomaticheskiy Pistolet Stechkina (APS) 81, 137, 149*, **149**

B

Baader-Meinhoff gang: 84
'Baby Beretta': **46**
'Baby Nambu': 16
'Bang' system: 114
BAR (see Browning Automatic Rifle)
BAR M1918 (see Browning Automatic Rifle)
Bastico, General: **78**
BAT Riot Munitions: 280*, **280**
BDA-9 Browning Compact (see FN)
Beaufort Castle, storming of: 91, 92
BEF (British Expeditionary Force) 101, 107, 125, 126
Belgium
   Army: 106, 185, 204
   Gendarmerie: 106
Belholla-Selbsladepistole: 18
Bell UH-1 'Huey': **159, 160**, 238, **238, 243**, 262

Bené-Mercié Machine Rifle Model 1909 (see Hotchkiss mle 1909)
Berdan rifle: 110, 120
Beretta
   AR70: 171*, **171**
   BM59: 151*, **151**
   Brigadier': 47
   Model 1: 78
   Model 12: 93*, **93**
   Model 38/42: 78
   Model 81: 48
   Model 92 series: 48*, **48, 49, 50**, 51, **51**
   Model 93R: 48*
   Model 98: 48
   Model 99: 48
   Model 951: 47
   Model 1938A: 78, **78**
   Model 1951: 47*, **47**, 48
   Pistola Automatica modello 1915: 11*
   RS200 and RS202P: 255*, **255**, 256*, **256**
   Sniper: 174*
   sub-machine guns: 78*
Bergmann brothers: 73
Bergmann MP34 and MP35: 67, 73*, 206
Berthier
   Fusil d'infanterie mle 07/15: 130
   Fusil d'infanterie mle 1916: 130
   Fusil mle 1907: 105*, **106*, 106**, 130
   mle 1890 (see Mousqueton)
   mle 1892 (see Mousqueton)
Besa machine-gun: 220
Biafran War: 151
Bingham PPS-50 Carbine: 272*, **272**, 273*
'Bisley School': 98, 99, 127
Blackhawk (see Ruger)
'Bloop gun' (see M79 grenade launcher)
Boer War: 123
'Bolo' (see Mauser C/96)
Borchardt (see Luger Pistole '08)
Borchardt, Hugo: 26
BM59 (see Beretta)
Bradley ICV (see M2)
Breda
   machine-guns: 210*, 211*, **211**
   modello 1930: 209
Bren gun: 63, 85, 150, 209, **209**, 210, **217, 218**, 219*, **219**, 221, 229, **231**, 235, **242**, 245*, **245**
'Brigadier' (see Beretta)
Brixia (see Glisenti Pistola Automatica modello 1910)
Browning, John Moses: 14, 32, 54, 197, 212, 254
Browning
   0.3-in heavy machine-gun: **208**, 209, 213*, **213**, 214*, 216, 226, 230, **233**, 236
   A5: **254**
   Automatic Rifle (BAR) 198*, **198, 208**, 212*, **212**, 213, 214, **215**
   Automatic series: 254*, **254**
   High power pistol: **41**, 54, 166
   M1917: 196*, 196, 197*, **197**, 198, 213, 214
   M1919: 209, 213*, **213, 215**, 216
   Modèle 1900: 14, **14**
   Modèle 1903: 14
   Modèle 1922: 14
   Pistole Automatique modèle 1910: 14, 32*, **32**
   Pistole Automatique modèle à Grande Puissance: 32*, **32**
   pistols: 14*
Brusilov, General: 110
Buffel armoured vehicle: 242
Bulgaria
   Army: 63
Bulge, battle of the: 23
Bullpup 12 (see Mossberg 500 series)
'Busting Caps' – The M60 in Vietnam: 235

C

C1 (see L23A Sterling)
Cadet Training Rifle L81A1 (see Parker-Hale Model 82)
Cadillac-Gage Stoner 63 System: 137, 141*, **141, 143**, 145
Camel (see Sopwith)
Canada
   Army: 98, 176
Caporetto, battle of: 111
Carabina Automatica (see LAPA Model 02)
Carabina Esportiva (see LAPA Model 02)
Carabine FN-Mauser mle 1889: 106

Carbine, Caliber .30, M1, M1A1, M2 and M3: 113, **113**, 114, 119, 134*, **134, 136**, 139, 140, 259
Carbine Model 1910 (see Mosin-Nagant)
Carbine Type 38 (see Rifle type 38)
Carbine UZI (see Mini-UZI)
Carcano, Salvatore: 110
Carl Gustav (see Model 45)
Cassino, battle for: 61, 70
CAWS (see Close-Assault Weapon Systems)
CAWS programme: 264
CETME Modelo 58: 138*, **138**
Chad
   Armée du Nord: 168
Chauchat machine-gun: 191, 193*, **193**, 198
Chiang Kai Shek, General: 210
China
   Army: 212, 219
Churchill, Winston S: 19
CIS Ultimax 100: 240*, **240**
Close Assault Weapon (CAW) (see Heckler und Koch)
Close Assault Weapon Systems (CAWS) 269
Colt
   Commando: 158
   Lawman: 52, 53, **53**
   M1892 revolver: **10**
   M1911 and M1911A1: 10, 25, 32, 33*, **33**, 34, 35, **35**, 38, 49, 50, **50**
   Model SSP: 50
   'Peacemaker': 52
   Python: 52, **52**
   revolvers: 52*, 53*
   SSA: 51
   Trooper: 52, 53, **53**
Colt M1911 and M1911A1, The: 34-35
Colt-Browning
   Model 1895: 196, 197*, **197**
   Model 1900: 33
Combat Scatterguns in Action: 257-262
Combat Shotguns: 252
'Combat Trombone' (see Winchester Model 1897)
Commando (see Colt)
CSRG (see Chauchat machine-gun)
Cutaway drawings
   AK-47 assault rifle: **144-145**
   Beretta Model 92: **51**
   Bren light machine-gun: **218-219**
   Colt M1911 pistol: **34-35**
   Heckler und Koch G3 SG/1: **178-179**
   Lebel mle 1886: **102-103**
   Lee-Enfield Rifle No. 4 Mk I: **126-127**
   M16A1 rifle: **160-161**
   M60 GPMG: **238-239**
   MAS Model 1938: **67**
   Mauser C/96 'Broomhandle': **21**
   MP38: **74**
   Thompson M1928: **70-71**
   Vickers Gun Mk I: **200-201**
   Walter P 38 pistol: **30-31**
   Winchester Model 12: **260-261**
Cutt's Compensator: 70, 71, 270
Czechoslovakia
   Army: 39, 63, 115, 150, 210, 229

D

DA 140 (see FN)
Darne light machine-gun: 223
DDA (see FN)
'D-Day': 132
'Deer Gun': 33
Defender (see Winchester)
Degtyayrov light machine-gun: 120
Degtyarev DP Model 1928 (see DShK 1938)
De Lisle, William Godray: 128
De Lisle carbine: 128*, **128**, 129
Desert Eagle (see IMI)
Development of the German Assault Rifle: 119
DP (see Ruchnoy Pulemyot Degtyarev)
DPM (see Ruchnoy Pulemyot Degtyarev)
Dragoon Rifle Model 1891 (see Mosin-Nagant)
Dragunov (see SVD)
Dreyse machine-gun: 206
DS (Deer Slayer) (see Ithaca 37 M & P)
DShK 1939, SG43 and other Soviet machine-guns: 226*, **226**
Dunkirk, evacuation from: 64, 66, 219, 220

E

EM-1 (see Enfield EM-2)
EM-2 (see Enfield)
Enfield
   EM-2: 139*, **139**, 144, 157
   Individual Weapon (IW) XL70E3: 80, 81, 144, 157*, **157**, 158, 233, 245, 246
   No. 2 Mk 1 pistol: **23**, 24*, **24**
Enforcer (see Lee-Enfield L42A1)
Envoy (see Lee-Enfield L42A1)

F

F1 sub-machine gun: 82*, **82**
Fairey Swordfish: 221
FAL (Fusil Automatique Legère) (see FN)
Falklands war: 80, 175, 228, 231, 242
Fallschirmjägergewehr 42 (see Rheinmetall)
FA MAS: 83, 149, 154*, **154**, 155*, **155**
FAO (see Lehky Kulomet ZB vz.26 and vz.30)
Federal Riot Gun: 273*, **273**
Feederle brothers: 18
FFV 890C (see Galil and R4)
FG 42 (see Rheinmetall)
Fiat modello 1914: 210
Finland
   Army: 63, 146
Flare Pistol M1942: 33
FN (Fabrique Nationale)
   BDA-9 Browning Compact: 54, **54**
   DA 140: **54**
   DDA: 51
   FAL and L1A1: 139, **153**, 155*, **155, 156**, 158, 166, 172
   Fusil Automatique modèle 49: 139*, **139**, 149
   'Grand Puissance': 54
   High-power pistol: 54*, **54**, 166
   MAG: 228*, **228**, 229, 230, **230, 231**, 233, 242, 244, 245
   Minimi: 229*, **229**, 233, 234, 235
   Model 30-11: 184*, **184**, 185*, **185**
   Riot Shotgun: 254*, **254**, 255*, **255**
FNC (see FN FAL and L1A1)
Fokker triplane: 199
Fosbery, Colonel G.V.: 14
France
   Army: 30, 42, 67, 72, 83, 104, 108, 130, 149, 155, 175, 192, 193, 196, 214, 225, 246
   Foreign Legion: 30, 44, 131, 246
      2nd REP: 149
      13th Brigade: 131
Franchi, Luigi: 256
Franchi
   SPAS Model 11: 256
   SPAS Model 12: 256*, **256**, 260
'Frederick Hill' operation: 262
Free French: 130
French automatic pistols: 42*
French carbines: 105*, **105**
FR-F1 and FR-F2: 175*, **175**, 180
Frontiers, battle of the: 104, 107
Fucile Mitriagliatori modello 30 (see Breda machine-guns)
Fucile modello 91 (see Mannlicher-Carcano)
Fusil Automatique Legère (see FN FAL)
Fusil Automatique modèle 49 (see FN)
Fusil d'infanterie mle 07/15 (see Berthier)
Fusil d'infanterie mle 1916 (see Berthier)
Fusil FN-Mauser mle 1889: 106*, **106**, 110
Fusil Gras mle 1874 (see Mousqueton)
Fusil MAS36: 130*, **130, 131**
Fusil-mitrailleur Hotchkiss mle 1909 (see Hotchkiss mle 1909)
Fusil-Mitrailleur mle 1915 (see Chauchat)
Fusil Mitrailleur Modèle 49 (MAS 49) 149*, **149**
Fusil Mitrailleur modèles 1924/29 and Mitrailleuse 1931: 214*, **214**
FV432 APC: **153**

G

G3 (see Heckler und Koch)
G3 A3ZF (see Heckler und Koch)
G3 SG/1 (see Heckler und Koch)
G11 (see Heckler und Koch)
Gail, Lieutenant Uziel: 88, 89
Gail and R4: 170*, **170**, 171*, **171**
Galil and R4: 170*, **170**, 171*, **171**
Galil sniping rifle: **173**, **181**, 182, 184*, **184**, 185
Garand, John C: 132
Garand (see Rifle, Caliber .30, M1)
Gatling Gun: 197
GB (see Steyr)
German pistols: 17*, 18*
Germany
  Air force: 20
  Army: 17, 18, 19, 20, 26, 28, 30, 39, 46, 63, 70, 73, 75, 76, 77, 78, 98, 108, 113, 114, 115, 116, 118, 119, 135, 153, 195, 205, 202, 212, 224, 234
    Afrika Korps: 30, 222
    Feldgendarmerie: 30
    Gebirgsjäger: 120, 225
    Panzergrenadiers: **73**, 74
    Schüztruppen: 195
  Hitler Youth: 20
  Luftwaffe: 28, 29, 32, 115, 119, 222
    Fallschirmjäger: 224
  National Socialists: 28
  Navy: 17, 20, 30
  Volkssturm: 130
  Waffen-SS: 20, 23, 29, 30, 32, 38, 61, 62, 63, 73, 114, 118, 119, 210
Gewehr 242(f) (see Fusil MAS36)
Gewehr 252(r) (see Mosin-Nagant rifles)
Gewehr 254(r) (see Mosin-Nagant rifles)
Gewehr 1898 (see Mauser)
Glisenti Pistola Automatica modello 1910: 11*, **11**
Goryunov, P.M: 226
GP 35: 32
'Grand Puissance' pistol (see FN)
Gras mle 1874 (see Mousqueton)
'Grease Gun' (see M3 and M3A1)
Green Beret Ambush: 259-260
Greener GP (see Webley)
Grenade Discharger L1A1: 278*, **278**

H

Haile Selassie, Emperor: **20**
Halcon (see PA3-DM)
Handgrip Model 37 (see Ithaca)
Heckler und Koch
  Close Assault Weapon: 262
  G3: 84, 138, 168, **169**, 172*, **172**
  G11: 172*, 269
  HK4: 55
  machine-guns: 247*, **247**
  MP5: 84*, **84**
  P7A13: 51
  P7 K3: **46**, 55, **55**
  P7M13: 51, 55
  P9S: 55, **55**
  pistols: 55*
  sniper rifles: 178*, **178, 179**
  TRGG Portable Irritant Agent Projector: 279*
  VP-70: **81**
  VP70M: 56*, **56**
Heeres Pistole (see Walther P 38)
Hermes, HMS: 156
High-power 9-mm pistol (see FN)
Hill, Warrant Officer 2 Steven: 262
Hilton anti-riot gun: **275**
Hitler, Adolf: 29, 118
HK4 (see Heckler und Koch)
HK 11E (see Heckler und Koch)
HK 13E (see Heckler und Koch)
HK 21 (see Heckler und Koch G3)
HK 21A1 (see Heckler und Koch)
HK 21E (see Heckler und Koch)
HK 23E (see Heckler und Koch)
HK 33 (see Heckler und Koch G3)
Hotchkiss
  medium machine-guns: 192*, **192**, 193*, **193**, 194
  Mk 1 (see Hotchkiss mle 1909)
  mle 1900: 191
  mle 1909: 192*, **192**
How machine-guns work: 218
HP pistol: 28, 29

Hyde, George: 69
Hyde M2: 69

I

Ilyin, Nikolai: **121**
IMI Desert Eagle: 47*, **47**
India
  Army: 191, 195, 220, 221
  Individual Weapon (IW) XL70E3 (see Enfield)
Indo-China War: 67, 225, 246
Ingram, Gordon B: 87
Ingram
  Model 10: 81, 87*, **87**
  Model 11 (see Ingram Model 10)
Into the Unknown: 107-109
IRA (see Irish Republican Army)
Ireland
  Royal Irish Constabulary: 260
  Irish Republican Army: 134, 158, 163, 239, 242
Israel
  Army: 88, 89, 184
Italy
  Army: 11, 40, 48, 78, 93
    35th Italian Division: 111
    Parachute Brigade: 93
    Special Troops: 93
  Air Force: 40
  Navy: 40
Ithaca
  37 M and P: 259, 261, 265*, **265**, 266
  Handgrip Model 37: 266, **266**
  Mag-10 Roadblocker: 266*, **266**
  Stakeout: 266*
Iver-Johnson Model 300 Multi-Caliber Rifle: 173, 182, 186*, **186**

J

Jackhammer (see Pancor)
Japanese pistols: 16*
JS-2 heavy tank: 226

K

Kahles Helia ZF69 telescopic sight: 174, **174**, 176
Kalashnikov, Mikhail: 164
Kalashnikov
  AK-47: 91, 120, 137, 144, **144, 145**, 146, 147, 148, 151, 158, 163, 164*, **164**, 165, **165**, 167, **167**, 168, **168**, 169, 170, 183, 240, 262
  AK-74: 167, 170*, **170**, 241
  AKM: 148, 164, **164**, 167, **167, 169**, 170, **170**, 187, 233, 241
Karabiner 43 (see Walther Gewehr 43)
Karabiner 98K (see Mauser)
karabin wz 91/98/25 (see Mosin-Nagant rifles)
Korean War: 112, 132, 144, 198, 258
Kpfw MG 331(f) (see Mitrailleuse 1931 machine-gun)
Krag-Jorgensen Model 1896: 112, 132, 257
Krummlauf curved barrel: 118

L

L1A1 (see FN FAL)
L1A1 (see Grenade Discharger L1A1)
L2A3 Sterling: 66, 80*, **80**, 81*, **81**, 82
L4A2 (see Bren gun)
L4A4 (see Bren gun)
L7A1 (see FN MAG)
L7A2 (see FN MAG)
L20A1 (see FN MAG)
L34A1 (see L2A3 Sterling)
L39A1 (see Lee-Enfield L42A1)
L42A1 (see Lee-Enfield)
L67A1 Riot Gun: **275**, 278
Lafette
  34 tripod: **222**
  42 tripod: **223**
Lanchester, George: 66
Lanchester sub-machine gun: 66*, **66**
Langenhan pistol: 18, **18**

LAPA
  Model 02 Carabina Automatica: 281*, **281**
  Model 03 (see LAPA Model 02)
LAPD (see Ithaca 37 M and P)
Laser Lok sighting system: 272
Lawman (see Colt)
Lebel and Berthier rifles: 130*, **130**
Lebel
  Fusil mle 1886: 102, **102**, 103, **103**, 104*, 105, 130
  Fusil mle 1886/93: 97, 104, **104**, 130
  revolver: 22, **22**
Lee, James Paris: 101, 123
Lee-Enfield
  No. 1 rifle: 66, 200
  No. 4 rifle: 64
  Rifle L39A1: 127
  Rifle L42A1: 127, 173, 175*, **175**
  Rifle No. 1 Mk III: 97, **97**, 99, 101*, **101, 122**, 123, 124, 125, **125**, 126, 127, 128
  Rifle No. 4 Mk I: 114, **122, 123, 124**, 125*, **125**, 126, **126**, 127, **127**, 128, **135**, 175
  Rifle No. 5 Mk I: 127, 128*, **128**
Lee-Enfield Story, The: 123-127
Lee-Metford rifle: 123
Lehky Kulomet
  vz 52 and vz 59: 150*, **150**
  vz 52/57 (see vz 52 and vz 59)
  ZB vz. 24 (see Lehky Kulomet ZB vz. 26 and vz. 30)
  ZB vz. 26 and vz. 30: 210*, **210**, 212, 219, 229, 242
Leichte MG 116(f) (see Fusil Mitrailleur modèles 1924/29)
Leichte MG 138(e) (see Bren gun)
Leningrad, siege of: 77
Leopard tank: 92, 225, 228
Leupold telescopic sight: 186
Lewis, Colonel Isaac: 204
Lewis Gun: 194, **194**, 195, **195**, 200, 204*, **204**, 219
Liberator M1942: 33*, **33**
Light Machine-Gun Tactics 1915-1918: 194-195
Light Support Weapon (LSW) 233, 245*, **245**, 246*, 246
Little, Captain: 13
LMG 08/15 (see Maschinengewehr 08/15)
Loos, battle of: 199, 205
LSW (see Light Support Weapon)
Luger, Georg: 17, 26
Luger Pistole P '08: 9, 10, 17*, **17**, 26*, **26**, 28, 29, 30, 72
Lynx (see Westland)

M

M1 (see Carbine, Caliber .30)
M1 (see Rifle, Caliber .30, Garand)
M1 and M1A1 (see Thompson)
M1 carbine: 34, 145
M2 (see Browning 0.5-in HMG)
M2 (see Browning M1919)
M2 (see Carbine, Caliber .30)
M2 Bradley ICV: **162**
M2 HB (see Browning 0.5-in HMG)
M3 (see Carbine, Caliber .30)
M3 and M3A1 'Grease Gun': 61, 69*, **69**, 71, 77, 80, 147
M3 half-track: **90**
M3 sub-machine gun: 35
M10 shotgun (see Remington)
M11 riot gun (see Remington)
M14 rifle: 132, 140*, **140, 142, 152**, 159, 168, 185, **185**, 186, 259
M16 and M16A1: 82, 141, 145, 146, **152, 153**, 155, 157, 158*, **158**, 159, **159**, 160, **160**, 161, **161**, 162, **162**, 166, 167, 168, **169**, 171, 229, 233, 238, 240, 263, 270
M16 in Action, The: 159-162
M21 (see M14 rifle)
M26 sniping rifle: 184
m/27 (see Mosin-Nagant rifles)
m/28/30 (see Mosin-Nagant rifles)
m/39 (see Mosin-Nagant rifles)
M40A1 (see Sniping Rifle M40A)
m/45 (see Madsen)
M45 Maxson Mount: **214**
m/46 (see Madsen)
m/50 (see Madsen)
m/53 (see Madsen)
M53 (see Maschinengewehr 42)
m/59 (see Samozaryadnyi Karabin Simonova)

m/60 and m/62 (see Valmet)
M60 GPMG: 153, 161, 227, **227, 232**, 233, 234*, **234, 235-239**, 242, **243**
M63A1 (see Stoner 63 System)
M65 pistol (see Tokarev TT-33)
M68 pistol (see Tokarev TT-33)
M70B1 assault rifle: 187
M76: **173**, 187*, **187**
M79 40-mm grenade launcher: 262
M113 APC: 92
M203 grenade launcher: 158, **158, 161**, 161
M249 Squad Automatic Weapon (see FN Minimi)
M/908 (see Savage Model 1907 & 1915)
M/915 (see Savage Model 1907 & 1915)
M1897 shotgun (see Winchester)
M1903 (see Model 1903 Springfield)
M1903 pistol (see Mannlicher)
M1910 Maxim gun (see DShK 1938)
M1911 and M1911A1 (see Colt)
M1912 shotgun (see Winchester)
M1917 (see Browning)
M1917 (see Rifle No. 3 Mk I)
M1917 revolver: 10, 38
M1919 (see Browning M1917)
M1921 (see Browning 0.5-in HMG)
MAB 38/49: 93
Machine-Gun, Caliber .30, M1917 (see Browning M1917)
Machine-Guns of World War I: 191
Machine-Guns of World War II: 209
Machine-Gun Tactics: 230-233
Machine Pistols: 81
Maclean, Samuel: 204
Madsen
  machine-guns: 203*, **203**, 206
  sub-machine guns: 147*, **147**
MAG (Mitrailleuse d'Appui Général) (see FN)
Mag-10 Roadblocker (see Ithaca)
Maginot Line: 214
Makarov 9-mm pistol: 25, 57*, **57**
Malayan Emergency (1948-60) 254, 263
Mannlicher, Ferdinand von: 111
Mannlicher
  M1903 pistol: **15**
  Modell 1890: 111
  Modell 1895: 97, 111*, **111**
Mannlicher-Carcano
  Fucile modello 91: 97, **97**, 110*, **110**, 111*, **111**
  Moschetto modello 91: **110**
Marcos, President: 140
Maremount Lightweight Machine-Gun (see M60 GPMG)
'Market Garden' operation: 24
Marlin Gun (see Colt-Browning Model 1895)
Marlin UD M42: 68*, **68**, 69
MAS 46 (see Fusil Mitrailleur Modèle 49)
MAS 49 (see Fusil Mitrailleur Modèle 49)
MAS 49/56 (see Fusil Mitrailleur Modèle 49)
Maschinengewehr 08: 205*, **205**, 206
Maschinengewehr 08/15: **194**, 195, **195**, 206*, **206, 207**
Maschinengewehr 34: 26, 209, **209**, 221*, 222*, **222**, 223, 224, 225, 230, 242
Maschinengewehr 42: 209, 223*, **223**, 224, **224**, 225, 230, 233, 234, 235, 243, 244, 248, 249
Maschinenpistole 43 and Sturmgewehr 44: 118*, **118**, 119, **119**, 120
MAS Model 1938: 66*, **66**, 67, **67**, 83
MAT 49: 83*, **83**, 149
Matilda tank: 220
Mauser
  C/96: 9, 15, 18*, **18**, 19*, **19**, 30, 81
  Gewehr 98 and Karabiner 98k: 113, 114*, **114, 115, 116**
  Gewehr 1898: 97, 98*, **98**
  Model 712 Schnellfeuer: 20
  Modell 1888: 98
  SP 66 and SP 86: 173, 176*, **176**, 177*, **177**
  Sturmgewehr 45: 138, 234
  T-Gewehr anti-tank rifle: 214
Mauser: the story continues: 19-21
Maxim, Hiram: 85, 197, 199, 205
Maxim Gun: 198, 199, 203, 206, 220, 235
Mayaguez incident: 268
MECAR 40-mm rifle grenade: 154, 171
MEMS (see PA3-DM)
Mesrine, Jacques: 46
Mexico
  Navy: 85
MG 08/15 (see Maschinengewehr 08/15)
MG 08/18 (see Maschinengewehr 08/15)
MG 1 (see Maschinengewehr 42)

Index

MG 2 (see Maschinengewehr 42)
MG 3: 227, 235, 243, 244, 248*, **248, 249**
MG 15 (see Maschinengewehr 34)
MG 26(t) (see Lehky Kulomet ZB vz.26 and vz.30)
MG 30(t) (see Lehky Kulomet ZB vz.26 and vz.30)
MG 34 (see Maschinengewehr 34)
MG 39/41 (see Maschinengewehr 42)
MG 42 (see Maschinengewehr 42)
MG 42/59 (see Maschinengewehr 42)
MG 42 in Action, The: 224-225
MG 45 (see Maschinengewehr 42)
MG Model 07/16 (see Schwarzlose machine-guns)
MG Modell 08 (see Schwarzlose machine-guns)
MG Modell 12 (see Schwarzlose machine-guns)
Mini-14 (see Ruger)
Mini-14/20GB (see Ruger Mini-14)
Minigun: 160
Minimi (see FN)
Mini-UZI: 81, 88*, **88**
Mitrailleuse Hotchkiss mle 1897 (see Hotchkiss medium machine-guns)
Mitrailleuse Hotchkiss mle 1900 (see Hotchkiss medium machine-guns)
Mitrailleuse Hotchkiss mle 1914 (see Hotchkiss medium machine-guns)
Mitrailleuse mle 1907 (see Saint-Etienne)
Mitraglice Fiat modello 1914/35: 210
Mitraglice modello 37 (see Breda)
Mitraglice modello 38 (see Breda)
Mitragliera RM modello 31 (see Breda)
mle 1866 Chassepot rifle: 130
mle 1889 (see Fusil FN-Mauser mle 1889)
mle 1905 (see Saint-Etienne)
mle 1907 (see Fusil Berthier)
mle 1907/15 (see Fusil Berthier mle 1907)
mle 1909 (see Hotchkiss)
mle 1916 (see Fusil Berthier mle 1907)
mle 1950 MAS pistol: 42, **42**
MM-1 Multi-Round Projectile-Launcher: 276*, **276**
Model 1 (see Beretta)
Model 12 (see Beretta)
Model 12 (see Winchester)
Model 30-11 (see FN)
Model 37-39 (see Suomi)
Model 38/42 (see Beretta)
Model 45: 82*, **82**, 83*, **83**, 137, 280
Model 50 and Model 55 (see Reising)
Model 61 Skorpion: 81, 86*, **86**
Model 63 (see Model 61 Skorpion)
Model 68 (see Model 61 Skorpion)
Model 75: 42
Model 77E (see Savage)
Model 81 (see Beretta)
Model 82 (see Parker-Hale)
Model 83 (see Parker-Hale Model 82)
Model 85 (see Parker-Hale Model 82)
Model 92 (see Beretta)
Model 93R (see Beretta)
Model 98 (see Beretta)
Model 99 (see Beretta)
Model 300 (see Iver Johnson)
Model 459M (see Smith & Wesson)
Model 469 (see Smith & Wesson)
Model 500 (see Iver Johnson Model 300)
Model 520 (see Savage Model 77E)
Model 620 (see Savage Model 77E)
Model 712 Schnellfeuer (see Mauser)
Model 870R (see Remington)
Model 912 (see Smith & Wesson)
Model 951 (see Beretta)
Model 1200 (see Winchester)
Model 1891 (see Mosin-Nagant)
Model 1891/30 (see Mosin-Nagant)
Model 1895 (see Nagant)
Model 1897 (see Winchester)
Model 1903 Springfield: 112*, **112**, 114, 132*, **132**, 197, 198
Model 1910 (see Mosin-Nagant)
Model 1930 (see Mosin-Nagant)
Model 1938 (see Mosin-Nagant)
Model 1938A (see Beretta)
Model 1944 (see Mosin-Nagant)
Model 1951 (see Beretta)
Model 3000 (see Smith & Wesson)
Model ATP-8SP (see Mossberg 500)
Model D MAB: 42
modèle 30 (see Browning Automatic Rifle)
Modèle 1873 revolver: 22
Modèle 1874 revolver: 22
Modèle 1900 (see Browning)
Modèle 1903 (see Browning)
Modèle 1910 (see Browning)
Modèle 1922 (see Browning)
Modèle 1936 (see FR-F1 and FR-F2)

Modèle d'Ordnance (see Lebel revolvers)
Modell 1888 (see Mauser)
Modell 1890 (see Mannlicher)
Modell 1895 (see Mannlicher)
modello 12 (1912) (see Glisenti Pistola Automatica modello 1910)
modello 30 (see Breda)
modello 38 (see Breda)
modello 1930 (see Breda)
Modello 58 (see CETME)
Model SSP (see Colt)
Modern Assault Rifles: 153
Modern Combat Pistols: 41
Modern Machine-Guns: 227
Modern Sniping Rifles: 173
Modern Sub-Machine Guns: 79
MOD-T-22 CS Rocket-Launcher: 276*
Monitor (see Browning Automatic Rifle)
Mons, battle of: 107
Moro Insurrection: 257
Moschetto modello 91 (see Mannlicher-Carcano)
Mosin, Captain Sergei: 110, 120
Mosin-Nagant
    Carbine Model 1910: 110
    Dragoon Rifle Model 1891: 110
    Model 1891: 97, 110*, **110**, 120
    Model 1891/30: 110, 120, **121**
    Model 1930: 135
    rifles: 120*, **120**, 240
Mossberg 500 series shotgun: **261**, 262, 264*, **264**
Mousqueton Berthier
    mle 1890: 105, **105**, 106, 130
    mle 1892: 105, **105**, 106, 130
Mousqueton Fusil Gras mle 1874: 104, 105, 130
MP2 (see UZI)
MP5 (see Heckler und Koch)
MP18: 61, 67, 70, 72*, **73**, 74
MP28: 66, 72*, **72**, 73, 74
MP34 and MP35 (see Bergmann)
MP34(ö) (see Steyr-Solothurn S1-100)
MP38, MP38/40 and MP40: 61, **61**, 64, 69, 73*, 74*, **74**, 75, 89, 223, 224
MP48 (see SIG)
MP310 (see SIG)
MP-K and MP-L (see Walther)
Mussolini, Benito: 115

N

Nagant brothers: 110, 120
Nagant Model 1895: 16*, **16**, 25
Nambu, General Kijiro: 16, 211
Nambu: 16, 39
Nambu Type 100: 67, 68*, **68**
NATO (North American Treaty Organization) 49, 139, 140, 145, 146, 157, 225, 235, 243, 244, 248
NATO L1A1 rifle: 82
Netherlands
    Army: 228
neue Sicherung 1912 (see Mauser C/96)
Neuve Chapelle, battle of: 205
NF-1 (see AA 52)
Nieuport 10: **12**
No. 29 reolver (see Smith & Wesson)
No.38 revolver, Bodyguard (see Smith & Wesson)
No.49 revolver (see Smith & Wesson)
No.57 revolver (see Smith & Wesson)
No.209 gas pistol (see Smith & Wesson No.210)
No.210 shoulder gas gun (see Smith & Wesson)
Northern Ireland
    Royal Ulster Constabulary: 134
    Ulster Defence Regiment: 28

O

obr 1910 (see Pulemet Maksima obrazets 1910)
Oerlikon 20-mm cannon: 216
Olin/Heckler und Koch CAWS: 269, **269**
OSS pistol: 33
Owen, Lieutenant Evelyn: 62, 82
Owen Gun: 62*, **62**, 82

P

P1 and P5 pistol (see Walther)
P4 pistol (see Walther)
P6 pistol: 42
P7A13 (see Heckler und Koch)
P7 K3 (see Heckler und Koch)
P7M13 (see Heckler und Koch)
P9S (see Heckler und Koch)
P.13/P.14 (see Rifle No.3 Mk I)
P.17 (see Rifle No.3 Mk I)
P17 Artillerie (see Luger P 08)
P/39 pistol: 29
P-64 (see Makarov 9-mm pistol)
P88 (see Walther)
P226 (see SIG-Sauer)
PA3-DM: 80*, **80**
PA 15 MAB: 42, **44**
Pakistan
    Army: 220
Palestine Liberation Organization (PLO) 86, 90, 91, 92, 148, 167, 169, 185
PAM 2 (see PA3-DM)
Pancor Jackhammer: **253**, 268*, **270**
Panther tank: 224, 225
Parabellum 9-mm pistol: 10, 44
Parachutist's Rifle Type 2 (see Rifle Type 38)
Parker-Hale Model 82: 176*, **176**
Patchett (see L2A3 Sterling)
'Peacemaker' (see Colt)
Pedersen Device: 112
Pistol, Browning, FN, 9-mm, HP No.1: 32
Pistola Automatica Beretta modello 1934: 40*, **40**
Pistola Automatica modello 1915 (see Beretta)
Pistola Automatica modello 1910 (see Glisenti)
Pistol Automatic, Caliber .45, M1911: 33
Pistol, Automatic L9A1: 32
Pistol Automatic Type 4: 16, **16**
Pistole 75: 42
Pistole M (see Makarov 9-mm)
Pistole P 08 (see Luger)
Pistole P 35(p): 38
Pistole P 39(t): 39
Pistole P 620(b): 32
Pistole P 621(b): 32
Pistole P 671(i): 40
Pistolet Radom wz.35: 38*, **38**
Pistol revolver Type 26: 16
Pistol Revolveur Modele 1892: 32
Pistols of the Great War: 9
Pistols of World War II: 23
Pistol Type 94: 39
PK 7.62-mm series: 229, 240*, 241*, **241**, 244
PLO (see Palestine Liberation Organization)
PM1910 (see Pulemet Maksima obrazets 1910)
Poland
    Army: 38
'Port Said' (see Model 45)
Post-War Infantry Weapons: 137
Power-Staf/KA-1 Impact Weapon: 276*
PM (Pistole Makarov) (see Makarov)
PP and PPK (see Walther)
PPD-1934/38: 74*, **74**
PPD-1940: 74
PPS-42 and PPS-43: 30, 77*, **77**, 85
PPS-50 Carbine (see Bingham)
PPSh-41: 30, 61, 75*, **75, 76**, 77, **77**, 120, 272
PSG-1 (see Heckler und Koch sniper rifles)
PSM: **44**
PSO-1 telescopic sight: 183, 187
Pulemet Maksima obrazets 1905: 203
Pulemet Maksima obrazets 1910: 191, 203*, **203**
Puteaux (see Saint-Etienne)
Python (see Colt)

R

Rast und Gasser Revolver M.1898: 15
Reagan, President Ronald: 79, 91
Redfield telescopic sight: 186
Reichs-Commissions-Revolver Modell 1879: 17
Reichs-Commissions-Revolver Modell 1883: 18
Reichstag: 30
Reising Model 50 and Model 55: 72*, **72**

Rekytgevaer M1903 (see Madsen machine-guns)
Remington
    M10 shotgun: 257, 261
    M11 riot gun: 258, 261
    Model 11A (see Browning Automatic series)
    Model 12 (see Browning Automatic series)
    Model 700 (see Sniping Rifle M40A)
    Model 870 shotguns: 254, **257, 259**, 261, 268*, **268, 274**
Renault FT17 tank: 192
Repetier Gewehr Modell (1895 (see Mannlicher Modell 1895)
Repetier-Stutzen-Gewehr (see Mannlicher Modell 1895)
Replacing a Legend: 49-51
Revolver, Caliber .45, Colt New Service, M1917: 38
Revolver, Caliber .45, Smith & Wesson Hand Ejector, M1917: 38
Revolver No.2 Cal .380: 36
Rheinmetall
    Fallschirmjägergewehr 42 (FG 42) 113, 115*, **115**, 119
    MG 08/15: **194**, 195, **195**
Richthofen, Manfred von: 13, 199
Rifle 7.62-mm C3 (see Parker-Hale Model 82)
Rifle 7.62-mm L39A1 (see Lee-Enfield)
Rifle 7.62-mm L42A1 (see Lee-Enfield)
Rifle 7.62-mm M14 National Match (Accurised) (see Rifle M21)
Rifle, Caliber .30, M1 (Garand): 132*, **132, 133**, 134*, **134**, 142, 150, 151, 159, 163, 238
Rifle, Caliber .30, Model 1903 (see Model 1903 Springfield)
Rifle M21: 185*, **185**
Rifle No.1 Mk III (see Lee-Enfield)
Rifle No.3 Mk I: 97, 99*, **99**
Rifles of the Great War: 97
Rifles of World War II: 113
Rifle Type 38: 129*, **129**
Rifle Type 99 (see Rifle Type 38)
Riot Control Grenades: 274-275
Riot Control Weapons: 271
Riot Gun (see Federal)
Riot Pac (see Power-Staf/KA-1)
Riot Shotgun (see FN)
RM & M 'Dreyse' pistol: **17**, 18
Role of the Sniper, The: 135
Ross, Sir Charles: 98
Ross rifles: 97, 98*, **99**, **99**
Roth-Steyr Repetierpistole M.07: 15
RP46 (see Ruchnoy Pulemyot Degtyarev)
RPD (see Ruchnoy Pulemyot Degtyarev)
RPG-7 anti-tank rocket launcher: 167
RPK: 148, 233, 241*, **241**, 244
RPK-74 (see RPK)
RS200 (see Beretta)
RS202P (see Beretta)
Ruchnoy Pulemyot Degtyarev (RPD) 148*, **148**, 167, **232**
Ruger, William B: 53
Ruger
    Blackhawk: 53
    Mini-14: 163*, **163**
    revolvers: 53*
    Security-Six: 53
    Service-Six: 53
    Speed-Six: **53**
Russia
    Army: 110, 112, 120, 203
    Civil War: 20

S

S1-100 (see Steyr-Solothurn)
Saint-Etienne machine-gun: 196*, **196**
Saive, Dieudonné J: 139
Samonabiject Puska vz 52: 150*, **150**
Samozaryadnyi Karabin Simonova (SKS) rifle: 137, 144, 148*, **148**
Samozariyadniya Vintokvka Dragunova (see SVD)
Samson, Wing Commander Charles R: **12**
SARAC M1953 (see MG3)
Savage
    Automatic: **10**
    Model 77E: 270*
    Model 1907 and 1915 pistols: 10*
SC70 (see Beretta AR70)
SC70 Short (see Beretta AR70)
Schermuly Multi-purpose Gun: 277*, **277**

chmeisser, Hugo: 72, 74
chmeisser, Louis: 118, 119
chmidt und Bender telescopic sight: 177
chnellfeuer pistols: 81
chwarzlose, Andreas: 206
chwarzlose
  machine-guns: 206*, **206, 207**
  Maschinengewehr Modell 07: 206
chwere Maschinengewehr 08: 205*, **205**
ecurity-Six revolver (see Ruger)
elbstladegewehr 258(r) (see Tokarev
    rifles)
elbstladegewehr 259(r) (see Tokarev
    rifles)
elbstladekarabiner 455(a): 134
ervice-Six revolver (see Ruger)
G 43 (see DShK 1938)
G 510 series (see SIG assault rifles)
GM (see DShK 1938)
hepherd, Major R.V: 64
hort Magazine Lee-Enfield (see SMLE)
G
  710-3 7.62-mm: 234*, **234**
  AK-53: **151**
  assault rifles: 151*, 234
  sub-machine guns: 138*, **138**
G-Sauer
  P220: 42*, **42**
  P225: 42
  P226: 51
imonov, Sergei G: 118, 148
korzeny, Colonel Otto: 115
KS (see Samozaryadnyi Karabin
    Simonova)
MG 08 (see Maschinengewehr 08)
mith & Wesson
  0.38/200 Revolver: 36*, **36, 37**
  AS shotgun: 264, **264**
  M1917: 38*, **38**
  Magnum: **45**
  Model 459M: 51
  Model 469: 50
  Model 912: 264
  Model 3000: 264
  No.29: 52
  No.38: 52, **52**
  No.49: 52
  No.5?: 52
  No.210: **271**, 272*, **272**
  revolvers: 52*
  shotguns: 264*
MLE (Short Magazine Lee-Enfield): 99,
    100, 101, **101, 122**, 123, **123**, 125, 126
niper (see Beretta)
nipers in Action: The Tangling
    Machine: 180-182
niper's Rifle Type 97 (see Rifle Type 38)
niping rifle M40A: 173, 182, 186*, **186**
olothurn Modell 1929 (see
    Maschinengewehr 34)
OS shotgun (see Viking Arms)
omme, battle of the: 107, 108, 200, 205
opwith Camel: 13
outh Africa
  Army: 227
oviet Union
  KGB: 165
  Red Army: 25, 30, 38, 74, 75, 77, 110,
      120, 135, 164, 170, 183, 212, 226, 233,
      240, 243, 244
  Marines: 120
  Navy:
    Baltic Fleet: 120
    Black Sea Fleet: 77
    Naval Infantry: 57
P 66 and SP 86 (see Mauser)
pain
  Army: 138
panish Civil War: 63, 73
pandau' (see Maschinengewehr 08)
PAS
  Model 11 (see Franchi)
  Model 12 (see Franchi)
peed-Six revolver (see Ruger)
pringfield (see Model 1903)
SA (see Colt)
SG 69 (see Steyr)
SG 2000 (see Steyr)
takeout (see Ithaca)
tandard (see Mauser Gewehr 98)
tar automatic: **51**
tarlight night sight (see AN/PVS-2)
tarlight night sight (see AN/PVS-2)
techkin (see Avtomaticheskiy Pistolet
    Stechkina)
ten guns: 61, 62, 64*, **64, 65**, 66, 69, 71,
    75, 77, 80, 81, 88, 89, 127, 147, 258
teyr
  AUG: 154*, **154**, 180
  GB: 43, 51
  SSG 69: 174*, **174**, 182

SSG 2000: **182**
Steyr-Hahn Repetierpistole M.12: 15, **15**
Steyr-Solothurn S1-100: 67*, **67**
Stielgranate 35 grenades: 26, 31, 224
Stoner, Eugene: 141, 146, 158
Stoner 63 System (see Cadillac-Gage)
Stopper riot gun: 280*, **280**
Stug 111: **26**
Sturmgewehr 45 (see Mauser)
Sturmgewehr Modell 57 (see SIG assault
    rifles)
Sub-machine guns of WWII: 61
Sudarev, A.I: 77
Suez War (1956): 90
Suomi
  m/1931: 63*, **63**, 74
  Model 37-39: 82
SUSAT optical sight: 157, 245
SVD (Samozariyadniya Vintokvka
    Dragunova) 173, 182, 183*, **183**, 187
SVT (see Tokarev rifles)
SVT40 (see Tokarev rifles)
SWAPO guerrillas: 242
Sweden
  Army: 29
Switzerland
  Army: 26, 42, 63, 151
Swordfish (see Fairey)

T

T-34/76 tank: 75
T44 (see M60 GPMG)
Tank Machine-Gun Type 91 (see Type 11
    and Type 96 light machine-guns)
Tannenberg, battle of: 107, 112
T-Gewehr anti-tank rifle (see Mauser)
Thompson, General John: 70
Thompson
  M1 and M1A1: 69, **70**, 71, **71**
  M1928: 70, **70**, 71, **71**
  sub-machine guns: 61, **61**, 67, 69, 70*,
      70, 71*, **71**, 87, 217
Tiger tank: 224
Tikagypt (see Tokarev TT-33)
TN$_2$1 night sight: **155**
Tokarev, F.V: 118
Tokarev
  rifles: 114, 115, 118*, **118**, 120*, **120,
      121**
  TT-30: 25
  TT-33: 25*, **25**, 38
'Tommy Gun': 70, 71
TRGG (see Heckler und Koch)
Trooper (see Colt)
Turkey
  Army: 109
Turpin, H.J: 64
Type 10 (see Nieuport)
Type 11 and Type 96: 211*, **211**, 212*, **212**
Type 43: 85
Type 51 (see Tokarev TT-33)
Type 56 (see Kalashnikov AK-47)
Type 56 (see Ruchnoy Pulemyot
    Degtyarev)
Type 56 (see Samozaryadnyi Karabin
    Simonova)
Type 59: (see Makarov 9-mm)
Type 64: 85*, **85**
Type 74: (see RPK)
Type 80 machine gun: 240
Type 80 machine pistol: 21, **21**
Type 99 (see Type 11 and Type 96)
Type 100 (see Nambu)

U

UD M'42 (see Marlin)
UH-1 'Huey' (see Bell)
Uirapuru Mekanika: 248*, **248**
Ultimax 100 (see CIS)
Unimog 4×4 light truck: 169
United Kingdom
  Army: 13, 24, 32, 36, 38, 62, 64, 80, 81,
      98, 101, 123, 127, 129, 139, 145, 157,
      158, 175, 192, 194, 198, 199, 203, 204,
      219, 220, 221, 230, 233, 242, 245, 254,
      258, 272, 273, 275, 278
    1/7th Lancashire Fusileers: 192
    5th Hampshire Regiment: 122
    6th Airborne Division: 127
    8th Rifle Brigade: **125**

18th Independent Brigade: 254
58th (London) Division: 105
100th Machine Gun Company: 200, 201
Air Corps: 230
ATS (Auxiliary Territorial Service) **37**
Cheshire Regiment: 220
Eighth Army: 217
Gordon Highlanders: 195
Long Range Desert Group: 213, 220
Machine Gun Corps: 194, 198, 200,
    202, 207
Parachute Regiment: 242
'Popski's Private Army': 221
Royal Artillery: 245
Royal Horse Artillery: 12
Royal Signals: 245
SAS (Special Air Service) 84, 87, 221,
    265
Worcesters: 9
Home Guard: 38, 70, 99, 132, 203, 204,
    212
Royal Air Force: 66, 108, 204, 221, 245
Royal Flying Corps: 12, 14
Royal Naval Air Service: 13
Royal Navy: 9, 12, 38, 66, 123, 219, 220,
    245
  Fleet Air Arm: 221
  Royal Marine Commandos: 231
  Royal Marines: 12, 156, 175, 220
  Second Naval Brigade: 109
United Nations Organization: 89
United States
  Air Force: 50, 158, 159, 213
  Army: 10, 33, 34, 35, 38, 41, 48, 49, 53,
      69, 70, 71, 99, 106, 112, 132, 134, 140,
      145, 158, 159, 160, 161, 162, 192, 193,
      196, 197, 198, 204, 212, 213, 225, 229,
      233, 234, 235, 238, 239, 254, 257, 258,
      259, 262, 264, 265, 269, 270, 277
    4th Armored Division: 134
    82nd Airborne Division: 162, 243
    101st Airborne Division: 134
    176th Aviation Company: 262
    331st Infantry Regiment: 215
    Allied Mobile Force (Land): 243
    Green Berets: 259
    National Guard: 140
    Ordnance Board: 69
    Special Forces: 82, 159, 196, 259
  Army Air Force: 34
  CIA (Central Intelligence Agency) 82
  Coast Guard: 49, 257
  Marine Corps: 34, 72, 133, 134, 135, 136,
      141, 186, 197, 232, 239, 257, 260, 261,
      268, 270, 274
  Navy: 35, 70, 141, 145, 197, 213, 214
    SEALS (Sea-Air-Land) forces: 141, 143,
        145, 268
  Rapid Deployment Force: 162, 229
UZI: **79**, 88*, **88, 89-92**
UZI in action, The: 89-92

V

Valmet m/60 and m/62: 146*, **146**, 147*,
    147, 164
Vampir infra-red sight: 118
Verdun, battle of: 108, 194
Versailles Treaty (1919): 67, 221
Vickers Gun: 191, 194, 196, 198*, **198, 199-
    202**, 204
Vickers in Action, The: 199-202
Vickers machine-guns: 220*, **220**, 221
Vickers-Berthier
  K gun (see Vickers-Berthier light
      machine-gun)
  G.O (see Vickers-Berthier light machine-
      gun)
  light-machine gun: 213, 221
Vielle, Paul: 104
Viet Cong: 159, 163, 214, 232, 235, 259
Vietnam War: 43, 82, 137, 141, 148, 153,
    159, 235-238, 260, 261, 262, 268, 269,
    270
Viking Arms SOS shotgun: 263*, **263**
Villa-Perosa: 61, 72
Volkpistole: 55
VP-70 (see Heckler und Koch)
VP-70M (see Heckler und Koch)
vz 9: 63
vz 23: 80, 88, 89
vz 24: 89
vz 25: 89
vz 26: 89
vz 52 (see Samonabiject Puska vz 52)

vz 52 (see vz 59)
vz 52/57 (see Samonabiject Puska vz 52)
vz.58: 163*, **163**
vz.59: 150, 229*, **229**

W

WA2000 (see Walther)
Walther
  Gewehr 41(W) and Gewehr 43: 114*,
      115, 117
  MP-K and MP-L: 85*
  P1 and P5: 28, 30, 51, 56*, **56**
  P4: **57**
  P38: 26, **27**, 28*, **28**, 29, 30, **30, 31**, 56,
      56
  P88: 51
  PP and PPK: 28*, **28**, 57
  WA2000: 173, 177*, **177**, 182
Walther P38 in Action: 29-31
War of Independence (1948): 88, 89
Warsaw Pact: 24, 45, 86, 146, 148, 149,
    163, 164, 170, 183, 235, 240, 241
Water Cannon: 281*
Weaver telescopic sight: 132
Webley
  0.455-in revolver: 9, **9**, 10, 13*, **13**, 24
  Fosbery revolver: 9, 14*, **14**, 268, 270
  Greener GP: 254, 263*, **263**
  Mk 4: 24*, **24**
  Self-Loading Pistol Mk I: 12
Webley & Scott self-loading pistols: **9**, 12*
Western Somali
  Liberation Front forces: 168
West Germany
  Army: 30, 55, 92, 179, 235, 243
    305th Panzer Artillery: 92
    Gebirgsjäger: 243
  GSG-9 border police: 55
  Navy: 85
Westland Lynx: 230
What use is a pistol in combat?: 27
Wilhelm II, Kaiser: 205
Wilniewicz, Piotr: 86
Winchester
  Defender: 267, **267**
  M1897: 257, 260, **260**, 261
  M1912: 261
  Model 12: **260, 261**, 267
  Model 1200: 267, **267**
  Model 1895: 112*, **112**
  shotguns: 267*, **267**
wz 63 (PM-63): 81, 86*, **86**, 87

X

X3: 62, **62, 82**
XL47E1 (see Walther PP and PPK)
XL65E5 (see Enfield Individual Weapon)
XL70E3 (see Enfield Individual Weapon)
XL73E2 (see Light Support Weapon)
XM9: 35, 50

Y

Yom Kippur War (1973): 164
Ypres, battle of: 107
Yugoslavia
  Army: 187

Z

ZB vz.26 (see Lehky Kulomet)
ZB vz.27: 219
ZB vz.30 (see Lehky Kulomet)
ZB vz.32: 219
ZB vz.33: 219
Zeiss
  Divari Z telescopic sight: 174
  Divari ZA telescopic sight: 176
ZK 383: 62*, **62**, 63

Picture acknowledgements

The publishers would like to thank the following organisations and individuals for their help in supplying photographs for this book. We are also grateful to the Pattern Room, Royal Ordnance Factory Enfield, and to the Weapons Museum, School of Infantry, Warminster for their kind permission to photograph weapons from their collections.

IWM = Imperal War Museum

Page 9: IWM (both). **12:** IWM. **13:** IWM. **16:** T.J. O'Malley. **18:** T.J. O'Malley. **20:** IWM. **21:** T.J. O'Malley. **22:** IWM. **23:** IWM (both). **24:** IWM. **25:** Robert Hunt Library. **26:** Robert Hunt Library (both). **29:** Robert Hunt Library/MacClancy Collection. **30:** Robert Hunt Library/T.J. O'Malley. **31:** IWM. **34:** US National Archives. **37:** IWM. **40:** MacClancy Collection. **41:** Portuguese Army/Fabrique Nationale. **43:** Associated Press/US Navy. **44:** Associated Press (both). **45:** Associated Press. **46:** Associated Press (all). **47:** Israel Military Industries. **49:** Beretta (both). **50:** US Army. **54:** Fabrique Nationale (two, bottom). **61:** MacClancy Collection/IWM. **62:** T.J. O'Malley. **63:** T.J. O'Malley. **64:** T.J. O'Malley/IWM. **65:** IWM. **66:** T.J. O'Malley. **67:** T.J. O'Malley **70:** T.J. O'Malley. **71:** IWM. **73:** Robert Hunt Library. **64:** Imperial War Museum. **75:** IWM/Robert Hunt Library. **76:** MacClancy Collection. **77:** MacClancy Collection. **78:** Robert Hunt Library (both). **79:** Herman Potgieter/Associated Press. **80:** MoD/MARS, Lincs. **82:** Australian Defence Department/T.J. O'Malley. **83:** FFV/MARS, Lincs. **85:** T.J. O'Malley. **89:** Herman Potgieter/Robert Hunt Library. **90:** MARS, Lincs/Associated Press. **91:** Israel Military Industries/Associated Press. **92:** MARS, Lincs/Robert Hunt Library. **93:** Beretta (all). **97:** IWM (both). **98:** IWM. **99:** IWM (both). **100:** MacClancy Collection. **101:** IWM. **102:** IWM. **103:** MacClancy Collection. **104:** Robert Hunt Library/IWM/IWM. **105:** IWM (both). **106:** IWM. **107:** IWM (all). **108:** IWM (both). **109:** IWM (all three). **110:** Robert Hunt Library/IWM. **111:** IWM/Robert Hunt Library. **112:** IWM. **113:** T.J. O'Malley/IWM. **114:** MacClancy Collection/IWM/IWM. **115:** T.J. O'Malley. **116:** MacClancy Collection. **117:** MacClancy Collection/MacClancy Collection. **118:** IWM. **119:** IWM/T.J. O'Malley/IWM. **120:** IWM. **121:** T.J. O'Malley/Novosti Press Agency. **122:** MacClancy Collection/IWM. **123 (both).** **124:** IWM (both). **125:** IWM. **127:** IWM. **128:** T.J. O'Malley. **129:** IWM. **130:** MacClancy Collection. **131:** MacClancy Collection (both). **132:** T.J. O'Malley. **133:** US Marine Corps. **134:** IWM/US Marine Corps. **135:** IWM/US Marine Corps/IWM. **136:** US Marine Corps. **138:** MARS, Lincs. **140:** Associated Press. **142:** US Army.

143: US Navy. **144:** MoD. **145:** US Navy. **146:** T.J. O'Malley. **147:** T.J. O'Malley (both). **149:** ECP Armées. **150:** T.J. O'Malley. **152:** US Army. **153:** US Army/COI. **154:** Steyr/Steyr/T.J. O'Malley. **155:** T.J. O'Malley/Australian Defence Department. **156:** Associated Press. **158:** US Air Force. **159:** US Army. **160:** US Army. **161:** US Army (all four). **162:** US Army (both). **163:** T.J. O'Malley. **164:** Gamma. **165:** MacClancy Collection/US Department of Defense. **166:** Associated Press (both). **167:** Associated Press/Duncan Mil. **168:** Associated Press (all). **169:** Associated Press (all). **170:** Duncan Mil/Duncan Mil/Israel Military Industries. **171:** Armscor/Beretta/Beretta/Beretta. **172:** T.J. O'Malley (both). **173:** Zavodi Crvena Zastava/Israel Military Industries. **174:** Steyr. **175:** ECP Armées. **177:** Walther (all). **180:** Steyr/ECP Armées. **181:** Israel Military Industries. **182:** SIG-Sauer. **183:** T.J. O'Malley (both). **184:** Israel Military Industries/Israel Military Industries/Fabrique Nationale. **185:** Fabrique Nationale. **186:** T.J. O'Malley. **187:** Zavodi Crvena Zastava (both). **191:** IWM (both). **192:** IWM (both). **194:** IWM. **195:** IWM (both). **196:** IWM. **197:** IWM/Bruce Robertson. **199:** IWM (both). **202:** IWM (all). **204:** IWM (both). **205:** IWM. **207:** MacClancy Collection (both). **208:** US Army. **209:** MacClancy Collection/IWM. **210:** T.J. O'Malley/IWM. **212:** IWM. **213:** IWM. **214:** US Army. **215:** US National Archives (both). **216:** US National Archives (both). **217:** IWM. **220:** T.J. O'Malley/IWM. **221:** IWM. **222:** T.J. O'Malley/MacClancy Collection. **223:** IWM. **224:** IWM (all). **225:** Robert Hunt Library. **226:** T.J. O'Malley/Novosti Press Agency. **227:** US Army/Herman Potgieter. **228:** MARS, Lincs. **230:** MARS, Lincs/COI. **231:** Royal Marines. **232:** MacClancy Collection/US Marine Corps. **233:** Fabrique Nationale/US Army. **234:** T.J. O'Malley. **235:** Edward Rasen. **236:** US Army. **237:** US Army. **238:** US Army. **239:** US Army. **240:** Chartered Industries of Singapore (both). **242:** Herman Potgieter. **243:** MARS, Lincs/US Army/US Army. **244:** MARS, Lincs/Associated Press. **245:** T.J. O'Malley/MARS, Lincs/British Army. **249:** Pakistan Army. **253:** Ian V. Hogg/Associated Press. **254:** Fabrique Nationale. **255:** Fabrique Nationale/Beretta/Beretta/Beretta. **256:** Beretta/Swearingen/Swearingen. **257:** US Coast Guard. **258:** US National Archives. **259:** Swearingen. **260:** Ian V. Hogg. **261:** Swearingen. **262:** Swearingen/Associated Press. **263:** Ian V. Hogg. **264:** Swearingen (both). **265:** Swearingen (all). **266:** Ian V. Hogg (both). **267:** Ian V. Hogg/Winchester/Winchester. **268:** Associated Press. **269:** Ian V. Hogg/Ian V. Hogg/Swearingen. **270:** Ian V. Hogg (both). **271:** Associated Press/Hotspur. **272:** Ian V. Hogg (all). **274:** Associated Press/Ian V. Hogg. **275:** Ian V. Hogg/Associated Press. **276:** Associated Press. **277:** T.J. O'Malley (both). **278:** T.J. O'Malley. **280:** BAT. **281:** Associated Press/Ian V. Hogg.